# DISCOUNTS AND DEALS

## AT THE NATION'S 360 BEST COLLEGES

# DISCOUNTS AND DEALS

## AT THE NATION'S 360 BEST COLLEGES

The  Financial Aid
and College Guide

## BRUCE G. HAMMOND

St. Martin's Griffin
New York

# TO MRS. FAYE TROUTMAN,
## MY UNFORGETTABLE THIRD-GRADE TEACHER

The 1999–2000 CSS/Financial Aid PROFILE Form is reprinted with permission of the College Board. College Board, CSS, CSS/Financial Aid Profile, and the acorn logo are registered trademarks of the College Entrance Examination Board.

College Data is provided by Wintergreen/Orchard House, an imprint of Riverside Publishing. Copyright 1998 by The Riverside Publishing Company. Reproduced with permission. All rights reserved.

Designed by Meryl Sussman Levavi/digitext, inc.

ISBN 1-58238-030-9

First Edition: August 1999

10 9 8 7 6 5 4 3 2 1

# CONTENTS

# INTRODUCTION

The need for this book hit home as I was peering around a corner watching unsuspecting families get scammed. I was director of college counseling at a small private school at the time, and the parents of a number of my eleventh graders had received a direct mail solicitation from a group cultivating the look and feel of a charitable foundation, inviting them to attend a "seminar" about ways of getting "free money." I also wrote a column about college admission for a local newspaper, so with a mixture of journalistic interest and personal indignation, I had gone to take a peek for myself.

The written solicitation was classic scam material. "I am pleased to inform you that your child has been selected as one of the local area students that is eligible to apply for scholarships, grants, and other financial assistance through our center," the letter began. It went on to promise that families would "learn how to reduce or even eliminate your out-of-pocket cost of education." And then came the kicker: "A licensed representative of the _____ Life Insurance Company will be available to explain how using financial programs like annuities and life insurance can help secure your son or daughter's future education."

I didn't need a Ph.D. in counseling to realize that these families were being set up for one of the oldest cons in financial aid—the promise-'em-aid-and-sell-'em-life-insurance scam. On the appointed Saturday afternoon, I arrived outside the scam outfit's headquarters, a hotel conference room, in time to watch the unsuspecting prospects file in.

The song and dance was predictable: vague talk about scholarships, then the hard sell. After observing the scene unfold for about an hour, I suddenly realized that I had no idea what to do next. If only I had a cameraman from *60 Minutes*, with whom I could barge in and shoot footage of them running away, hiding their faces, or trying to cover the lens with their hands. So much for fantasy. Their scam was probably legal, if misleading. I soon left, wrote my column on scholarship scams, and ultimately had the satisfaction of shutting down one of their local sites.

But what sank in for me was the sorry state of public information about financial aid. Even some of the parents at my school, savvy and well-informed as they were, had been taken in. Part of my frustration was knowing that hundreds of other families in the Cleveland area, and thousands nationwide, would continue to be fleeced by the multimillion-dollar "business" of scholarship scams.

But why should I have been surprised? Of all the Byzantine shell games this side of the federal tax code, what is more confusing than college financial aid? Unfathomable rules, a labyrinth of mumbo jumbo and acronyms, layer upon layer of complexity, and to top it all off, a financial aid scene that is changing at warp speed. Who translates it all into plain English? The federal government is no help, and though financial aid officers are a decent group, their bottom line is serving the interests of their college, not your interest.

My desire to reach a wider audience with the real story on college financial aid is a big reason why I joined Parent Soup, the leader in family programming on America Online (Keyword: Parent Soup) and the World Wide Web (www.parentsoup.com). In my two years as Parent Soup's school and college counselor, I have experienced the remarkable power of the Internet to create real communities in cyberspace. I have chatted several times per week with parents in all corners of the nation—and the world—many of whom are now good friends. I have answered thousands of questions posted on Parent Soup's message boards, including some that are in this book. I have been challenged and inspired by the many wonderful folks I have met at Parent Soup, who have helped in the writing of this book in countless ways. But working with them has further highlighted the confusion that is rampant when the subject turns to college financial aid.

*Discounts and Deals at the Nation's 360 Best Colleges* is an attempt to cut through the myths and misinformation. It is a straightforward guide to financial aid in the twenty-first century—a system far different from what existed even a decade ago.

My work at Parent Soup has heightened my appreciation of the importance of parents in the college search, and this book is the first guide to colleges written specifically for them. The conventional wisdom used to be that the only role for parents was to pay for college. The students were supposed to pick which one. Good parents, so the thinking went, would find a way to foot the bill for any school the student wanted to attend.

Colleges have benefited handsomely from the pay-any-price mentality, but with higher education now rivaling home ownership on the list of life's most expensive purchases, a new model is needed. Finances can and must play a role in the decision, and parents must be there side by side with students to help weigh the alternatives and cut through the baloney. Colleges no longer separate admission and financial aid, and it makes no sense for families to do so, either. After years of grim sacrifice, there is finally some good news for the middle class on the subject of paying for college. But the new opportunities come at the price of new complexity, and only savvy families will get the full benefit.

Admittedly, the new rules put pressure on parents to know when to be involved and when to step back. Is there an issue more fundamental to good parenting? Parents should contribute their love, support, insight, and when necessary, some financial parameters for the search. Students should retain the right to determine their fate to the largest degree possible. I think most parents will know instinctively where to draw the line, and it is my hope that this book can be part of a shared college search that deepens familial bonds. Though written ostensibly to the older generation, I encourage students to read it too.

It is important to be clear at the beginning that our fundamental purpose in the college search is to help a young person get a head start on a happy life. College admission and financial aid is a crucial topic to today's families, and we'll soon be knee-deep in strategizing. But let's keep in mind that the game we're playing does not have ultimate importance. A merit scholarship or an offer of admission is not a ticket to paradise. There are a lot of desperately unhappy people at the Harvards of the world, and thousands more at colleges most of us have never heard of who are on their way to fulfilling lives.

The college search can be a time full of anxiety and strain or a time when the bonds between parent and student are deepened as they enter a new phase. As college looms on the horizon, we should remind our children how much we love them, how badly we want what is best for them, and how much we will still love them no matter where life may take them. They will be successful and happy because of who they are, not which college they attend.

# PART I

# INSIDE THE
# AID PROCESS

# 1.

# SEPARATING FACT
# FROM FICTION

Small wonder that today's parents are petrified by college costs. The reality of all those bills is frightening enough, but many parents feel a keener sense of dread because they don't understand how financial aid works. They only know what they hear. One friend says that middle-income people never get anything, so don't even bother applying. Another tells about a next-door neighbor whose daughter got a full scholarship. Announcers blare about tuition and fees topping $30,000 a year—then commercials advertise billions of unclaimed aid waiting for the lucky parent who looks beneath the right rock. Most people can reconcile themselves to paying huge bills, but the nagging thought that money is out there, somewhere, if only you knew how to find it... That's enough to drive anyone crazy.

Here's a pain reliever designed to work on your financial aid headaches in five minutes—without a prescription. This chapter conveys the essence of what you need to know about paying for college. The rest of the book takes you through the process from A to Z and offers an overview of the aid situation at 360 of the nation's best colleges.

> FICTION: The financial aid process is like a scavenger hunt for scholarships hidden in dusty corners.
> FACT: 95 percent of aid comes through colleges, the federal government, and the states.

If you want financial aid, your first move is to learn about the colleges and their aid policies. Some offer only need-based aid; others give hundreds of merit scholarships and talent awards. The most expensive colleges tend to combine a high price tag with hefty aid packages. Other colleges may have lower sticker prices, but then pile on the loans or do not fully meet need. In addition to doling out their own money, the college aid offices provide points of access for most federal and state money.

One of the most enduring myths of financial aid is the idea that private organizations sponsor scholarships that nobody applies for. Let's think for a minute. How many families do you know who brag about finding these mystery scholarships? And if these sources are really so secret, why has the same sales pitch been airing since the 1980s? The scholarship search industry is a mostly bogus, multimillion-dollar money grab that peddles everything from useless books to overpriced investment accounts to pay for its "services." The best scholarship search programs are available on the Internet for free (see chapter 6).

---

### THE MYTH OF UNCLAIMED AID

This myth dates back to a study in the early 1980s that counted the tuition benefits that private corporations offer their employees as "aid," according to Tim Christensen of the National Association of Student Financial Aid Administrators. Since most people in the workforce don't take advantage of those benefits, it was possible to knit the yarn of "unclaimed aid."

---

Families can and should search these databases for private awards—you may get lucky and find an endowment for Concert Harpists from Montana or Second Generation Ukrainian Glassblowers. But scholarships like these are not plentiful and usually amount to no more than a few hundred dollars. Most national scholarship contests are incredibly competitive—winning one of the big ones is tougher than getting into Harvard. A better strategy is to look locally, where the community Elks Club or Daughters of the American Revolution chapter just might have an award with your student's name on it. The school counselor will probably have a list of these opportunities, or know where to get one. If not, check with area foundations or civic groups.

FICTION: Middle-class families never qualify for aid.
FACT: New aid programs target millions of middle-income students.

Call it the great middle-class aid giveaway. With all the subtlety of a K-Mart blue-light special, private colleges have poured millions into discounts and give-backs to woo middle-class customers away from cheaper public university competitors. Though often dressed up in the glitzy garb of merit scholarships, these awards benefit average and good students whose families can pay the balance of the bill. The popularity of merit scholarships and middle-class tuition relief has not been lost on the state legislatures, which have been falling all over themselves to create new programs. In 1998, the federal government jumped on the bandwagon, implementing the highly popular Hope Scholarship tax credit and Lifetime Learning Credit, which will shave up to $1,500 off the tuition bill of a middle-class family. More recently, some of the nation's most elite colleges have announced major changes in their aid formula to make it more favorable to the middle class.

Aid aside, families have more choices than they realize in the sticker price of college. Two-year institutions are a guaranteed bargain; the sticker price is generally less than $2,500, and with the new federal tax breaks a typical family's bill for the year may be less than $1,000.

At public universities, the average sticker price, including room and board, is about $10,500, while private colleges cost about $22,500. Alas, the horror stories are true for parents of Ivy League hopefuls who don't qualify for aid—they get walloped to the tune of nearly $35,000 per year. But even families with incomes of $100,000 or more can sometimes qualify for need-based aid at these expensive schools.

> FICTION: Need-based aid packages depend only on a need-based formula.
> FACT: Colleges give better need-based aid packages to the students they want most.

No need to adjust your reading glasses—I meant it when I said that need-based aid packages don't necessarily depend only on need. The first trick is to understand that need-based packages include government money, which *is* distributed exclusively by a need-based formula, and money from the college's own coffers, which can be given away by any rationale so long as the total package does not exceed a student's need. Top students, recruited athletes, and other hot prospects are much more likely

---

### MERIT MONEY FROM THE STATES

In 1997, the State of Florida launched the Florida Bright Futures Scholarship Program, which offers students with a 3.5 grade-point average (GPA) and a combined 1270 on the SAT (or 28 on the ACT) a full-tuition scholarship plus $600.00 at an in-state public university, or an equal amount toward the expenses at a Florida private college. Students with lower credentials qualify for a lesser amount.

---

### THE IVY LEAGUE FEELS MIDDLE-CLASS PAIN

An important sign of the times was a recent move by Princeton University to sweeten need-based aid packages for lower- and middle-income families. Harvard, MIT, Yale, and Stanford quickly announced similar changes, and the impact is still rippling through the private university world (see chapter 4). The elite colleges are concerned because more cash-strapped families are opting for low tuition and merit scholarships at public universities. Princeton's announcement was revealing because it caught other Ivy League schools off guard. Ten years ago, they would have coordinated. Today, they're competing.

to see large grants with funds from the latter category, while borderline students are more often saddled with large loans or aid packages that don't fully meet need. Colleges call it "preferential packaging" or "merit-within-need." The practice is nearly universal at private colleges, which use millions of their own money to woo the most desirable students.

FICTION: Aid awards are nonnegotiable.
FACT: Aid awards can (sometimes) be negotiated.

Persistent yet reasonable advocacy can get you a better aid package. But the process has less to do with bargaining bravado than with careful preparation, such as applying to an intelligent mix of colleges and thoroughly documenting any special circumstances that might increase an award. Private colleges are far more likely to give a little when push comes to shove; a few openly advertise that they will match better offers from competing institutions. Others have a policy against bargaining and stick to it. Still others absolutely, positively wouldn't think of negotiating—at least not usually, by which I mean in no case whatsoever except for a few special situations. Chapter 4 covers the art of appealing for more aid in detail, including what kinds of colleges are most likely to negotiate, what's negotiable and what isn't, and how to maximize your chances of success.

## THE RULES HAVE CHANGED

The Communist world isn't the only one that has fallen to free-market competition. The world of financial aid, under pressure for years, has also given way to competitive forces. At today's selective colleges, financial aid is less about helping the needy than the never-ending drive for students and tuition revenue. Education consumers can reap the benefits, but only if they have the necessary information to take advantage of the explosion in new opportunities to cut education costs. That's why the heart of this book is a first-of-its-kind look at the aid policies of 360 of the nation's best colleges. Which ones offer the biggest academic merit scholarships? Which offer the best need-based aid packages? Which give scholarships for artistic talent, leadership, or community service? Which offer awards for good-but-not-great students who don't have financial need? Browse the profiles in Part II, scan the lists and rankings, and encourage your child to do the same.

The remainder of the book is an inside look at the financial aid search. Chapter 2, "Behind the Ivy Façade," describes the hidden pressures that drive today's financial aid process. Chapter 3, "The College Application Portfolio," provides you with a strategy for success in the application process. Chapter 4, "Getting Need-Based Aid," gives a detailed look at the various forms of aid while debunking more myths. Chapter 5, "The Forms," is an extra-strength chapter designed to help you fill out the forms and fend off migraines during those lonely nights at the dining room table. In chapter 6, "Savvy Books and Links," you'll find a complete guide to college and financial aid sources, including all the best from the world of cyberspace. Whether your child is a toddler or an eighteen-year-old, chapter 7, "The College Planning Timeline," will give you a year-by-year, month-by-month look at where you are and what happens next.

We begin with an examination of the forces that have shaped today's aid system—and what the future may hold.

# 2.

# BEHIND THE IVY FAÇADE

A glance at the headlines tells the grim story of college costs. "Tuition, room, board—every campus expense keeps climbing in a spiral that seems endless," declares one article from *U.S. News & World Report*, with a sense of despair that captures the mood of many families. "If you are shocked by the cost of sending your son or daughter to college, brace yourself for more bad news. Latest official figures show that still another boost in college bills, averaging 4 to 5 percent, is in store for the next school year. All this comes on top of a rapid climb in college expenses that, over the last decade, has far outstripped the rise in most other living costs."

Nothing here should come as a surprise to families of college-bound students—except that this particular article is dated March 4, 1968. That year, the average total cost of a year at a public university had skyrocketed to $1,110, while private college expenses had reached the then-astronomical total of $2,266. Little did anyone dream that the next three decades would bring a breathtaking acceleration of the increases that would reach double digits in the 1980s. The article's observation that "college bills can amount to a small fortune" seems quaint in retrospect. The spooky part is that virtually every word could be printed in this week's magazine, right down to the fact that current tuition increases have been in the 4 to 5 percent range, roughly double the rate of inflation.

Why is the price of college so high? And why has the bill climbed so fast, without a break, for four decades? The litany of reasons boils down to two biggies: the colleges' inability to contain costs, and the decline of federal and state support. Though adminstrators have fretted for decades about runaway tuition increases, the incentives to raise tuition yet another year have always outnumbered those for keeping the price in check.

The college-paying public has been a willing accomplice. Howls of protest notwithstanding, the percentage of the population attending college has risen substantially, and the public is more convinced than ever that higher education is a good investment. At the heart of it all is the seemingly effortless way colleges and universities are able to market their product—especially the most prestigious schools, who have skillfully parlayed their brand names into a universal measure of success and accomplishment for young people. What other industry could double and triple its price while attracting twice as many applicants desperate for the privilege to pay the bill?

But the four decades of hyper-inflation have taken their toll. While extracting huge sums from those able to pay, colleges have been forced to dramatically increase their financial aid to the families who can't. The prestigious ones can still charge any price they wish and be swamped with applicants, most of whom can afford to pay. State universities, with lower sticker prices and growing reputations, are also doing just fine. Most private colleges, especially the small ones, are feeling the pinch. In their increasingly urgent attempts to generate tuition revenue, they have discovered the factory rebate theory of pricing that has worked so well in the automobile industry. People are more likely to sign on the dotted line if

### INFLATIONARY SPIRAL

| | 1968 price | 1998 price | Increase |
|---|---|---|---|
| Dozen eggs | 50 cents | 90 cents | 80% |
| Washing machine | $210.00 | $500.00 | 140% |
| Gallon of gas | 35 cents | $1.10 | 240% |
| Luxury car | $7,000 | $40,000 | 470% |
| Four-year public college | $1,110 | $10,500 | 850% |
| Four-year private college | $2,266 | $22,500 | 900% |

Sources: College Board, Consumer Reports, U.S. Department of Labor, U.S. News & World Report

they think they're getting a special deal, and particularly if they think they've won something. Rather than limit price increases, many colleges have chosen to maximize revenue by raising tuition in combination with scholarships and give-backs.

Though they rarely hire announcers to hawk their product over the air waves, colleges compete as intensely as any cut-rate discounters. But it is more prestige than price that drives the market, as measured largely by the ability to attract top students. This chapter offers a peek inside the ivy-covered walls to reveal an industry that is much more competitive than it seems on the surface. It shows how colleges use SAT scores and acceptance rates in a dog-eat-dog fight for the next rung on the prestige ladder, and how financial aid became one more weapon in the fight. Finally, this chapter gives a systematic overview of the tangle of policies that crisscross today's aid scene. By learning about each policy, families can begin to understand which colleges may provide their best chances at scholarships and aid.

To understand the financial aid scene at the dawn of a new century, it is necessary to take a glance back. Like so many of today's public institutions, modern college financial aid has its roots in the 1960s.

## HOW EXCLUSIVITY FOUND MASS APPEAL

There is no better benchmark in the selling of higher education than Thurston Howell III, the blue-blooded millionaire from *Gilligan's Island*. The show first aired in 1965, and Mr. Howell fit the country's image of a "Hahvahd" man. He was filthy rich but not particularly smart, a bumbling country-clubber who snorted "must be a Yale man" at anyone who violated his warped sense of the social graces. Harvard was something a little un-American back then—an island of privilege seemingly beyond the reach of the average person, no matter how intelligent.

There was certainly an element of altruism in the decision to open elite institutions to women, minorities, and those of humble means beginning in the 1960s, but it set in motion one of the greatest marketing campaigns of the late twentieth century. In a nation without an aristocracy, college admission became the new standard of distinction. Anybody could aspire to go to Harvard if their grades and test scores were good enough, and students everywhere rose to the bait. Where once the best and brightest had scattered themselves across institutions nationwide, more and more began to hone in on the short list of the nation's most prestigious. The trend has grown stronger with each passing decade, reinforced now by national rankings in publications ranging from *U.S. News & World Report* to *Yahoo! Internet Life*. The coat of arms on the castle gate has been replaced by the window decal on the family car.

Collectively, the 360 colleges profiled in this book comprise approximately the most prominent 15 percent of the four-year colleges nationwide. The majority are more selective than they were ten or twenty years ago, and all have substantially increased their inflation-adjusted price. The competition for admission—and the price increases—have been greatest at the top perch of the Ivy League and its cousins. This leads to the first rule of college finance: You'll pay for prestige.

For good students, and even average ones, the price tag of a college education is likely to be thousands cheaper for those willing to consider less selective options. These colleges are increasingly determined to enroll students with high grades and standardized test scores, and money is their incentive of choice. But before we turn to merit scholarships and tuition discounts, let's get up to speed on how the modern aid system took shape.

# A DREAM DENIED

The same year Mr. Howell and company arrived on Gilligan's Island, President Lyndon Johnson was at work on weightier stuff. The Higher Education Act of 1965 created the modern federal need-based aid system, with an infusion of 1960s idealism and millions of dollars from the federal till to back it up. "To thousands of young men and women, this act means the path of knowledge is open to all that have the determination to walk it," said Johnson as he announced the act. "It means that a high school senior anywhere in this great land of ours can apply to any college or any university in any of the 50 states and not be turned away because his family is poor."

It was a far-reaching commitment. The act authorized grants of up to $1,000, good enough to cover the entire cost of a public college education and half of a private one. Work study of up to $500 per year allowed students to earn money for tuition, and low-interest loans were also available. The entry of the federal government was a necessary step in transforming college admissions from a matter of social status into a national contest. Though it might not have been clear at the time, the greatest beneficiaries were the elite institutions that had formerly defined themselves mainly in terms of wealth and class. In their increasingly selective admissions processes, these colleges now offered a vehicle for demonstrating merit that proved irresistible.

The modern need-based financial aid system was one of the most important legacies of Lyndon Johnson's Great Society Program. With the infusion of government funding came a federal need assessment formula that defined the rules for distributing the money, and most colleges used the same standards to give out their own funds. At selective private colleges, a policy of "need-blind admissions"—the practice of judging applicants without respect to their ability to pay—was combined with a pledge to meet the full financial need of each applicant who was admitted.

But the philosophical commitment to need-based aid was destined to outlive the availability of cash to pay for it. By the late 1970s, federal aid was in decline, its purchasing power sapped by mushrooming inflation and waning political will. And the real tuition increases were only beginning. "Now, a $30,000 Diploma," fretted *Time* magazine in 1978. "College costs, up 77 percent in a decade, are still soaring." With middle-income families complaining loudly, Congress and President Carter produced several measures to extend more aid, but they succeeded only in creating a spurt of red ink that made student aid ripe for the chopping block when Ronald Reagan took office in 1980. The stagnation in government support continued throughout the 1980s and early 1990s as the grant programs hemorrhaged and student debt rose. By the late 1980s, states were also slashing their support. Meanwhile, college costs went on a staggering rise, at more than twice the rate of inflation as measured by the consumer price index.

College administrators recite a host of reasons for the dramatic rise in recent decades, including a loss of federal subsidies, rising maintenance costs, expensive new technology, poor endowment performance in the 1970s, an upward spike in the price of books and paper, rising demand for student services, the growth of health-care costs for a people-intensive industry, and the pressure to match anything and everything at competitor institutions. Colleges today offer a profusion of amenities unheard of a generation ago: arts centers, cultural houses, apartment-style dorms, food courts, and fitness centers, to name a few. As one administrator told *The Chronicle of Higher Education*, "There are unlimited opportunities to improve what we're doing. We don't try to minimize costs—we try to maximize what we spend."

Another factor is the presence of a firmly entrenched white-collar workforce, the faculty, who strongly resist any efforts at restructuring. When a private corporation can't sell a product, the item is discontinued. But if a college major falls out of favor, woe to the university president who tries to cut faculty positions, especially tenured ones.

Perhaps the most interesting reason why college costs keep rising is the reluctance to be perceived as cut-rate. Economists call it the Chivas Regal effect—with liquor and colleges, people associate quality with a higher price. It certainly seemed so in the 1980s and 1990s, when the only thing that grew faster than tuition were the eager hordes of students clamoring for admission. As costs continued to rise, colleges merely forwarded the bill to students and parents.

Everybody in higher education knew that the party could not last, and by the mid-1990s it was clear that the bank accounts of the college-going public had been stretched to the breaking point. The press was in an uproar, the middle class was angry, and on Capitol Hill critics were talking ominously about regulation and even price controls. It was déjà vu all over again, but this time the colleges seemed to get the message. "I think there's a collective sense that we've gone too far," observed one director of financial aid. The situation was particularly acute at private colleges, which saw a growing percentage of their market defect to cheaper public institutions. A few, notably Muskingum College in Ohio and North Carolina Wesleyan University, seized the moment and slashed tuition by approximately one-third, proving if nothing else that it could be done. Under the watchful eyes of Congress and a skeptical public, most colleges held their price increases to the 5 percent range—still significantly higher than inflation, if far below earlier levels. But the aid system proclaimed with such fanfare by President Johnson was a dim shadow of the original vision.

## THE BRAVE NEW WORLD OF NEED ASSESSMENT

The most crucial event in shaping the new aid process at highly selective colleges occurred in the early 1990s. Previously, officials from elite institutions met annually to discuss the determination of need for students who applied to more than one of the participating institutions. The idea was to coordinate aid so that each package was roughly the same, ensuring that students chose their ultimate college destination based on educational factors rather than financial ones. It all seemed a little too cozy for the Bush administration's Justice Department, which smelled price-fixing and moved in to break up the meetings. "An Ivy League Cartel," clucked *Newsweek* when the probe was made public. Feeling the heat, the colleges reluctantly ended their "overlap" meetings and set the stage for competition in financial aid.

Another defining event was the federal government's decision to rewrite the need formula in 1992. With visions of middle-income voters dancing in its head, Congress removed home equity from the need assessment formula, opening the door to thousands of families who would not have qualified for aid under the old rules. That was fine for the portion of the pie that consisted of federal money, but many expensive colleges balked at the idea of raiding their own treasuries to subsidize the new formula. It was unfair, they argued, to give the same aid to a family living in a $200,000 home as to one who was renting—even if both earned the same income. Rather than fork over millions more of their own cash, a few hundred of the most selective colleges banded together with the College Scholarship Service, a division of the College Board, to create a new need assessment form known as the CSS/Financial Aid PROFILE. Used in combination with the Free Application for Federal Student Aid (FAFSA), the CSS PROFILE allows colleges to consider criteria not encompassed by the federal aid formula when distributing their own need-based funds. The CSS PROFILE is an especially intriguing instrument because unlike earlier forms, each college has the prerogative to add its own institutional questions, ranging from the value of household retirement savings to whether parents receive free housing or food as a job benefit. Each college that uses the PROFILE, or a form of its own, creates its own standard of need with its own "institutional methodology," as distinguished from the "federal methodology" that underlies the FAFSA.

Thus was born the two-tier need assessment system that so befuddles families today. For a detailed explanation on how they work, turn to chapter 4. The following thumbnail sketches explain the basics.

## THE FREE APPLICATION FOR FEDERAL STUDENT AID

*Who must file it?* Every applicant seeking need-based aid at any college.

*What does it do?* The FAFSA computes an expected family contribution (EFC) according to federal methodology. If your EFC is less than your cost of attendance (COA), the total bill for a year at college, then you qualify for aid.

*Where can I get it?* Paper copies of the FAFSA are available in high school guidance offices and college financial aid offices beginning around December 1 for students planning to enroll the following fall. It is also available on the World Wide Web at www.fafsa.ed.gov.

*What's the deadline?* Federal rules prohibit filing the FAFSA before January 1. Selective colleges usually want it as soon as possible thereafter, usually no later than March. Check the listings in Part II for college-by-college deadlines.

## THE CSS/FINANCIAL AID PROFILE

*Who must file it?* Of the 360 colleges in this book, about 110 require the CSS PROFILE. The vast majority are private universities.

*What does it do?* The PROFILE allows the expensive colleges which require it to add additional items into the need assessment formula, including home equity, the finances of noncustodial parents, trust funds held by siblings, an expectation for summer earnings, private school tuition, the value of life insurance and pension plans—even the make and model of the cars you drive.

*Where can I get it?* PROFILE registration forms are available at high school guidance offices and college financial aid offices. Families can also complete it on-line at www.collegeboard.org. Since the PROFILE includes supplemental questions requested by particular colleges, students must designate which colleges are to receive it on the registration the form. The CSS then generates an individualized PROFILE form for each family, including all supplemental questions requested by any of those colleges.

*What's the deadline?* Filing deadlines for the PROFILE run on approximately the same schedule as those for the FAFSA, with the exception of students who are applying via an early decision or early action program.

In addition to the FAFSA and CSS/Financial Aid PROFILE, or sometimes instead of the latter, many colleges in this book also require families to complete the college's own aid form, referred to as an "institutional" form. Institutional forms can be used to supplement information from the FAFSA and PROFILE. Few things are as confusing as the need-assessment process, but there is at least one: the myriad policies and procedures governing how aid is distributed.

## THE COLLEGES DECIDE TO PLAY BALL

Anyone who has written a tuition check lately will tell you that these aren't the best of times to be paying college bills. But neither are they the worst—at least for the middle-income family. Sticker prices are in the stratosphere and need-based aid has stagnated, but new sources have risen to take their place. Government money has been beefed up at both the state and federal level. Colleges now offer merit scholarships, incentive plans, discounts made to look like scholarships, and competitive aid packaging as a major part of the mutual pursuit. Though the average tuition keeps going up, the average total discount is rising even faster.

No less significant has been the blurring of the line between need-based aid and merit scholarships. With the reputation and livelihood of the college depending on the quality of students it is able to attract, financial aid policy has become a crucial element of what is now called "enrollment management," the process of competing for the best students, or sometimes merely filling the beds. The bottom line is that stronger applicants now get better need-based aid as well as more merit scholarships.

The flip side of sweetening the pot for middle-income families is that poorer families are sometimes left out in the cold. To illustrate the problem from the colleges' perspective, suppose that Low-Income Lucy applies to Expensive U, which determines through the aid forms that she will need a grant of $20,000 per year to attend. Over four years, that's an $80,000 raid on its treasury. The college could use that money to pay Lucy's way, but suppose four middle- and upper-middle-income students also apply for admission, and they are all reasonably good students who will also be admitted by competitor schools. Instead of lavishing $20,000 per year on Lucy, the university decides to offer $5,000 discounts to the other four.

It is not hard to imagine their acceptance letters: "Congratulations! We are pleased to announce that you are the winner of the $5,000 Worthington B. Snodgrass Award for All-Around Excellence." Since our four students have

# THE SELECTIVITY GAME

Tom Anthony saw firsthand how competitive pressures shape admissions and financial aid policy. He worked in the admissions office at Colgate University for twenty-five years, the last seven as dean of admissions. In an interview, he spoke to me about the two biggest pressures facing college admissions offices: the need to maintain selectivity and the push for tuition revenue.

<u>Colleges are very concerned with maintaining their selectivity. Why?</u> It's the guidebook syndrome, and by that I mean not just the guidebooks, but the public desire for quick and easy measurements of quality. Colleges are under great pressure to have the kind of student profile that is going to move them up a couple of notches in the rankings. I think admissions people are universal in their dislike of the rankings, but they're hostage to them. You know what happens every fall when the <u>U.S. News & World Report</u> ratings come out. It's the best-selling issue, and the colleges know that they've got to be in there.

<u>Does the guidebook syndrome affect admissions decisions?</u> It causes admissions offices to put more emphasis on things like test scores, because they know that's one of the elements that has to look good in the guidebooks. Pitted against that is the pressure to enroll more students from disadvantaged backgrounds who may not have competitive scores, or students with special talents or connections. They really have to limit the number of places in the class given to students with lower scores.

<u>And some of those might be athletes, legacies, and disadvantaged students?</u> Yes. And if you ever let that percentage creep toward half the class, you begin to have a problem. Using medians instead of means will cover that, as long as you keep those kids to slightly less than half of the class. A lot of pressure there. One thing that helps is that many of the high schools are deciding not to rank students. The percentage in the top 20 percent or top 10 percent of the high school class used to be a big credential, but it's losing its power now.

(continues)

won something, they're more likely to enroll. Let's suppose, for the sake of argument, that all four do decide to go to Expensive U—bragging to their friends that they won a merit scholarship. The college is the real winner, having snagged four students who can pay the balance of the $30,000 per year total bill. Even with the $5,000 discount, the college will still rake in up to $100,000 in tuition revenue for every year that they're enrolled.

If Lucy is a stellar applicant or member of an underrepresented minority group, Expensive U might be willing to swallow hard and cough up the aid. But

Does that make the SAT even more important? Yes, it may. And there are other pressures. You need a national student body, and international students, and all these other kinds of special groups. You just can't satisfy everybody. As my former boss used to say, "A successful admissions year is when everybody is just a little bit unhappy."

Tell me about how colleges use admissions to bring in tuition dollars. One of the things they do is buy wealthy kids. Let's say a college admits a student who needs $20,000—they're going to have to pay him that amount to come. But if they can fill that bed with someone who needs only $10,000, they've made money on the deal.

Because he's bringing his tuition dollars? Right. And if you can admit somebody who can pay most or all of the bill, it's a good investment on your part...

More of the wealthy students are choosing public universities. What's driving that? My impression is that these are not the students at the very top of the academic heap—they're good students, but not necessarily the best. Let's assume the parents look around and see that it costs $10,000 to go to a state college. So they say to their kids, "I don't really think there's any difference between the state school and a private college. Why don't you go to the state school, and I'll buy you a car?"

How do the private colleges fight that mentality? They have to be competitive in terms of money by giving discounts. And at many private colleges, the discount rate is getting very high. I've heard of places where the discount rate is over 50 percent, and it's not uncommon to be at 35 or 40 percent.

Is that sustainable? You're okay at that rate but it's difficult to sustain. Let's say you had a drop in enrollment due to a decline in population or a major new expense that emerges on campus. That would be tough. The problem at some private schools is that they're already aiding such a high percentage of their students—80 to 90 percent. There's no upside advantage—you're running out of students.

It seems as if colleges aren't keen on talking about their discount rate. No, they aren't. Because if anybody thinks about it, they realize, "Hey, I'm Mr. High Income and I'm paying for financial aid for some kid who isn't even mine." Yet almost every high cost college in the country sets aside a portion of its tuition income for financial aid.

if she is an average applicant, one of two things will happen: either she'll be admitted without enough aid to enroll without piling up huge debts, or she'll be denied admission. In today's competitive admissions climate, it is more and more likely that the latter will happen. Reason? Colleges know that if they admit an applicant without the necessary aid, that student is unlikely to enroll. That's a wasted acceptance letter that will drive up the university's admittance rate and lower its selectivity. The savvy thing to do is to deny her admission, because the university can save its money and control its acceptance rate.

The question of whether particular colleges consider need in their admission decisions, and deny admission to some needy students, is often murky. Private colleges face clear incentives to do so, especially when filling the final few spaces on the acceptance list. Yet the moral taboo against denying needy students is strong, and the National Association for College Admission Counseling frowns on the practice. At colleges that do consider need in borderline admission decisions, a public declaration that they do so can lead families to erroneously conclude that only wealthy students will be admitted. Some colleges skirt the issue, a few are less than candid, and most colleges are being honest (for the most part) if they say they don't consider need.

Many parents are rightfully concerned about harming their son or daughter's chances for admission by applying for aid. In the vast majority of cases, an aid application is the right move. For families with significant need, there is little choice. Even if you don't qualify, there is usually no harm in communicating the expectation of receiving aid. In addition, some non-need awards require filing of a need-based application. But the picture gets fuzzy for upper-middle- and high-income families where the student is a borderline applicant at a selective private college. "If you feel that there is a strong likelihood that you will not get any aid, then my recommendation is that you not apply for aid—simply because if your child is on the bubble for admission, that could have an impact," says Don Dietrich, a former dean of admissions at Amherst and Trinity Colleges, who is now a college counselor. Dietrich notes that "almost no candidates who get in off the waitlist are financial aid candidates."

Once upon a time, there was a fire wall between admissions and financial aid at most colleges. Admissions brought in the students; financial aid determined how much aid they got. Today, financial aid is a tool of the admissions office, and aid policies at each college are shaped largely by its place in the prestige pecking order.

## THE NITTY-GRITTY ON NEED-BASED AID POLICIES

Financial aid was never the easiest topic to understand, but today's competitive climate has added new layers of complexity. Competitive pressures have pushed colleges in different directions, and confusion reigns in the public mind about the jumble of terms used to describe aid policies. To help sort it out, the rest of this chapter takes a closer look at what the buzz words mean and how the policies work. To assist the comparison shopper, I have framed the issues with questions that savvy parents might ask an admissions or aid officer. For a snapshot of the policies at colleges in this book, consult the college listings in Part II.

*Is the admission process need-blind?* Of the 360 colleges in this book, 312 say they're need-blind. If need-blind status is of particular concern, be sure to flesh out the issue with an admissions officer (or suggest that your student do so) on a campus visit. At those colleges which advertise need-blind status, an inquiry about whether the policy holds on the waitlist is a good follow-up. Be aware that many colleges don't include foreign students or other special categories while claiming to be need-blind. The list of colleges that publicly admit to considering need for a portion of their admission decisions is growing and includes highly selective institutions such as Brown University, Bryn Mawr College, Carleton College, Johns Hopkins University, Smith College, and Washington University.

*...If not, for what portion of admission decisions is financial need considered?* Sometimes, colleges will specify a percentage.

*Does the college meet demonstrated full need?* The second part of the need-based equation is no less important than the first. The number of colleges that are still need-blind in admissions AND meet full need is dwindling fast. They're listed on page 114. Many more colleges are need-blind in admissions but don't meet full need. Instead, they leave a gap between the total aid package and the total need. This practice—called "gapping" or "admit/deny"—is common across a broad spectrum of public and private institutions.

*...If not, what proportion of accepted applicants with need receive a package that meets it fully?* Some colleges meet the full need of a percentage of accepted applicants and gap the rest; others have a standard percentage of need that they usually meet. Still others offer no aid at all to some admitted students and/or have a financial aid waiting list. In every case, stronger applicants are more likely to get the best deal.

*Does this college use federal or institutional methodology?* Most public universities and less selective private ones use the federal formula, while highly selective private institutions generally add the CSS PROFILE or their own form to create institutional methodology. A college that meets full need under federal methodology will probably offer a better package than one that meets full need under its own methodology. For schools in the latter category, try to find out their major points of difference with the federal formula and/or with the institutional methodologies of other colleges. Traditionally, information of this sort has not been widely circulated, but more colleges are now competing on the basis of how they calculate need.

*Does the college use preferential packaging?* The overwhelming majority of colleges use this practice to benefit the top students in an applicant pool. A typical aid package includes a mix of three elements: grants that you don't pay back, loans that you do pay back, and a work study job that will yield wages to help pay the bill. Preferential packaging, also called differential packaging,

# INSIDE THE NEW FINANCIAL AID GAME

Most people in higher education mourn the decline of need-based aid. But Peter Van Buskirk, Dean of Admissions at Franklin and Marshall College, makes the case that the trend toward "resource-aware" admissions and the rise of merit scholarships may actually be good for both colleges and applicants. He spoke to me about the way aid works at a highly selective private college:

How do you use financial aid to help bring in the class? In higher education circles, colleges now talk about leveraging enrollment with financial aid. That aid can be either merit-based or need-based.

What does that mean? Leveraging means using available financial resources strategically to influence enrollment. Let's suppose that we're dealing with a well-known college or university with a very strong program in business. They're just swamped with applications. That school is much more likely to give a generous financial aid package—need-based or merit-based—to a student at the top of the applicant group than to a student in the middle or at the bottom. That's leveraging— using money to go after the top kids and assuming that those who are good but not great, if they want you badly enough, will figure out a way to make it happen. Conversely, let's suppose that the same university has a classics program it really wants to push, and not many prospective classicists apply. It might target the classics students with richer financial aid awards, even if they have more modest credentials.

So the institution can target aid to areas that need to be shored up. Absolutely. The notion of need-based aid grew out of the desire to create opportunities for students who were at a disadvantage. Initially, the federal and state governments led the way with a lot of money for need-based aid. Approximately 75 percent of financial aid dollars came from the government. But over the years, the government has backed out and now only about 20 percent of the money that goes to need-based aid at colleges like Franklin and Marshall comes from the government. That's put the onus on private colleges in particular to come up with more aid. After twenty years of playing the game, private colleges now are saying, "Hey, wait a minute. If this is our money, why don't we use it the way we want to instead of the way somebody tells us we should?" A particular college can't be obligated to provide an opportunity for every person who wants an education. It must operate within the constraints of its own mission and resources.

And so you are rewarding merit. Absolutely. Let's consider a student in the middle of the class at a strong high school. He is of good character and can definitely do the work. But this student also experienced some ups and downs academically. Let's say

(continues)

he's a contributor but not a leader, and made a good impression during the interview. In discussing his admission, there are people saying, "This is a really neat kid. We get diversity because he comes from a different part of the country and he's coming from a really strong school, etc., etc. So what if his grades aren't the best?"

But then somebody else says, "Whoa, it looks like this kid is probably going to require a lot of financial aid." At this point, a check of his financial aid status reveals a documented need of $22,000.

<u>Is that going to give you pause?</u> A lot of admission committees will consider this candidate carefully, especially if there are others with similar credentials who require no assistance. The question becomes, "Do I really want to give the kid who is in the middle of the class a scholarship two or three times greater than the amount we could give the student who is number one in the class?" That's the kind of logic that a lot of colleges are using. At Franklin and Marshall, we've realized that a merit scholarship program gives us a chance to leverage the student who has high ability but may come from a family situation where there is no need. We would rather go after that candidate than one who is on the "bubble" and has high need.

<u>So what does that mean in practical terms?</u> At Franklin and Marshall, it means that we have a degree of resource awareness in making admission decisions and that we are using our aid money strategically to bring in the best class we can. We are guided by a set of values that begins with the fact that we want the best academic class possible. We have also given priority to getting the most diverse class possible. Many people will say that if you're not need-blind, you're hurting the kid who comes from a disadvantaged background. I would argue that resource aware admissions allows an institution to exercise greater choice in supporting its values.

<u>How so?</u> If you're practicing need-blind admission in all cases, you're not necessarily doing anything strategic for the young person who needs help. If you're resource aware, you can identify the students who need help and make sure you direct necessary resources in their direction.

<u>So if you're need-blind, that doesn't mean that you're meeting the need.</u> Right...

<u>And so you'd rather be need-sensitive on the front end and take care of everybody you admit?</u> I'd rather take care of everybody I admit and I'd rather take care of the people who are most compelling to me, given the values of the institution. What's interesting is that since Franklin and Marshall has become resource aware, our multicultural profile has increased. It hasn't edged forward—it has jumped. Our overall academic profile has reached new heights as well.

<u>Why do you think that is?</u> Because we've been able to target our resources to the best students.

refers to colleges that sweeten need-based aid awards by substituting grants for loans to create a better package. In the arcane world of aid accounting, a grant and a loan meet the same need. Two aid packages can thus both meet full need, even if one is chock-full of loans and the other includes mainly grants.

*Is there a standard expectation for loans and work study?* Taken together, loans and work study are called "self-help." Some colleges have a standard yearly self-help expectation that they build into most or all of their aid packages. A related question: *What is the expectation for summer earnings?*

*What is the average indebtedness of aid recipients when they graduate?* This average is a good indication of whether your child can expect a mountain of debt along with a degree. The figures for the colleges in this book are listed in the college profiles. Another good question: *Are parent loans or unsubsidized loans used to meet need?* The more supplemental loans that families at a particular college are forced to take out, the less likely that their aid packages include generous amounts of grant money.

In addition to those listed above, I can't resist mentioning one commonly asked question that is often misleading: *What percentage of your students receive aid?* The answer is more a function of the sort of students who enroll than the ability of the college to provide aid. One of the harsh truths of admission from the college perspective is that applicants from wealthier families tend to apply to more selective schools. Some of the lowest percentages of students on aid are at Ivy League schools—the colleges with the most need-based money. A big reason why the prestige game has such a desperate edge is that the price of losing includes the wealthy applicants whose tuition pays the bills.

## MERIT SCHOLARSHIPS AND NON–NEED-BASED AWARDS

With all the murky terminology that surrounds need-based aid and merit-within-need, merit scholarships and other non-need awards are relatively straightforward. The college offers money in hopes of enticing students to enroll, usually bestowing it with as much fanfare as possible. Some merit scholarships—the more lucrative ones—are genuinely competitive, with many applicants for few awards. But many private colleges now give smaller "merit" awards to at least half their applicants, and public universities are also joining the party. Statewide merit scholarship programs, immensely popular with voters, are also on the rise. The most famous is Georgia's HOPE Scholarship program, the original model for the federal version. For students who have earned a 3.0 in high school, it provides full tuition at in-state public universities or about $3,000 toward tuition at in-state private colleges.

Programs such as Georgia's HOPE have put even more intense pressure on private colleges to throw merit money at any applicant with a pulse. In a recent survey of 232 colleges, more than half gave need-based or non-need grants to 75 percent of their students, and at three of these colleges, not a single freshman paid the full sticker price. As a college counselor at a private school, I saw many instances where students at the absolute bottom of the class—C's and D's and middling SAT scores—received "merit" awards. Some colleges couldn't bring themselves to describe these awards as academic scholarships; community service was a common rationale even if the student had no particularly significant involvement. But such awards do make the recipients feel good, and money is money.

Merit scholarships can play an important role in making college affordable. The following questions should be considered.

*Do you offer merit scholarships?* The combination of competitive pressures and the budget squeeze have dramatically increased the number of colleges that do so. The list of about 50 in this book that don't is in Part II. Most of the holdouts are among the nation's most selective colleges, which remain committed to the old system of need-blind admissions and meeting full need (though keep in mind that virtually all use preferential packaging to reward merit within need).

*Are there awards based on other factors?* Athletic scholarships generally top the list, but colleges also offer non-need awards based on leadership, service, artistic talent, minority status, intended major, place of birth, and a range of other characteristics.

*What percentage of freshmen get non–need-based awards?* While lots of schools advertise big-ticket scholarships, the bottom line for most students is the number of awards made annually. This percentage is the best indicator of the typical applicant's likelihood of getting a tuition discount.

---

### PARENT SOUP Q&A

Q: How do the SAT scores correspond to ACT scores? I grew up in SAT country and can't quite grasp this ACT business!!

A: This question is crucial to the merit scholarship hopes of many applicants. The SAT (now divided into SAT I and II) is more prevalent on the coasts. The SAT I includes the basic verbal and math. SAT IIs are hour-long subject tests that were once called Achievement Tests. The SAT scale is 200 (lowest) to 800 (highest) for verbal and math. The ACT is more common in the country's midsection and features English, Math, Reading, and Science. The ACT scale is 1 to 36. Most colleges will accept either the SAT I or ACT for admission, though the highly selective colleges favor the SAT (even if they don't say so). A conversion chart published by the College Board (maker of the SAT) reveals the following relationship between ACT and SAT I (combined verbal and math) scores:

| ACT | | SAT |
|-----|---|------|
| 36 | = | 1600 |
| 33 | = | 1470 |
| 30 | = | 1340 |
| 27 | = | 1220 |
| 24 | = | 1110 |
| 21 | = | 990 |
| 18 | = | 870 |
| 15 | = | 740 |

*Is there an early deadline for merit scholarships?* Deadlines for top merit awards come as early as October. Some colleges merely require that a student apply for admission; others ask for a special scholarship application. See the Early Bird Scholarship Deadlines list at the beginning of Part II.

## THE NATIONAL MERIT PROGRAM

Among the 1 to 2 percent of the total aid pie that consists of scholarships not offered by colleges or the government, the most famous is the National Merit Scholarship Program. For some honorees, the program means big money. For others, it offers nice recognition or a token award.

The gateway to the National Merit Program is the College Board's Preliminary SAT (PSAT), which is administered to eleventh graders in October. Though tenth graders sometimes take the PSAT for practice, their scores don't count in the scholarship programs. In the National Merit Program, each PSAT test-taker is assigned a Selection Index that is the sum of the scores on the test's three parts: verbal, writing skills, and math. On that basis alone, approximately 15,000 Semifinalists are chosen, based on a state-by-state quota. That's good news if you're from a state like Mississippi, where scores tend to be low, and bad news if you hail from a brainy place like Massachusetts. For students who score high but don't make the Semifinalist cut-off, there is a Commended Student designation that comes with a certificate.

After a review of their academic record, approximately 90 percent of the Semifinalists advance to the finalist stage and are eligible for scholarships. Of the 14,000 Finalists, approximately 2,400 of the highest scorers get $2,000 directly from National Merit. An additional 1,200 students get scholarships if they happen to have a link to one of the private corporations that sponsors the awards (such as a mom or dad who works there). The major dollars usually come when a student attends one of the colleges that sponsor National Merit awards. Some of these offer only a token award of $2,000 or less, but many lavish huge awards on these students as an incentive to enroll. (Often, students must inform National Merit that a participating college is their first choice in late winter or early spring of twelfth grade.) The nation's most selective colleges generally don't fund National Merit Scholars, so nearly half of

---

### IT'S A MERIT SCHOLARSHIP (SORT OF)

One director of admissions who asked not to be identified describes a new scholarship aimed at out-of-state students, most of whom come from affluent families. "They have a country club mentality and they need their students to receive a scholarship," she says. Does it reward merit? To a degree, but the main purpose is to encourage more families to sign on the dotted line. "It's got a name and it's something the parents can talk about." The amount is $2,000— "to give them four figures for every semester."

the Finalists come away with only recognition. A list of the colleges that give awards to National Merit Finalists appears in Part II.

The National Merit folks sponsor a second scholarship program, the National Achievement Scholarship Program for Outstanding Negro Students, which operates with a similar selection process. Also connected to the PSAT is the National Hispanic Scholar Recognition Program, which can qualify students for scholarships from the colleges.

## LETTING IT SINK IN

Any parent who gets a handle on even a fraction of the information in this chapter deserves an A for effort. The rest will become clear as the college search unfolds. For a look at the policies of each college, consult the profiles and lists in Part II of this book. College Web sites and brochures are also fertile sources of information. With public scrutiny at an all-time high, there has been a notable increase in candor from the colleges about their policies. Other sources that are independent of the colleges can provide a reality check—the best of these are listed in chapter 6. A college visit is a good time to reach clarity with admissions or financial aid staff about unresolved issues. Many colleges offer group information sessions where students and parents can ask questions of admissions officers. If the student has a personal interview with the admissions office, the parent may want to take that time to visit the financial aid office. If no other opportunities offer, lingering questions can always be answered by phone.

Understanding the policy differences that divide today's aid offices is at least half the battle. The purpose of chapter 3 is to help you and your child win the war by converting this knowledge into a well-conceived college application strategy.

# 3.

# THE COLLEGE APPLICATION PORTFOLIO

Applying to college is like managing investments. There are safe bets and long shots. Some colleges get tens of thousands of applicants and accept a tiny fraction; others enroll virtually anyone who sends a check. Some advertise a sticker price of over $30,000 for one year; others charge as little as $20,000 for four years. The most expensive schools dangle huge amounts of financial aid—need-based, merit-based, middle-class discounts, awards for multicultural students, community service,—name your category and there's a scholarship. But will your son or daughter actually get one? And if so how much? Nobody can say for sure.

That's why every student needs an application portfolio, a carefully chosen mix of colleges that maximizes aid and admission possibilities at colleges in various categories. Traditionally, students and their guidance counselors have thought mainly in terms of selectivity when making application choices. But today's financial aid scene makes it imperative for many families to construct an application portfolio with affordability as a determining factor. By applying to schools with aid programs that play to their strengths, students can maximize their chances of getting a degree without a mountain of debt.

That doesn't mean that finances should dictate the choice of a particular college. The paramount objective of the college search must always be to find a place that meets the student's academic and personal needs. Students should be encouraged to explore the rich variety of institutions in the United States—there are more than 2,200 of them at last count—and to go on a journey of self-exploration as they try to find the ones that make the best match. But with so many superb institutions across the spectrum of price and aid categories, it is often possible to find excellent options that are also easy on the pocketbook. For many students, a necessary step is to get beyond the notion that only the most prestigious (and most expensive) colleges are worthy of consideration. There are many fine schools that are not household names but deliver the same quality of education—and usually at a much lower sticker price than the designer label schools. Such colleges may also be more likely to bestow a merit scholarship or give preferential need-based packages to a good student who may not be an academic superstar.

For parents, the first step in creating an application portfolio is to think hard about how much the family can afford. Do it early—the fall of eleventh grade is a good time—before your child has a chance to fall in love with a school that may be out of your price range. Ten or twenty years ago, parents could reasonably tell a child to pick any college no matter what the cost and no matter how much aid was forthcoming. But with the sticker price at the most expensive schools soon to eclipse $150,000 for four years, it takes a hefty bank account to choke out those words without getting a lump in your throat. Is a Princeton degree really worth $100,000 more than one from Ohio State? Or the University of Arizona? Or the University of Georgia's Honors Program? You don't need a definitive answer now. Instead, try to arrive at a rough idea of how much you can afford and then have a talk with your student about his or her aspirations. If the child knows your financial bottom line from the beginning, there is much less chance for heartache at the end.

Keep in mind that setting tentative financial parameters is not the same thing as declaring particular colleges off-limits. Suppose the family can afford about $10,000 per year. That doesn't mean your child should consider only colleges with a sticker price below that amount. Rather, it means that after all the aid offers come in, he or she must choose one near that figure or below. If a student applies to three colleges—one that costs $20,000, another at $15,000, and a third that costs $10,000—the college with the $20,000 sticker price may turn out to be the cheapest. The more expensive colleges are often the ones that offer the most aid.

The time to make the choice is at the end of the process when all of the aid offers are on the table. I'm a firm believer that students should make the final decision on where to attend, but just as convinced that parents have the right to set parameters when it comes to cost. The purpose of a good application portfolio is to guarantee a variety of appealing alternatives. Parents should keep in mind that spending a few thousand dollars may be a small price to pay if there is a more

**PARENT SOUP Q&A**

Q: Is it possible to apply to too many colleges?

A: Absolutely. I recommend eight as a maximum. That's enough to cover all the bases without spreading yourself too thin. Applicants who apply to ten or more colleges can't possibly devote adequate attention to each one. They generally end up overwhelmed, confused, and stressed out.

expensive college that is a student's first choice; students should understand that a differential of tens of thousands may mean that the low cost option is the best choice. But the final decision is a topic for chapter 4. The first order of business is to learn the portolio strategy for applying.

## THE FINANCIAL AID CATEGORIES

Colleges like to confuse the issue by talking about aid as if it were a heart-felt gift. (Imagine if General Motors or Ford carried on the same way about their factory rebates.) Edu-babble aside, scholarship policies are dictated by each college's enrollment management strategy. Within the context of schools that are appropriate for the student's needs, the goal is to make a match between the policies of the college and the strengths and/or needs of the applicant. After some preliminary thinking about how much your family can afford, the next step is to learn about the four financial aid categories that cut across the entire spectrum of higher education. By understanding a college's place in the pecking order, you'll go a long way toward figuring out its aid policies.

### 1. Colleges That Emphasize Need-Based Aid

The nucleus of this group are the few dozen schools rich enough to continue the need-based aid system of a generation ago. You'll probably feel queasy when you see the sticker price, but millions of dollars in aid assure that many people don't pay the whole bill. Top students with major financial need should look seriously at colleges like these. Such schools are likely to offer excellent aid packages and won't discriminate (much) against needy students in the admissions process. High income families are the big losers—their full-pay tuition dollars help subsidize the needy ones.

### 2. Colleges That Emphasize Merit Scholarships

This group is larger and includes colleges that are struggling to compete with Group 1. Merit scholarships are their best weapon for enticing students who would otherwise climb higher on the prestige ladder. Students with good grades (A's and B's) and good scores (roughly 1200 to 1600 on the SAT I) can haul in major merit money. Less stellar students can also expect a discount, so long as their families can cough up the rest.

### 3. Colleges with Low Sticker Prices

Most of the nation's public colleges and universities are here. They dispense the same proportion of Uncle Sam's need-based aid as colleges in Groups 1 and 2 but offer relatively little of their own. These institutions also have less merit money than those in Group 2, but to snag the top students, they can be just as lavish in their offers. Because the low price is guaranteed, Group 3 schools are always the safest bets for low income students. High-achieving bargain hunters—especially if they have National Merit status—can make out like bandits.

## 4. Colleges with Scholarships for Athletic Ability and Other Special Talents

This is the only category that cuts across the other three. The big money is in athletics, where schools that compete in NCAA Division I or II offer lucrative awards. Most such places are middle-sized or large universities. With a few exceptions, small colleges rarely offer scholarships based solely on athletic achievement, though they often sweeten the pot with better need-based packages, or with a "leadership" or "community service" award to athletes who are particularly hot prospects. The other primary special talent category is the arts, most notably music. Depending on the college, miscellaneous scholarships can be found for anything from chess to community service.

---

### AND YOU THOUGHT HARVARD IS SELECTIVE...

❦

In addition to merit scholarships from the colleges, many students apply for national awards sponsored by private corporations. Nothing should discourage outstanding candidates, but don't start counting the money until the award letter arrives in the mailbox. Here are the odds of winning scholarships through a few of the nation's best known programs compared to those for admission to Harvard:

| | Applicants | Awards | Percent who win (or get in) |
|---|---|---|---|
| Coca-Cola Scholars Program | 129,000 | 150 | 0.1 |
| Ron Brown Scholar Program | 4,500 | 20 | 0.4 |
| Toyota Community Scholars | 10,000 | 100 | 1.0 |
| Tandy Technology Scholars | 8,000 | 100 | 1.3 |
| Intel Science Talent Search (formerly Westinghouse) | 1,600 | 40 | 2.5 |
| Discover Card Tribute Awards | 11,000 | 479 | 4.3 |
| Harvard University | 16,800 | 2,100 | 12 |

---

# THE "GETTING IN" CATEGORIES

This is the part that turns otherwise confident eighteen-year-olds into scared rabbits. As more of the best and brightest aim for elite colleges, competition to get in has gone from intense to outrageous—and has sent shock waves through the student lounges and school cafeterias of America. The good news is that 90 percent of the nation's 2,200 four-year colleges are hungry for smart students—or any students—as shown by the rise of discounting. But that's small consolation to the thousands who've slogged through mountains of homework to make the grade at Duke or Princeton. I'm not suggesting that these students abandon their dreams, but I do urge everyone in this category to hedge their bets by applying to half a dozen colleges, including at least one where the odds of success are excellent. The soundest strategy is to choose at least two schools from each of these categories:

Dream schools       Where admission is a long shot
Possible schools     Where the odds are good
Likely schools       Where admission is (nearly) certain

Think of them as rungs in a ladder. If the top one is missing, applicants will never know how high they could have climbed. If the bottom rung is gone, they risk falling flat on their faces.

Since each applicant has a unique mix of qualifications, it is a ticklish business to decide which colleges fit into each of the categories. If you're lucky enough to have a college counselor at school, ask for a meeting to discuss your selections. The good ones will have records of how students with similar credentials fared at those same colleges in years past. Colleges themselves publish admissions profiles that offer data on the acceptance rate, SAT scores, and class rank of those accepted, but be aware that most colleges tinker with these numbers to make themselves appear more selective. (I'm not suggesting that they're dishonest about it, exactly, but sometimes their creative accounting gets the best of them.) At colleges with a high acceptance rate—say, 75 percent—students who match the profile are almost assured admission.

At the opposite end of the spectrum, some highly selective colleges actually downplay the difficulty of admission to avoid scaring away potential applicants. The averages at these colleges are often misleading because various "special admits," such as athletes and children of alumni, will account for most of those who get in with scores and grades below the averages. When a college's accep-

---

## ADVICE ON ATHLETIC SCHOLARSHIPS

The first move for the college-bound athlete is to visit the NCAA's Web page at www.ncaa.org. The site provides a rundown on the rules as well as lists of the colleges that have teams in each sport and division. Students who want to play in Division I or II must be certified by the NCAA's Clearinghouse, where the basic requirements are completion of 13 core courses with a 2.5 average and an 820 on the SAT or a sum of 68 across the ACT's four subscores. (Those with a lower GPA can qualify with higher scores.) To avoid any chance of getting caught in the NCAA's bureaucratic net, begin the certification process in the fall of twelfth grade. Your high school guidance counselor will have the form you need.

The most important task for college-bound athletes is to get the attention of coaches. Summer camps or community leagues can boost exposure and promote relationships with coaches who have college contacts. When college visits are on the horizon, students should write a letter to the college coaches on their list and include a résumé of their awards or competitions. They should then ask the high school or community league coach to draft a cover note or phone the college coaches to make contact and tell them that the letter is on its way. Some athletes also make a videotape, which may include drills and game highlights. On the college tour, a meeting with the coach or a representative should take place in addition to any interviews in the admissions office. Even at colleges with no athletic scholarships, coaches can have a major influence on who gets in.

tance rate is low—say, 25 percent—the "typical" applicant will need to present scores and grades significantly above the averages to get in.

While I'm on the subject of highly selective admissions, a note of caution. Many parents are gung ho for Prestige U—a little too gung ho. If too many thoughts creep in about "having a Yalie in the family," that's a sign that the student's interests are being subsumed beneath the family's greater glory. Take a step back and listen to your son or daughter. Make sure that you are supporting your child's dreams rather than vice versa.

---

**HOW COLLEGES PLAY WITH NUMBERS**

❦

Suppose Second Choice U says that it "chooses a class of 2,000 from a pool of 10,000 applicants." What's the acceptance rate? If you said 20 percent...you're wrong! This equation, commonly repeated in college brochures, leaves out the fact that less than half of those admitted at most colleges actually enroll. In truth, Second Choice probably accepts 6,000, or 60 percent, approximately one-third of whom enroll to make the class of 2,000.

---

# BUILDING YOUR PORTFOLIO

Now comes the hard part: putting together a list of colleges with varying degrees of selectivity that maximizes your chance for aid. Even with the big picture in your head, naming names can be a white-knuckle experience. Does my daughter really have a shot at Stanford? Is Wake Forest likely to come through with a merit scholarship? Is the University of Michigan a safe option? Small wonder that many families turn to high-priced consultants for the answers—and pay them thousands of dollars for a little peace of mind.

The purpose of this book is to save you all that money. In the pages that follow, I offer eight case studies that illustrate how to build a college application portfolio for students with various credentials and goals. Each of the students described below has chosen a mix of colleges from across the aid categories that I have outlined in this chapter. Though the students are fictitious, the colleges are real, and the scenarios describe judgments that actual applicants might make after reading this book (with a little help from Mom and Dad).

Once you've read these sample portfolios, move on to the Part II for the inside information on the colleges you'll need to begin building your own.

# MICHAEL: DEALING WITH DIVORCE

Classmates would not be surprised to see Michael emerge from a phone booth with a big red "S" on his chest. In no particular order, Michael is a straight A student, homecoming king, senior class president, and an all-state tennis player. His combined SAT score is 1520. Michael's college prospects look rosy—except for one major problem. His parents divorced six years ago, and the agreement specified that his mom would pay for college. (Dad paid Michael's hefty private school tuition bills.) Though Michael and his mom live in a beautiful house, her income is only $42,000 per year. Dad is a multimillionaire but firmly maintains that he has done his share for Michael's education.

| Application Portfolio | Financial Aid Category |
| --- | --- |
| Princeton University (NJ) | Need-Based |
| Stanford University (CA) | Need-Based |
| Emory University (GA) | Merit Scholarship and Need-Based |
| Johns Hopkins University (MD) | Merit Scholarship and Need-Based |
| University of Chicago (IL) | Merit Scholarship and Need-Based |
| Washington University (MO) | Merit Scholarship and Need-Based |
| University of Virginia Echols Scholars | Merit Scholarship and Low Sticker Price |
| University of Massachusetts Honors Program | Merit Scholarship and Low Sticker Price |

## Comments

Michael is determined to go to an elite college. He hopes to get substantial need-based aid from one or more of them, but eligibility is doubtful because of his father's wealth and the fact that highly selective colleges may factor in his mother's equity in their home. His mom plans to write letters to the aid offices pleading their case. Her lifestyle has already suffered a severe blow from the divorce and she can't afford huge tuition bills. At Princeton and Stanford, need-based aid is the goal, and the family is hoping for help from recent changes in their policies for aid to middle-income families (see chapter 4). Though Stanford offers athletic scholarships, Michael is realistic enough to know that he isn't the next John McEnroe. He will also make a bid for three of the most prestigious merit scholarships in higher education: the Beneficial-Hodson at Johns Hopkins, the Emory Schol-

---

**PARENT SOUP Q&A**

Q: When looking at a school such as Duke or Georgetown, is it better to take the hardest courses and get lower grades or to take a few easy courses to help increase your GPA?

A: Nine times our of ten, the hardest courses are best. Selective private colleges look less at students' overall GPA than the grades they get in each of the courses they take. A B in an advanced course beats an A in an easy one, although colleges as selective as Duke or Georgetown generally want both top grades and the most challenging courses.

arships program, and the College Honor Scholarship at the University of Chicago. Washington University, a private institution with prestige but not quite so selective, is likely to offer at least some merit money. Michael has also set his sights on the University of Virginia and its honors program. The sticker price is about half that of private institutions and he has secured his school's nomination for the prestigious Jefferson Scholarship. If all else fails, Michael has decided that he could be happy at nearby University of Massachusetts at Amherst, where he has several friends enrolled in the honors program.

## JUDY: LOOKING FOR MERIT MONEY

Judy calls to mind the Peanuts comic strip where Lucy hangs out a sign that says, "Psychiatry: Five Cents." Having psychoanalyzed her friends and family for years, she plans to go to medical school and then open a private practice. Judy's parents, with a combined income of $95,000, have told her that they are willing to contribute a total of $50,000 to her educa-

### THE TROUBLE WITH THE RANKINGS

When it comes to picking colleges, the most widely used resource is the annual rankings guide published by U.S. News & World Report. Since the first issue burst onto the college scene in 1983, college officials have reacted in horror as families gobble it up. The original version consisted solely of a poll of university presidents. In response to ongoing criticism, U.S. News has added layer upon layer of complexity to its calculations. College administrators continue to disdain the rankings—unless their college happens to place highly, in which case they hustle out a new brochure trumpeting the results. Presidents, provosts, and deans of admission are asked to rate other institutions, which often puts them in the position of judging schools that they know little or nothing about. In a bizarre twist, administrators are now targeted by public relations campaigns from competing institutions hoping to curry favor.

The rankings frenzy would be comical if it weren't such a high stakes game. A decline can send alumni into an uproar, while an advance can signal that a college is "on the move." (Never mind that meaningless statistical blips are often responsible for the moves.) So the colleges form committees and conduct studies to find out what determines the rankings and how they can package their numbers to look better. A tried and true strategy is to omit selected groups from the SAT profile: international students, minorities, alumni children, etc. Upon learning that U.S. News gives weight to small classes, one university declared that its laboratory sections, formerly considered components of larger classes, were in fact separate classes. The cat-and-mouse game continues, and the colleges recently acquired a new ally in the person of the former managing editor of the rankings issue, who left the magazine to become a consultant to colleges.

tion. With one eye on medical school, Judy has decided to save the $50,000 and go for the biggest merit scholarship she can find. Judy has a 3.8 grade-point average, and her combined SAT I score of 1320 is excellent but short of the level that would guarantee a lucrative award. The family is also applying for need-based aid, and her parents are urging her to consider Penn State's superb honors program.

# PUBLIC UNIVERSITY HONORS PROGRAMS

For some of the best deals in higher education today, look no further than your local state university. With the sky-high price of private education, more and more of the nation's best students are flocking to public university honors programs. The trend has been particularly strong among upper-middle-class families who don't qualify for need-based aid at front-rank private colleges.

There are strong honors programs at virtually every state university in this book. Almost without exception, they offer small classes with top faculty and enhanced access to the best that the university has to offer. In states like Georgia and Florida, the whole package is virtually free because of state-sponsored merit scholarships. Though most public honors programs attract mainly state residents, a few have gained national prominence. At the pinnacle of public university honors prestige are the University of North Carolina, the University of Virginia, the University of Texas, and the University of Michigan. They share Ivy League–quality applicants but illustrate varied approaches to honors education.

At Virginia and North Carolina , the honors programs are akin to VIP programs. Students in UVA's Echols program are given first crack at course selection, they are freed from distribution requirements, and funneled directly into advanced courses. UNC honors includes special seminars and a senior thesis. Both offer enriched opportunities for honors students and self-consciously avoid separating students from their classmates outside the program.

The renowned Plan II program at the University of Texas is much more like a college within a college, with separate classes, a full range of extracurricular activities, and a focus on the liberal arts that sets it apart from the mainstream of the university. At the University of Michigan, students in the honors program divide their time between honors and nonhonors courses in the first two years, then complete an upper level Honors Concentration (major). The program's lofty admissions standards are like those of the other three: average credentials include an SAT I score of 1410, a 32 on the ACT, and a 3.8 high school GPA.

With numbers like these, it won't be long before public university honors programs have an ivy league of their own.

| Application Portfolio | Financial Aid Category |
| --- | --- |
| Albright College (PA) | Merit Scholarship and Need-Based |
| Dickinson College (PA) | Merit Scholarship and Need-Based |
| Gettysburg College (PA) | Merit Scholarship and Need-Based |
| St. Lawrence University (NY) | Merit Scholarship and Need-Based |
| Muhlenberg College (PA) | Merit Scholarship and Need-Based |
| Penn State University (PA) Schreyer Honors College | Merit Scholarship and Low Sticker Price |

## Comments

Since Judy is unlikely to get a free ride at an elite college, she has concentrated on less selective ones that offer merit awards, and she showed insight by picking from a cluster of competing institutions. Gettysburg and Dickinson go head to head for many of the same students, and St. Lawrence and Muhlenberg are private colleges of a similar stripe. Dickinson is her first choice, and if it does not come through with the best offer, her parents will use other awards in an attempt to sweeten the deal. Albright, in central Pennsylvania, is the least selective of the group, and Judy is not likely to consider it without a full ride or something close. With a $95,000 income and Judy the only child in school, the family may qualify for a smattering of need-based aid but not enough to be significant in their eyes. As an in-stater, Judy is all-but guarenteed admission to Penn State, but its Schreyer Honors College honors program turns out to be more selective than any of the colleges on her list. To get in, Judy will need a killer essay.

# PETE: NO NEED, WEAK GRADES

Pete is a quiet young man, the kind whose conversations with his parents are usually limited to words like "fine" and "nothing" (as in "How are you?" and "What did you do today?"). Pete spends most of his free time wearing headphones or jamming with three other friends who have formed a band. He plays bass. Never particularly serious about school, he dazzles his teachers when piqued. If asked where he wants to attend college, he shrugs. Pete's family has already invested a huge sum in his private school education. Though they can afford more for college, his dad is reluctant to shell out big bucks to educate a boy with so little interest in school.

| Application Portfolio | Financial Aid Category |
| --- | --- |
| Denison University (OH) | Merit Scholarship/Tuition Discount |
| Ohio Wesleyan University (OH) | Merit Scholarship/Tuition Discount |
| Wittenberg University (OH) | Merit Scholarship/Tuition Discount |
| Miami University (OH) | Low Sticker Price |
| University of Cincinnati (OH) | Low Sticker Price |

## Comments

Despite his relatively weak academic record (B's and a few C's), Pete is a prime candidate for a merit scholarship or discount award. He is also lucky to live in

Ohio, a state with as many good colleges per capita as any in the nation. Private institutions such as Denison, Ohio Wesleyan, and Wittenberg are similar schools in close proximity, which compete on the basis of their SAT profiles. With Pete's excellent scores (760 verbal and 580 math), they might be willing to overlook his spotty record. Added incentive to cough up a merit award comes from a fourth competitor in the neighborhood: Miami University, a fine state university with a sticker price of approximately $12,000 for in-staters, less than half that of its private counterparts. Pete includes the University of Cincinnati as an additional low cost option.

## AMY: TRYING NOT TO BANKRUPT THE FAMILY

Amy wants to be the first person in her family to attend college. Her mother is a single parent who has worked long and hard as a secretary and part-time sales clerk to save a nest egg for college. Her combined income from two jobs is $19,000. Amy has been a model child all her life and in recent years has been the primary caregiver for her twelve-year-old brother. She has never excelled in school, but she is a hard worker and determined to get at least an associate's degree in a business-related field. She plans to explore a variety of four-year institutions but will consider the possibility of two years at a nearby community college to save money. Her combined SAT I score is 970 and she got a 21 on the ACT.

| Application Portfolio | Financial Aid Category |
|---|---|
| St. Louis University (MO) | Need-Based |
| University of Missouri/ Columbia (MO) | Need-Based and Low Sticker Price |
| Southeast Missouri State University (MO) | Need-Based and Low Sticker Price |
| St. Louis Community College (MO) | Need-Based and Low Sticker Price |

## Comments

Amy wants to stay in Missouri to be near her family. She has included one expensive private college (in hopes of getting need-based aid), one major state university (less expensive), one regional state school (cheaper still), and one community college (the bargain rack). With her less-than-stellar academic record and test scores, Amy is not a strong candidate for any aid but Uncle Sam's. She'll probably qualify for grant money from the Pell program and also receive some subsidized loans. Amy plans to work throughout her academic career—she might be required to do so as part of the Federal Work Study program. If finances at the four-year schools don't work out, she plans to enroll at nearby St. Louis Community College and live at home to save money. After two years, she can transfer to one of the four-year institutions and get her degree at a substantial savings. She is also considering the option of part-time attendance to cut the tuition bill and create more time for a job. The disadvantage of studying part-time is that the degree will take longer and her aid eligibility will go down.

# LISA: THE DILEMMA OF AN UPPER-MIDDLE-INCOME FAMILY

Whenever school administrators need a student representative to speak at a program or to schmooze dignitaries, Lisa inevitably gets the call. With the poise of a person twice her age, she is equally at home with adults and classmates. Voted "Best All-Around" by the senior class, she is a three-sport athlete and a fine student, with A's and B's in the school's most challenging courses. Her SAT I score is 1310, and she got a 29 on the ACT. Her parents are confident that she will find a good college but confused about their prospects for aid. College reps have assured them that money is available; friends warn them not to count on it. Her parents don't want to limit Lisa's choices but don't think they can afford the most expensive schools. The family's annual income is $82,000. In addition to her school shopping, Lisa is considering the Army ROTC program and its promise of big bucks for college.

| Application Portfolio | Financial Aid Category |
|---|---|
| Dartmouth College (NH) | Need-Based |
| Davidson College (NC) | Merit Scholarship and Need-Based |
| Furman University (SC) | Merit Scholarship and Need-Based |
| Rhodes College (TN) | Merit Scholarship and Need-Based |
| Trinity University (TX) | Merit Scholarship and Need-Based |
| University of Richmond (VA) | Merit Scholarship and Need-Based |
| University of South Carolina (SC) | Merit Scholarship and Low Sticker Price |

## Comments

Since Lisa has decided that she wants a private college, she will pursue a three-track strategy. She will seek need-based aid at her two most selective choices: Dartmouth College and Davidson College. (Merit money is also a possibility at the latter.) If she gets in, the family will probably qualify for need-based aid but still be expected to pay about $15,000 to $20,000 per year. Her second track consists of less choosy private alternatives: Trinity University (TX), Rhodes College, the University of Richmond, and Furman University. Though the family is hoping against hope for a large merit award from one of these schools, a more likely scenario is a scholarship in the $5,000 range. Though tempting, the ROTC option has one significant drawback—service in the reserves for eight years after graduation. In the absence of major awards from the private colleges, Lisa will also look hard at the University of South Carolina's well-known honors program, with a price tag of approximately $8,000 per year.

## STEVE: LOOKING AT STICKER PRICES

Steve is a quiet young man who works hard in school but has never excelled. His suburban high school includes many students on the fast track, and in retrospect his parents realize that he has probably taken a few too many honors courses. Though he has managed mainly B's, his confidence needs a boost. Steve's mother hopes that he will find a college that will offer enough challenge but also allow him to excel. Though Steve's interests range from politics to environmental studies, the family already has an eye on graduate school and doesn't want to break the bank. Since Steve won't be admitted to a highly selective college, there is limited incentive to fork over big bucks. The greatest passion in Steve's young life is sailing. Though he doesn't have a great deal of competitive experience, he is among the finest sailors in his age group at the yacht club and would like to join a college team (preferably at a small- or medium-sized institution rather than a mega-university). With a GPA just under 3.0, Steve got a 1060 on the SAT I. His parents are not in the ballpark for need-based aid.

| Application Portfolio | Financial Aid Category |
|---|---|
| Hobart and William Smith Colleges (NY) | Merit Scholarship/Tuition Discount |
| College of Charleston (SC) | Low Sticker Price |
| University of Maine/Orono | Low Sticker Price |
| University of Rhode Island | Low Sticker Price |
| St. Mary's College (MD) | Low Sticker Price |
| State University of New York —Stony Brook | Low Sticker Price |

## Comments

Since Steve is not a strong candidate for merit scholarships and doesn't qualify for need-based aid, he has selected mainly middle-sized public colleges that have excellent sailing programs (or at least are on the water). Hobart and William Smith in the New York Finger Lakes is the only expensive private college on the list. A sailor friend is there and has urged Steve to apply. St. Mary's College is probably the most selective college on his list, given its growing reputation as a public college bargain. College of Charleston in historic Charleston has an excellent sailing team and strong programs in the sciences, the probable area of Steve's major. The University of Rhode Island and the University of Maine are both near the water and of moderate size, given that they are the flag-ship public universities of their respective states. SUNY/Stony Brook is a fifteen minute drive from his house, although Steve would prefer to go away to college.

## JOHN: HIGH AMBITIONS, HIGH NEED

In the rough-and-tumble world of Central High School, John has answered every challenge. As star basketball player and student council president, he has the respect of everyone from school administrators to gang members. His mother, a single parent, works as a secretary, earning $17,000 per year. She has pinned her hopes on a basketball scholarship, preferably to the nearby University of Hartford, but John's counselor has strongly encouraged him to apply to some elite private colleges. John has a 3.8 grade-point average and scored a combined 1180 on his SAT I.

| Application Portfolio | Financial Aid Category |
| --- | --- |
| Yale University (CT) | Need-Based |
| Wesleyan University (CT) | Need-Based |
| Columbia University (NY) | Need-Based |
| Trinity College (CT) | Need-Based |
| University of Hartford (CT) | Athletic Scholarship |
| Central Connecticut State University | Athletic Scholarship |

## Comments

John has a chance for at least three different types of financial aid: need-based, athletic, and academic merit. Yale, Wesleyan, and Columbia are highly selective schools with generous need-based aid. But each may expect him to carry a part-time job and take out significant loans in addition to playing basketball. By applying to a cohort of three, he may be able to do some comparison shopping if admitted to more than one. He is virtually guaranteed admission to the University of Hartford, whose coaches are eagerly pursuing him. He could also play ball on scholarship for Central Connecticut State, a school ten miles down the road where one of his former teammates is playing. He included Trinity at the last minute because he liked the campus and the people he met there. Although Trinity doesn't offer athletic scholarships, John would be a strong candidate for sweetened need-based aid.

Assuming that he gets in at most or all of them, John will have the choice of either a prestigious degree plus approximately $10,000 to $20,000 in loans or an all-expenses-paid education at the University of Hartford or Central Connecticut State.

## TONY: THE PASSIONATE PERFORMER

Call him "The Music Man." Tony does it all: He sings, dances, has played the piano since age four, and is the perennial lead in school dramatic productions. Although Tony is a bright young man (1140 on his SAT I), his grades have been nothing to sing about (B's and C's). He means to devote more time to his academics in college but is undecided about a major. His heart says be a performer; his head knows that a business major would be more practical. His parents' combined income is about $65,000.

| Application Portfolio | Financial Aid Category |
|---|---|
| California Institute of the Arts | Need-Based |
| San Francisco Conservatory of Music (CA) | Need-Based |
| Santa Clara University (CA) | Need-Based and Merit Scholarship |
| Southern Methodist University (TX) | Need-Based and Merit Scholarship |
| Arizona State University | Low Sticker Price |
| California State University at Long Beach | Low Sticker Price |

## Comments

Tony is torn between studying voice or piano, with a third option of majoring in something else and pursuing music on the side. His portfolio includes three different types of colleges: arts specialty schools, comprehensive private institutions that are strong in the arts, and public universities with low sticker prices. His parents will qualify for some need-based aid, but the family EFC is likely to be over $10,000. A key question is how much the aid offers from the expensive private colleges will narrow the price differential with the less expensive options, Arizona State and Cal State. (Although Tony's mom wants him to choose the best program, his dad still needs convincing that the expensive colleges are really worth thousands more.)

As a resident of the San Francisco Bay area, Tony prefers to stay in a warm-weather spot. California Institute of the Arts and San Francisco Conservatory are two of the most prestigious arts schools in the region. Both are expensive, however, and would close off the option of majoring in a non-arts field. SMU and Santa Clara are comprehensive universities with well-known arts programs. Tony will audition for scholarships at both, but the competition will be fierce.

# 4.

# GETTING NEED-BASED AID

Now that we've seen financial aid from the perspective of the colleges, and examined how families can choose the right ones, it's time for a closer look at the process that distributes the goods. Fasten your seat belt. There is deceptive simplicity in the aid package that comes neatly gift-wrapped from the financial aid office. Money is money, but how the dollars get there is a tale that has many story lines, not just one.

Financial aid was complicated when most colleges played by the same rules; today it can be downright bewildering. Merit scholarships, merit-within-need awards, and tuition discounts depend completely on the policies of each college, and the standards for calculating and meeting need also vary. This chapter begins with the only constant across the aid universe—Uncle Sam's rules for distributing federal funds.

## HOW THE FAFSA DETERMINES NEED

Every college in this book requires students seeking need-based aid to file the FAFSA, the federal government's instrument for finding out how much each family can pay for college. The FAFSA generates an expected family contribution (EFC) that guides colleges in the distribution of federal funds and serves as a baseline for colleges in calculating eligibility for their own need-based funds. Because aid is limited, the standard for need is high, especially when it comes to getting grants. For every family that is pleasantly surprised by the size of its award, another one comes away feeling disillusioned or even betrayed. The most common source of frustration, say financial aid officers, is when upper-middle-income families expect to maintain their lifestyle and still qualify. The fact that you're still paying off the family Lexus won't stir any sympathy, and if you own a vacation home in the mountains, your EFC will definitely show it.

I'm not suggesting that families in this situation are being frivolous. The real truth is that need-based aid can meet your need but not meet your NEED. That why it's necessary to shop around and compare offers.

The fundamental premise of the need-based aid system has always been that parents are

## ESTIMATING YOUR EFC

The first move in understanding your prospects is to try out one of the EFC estimator programs commonly available on the World Wide Web. Among the sites listed in chapter 4, you'll find one at www.collegeboard.org (the College Board), www.finaid.org (the Financial Aid Information Page) and www.salliemae.com (Sallie Mae). These programs mimic the aid formula, allowing you to enter your financial data anonymously and get a ballpark estimate of your eligibility. Be sure to distinguish between federal and institutional methodology calculations, and be aware that special circumstances or complicated financial situations lessen the predictive power of the estimators.

responsible for paying for college to the extent that they are able. College is expensive, but even at today's prices, it is still a good investment. Most need-based aid goes to people who have already sacrificed significantly, or who simply don't have the money to make those choices.

The federal formula for need is relatively simple. It tallies a combination of income figures from the calendar year prior to enrollment (called the "base year") and assets held at the time the form is filed. The calculations yield an expected contribution in each of four categories: parental income, parental assets, student income, and student assets. The total cost of attendance (COA)—including everything from tuition to travel and expenses—minus the EFC yields need. Note that the formula considers the financial information of any adults who live in the household with the student. Noncustodial parents are excluded.

Here's an inside look at how the formula works. (Don't worry if your eyes glaze over—there won't be a quiz.)

## PARENTAL CONTRIBUTION

Income: The formula begins by summing all taxed and untaxed income, including child support, social security benefits, and payments to retirement plans. From this total come the following deductions:

- ◆ Federal income taxes paid
- ◆ 3 to 10 percent of income for state taxes, depending on where the family lives
- ◆ Approximately 7.65 percent of income for social security taxes (less for those with higher incomes)

◆ An income protection allowance based on the family's size and the number of members in college (see table)

## PARENTAL INCOME PROTECTION ALLOWANCE
### 1998–99 Award Year

| Number in parents' household, including student | number of college students in household | | | | |
|---|---|---|---|---|---|
| | 1 | 2 | 3 | 4 | 5 |
| 2 | $12,030 | $9,980 | — | — | — |
| 3 | 14,990 | 12,940 | $10,880 | — | — |
| 4 | 18,510 | 16,450 | 14,400 | $12,340 | — |
| 5 | 21,840 | 19,780 | 17,730 | 15,670 | $13,630 |
| 6 | 25,550 | 23,490 | 21,440 | 19,380 | 17,330 |

Note: For each additional family member, add $2,880. For each additional college student, subtract $2,050

An employment expense allowance if all parents in the household work ($2,800 maximum)

Total income minus the deductions equals available income.

Assets: Net worth is determined by summing the total value of:

◆ cash, savings, and checking accounts
◆ real estate not including the primary residence
◆ the net value of a business or investment farm (adjusted by up to 60 percent)

The asset calculations do not include personal or consumer debt, or the value of life insurance policies or retirement plans.

From the total net worth, a protection allowance is subtracted according to the table below. The resulting total is multiplied by 12 percent to yield the contribution from assets. Finally, the available income is added to the contribution from assets to yield an adjusted available income (AAI), from which parents' contribution is calculated according to the next table.

## EDUCATION SAVINGS AND ASSET PROTECTION ALLOWANCE
### 1998–99 Award Year

| Age of older parent* | Allowance if there are two parents | Allowance if there is only one parent | Age of older parent* | Allowance if there are two parents | Allowance if there is only one parent |
|---|---|---|---|---|---|
| 25 or less | 0 | 0 | 31 | 14,500 | 9,800 |
| 26 | 2,400 | 1,600 | 32 | 16,900 | 11,500 |
| 27 | 4,800 | 3,300 | 33 | 19,400 | 13,100 |
| 28 | 7,300 | 4,900 | 34 | 21,800 | 14,800 |
| 29 | 9,700 | 6,600 | 35 | 24,200 | 16,400 |
| 30 | 12,100 | 8,200 | 36 | 26,600 | 18,000 |

(continues)

| Age of older parent* | Allowance if there are two parents | Allowance if there is only one parent | Age of older parent* | Allowance if there are two parents | Allowance if there is only one parent |
|---|---|---|---|---|---|
| 37 | 29,000 | 19,700 | 52 | 49,400 | 32,200 |
| 38 | 31,500 | 21,300 | 53 | 50,900 | 33,000 |
| 39 | 33,900 | 23,000 | 54 | 52,100 | 33,800 |
| 40 | 36,300 | 24,600 | 55 | 53,700 | 34,700 |
| 41 | 37,300 | 25,200 | 55 | 53,700 | 34,700 |
| 42 | 38,200 | 25,700 | 57 | 57,100 | 36,400 |
| 43 | 39,200 | 26,300 | 58 | 58,800 | 37,500 |
| 44 | 40,200 | 26,900 | 59 | 60,600 | 38,500 |
| 45 | 41,200 | 27,400 | 60 | 62,400 | 39,400 |
| 46 | 42,300 | 28,100 | 61 | 64,500 | 40,500 |
| 47 | 43,300 | 28,800 | 62 | 66,800 | 41,700 |
| 48 | 44,400 | 29,300 | 63 | 68,700 | 42,900 |
| 49 | 45,500 | 30,000 | 64 | 71,100 | 44,000 |
| 50 | 46,700 | 30,700 | 65 or more | 73,500 | 45,500 |
| 51 | 48,100 | 31,500 | | | |

*Age of older parent is FAFSA/SAR #82; if blank, use age 45 on table.

## PARENTS' CONTRIBUTION FROM ADJUSTED AVAILABLE INCOME
### 1998–99 Award Year

| If parents' AAI is— | The parents' contribution from AAI is— |
|---|---|
| Less than -$3,409 | -$750 |
| -$3,409 to $10,800 | 22% of AAI |
| $10,801 to $13,500 | $2,376 + 25% of AAI over $10,800 |
| $13,501 to $16,200 | $3,051 + 29% of AAI over $13,500 |
| $16,201 to $19,000 | $3,834 + 34% of AAI over $16,200 |
| $19,001 to $21,700 | $4,786 + 40% of AAI over $19,000 |
| $21,701 or more | $5,866 + 47% of AAI over $21,700 |

## STUDENT CONTRIBUTION

Calculation of the student's available income follows the same rules, except for the fact that the protection allowance is a standard $2,200. The total available income is multiplied by 50 percent to yield the contribution from income. Student assets are multiplied by 35 percent to determine the contribution from assets.

## THE EXPECTED FAMILY CONTRIBUTION

The EFC is the sum of the parent and student contributions, though the parental EFC is divided by the number in the family who are in college to determine how much is available to pay the costs of each.

For some middle- and low-income families, there are two additional wrinkles that help lower EFC. The first is called the "Simplified Formula" provision. If your family's adjusted gross income is less than $50,000, and if you were eligible to file the 1040A or 1040 EZ, the EFC will be calculated without regard to parental or student assets. (If you are eligible to file the 1040A or 1040EZ for a base year, it is a good idea to do so.) The second is known as "Automatic Zero." If the parents' adjusted gross income is less than $12,000 and they're not required to file the 1040, there is no EFC.

## WHEN THE CSS/FINANCIAL AID PROFILE IS ALSO REQUIRED

At the colleges that require the CSS/Financial Aid PROFILE or a form of their own, the fun doesn't stop with the FAFSA. The PROFILE duplicates much of the information on the FAFSA and then probes deeper. There's no beating around the bush—the main purpose of the PROFILE is to ferret out additional ability to pay, which might not show up in the FAFSA. (It is most commonly used at colleges that attract large numbers of affluent applicants and give away large amounts of aid.) But the PROFILE also allows consideration of special circumstances that may work in your favor. Unlike the FAFSA, the PROFILE isn't free. The processing fee is $6.00 ($5.00 if you register online) with an additional $15.00 for every college designated to receive it. Colleges that require their own forms instead of the PROFILE do so in part to save you some lunch money.

The PROFILE allows colleges to calculate their own figure for EFC, which is generally higher than that yielded by the federal formula. Major criteria included in the PROFILE but not the FAFSA include:

- *Home equity.* The percentage of its value factored into the asset equation varies from college to college and student to student.
- *Whether family members in college are children or parents.* Since a parent in college costs less than a child going away, some colleges modify the EFC accordingly.
- *Assets held in the names of other children.* Consider this loophole closed.
- *An expectation for summer earnings.* Some colleges require the student to earn $1,500 or more.
- *Other sources of assistance such as relatives, employers, or outside scholarships.* The PROFILE colleges want to know about any sources of help waiting in the wings.
- *Medical and dental expenses not covered by insurance.* At last, something in the plus column.
- *Private school tuition.* Colleges differ on whether they'll give credit on this one.

# WHY ONE COLLEGE PRESIDENT DEFENDS
## NEED-BASED AID

With the rise of merit scholarships and discounting, some administrators have pre-dicted the end of need-based aid at most private colleges in the foreseeable future. A staunch defender of the need-based system is Nancy S. Dye, president of Oberlin Col-lege. Oberlin is among the nation's best-known liberal arts colleges and was the first to admit women and African Americans. In an interview, Dr. Dye reflected on today's aid climate and why Oberlin remains committed to need-based aid.

<u>From a president's point of view, what are some of the changes that you've seen in admissions and financial aid?</u> The biggest change has been a move away from need-based aid to merit aid—or at least something called "merit aid." That change seems to me to be largely enrollment driven and market driven. For a variety of reasons, pri-vate higher education is in something of a fiscal crisis. Over a period of twenty years, tuition has gone up faster than people's ability to pay. Throughout the 1970s and 1980s (first because of poor return on endowment in the seventies, and then trying to catch up with things like faculty salaries and maintenance deferments) private institutions chose to maximize tuition revenue and raised tuition every year by an amount consid-erably greater than the rate of inflation. Now we've hit a wall, with a comprehensive fee that is more expensive than a critical number of American families can pay or are willing to pay. Over much of this period, we've also seen a shrinkage in the market.

<u>You mean a drop in the number of eighteen-year-olds?</u> Yes. And for many institutions it has become an issue of trying to fill their beds. Let's say a college has a physical plan that is designed to teach and house 2,000 students—it's up to the director of admis-sions to bring in the number of students they need. What some colleges have discov-ered is that they can't do it at their set price, so they've dropped their price in much the same way that airlines drop prices on seats or dealers drop prices on cars. They cut the price on an individual basis.

<u>You mean colleges keep the high sticker price and then discount?</u> Like airfares, or cars, or anything else. So instead of everyone paying one tuition, different people actually end up paying many different tuitions.

<u>And why is that more efficient that simply cutting the sticker price?</u> If it were up to me—if I were the czar of higher education—I would say that there is one tuition with the exception that if we admit a student who demonstrably can't pay, we give that stu-dent a scholarship for the amount of their need. But institutions like ours that have been very pleased with the need-based system now find themselves swimming against the tide, so that we're at a competitive disadvantage. It has become harder and harder to hold on to need-based aid because we've got too many families who are not truly rich but do not qualify for need-based aid. And they're saying, "We can't

(continues)

(continued from p. 51)

afford it." And they can't. And they're also saying, "How come all these other schools can offer merit scholarships?" So then you think, "Gee, if we're just going to stick with this need-based system, we're going to see many of the people who are bringing in a lot of tuition revenue go somewhere else. Maybe we better do this, too..."

And yet Oberlin is still committed to need-based aid... We are very committed to need-based aid. We do have some merit scholarships, I will admit—though I'm harder-nosed on this topic than most presidents.

You mean you've got fewer merit scholarships? We've got fewer, though we do have some.

Why aren't you interested in having more merit scholarships? What colleges do with merit aid, it seems to me, is put the director of financial aid in the position of being a used car dealer. And then a family calls and says, "Gee, you've given us $5,000, but some other school has given us $10,000. Why won't Oberlin give us $10,000?"

How do you respond to that? We say no. We'll make a change only if we look again and decide that we've made a mistake—missed something... What families don't understand is that merit scholarships drive up tuition. The more a college gives away in discounts, the higher its sticker price will have to be—unless you have an endowment large enough to fill the gap. And that's not true of many places. At Oberlin, we sit on top of an endowment of about $410,000,000, a handsome endowment, though not as large as some of our competitors. For us to layer on major merit money in addition to need-based aid would do nothing but push tuition up.

Or diminish need-based aid? That's right. And I don't think there is any institution that would tell you it is ready to get rid of need-based aid. Now, there are schools who could probably fill their classes only with people who got something called merit aid because those schools tend to attract a pretty wealthy student body. That's not true of Oberlin and never has been. Central to Oberlin's mission has been the notion of access for all students. Oberlin's prestige has never rested on having an affluent student body or a socially prestigious student body. It's been based on other things, including a commitment to diversity that started way before anybody else ever imagined diversity or interracial education. And Oberlin will not waver from that commitment.

In addition to all its questions, the PROFILE includes a space where you can write about special circumstances. It also has two supplemental forms that many colleges request: the Business/Farm Supplement for those who own a business, and the Noncustodial (Divorced/Separated) Parents Statement. The latter is a particularly significant item for the families to whom it applies. Many private colleges are sticklers for a contribution from the noncustodial spouse, regardless of any legal agreements that may say otherwise. If you're the custodial spouse in a situation where the noncustodial parent is not cooperating, plead your case to the financial aid offices. (It may be necessary to get corroboration from a social worker or clergy member about a domestic situation that precludes support from the noncustodial parent.)

The PROFILE also includes dozens of institutional questions that are requested by some colleges but not others. Subjects include:

- The value of tax deferred pensions, annuities, and savings plans
- Assets that were liquidated in the year prior to the base year
- Motor vehicles owned or leased, including the make and model
- Additional information about real estate other than the primary home
- Information about interest in a corporation, partnership, or Schedule C business
- Consumer debt
- Amount paid to support relatives who are not immediate family members

When you receive your copy of the PROFILE, the form will tell you which colleges requested each of the institutional questions. When colleges use the PROFILE to create an institutional methodology, the typical family's EFC will rise by about $1,000 to $2,000. (Though bear in mind that results vary. It may be dramatically higher in cases of divorce, for instance, or lower where there are special circumstances.)

Scary as all this may sound, there are signs that the most expensive PROFILE colleges are softening the blow for families of limited means. A 1998 policy change by Princeton University set off a move by many PROFILE colleges to ease the need formula and beef up aid to families of modest means. Princeton's new policies include:

- Elimination of home equity as an asset in the calculation of need for most families earning less than $90,000 per year, and reduction of the percentage of the value that is included for others

## FINALLY, SOME GOOD NEWS FROM UNCLE SAM

At least there is if you're middle-income or below. The new Hope Scholarship gives families a tax credit of up to $1,500 for education expenses in the first two years of college. For families with a college junior or senior, the new Lifetime Learning Credit is currently capped at $1,000 but will rise to $2,000 in 2003. Details are available at the Education Department's Web site at www.ed.gov/inits/hope/tax_qa. Both programs begin to phase out for married couples earning $80,000 or more per year (or single parents who earn $40,000). The only fly in the ointment is that some colleges may diminish their need-based aid packages to families who get these awards. But under pressure from the federal government and a wary public, many schools have pledged to keep their hands off.

- Replacement of loans with grants in aid packages for families with incomes below $40,000
- Reduction of loans for families with incomes between $40,000 and $57,000

The recent developments underscore how need analysis is now used as another leg up in attracting the best students. Such changes also point to the importance of a huge endowment to finance multimillion-dollar aid budgets. Only the richest colleges have been able to follow Princeton's lead for all students.

## MAXIMIZING YOUR AID ELIGIBILITY

Congratulations to anyone who has made it this far in a state of reasonable alertness. There is a bottom line: In most cases, the primary determinant of aid eligibility is family income in the base year before enrollment. Whatever reduces your income in the base year will enhance your eligibility.

The year that determines your fate begins in January of eleventh grade and ends in December of twelfth grade (assuming that the student goes directly to college). If you've got time before that, you may want to accelerate some discretionary income. The most obvious example would be a bonus or other compensation that you could get under the wire before January 1 of the base year. Gains from the sale of stock or other assets might also be moved up. If you're already into a base year—which most readers probably are — you can still defer items like these. Though you have to reapply for aid every year, it is a good strategy to show the highest possible amount of need in the first base year. While most colleges will increase your award if you show more need in later years, this is not always guaranteed.

Although income is generally the most important determinant of aid, assets also play a role and families have more latitude in shifting them around. There is one ironclad law of asset management for college financial aid: Don't save in your child's name. Accountants frequently advise parents to save for college under the Uniform Gifts and Transfers to Minors Acts (UGMA and UTMA) for the tax advantage, but those gains are usually overwhelmed by the aid formula's 35 percent "tax" on student assets versus only about 5.65 percent (after exclusions) on parental ones. Since a gift must be irrevocable in order to get the tax benefit,

**PARENT SOUP Q&A**

Q: Given the many risks to saving for college in our childrens' names, could the Roth IRA be an option for us to save "protected" money for our kids' college?

A: Many financial planners recommend this strategy. Retirement accounts are among the few places to put money that won't lower your aid eligibility at most colleges. Yet the money is available penalty-free to pay tuition bills.

there's no easy way to put the tooth-paste back in the tube once money is placed in a student's name. The best bet is to spend some of the money on the student before filling out the aid forms, where possible, and to use the student assets to pay the bills for the freshman year to increase aid prospects later.

A key variable in the asset game is home equity. At public institutions and private colleges that don't require the PROFILE, home equity doesn't reduce eligibility. Therefore, it may be wise to cash in other assets to pay down your mortgage. At colleges that do require the PROFILE, virtually all of which consider home equity as an asset that is "taxable" by the aid formula, families may want to go the other way and take out a home equity loan. The debt counts toward reducing the value of the home as an asset, and the loan may be tax deductible.

It is possible to go to great lengths in order to keep your money away from the long arm of the aid office. You might, for instance, liquidate some assets and stick them in a tax-deferred annuity, out of the reach of need analysis at all but a handful of schools. You might start a new business or invest in an existing one. But be careful about maneuvering that is too complicated or doesn't make sense outside the context of your long-term financial outlook. Financial aid differs from tax law in that behind all the rules is a human being (the aid officer) trying to apply those rules in a fair and equitable way. In part, aid officers depend on your portraying your situation accurately. But they also have finely tuned radar to detect "miracle" applications where the lifestyle doesn't match the reported financial information. Particularly at the colleges that use the PROFILE or an institutional form, it is not always possible to know in advance exactly what information will be considered. Just ask the hapless aid applicant at one highly selective college who was headed for a need-based award, but made the mistake of writing her essay about the joys of riding in the family's two thirty-foot sailboats.

If you're contemplating money moves, it is always a good idea to consult a financial planner, especially one with experience in college financial aid. A growing number specialize in assisting families through the aid process. If you're signing on with someone new in hopes of getting more aid, proceed with caution. Don't be too impressed if he or she offers to estimate how much aid you'll get. That can be done on the Web, as noted earlier. Make sure you know whether the person is going to sell you anything other than advice. Be aware that having pocketed your money, the adviser may feel pressure to devise an intricate asset shell game. Such strategies can backfire if you get more aid at the price of tying your finances into knots. Finally, if a planner suggests that he or she has influence in the aid offices or can get you a particular dollar figure in aid, move on to the next prospect. Aid consultants are the last people that financial aid officers want to cozy up to.

## APPLICATION ANXIETY AND EARLY DECISION

Few seasons in the life of an ambitious young person are as stressful as the fall and winter of twelfth grade. As the admission gods loom on the horizon, the student must give heart and soul to the application process while balancing the rigors of college-level academic work and a slate of extracurricular activities. Parents can help by reminding the student—repeatedly if necessary—of their support (and love) no matter where he or she goes to college. When the student is stressed out, the parental role is to stay calm.

With the student otherwise occupied, parents should be prepared to assume control of the aid process. The first push will come if the student decides to apply for early decision or early action, programs that allow students to receive a yes, no, or maybe by around December 15. (Early decision is the more common of the two and entails a binding commitment to attend if accepted. Early action allows the student to weigh other options until April.)

Many colleges in this book use the CSS/Financial Aid PROFILE (or their own form) to generate a tentative aid offer for early applicants by December. With deadlines popping up as early as October 15, students should get registration forms in the high school guidance office (or register at on-line www.collegeboard.org) by late September. If there is no early application in the offing, registration should probably be held off until November because applicants must list all the PROFILE colleges where they intend to apply. Completing the PROFILE means preparing estimated taxes for a year that has not yet ended, a task that will involve some guesswork. The best approach is to go over last year's tax return item by item and multiply your salary by the percentage of this year's raise. Colleges understand that estimated figures are subject to change—that's why the award in December will be tentative. Even if your child will not be an early candidate, you should lay the groundwork for doing your taxes as soon as possible after January 1.

In recent years, highly selective private colleges have been awash with early applicants seeking an extra advantage in the ever-intensifying competi-

---

### IF GRANDMA IS YOUR CHILD'S GUARDIAN ANGEL

Don't let her make a deposit in the child's account to help pay for college (and where the aid formula will take 35 percent of the money per year). You'll get more bang for her buck by asking her to keep the money in her name until the tuition bill arrives. At colleges that require the PROFILE—which asks about contributions from family members—her best move may be to help pay off loans after college.

---

tion. Early decision, the variant that requires a commitment to attend if admitted, is not to be taken lightly. Colleges love early decision applicants because they've got them in the bag, and some schools offer financial aid incentive programs to encourage early applications. But outside of that, colleges may be less likely to offer tuition discounts or merit money to students in the early round because they've already signed on the dotted line. Also, families lose the chance to compare offers that is enjoyed by regular applicants.

But the more crucial issue is whether the early choice is right for the student. Under the pressures of the admission process, some students consider early decision because of the overwhelming desire to get it over with, or in the belief that there's no way they'll get in unless they "apply early somewhere." Under these circumstances, parents can help by gently putting on the brakes. Applying early does give an incremental advantage at most colleges, but it's not worth making a hasty or ill-considered choice.

## FILING THE FORMS

The dead of winter is when the aid process heats up. If the student is applying to colleges that require the PROFILE, the registration should be completed by early December so the actual form can be received by the holidays. Paper copies of the FAFSA arrive in the high school guidance office by about December 1. The electronic version is posted on the Web at www.fafsa.ed.gov on January 1 of the new year. It is against the rules to file the FAFSA before that date.

The advantage of using the electronic versions of the FAFSA and PRO-FILE is that they catch common mistakes before you send in the form. Electronic transmission speeds processing though the FAFSA requires students to mail a signed signature page.

The best strategy is to fill out the FAFSA and PROFILE together to avoid discrepancies (though in a few cases, an early PROFILE deadline may make it impossible to do so). Most of the questions are the same. The main decision is whether to file on the basis of estimates or a completed tax return. The latter is ideal but a squeeze since the deadline for filing both forms at highly selective colleges is usually February 1 or 15. But if the choice is between missing a deadline or filing with estimates, choose the latter. You'll have at least one chance to make corrections, as noted later. The downside of estimating is that your aid award may be delayed if there is a significant discrepancy between your projections and the completed tax returns (which many colleges will require).

No matter what your choice, take your time and try to avoid bonehead mistakes. At the top of the FAFSA, it says that "you" means the student. Keep that in mind when you get to question 16 and the form asks for "marital status as of today." For line-by-line advice on filing the FAFSA and PROFILE, go to chapter 5. Next to scrupulous attention to accuracy, the most important rule is to photocopy, or save and print, everything.

In addition to the FAFSA, PROFILE, and institutional forms, some states also require a separate form to qualify for state aid. (The others, about half, get the necessary data from the FAFSA.) Many state awards are based on need or go to every student who attends an in-state school, though some states do offer awards that can be transferred to out-of-state schools. In recent years, the number of state-sponsored merit scholarships is on the rise. Georgia's HOPE Scholarship program, the original model for the federal version, is the most famous. For students who have earned a 3.0 or higher in high school, it provides full tuition at in-state public universities or about $3,000 toward in-state private college tuition. The states also administer the federally funded Robert C. Byrd Honors Scholarships and various other awards based on merit and need. For more information, talk to your guidance counselor or visit www.easi.ed.gov/studentcenter/html/apply/state.html on-line and find the link to your state's education department.

In cases where there are special circumstances related to income or expenses, families should appeal directly to the college aid offices via a carefully written letter. If Dad just lost his job, that's a special circumstance. Ditto if a grandparent has advancing Alzheimer's and needs financial support. If Mom's business was flying high last year and is now on the skids, that also qualifies, although it may be a bit harder sell.

## THE WAITING

Once the forms are on their way, attention shifts to the mailman, who should arrive with letters bearing your child's name within four weeks. Be sure they don't get lost in a pile of college junk mail. The FAFSA processor will respond in the form of a Student Aid Report (SAR). If there's a tiny drumroll in your head as you crack the envelope, it might be because your EFC, according to the federal methodology, will be printed in the upper-right-hand corner of page 1. (Remember that if you are applying to a PROFILE college or one that uses an institutional form, the number will probably change.) No EFC means your application has landed in the reject pile because of omissions or mistakes, an invalid social security number, failure to register for the selective service, or other bad stuff that surfaces through a "database match." If this is you, get to work right away on the enclosed

Information Request Form or call the Federal Student Aid Information Center at (800) 433-3243. Even if the SAR is in good order, be sure to review your information and send in corrections if necessary. (This includes estimate filers who have now completed their tax forms.) Take particular care to note that all the colleges that you intended to receive the report are listed in Section G.

The fallout from the SAR can include one other less-than-pleasant detail known as "verification," the financial aid equivalent of a tax audit. (If your EFC has an asterisk beside it, you win the booby prize.) Each year, the federal government mandates that approximately 30 percent of EFCs be verified. (Many private colleges choose to verify all aid applications on their own.) To comply with verification, you'll need to complete an additional form confirming key financial data, the size of the household, and the number of family members in college. Required paperwork will include completed tax returns, copies of W-2s, and any documents pertaining to special circumstances. Some families are chosen randomly for verification, but the odds are heightened if you file on the basis of estimated figures or if there is something fishy in your FAFSA. If you're subject to verification, or if you merely filed on the basis of income estimates, there is $400 of wiggle room between the income numbers you recorded on the FAFSA and the reality shown on your completed tax return. If you missed by more than that, you'll need to submit corrected figures and get a new EFC. Whether or not you are officially selected for verification, many colleges will check at a later date to confirm that members of the household reported to be attending college more than half-time are actually doing so.

The procedure for the PROFILE is similar. The College Scholarship Service will send you an acknowledgment that includes the list of colleges that will receive the report, the list of questions and your responses, and messages about anything that may be amiss. If there are corrections or changes, families should write them in, photocopy the form, and send it directly to the colleges.

## THE OFFERS

Teddy Roosevelt once described his charge up San Juan Hill as "my crowded hour." There is certainly no more crowded hour in the life of college-bound families than late March and April of twelfth grade. To students, it's a time when admissions offices seem to render a final grade on the first eighteen years of their lives. With good news comes exultation. With bad news comes hurt that cuts to the core. It is natural for parents to get caught up in the emotion—how could you not?—but your main priority should be to keep both feet on the ground, especially when wearing your grief counselor hat.

With any luck, your son or daughter will have gained admission to one or several excellent colleges. If the family has followed the advice in chapter 3, he or she will have a menu of options. Now is the time for parents to take a close look at each of the aid offers. Bargaining power is at a maximum before you sign on the dotted line. Even if there is an obvious first-choice college, other offers may provide grounds to question the aid award and possibly increase it.

Each college uses the data from your aid forms to build a package that includes any available federal and state money plus a helping of the college's own. As noted in chapter 2, the amount of the latter may depend on how badly the college wants you and how much money it has available. No two aid packages are likely to be the same. Yet all include standard building blocks.

## Grants

At private colleges, most grant money is likely to come from the institution's own coffers. Such grants often have prestigious-sounding names even though they're based on need. The federal government kicks in Pell grants and Supplemental Educational Opportunity grants, though significant dollars from these go only to families of modest means. Some state money may also be included. Aside from merit scholarships, public universities generally do not offer large amounts of their own grant money.

## Loans

Most of these will come courtesy of federal programs, though colleges and states also have loan programs. The most desirable of these is the Perkins loan, which features no interest until graduation, no loan fees, and a bargain-basement rate of 5 percent. Next on the list is the subsidized Stafford, similar to the Perkins except with a variable interest rate. Stafford loans also come in the unsubsidized variety, which begin accruing interest immediately. Some loans come directly from the U.S. Department of Education; others must be arranged through a private lender.

## Work Study

The Federal Work Study Program dates from the earliest origins of federal aid. In exchange for working approximately 10 hours per week in a campus job, students earn good wages that can be applied toward their tuition bills. A typical student might earn about $2,000 per year, and there is good evidence that work study does not harm grades or take away too much free time. Just remember that the funds budgeted for work study don't come at the beginning, but in a stream throughout the year.

As you compare offers, the best approach is to tally the costs of attendance for each college and then take a close look at each of the components of the packages. Pay less attention to how much of your need the college says it is meeting—that calculation is subjective. Don't get too caught up in the total size of the award. A $10,000 package that includes a large grant could be better than a $12,000 offer that is mainly loans and work study.

On the cost side of the ledger, the equation to keep in mind is:

Cost of Attendance = tuition + room and board + fees + books and supplies + living expenses + transportation

Remember that the cost of living is likely to be higher in a northeastern city than out in the Iowa cornfields. When you've got a handle on how much each college will cost, check out how each of the packages stack up, including the proportion of them that are (a) grants, (b) subsidized loans, (c) unsubsidized loans, and (d) work study. Most important, be sure you are very clear as to whether the offer is renewable. Aid officers can't guarantee the same need-based awards every year, but they can commit to meeting the same level of need. Be aware that it is standard procedure for loans to increase at many colleges from freshman to senior year. Families should be on guard for one-time merit awards that may be withdrawn after the freshman year, or scholarships that have unreasonably high academic standards for renewal. Most of the colleges in this book won't pull a bait and switch, but there are some that do.

---

### COULD YOU REPEAT THAT?

I wonder what would happen if acceptance letters came with subtitles for parents.

"Congratulations! You've earned a place in the Class of '04."
[Congratulations! Your parents have earned the right to pay us $100,000 of their money.]

"The college has reviewed your credentials and is confident of your potential for success."
[The college has reviewed your parents' net worth and will leave them just enough assets to maintain the lifestyle of a hunter/gatherer.]

"In the weeks ahead, you'll receive an official welcome to the college community."
[It will include an official envelope in which to enclose your check. Payment is due in July.]

I probably sound like Scrooge McDuck. But what other industry succeeds in making us feel so lucky for the right to spend so much money?

---

## APPEALING FOR MORE AID

One of my former students found out firsthand that a little negotiating can pay big dividends. A partial list of his acceptances included Princeton University, the University of Pennsylvania, the University of Chicago, Carnegie Mellon University, Washington University, and Wake Forest University. Armed with aid packages from each, he decided to ask for more. At Princeton, Penn, and Chicago, the answer was no. But Carnegie Mellon sprang into action, hiking its offer approximately $10,000 with grants substituted for loans. The offer from Washington U of full tuition plus $2,500 was looking good. But after several discussions with Wake Forest, the university upped its offer from full tuition to full expenses, and today my student has a new home down on Tobacco Road.

It's a fact that you can sometimes get a better deal by being a squeaky wheel. But there's a right way and a wrong way. Anyone who goes in with guns blazing and starts naming figures out of thin air will only succeed in shooting themselves in the foot. The first order of business is to understand what might be negotiable and what definitely isn't. Only the college's own funds are up for discussion. At institutions that give mainly federal funds, including the majority of state institutions, negotiating for more aid is a faint hope.

There are three rationales that give a reasonable chance for success:

- A better offer from a similar college that is a close competitor
- A special circumstance that other colleges treated more generously
- A new circumstance that has come up since the aid forms were filed

The competing college rationale works for two reasons. First, a competitor school probably calculates aid by similar ground rules. The process is as much an art as a science, and with judgment calls built into many awards, the actions of another aid office can carry significant weight. Second, colleges hate losing students to close competitors. In the absence of a better offer—or even if there is one—be sure to highlight anything unusual that might need explaining. Families with circumstances like high medical bills, unusual nondiscretionary expenses, debts or sudden changes in job status should actively bring these to the attention of the aid office.

The most important rule of negotiation is to know who you're dealing with. That's true in spades for financial aid. The typical aid officer is an idealist who takes seriously the responsibility of delivering limited funds to the people who need it most. Most aid officers don't like the idea of sweetening aid packages for top students—or anything else that deviates from awarding aid on the basis of need—but they don't make the rules.

So here's a tip: Always couch your appeal in terms of a request to see if anything was missed. Don't ask: "How much more can you give?" Take the latter

---

### WHERE DEALING ISN'T A DIRTY WORD

Carnegie Mellon University is one of the few selective colleges that is up-front about its willingness to sweeten aid packages in response to competing offers. While most institutions pooh-pooh the idea, Carnegie Mellon sends a letter to accepted applicants inviting them to send in copies of competing offers. "We call it a reaction process rather than a negotiation process," says director of admissions Michael Steidel. "Until May 1, we take off the gloves and say, 'Hey, we want to try to come closer if you're getting a better offer.'" CMU is most likely to react to the offer of a competing institution—"private urban research universities," according to Steidel. But he adds that "we don't react to all institutions, and we don't react to all students who are coming back with other offers."

approach and you can be sure of a polite response—through clenched teeth—but that sort of talk shows contempt for their need-based process. Instead, merely ask if they can take another look at your case while highlighting anything close to a special circumstance and making them aware of better offers. Although Carnegie Mellon is an exception, colleges are less likely to come back and say, "We'll match the offer," than they are to say, "We've taken another look and are willing to make an adjustment." The end result will be the same without needless antagonism, which might lower your chances of success.

Since aid officers know your salary, it might help to know theirs. Most earn in the $20,000 to $35,000 range. If you happen to be talking to the director of financial aid, his or her salary is probably about $40,000 to $50,000. If you yourself sat in the director's chair, you'd be amazed at the number of people who earn double or triple your income but plead financial hardship, or who simply want to browbeat you to get more aid. People with wealth and savvy are often the ones who question aid awards, an irony that does not go unnoticed.

When you're ready to pick up the phone, a little humility is in order. Rest assured that your aid package is more important to you than it is to the aid officer or his institution, no matter how much leverage you have or think you have. With supporting documentation in hand, place a call to the director of financial aid. Most likely, the person at the other end of the line will want to take your name and number. If you reach the director's administrative assistant, have a brief chat and ask about the preferred procedure for appeals. When you do connect with the director or someone of comparable authority, stay calm and genial. Remember, you're not bargaining so much as appealing. Be prepared to summarize your case in a concise letter that talks about your circumstances without conveying a pushy sense of entitlement. Overnight mail is the cleanest way of getting it there. Use a fax machine if time is of the essence.

In some cases, it may be a good idea to let your son or daughter make the contacts. Colleges are generally more receptive to inquiries from students than parents. The student whom I described at the beginning of this segment carried off the negotiation process on his own with great aplomb, no doubt winning points for tact and maturity.

## FIGHTING FOR THE RIGHT TO KEEP OUTSIDE SCHOLARSHIPS

Prominent among potential topics for negotiation are scholarships bestowed by private organizations. Colleges routinely subtract from the need-based aid packages of students who win such awards, due in part to federal rules stipulating that aid should not exceed need as dictated by federal methodology. But the colleges do have discretion about whether the subtraction is made from grants (bad), or loans and work study (good), or whether the money is applied to reducing the family's EFC to the extent that federal rules allow (best of all). Less-selective institutions often let students keep most or all of such awards when possible. But many highly selective colleges skim off a significant percentage, while leaving the student with thousands in loan and/or work requirements.

That doesn't sit well with Michael Mallory, executive director of the Ron Brown Scholarship Program, one of the nation's most prestigious for African Americans. He takes offense at the amount of his foundation's scholarship money that ends up in the coffers of the elite colleges where most of his scholars enroll. "If scholarship programs knew what was going on with their money, they'd cry foul," he says.

So Mallory travels the circuit of highly selective colleges, pleading the case for Ron Brown Scholars and for lenience in allowing students to reap more rewards from outside scholarships. "If I don't go and fight for the kids, the parents in most cases don't know what to do. They're given a package and they're just going to eat it," he says.

Mallory and other like-minded advocates won a major victory in 1998 when Harvard University, an important barometer for the rest of the nation's colleges, decided to change its policy to allow students on need-based aid to keep more of their outside scholarship winnings. Where previously Harvard had deducted 60 percent of the amount from its grants, the university now subtracts the entire total from the loan portion of the package. Watch for many other colleges to follow suit. Students who receive an outside scholarship are required to report that fact to the college where they plan to enroll. Though most colleges have a standard policy for dealing with outside scholarships, some are willing to negotiate on a case-by-case basis. Students should not hesitate to shop around, compare policies, and tactfully ask for better terms if First Choice U doesn't match the most lucrative offer.

## FINAL DECISIONS

While students dream of the day when acceptance letters arrive, parents may find the real work of paying for college is only beginning. The purpose of this book is to help minimize the price tag, but tuition bills are still likely to take a significant bite out of your family budget. Although the aid award letter will outline your main sources of help, there are other avenues available to soften the blow.

One popular option is to pay by the installment plan. Most colleges offer a monthly arrangement with a nominal fee or none at all. There is also the opportunity to pay all four years up-front, although this arrangement is no panacea now that average tuition increases have slowed to the 4 to 5 percent range, a lower return than can be had in other investments.

Some families may want to investigate the possibility of a supplemental loan. The most universal of these is the PLUS, an unsubsidized program that allows parents to borrow a sum equal to the total costs of attendance minus the aid received. Information about PLUS will be available from your aid officer. (Some colleges will include PLUS loans as part of the aid package, though such loans are available to anyone for whom the aid package does not cover the full cost of attendance.) Many colleges have special deals with lenders to provide additional supplemental loans. Because the schools in this book attract credit-worthy customers, they can generally offer favorable terms. For web links to lenders offering supplemental loans, turn to chapter 6. Parents may want to weigh these options against the possibility of a home equity loan, which can provide a reasonable rate and a tax deduction.

Even after every angle for aid has been exhausted, many families face the prospect of hefty tuition bills. The choice often comes down to swallowing hard for an expensive college—usually a prestigious one—versus opting for a less expensive alternative without the gilded diploma. People ask me all the time: Is an elite college really worth thousands more?

Popular sentiment to the contrary, there is little hard evidence to confirm that a prestige degree has economic value. Graduates of selective colleges are certainly prominent in the corporate boardrooms and corridors of power, but is that because of the prestigious colleges they attended? Or do those students bring with them extraordinary qualities that ensure success after graduation? When the time comes for graduate school, top grades at a regional college are often just as good as average ones from a more selective institution. Add in the extra attention that a student gets from being a "big fish in a little pond" or part of an elite honors program, and the less expensive institutions offer an increasingly compelling alternative.

The case for an expensive private college boils down to the opportunity to rub shoulders with the nation's brightest students, and the chance for a life-time affiliation that will open doors. I myself was an undergraduate at Yale University who wrote for the campus newspaper, and in later years I've enjoyed watching friends and acquaintances write for publications such as the *New York Times*, *Time*, *The New Republic*, and a slew of others. They might have gotten those jobs without Yale; no one can say for sure. I should add that my introduction into the college guide world—and the indirect reason I am writing this now—came because the *Yale Daily News* publishes a book called *The Insider's Guide to the Colleges*.

Ivy League tuition has nearly tripled since I attended, and I am not sure my family would make the same decision today. More and more families now choose the less expensive alternatives—one reason for the policies at private colleges described in this book, which aim to lure them back. If your family has followed the advice herein, a menu of offers will come your way. But there is no rule book to help make the final decision beyond careful consideration of your son's or daughter's hopes and dreams along with the financial bottom line. Students have a right to attend a college they choose, but parents can still be good parents if there is an outer limit to what they feel they can afford. Hopefully, all can agree on a choice that is appropriate for the student and sensible for the family.

# 5.

---

# THE FORMS

---

Got a pot of coffee handy? You're going to need something to keep you awake as we enter the most tedious part of the aid process—a line-by-line overview of the FAFSA and CSS/PROFILE. Boring though it may be, this phase is crucial. According to one aid officer, 60 percent of FAFSAs include at least one error. Most of the mistakes are minor, but catastrophic ones are no less easy to make.

As noted in chapter 4, try to complete all your aid forms as close to the same time as possible to ensure consistency. (When completing each form, be sure to refer to those done earlier.) The most time-consuming part of the process may be pulling together all the supporting documentation you'll need. Be sure to give yourself enough time.

The ideal is to work from a completed tax form with all the supporting documentation. If that's not possible, gather as much of the paperwork as you can and get last year's tax material as well as records on untaxed income for that year. (The PROFILE requires data from the year before the base year.) You'll need records on items such as Social Security benefits, welfare payments, child support, tax-exempt interest, payments to retirement accounts, worker's compensation or other benefits, and any food or living allowances. You'll also need all current information related to your assets, home or other properties, business or partnership, and trust funds. Most important of all, you'll need the student's Social Security card and driver's license. If the student has no Social Security number, apply for one pronto. (You can't get aid without one.) Lack of a driver's license will not jeopardize aid.

If you are estimating income, you should use a combination of last year's tax return and the amount of your (and your spouse's) pay raise along with W-2 and 1099 forms. If your son or daughter is applying to one or more colleges that require the CSS/PROFILE, you'll need even more material along the lines discussed in chapter 4. You won't want to forget information related to out-of-pocket dental or medical bills, or documentation of any extraordinary expenses that might help you qualify for more aid.

After assembling the necessary supporting material, you're ready to begin. If you're like most people, you'll sharpen a #2 pencil and start blackening ovals and filling in boxes. But those who are technically savvy should give serious consideration to filing the electronic version because of its automatic editing function. Located at www.fafsa.ed.gov, FAFSA on the Web operates by a password system whereby families can complete their form on-line (after as many sessions as they need) and then submit the form electronically when they are ready. An electronic version of the PROFILE works in a similar way and is available at www.collegeboard.org. It may help to have the paper version on hand for reference, or to consult the sample forms in this book. If you use paper, I recommend doing your initial work on a photocopy

and then transferring the figures to the real thing. Aside from the neatness factor, you'll have one more chance to check your work. Finally, *PLEASE NOTE THAT THE FOLLOWING DESCRIPTIONS OF THE FAFSA AND CSS/PROFILE APPLY TO THE 1999–2000 FORMS.* If you're seeking aid for a different year, be aware that the forms may vary.

# THE FAFSA

The first rule of the FAFSA is to remember where you're sending it: the Central Processing System (CPS). It would be easy to make fun of a faceless bureaucracy, but given that the CPS processes about six million aid applications a year, we should probably forgive the fact that it is a wee bit literal-minded. The imperative for families is simple: Don't count on the processor to put two and two together. The simple stuff is where the most devastating errors occur.

It is worth repeating the crucial instructions at the top of the form:

- use black ink or a #2 pencil and fill in ovals completely
- print clearly in *capital* letters and skip a box between words
- report figures in even dollar amounts (no cents)
- write numbers less than ten with a zero (0) first

There are 99 items on the FAFSA, and most of them can be handled by anyone smart enough to have parented a college applicant. Here is some advice for the ones that might cause problems:

## Step One

This section solicits biographical and financial information about the student. Be on guard against careless mistakes—they're most likely to occur here.

Questions 1–3. *Your name.* Do you know what your name is? Don't speak too soon, because as long as you're working on the FAFSA, "you" means "your son or daughter." It's just the federal government's friendly way of keeping You (the parent) on your toes. Write in the student's full name exactly as it appears on their social security card.

Question 8. *Your Social Security number.* This is the most important item on the form. Don't write in your own number. Don't write in baby sister's number. Don't go by your memory. Write the number exactly as it appears on the card. If you get it wrong, you'll eventually have to start over with a new application—after a delay. Also, if the student happens to have changed her (or his) name, possibly from a marriage, make sure that fact has been communicated to the Social Security Administration. Otherwise, the name and the number won't match, and there won't be any aid.

Question 9. *Your date of birth.* Be sure not to write in the current year, and be sure not to write in your own birth date. This item is also the first test of the zero rule for numbers less than ten. The birth date of a student born on May 3, 1981 is 05-03-81.

Question 16. *Marital status as of today.* One more reminder about who "you" is...

Questions 18–22. These questions concern the student's expected enrollment status. Aid eligibility depends in part on which portions of the year a student will be enrolled and whether it will be part-time or full-time. Where applicable, be sure to blacken "Full-time."

Question 32. *Will you have a high school diploma or GED before you enroll?* Students are normally required to have one of the two in order to qualify for aid.

# Free Application for Federal Student Aid

OMB 1840-0110

*July 1, 1999 — June 30, 2000 school year*

**Step One:** For questions 1-37, leave blank any questions that do not apply to you (the student).

SAMPLE DO NOT USE

**1-3.** Your name

1. LAST NAME  2. FIRST NAME  3. M.I.

**4-7.** Your permanent mailing address

4. NUMBER AND STREET (INCLUDE APARTMENT NUMBER)

5. CITY (AND COUNTRY, IF NOT U.S.)  6. STATE  7. ZIP CODE

**8.** Your Social Security Number

**9.** Your date of birth — MONTH / DAY / YEAR 1 9

**10.** Your permanent telephone number — AREA CODE

**11.** Do you have a driver's license?  Yes ○ 1  No ○ 2

**12-13.** Driver's license number and state

12. LICENSE NUMBER  13. STATE

**14.** Are you a U.S. citizen? Pick one. **See Page 2.**

a. Yes, I am a U.S. citizen. .................... ○ 1

b. No, but I am an eligible noncitizen. **Fill in question 15.** ○ 2

c. No, I am not a citizen or eligible noncitizen. .............. ○ 3

**15.** ALIEN REGISTRATION NUMBER  A

**16.** Marital status as of today

I am single, divorced, or widowed. ○ 1

I am married. ○ 2

I am separated. ○ 3

**17.** Month and year you were married, separated, divorced, or widowed — MONTH / YEAR

For each question (18 - 22), please mark whether you will be <u>full time</u>, <u>3/4 time</u>, <u>half time</u>, less than half time, or not attending.  Mark "Full time" if you are not sure.  See page 2.

**18.** Summer 1999  Full time ○ 1  3/4 time ○ 2  Half time ○ 3  Less than half time ○ 4  Not attending ○ 5

**19.** Fall semester or quarter 1999  Full time ○ 1  3/4 time ○ 2  Half time ○ 3  Less than half time ○ 4  Not attending ○ 5

**20.** Winter quarter 1999-2000  Full time ○ 1  3/4 time ○ 2  Half time ○ 3  Less than half time ○ 4  Not attending ○ 5

**21.** Spring semester or quarter 2000  Full time ○ 1  3/4 time ○ 2  Half time ○ 3  Less than half time ○ 4  Not attending ○ 5

**22.** Summer 2000  Full time ○ 1  3/4 time ○ 2  Half time ○ 3  Less than half time ○ 4  Not attending ○ 5

**23.** Highest school your father completed  Middle school/Jr. High ○ 1  High school ○ 2  College or beyond ○ 3  Other/unknown ○ 4

**24.** Highest school your mother completed  Middle school/Jr. High ○ 1  High school ○ 2  College or beyond ○ 3  Other/unknown ○ 4

**25.** What is your state of legal residence?  STATE

**26.** Did you become a legal resident of this state before January 1, 1994?  Yes ○ 1  No ○ 2

**27.** If the answer to question 26 is **"No,"** give month and year you became a legal resident.  MONTH / YEAR

**28.** Most male students must register with Selective Service to get federal aid.  Are you male?  Yes ○ 1  No ○ 2

**29.** If you are male (age 18-25) and not registered, do you want Selective Service to register you?  Yes ○ 1  No ○ 2

**30.** What degree or certificate will you be working towards during 1999-2000?  **See page 2** and enter the correct number in the box.

**31.** What will be your grade level when you begin the 1999-2000 school year?  **See page 2** and enter the correct number in the box.

**32.** Will you have a high school diploma or GED before you enroll?  Yes ○ 1  No ○ 2

**33.** Will you have your first bachelor's degree before July 1, 1999?  Yes ○ 1  No ○ 2

**34.** In addition to grants, are you interested in student loans (which you must pay back)?  Yes ○ 1  No ○ 2

**35.** In addition to grants, are you interested in "work-study" (which you earn through work)?  Yes ○ 1  No ○ 2

**36.** If you receive veterans' education benefits, for **how many months** from July 1, 1999 through June 30, 2000 will you receive these benefits?

**37. Amount per month?**  $

Page 2

**For 38-52, if you are now married (even if you were not married in 1998), report both your and your spouse's income and assets. If you are not married, answer these questions about you and ignore the references to "spouse." If the answer is zero or the question does not apply to you, enter 0.**

38. For 1998, have you filed your IRS income tax return or a tax return listed in **question 39**?

   **a.** I have already filed. ○ 1     **b.** I will file, but I have not yet filed. ○ 2     **c.** I'm not going to file. **(Skip to question 45.)** ○ 3

39. What income tax return did you file or will ~~you file for 1998~~?  *SAMPLE DO NOT USE*

   **a.** IRS 1040 ...............................................    **c.** A foreign tax return. **See Page 2.** ..................................... ○ 3

   **b.** IRS 1040A, 1040EZ, 1040Telefile ...... ○ 2    **d.** A tax return for Puerto Rico, Guam, American Samoa, the Virgin Islands, Marshall Islands, the Federated States of Micronesia, or Palau. **See Page 2.** ...... ○ 4

40. If you have filed or will file a 1040, were you <u>eligible to file a 1040A or 1040EZ</u>? **See page 2.**    **Yes** ○ 1 **No/** ○ 2 don't know

41. What was your (and spouse's) adjusted gross income for 1998? Adjusted gross income is on IRS Form 1040–line 33; 1040A–line 18; or 1040EZ–line 4.    $ ⬚⬚⬚ , ⬚⬚⬚

42. Enter the total amount of your (and spouse's) income tax for 1998. Income tax amount is on IRS Form 1040–line 49; 1040A–line 32; or 1040EZ–line 10.    $ ⬚⬚⬚ , ⬚⬚⬚

43. Enter your (and spouse's) exemptions. Exemptions are on IRS Form 1040–line 6d, and on Form 1040A–line 6d. For Form 1040EZ, **see page 2.**    ⬚⬚

44. Enter your Earned Income Credit from IRS Form 1040–line 59a; 1040A–line 37a; or 1040EZ–line 8a.    $ ⬚⬚⬚ , ⬚⬚⬚

45-46. How much did you (and spouse) earn from working in 1998? Answer this question whether or not you filed a tax return. This information may be on your W-2 forms, or on IRS Form 1040–lines 7, 12, and 18; or on 1040A–line 7; or on 1040EZ–line 1.

   **You (45)** $ ⬚⬚⬚ , ⬚⬚⬚

   **Your Spouse (46)** $ ⬚⬚⬚ , ⬚⬚⬚

47. Go to page 8 of this form; complete the column on the left of **Worksheet A**; enter student total here.    $ ⬚⬚⬚ , ⬚⬚⬚

48. Go to page 8 of this form; complete the column on the left of **Worksheet B**; enter student total here.    $ ⬚⬚⬚ , ⬚⬚⬚

49. Total current balance of cash, savings, and checking accounts    $ ⬚⬚⬚ , ⬚⬚⬚

**For 50-52, if net worth is one million or more, enter $999,999. If net worth is negative, enter 0.**

50. Current <u>net worth</u> of <u>investments</u> (<u>investment value</u> minus <u>investment debt</u>) **See page 2**.    $ ⬚⬚⬚ , ⬚⬚⬚

51. Current <u>net worth</u> of business (<u>business value</u> minus <u>business debt</u>) **See page 2**.    $ ⬚⬚⬚ , ⬚⬚⬚

52. Current <u>net worth</u> of investment farm (Don't include a farm that you live on and operate.)    $ ⬚⬚⬚ , ⬚⬚⬚

## Step Two: If you (the student) answer "Yes" to any question in Step Two, go to Step Three. If you answer "No" to every question, skip Step Three and go to Step Four.

53. Were you born before January 1, 1976? ........................................................................... **Yes** ○ 1 **No** ○ 2

54. Will you be working on a degree beyond a bachelor's degree in school year 1999-2000? ........... **Yes** ○ 1 **No** ○ 2

55. As of today, are you married? (Answer yes if you are separated, but not divorced.) ..................... **Yes** ○ 1 **No** ○ 2

56. Are you an orphan or ward of the court or were you a ward of the court until age 18? ................ **Yes** ○ 1 **No** ○ 2

57. Are you a <u>veteran</u> of the U.S. Armed Forces? **See page 2.** ..................................................... **Yes** ○ 1 **No** ○ 2

58. Answer **"Yes"** if: (1) You have children who receive more than half of their support from you; **or**
   (2) You have dependents (other than your children or spouse) who live with you and receive more than half of their support from you, now and through June 30, 2000. ...... **Yes** ○ 1 **No** ○ 2

## Step Three: Complete this step only if you answered "Yes" to any question in Step Two.

59. How many people are in your (and your spouse's) <u>household</u>? **See page 7.**    ⬚⬚

60. How many in question 59 will be <u>college students</u> between July 1, 1999, and June 30, 2000? **See page 7.**    ⬚

## Now go to Step Five. (If you are a graduate health profession student, you may be required to complete Step Four even if you answered "Yes" to any questions in Step Two.)

~~Page 4~~

# Step Four: Please tell us about your parents. See page 7 for who is considered a parent.

## Complete this step if you (the student) answered "No" to all questions in Step Two.

**For 61 - 75, if the answer is zero or the question does not apply, enter 0.**

**61.** For 1998, have your parents filed their IRS income tax return or a tax return listed in **question 62**?

    **a.** My parents have already filed. ○ 1     **b.** My parents will file, but they have not yet filed. ○ 2     **c.** My parents are not going to file. **(Skip to question 68.)** ○ 3

*SAMPLE DO NOT USE*

**62.** What income tax return did your parents file or will they file for 1998?

    **a.** IRS 1040 ............................ ○ 1     **c.** A foreign tax return. **See Page 2.** ................................. ○ 3

    **b.** IRS 1040A, 1040EZ, 1040Telefile ...... ○ 2     **d.** A tax return for Puerto Rico, Guam, American Samoa, the Virgin Islands, Marshall Islands, the Federated States of Micronesia, or Palau. **See Page 2.** ...... ○ 4

**63.** If your parents have filed or will file a 1040, were they eligible to file a 1040A or 1040EZ? **See page 2.**   Yes ○ 1  No/don't know ○ 2

**64.** What was your parents' adjusted gross income for 1998? Adjusted gross income is on IRS Form 1040–line 33; 1040A–line 18; or 1040EZ–line 4.   $ ☐☐☐ , ☐☐☐

**65.** Enter the total amount of your parents' income tax for 1998. Income tax amount is on IRS Form 1040–line 49; 1040A–line 32; or 1040EZ–line 10.   $ ☐☐☐ , ☐☐☐

**66.** Enter your parents' exemptions. Exemptions are on IRS Form 1040–line 6d and on Form 1040A–line 6d. For Form 1040EZ, **see page 2.**   ☐☐

**67.** Enter your parents' Earned Income Credit from IRS Form 1040–line 59a; 1040A–line 37a; or 1040EZ–line 8a.   $ ☐☐☐ , ☐☐☐

**68-69.** How much did your parents earn from working in 1998? Answer this question whether or not your parents filed a tax return. This information may be on their W-2 forms, or on IRS Form 1040–lines 7, 12, and 18; or on 1040A–line 7; or on 1040EZ–line 1.

    **Father/Stepfather (68)** $ ☐☐☐ , ☐☐☐

    **Mother/Stepmother (69)** $ ☐☐☐ , ☐☐☐

**70.** Go to page 8 of this form; complete the column on the right of **Worksheet A**; enter parent total here.   $ ☐☐☐ , ☐☐☐

**71.** Go to page 8 of this form; complete the column on the right of **Worksheet B**; enter parent total here.   $ ☐☐☐ , ☐☐☐

**72.** Total current balance of cash, savings, and checking accounts   $ ☐☐☐ , ☐☐☐

**For 73–75, if net worth is one million or more, enter $999,999. If net worth is negative, enter 0.**

**73.** Current net worth of investments (investment value minus investment debt) **See page 2.**   $ ☐☐☐ , ☐☐☐

**74.** Current net worth of business (business value minus business debt) **See page 2.**   $ ☐☐☐ , ☐☐☐

**75.** Current net worth of investment farm (Don't include a farm that your parents live on and operate.)   $ ☐☐☐ , ☐☐☐

**76.** Parents' marital status as of today? (Pick one.)   Married ○ 1   Single ○ 2   Divorced/Separated ○ 3   Widowed ○ 4

**77.** How many people are in your parents' household? **See page 7.**   ☐☐

**78.** How many in question 77 will be college students between July 1, 1999, and June 30, 2000? **See page 7.**   ☐☐

**79.** What is your parents' state of legal residence?   STATE ☐☐

**80.** Did your parents become legal residents of the state in question 79 before January 1, 1994?   Yes ○ 1  No ○ 2

**81.** If the answer to question 80 is "No," enter month/year for the parent who has been a legal resident the longest.   MONTH ☐☐ / YEAR ☐☐☐☐

**82.** What is the age of your older parent?   ☐☐

# Step Five:  Please tell us which schools should receive your information.

For each school (up to six), please provide the federal school code and indicate your housing plans.  Look for the federal school codes at your college financial aid office, at your public library, on the internet at http://www.ed.gov/offices/OPE, or by asking your high school guidance counselor.  If you cannot get the federal school code, write in the complete name, address, city, and state of the college.

| | Federal school code *OR* Name of college | College street address and city | State | Housing Plans |
|---|---|---|---|---|
| 83. | | | | 84. on campus ○ 1 / off campus ○ 2 / with parent ○ 3 |
| 85. | | | | 86. on campus ○ 1 / off campus ○ 2 / with parent ○ 3 |
| 87. | | | | 88. on campus ○ 1 / off campus ○ 2 / with parent ○ 3 |
| 89. | | | | 90. on campus ○ 1 / off campus ○ 2 / with parent ○ 3 |
| 91. | | | | 92. on campus ○ 1 / off campus ○ 2 / with parent ○ 3 |
| 93. | | | | 94. on campus ○ 1 / off campus ○ 2 / with parent ○ 3 |

SAMPLE DO NOT USE

# Step Six:  Please read, sign, and date.

By signing this application, you agree, if asked, to provide information that will verify the accuracy of your completed form. This information may include a copy of your U.S. or state income tax form.  Also, you certify that you (1) will use federal student financial aid only to pay the cost of attending an institution of higher education, (2) are not in default on a federal student loan or have made satisfactory arrangements to repay it, (3) do not owe money back on a federal student grant or have made satisfactory arrangements to repay it, and  (4) will notify your school if you default on a federal student loan.  If you purposely give false or misleading information, you may be fined $10,000, sent to prison, or both.

**95.** Date this form was completed.

MONTH    DAY

[ ] / [ ] / 1999 ○   or 2000 ○

**96. Student** signature

[ 1 ]

**Parent** signature (one parent whose information is provided in Step Four.)

[ 2 ]

**If this form was filled out by someone other than you, your spouse, or your parent(s), that person must complete this part.**

Preparer's
Name and Firm _____

Address _____

**97.** Social Security # [ ] [ ] – [ ] [ ] – [ ] [ ] [ ] [ ]

**OR**

**98.** Employer ID # [ ] [ ] – [ ] [ ] [ ] [ ] [ ] [ ]

**99.** Signature and Date 1 _____

SCHOOL USE ONLY

D/O ○ 1    Federal School Code [ ] [ ] [ ] [ ]

FAA Signature

[ 1 ]

MDE USE ONLY

Special Handle [ ] – [ ] [ ] [ ] [ ] [ ]

Question 33. *Will you have your first bachelor's degree before July 1, 1999?* If you have a child in high school, the answer is "no." Most federal grants are available only to undergraduates.

Questions 34. *In addition to grants, are you interested in student loans (which you must pay back)?* The best move is to say yes. Most financial aid loans are a good deal, and you can always decide later that you don't want them after you've seen the award. The same applies for work-study opportunities in Question 35.

Questions 38–52. This section creates more potential for confusion because it concerns the *student's* income and assets, not the parents'. (The latter is addressed on the following page in Questions 61–75.) Be sure not to under-report assets held in the student's name, but also remember to write in "0" in cases where the answer is zero or the question does not apply.

### REMEMBERING WHAT YEAR IT IS

It's no joke. If you're completing aid forms in January of 2000 for the following fall, don't file the 1999–2000 aid form. You need the one for 2000–2001. Filing for the wrong year can cause major confusion and delays.

## Step Two

The purpose of this section is find out whether the student is dependent for the purposes of financial aid. A yes to any of these questions gets the student independent status. To be independent, a student needs to be at least one of the following: (a) twenty-four years old by December 31 of the award year; (b) a veteran of the U.S. Armed Forces, including anyone who was enrolled at one of the military academies; (c) a graduate student; (d) married; (e) an orphan or ward of the court; or (f) a person with legal dependents other than a spouse.

Parents may remember when students could move out and declare independent status, but the federal government closed that loophole in the early 1990s. If a student doesn't fit the federal criteria but wants to claim independence, the appeal should go directly to the financial aid offices. In most cases, it will be an uphill climb.

## Step Three

This section applies only to independent students. Families with dependent students do not answer these questions.

## Step Four

This section addresses parental financial information. When the FAFSA says "parent," it means the custodial parent(s), and in cases of divorce, the person who is currently married to the custodial parent. These persons are considered financially responsible for the student's education, notwithstanding any legal agreements to the contrary. For the purposes of federal financial aid, the non-custodial parent does not exist. In cases of joint custody, the household where the student resided most of the time during the twelve months prior to filing the form is the one to which the form applies. In cases where a student spent an equal amount of time in two households, the household that provided the most financial support is the one to which the form applies. As a reminder, be sure to write in "0" in cases where the answer is zero or the question does not apply.

Question 62. *What income tax return did you parents file or will they file?* Choose the appropriate form. Remember that parents with income of less than $50,000 who file the 1040A or 1040EZ can have their assets omitted from the need calculations via the Simplified Formula. The rule technically says that you qualify for the Simplified Formula if you were eligible to file the 1040A or 1040EZ (even if you didn't), but it is best to do so for those who qualify in order to minimize any confusion.

Question 64. *What was your parents' adjusted gross income?* Parents who will file jointly with a former spouse in the base year should report only the information that applies to them. For current spouses who file separately, the information should reflect the sum of both incomes, even if they were not married in the base year.

Question 65. *Enter the total amount of your parents' income tax.* Note that this question refers to the amount paid rather than the amount withheld. Estimate filers should not merely copy the amount that appears on their W-2, which is the amount withheld. The relevant figure is the amount withheld plus any additional payments or minus any refund. This item does not include Social Security tax (F.I.C.A.).

Question 68–69. *How much did your parents earn from working?* This one earns points in your favor. By asking for your income from work, the formula will compute a F.I.C.A. allowance that will lower your EFC.

Question 70. This question refers to an attached worksheet to calculate untaxed income and benefits. Note that deductible IRA and Keogh payments during the base year are included, but not the accumulation in those accounts. Make sure that the figure for child support reflects payments actually received when it differs from the amount that is supposed to be forthcoming. (Accurate records are important if the two differ substantially.)

Question 72. *Total current balance of cash, savings, and checking accounts.* Asset information in the FAFSA should be accurate as of the date you file. If you are contemplating major purchases or other ways of diminishing assets, do it before you complete the form. You can make corrections to the FAFSA at a later time, but you're not allowed to update.

Question 73. *Current net worth of investments (investment value minus investment debt).* This total should include all real estate and investments but not the family's principal residence or the value of life insurance policies, retirement plans, and prepaid tuition plans. Note the assets held in trust funds *are* included.

Question 74. *Current net worth of business (business value minus business debt).* Be forewarned that private colleges are likely to give this special scrutiny and may require the relevant tax forms.

Question 76. *Parents' marital status as of today.* Remember the definition of parent from the beginning of Step Four. If the student's biological parents are divorced but the custodial parent has remarried, the correct response is "married."

Question 77. *How many people are in your parent(s)' household?* Include everyone who lives in the household more than half of the time and gets more than half of their support from it.

Question 78. *How many in question 77 will be college students?* Anyone counted here must be working toward a degree or certificate and be attending at least half-time during the award year. If there is confusion about what constitutes half-time, talk to the college where the household member is enrolled.

Question 82. *What is the age of your older parent?* For once, being old is good. The less time an older parent has until retirement, the more family assets will be protected in the aid formula.

## Steps Five and Six

These sections include the basics of signing and dating the forms and preparing them to be sent to the appropriate colleges.

Questions 83–94. *Please tell us which schools should receive your information.* Now that you've gone to all the trouble of applying for aid, you need to make sure the

### HEADING OFF FAFSA FRAUD

The federal government appears to be getting serious about the longstanding problem of families who cheat on their application for federal aid. Prosecutions have accelerated, and there is a move afoot to use income tax forms and other databases to upgrade verification procedures. Many of those convicted had been led astray by unscrupulous aid consultants. When it comes to aid fraud, the fact that someone else suggested it won't get you off the hook.

right colleges get the report. Even though there are blanks to write in their names, the recommended procedure is to enter a six digit code instead—each college has a unique one. Known as Title IV School Codes, they are available from the financial aid offices, your high school guidance office, or on-line at www.ed.gov/BASISDB/TITLEIV/search/Sf. On the other hand, your application may be disastrously delayed if you enter only the wrong code. Be aware that these aren't the same codes used for test registration by the College Board.

You may also choose to write out the names and addresses of the colleges, but print neatly in capital letters to avoid confusion. In this book alone, there are three St. John's, two Cornells, two Trinitys, and two Wheatons, not to mention the confusion between St. Lawrence, Sarah Lawrence, Lawrence, and dozens of state universities with more than one branch.

One potential sticking point is that the FAFSA includes space for only six college choices. Students who are applying to more than six should list those with the earliest aid deadlines and then contact the remaining colleges for instructions. (In cases where the returned Student Aid Report requires no corrections, students can amend the SAR to include the additional colleges, replacing others that were listed on the first submission, and send it back to the processor.)

## DOUBLE-CHECKING THE FAFSA

The following items are the most common sources of catastrophic FAFSA errors. Be sure that:

♦ Student's name exactly matches Social Security card
♦ Student's Social Security number is correct
♦ Student's date of birth is correct
♦ All relevant lines are completed (with zeros where appropriate)
♦ Title IV School Codes are correct
♦ The student and a parent sign the form

When you're ready to send the form, it is a good idea to sit down with your son or daughter to discuss its significance. Students should be aware of the financial sacrifice you are prepared to make—and the fact that the aid application is the first step toward financial obligations for them that may last well in their adult lives. They should also understand that financial aid, like admission, is an application process with uncertain results. In some cases, the college they attend may depend on the result of the financial aid process as well as the admission process.

It's all for naught if the student and a parent don't sign the form. Electronic filers should not forget that they must print, sign, and mail the signature page.

Here's a detail that's worth highlighting: *be sure to make a copy of the form before you send it.* Keep it in a safe place with the instructions and your supporting material. Don't send anything but the form to Central Processing. Tax forms, appeal letters, or other documentation should go directly to the colleges. One last detail for the FAFSA's paper version: There is a return postcard in the application for the processor to acknowledge receipt of your form, but you need to affix a first class postcard stamp to get it back.

# THE CSS/FINANCIAL AID PROFILE

There's at least one good thing about the PROFILE: it doesn't include those troublesome "yous" that cause such confusion. As with the FAFSA, don't leave items blank. If the value is zero, write it in. If you've already completed the FAFSA, have a copy on hand to work from. A lot of the questions are the same, and consistency is crucial.

Since the PROFILE is customized for each student, the form will include instructions at the top about which questions must be answered.

Here is an overview of the PROFILE:

## Section A: Student's Information

Only independent students will be asked to answer questions 1 and 2 about how many people the student will support. The other questions deal with residency status.

## Section B: Student's Income and Benefits

Much of this can be lifted from relevant lines in Section E of the FAFSA. Since this is the student section, there will probably be a lot of zeros.

## Section C: Student's Assets

This section differs from the one in the FAFSA in that it has a separate line for Uniform Gifts to Minors, custodial accounts held in the student's name to get a tax advantage. As with Section B, most of the answers in this section are likely to be zero. Question 18 asks for a valuation of the student's home, but that's only if the student owns one. (Information on your home comes later.)

## Section D: Student's Trust Information

Question B asks, "Is any income or part of the principal currently available?" Unfortunately, these funds are likely to be included in the calculations regardless of your answer.

## Section E: Student's Expenses

May be omitted for dependent students. The query in Question 25 about medical and dental expenses not covered by insurance does not include those paid for by the parents.

> ### CREDIT FOR PRIVATE SCHOOL TUITION
>
>
> Religiously affiliated colleges are much more likely to allow a reduction in EFC for private school tuition payments. Much of their constituency attends such schools.

# CSS/FINANCIAL AID PROFILE 1999-2000

## Application

## Section A - Student's Information

**1.** How many family members will the student (and spouse) support in 1999-2000? <u>Always include the student and spouse.</u> List their names and give information about them in Section M. See instructions.

**2.** Of the number in 1, how many will be in college at least half-time for at least one term in 1999-2000? Include yourself.

**3.** What is the student's state of legal residence?

**4.** What is the student's citizenship status?

a. ₁ ⚪ U.S. citizen (Skip to Question 5.)

₂ ⚪ Permanent resident (Skip to Question 5.)

₃ ⚪ Neither of the above (Answer 'b' and 'c' below.)

b. Country of citizenship?

c. Visa classification?

₁ ⚪ F1  ₂ ⚪ F2  ₃ ⚪ J1  ₄ ⚪ J2  ₅ ⚪ G  ₆ ⚪ Other

## Section B - Student's 1998 Income & Benefits

If married, include spouse's information in Sections B, C, D, and E.

**5.** The following 1998 U.S. Income tax return figures are (Fill in only one oval.)

₁ ⚪ estimated. Will file IRS Form 1040EZ, 1040A, or 1040TEL. Go to 6.

₂ ⚪ estimated. Will file IRS Form 1040. Go to 6.

₃ ⚪ from a completed IRS Form 1040EZ, 1040A, or 1040TEL. Go to 6.

₄ ⚪ from a completed IRS Form 1040. Go to 6.

₅ ⚪ a tax return will not be filed. Skip to 10.

*Tax Filers Only*

**6.** 1998 total number of exemptions (IRS Form 1040, line 6d or 1040A, line 6d or 1040EZ - see instructions.)

**7.** 1998 Adjusted Gross Income from IRS Form 1040, line 32 or 1040A, line 16 or 1040EZ, line 4 (Use the worksheet in the instructions, page 3.) $ .00

**8.** a. 1998 U.S. income tax paid(IRS Form 1040, line 46 or 1040A, line 25 or 1040EZ, line 10) $ .00

b. 1998 Hope Scholarship Credit and Lifetime Learning Credit from IRS Form 1040, lines xx and xx (Use the worksheet in the instructions, page x.) $ .00

**9.** 1998 Itemized deductions (IRS Form 1040, Schedule A, line 28. Write in "0" if deductions were not itemized.) $ .00

**10.** 1998 income earned from work by student (See instructions.) $ .00

**11.** 1998 income earned from work by student's spouse $ .00

**12.** 1998 dividend and interest income $ .00

**13.** 1998 untaxed income and benefits (Give total amount for year.)

a. Social security benefits (See instructions.) $ .00

b. AFDC/ADC or TANF (See instructions.) $ .00

c. Child support received for all children $ .00

d. Earned Income Credit (IRS Form 1040, line 56a or 1040A, line 29c or 1040EZ, line 8a) $ .00

e. Other - write total from instruction worksheet, page 4. $ .00

**14.** 1998 earnings from Federal Work-Study or other need-based work programs plus any grant and scholarship aid required to be reported on your U.S. income tax return $ .00

## Section C - Student's Assets

Include trust accounts only in Section D.

**15.** Cash, savings, and checking accounts $ .00

**16.** Total value of IRA, Keogh, 401k, 403b, etc. accounts as of December 31, 1998. $ .00

**17.** Investments (Including Uniform Gifts to Minors. See instructions.)

| What is it worth today? | What is owed on it? |
|---|---|
| $ .00 | $ .00 |

**18.** Home (Renters write in "0".) $ .00     $ .00

**19.** Other real estate $ .00     $ .00

**20.** Business and farm $ .00     $ .00

**21.** If a farm is included in 20, is the student living on the farm? Yes ⚪ ₁     No ⚪ ₂

**22.** If student owns home, give

a. year purchased | 1 9 |     b. purchase price $ .00

## Section D - Student's Trust Information

**23.** a. Total value of all trust(s) $ .00

b. Is any income or part of the principal currently available? Yes ⚪ ₁     No ⚪ ₂

c. Who established the trust(s)? ₁ ⚪ Student's parents   ₂ ⚪ Other

## Section E - Student's 1998 Expenses

**24.** 1998 child support paid by student $ .00

**25.** 1998 medical and dental expenses not covered by insurance (See instructions.) $ .00

## Section F - Student's Expected Summer /School-Year Resources for 1999-2000

| | Amount per month | Number of months |
|---|---|---|
| 26. Student's veterans benefits (July 1, 1999 - June 30, 2000.) | $ .00 | ⊔ |

27. Student's (and spouse's) resources
(Don't enter monthly amounts.)

| | Summer 1999 (3 months) | School Year 1999-2000 (9 months) |
|---|---|---|
| a. Student's wages, salaries, tips, etc. | $ .00 | $ .00 |
| b. Spouse's wages, salaries, tips, etc. | $ .00 | $ .00 |
| c. Other taxable income | $ .00 | $ .00 |
| d. Untaxed income and benefits | $ .00 | $ .00 |
| e. Grants, scholarships, fellowships, etc. from sources other than the colleges or universities to which the student is applying (List sources in Section P.) | | $ .00 |
| f. Tuition benefits from the parents' and or the student's or spouse's employer | | $ .00 |
| g. Contributions from the student's parent(s) for 1999-2000 college or university expenses | | $ .00 |
| h. Contributions from other relatives, spouse's parents, and all other sources (List sources in Section P.) | | $ .00 |

SAMPLE–DO NOT USE

## Section G - Parents' Household Information - See page 5 of the instruction booklet.

28. How many family members will your parents support in 1999-2000?
Always include the student and parents
List their names and give information about them in Section M.  ⊔

29. Of the number in 28, how many will be in college at least half-time for at least one term in 1999-2000? Include the student.  ⊔

30. How many parents will be in college at least half-time in 1999-2000?
(Fill in only one oval.)
1 ○ Neither parent    2 ○ One parent    3 ○ Both parents

31. What is the current marital status of your parents?
(Fill in only one oval.)
1 ○ single    3 ○ separated    5 ○ widowed
2 ○ married    4 ○ divorced

32. What is your parents' state of legal residence?  ⊔⊔

## Section H - Parents' Expenses

| | | 1998 | Expected 1999 |
|---|---|---|---|
| 33. | Child support paid by the parent(s) completing this form | 33. $ .00 | $ .00 |
| 34. | Repayment of parents' educational loans (See instructions.) | 34. $ .00 | $ .00 |
| 35. | Medical and dental expenses not covered by insurance (See instructions.) | 35. $ .00 | $ .00 |
| 36. | Total elementary, junior high school, and high school tuition paid for dependent children | | |
| | a. Amount paid (Don't include tuition paid for the student.) | 36. $ .00 | $ .00 |
| | b. For how many dependent children? (Don't include the student.) | ⊔ | ⊔ |

## Section I - Parents' Assets - If parents own all or part of a business or farm, write in its name and the percent of ownership in Section P.

| | | What is it worth today? | What is owed on it? |
|---|---|---|---|
| 37. Cash, savings, and checking accounts | $ .00 | 41. Business $ .00 | $ .00 |
| 38. Total value of assets held in the names of the student's brothers and sisters | $ .00 | 42. a. Farm $ .00 | $ .00 |

| | What is it worth today? | What is owed on it? | |
|---|---|---|---|
| 39. Investments | $ .00 | $ .00 | b. Does family live on the farm? Yes ○ 1   No ○ 2 |
| 40. a. Home (Renters write in "0". Skip to 40d.) | $ .00 | $ .00 | 43. a. Other real estate $ .00   $ .00 |

40. b. year purchased |1|9| | |    c. purchase price $ .00

43. b. year purchased |1|9| | |    c. purchase price $ .00

40. d. Monthly home mortgage or rental payment (If none, explain in Section P.) $ .00

CSSBV2 4-15-98

## Section J - Parents' 1997 Income & Benefits

**44.** 1997 Adjusted Gross Income (IRS Form 1040, line 32 or 1040A, line 16 or 1040EZ, line 4)    $ _____ .00

**45.** 1997 U.S. income tax paid (IRS Form 1040, line 46, 1040A, line 25 or 1040EZ, line 10)    $ _____ .00

**46.** 1997 itemized deductions (IRS Form 1040, Schedule A, line 28. Write "0" if deductions were not itemized.)    $ _____ .00

**47.** 1997 untaxed income and benefits (Include the same types of income & benefits that are listed in 55 a-k.)    $ _____ .00

## Section K - Parents' 1998 Income & Benefits

**48.** The following 1998 U.S. income tax return figures are (Fill in only one oval.)

1. ○ estimated. Will file IRS Form 1040EZ, 1040A, or 1040TEL. Go to 49.
2. ○ estimated. Will file IRS Form 1040. Go to 49.
3. ○ from a completed IRS Form 1040EZ, 1040A, or 1040TEL. Go to 49.
4. ○ from a completed IRS Form 1040. Go to 49.
5. ○ a tax return will not be filed. Skip to 53.

*Tax Filers Only*

**49.** 1998 total number of exemptions (IRS Form 1040, line 6d or 1040A, line 6d or 1040EZ - see instructions)    **49.** ⌊_⌋

**50.** 1998 Adjusted Gross Income (IRS Form 1040, line 32 or 1040A, line 16 or 1040EZ, line 4)    **50.** $ _____ .00

   Breakdown of income in 50

   a. Wages, salaries, tips (IRS Form 1040, line 7 or 1040A, line 7 or 1040EZ, line 1)    **50. a.** $ _____ .00

   b. Interest income (IRS Form 1040, line 8a or 1040A, line 8a or 1040EZ, line 2)    **b.** $ _____ .00

   c. Dividend income (IRS Form 1040, line 9 or 1040A, line 9)    **c.** $ _____ .00

   d. Net income (or loss) from business, farm, rents, royalties, partnerships, estates, trusts, etc. (IRS Form 1040, lines 12, 17, and 18). If a loss, enter the amount in (parentheses).    **d.** $ _____ .00

   e. Other taxable income such as alimony received, capital gains (or losses), pensions, annuities, etc. (IRS Form 1040, lines 10, 11, 13, 14, 15b, 16b, 19, 20b and 21 or 1040A, lines 10b, 11b, 12, and 13b or 1040EZ, line 3)    **e.** $ _____ .00

   f. Adjustments to income (IRS Form 1040, line 31 or 1040A, line 15)see instructions.    **f.** $ _____ .00

**51.** a. 1998 U.S. income tax paid (IRS Form 1040, line 46, 1040A, line 25 or 1040E... line 10)    **51. a.** $ _____ .00

   b. 1998 Hope Scholaship Credit and Lifetime Learning Credit from IRS Form 1040, lines xx and xx (use the worksheet in the instructions, page x.)    **b.** $ _____ .00

**52.** 1998 itemized deductions (IRS Form 1040, Schedule A, line 28. Write in "0" if deductions were not itemized.)    **52.** $ _____ .00

**53.** 1998 income earned from work by father/stepfather    **53.** $ _____ .00

**54.** 1998 income earned from work by mother/stepmother    **54.** $ _____ .00

*SAMPLE DO NOT USE*

**55.** 1998 untaxed income and benefits (Give total amount for the year. Do not give monthly amounts.)

   a. Social security benefits received    **55. a.** $ _____ .00

   b. AFDC/ADC or TANF (See instructions.)    **b.** $ _____ .00

   c. Child support received for all children    **c.** $ _____ .00

   d. Deductible IRA and/or Keogh payments (See instructions.)    **d.** $ _____ .00

   e. Payments to tax-deferred pension and savings plans (See instructions.)    **e.** $ _____ .00

   f. Amounts withheld from wages for dependent care and medical spending accounts    **f.** $ _____ .00

   g. Earned Income Credit (IRS Form 1040, line 56a or 1040A, line 29c or 1040EZ, line 8a)    **g.** $ _____ .00

   h. Housing, food and other living allowances (See instructions.)    **h.** $ _____ .00

   i. Tax-exempt interest income (IRS Form 1040, line 8b or 1040A, line 8b)    **i.** $ _____ .00

   j. Foreign income exclusion (IRS Form 2555, line 43 or Form 2555EZ, line 18)    **j.** $ _____ .00

   k. Other - write in the total from the worksheet in the instructions, page 7.    **k.** $ _____ .00

WRITE ONLY IN THE ANSWER SPACES. DO NOT WRITE ANYWHERE ELSE.

## Section L - Parents' 1999 Expected Income & Benefits

If the expected total income and benefits will differ from the 1998 total income by $3,000 or more, explain in Section P.

**56.** 1999 income earned from work by father    $ _____ .00      **58.** 1999 other taxable income    $ _____ .00

**57.** 1999 income earned from work by mother    $ _____ .00      **59.** 1999 untaxed income and benefits (See 55a-k.)    $ _____ .00

CSS8V3 6-2-98

## Section M - Family Member Listing - Give information for all family members entered in question 1 or 28. List up to seven family members in addi to the student. If there are more than seven, list first those who will be in school or college at least half-time. List the others in Section P. Leave shaded sections b

| 60. | Full name of family member | Use codes from below. | Age | Claimed by parents as tax exemption in 1998? Yes? | No? | 1998-99 school year Name of school or college | Year in school | Scholarships and grants | Parents' contri-bution | 1999-2000 school year Attend college at least one term full-time | half-time | College or university Type | Name |
|---|---|---|---|---|---|---|---|---|---|---|---|---|---|
| 1 | **You - the student applicant** | | | ○ | ○ | | | $ | | | | | |
| 2 | | | | ○ | ○ | | | $ | | 1 ○ | 2 ○ | | |
| 3 | | | | ○ | ○ | | | $ | | 1 ○ | 2 ○ | | |
| 4 | | | | ○ | ○ | | | $ | | 1 ○ | 2 ○ | | |
| 5 | | | | ○ | ○ | | | $ | | 1 ○ | 2 ○ | | |
| 6 | | | | ○ | ○ | | | $ | | 1 ○ | 2 ○ | | |
| 7 | | | | ○ | ○ | | | $ | | 1 ○ | 2 ○ | | |
| 8 | | | | ○ | ○ | | | $ | | 1 ○ | 2 ○ | | |

Write in the correct code from the right. → 1 - Student s parent  2 - Student s stepparent  3 - Student s brother or sister  4 - Student s husband or wife  5 - Student s son or daughter. 6 - Student s grandparent  7  Student s stepbrother or stepsister. 8  Other

Write in the correct code from instructions on page 8.

## Section N - Parents' Information (to be answered by the parent(s) completing this form)

**61.** Fill in one: ○ Father  ○ Stepfather  ○ Legal guardian  ○ Other (Explain in P.)

a. Name _____ Age | |

b. Fill in if: ○ Self-employed  ○ Unemployed - Date: _____

c. Occupation _____

d. Employer _____ No. years _____

e. Work telephone | | | | – | | | | – | | | |

f. Retirement plans:  ○ Social security  ○ Union/employer  ○ Civil service/state  ○ IRA/Keogh/tax-deferred  ○ Military  ○ Other

**62.** Fill in one: ○ Mother  ○ Stepmother  ○ Legal guardian  ○ Other (Explain in P.)

a. Name _____ Age | |

b. Fill in if: ○ Self-employed  ○ Unemployed - Date: _____

c. Occupation _____

d. Employer _____ No. years _____

e. Work telephone | | | | – | | | | – | | | |

f. Retirement plans:  ○ Social security  ○ Union/employer  ○ Civil service/state  ○ IRA/Keogh/tax-deferred  ○ Military  ○ Other

## Section O - Information About Noncustodial Parent (to be answered by the parent who completes this form if the student's biological or adoptive parents are divorced, separated, or were never married to each other)

**63.**

a. Noncustodial parent's name: _____
Home address _____
_____
Occupation/Employer _____

b. Year of separation | | | |  Year of divorce | | | |

c. According to court order, when will support for the student end? | |  | |  Month  Year

d. Who last claimed the student as a tax exemption? _____
_____ Year? | | | |

e. How much does the noncustodial parent plan to contribute to the student's education for the 1999-2000 school year? (Do not include this amount in 27g.) $ _____ .00

f. Is there an agreement specifying this contribution for the student's education?  Yes ○  No ○

## Section P - Explanations/Special Circumstances  Explain any unusual expenses such as high medical or dental expenses. educational and other debts, child care, elder care, or special circumstances Also. give information for any outside scholarships you have been awarded If more space is needed  use sheets of paper and send them directly to your schools and programs. (please print)

SAMPLE DO NOT USE

## Certification:

All the information on this form is true and complete to the best of my knowledge  If asked. I agree to give proof of the information that I have given on this form I realize that this proof may include a copy of my U S state. or local income tax returns  I certify that all information is correct at this time. and that I will send timely notice to my schools programs of any significant change in family income or assets. financial situation college plans of other children. or the receipt of other scholarships or grants

1. Student's signature _____

2. Student's spouse's signature _____

3. Father's (stepfather's) signature _____

4. Mother's (stepmother's) signature _____

MAIL COMPLETED APPLICATION TO:  COLLEGE SCHOLARSHIP SERVICE P.O. BOX 4004 MOUNT VERNON, IL 62864-8604

Date completed: | | | |  Month  Day

1 ○ 1998
2 ○ 1999

| CSS Use Only |
|---|
| W |
| Y |
| P |
| S |

## Section F: Student's Expected Summer/School Year Resources

This section is among the most bothersome on the PROFILE. It puts the cart before the horse by asking how much the student, parents, and others are expecting to contribute to education in the coming year—a question the need-analysis process is supposed to decide. Here is a run-down:

**PARENT SOUP Q&A**

Q: Would a car have less significance than assets when need is determined? I am a student who is contemplating selling my car when I leave to go to college.

A: Most definitely. Your best move is to wait until after you complete the aid forms to sell the car. Any cash you receive beforehand would lessen your aid award. Only a few highly selective colleges include cars in the aid equation.

Question 27a asks for the student's expected earnings and income for the summer prior to enrollment and the freshman year. One of the ways that the PROFILE hikes the EFC is by allowing the colleges to factor in an expectation for summer earnings. $1,600 is the highest I have encountered for the summer prior to enrollment, though the total often climbs above that figure for succeeding years. The summer earnings expectation may not change regardless of your estimate, but there's no reason to be high in your projection of what you think your son or daughter can earn. The colleges will use your figure as they choose. The estimated earnings for the freshman year should be zero in most cases; they aren't supposed to include work study.

Question 27e asks for disclosure of outside scholarships. Don't list anything here unless you've been notified officially that you will receive an award. Most outside scholarship programs don't designate winners until after the aid forms have been filed. Students must report outside scholarships to the school where they enroll, but the preferred scenario is to get the need-based aid offer first. Policies differ as to how an outside award may affect a need-based package (see chapter 4).

Question 27g asks for "Contributions from the student's parent(s) for 1999–2000 college or university expenses." In effect, the PROFILE wants you to guess how much you'll be expected to contribute to the combined costs of college, or at least how much you feel able to contribute. Consult the formulas in chapter 4 to estimate an amount, though it makes sense to err on the low side when in doubt.

Question 27h asks for "Contributions from other relatives, spouse's parents, and all other sources." This question represents a tough moral dilemma for families with grandparents waiting in the wings to help with college costs. The

FAFSA takes no account of money that may come in after the forms are filed to help pay the bills. The PROFILE colleges want to know about such funds in advance, and they will adjust their aid packages accordingly.

## Section G: Parents' Household Information

Most of these questions mirror those in Section D of the FAFSA. Question 30 asks about any parents that are included among those attending college. The PROFILE institutions are not likely to count a back-to-school parent in the same way that they do a second child who is enrolled. For Question 31, keep in mind that marital status refers to the student's current household, not necessarily the biological parents.

## Section H: Parents' Expenses

Questions 33–36 chalk up a few items in your favor: child support paid to others, repayment of educational loans, medical and dental expenses not covered by insurance, and private school tuition for children other than the student.

## Section I: Parents' Assets

The asset questions are similar to those in the FAFSA's Section F with two additional items: total value of assets held in the names of the student's brothers and sisters, and information on the family home. Along with the value of the home, the amount of the mortgage, and the monthly payment, the form asks for the purchase price and the year purchased. Such information allows aid officers to eyeball whether your valuation is consistent with what they would expect in light of the original price and the date you bought the home.

Parents who own a business or farm can count on additional scrutiny. Many PROFILE colleges require a Business/Farm Supplement that should be mailed directly to them, along with relevant tax forms.

## Section J: Parents' Income & Benefits in the Year Prior to the Base Year

With these questions, the long arm of the need assessment formula reaches back to the calendar year that began in the winter when your child was in tenth grade. The items requested are adjusted gross income, U.S. income tax paid, itemized deductions, and untaxed income and benefits.

## Section K: Parents' Income & Benefits

All of the information solicited by the FAFSA is also requested here, but the PROFILE delves deeper into the configuration of income: interest and dividends are broken out, as are itemized deductions and adjustments to income.

## Section L: Parents' Expected Income & Benefits

This is your projection of income for the current calendar year. Be accurate but not overly generous in counting income that may or may not be there.

---

**TOUGH CALLS**

Need assessment is full of borderline judgments, including special consideration (or not) for certain situations. If any of these apply to you, write a letter stating your case to the aid offices:

- Orthodontic care or eye surgery for an adult
- Tuition payments for a handicapped or learning disabled sibling
- Debts related to a parent's graduate or professional education
- A parent who was recently diagnosed with a serious illness

---

## Section M: Family Member Listing

All family members supported by the parents (or student) are listed in this section, along with those in college at least half-time. But unlike the FAFSA, the PROFILE asks you to specify the colleges. Count on the fact that this information will be verified sooner or later.

## Section N: Parents' Information

This section includes straightforward questions about parents' occupations and retirement plans.

## Section O: Information about Noncustodial Parent

In addition to the noncustodial parent's name, address, and employer, the form asks for the year of separation, year of divorce, court stipulations about support, which parents claimed the student as a tax exemption, whether the noncustodial parent plans to contribute, and whether there is a (legally binding) agreement about who pays. Not all PROFILE colleges require the noncustodial spouse to contribute, but many do. As before, your answers to the questions may have no bearing on whether and to what extent the noncustodial spouse is included in the calculations.

Naturally, this is a gray area. Colleges are more likely to insist that the noncustodial parent from a recent divorce pay college expenses than they are to track down a long-lost parent who has not seen the child in fifteen years. Divorce is one of the most difficult issues in financial aid, and students can be caught in the middle between parents who don't want to pay and colleges that insist they must.

## Section P: Explanations/Special Circumstances

The form offers a space of approximately two inches to explain unusual circumstances such as "high medical or dental expenses, educational and other debts, child care, elder care, or special circumstances." This is also the place to talk about fluctuating income and to explain assets jointly held with other parties. Although it makes sense to complete this section, families should also write a letter to each of the colleges on the application list and send it directly to them.

## Section Q: Institutional Questions

Some colleges require the answers to one or more additional questions that are appended to the PROFILE Section Q. This is why the PROFILE registration process asks that students list the colleges to which they will apply. When the College Scholarship Service sends the form, it includes all the supplemental questions the colleges requested with a note as to which college requested each. The institutional questions solicit a wide variety of information, ranging from detail about assets and divorce to whether the student plans to have a car on campus.

When you're finally finished, your first impulse may be to run to the mailbox and never look back. A better move is to set the form aside and then double-check everything—yet again—when you have a clear head. And remember, the main form should be sent to the College Scholarship Service, but the Business/Farm Supplement and the Noncustodial Parent's Statement go directly to each college (photocopies are fine) along with any letters about special circumstances. Once the forms are sent, you'll join your son or daughter in a time-honored ritual of early spring—waiting for the mailman.

# 6.

# SAVVY BOOKS AND LINKS

Nobody who applies to college can complain about a lack of information. Any bookstore has shelves full of college offerings, the Internet is plastered wall-to-wall with college information, and most applicants get enough material in the mail to start a small library. A typical family doesn't have time for even a glance at all this stuff, let alone enough time to separate the good from the bad.

This chapter is a one-stop guide to the best information about financial aid and college available on the Internet and in print. It doesn't list everything—just the sources I think are most useful. Where two or more offer roughly the same information, I've tried to choose the best one. No doubt there will be some material I have not listed that other well-informed people might choose, but I think choices are necessary given the huge quantity of information.

I have divided this chapter into two primary parts: financial aid and college selection.

## FINANCIAL AID

This is a topic uniquely suited to the power of the World Wide Web for interactivity and information retrieval. The Web sites in this section have a variety of calculator and estimator programs that deal with saving, borrowing, EFC, and many more. Scholarship search is another of the Web's fortes. There is no reason in the world to buy a book that lists scholarships (unless they're local) or to pay someone else to do a search for you. The programs listed below offer this service for free. Just keep in mind that noncollege, nongovernment scholarships account for only about 1 percent of all aid. Most of the books listed in this section address the topic of saving for college.

## General References

www.parentsoup.com—American Online (AOL) Keyword: Parent Soup. This is my Internet home, but that's only part of the reason why I list it first. (Honest.) I'm there every day to chat and answer messages, but the most important part of Parent Soup is the chance to bond with others who are in the same boat. On AOL and the Web, Parent Soup is among the most active communities of parents of the college-bound in cyberspace. My screen name is PSWN Bruce.

www.finaid.org—The granddaddy of aid sites is the Financial Aid Information Page. Every facet of financial aid is covered here in a depth unrivaled anywhere else on-line or off. The site is particularly good on specialized topics ranging from prepaid tuition to scholarship scams.

www.collegeboard.org—Registration for tests is only the beginning of what the College Board's site offers. It features a full complement of calculators, including ones for EFC, savings, debt management, and loan repayment. The site also offers a scholarship search feature.

www.petersons.com—For anyone overwhelmed by finaid.org, this site offers the fundamentals of financial aid in a boiled-down format. Much more is available from this giant of the college search.

www.review.com—There's plenty of good stuff at the Princeton Review's site, including some interactive programs that allow students to match themselves to colleges by their interests and qualifications. But watch out for the cutsie rankings.

*Don't Miss Out: The Ambitious Student's Guide to Financial Aid*—This classic among financial aid books includes a concise but comprehensive overview of the subject. Anna and Robert Leider, Octameron Associates.

*Paying for College Without Going Broke*—Published under the Princeton Review's brand, this book on the financial aid process merits special consideration from families with complicated finances or those who are looking to reposition assets or income stream to qualify for more aid. Kalman Chany, Random House.

## Saving

*Financing College*—Written by a reporter for *Kiplinger Personal Finance* magazine, this excellent book contains user-friendly material on saving for college as well as the aid process. Kristin Davis, Random House.

*Making the Most of Your Money*—For those who want a book about saving and investing they can sink their teeth into, Jane Bryant Quinn's tome of nearly 1,000 pages will fill the bill. Simon and Schuster.

*Guide to Planning Your Financial Future*—If you want to start saving and don't have a clue where to begin, this *Wall Street Journal* guide is a highly readable overview. Lightbulb Press.

## Borrowing

www.finaid.org—Numerous financial institutions offer student loans, and the Financial Aid Information Page is the best place I know to begin sorting through them. The site includes information on every facet of the loan process and links to dozens of lenders.

www.salliemae.com—Of the many lender-sponsored Web sites, Sallie Mae's is probably the most useful. There are a number of calculators to help plan saving and debt, as well as information about the borrowing process. The site also offers the scholarship search program listed below.

## Federal Aid

www.easi.ed.gov—Project EASI is more than just the federal government's idea of a clever acronym. It stands for Easy Access for Students and Institutions and is the gateway to information on federal aid programs and the on-line version of the FAFSA.

www.fafsa.ed.gov—The electronic version of the FAFSA is described and linked here.

www.ed.gov/BASISDB/TITLEIV/search/Sf—When you fill out the FAFSA, you'll need to enter a Title IV code for each one. This link has the list.

*Loans and Grants for Uncle Sam: Am I Eligible and for How Much?*—This short book tells you everything you need to know about federal aid. Anna Leider, Octameron Associates.

www.ed.gov/inits/hope/tax_qa—This page includes a complete rundown on the goodies included in the Taxpayer Relief Act of 1997, including the Hope Scholarship and Lifetime Learning tax credits, the Education IRA, the waiver of the early withdrawal penalty for IRA funds used to pay for education, and the deductibility of interest on student loans.

## State Aid

www.easi.ed.gov/studentcenter/html/apply/state.html—This link features a clickable map of all fifty states with links to their higher education agency Web sites, which include information on state scholarship and loan programs.

## Athletic Scholarships

www.ncaa.org—This site gives a rundown on the rules for eligibility and the recruiting process and a list of the colleges that offer each sport.

*The Winning Edge: The Student Athlete's Guide to College Sports*—Includes a concise summary of the college selection process for athletes, then lists all the colleges in the various National College Athletic Association (NCAA) divisions. Frances and James Killpatrick, Octameron Associates.

*The Road to Athletic Scholarships*—Author Kim McQuilken is a former NFL quarterback and his book is most useful for those interested in big-time sports. New York University Press (ISBN 0-8147-5546-1).

## The Armed Forces

www.myfuture.com—The armed forces have teamed up to create this site, which includes information about their various money-for-college programs. The site also includes links to the service academies and ROTC programs.

## Scholarship Searches

www.fastweb.com—FastWEB is the Internet's most popular scholarship search site. In exchange for your name and personal information, it sends a list of possibilities with updates of new sources that fit the student's criteria.

www.collegeboard.org/fundfinder/html/SSrchtop.html—Unlike fastWEB, the College Board's scholarship search allows students to preserve their anonymity. The database is not nearly as big but includes the major national programs.

www.rams.com/srn—Sponsored by the Scholarship Resource Network, this useful site focuses mainly on private sector non-need scholarships. The search process is easy and anonymous.

www.collegenet.com/mach25—Operated by CollegeNet. After a quick registration process, this site allows anonymous searching for scholarships using criteria in five personal and academic categories.

scholarships.salliemae.com—In exchange for a detailed personal questionnaire, Sallie Mae offers its College Aid Sources for Higher Education database. After you input your data, the program sends you scholarship information via e-mail.

## COLLEGE SELECTION

Despite its profusion of sources, the Web is a mixed bag when it comes to college selection. The main problem is quality control. The Web sites of the colleges themselves can be a useful beginning, and be sure not to overlook the affiliated student publications, such as the school newspaper, which often provide a candid view of what life is like on campus. At the dozens of general-interest sites devoted to college selection, the most common offering is a college search program that allows students to generate a list according to their preferences for criteria such as total enrollment, location, etc. At the click of a mouse, the site produces a list of all the colleges that match. College Board, Peterson's, and Princeton Review offer this feature. Others among the multitude include www.collegeview.com, www.collegeedge.com, and www.collegenet.com.

College search programs on the Web or in the guidance office can be useful for students whose preferences will yield a manageable list—like the student who wants to major in mining engineering at a school in Montana. Such programs are less useful for prospective English majors who want an excellent small college on the East Coast. They also do not convey a sense of the college's personality or its place in the higher education universe. That information is still the domain of books, and such will be the case until someone figures out how to make money on-line with copyrighted material.

The lists below consist entirely of books with special emphasis on evaluative guides that try to convey the tenor of life at the colleges and/or make judgments about their quality. As such, they are subjective and should be read with a critical eye. I recommend buying more than one, when possible, to make comparisons. Evaluative guides tend to have a large amount of information about the colleges they cover, but they are often limited to the most selective ones or some other subset.

The other kind of guide is statistical, often mistakenly referred to as "objective." You may need a forklift to carry one of them home. They usually cover thousands of schools and look impressive on the bookstore shelf. But at least in my opinion, the value of statistics is limited unless the book can offer a context in which to view them. Some statistics are accurate and useful, others are accurate and meaningless, still others are accurate but misleading, and then there's the cohort that's simply inaccurate. Furthermore, the evaluative guides generally have a selection of the most useful statistics at the top of each article.

The primary benefit of statistical guides is that they offer broader coverage of the nation's colleges, but I don't see the need to buy one unless the primary evaluative guides don't include institutions that are under considera-

tion. As statistical guides go, Peterson's is probably the best. The omnibus *Four Year Colleges* includes more than 3,000 pages and 2,000 colleges, but beware that the back half of the book consists of public relations material written by the schools. *Competitive Colleges* includes a statistical snapshot of about 375 of the nation's most selective schools.

Lastly, there is the subject of getting into college. There are many books available, including one that I co-authored with

**PARENT SOUP Q&A**

Q: I was wondering if you know of any good resources to help with college visits.

A: I recommend that you check out <u>Visiting College Campuses</u> by Janet Spencer and Sandra Maleson (Princeton Review, Random House, ISBN 0-375-75088-6). It includes complete directions and visit information for about 250 of the nation's more prominent colleges.

Edward B. Fiske titled *The Fiske Guide to Getting Into the Right College.* In addition to offering advice on the college search, the book provides lists of selective colleges in various categories.

## General Guides

*America's Best Colleges*—The reputations of colleges rise and fall with every issue of *U.S. News & World Report*'s rankings, published annually in August. But don't pay too much attention to the numerical order of the colleges, which fluctuates randomly. I recommend probing the various lists for new prospects. You can access the rankings year-round at www.usnews.com.

*Cass and Birnbaum's Guide to American Colleges*—An old favorite among high school counselors, this book combines coverage of 1,500 colleges with prose descriptions that are informative but do not make judgments about quality. By Julia Cass-Liepmann, HarperCollins.

*The College Finder*—Lists compiled by author Steven Antonoff, which include dozens of academic, extracurricular, and institutional categories. Fawcett Columbine.

*Colleges That Change Lives*—This book profiles approximately forty private colleges that are well known but not, in most cases, highly selective. The author is a believer in small colleges, and so am I, but the book often exaggerates the quality of its subjects. Loren Pope, Penguin Books.

*The Fiske Guide to Colleges*—I was managing editor for four editions of this book in the late 1980s and more recently a contributing editor. It includes evaluative essays on nearly 300 of the nation's "best and most interesting" colleges. Edward B. Fiske, Times Books.

*The Insider's Guide to the Colleges*—Student editors at the *Yale Daily News* (including me, in the early 1980s) have been editing this book for nearly 30 years. Despite constant turnover among the editorship, it remains a solid book. Covers approximately 300 colleges. St. Martin's Press.

*The Best 311 Colleges*—A useful book in an easy-to-use format, although compromised by a bogus "what's hot, what's not" feature used to grab headlines and generate equally bogus rankings. The Princeton Review/Random House.

*Rugg's Recommendations on the Colleges*—This book consists solely of lists of colleges judged to be strong in various majors. The author travels the country meeting with guidance counselors to maintain his lists. Frederick E. Rugg, Rugg's Recommendations.

*100 Colleges Where Average Students Can Excel*—This book includes a less selective list than the one in *Colleges That Change Lives*. Joe Anne Adler, Arco/Macmillan.

## Guides for the Cost-Conscious

*Barron's Best Buys in College Education*—An evaluative guide to 300 of the nation's lowest-priced institutions. Though a good reference for the colleges it includes, the book is flawed because it doesn't feature high-sticker-price colleges that discount. Lucia Solorzano, Barron's Educational Series.

*Ivy League Programs at State School Prices*—An evaluative look at 55 of the nation's best public university honors programs. A good book, though last published in 1994. Robert R. Sullivan and Karin R. Randolph, Arco/Prentice Hall.

*Peterson's Honors Programs*—This large volume includes detailed descriptions of the honors programs at 350 colleges. Useful for those that are included, but coverage is spotty and the program descriptions are written by the colleges themselves. Dr. Joan Digby, Peterson's Guides.

## Niche Guides

*Art Student's College Guide*—Offers factual profiles of 225 visual arts programs with an evaluative comment at the end of each. Linda Sweetow and Carol Brown, Arco/Macmillan.

*Colleges With Programs for Students With Learning Disabilities and Attention Deficit Disorders*—Includes factual profiles of the programs at more than 800 colleges. Charles Mangrum and Stephen Strichart, Peterson's Guides.

*The Complete Guide to American Film Schools*—Provides mainly statistics, but also some evaluative material for 600 programs in media and film. Ernest Pintoff, Penguin Books.

*The Complete Guide to Animation and Computer Graphics Schools*—Also by Ernest Pintoff, this book is written in a similar format to his film school book. Watson-Guptill Publications.

*Education for the Earth: The College Guide for Careers in the Environment*— There is mainly factual and statistical information in this book profiling 200 environment-related programs. Peterson's Guides.

*Film School Confidential*—Evaluative profiles of 26 top film schools by two alumni of NYU's Tisch School of the Arts. Geared toward graduate students, but offers good insider information for anyone contemplating film. Karin Kelly and Tom Edgar, Perigee Books.

*The K&W Guide to Colleges for the Learning Disabled*—Offers more detail on fewer colleges than the Peterson's book. Includes just over 300 schools. Marybeth Kravets and Imy F. Wax, The Princeton Review/Random House.

*Making A Difference College Guide*—Budding idealists can read about 100 schools with programs that foster service and civic-mindedness. Miriam Weinstein, The Princeton Review/Random House.

*The Multi-Cultural Student's Guide to Colleges*—An in-depth, evaluative guide for minority students to more than 200 selective colleges. The best book of its kind. Robert Mitchell, Noonday Press.

*Guide to Performing Arts Programs*—Written by a former admissions dean at the Juilliard School, this book is especially helpful for its lists of colleges that are strong in various academic disciplines. Carole J. Everett and Muriel Topaz, The Princeton Review/Random House.

*Professional Degree Programs in the Visual and Performing Arts*—Factual and statistical profiles of arts programs at 650 institutions. Peterson's Guides.

*Top Colleges For Science*—Factual and statistical profiles of 190 programs in the sciences. Peterson's Guides.

*Women's Colleges*—Features in-depth profiles of the nation's women's colleges. Joe Anne Adler, author of *Where Average Students Can Excel*. Arco/Macmillan.

## Applying

More and more college applicants are foresaking the typewriter in favor of the computer. Many schools offer their applications on disk, CD-ROM, or on the Internet. But the advantage of the following programs is that they allow students to enter the core data only once. Two caveats for electronic filers: (a) always carefully scrutinize a printout before sending, since that's what the admissions officers will being looking at, and (b) be sure to file any supplements that may be required by the colleges.

www.collegequest.com—This site is Peterson's bid for a slice of the electronic application market. It allows you to apply to more than 1,000 colleges via a "Universal" electronic application. Time will tell whether this catches on. Free.

www.collegelink.com—Allows electronic processing of applications to hundreds of colleges, although there is a fee. Data must be submitted to the company for processing, an extra step that takes time but allows double-sided printing.

www.weapply.com—Apply Technology and Princeton Review offer software including applications to more than 500 colleges, available for download. Free.

# 7.

# COLLEGE PLANNING TIMELINE

This chapter offers peace-of-mind to every parent who wakes up in a cold sweat worrying about missed deadlines. Much of the material here has been discussed elsewhere, but the pages that follow cover the whole process in a month-by-month, year-by-year sequence. Saving for college is the focus of the initial section, while later parts cover the mechanics of getting in and getting aid. Read the whole thing if you like, or go straight to the part that deals with your son's or daughter's current stage of the process.

## THE ELEMENTARY GRADES

Although saving for college lacks the urgency of, say, an ear infection or a skinned knee, it is never too early to think about how to pay for the second most expensive purchase of your life. An early start is crucial. Because of compounding, money you save today will probably be worth twice as much as the same amount saved ten years from now. Heed the Rule of 72: if you want to find out how long it will take for your money to double, divide 72 by the rate of return. A very do-able 7.2 percent rate of return will double your nest egg after a decade, not counting inflation.

Another fundamental rule: Buy stock mutual funds. The most common college saving mistake is to put too much money in conservative investments such as bonds or CDs. Historically, stocks have gained more than 10 percent per year, and in the past 20 years that figure has been closer to 15 percent. With 10 years or more until you need the money, most financial pros would recommend keeping at least three quarters of your college kitty in stocks, and preferably growth-oriented accounts. A few other tips:

*Don't Skimp on Retirement Saving.* Put away as much as possible in tax-preferred retirement plans, especially if your employer will match the contribution, as in a 401(k) or 403(b) plan. As noted in chapter 3, retirement accounts are among the few places to put money that won't affect your ability to qualify for need-based aid. You can usually borrow against the accumulation, or in the case of an IRA, make penalty-free withdrawals to pay for education.

*Don't Save in Your Child's Name.* A reminder to keep the money in your name, even if means a larger tax bill—at least if you harbor hopes of getting need-based aid. The federal aid formula takes 35 percent of assets in the child's name versus only 5.65 percent (after exclusions) of those belonging to the parents. Trusts are no good either. The only caveat is to watch Congress in the years ahead. The rules may change.

*Avoid the Education IRA.* It's a lousy deal in its current form. It allows parents to put away up to $500 in an account where the earnings are tax free if used to pay for education, but it doesn't allow use of the funds in the same year as a Hope Scholarship or Lifetime Learning tax credit. Just as bad, these funds may be considered student assets—and thereby run afoul of the 35 percent rule for funds held in the student's name. Stay tuned to see if changes are forthcoming.

---

### PARENT SOUP Q&A

Q: We have twin babies. How much should we be planning to fork out in 18 years?

A: What you'll pay depends most of all on which type of institution they choose. Today's sticker prices range from $2,000 per year for commuters at the cheapest public universities to over $30,000 for an expensive private institution. But remember, many people don't pay the sticker price, especially at the expensive colleges. Here are some projections for the total annual bill at various kinds of colleges, assuming a 5 percent per year increase in costs:

| | 1998–99 | 2008–09 | 2016–17 |
|---|---|---|---|
| Public university (in-state) | $10,500 | $17,000 | $25,500 |
| Private college | $22,500 | $36,500 | $54,000 |
| Ivy League college | $33,500 | $54,500 | $81,000 |

---

*Be Wary of Prepaid Tuition.* About 40 states either have, or are considering, accounts that allow parents to lock in tomorrow's tuition at today's prices. That may sound good, but now that annual tuition hikes have slowed to the 5 percent range, the deal is unlikely to be a good one for parents with more than five years before the tuition bills.

A better idea than either of the latter two is to investigate a new kind of account being developed by a number of states, known as savings trusts or 529 accounts after the section of the tax code permitting them. The accounts allow tax-preferred savings with much higher deposit limits than the Education IRA. They're a new idea brought forth by recent changes in the tax law that is rapidly gaining momentum. For additional resources on saving and investing, turn to chapter 6.

It is never a bad idea to consult a financial planner if you are at all in doubt. The most important criterion is trust, and the best recommendation is word of mouth. Find out if any friends or relatives have worked with someone they would recommend.

## MIDDLE SCHOOL

By the middle grades, more and more parents begin thinking about how to give their kids a leg up on college. The main priority is to ensure that your child is placed in the most challenging courses that are appropriate, especially in math. Placement in seventh and eighth grade sets the stage for the courses to be taken in high school.

Outside activities are important, but ambitious parents should resist the impulse to overprogram. Too many children lead pressure-cooker lives because their parents want them to do everything. A better strategy is to encourage children to pursue a manageable list of activities to distinction. Kids need time to be kids, and colleges prefer students who excel in a few areas to those who dabble in many.

On the college saving front, middle school is the time to begin shifting your money to safer vehicles to guard against a prolonged stock market down-turn. Mutual funds that feature large "blue chip" companies are less risky than small company or international stocks. Corporate bond funds are safer still. For maximum safety, turn to money market funds, treasury bills, U.S. savings bonds, and certificates of deposit. With investments that have a fixed maturity, try to make the date coincide as closely as possible with the time when the tuition bills arrive. A common strategy is "laddering" the maturity dates, one in the summer before each academic year that the child will be in college. By the time high school begins, college funds should be invested approximately 50 percent in the stock market and 50 percent in safer holdings.

## NINTH GRADE

Help your student look ahead to a challenging high school curriculum, and make sure that he or she is on course for advanced work as a junior and senior. Encourage continuation of extracurricular activities where your student shows promise for distinction and leadership. Ninth grade is the year when report card results begin to appear on the high school transcript—make sure they study hard!

College investors should continue to shift their holdings. Now is also the time to begin learning about college financial aid with an eye toward positioning assets and planning income to qualify for maximum aid. Since many private colleges require financial information from as far back as the calendar year that begins in the winter of tenth grade, this year may be the last that you can make moves that won't leave footprints on your aid forms (see chapter 4).

Advanced students may want to consider taking one of the SAT II Subject Tests in June. Formerly known as the Achievement Tests, they measure performance in particular academic subjects. Biology is the one most commonly taken by freshmen. Such tests are required only at highly selective colleges, and in any case a ninth grade sitting is optional. If you have questions, talk to the high school guidance counselor for details.

One other miscellaneous note: make sure your son or daughter has a Social Security number. He or she will need one to qualify for aid.

## TENTH GRADE

Tenth grade is the college search equivalent of the calm before the storm. For students, the main priority is to enroll in challenging courses and make plans for honors and/or advanced placement (AP) work in grades 11 and 12. Some schools offer sophomores an early administration of the Preliminary SAT in October, though such students are not eligible for National Merit Scholarship consideration until eleventh grade. Other schools administer the ACT's PLAN test, which assesses achievement and aptitude. SAT II Subject Tests will once again be an option in the spring.

Parents should continue to bone up on the financial aid process and execute any last minute asset shifting that might result in income that would diminish aid eligibility.

## ELEVENTH GRADE

Eleventh grade is the official beginning of white-knuckle time for parents of college-bound students. The questions come thick and fast: What should I be doing to help my son or daughter? Where can I get information about admission and financial aid? How can I avoid missing deadlines? And perhaps the most popular question on the eleventh grade FAQ: How can I get my child to focus on college?

For parents, the college search is like teaching a teen to drive. From the passenger's seat, obstacles in the road always loom large. But instead of making a lunge for the steering wheel at the first sign of trouble, parents should take a deep breath and stay calm. Feel free to drop hints, encourage, and cajole as needed, but the most important task in eleventh grade is to help your son or daughter feel comfortable in the driver's seat. Communicate clearly the expectation that he or she will assume responsibility for the college search. (You'll be there to help, especially with the financial aid part.) When teens know that Mom or Dad won't immediately jump in after every little bump in the road, they're more likely to meet the challenge. A few false starts are a small price to pay for establishing a pattern of responsibility.

Here is a list of other priorities for eleventh grade:

*Discuss Financial Parameters.* All the advice from chapter 3 applies here. It is too early to eliminate colleges based on cost—you never how much financial aid will be available—but straight talk now about finances can help students make realistic choices about where to apply among schools with various price tags. Will the student be looking primarily at colleges that offer need-based aid? Or is winning a merit scholarship part of the plan? Is there a ceiling on how much the family feels it can spend?

*Plan for Standardized Tests.* Before choosing a college, students must do battle with standardized tests. When school starts in the fall, be sure your son or daughter is registered with the guidance office to take the PSAT in October. Beginning in January, every student should consider taking the SAT I or ACT one or more times in the winter and spring of eleventh grade. The SAT I is usually administered in January, March, May, and June, while the ACT is offered in February, April, and June. Registration forms are available in the high school guidance office and must be mailed about 40 days in advance of the requested test date. Applicants to selective colleges should also consider taking the SAT II Subject Tests in either May or June. For information or to register on-line, visit www.collegeboard.org or www.act.org.

*Make a Tentative College List.* By the summer after eleventh grade, students should have a working list of about ten colleges. For a list of resources, see "Savvy Books and Links."

*Begin College Visits.* The most important part of the college search is visiting the campuses. Your son or daughter need only call to find out the schedule of tours and information sessions and then show up (with you) on the appointed day. A good initial strategy is to visit various types of institutions—a large, urban university; a small, rural private college, etc.—to get a sense for the variety of options. Visits should continue throughout the spring and summer. Where possible, later visits should include an interview with an admissions representative.

*Keep Your Child Working Hard!* Prospects for both admission and financial aid depend heavily on your son's or daughter's academic performance in eleventh grade and the first semester of twelfth grade. A few more A's this year can mean thousands of dollars in financial aid.

## TWELFTH GRADE

The senior year is all about the "D word" — deadlines, deadlines, deadlines. The following is a month-by-month overview of the twelfth grade timetable.

### September

The fall's first question is whether the student should apply via an early decision or early action program. Deadlines are as a early as October 15. Students should be wary of early decision, which entails a binding commitment to enroll if accepted. Early action requires no such commitment. For details, see chapter 4. An early application will require students to tend to details like getting teacher recommendations and reviewing transcripts as soon as possible after school begins.

If applying early to a college that requires the CSS/Financial Aid PRO-FILE, students should register to receive it using a paper registration packet available in the guidance office or on-line at www.collegeboard.org. The PRO-FILE often provides the basis for a preliminary aid offer to early applicants. Students applying in the regular admission pool should wait until November to register to receive the PROFILE form and file it in January with the Free Application for Federal Student Aid (FAFSA).

All students should plan a standardized testing schedule for the senior year. The SAT I & II are administered in October, November, and December, while the ACT is offered in October and December. (An additional ACT date in late September is available in some states with a registration deadline in late August.)

September is also a good time to focus on the search for outside scholarships, with local sources the most likely. Many high school guidance offices offer scholarship search resources, as do a variety of sites on the Internet. Families should continue college visits and send away for applications if they have not already received them.

### October

Students should file early applications, if applicable, and settle on a list of approximately five to eight colleges. Students should visit the guidance office to review their academic transcript and talk with the guidance counselor about the logistics of the application process. Students should ask teachers to write recommendations and provide those teachers with the necessary forms and envelopes. Students should take the SAT I or II, or ACT, if scheduled. This is the last date that will serve for those applying in an early program.

## November

Students should continue distributing teacher recommendation forms and filing applications. Double-check with the guidence counselor to make sure that final selections are appropriate. Add or subtract additional choices as needed. Take the SAT I or II if scheduled. Where applicable, students should register to receive the PROFILE form, which should be filed with the FAFSA after January 1.

## December

Students should file applications with January deadlines and politely check with teachers and counselors to ensure that recommendations and transcripts have been sent. Families should also be sure to get a copy of the FAFSA from the guidance office. The electronic version will be available on-line at www.fafsa.ed.gov, but not until January 1. Parents should begin collecting tax information and prepare to complete tax forms as soon as possible after January 1. December is the last date that students may take the SAT I or II or ACT for consideration by colleges with January and February application deadlines.

## January–February

Parents should complete the FAFSA form and file it as soon as possible after January 1. If necessary to meet a deadline, they should file on the basis of estimated tax figures rather than completed tax forms. Where applicable, parents should file the CSS/PROFILE form. Parents should review return correspondence regarding both forms and promptly make corrections or changes where necessary. Parents should also complete institutional forms required by the colleges and forward any supporting documentation that may be required, including tax forms, the PROFILE's Noncustodial Parent and Business/Farm supplements, and letters regarding special circumstances.

Students should continue filing applications for admission. About two weeks after sending their material, students should contact each office to verify that their application is complete.

## March–April

Hopefully, your son or daughter will be blessed with many fat letters of congratulations. Pay close attention to each college's financial aid package and the breakdown of grants, loans, and work study jobs. If First Choice U doesn't come through with the best offer, ask it (politely) to take another look at its calculations in light of any awards that are more favorable.

Where students have been put on the waitlist, follow up with a letter expressing continued interest. Consult with your guidance counselor about the possibility of sending an additional recommendation. Regardless of whether the student has been waitlisted, send a deposit to the first choice college among those who offered admission by the May 1 reply date.

## May

The finish line! But will the college search marathon now over, the reality will soon dawn that no matter where a student goes to college, admission is only the beginning.

# PART II

# FINDING A COLLEGE

# 8.

# A Road Map for
# the College Search

$O$f all the misconceptions that surround the college search, one of the most pervasive might be called "the myth of the perfect school." Like Cinderella trying on the glass slipper, there is supposed to be one perfect fit for everyone. When students arrive on the campus of Dream U, so the theory goes, they know immediately that they have reached the promised land. Lightning strikes, the earth moves, magic wands wave, and the student lives happily ever after.

Though some students do have a love-at-first-sight college search, many more successful searches are the product of careful reflection and thorough investigation. A good college search generally uncovers not one, but a number of excellent alternatives, allowing the student and parents to weigh the pluses and minuses of competing colleges. The purpose of this book is to show that when students keep an open mind, they can uncover outstanding colleges across a variety of price ranges.

The purpose of this section is to provide a road map for the college search—from the high rent district to the bargain colleges hidden off the beaten path. The book's point of view comes from my sixteen years as a college counselor and college guide editor, and I hope to convey the sort of broad brush picture of the higher education landscape that families might get at the knee of a good counselor.

A cursory glance a Part II will illustrate one of the book's core principles: the better a student's grades and test scores, the more likely that he or she will get a scholarship. Colleges usually express grade point average (GPA) in terms of a 4.0 scale, where A = 4.0, B = 3.0, C = 2.0, and so on. Many colleges do their own calculation of GPA, regardless of what the high school may report, and they frequently include only academic courses. Standardized testing is also crucial, and scholarship aspirants should strongly consider taking both the SAT I and the ACT. (For an explanation of how these tests relate, turn to page 29.) Be aware that there is sometimes flexibility in the printed standards for scholarship consideration, and students are recommended to inquire if they are near the threshold for consideration or short in only one particular area. Many colleges purposely avoid publishing GPA or testing standards, either from a philosophical commitment to considering the whole applicant or to preserve flexibility.

Some other pointers to keep in mind as you're leafing the profiles:

*Schools in your state may be cheaper:* The differential in sticker price between in-state and out-of-state costs at public institutions leaps off the page. The gap is accentuated by the fact that state-sponsored scholarships are generally good at all in-state institutions, public and private, but often cannot be transported out of state.

*Consider competing institutions:* The profiles often identify competitor schools. At private colleges in particular, applying to several similar ones may give you more leverage to get a better need-based package.

*Look at less selective colleges:* Students who are near the top of a college's applicant pool are more likely to get merit scholarships and better need-based packages, particularly at private colleges.

*Explore varied options:* It pays to consider as many different kinds of appropriate institutions as possible. If you can identify six or seven choices, you'll have more opportunities for aid than if you only apply to three or four.

*Apply early:* The best scholarships usually have the earliest deadlines, and students who apply well before a deadline for admission or aid can sometimes get extra consideration. (See page 22 for a list of colleges in this book with early deadlines for merit scholarships.)

## UNDERSTANDING THE PROFILES

The profiles describe each college and university, with roughly equal space devoted to general characteristics of the institution and scholarship opportunities. Needless to say, the profiles are a brief introduction to large and complex institutions—an appetizer that should leave readers hungry for more information. Unless otherwise noted, readers should assume that every college offers need-based aid distributed along the general guidelines discussed in chapter 4.

Information about need-based aid is included in the statistics and described more fully in some cases. But with limited space, the primary focus of most of the profiles is on merit scholarships and non–need-based aid, where each college's policies are unique. Although the profiles summarize the largest and most lucrative scholarship programs at each college, they should not be viewed as a comprehensive listing unless noted as such.

Scholarships are typically divided into two categories. The first, general recognition scholarships, are usually the largest and frequently offered to incoming students across all divisions of the college or university. These are the ones used to attract top students—and the ones most likely to be noted in the profiles. The second category consists of awards with specific restrictions mandated by the donor, designating the award for students in particular majors, from particular cities or states, or who meet other specific qualifications. These awards are usually small and are often reserved for students with need or for returning students. In some cases, such awards are given by academic departments rather than the admissions or financial aid office. Public universities generally have hundreds of such awards. Private colleges tend to concentrate most of their merit money into general recognition awards, although they may also have restricted merit awards.

Unless otherwise noted, scholarships are renewable and the figure quoted is the annual amount of the award. Colleges generally require a minimum GPA for renewal of merit scholarships—often 3.0—and such terms are an important item to investigate before signing on the dotted line.

## TODAY'S COLLEGE SCENE

At least five major trends are shaping college admissions as we look toward a new millennium. Taken together, they help explain why many colleges in this book are awash with applicants, while others are struggling:

1. <u>Universities are hot and small colleges are not.</u> Bigger is definitely better in the eyes of today's college applicants. Maybe it's the halo effect from graduate programs, or maybe just the fact that students want a college that other people have heard of. On the flip side, more students can gain admission to excellent small colleges.

2. <u>The power of prestige.</u> Most of the nation's elite universities are attracting 50 percent more applications than a decade ago, and some have nearly doubled their total. With the number of eighteen-year-olds rising, the trend is likely to continue.

3. <u>Public institutions attract the budget-conscious.</u> Don't assume that a son or a daughter can get into State U just because a parent did. Standards are rising, especially at the leading campuses, and the honors programs are sizzling.

4. <u>The major cities are hot.</u> I'm talking about chic places like Boston, New York, Washington, D.C., and San Francisco. Everybody wants to go where the action is. Thinking deep thoughts on a rural hilltop surrounded by cows is out of style—at least for the moment.

5. <u>The heartland hustles for applicants.</u> While the coasts are attracting students in droves, the Midwest has many outstanding institutions that are fighting to maintain their selectivity. Aspiring students will have an easier time gaining admission to one of these schools.

Where scholarship deadlines occur before the admission deadline, every effort has been made to note that fact. While many scholarships require only an application for admission, others stipulate either a general scholarship application (often included in the admission packet) or a separate application that must be specifically requested. In some cases, students must contact particular departments or academic divisions for scholarship information. Where an early deadline is mentioned, students are strongly recommended to contact the college for details. PLEASE KEEP IN MIND THAT PROGRAMS AND POLICIES ARE CONSTANTLY CHANGING, AND THAT INFORMATION RELATED TO DEADLINES, REQUIREMENTS, AND SCHOLARSHIP AMOUNTS SHOULD ALWAYS BE VERIFIED WITH THE COLLEGES.

In order to help families zero in on desirable colleges, Part II begins with selected lists and rankings that offer insight about key criteria that underlie the profiles: Which colleges are the most selective? Which ones have the lowest sticker price? Which ones offer merit scholarships? Which ones have the best need-based aid? And so on. I encourage readers to browse them as they search the profiles. These lists include only institutions that are described in the profiles.

## HOW THE COLLEGES WERE SELECTED

Out of more than 2,200 four-year colleges in the United States, the profiles include 360 of the very best. All of the colleges that attract a national student body are listed, as well as the most prominent of those with regional appeal. Selectivity was the most important criterion for inclusion, both as an indicator of institutional resources and reputation and as a measure of success in attracting the best students. More than any other variable, the quality of the student body dictates the quality of the learning environment. The tenor of campus life, the level of intellectual discourse, and the opportunities after graduation are all linked to a college's success in attracting good students. By contrast, quality of the faculty does not vary so systematically across high education. Teaching ability is not the primary consideration in most hiring decisions, and the overabundance of Ph.D.s for the past twenty years has meant that even little-known institutions have had their pick of top faculty candidates.

In rounding out the list, every effort was made to encompass the rich diversity of American higher education. I included some additional large public universities, mainly because they are of interest to more applicants than smaller institutions. Colleges known for low tuition or hefty scholarship programs seemed a natural fit, and I made sure to include a number of outstanding schools that specialize in the arts. Geographical diversity was also a factor, especially in regions that do not have a large number of selective schools. A number of colleges made the list because I think they are noteworthy even if not well known. In the end, assembling the colleges for this book was a lot like the admissions process at a highly selective college. There was nothing scientific about it, but I am confident that I have included the vast majority of schools that will interest ambitious students.

Information about scholarships and aid policies was provided by the colleges themselves or gleaned from their published materials. I also drew liberally from the rich body of facts and information known as the Common Data Set, a database jointly developed by the College Board, major guidebook publishers, and the colleges themselves.

# THE STATISTICS

Most of the statistical data applies to the 1997–98 academic year, with the exception of the sticker price figures, which are for 1998–99. The following is a point-by-point summary of the factual data:

*Enrollment:* This represents the total enrollment of all students in all programs.

*Undergraduate:* The number of undergraduate students enrolled.

*Acceptance Rate:* The percentage of applicants for first-year admission who are accepted. Combined with the SAT range, this figure provides an approximate measure of the selectivity of each college. (See Where the Competition Is Keenest on page 112.) Note that figures for pubic institutions apply to a combination of in-state and out-of-state applicants, and that acceptance rates for those in each category may vary.

*SAT Range:* A few years ago, some colleges began to rebel at the prospect of reporting average SAT I scores. The rationale was that such figures might be mistaken for cutoffs and thereby cause confusion. The SAT range represents the scores of the middle 50 percent of students who enrolled: the score in the 25th percentile and the score in the 75th percentile. (A few colleges do report an average, which I offer in cases where the range is not available.) Note the word *enrolled.* The SAT range of accepted students is somewhat higher, in most cases, because fewer accepted applicants with high SAT scores enroll due to the fact that they are the ones most likely to have other options. In a few instances where an SAT range was not available, I have included an ACT range.

*Sticker Price:* This figure is for the annual sum of tuition, room and board, mandatory fees, and books and supplies, rounded down to the nearest thousand. In the case of public institutions, there is an in-state and out-of-state figure. The reason for the "+" is that families should factor in at least $1,000 additional dollars for personal expenses and travel. (Add in another $1,000 if the college is a plane ride away.)

*Need-Blind:* This brings us deep into fudge territory. Of the 357 colleges who responded to this item on the Common Data Set, 312 said they are need-blind, 29 said they are not, and 16 declined to answer the question. Unfortunately, I can't claim to be convinced that all the responses are entirely accurate, but such are the pitfalls of self-reported data. The colleges that are not need-blind typically consider need when evaluating the applications of some candidates in the final stages of their deliberations. Many needy students are admitted to such colleges, but those who are borderline candidates with high need are less likely to be admitted.

*Need Met:* Taken from the Common Data Set, this figure refers to the average percentage of need that was met for students who received need-based aid. A number of colleges did not report this item, and due to definitional difficulties and the fudge factor, these percentages seem high in some cases. The core distinction is between those colleges that meet 100 percent of need and those that do not. Any figure below 75 percent means that need-based aid is limited.

*Average Student Debt:* This figure is the average cumulative indebtedness of graduates who were borrowers. Overall, it's a good piece of data, though the percentage is apt to be somewhat higher for institutions that enroll high need students or enroll students who tend to borrow more. Nevertheless, it's a reliable indicator of whether students are being saddled with lots of loans. Any figure over $20,000 is high, while a number below $10,000 is low.

*Merit Scholarships:* The ratings are few, many, and none. Few refers to institutions with limited offerings, such as those that honor National Merit Scholars but have no programs of their own, or those with only a handful of programs that give a modest number of awards to less than 5 percent of the entering students. Most colleges in the book received the Many rating. Where available, I have included an upper end *Range* for the awards. Full costs refer to scholarships that cover the entire cost of attendance, including room and board and usually fees, too. Full tuition refers to awards that cover instructional fees but not living expenses.

*Athletic Scholarships:* This item is limited to yes and no. Cases where scholarships are offered in only one or two sports are noted in the profiles. Athletic scholarships range up to full costs, although amounts vary depending on the college and the sport.

*ROTC:* Institutions with this listing sponsor programs for recipients of Reserve Officer Training Corps Scholarships in one or more of the Army, Navy, and Air Force. (Marine Corps ROTC is an option within the Navy program.) Note that the programs may be offered on campus, or they may be hosted by neighboring institutions. Students apply for the scholarships through ROTC, although the colleges sometimes add in funds of their own.

*Deadlines:* Each college has various deadlines. *Early Decision* and *Early Action* refer to those programs, respectively. *Admission* refers to the regular admission deadline. In cases where a priority deadline is noted, applications may be considered after that date. *FAFSA* is the deadline for the Free Application for Federal Student Aid, required of all aid applicants except in isolated cases as noted. A significant portion of the colleges in this book also ask for the *CSS PROFILE*. Be aware that financial aid deadlines sometimes precede admission deadlines. A rolling designation signifies that applications are processed on a first-come, first-served basis. Families should check with the schools to verify deadlines and find out if additional material is mandatory. Many colleges require submission of a state financial aid form (depending on place of residents), an application for institutional need-based aid, a scholarship application for merit awards, and/or relevant tax documents and other documentation.

# 9.

# Lists and Rankings

This chapter is designed as an index to the College Profiles. The material is divided into four categories: Admission and Need-Based Aid, Sticker Price, The Scholarship Search, and Colleges with the Most Money.

## ADMISSION AND NEED-BASED AID

### Where the Competition Is Keenest

Measurement of selectivity is an inexact science. A college's acceptance rate is one obvious indicator, and the majority of those on all three lists below admit less than 50 percent of the students who apply. But just as important is the strength of a college's applicant pool and its success in persuading accepted applicants to enroll. An institution such as Grinnell College, for instance, has an acceptance rate of about 69 percent but attracts some of the nation's top students, with average SAT I scores above 1300. Though more than two-thirds of its applicants get in, Grinnell is more selective than other institutions that accept a lower percentage of applicants from a less distinguished pool.

The colleges on these lists were chosen on the basis of their overall selectivity as measured by their acceptance rates, the percentage of accepted applicants who enroll, and the class rank and standardized test scores of entering students. State institutions are classified primarily on the basis of their selectivity for out-of-staters. For individual students, the odds for admission at each college will vary depending on a host of factors ranging from intended major to place of residence.

By now you know the bad news: the nation's elite institutions are generally more selective now than they were ten or twenty years ago, with especially tough competition at universities in major cities. The silver lining is that there are more than 200 colleges in this book not listed below. While some of them offer particular programs that are very selective, most admit the overwhelming majority of qualified applicants.

## INTENSELY COMPETITIVE

Amherst College
Bowdoin College
Brown University
California Institute of Technology
University of California/ Berkeley
Columbia University
Cooper Union
Cornell University (NY)
Curtis Institute of Music
Dartmouth College
Deep Springs College
Duke University
Georgetown University
Harvard University
Haverford College
Johns Hopkins University

Juilliard School
Massachusetts Institute of Technology
Middlebury College
University of North Carolina/Chapel Hill
Northwestern University
University of Pennsylvania
Pomona College
Princeton University
Rice University
Stanford University
Swarthmore College
University of Virginia
Wesleyan University
Williams College
Yale University

## HIGHLY COMPETITIVE

Barnard College
Bates College
Boston College
Bryn Mawr College
Bucknell University
California Institute of the Arts
University of California/Los Angeles
Carleton College
Carnegie Mellon University
University of Chicago
Claremont McKenna College
Colby College
Colgate University
Davidson College
Eastman School of Music
Emory University

Franklin and Marshall College
Grinnell College
Hamilton College
Harvey Mudd College
College of the Holy Cross
Lafayette College
Lehigh University
Macalester College
Manhattan School of Music
University of Michigan
New College of the University of South Florida
New England Conservatory of Music
New York University
University of Notre Dame
Oberlin College

Peabody Conservatory of Music
Reed College
University of Richmond
Smith College
Trinity College (CT)
Tufts University
Vanderbilt University

Vassar College
Wake Forest University
Washington and Lee University
Washington University in St. Louis
Webb Institute
Wellesley College
College of William and Mary

## VERY COMPETITIVE

College of the Atlantic
Babson College
Bard College
Berea College
Boston University
Brandeis University
University of California/San Diego
Case Western Reserve University
Cleveland Institute of Music
Colorado College
Connecticut College
University of Florida
George Washington University
Georgia Institute of Technology
University of Illinois/Urbana-Champaign
Kenyon College
Lewis and Clark College
Maryland Institute, College of Art
McGill University
Morehouse College
Mount Holyoke College
College of New Jersey
North Carolina School of the Arts

College of the Ozarks
Parsons School of Design
Pennsylvania State University
Rensselaer Polytechnic Institute
Rhode Island School of Design
Rhodes College
University of Rochester
St. Mary's College of Maryland
San Francisco Conservatory of Music
Sarah Lawrence College
Skidmore College
University of the South (Sewanee)
University of Southern California
Spelman College
State University of New York/Binghamton
University of Texas/Austin
Tulane University
Union College
Wheaton College (IL)
Whitman College
University of Wisconsin/Madison
Worcester Polytechnic Institute

## Colleges That Are Need-Blind and Meet Full Need

This list and the one that follows are based on self-reported data from the colleges.

Agnes Scott College
Amherst College
Arizona State University
University of Arizona
Barnard College

Bates College
Beloit College
Bowdoin College
California Institute of Technology
Case Western Reserve University

University of Chicago
City University of New York/
    Brooklyn College
Claremont McKenna College
College of the Holy Cross
Colorado College
Colorado School of Mines
Columbia University
Cooper Union
Cornell University (NY)
Dartmouth College
Davidson College
Duke University
Georgetown University
Goucher College
Grinnell College
Hampshire College
Harvard University
Haverford College
College of the Holy Cross
Illinois Wesleyan University
Iowa State University
Knox College
Lake Forest College

Lawrence University
Macalester College
Massachusetts Institute of Technology
Middlebury College
University of Minnesota/Twin Cities
Northwestern University
University of Oklahoma
University of Pennsylvania
Pomona College
Princeton University
Rice University
St. John's University (NY)
St. Olaf College
University of the South (Sewanee)
Stanford University
Swarthmore College
Trinity College (CT)
Wabash College
Washington and Jefferson College
Webb Institute
Wellesley College
Wesleyan University
Williams College
Yale University

## Colleges That Are not Need-Blind in Admission

The colleges on this list acknowledge that ability to pay is a factor in some admission decisions and generally show preference for students without financial need in borderline cases. Some administrators at these colleges say privately that there are many others not listed here, most of them nonpublic, that also consider need in admission. As noted in chapter 2, most colleges show preference on the waitlist for applicants who do not need aid. (Nearly two dozen colleges in this book did not answer a survey question about need-blind status and are listed with an NA for that item in the profiles.) Though needy students face a slightly higher standard for admission, the colleges that are not need-blind often deliver better aid packages than competitor schools because they target money to the applicants they want most. On the list below, nearly two thirds report that they meet the full need of all students who are accepted.

Allegheny College
Brown University
Bryn Mawr College
Bucknell University

Carleton College
The Catholic University of America
Colby College
Colgate University

Connecticut College
Florida Institute of Technology
Franklin and Marshall College
Hamilton College
Harvey Mudd College
Johns Hopkins University
Lehigh University
Manhattan School of Music
Mount Holyoke College
Oberlin College

Pitzer College
Rhodes College
St. Lawrence University
Sarah Lawrence College
Skidmore College
Smith College
Union College
Vassar College
Washington University

## Colleges That Award Aid Only to Students Who Show Need

These colleges are the last hold-outs against merit scholarships, but many of them find alternative ways to entice the top students with extra goodies. The loot can include aid packages with beefed up grants and no loans, summer internships and research stipends, and named awards for the most meritorious of the needy. *

Amherst College
Art Center College of Design
Barnard College
Bates College
Bowdoin College
Brown University
Bryn Mawr College
Bucknell University
Colby College
Colgate University
Columbia University
Connecticut College
Cornell University (NY)
Curry College
Dartmouth College
Eugene Lang College
Georgetown University **
Harvard University
Haverford College
Massachusetts Institute of Technology
Middlebury College

Mount Holyoke College
University of Notre Dame**
Parsons School of Design
University of Pennsylvania
Princeton University
Reed College
College of Santa Fe
St. John's College (MD and NM)
San Francisco Conservatory of Music
Sarah Lawrence College
Smith College
Stanford University **
Thomas Aquinas College
Trinity College (CT)
Tufts University
Union College
Vassar College
Wellesley College
Wesleyan University
Williams College
Yale University

*Two additional colleges, Berea College and College of the Ozarks, accept only students who demonstrate need.
**These colleges offer athletic scholarships but no academic merit scholarships.

# Colleges That Require the CSS/Financial Aid PROFILE

This list includes the colleges that require the PROFILE from all financial aid applicants. Additional schools may require it of certain applicants, such as those applying for early decision. Families are advised to confirm requirements with each college.

Agnes Scott College
Amherst College
Babson College
Bard College
Barnard College
Bates College
Boston College
Boston University
Bowdoin College
Brandeis University
Brown University
Bucknell University
California Institute of Technology
Carleton College
Case Western Reserve University
University of Chicago
Clark University
Cleveland Institute of Music
Colgate University
Colorado College
Columbia University
Connecticut College
Cooper Union
Cornell University (NY)
Dartmouth College
Davidson College
Depauw University
Dickinson College
Duke University
Emory University
Eugene Lang College
Fairfield University
Fordham University
Franklin and Marshall College
George Washington University
Georgetown University

Gettysburg College
Gordon College
Goucher College
Guilford College
Hamilton College
Hampden-Sydney College
Hampshire College
Hanover College
Hartwick College
Harvard University
Harvey Mudd College
Haverford College
Hillsdale College
Hobart and William Smith Colleges
College of the Holy Cross
Hope College
Illinois Wesleyan University
Kalamazoo College
Kenyon College
Lafayette College
Lehigh University
Loyola College (MD)
Loyola University/ Chicago
Macalester College
Manhattan School of Music
Manhattanville College
Marlboro College
Massachusetts Institute of Technology
Middlebury College
Muhlenberg College
Northeastern University
Northwestern University
University of North Carolina/Chapel Hill
University of Notre Dame
Oberlin College
Occidental College

Parsons School of Design
University of Pennsylvania
Pitzer College
Pomona College
Princeton University
Providence College
Reed College
Rhode Island School of Design
University of Rochester
St. John's College (MD and NM)
Santa Clara University
Sarah Lawrence College
University of Scranton
Scripps College
Simon's Rock of Bard College
Skidmore College
Smith College
Stanford University
Susquehanna University
Swarthmore College
Trinity College (CT)
Tufts University

Tulane University
Union College
Ursinus College
Vanderbilt University
Vassar College
Wabash University
Wake Forest University
Washington and Lee University
Washington University in St. Louis
Wellesley College
Wells College
Wesleyan University
Wheaton College (MA)
Whitman College
Whittier College
Willamette University
College of William and Mary
Williams College
Wofford College
College of Wooster
Worcester Polytechnic Institute
Yale University

## STICKER PRICE

Families should always proceed with caution when investigating colleges based on their published prices. As this book shows, such figures may not reflect the ultimate out-of-pocket expense after the scholarships, discounts, and financial aid has been added up. Nevertheless, sticker price can be an important indicator of affordability. The first two lists feature my picks for the best values among small colleges and major universities. The other four include all colleges in the designated sticker price categories based on figures from the 1998–1999 academic year.

### The Best Bargains—Small Colleges

Evergreen State College
Grove City College
Hendrix College
Mary Washington College
University of Minnesota/Morris
Morehouse College

New College of the University of South
    Florida
College of New Jersey
North Carolina School of the Arts
University of North Carolina/Asheville
St. Mary's College of Maryland

Spelman College
Thomas Aquinas College

Truman State University
College of William and Mary

COMMENTS:

With an elite reputation and an out-of-state sticker price of just over $15,000,
New College of the University of South Florida is my choice as the nation's
best small-college bargain. New College is the leader in a category that has gotten more attention in the past ten years: the public liberal arts colleges. Others
in a similar price range include Evergreen State, Mary Washington, St. Mary's,
Minnesota/Morris, College of New Jersey, UNC/Asheville, and Truman State.
With favorable press and increasing applications, the reputation of these
schools will continue to grow. Among private colleges, Grove City stands out
for its remarkably low price tag of about $12,000. Hendrix is an excellent pri-
vate college in the $16,000 range, and Thomas Aquinas is a distinctive
Catholic college with a Great Books curriculum. Morehouse and Spelman,
two prestigious historically black institutions, deliver their goods for about
$18,000. William and Mary is actually a medium-sized public university, but it
offers prestige and a small-college atmosphere. Name-brand private colleges
begin at about $20,000, with the least expensive ones generally in the South
and the Midwest. Aside from Curtis Institute of Music (listed below in Six
Where Tuition Is Free), North Carolina School of the Arts is the nation's best
bargain among arts specialty schools.

## The Best Bargains—Major Universities

University of Florida
Georgia Institute of Technology
University of Georgia
University of Illinois/Urbana-Champaign
University of Kansas
Miami University (OH)

University of North Carolina/Chapel Hill
Rice University
State University of New York/Binghamton
University of Texas/Austin
University of Virginia
University of Wisconsin/Madison

COMMENTS:

A number of major universities combine an in-state sticker price of about
$8,000 with an out-of-state tab of about $16,000. A few of the most attractive
include Florida, Georgia, Illinois, Kansas, Wisconsin, UNC/Chapel Hill,
SUNY/Binghamton, and UT/Austin. As noted in chapter 3, the best way to
partake of these plus-sized institutions is usually to enroll in an honors program or other special opportunity. Georgia Tech is a prestigious science/engi-
neering school in the same price range. UVA and Miami are more expensive
but offer prestige and a private college atmosphere. Rice is the nation's preeminent bargain among elite private universities.

## Six Where Tuition Is Free

Berea College
Cooper Union
Curtis Institute of Music

Deep Springs College
College of the Ozarks
Webb Institute

COMMENTS:

Perhaps the most remarkable member of this group is Deep Springs College, where twenty-six of the nation's brightest college men pay nothing at all to live and learn in a remote desert hideaway. Berea and College of the Ozarks are small liberal arts colleges that waive tuition but require work, and only students with high need are admitted. Curtis is one of the nation's finest conservatories; Cooper Union offers outstanding programs in art, architecture, and engineering; and Webb is a tiny place that focuses solely on naval architecture and marine engineering.

## Private Colleges with a Sticker Price of Less Than $20,000

Alverno College
Austin College
Baylor University
Berea College
Bradley University
Brigham Young University
Calvin College
Cooper Union
Creighton University
Curtis Institute of Music
University of Dallas
Deep Springs College
Florida A&M University
Grove City College
Hampton University
Hanover College
Hendrix College

Hillsdale College
Houghton College
Kettering University
Morehouse College
Muskingum College
North Carolina Wesleyan College
College of the Ozarks
Prescott College
St. John's University (NY)
College of Santa Fe
Spelman College
Texas Christian University
Thomas Aquinas College
University of Tulsa
Warren Wilson College
Wells College
Webb Institute

## Public Institutions with an Out-of-State Sticker Price of Less Than $15,000

University of Alabama
Arizona State University
University of Arizona
University of Arkansas
Auburn University

California Polytechnic State University/
    San Luis Obispo
College of Charleston
City University of New York/Brooklyn
    College

City University of New York/City College
City University of New York/Hunter College
City University of New York/ John Jay
    College of Criminal Justice
City University of New York/Queens College
Clemson University
Evergreen State College
Florida State University
University of Florida
University of Houston
Iowa State University
Kansas State University
University of Kansas
Louisiana State University/Baton Rouge
University of Minnesota/Morris
Montana Tech of the University of Montana
Morgan State University

University of Nebraska/Lincoln
College of New Jersey
New Mexico Institute of Mining and
    Technology
University of New Mexico
University of North Carolina/Asheville
University of Oklahoma
University of South Carolina
State University of New York College/
    Geneseo
Texas A&M University
University of Texas/Austin
University of Toronto
Truman State University
University of Utah
West Virginia University

## Colleges with a Sticker Price over $30,000

Amherst College
Bard College
Barnard College
Bates College
Boston College
Boston University
Bowdoin College
Brandeis University
Brown University
Bryn Mawr College
University of Chicago
Colby College
Colgate University
Columbia University
Connecticut College
Cornell University (NY, private divisions)
Dartmouth College
Duke University
Emory University
George Washington University
Hamilton College
Hampshire College
Harvard University

Haverford College
Hobart and William Smith Colleges
Johns Hopkins University
Massachusetts Institute of Technology
Middlebury College
Mount Holyoke College
New York University
Northwestern University
Oberlin College
University of Pennsylvania
Pitzer College
Princeton University
Reed College
Rensselaer Polytechnic Institute
University of Rochester
Sarah Lawrence College
Skidmore College
Smith College
Stanford University
Trinity College (CT)
Tufts University
Tulane University
Union College

Vassar College
Washington University in St. Louis
Wellesley College

Wesleyan University
Williams College
Yale University

# THE SCHOLARSHIP SEARCH

## Early Bird Scholarship Deadlines

Failure to meet deadlines is the number one reason why qualified students miss out on scholarships. The following list includes colleges with a scholarship deadline that precedes the admission deadline and is before March 1. Some deadlines are for a particular highly competitive scholarship; others are general deadlines for some or all of the merit scholarships that an institution offers. Consult the college profiles for details; only the earliest deadline at each institution is listed here. There may be additional scholarships with early deadlines, including awards offered by particular academic departments and those that feature a nomination process controlled by the high school. Deadlines constantly change, and the best move is always to contact the colleges for the latest information.

| DEADLINE | COLLEGE OR UNIVERSITY | SCHOLARSHIP |
|---|---|---|
| October 1 | Miami University | Harrison Scholarship |
| October 9 | Michigan Technological University | University Scholar Award |
| October 15 | Whittier College | John Greenleaf Whittier Scholarship |
| October 31 | Georgia Institute of Technology | Presidential Scholarship |
| November 1 | Boston College | Presidential Scholarship |
| | Howard University | General |
| | Kansas State University | General |
| | Michigan State University | Alumni Distinguished Scholarship |
| | University of Missouri/Rolla | General |
| | University of Oklahoma | General |
| | University of South Carolina | General |
| November 3 | University of Connecticut | Nutmeg Scholarship |
| November 15 | Emory University | Emory Scholars |
| | North Carolina State University | General |
| | University of North Carolina/Chapel Hill | General |
| | Truman State University | General |
| November 26 | Lake Forest College | Founder's Scholarship |
| November 30 | University of Georgia | Foundation Fellowship |

|  | Pennsylvania State University | Academic Excellence Scholarship |
|---|---|---|
| December 1 | University of Alabama | General |
|  | Auburn University | General |
|  | Bennington College | Bennington Scholars |
|  | Boston University | Trustee Scholarship |
|  | Butler University | General |
|  | Depaul University | General |
|  | University of Iowa | Presidential Scholarship |
|  | Loyola University/New Orleans | General |
|  | University of Maryland/College Park | General |
|  | University of Missouri/Columbia | General |
|  | University of New Mexico | Regents and Presidential Scholarships |
|  | Purdue University | School of Science Distinguished Scholar |
|  | Rhodes College | Bellingrath and Hyde Scholarships |
|  | Saint Louis University | General |
|  | University of San Francisco | University Scholars |
|  | University of Texas/Austin | General |
|  | Tulane University | Dean's Honor Scholarship |
|  | Villanova University | Presidential Scholarship |
|  | Wabash College | President's Scholarship |
|  | Wake Forest University | Reynolds Scholarship |
|  | Wofford University | Wofford Scholars |
| December 4 | University of North Carolina/Asheville | General |
| December 5 | Presbyterian College | General |
| December 10 | University of Southern California | General |
| December 15 | City University of New York/Brooklyn College | Honors Scholarship |
|  | Florida State University | General |
|  | Kenyon College | Kenyon Honor and Science Scholarships |
|  | Louisiana State University/Baton Rouge | General |
|  | Ohio Northern University | General |
|  | Ohio State University | University Scholar Maximus Program |
|  | University of Redlands | General |
|  | University of Rhode Island | Centennial Scholars |
|  | Randolph-Macon Woman's College | Gottwald Scholarship |
|  | Rutgers, The State University of New Jersey | General |

| | | |
|---|---|---|
| | State University of New York/Albany | General |
| | State University of New York/Purchase | General |
| | State University of New York/ Stony Brook | Presidential Achievement Scholarship |
| | Villanova University | Presidential Scholarship |
| | Washington and Lee University | Honor Scholarships |
| | University of Wisconsin/Madison | General |
| December 31 | Clemson University | General |
| January 1 | University of Delaware | General |
| | Denison University | General |
| | Fairfield University | University Fellowship |
| | Guilford College | General |
| | Hillsdale College | General |
| | Hobart and William Smith Colleges | Trustee Scholarship |
| | Lawrence University | (Scholarship competition in Jan.–Feb.) |
| | Northeastern University | General |
| | Oregon State University | General |
| | University of Richmond | Oldham Scholars |
| | University of the South (Sewanee) | General |
| | University of Tennessee/Knoxville | Whittle Scholarship |
| | Vanderbilt University | General |
| First Friday in January | University of Kentucky | General |
| January 5 | George Mason University | General |
| January 8 | Texas A&M University | General |
| January 10 | Pacific Lutheran University | Regents' Scholarship |
| | Seton Hall University | Martin Luther King, Jr. Scholarship |
| | State University of New York/Buffalo | Distinguished Honors Scholars |
| January 15 | Agnes Scott College | General |
| | Austin College | Presidential Scholarship |
| | Beloit College | Presidential Scholarship |
| | Birmingham-Southern College | General |
| | Bradley University | General |
| | Brigham Young University | Gordon B. Hinckley Scholarship |
| | College of Charleston | General |
| | University of Cincinnati | Cincinnatus Scholarship Competition |
| | University of Dayton | General |
| | Hanover College | General |
| | Hendrix College | General |

| | | |
|---|---|---|
| | Illinois Institute of Technology | General |
| | University of Kansas | General |
| | University of Kentucky | President's and Chancellor's Scholarships |
| | Mary Washington College | Alumni Scholarship |
| | University of Michigan | Bentley and Shipman Scholarships |
| | University of Minnesota/Twin Cities | U2000 Scholarship |
| | University of Nebraska/Lincoln | General |
| | University of North Carolina/Greensboro | General |
| | University of Pittsburgh | General |
| | Siena College | Presidential Scholarship |
| | Southern Methodist University | General |
| | Stetson University | Edmunds Distinguished Scholarship |
| | Sweet Briar College | General |
| | Texas Christian University | General |
| | Valparaiso University | Founders Scholarship |
| | Virginia Polytechnic Institute and State University (Virginia Tech) | General |
| | College of Wooster | General |
| January 20 | Hope College | Trustee Scholarship |
| January 22 | Loyola University/Chicago | University Scholar Award |
| February 1 | University of Arkansas | Sturgis Fellowships |
| | Calvin College | General |
| | Creighton University | General |
| | Florida Institute of Technology | General |
| | Furman University | General |
| | Gordon College | A .J. Gordon Scholarship |
| | Hiram College | General |
| | Hollins University | Hollins Scholars |
| | University of Maine/Orono | General |
| | Marquette University | General |
| | University of Oregon | General |
| | University of Puget Sound | General |
| | Rochester Institute of Technology | General |
| | Rollins College | General |
| | St. John's University and College of St. Benedict (MN) | General |
| | Southwestern University | General |
| | University of Utah | General |
| | School of Visual Arts | Rhodes Scholarship |

| February 15 | Adelphi University | General |
| | Alverno College | Ellen Harcourt Scholarship |
| | Eckerd College | Presidential Scholarship |
| | John Carroll University | President's Honor Award |
| | University of Minnesota/Morris | Presidential Scholarship |
| | Montana Tech of the University of Montana | General |
| | West Virginia University | General |
| | Wittenberg University | General |
| February 28 | Hampton University | Presidential Scholars |
| | Warren Wilson College | General |

## The Nation's Most Prestigious Merit Scholarships

Top students are often disappointed when they find out that Ivy League and similar schools offer only need-based aid. This list is designed to take away some of the sting. It features my choices of the sweetest deals in higher education. The two criteria for inclusion are the size of the award and the desirability of the institution. Most of the scholarships cover at least full tuition, and all come with admission to one of the nation's best colleges. Readers will note that southern universities offer a disproportionate share of them. The most prestigious northeastern universities have generally followed the lead of the Ivy League in sticking to need-based aid, although more merit awards pop up north of the Mason-Dixon line with each passing year.

Every scholarship on this list is awarded on the basis of all-around excellence, which begins with excellence in the classroom. Needless to say, all are intensely competitive.

California Institute of Technology—Caltech Merit Scholarship—
Up to full tuition

> These coveted prizes represent the pinnacle of achievement for students in science and technology. Awarded at increments of $10,000, $15,000 and full tuition.

University of Chicago—College Honor Scholarship—Up to full tuition

> The U of C's main weapon in luring the crème de la crème away from the Ivy League. Approximately thirty-five are awarded for "outstanding academic and extracurricular achievement, demonstrated leadership, and commitment to the community."

Davidson College—Special Competition Scholarships—From $15,000 to "comprehensive costs"

> Davidson puts several named awards under the Special Competition

umbrella that together include about a dozen scholarships. Criteria vary but emphasize all-around excellence.

Duke University—Angier B. Duke Memorial Scholarship—
Full tuition plus summer at Oxford

It doesn't get any better than free tuition at Duke. Fifteen Duke Scholarships per year are awarded on the basis of "outstanding academic and leadership qualities."

Emory University—Emory Scholars Program—Ranges from full tuition to tuition, room and board, and fees.

Emory's deep pockets may account for the fact that there are seventy Emory Scholars each year. Students must be nominated by their school. And watch the deadline: November 15.

Johns Hopkins University—Beneficial-Hodson Scholarship—
$17,000 per year

The Hop awards fifteen of these a year for "academic excellence, personal achievement, and demonstrated leadership qualities." In a recent year, there were 800 nominees.

University of North Carolina/Chapel Hill—Morehead Scholar—Tuition, room and board, fees, and summer stipend

With UNC's booming popularity, the Morehead is a sought-after prize. A total of sixty scholarships are given each year. Students must be nominated in the fall of twelfth grade by a participating school, which include all those in North Carolina and sixty-four selected out-of-state high schools. (A small number of at-large nominees are chosen from the regular applicant pool.)

Rice University—Merit scholarships up to full tuition

Rice doesn't make a big deal out of its merit scholarships and they require no special application. Awards of up to full tuition are parceled out to the most outstanding students in its applicant pool.

Swarthmore College—McCabe Scholarship—Full tuition

Swarthmore is the only one of the Northeast's most prestigious liberal arts colleges to offer a major merit award. Just two are available to students nationwide, with several more reserved for students from Delaware County, Pennsylvania, and the Delmarva Peninsula.

Vanderbilt University—Harold Stirling Vanderbilt Honor Scholarship—Full tuition and summer foreign study stipend

Vandy awards twelve Stirling Honor Scholarships each year for "exceptional accomplishment and high promise in academic endeavors." A separate program gives the same package to minority students. Apply by January 1.

University of Virginia—Jefferson Scholars—Full tuition, room, board, expenses, and opportunity for summer stipend

UVA bestows twenty-five Jefferson scholarships each year to students who have "excelled as scholars, leaders, and citizens." Students from 1,300 participating high schools are eligible to be nominated by a November deadline. Other students may be considered on an at-large basis from the regular applicant pool.

Wake Forest University—Reynolds Scholarship—Full tuition, room, board, expenses, and opportunity for summer stipend

Only five of these coveted awards are made available each year, though Wake does have a number of other attractive scholarships in lesser amounts. Apply by December 1.

Washington University in St. Louis—Honorary Scholarships—Up to full tuition plus a $2,500 stipend

Wash U awards thirty scholarships per year of at least full tuition through its various academic divisions. A separate program honors outstanding African Americans.

Washington and Lee University—Honor Scholarships—Up to full tuition

W&L's Honor Scholarships include various named awards, some that cover full tuition and others of lesser amounts. Apply by December 15.

## More Highly Selective Colleges That Offer Academic Merit Scholarships

Of the colleges in this book, 318 of them offer scholarships based on academic merit. Most of the institutions in the previous list give awards of lesser amounts in addition to those that were described. The following is a list of more highly selective colleges that give merit money.

| | |
|---|---|
| College of the Atlantic | University of California/Berkeley |
| Babson College | University of California/Los Angeles |
| Bard College | University of California/San Diego |
| Berea College | Carleton College |
| Boston College | Carnegie Mellon University |
| Boston University | Case Western Reserve University |
| Brandeis University | Claremont McKenna College |
| California Institute of the Arts | Colorado College |

Cooper Union
Curtis Institute of Music
Eastman School of Music
University of Florida
Franklin and Marshall College
George Washington University
Georgia Institute of Technology
Grinnell College
Hamilton College
Harvey Mudd College
College of the Holy Cross
University of Illinois/Urbana-Champaign
Juilliard School
Kenyon College
Lafayette College
Lehigh University
Lewis and Clark College
Macalester College
Manhattan School of Music
Maryland Institute, College of Art
McGill University
University of Michigan
Morehouse College
New College of the University of South Florida
New England Conservatory of Music
College of New Jersey
New York University

North Carolina School of the Arts
Oberlin College
College of the Ozarks
Peabody Conservatory of Music
Pennsylvania State University
Pomona College
Rennselaer Polytechnic Institute
Rhode Island School of Design
Rhodes College
Rice University
University of Richmond
University of Rochester
St. Mary's College of Maryland
Skidmore College
University of the South (Sewanee)
University of Southern California
Spelman College
State University of New York/Binghamton
University of Texas/Austin
Tulane University
Washington University in St. Louis
Wheaton College (IL)
Whitman College
University of Wisconsin/Madison
Worcester Polytechnic Insitute
College of William and Mary
Webb Institute

## Colleges That Offer Athletic Scholarships

Adelphi University
University of Alabama
Albertson College of Idaho
American University
Arizona State University
University of Arizona
University of Arkansas
Auburn University
Baylor University
Birmingham-Southern College
Boston College
Boston University

Bradley University
Brigham Young University
Butler University
California Polytechnic State University/ San Luis Obispo
University of California/Berkeley
University of California/Irvine
University of California/Los Angeles
University of California/Riverside
University of California/Santa Barbara
College of Charleston
University of Cincinnati

City University of New York/Queens College
Clarkson University
Clemson University
Colorado College
Colorado School of Mines
University of Connecticut
Creighton University
Davidson College
University of Dayton
University of Delaware
University of Denver
Depaul University
Drexel University
Duke University
Duquesne University
Eckerd College
Fairfield University
Florida A&M University
Florida Institute of Technology
Florida State University
University of Florida
Fordham University
Furman University
Georgetown University
George Mason University
George Washington University
Georgia Institute of Technology
University of Georgia
Hampton University
Hartwick College
University of Hawaii/Manoa
Hillsdale College
Hofstra University
College of the Holy Cross
Houghton College
University of Houston
Howard University
Illinois Institute of Technology
University of Illinois/Chicago
University of Illinois/Urbana-Champaign
Indiana University/Bloomington
Iowa State University
University of Iowa
James Madison University

Johns Hopkins University
Kansas State University
University of Kansas
University of Kentucky
Lafayette College
Lehigh University
Louisiana State University/Baton Rouge
Loyola College (MD)
Loyola Marymount University
Loyola University/Chicago
University of Maine/Orono
Marquette University
University of Maryland/College Park
University of Massachusetts/Amherst
Miami University (OH)
University of Miami (FL)
Michigan State University
University of Michigan
University of Minnesota/Twin Cities
University of Missouri/Columbia
University of Missouri/Rolla
Montana Tech of the University of Montana
Morehouse College
Morgan State University
University of Nebraska/Lincoln
University of New Hampshire
University of New Mexico
Northeastern University
Northwestern University
North Carolina State University
University of North Carolina/Asheville
University of North Carolina/Chapel Hill
University of North Carolina/Greensboro
University of Notre Dame
Ohio State University
Ohio University
University of Oklahoma
Oregon State University
University of Oregon
College of the Ozarks
University of the Pacific
Pennsylvania State University
Pepperdine University
University of Pittsburgh

Presbyterian College
Providence College
Purdue University
Rensselaer Polytechnic Institute
University of Rhode Island
Rice University
University of Richmond
Rollins College
Rutgers, The State University of New Jersey
St. John's University (NY)
St. Lawrence College
Saint Louis University
University of San Francisco
Santa Clara University
Seton Hall University
Siena College
University of South Carolina
University of Southern California
Southern Methodist University
Spring Hill College
Stanford University
State University of New York/Albany
State University of New York/Binghamton
State University of New York/Buffalo

State University of New York/Stony Brook
Stetson University
Syracuse University
Temple University
University of Tennessee/Knoxville
Texas A&M University
Texas Christian University
University of Texas/Austin
Truman State University
Tulane University
University of Tulsa
University of Utah
Valparaiso University
Vanderbilt University
University of Vermont
Villanova University
Virginia Polytechnic Institute and State
   University (Virginia Tech)
University of Virginia
Wake Forest University
West Virginia University
College of William and Mary
University of Wisconsin/Madison
Wofford College

## Colleges That Offer Scholarships in the Arts

The colleges below offer non-need awards for students who plan to pursue academic programs in one or more of the creative and performing arts, or for students with extracurricular talent in the arts.

Adelphi University
Agnes Scott College
University of Alabama
Albertson College
Albion College
Albright College
Alfred University
Alma College
Alverno College
Arizona State University
School of the Art Institute of Chicago
Augustana College (IL)
Austin College

Baylor University
Beloit College
Birmingham-Southern College
Boston Conservatory
Boston University
Bradford College
Bradley University
Brigham Young University
Butler University
California Institute of the Arts
Calvin College
Case Western Reserve University
The Catholic University of America

College of Charleston
University of Cincinnati
Cleveland Institute of Music
Cornell College (IA)
Curtis Institute of Music
Davidson College
University of Dayton
University of Delaware
University of Denver
Depaul University
Depauw University
Drew University
Drexel University
Duke University
Duquesne University
Eastman School of Music
Eckerd College
Emory College
Evergreen State College
University of Florida
Furman University
George Washington University
Georgia Institute of Technology
Gordon College
Goucher College
Gustavus Adolphus College
Hendrix College
Hillsdale College
Hiram College
Hobart and William Smith Colleges
Hofstra University
Hollins University
Hope College
Houghton College
University of Illinois/Chicago
Illinois Wesleyan University
Indiana University/Bloomington
Iowa State University
Ithaca College
Juilliard School
Kalamazoo College
University of Kansas
Knox College
Lawrence University

Lehigh University
Lewis and Clark College
Louisiana State University/Baton Rouge
Loyola Marymount University
Loyola University/Chicago
Loyola University/New Orleans
University of Maine/Orono
Manhattan School of Music
Marquette University
Maryland Institute, College of Art
University of Maryland/College Park
University of Massachusetts/Amherst
Miami University (OH)
University of Miami (FL)
Michigan State University
University of Michigan
Millsaps College
Morehouse College
Muskingum College
University of Nebraska/Lincoln
New England Conservatory of Music
College of New Jersey
North Carolina School of the Arts
University of North Carolina/Asheville
University of North Carolina/Chapel Hill
University of North Carolina/Greensboro
Northwestern University
Oberlin College
Oglethorpe University
Ohio Northern University
Ohio State University
Ohio University
Ohio Wesleyan University
University of the Pacific
Peabody Conservatory of Music
Pepperdine University
Pratt Institute
Presbyterian College
University of Puget Sound
Randolph-Macon Woman's College
University of Redlands
Rhode Island School of Design
Rhodes College
Rice University

University of Richmond
Rollins College
St. John's University and
    College of St. Benedict (MN)
St. Olaf College
Santa Clara University
College of Santa Fe
Simon's Rock of Bard College
Skidmore College
University of South Carolina
Southern Methodist University
State University of New York/Buffalo
State University of New York College/
    Geneseo
State University of New York/Purchase
    College
State University of New York/Stony Brook
Southwestern University
Stetson University
Susquehanna University
Sweet Briar College

Syracuse University
Temple University
Texas Christian University
University of Tennessee/Knoxville
Trinity University (TX)
Truman State University
University of Tulsa
Valparaiso University
Vanderbilt University
School of Visual Arts
Wabash College
Wake Forest University
Washington University in St. Louis
West Virginia University
Wheaton College (IL)
Whitman College
Whittier College
Willamette University
Wittenberg University
College of Wooster

## Colleges That Sponsor National Merit Scholarships

The following colleges award scholarships to students named as National Merit Finalists by the National Merit Scholarship Corporation (NMSC). Amounts range from a minimum of $250 up to the full costs of attendance, depending on the policies of each college. A few give scholarships only to Finalists who show financial need, and not all Finalists who enroll at these colleges are guaranteed a scholarship. Normally, students must designate the institution as their first choice with the NMSC in late winter or early spring of twelfth grade. For more information on the National Merit Scholarship Program, see page 28.

University of Alabama
Albion College
Alfred University
Allegheny College
Alma College
American University
Arizona State University
University of Arizona
University of Arkansas
Auburn University

Austin College
Baylor University
Birmingham-Southern College
Boston College
Boston University
Bowdoin College
Bradley University
Brandeis University
Brigham Young University
Bucknell University

University of California/Berkeley
University of California/Davis
University of California/Irvine
University of California/Los Angeles
University of California/Riverside
University of California/San Diego
University of California/Santa Barbara
University of California/Santa Cruz
Calvin College
Carleton College
Case Western Reserve University
Centre College
University of Chicago
University of Cincinnati
Claremont McKenna College
Clarkson University
Clemson University
Colorado College
University of Dallas
Davidson College
University of Dayton
University of Delaware
Denison University
Depauw University
Drexel University
Earlham College
Emory University
Florida State University
University of Florida
Furman University
George Washington University
Georgia Institute of Technology
University of Georgia
Grinnell College
Gustavus Adolphus College
Hamilton College
Harvey Mudd College
Hendrix College
Hillsdale College
College of the Holy Cross
Hope College
University of Houston
Illinois Wesleyan University
Iowa State University

University of Iowa
John Carroll University
Johns Hopkins University
Kalamazoo College
Kansas State University
University of Kansas
University of Kentucky
Kenyon College
Knox College
Lehigh University
Lewis and Clark College
Lousiana State University/Baton Rouge
Macalester College
Marquette University
University of Maryland/College Park
Miami University (OH)
University of Miami (FL)
Michigan State University
Michigan Technological University
University of Minnesota/Morris
University of Minnesota/Twin Cities
University of Missouri/Columbia
University of Missouri/Rolla
University of Nebraska/Lincoln
New York University
Northwestern University
Oberlin College
Occidental College
Ohio State University
Ohio University
University of Oklahoma
Oregon State University
University of Oregon
Pacific Lutheran University
Pennsylvania State University
Pepperdine University
Pomona College
University of Puget Sound
Purdue University
University of Redlands
Rensselaer Polytechnic Institute
Rhodes College
Rice University
University of Richmond

Rochester Institute of Technology
University of Rochester
Rose-Hulman Institute of Technology
Rutgers, The State University of New Jersey
Saint Louis University
St. Olaf College
Santa Clara University
Sarah Lawrence College
University of the South (Sewanee)
University of South Carolina
University of Southern California
Southern Methodist University
Southwestern University
State University of New York/Buffalo
University of Tennessee/Knoxville
Texas A&M University
University of Texas/Austin
Trinity University
Truman State University
Tufts University
Tulane University

University of Tulsa
Ursinus College
Valparaiso University
Vanderbilt University
Villanova University
Virginia Polytechnic Institute and State University (Virginia Tech)
Wabash College
Wake Forest University
Washington and Lee University
Washington State University
Washington University in St. Louis
University of Washington
West Virginia University
Wheaton College (IL)
Whitman College
Willamette University
University of Wisconsin/Madison
Wittenberg University
Wofford College
College of Wooster
Worcester Polytechnic Institute

Source: 1998 PSAT/NMSQT Student Bulletin

# COLLEGES WITH THE MOST MONEY
## (Endowment Per Student)

Endowment is a college's nest egg. It consists of money set aside that grows over time and earns income that the university can spend on its operations. Endowment is a particularly important barometer at private colleges, where it is linked to a college's ability to provide millions in financial aid. The relationship isn't ironclad, but colleges with the highest endowment per student frequently offer the best packages. Below are rankings for private and public institutions drawn from a 1998 study by the National Association of College and University Business Officers, which included 281 of the colleges in this book. (The numbers are rounded in $1,000 increments.) Investment values are constantly changing, but the figures provide a useful relative measure. Most notably, they show the extent to which resources are concentrated in the hands of a few institutions. Readers will find familiar names at the top of the lists—but also some surprises.

# Private Colleges and Universities

| College or University | Endowment ($) Per Student |
| --- | --- |
| Princeton University | 776,000 |
| Webb Institute | 639,000 |
| Agnes Scott College | 611,000 |
| Harvard University | 610,000 |
| Curtis Institute of Music | 610,000 |
| Rice University | 578,000 |
| Grinnell College | 565,000 |
| Yale University | 526,000 |
| Swarthmore College | 521,000 |
| California Institute of Technology | 514,000 |
| Juilliard School | 450,000 |
| Emory University | 421,000 |
| Pomona College | 411,000 |
| Berea College | 352,000 |
| Stanford University | 347,000 |
| Washington and Lee University | 319,000 |
| Massachusetts Institute of Technology | 310,000 |
| Wellesley College | 307,000 |
| Williams College | 302,000 |
| Amherst College | 300,000 |
| Wabash College | 284,000 |
| Washington University in St. Louis | 280,000 |
| Claremont McKenna College | 280,000 |
| Macalester College | 264,000 |
| Middlebury College | 251,000 |
| Dartmouth College | 249,000 |
| Earlham College | 246,000 |
| Southwestern University | 231,000 |
| Smith College | 221,000 |
| Bryn Mawr College | 218,000 |
| Harvey Mudd College | 215,000 |
| Bowdoin College | 214,000 |
| Vassar College | 208,000 |
| Trinity University (TX) | 196,000 |
| Cooper Union | 192,000 |
| Carleton College | 191,000 |
| Haverford College | 187,000 |
| Lafayette College | 187,000 |
| Scripps College | 180,000 |
| University of Chicago | 180,000 |
| Sweet Briar College | 179,000 |

| COLLEGE OR UNIVERSITY | ENDOWMENT ($) PER STUDENT |
|---|---|
| University of Richmond | 177,000 |
| Columbia University | 173,000 |
| Reed College | 167,000 |
| Mount Holyoke College | 160,000 |
| University of the South (Sewanee) | 155,000 |
| Hamilton College | 153,000 |
| Whitman College | 152,000 |
| Trinity College (CT) | 150,000 |
| Colorado College | 145,000 |
| Wesleyan University | 145,000 |
| University of Notre Dame | 145,000 |
| Randolph-Macon Woman's College | 143,000 |
| University of Tulsa | 140,000 |
| Case Western Reserve University | 138,000 |
| Occidental College | 137,000 |
| Wells College | 137,000 |
| Vanderbilt University | 137,000 |
| Oberlin College | 135,000 |
| University of Pennsylvania | 131,000 |
| College of the Ozarks | 131,000 |
| Davidson College | 130,000 |
| Brown University | 128,000 |
| Mills College | 127,000 |
| Depauw University | 127,000 |
| Rhodes College | 125,000 |
| Denison University | 124,000 |
| Centre College | 122,000 |
| University of Rochester | 121,000 |
| Franklin and Marshall College | 120,000 |
| Northwestern University | 118,000 |
| Colby College | 115,000 |
| Texas Christian University | 114,000 |
| Hanover College | 114,000 |
| Cornell University (NY) | 111,000 |
| Hendrix College | 111,000 |
| Wake Forest University | 107,000 |
| Johns Hopkins University | 104,000 |
| Goucher College | 104,000 |
| Duke University | 102,000 |
| Colgate University | 100,000 |
| College of the Holy Cross | 99,000 |
| Lawrence University | 96,000 |
| Hampden-Sydney College | 93,000 |

| College or University | Endowment ($) Per Student |
|---|---|
| Lehigh University | 93,000 |
| Union College | 89,000 |
| Yeshiva University | 88,000 |
| College of Wooster | 86,000 |
| St. Lawrence University | 85,000 |
| Spelman College | 84,000 |
| Southern Methodist University | 84,000 |
| Austin College | 84,000 |
| Bates College | 83,000 |
| Carnegie Mellon University | 82,000 |
| Albion College | 81,000 |
| Hollins University | 80,000 |
| Illinois Wesleyan University | 78,000 |
| Washington and Jefferson College | 76,000 |
| Bucknell University | 76,000 |
| Drew University | 74,000 |
| Wheaton College (IL) | 74,000 |
| Rose-Hulman Institute of Technology | 74,000 |
| Loyola University/New Orleans | 72,000 |
| Ursinus College | 71,000 |
| Dickinson College | 70,000 |
| Furman University | 70,000 |
| Rensselaer Polytechnic Institute | 69,000 |
| Wheaton College (MA) | 69,000 |
| Rhode Island School of Design | 67,000 |
| Birmingham-Southern College | 67,000 |
| Brandeis University | 65,000 |
| Alma College | 63,000 |
| Albertson College of Idaho | 62,000 |
| Millsaps College | 62,000 |
| Willamette University | 62,000 |
| Kalamazoo College | 62,000 |
| Saint Louis University | 59,000 |
| Connecticut College | 59,000 |
| Worcester Polytechnic Institute | 59,000 |
| Beloit College | 58,000 |
| Gettysburg College | 57,000 |
| Barnard College | 53,000 |
| Boston College | 52,000 |
| Presbyterian College | 52,000 |
| Hartwick College | 51,000 |
| California Institute of the Arts | 51,000 |
| Kenyon College | 50,000 |

Discounts and Deals at the Nation's 360 Best Colleges

| College or University | Endowment ($) Per Student |
|---|---|
| University of Southern California | 49,000 |
| Lake Forest College | 49,000 |
| University of Puget Sound | 49,000 |
| Hiram College | 47,000 |
| Allegheny College | 47,000 |
| Ohio Wesleyan University | 46,000 |
| Stevens Institute of Technology | 45,000 |
| Simmons College | 45,000 |
| Tulane University | 45,000 |
| Tufts University | 44,000 |
| Babson College | 44,000 |
| Pepperdine University | 43,000 |
| Cornell College (IA) | 43,000 |
| Pitzer College | 43,000 |
| Santa Clara University | 43,000 |
| Guilford College | 42,000 |
| Wittenberg University | 41,000 |
| Skidmore College | 40,000 |
| Loyola Marymount University | 40,000 |
| Susquehanna University | 40,000 |
| Stetson University | 40,000 |
| Baylor University | 40,000 |
| Knox College | 38,000 |
| Clark University | 37,000 |
| George Washington University | 37,000 |
| Rollins College | 35,000 |
| Rochester Institute of Technology | 35,000 |
| St. Olaf College | 34,000 |
| Clarkson University | 34,000 |
| Warren Wilson College | 34,000 |
| Valparaiso University | 33,000 |
| Morehouse College | 33,000 |
| Hope College | 32,000 |
| Lewis and Clark College | 31,000 |
| Illinois Institute of Technology | 31,000 |
| Creighton University | 30,000 |
| Loyola University/ Chicago | 30,000 |
| New York University | 30,000 |
| Muhlenberg College | 30,000 |
| Hampton University | 29,000 |
| Muskingum College | 28,000 |
| Butler University | 27,000 |
| University of Miami (FL) | 27,000 |

| College or University | Endowment ($) Per Student |
|---|---|
| Syracuse University | 25,000 |
| Ithaca College | 25,000 |
| Augustana College (IL) | 25,000 |
| University of Pittsburgh | 24,000 |
| John Carroll University | 24,000 |
| Sarah Lawrence College | 24,000 |
| Gustavus Adolphus College | 23,000 |
| Loyola College (MD) | 23,000 |
| Howard University | 23,000 |
| Boston University | 21,000 |
| Alfred University | 21,000 |
| University of Dayton | 21,000 |
| Marquette University | 20,000 |
| Bradley University | 20,000 |
| University of Dallas | 19,000 |
| Drexel University | 18,000 |
| Northeastern University | 17,000 |
| Fordham University | 16,000 |
| University of San Francisco | 15,000 |
| University of Denver | 13,000 |
| University of Redlands | 13,000 |
| University of Scranton | 13,000 |
| New School University (Eugene Lang College) | 13,000 |
| Villanova University | 13,000 |
| Fairfield University | 12,000 |
| Siena College | 12,000 |
| Seton Hall University | 11,000 |
| Calvin College | 10,000 |
| American University | 9,000 |
| Depaul University | 9,000 |
| Kettering University | 8,000 |
| Pratt Institute | 6,000 |
| St. John's University (NY) | 5,000 |

## Public Colleges and Universities

| College or University | Endowment ($) Per Student |
|---|---|
| Georgia Institute of Technology | 63,000 |
| University of Texas System | 62,000 |
| University of Virginia | 60,000 |
| University of Michigan | 45,000 |
| University of Delaware | 44,000 |
| Texas A&M University System | 44,000 |

| COLLEGE OR UNIVERSITY | ENDOWMENT ($) PER STUDENT |
|---|---|
| College of William and Mary | 41,000 |
| University of North Carolina/Chapel Hill | 36,000 |
| University of Kansas | 28,000 |
| University of Cincinnati | 26,000 |
| Colorado School of Mines | 24,000 |
| University of Oklahoma | 21,000 |
| University of California* | 20,000 |
| Purdue University | 18,000 |
| Washington State University | 17,000 |
| McGill University | 17,000 |
| University of Vermont | 17,000 |
| University of Washington | 17,000 |
| Ohio State University | 15,000 |
| University of Florida | 15,000 |
| State University of New York/Buffalo | 14,000 |
| University of Nebraska | 14,000 |
| University of Alabama System | 14,000 |
| University of Toronto | 13,000 |
| University of Wisconsin | 13,000 |
| Unversity of Iowa | 13,000 |
| University of Missouri System | 12,000 |
| Oregon State University | 12,000 |
| Virginia Polytechnic Institute and State University (Virginia Tech) | 11,000 |
| Clemson University | 10,000 |
| University of Houston System | 10,000 |
| University of Minnesota | 10,000 |
| University of Arkansas | 10,000 |
| University of Georgia | 9,000 |
| Auburn University | 9,000 |
| West Virginia University | 9,000 |
| University of Utah | 9,000 |
| Indiana University | 9,000 |
| University of Oregon | 9,000 |
| Rutgers, The State University of New Jersey | 8,000 |
| Pennsylvania State University | 8,000 |
| University of Tennessee System | 8,000 |
| Iowa State University | 8,000 |
| Miami University (OH) | 8,000 |
| University of New Mexico | 8,000 |
| Kansas State University | 7,000 |

*University of California campuses have additional endowment funds.

| College or University | Endowment ($) Per Student |
|---|---|
| University of North Carolina/Greensboro | 7,000 |
| University of Illinois | 7,000 |
| University of Colorado | 7,000 |
| Ohio University | 6,000 |
| Louisiana State University System | 6,000 |
| Florida State University | 5,000 |
| University of South Carolina | 5,000 |
| Michigan State University | 5,000 |
| University of Connecticut | 5,000 |
| Temple University | 5,000 |
| University of North Carolina/Charlotte | 5,000 |
| Michigan Technological University | 5,000 |
| University of Maryland System | 4,000 |
| North Carolina State University | 4,000 |
| University of Kentucky | 4,000 |
| University of North Carolina/Asheville | 4,000 |
| New Jersey Institute of Technology | 4,000 |
| University of Rhode Island | 4,000 |
| University of Hawaii | 4,000 |
| University of Arizona | 4,000 |
| University of Maine System | 3,000 |
| University of New Hampshire System | 3,000 |
| University of Illinois | 3,000 |
| University of Massachusetts | 2,000 |
| Arizona State University | 2,000 |
| State University of New York/Binghamton University | 2,000 |
| University of Wisconsin System | 2,000 |
| State University of New York/Stony Brook | 1,000 |

# 10.

# The College Profiles

## ADELPHI UNIVERSITY ✦ Garden City, NY 11530

| | |
|---|---|
| ENROLLMENT: | 5,700 |
| UNDERGRADUATE: | 3,300 |
| ACCEPTANCE RATE: | 64% |
| SAT RANGE: | 410–540 Verbal |
| | 460–588 Math |
| STICKER PRICE: | $20,000+ |
| NEED-BLIND: | Yes |
| NEED MET: | NA |
| AVERAGE STUDENT DEBT: | NA |
| MERIT SCHOLARSHIPS: | Many |
| RANGE: | Up to $13,500 |
| ATHLETIC SCHOLARSHIPS: | Yes |
| ROTC: | Army, Air Force |
| WEB SITE: | www.adelphi.edu |
| PHONE: | (516) 877-3050 |

Adelphi is on the comeback trail after firing a rogue president who incurred lavish expenses while the enrollment was in free fall. Now just over half the size it was ten years ago, Adelphi still offers credible preprofessional programs in areas such as business, education, and nursing. The university is nationally recognized for its programs for assisting learning disabled students. With dorm space in short supply, most of the students on this Long Island campus are commuters. Adelphi has a full stable of non-need scholarships, beginning with the Presidential Scholarship, which offers up to $13,500 to those with a superior high school record and a combined SAT I score of 1300 or higher. Two other scholarships have less exalted standards, the least competitive of which is the Adelphi University Scholarship, which gives up to $7,000 to students with a good academic record and an SAT score of at least 1000. Additional awards recognize artistic talent (up to $6,000) and athletic achievement (up to $12,800). Scholarship candidates should apply for admission by February 15 and must file the FAFSA.

*Deadlines:*
  ADMISSION: Mar. 1
  FAFSA: Feb. 15

## AGNES SCOTT COLLEGE ✦ Decatur, GA 30030

| | |
|---|---|
| ENROLLMENT: | 800 |
| UNDERGRADUATE: | 800 |
| ACCEPTANCE RATE: | 77% |
| SAT RANGE: | 560–670 Verbal |
| | 520–620 Math |
| STICKER PRICE: | $21,000+ |
| NEED-BLIND: | Yes |
| NEED MET: | 100% |
| AVERAGE STUDENT DEBT: | NA |
| MERIT SCHOLARSHIPS: | Many |
| RANGE: | Up to full costs |
| ATHLETIC SCHOLARSHIPS: | No |
| ROTC: | Navy, Air Force |
| WEB SITE: | www.agnesscott.edu |
| PHONE: | (800) 868-8602 |

This small Georgia women's college is sitting on top of a big secret: the largest endowment per student of any liberal arts institution in the nation except Princeton. With a student body of only 800, ASC offers a familylike atmosphere on its suburban Atlanta campus. Not just any college could afford ASC's current $100 million building campaign, and the college offers one of the nation's strongest financial aid programs. In addition to meeting full need, ASC offers ten categories of non-need awards, topped by three Presidential Scholarships that cover nearly the full costs of attendance. Other academic awards range down to the $8,500 Frances Winship Walters Scholarships for students with a 3.25 GPA and an SAT I score of 1180. Additional other scholarships honor musical talent and community service, and Georgia residents who qualify for the state's HOPE Scholarship get an additional $3,000 bonus. There's even a Middle Income Assistance award of up to $5,000 for families that don't qualify for significant need-based aid. Scholarship seekers must apply for admission and file a separate application by January 15.

*Deadlines:*
  EARLY DECISION: Nov. 15
  REGULAR ADMISSION: Mar. 1 (priority)
  FAFSA: Mar. 1

# UNIVERSITY OF ALABAMA ✦
## Tuscaloosa, AL 35487

| | |
|---|---|
| ENROLLMENT: | 18,300 |
| UNDERGRADUATE: | 14,400 |
| ACCEPTANCE RATE: | 81% |
| ACT RANGE: | 21–26 |
| STICKER PRICE: | In-state, $7,000+ |
| | Out-of-state, $11,000+ |
| NEED-BLIND: | Yes |
| NEED MET: | 52% |
| AVERAGE STUDENT DEBT: | $16,900 |
| MERIT SCHOLARSHIPS: | Many |
| RANGE: | Up to full costs |
| ATHLETIC SCHOLARSHIPS: | Yes |
| ROTC: | Army, Air Force |
| WEB SITE: | www.ua.edu |
| PHONE: | (800) 933-BAMA |

It should come as no surprise that one of the many scholarships at the University of Alabama is ear-marked for children of former players for the legendary coach Paul "Bear" Bryant. The football team has always been the biggest rallying point on this campus, but it is far from the only one. The University Honors Program is a highly selective option for approximately 700 students, and the even more elite Computer-Based Honors Program teaches students how to apply computers to their chosen field of study. Honors students are prime candidates for 'Bama's merit scholarships, which are headlined by 100 full-tuition Presidential Scholarships; for consideration candidates must have a minimum high school GPA of 3.0, and a combined SAT I score of 1170, and/or an ACT of 26. National Merit, National Hispanic, and National Achievement honorees are eligible for awards that cover full expenses. Additional scholarships recognize leadership, excellence in particular fields, and various other qualities. Students must file a scholarship application by December 1 to ensure consideration for all awards.

*Deadlines:*
  ADMISSION: Apr. 1 (priority)
  FAFSA: Mar. 1

# ALBERTSON COLLEGE OF IDAHO ✦
## Caldwell, ID 83605

| | |
|---|---|
| ENROLLMENT: | 700 |
| UNDERGRADUATE: | 700 |
| ACCEPTANCE RATE: | 86% |
| SAT AVERAGE: | 571 Verbal |
| | 562 Math |
| STICKER PRICE: | $20,000+ |
| NEED-BLIND: | Yes |
| NEED MET: | 70% |
| AVERAGE STUDENT DEBT: | $15,100 |
| MERIT SCHOLARSHIPS: | Many |
| RANGE: | Up to full tuition |
| ATHLETIC SCHOLARSHIPS: | Yes |
| ROTC: | No |
| WEB SITE: | www.acofi.edu |
| PHONE: | (800) 224-3246 |

A better name for Albertson might be *U.S. News* College of Idaho. With a string of number-one rankings from the magazine in its category for regional liberal arts colleges of the West, this erstwhile little-known school is now strutting like a peacock on the national stage. Its selling points include rising enrollment, a high graduation rate, and a major building program that has spruced up the academic facilities. Business and pre-med are the top-drawing programs, and with only 700 in the whole college, students get ample attention from faculty. A wide variety of merit scholarships are given for all-around academic achievement, including one worth up to full tuition for honorees in the National Merit Program. Other awards recognize students who excel in a particular academic field or who show artistic talent. Scholarships also target members of the Presbyterian Church (U.S.A.), and children of alumni get a 15 percent tuition discount. Unlike most colleges its size, Albertson offers 130 athletic scholarships per year.

*Deadlines:*
  EARLY ACTION: Nov. 15
  REGULAR ADMISSION: Feb. 15 (priority)
  FAFSA: Feb. 15

# ALBION COLLEGE ◆ Albion, MI 49224

| | |
|---|---|
| TOTAL ENROLLMENT: | 1,500 |
| UNDERGRADUATE: | 1,500 |
| ACCEPTANCE RATE: | 91% |
| SAT RANGE: | 530–660 Verbal |
| | 550–650 Math |
| STICKER PRICE: | $23,000+ |
| NEED-BLIND | Yes |
| NEED MET: | NA |
| AVERAGE STUDENT DEBT: | $15,900 |
| MERIT SCHOLARSHIPS: | Many |
| RANGE: | Up to full tuition |
| ATHLETIC SCHOLARSHIPS: | No |
| ROTC: | No |
| WEB SITE: | www.albion.edu |
| PHONE: | (800) 858-6770 |

Albion is a small college hustling for students in a state dominated by a certain Goliath-sized public university in Ann Arbor. Best known for its business and public affairs programs, Albion places strong emphasis on teaching and offers funds for selected students to do research alongside faculty members. To compete with the big boys and their low sticker prices, the college offers a whopping thirteen—count 'em—merit scholarship programs. For National Merit finalists who designate Albion as their first choice, the college gives a full-tuition award renewable for all four years. Other awards honor lesser levels of achievement, down to students with at least a 3.2 GPA and a 1020 on the SAT or 22 on the ACT, who get a renewable discount of $3,500–$4,500 per year. A $4,000-per-year award honors those who show "a commitment to enhancing the diversity of the college," and Albion also offers special scholarships for study in chemistry, math or physics, fine arts, speech communication, public service, and business management.

*Deadlines:*
  EARLY DECISION: Dec. 1
  REGULAR ADMISSION: Apr. 1 (priority)
  FAFSA: Feb. 15

# ALBRIGHT COLLEGE ◆ Reading, PA 19612

| | |
|---|---|
| ENROLLMENT: | 1,400 |
| UNDERGRADUATE: | 1,400 |
| ACCEPTANCE RATE: | 86% |
| SAT RANGE: | 460–590 Verbal |
| | 460–580 Math |
| STICKER PRICE: | $25,000+ |
| NEED-BLIND: | Yes |
| NEED MET: | 78% |
| AVERAGE STUDENT DEBT: | $18,100 |
| MERIT SCHOLARSHIPS: | Many |
| RANGE: | Up to $10,000 |
| ATHLETIC SCHOLARSHIPS: | No |
| ROTC: | No |
| WEB SITE: | www.alb.edu |
| PHONE: | (800) 252-1856 |

In a state chock-full of private liberal arts colleges, Albright has found its niche by turning out well-qualified business majors and other preprofessionals. Though not overly selective, Albright has enjoyed rising enrollment in recent years. Along with liberal arts and business, the college offers teacher certification and pre-law, pre-med, pre-dental, and pre-veterinary medicine programs. Topping the college's merit awards are the Jacob Albright Scholarships, worth $10,000 per year for students who rank in the top 5 percent of their high school classes. The Dean's and Presidential Awards of $5,000 or $7,500 per year emphasize participation in community service, activities, or employment. Additional awards honor academic achievement in a particular subject and artistic ability (both up to $1,500). Still others recognize students of color (up to $3,000), children of alumni ($1,000), students with Albright siblings ($500), and United Methodists (up to $1,000). Financial aid applicants may request a formal review of Albright's aid package versus that of another private college.

*Deadlines:*
  ADMISSION: Feb. 15 (priority)
  FAFSA: Mar. 1

# ALFRED UNIVERSITY ◆ Alfred, NY 14802

| | |
|---|---|
| ENROLLMENT: | 1,500 |
| UNDERGRADUATE: | 1,200 |
| ACCEPTANCE RATE: | 85% |
| SAT RANGE: | 470–580 Verbal |
| | 530–650 Math |
| STICKER PRICE: | $27,000+ |
| NEED-BLIND: | Yes |
| NEED MET: | 95% |
| AVERAGE STUDENT DEBT: | $21,000 |
| MERIT SCHOLARSHIPS: | Many |
| RANGE: | Up to full costs |
| ATHLETIC SCHOLARSHIPS: | No |
| ROTC: | Army |
| WEB SITE: | www.alfred.edu |
| PHONE: | (800) 541-9229 |

The way Alfred University carries on, you'd swear it has 15,000 students instead of only 1,500. With colleges of business, engineering, and liberal arts and sciences—plus state supported schools of art and design and ceramic engineering—Alfred has a wider variety of programs than some institutions ten times its size. World famous in ceramics, Alfred has an uncommonly diverse student body. The university is located in rural western New York. National Merit Finalists are eligible for a free ride at Alfred; those in the top 10 percent of their high school class are eligible for Presidential Scholarships of up to $13,000 in the private divisions and $5,500 in the public ones. Additional awards target western New York state residents, international students, and high school leaders with awards of varying amounts. A $500 per year scholarship goes to women who enroll in the School of Ceramic Engineering. Art portfolio awards yield up to $5,500 for nonresidents and $3,500 for New Yorkers. Alfred also hosts on-campus scholarship competitions in various fields in the fall and winter. Scholarship applicants must file the FAFSA.

*Deadlines:*
EARLY DECISION: Dec. 1
REGULAR ADMISSION: Feb. 1 (priority)
FAFSA: Rolling

# ALLEGHENY COLLEGE ◆ Meadville, PA 16335

| | |
|---|---|
| ENROLLMENT: | 1,900 |
| UNDERGRADUATE: | 1,900 |
| ACCEPTANCE RATE: | 82% |
| SAT RANGE: | 550–640 Verbal |
| | 550–630 Math |
| STICKER PRICE: | $25,000+ |
| NEED BLIND: | No |
| NEED MET: | 93% |
| AVERAGE STUDENT DEBT: | $15,600 |
| MERIT SCHOLARSHIPS: | Many |
| RANGE: | Up to $7,500 |
| ATHLETIC SCHOLARSHIPS: | No |
| ROTC: | Army |
| WEB SITE: | www.alleg.edu |
| PHONE: | (800) 521-5293 |

Allegheny College is as all-American as apple pie and football, which makes sense because its football team is an annual contender for the Division III national championship. Other private colleges deal in wealth and status, but Allegheny has always catered to more down-to-earth folks. Strong programs include English, biology, and psychology, and Allegheny is known for its highly accessible faculty. Located inside a geographical triangle formed by Buffalo, Cleveland, and Pittsburgh, Allegheny has broadened its geographic reach in recent years and now enrolls students from forty states. Allegheny offers two merit scholarships. The Presidential Scholar Awards provide up to $7,500 to students who are generally in the top 10 percent of their high school class. Dean's Achievement Awards of up to $5,000 target those in the top 20 percent. There is no separate application for merit scholarships, although finalists must come to the campus for an interview. One other stocking stuffer: Allegheny waives its application fee for prospective students who visit the campus.

*Deadlines:*
EARLY DECISION: Jan.15
REGULAR ADMISSION: Feb. 15
FAFSA: Feb. 15

# ALMA COLLEGE ◆ Alma, MI 48801

| | |
|---|---|
| ENROLLMENT: | 1,400 |
| UNDERGRADUATE: | 1,400 |
| ACCEPTANCE RATE: | 90% |
| ACT RANGE: | 23–28 |
| STICKER PRICE: | $20,000+ |
| NEED-BLIND: | Yes |
| NEED MET: | 87% |
| AVERAGE STUDENT DEBT: | $13,900 |
| MERIT SCHOLARSHIPS: | Many |
| RANGE: | Up to full tuition |
| ATHLETIC SCHOLARSHIPS: | No |
| ROTC: | Army |
| WEB SITE: | www.alma.edu |
| PHONE: | (800) 321-ALMA |

To locate Alma on a map, find the point that is smack in the middle of Michigan's mitten. Alma is a small college that is international in outlook, from its Scottish heritage to an academic calendar that allows students extra flexibility to travel with a one month term at the end of the school year. Business administration is the most heavily subscribed major at Alma, followed by biology and exercise/health sciences. Students looking for merit scholarships and tuition discounts will find plenty. A Distinguished Scholar Award of up to full tuition is available for selected National Merit finalists. Trustee Honors Scholarships of up to $7,000 are awarded to students with a 3.75 GPA in academic courses who score either 1250 on the SAT I or 28 on the ACT. The Tartan Award gives up to $4,500 for a rank in the top 25 percent and an 1140 or 25. Other scholarships are given for artistic talent (up to $1,500), achievement in science, religious leadership in any faith, and membership in the Presbyterian Church (U.S.A.). There's even a $500 award for skill in "Scottish Arts" such as fiddling, dancing, and bag-piping.

*Deadlines:*
  EARLY DECISION: Nov. 1
  REGULAR ADMISSION: Mar. 1 (priority)
  FAFSA: Feb. 15

# ALVERNO COLLEGE ◆ Milwaukee, WI 53234

| | |
|---|---|
| ENROLLMENT: | 2,100 |
| UNDERGRADUATE: | 2,000 |
| ACCEPTANCE RATE: | 65% |
| SAT RANGE: | NA |
| STICKER PRICE: | $15,000+ |
| NEED-BLIND: | Yes |
| NEED MET: | 76% |
| AVERAGE STUDENT DEBT: | $23,900 |
| MERIT SCHOLARSHIPS: | Many |
| RANGE: | Up to full tuition |
| ATHLETIC SCHOLARSHIPS: | No |
| ROTC: | Army, Air Force |
| WEB SITE: | www.alverno.edu |
| PHONE: | (800) 933-3401 |

A first glance at Alverno reveals a small, Roman Catholic women's college that serves an equal number of full- and part-timers in suburban Milwaukee. But scratch the surface and you'll find one of the nation's most innovative curriculums, an ability-based program that replaces memorization with hands-on work and intertwines the liberal arts with professional fields such as business, education, and nursing. Alverno is also known for teaching excellence and a bargain price. The college's richest merit scholarship is a single award for community involvement that provides full tuition. (The application deadline for this award is in March.) The Ellen Harcourt Scholarship offers $6,000 per year for applicants in nursing or liberal arts and has a mid-February deadline. Alverno awards $5,000 per year to high school valedictorians and salutatorians and at least $3,000 to students in the top 20 percent of their class with a 3.0 GPA or a 20 ACT composite. The college also sponsors a Scholarship Opportunity Day, when students can earn awards of up to $3,000 on the basis of an interview and essay.

*Deadlines:*
  ADMISSION: Aug. 1
  FAFSA: Apr. 1

# AMERICAN UNIVERSITY ◆ Washington, DC 20016

| | |
|---|---|
| ENROLLMENT: | 10,700 |
| UNDERGRADUATE: | 5,400 |
| ACCEPTANCE RATE: | 79% |
| SAT RANGE: | 550–660 Verbal |
| | 530–630 Math |
| STICKER PRICE: | $26,000+ |
| NEED-BLIND: | NA |
| NEED MET: | 73% |
| AVERAGE STUDENT DEBT: | $17,400 |
| MERIT SCHOLARSHIPS: | Many |
| RANGE: | Up to full tuition |
| ATHLETIC SCHOLARSHIPS: | Yes |
| ROTC: | Army, Air Force |
| WEB SITE: | www.american.edu |
| PHONE: | (202) 885-6000 |

When brochures for American University speak of "our campus," they don't mean grassy lawns and shady trees. Instead, they tout Washington, D.C., as American's true campus, and with good reason. Most students who come to AU have their sights set on Capitol Hill and the corridors of power, although the D.C. party scene is also a major attraction. Economics and politics are where the university excels, with international studies its most popular major. American's suburban campus is secluded from the hustle and bustle of downtown, in stark contrast to rival George Washington. American offers scholarships of up to full tuition to National Merit Finalists and other top students. Dean's Scholarships of $6,000 to $10,000 go to students who show "above average ability, accomplishments, and potential." An unusually large number of awards are targeted to minority students, including the Frederick Douglass Scholarship, which requires a special application. Leadership Scholarships of $1,000 to $6,000 go to students who don't qualify for other awards.

*Deadlines:*
EARLY DECISION: Nov. 15
REGULAR ADMISSION: Feb. 1
FAFSA: Mar. 1

# AMHERST COLLEGE ◆ Amherst, MA 01002

| | |
|---|---|
| TOTAL ENROLLMENT: | 1,600 |
| UNDERGRADUATE: | 1,600 |
| ACCEPTANCE RATE: | 20% |
| SAT RANGE: | 660–750 Verbal |
| | 670–740 Math |
| STICKER PRICE: | $31,000+ |
| NEED-BLIND: | Yes |
| NEED MET: | 100% |
| AVERAGE STUDENT DEBT: | $11,000 |
| MERIT SCHOLARSHIPS: | None |
| ATHLETIC SCHOLARSHIPS: | No |
| ROTC: | No |
| WEB SITE: | www.amherst.edu |
| PHONE: | (413) 542-2328 |

More well-rounded than Swarthmore and less isolated than Williams, Amherst stands at the pinnacle of small private college prestige. All the classic elements are here: a beautiful campus, small classes, and a handpicked student body with average SAT scores that top 1400. Yet Amherst's trump card is what lies beyond: the four affiliated colleges—Hampshire, Mount Holyoke, Smith, and the University of Massachusetts—that with Amherst make up the Five College Consortium. The combined resources of this dynamic group, plus the cosmopolitan surroundings of west-central Massachusetts, make for an unbeatable combination. Amherst is in a strong financial position due to the size of its endowment and the fact that its student body is among the wealthiest in the nation. During one recent year, only 37 percent of its students showed financial need, a figure less than half that of many private colleges. Though diversity advocates might raise eyebrows, Amherst's affluence leaves it with abundant resources to aid those students who do show need.

*Deadlines:*
EARLY DECISION: Nov. 15
ADMISSION: Jan. 1
FAFSA: Feb. 15
CSS PROFILE: Feb. 15

## ANTIOCH COLLEGE ✦
## Yellow Springs, OH 45387

| | |
|---|---|
| ENROLLMENT: | 600 |
| UNDERGRADUATE: | 600 |
| ACCEPTANCE RATE: | 81% |
| SAT RANGE: | 480–550 Verbal |
| | 480–600 Math |
| STICKER PRICE: | $21,000+ |
| NEED-BLIND: | Yes |
| NEED MET: | 88% |
| AVERAGE STUDENT DEBT: | $14,200 |
| MERIT SCHOLARSHIPS: | Many |
| RANGE: | Up to $6,000 |
| ATHLETIC SCHOLARSHIPS: | No |
| ROTC: | No |
| WEB SITE: | www.antioch-college.edu |
| PHONE: | (800) 543-9436 |

Parents may remember when Antioch was one of the hottest places in higher education. Antioch's brand of hands-on learning, which features work in the real world combined with academic study, is as relevant as ever today. But the marching, protesting, nonconformist part of the Antioch equation has not worn so well. Only a third of its size in the glory days, Antioch struggles mightily to attract able students. The college's trimester system facilitates alternating terms of work and study, although a high attrition rate shows that many students get sidetracked before completing their degrees. Antioch's merit scholarships include the Horace Mann, which offers $6,000 per year for students with a GPA of 3.8 or better; the $4,000 Arthur Morgan for those with a 3.5; and the $2,000 Rebecca Pennell for a 3.2 or better. (Awards can depend on additional factors such as leadership and extracurricular involvement.) The college also awards 50 Community Responsibility Scholarships of $5,000 to students "who demonstrate extraordinary involvement in, and responsibility for, the quality of their community."

*Deadlines:*
EARLY DECISION: Nov. 15
REGULAR ADMISSION: Feb. 1 (priority)
FAFSA: Mar. 1

## ARIZONA STATE UNIVERSITY ✦
## Tempe, AZ 85287

| | |
|---|---|
| ENROLLMENT: | 44,300 |
| UNDERGRADUATE: | 33,500 |
| ACCEPTANCE RATE: | 79% |
| SAT RANGE: | 480–600 Verbal |
| | 490–610 Math |
| STICKER PRICE: | In-state, $7,000+ |
| | Out-of-state, $14,000+ |
| NEED-BLIND: | Yes |
| NEED MET: | 100% |
| AVERAGE STUDENT DEBT: | $17,800 |
| MERIT SCHOLARSHIPS: | Many |
| RANGE: | Up to full in-state tuition |
| ATHLETIC SCHOLARSHIPS: | Yes |
| ROTC: | Army, Air Force |
| WEB SITE: | www.asu.edu |
| PHONE: | (602) 965-7788 |

In a metropolitan area that includes two million people, ASU is a thriving metropolis in its own right. Many a sun-starved northerner has fled the winter cold for this haven of year-round sunshine amid the palm trees. But ASU's academic reputation has also been on the rise in recent years, notably its Honors College, which enrolls approximately 1,800 students. In-staters need a rank in the top 25 percent, a 3.0 GPA, an SAT I of 1040, or an ACT of 22 for automatic admission to the university. Merit scholarship applicants must file the university's General Scholarship Application by March 1. Under the Regents Waiver Program, several scholarships cover in-state tuition for selected Arizona residents who rank in the top 15 percent of their high school classes or maintain a GPA of at least 3.0. The Regents General Non-Resident Scholarship gives partial nonresident tuition to students in the top 3 percent. Various academic divisions offer their own scholarships, and Private Donor Scholarships are earmarked for a variety of special interests. Freshmen received a total of 212 non-need-based awards in a recent year.

*Deadlines:*
ADMISSION: Rolling
FAFSA: Mar. 1

## UNIVERSITY OF ARIZONA ✦ Tucson, AZ 85721

| | |
|---|---|
| ENROLLMENT: | 33,700 |
| UNDERGRADUATE: | 25,600 |
| ACCEPTANCE RATE: | 85% |
| SAT RANGE: | 490–600 Verbal |
| | 490–610 Math |
| STICKER PRICE: | In-state, $7,000+ |
| | Out-of-state, $14,000+ |
| NEED-BLIND: | Yes |
| NEED MET: | 100% |
| AVERAGE STUDENT DEBT: | $16,900 |
| MERIT SCHOLARSHIPS: | Many |
| ATHLETIC SCHOLARSHIPS: | Yes |
| ROTC: | Army, Navy, Air Force |
| WEB SITE: | www.arizona.edu |
| PHONE: | (520) 621-9799 |

University of Arizona has one of the nation's leading astronomy programs, but it doesn't take a telescope to see why students flock to this desert oasis. Applications and selectivity have been on the rise, and out-of-staters account for nearly a fourth of the student body. Along with mountain views and breathtakingly clear skies, the university offers leading programs ranging from business and communications to architecture and engineering. With the prominence of Native American culture in the region, anthropology and archaeology are also strong. The university offers a broad range of merit awards based on particular academic interests, achievement in the arts, and a variety of other criteria. Approximately fifty students per year receive scholarships for National Merit Finalist status, and top-performing in-staters get full tuition bought and paid for by the Arizona Regents Academic Waiver. Arizona is one of the relatively few institutions to offer Army, Navy, and Air Force ROTC programs on campus.

*Deadlines:*
    ADMISSION: Apr. 1
    FAFSA: Mar. 1

## UNIVERSITY OF ARKANSAS ✦ Fayetteville, AR 72701

| | |
|---|---|
| ENROLLMENT: | 14,300 |
| UNDERGRADUATE: | 11,600 |
| ACCEPTANCE RATE: | 91% |
| ACT RANGE: | 20–26 |
| STICKER PRICE: | In-state, $7,000+ |
| | Out-of-state, $11,000+ |
| NEED-BLIND: | Yes |
| NEED MET: | NA |
| AVERAGE STUDENT DEBT: | $15,000 |
| MERIT SCHOLARSHIPS: | Many |
| RANGE: | Up to full costs |
| ATHLETIC SCHOLARSHIPS: | Yes |
| ROTC: | Army, Air Force |
| WEB SITE: | www.uark.edu |
| PHONE: | (800) 377-8632 |

Hollywood Boulevard it isn't, but students at the University of Arkansas have their own version of the Walk of Fame in the form of a five-mile stretch of sidewalk engraved with the name of every graduate since 1871. Many students can trace their whole family tree along the way, and Razorback pride runs deep. Although the college of arts and sciences is Arkansas' largest, its reputation lies in preprofessional programs such as business, architecture, and agriculture. (Marketing is the largest major.) Arkansas has more big-ticket merit scholarships than most state institutions, including the Sturgis Fellowships, which offer up to $11,000 per year to exceptional students headed for arts and sciences. Apply by February 1. The Chancellor's Scholarships offer a full ride to 100 students with an A average and an SAT I of 1470 or ACT of 33. Less lucrative awards target Arkansas residents with lower scores (down to 1110 and 24), and there are also multicultural, music, and alumni children awards. Aside from the Sturgis, most scholarships require a completed application by March 1.

*Deadlines:*
    ADMISSION: Mar. 1
    FAFSA: Apr. 1 (priority)

# ART CENTER COLLEGE OF DESIGN ✦
## Pasadena, CA 91103

| | |
|---|---|
| ENROLLMENT: | 1,300 |
| UNDERGRADUATE: | 1,200 |
| ACCEPTANCE RATE: | 61% |
| SAT AVERAGE: | 510 Verbal |
| | 525 Math |
| STICKER PRICE (COMMUTER): | $19,000+ |
| NEED-BLIND: | Yes |
| NEED MET: | 45% |
| AVERAGE STUDENT DEBT: | $16,100 |
| MERIT SCHOLARSHIPS: | None |
| ATHLETIC SCHOLARSHIPS: | No |
| ROTC: | No |
| WEB SITE: | www.artcenter.edu |
| PHONE: | (626) 396-2373 |

Art Center is no place for the dilettante artist or the student who *might* be interested in a design career. With an average age of twenty-four, most freshmen have already experienced the world of work and know what they want. Applicants apply directly to the department where they wish to study and must present a portfolio directed toward that major. Illustration is the most popular, followed by graphic and product design. High school students should be prepared to spend five years to complete a degree and are forewarned about the lack of a conventional college social life. (There is no campus housing.) Yet for those with unusual ability who could thrive on their own in Pasadena, there may be no better place to begin a career in design. All financial aid is need-based, and with only 45 percent of need met on average, there is not a huge amount available. Art Center awards its own funds partly based on the strength of a student's portfolio. The sticker price includes an estimated $2,400 for books and art supplies.

*Deadlines:*
  ADMISSION: Rolling
  FAFSA: Mar. 1

# SCHOOL OF THE ART INSTITUTE OF CHICAGO ✦
## Chicago, IL 60603

| | |
|---|---|
| ENROLLMENT: | 2,000 |
| UNDERGRADUATE: | 1,500 |
| ACCEPTANCE RATE: | 73% |
| SAT AVERAGE: | NA |
| STICKER PRICE: | $25,000+ |
| NEED-BLIND: | Yes |
| NEED MET: | NA |
| AVERAGE STUDENT DEBT: | NA |
| MERIT SCHOLARSHIPS: | Many |
| ATHLETIC SCHOLARSHIPS: | No |
| ROTC: | No |
| WEB SITE: | www.artic.edu/saic |
| PHONE: | (800) 232-7242 |

Located in the heart of America's Second City, the School of the Art Institute of Chicago is one of the nation's top art schools. Chicago's thriving arts scene offers many of the same opportunities as New York in a much more livable environment for those who hail from smaller cities and towns. Entering students are not expected to declare a major, but proceed en masse to the First Year Program, which features a broad range of studio work combined with courses in writing and a year-long survey of art history. From that foundation, students work with faculty to develop their own areas of concentration in the upperclass years. Along with need-based aid, SAIC gives merit awards in three categories: the Presidential Scholarship ($7,000), the Recognition Scholarship ($3,500), and the Incentive Scholarship ($2,000). Applicants for admission are automatically considered. In addition to its regular admission process, SAIC offers an Immediate Decision Option in which students can come for a day of interviews and portfolio review that culminates in a yes or no.

*Deadlines:*
  ADMISSION: Mar. 15 (priority)
  FAFSA: Apr. 1

## COLLEGE OF THE ATLANTIC ◆ Bar Harbor, ME 04609

| | |
|---|---|
| ENROLLMENT: | 300 |
| UNDERGRADUATE: | 300 |
| ACCEPTANCE RATE: | 60% |
| SAT RANGE: | 610–710 Verbal |
| | 560–650 Math |
| STICKER PRICE: | $24,000+ |
| NEED-BLIND: | Yes |
| NEED MET: | NA |
| AVERAGE STUDENT DEBT: | $17,100 |
| MERIT SCHOLARSHIPS: | Few |
| RANGE: | Up to $9,000 |
| ATHLETIC SCHOLARSHIPS: | No |
| ROTC: | No |
| WEB SITE: | www.coa.edu |
| PHONE: | (800) 528-0025 |

Though College of Atlantic has an air of the 1960s about it, COA's unique brand of environmental education is very much in tune with today. Founded in 1969 as an experiment in interdisciplinary learning, COA has only one degree program, human ecology, which entails study of the relationship between people and the environment. The college's campus in coastal Maine borders Acadia National Park and provides the perfect location for field work. COA is governed by a weekly All College Meeting, and everyone from the president to first year students participate. The college has a decidedly feminine aura—women outnumber men by more than 2 to 1. Applicants should take note that COA recommends interviews for all, and requires them in some cases. The lion's share of the college's financial aid is based on need, though a limited number of Presidential Scholarships of up to $9,000 are awarded for "superior academic achievement, positive citizenship, and leadership skills." Awards for international students are also available.

*Deadlines:*
  EARLY DECISION: Dec. 1, Jan. 1
  REGULAR ADMISSION: Mar. 1
  FAFSA: Feb. 15

## AUBURN UNIVERSITY ◆ Auburn, AL 36849

| | |
|---|---|
| ENROLLMENT: | 21,500 |
| UNDERGRADUATE: | 18,200 |
| ACCEPTANCE RATE: | 86% |
| SAT RANGE: | 520–620 Verbal |
| | 510–630 Math |
| STICKER PRICE: | In-state, $7,000+ |
| | Out-of-state, $13,000+ |
| NEED-BLIND: | Yes |
| NEED MET: | 44% |
| AVERAGE STUDENT DEBT: | $16,700 |
| MERIT SCHOLARSHIPS: | Many |
| RANGE: | Up to full tuition + $2,000 |
| ATHLETIC SCHOLARSHIPS: | Yes |
| ROTC: | Army, Navy, Air Force |
| WEB SITE: | www.auburn.edu |
| PHONE: | (334) 844-4080 |

Auburn was once known as Alabama Polytechnic Institute, and before that as the Agricultural and Mechanical College of Alabama. There's a lot more to today's Auburn than technology, but its strength still lies in fields like engineering, architecture, and agriculture. Another major draw is the university's honors program, which features small classes, priority registration, and access to a specially designed study abroad program in England. Auburn is best known among the general public for its football team, which commands a following every bit as rabid as one would expect in the heart of the rural South. Students seeking an academic scholarship should heed this wake-up call: only those who apply for admission by December 1 will be considered. Minimum eligibility requirements include a 3.5 GPA and an SAT I of 1220 or an ACT of 27. Students who meet that threshold are considered for awards that range from $4,000 up to full tuition. National Merit Scholars get full tuition plus an additional $750–$2,000, and academic departments also sponsor their own awards.

*Deadlines:*
  ADMISSION: Rolling
  FAFSA: Apr. 17

## AUGUSTANA COLLEGE ✦ Rock Island, IL 61201

| | |
|---|---|
| ENROLLMENT: | 2,200 |
| UNDERGRADUATE: | 2,200 |
| ACCEPTANCE RATE: | 81% |
| ACT RANGE: | 23–29 |
| STICKER PRICE: | $21,000+ |
| NEED-BLIND: | Yes |
| NEED MET: | 91% |
| AVERAGE STUDENT DEBT: | $14,400 |
| MERIT SCHOLARSHIPS: | Many |
| RANGE: | Up to full tuition |
| ATHLETIC SCHOLARSHIPS: | No |
| ROTC: | No |
| WEB SITE: | www.augustana.edu |
| PHONE: | (800) 798-8100 |

Old grads returning to Augustana College might not recognize the place. With the recent completion of a $40 million building campaign, Augustan's spiffy new additions include arts facilities, a student activities center, a technology center with a 300-seat auditorium, and a major science building. Founded by Scandinavian Lutherans in 1860, Augustana features a liberal arts core with career-oriented programs in business, education, pre-law, and health professions. The full-tuition Presidential Scholarship is Augustana's top award for all-around excellence; two other smaller scholarships of at least $1,500 are available. Separate awards are available in art (up to $2,000), debate (up to $2,000), music (up to $5,000), theater (up to $2,000), and writing (up to $1,000). Sons and daughters of alumni get a $1,000 discount. Students preparing for a career in the Evangelical Lutheran Church qualify for up to half-tuition, and other Lutherans can get a $1,000 scholarship with a letter from their church pastor. Families with more than one sibling enrolled qualify for a one-quarter reduction of their bill.

*Deadlines:*
   ADMISSIONS: Rolling
   FAFSA: Apr. 1

## AUSTIN COLLEGE ✦ Sherman, TX 75090

| | |
|---|---|
| ENROLLMENT: | 1,200 |
| UNDERGRADUATE: | 1,200 |
| ACCEPTANCE RATE: | 61% |
| SAT RANGE: | 540–660 Verbal |
| | 560–660 Math |
| STICKER PRICE: | $20,000+ |
| NEED-BLIND: | Yes |
| NEED MET: | 97% |
| AVERAGE STUDENT DEBT: | $19,300 |
| MERIT SCHOLARSHIPS: | Many |
| RANGE: | Up to full tuition |
| ATHLETIC SCHOLARSHIPS: | No |
| ROTC: | No |
| WEB SITE: | www.austinc.edu |
| PHONE: | (800) 442-5363 |

Austin College is not to be confused with the Texas-sized state university in the city of Austin. Located hundreds of miles to the north near the Oklahoma border, AC offers a rare package for these parts: liberal arts excellence in a small college. Business is the most popular major, but there are also plenty of aspiring doctors and lawyers. Although Austin's sticker price is a bargain by national standards, its average total debt for financial aid recipients is a relatively high $19,300. Approximately one third of entering students receive a merit scholarship, the most highly prized of which is the full tuition Presidential Scholarship, which requires a special application due January 15. The $10,000 Leadership Institute Award has the same early deadline. National Merit Finalists can rake in $6,000 to full tuition; other scholarships range downward to the Achievement Scholarship, valued at $2,000 to $5,000. There are also awards for performing artists (up to $6,000), members of the Presbyterian Church (U.S.A.) (up to $10,000), and for students who would "enhance the diversity" of the campus (up to $10,000).

*Deadlines:*
   EARLY DECISION: Dec. 1
   EARLY ACTION: Jan. 15
   REGULAR ADMISSION: Mar. 1
   FAFSA: Feb. 15

# BABSON COLLEGE ◆ Babson Park, MA 02157

| | |
|---|---|
| ENROLLMENT: | 3,300 |
| UNDERGRADUATE: | 1,700 |
| ACCEPTANCE RATE: | 50% |
| SAT RANGE: | 500–600 Verbal |
| | 600–700 Math |
| STICKER PRICE: | $29,000+ |
| NEED-BLIND: | Yes |
| NEED MET: | 96% |
| AVERAGE STUDENT DEBT: | 19,500 |
| MERIT SCHOLARSHIPS: | Few |
| RANGE: | Up to $5,000 |
| ATHLETIC SCHOLARSHIPS: | No |
| ROTC: | Army, Navy, Air Force |
| WEB SITE: | www.babson.edu |
| PHONE: | (800) 488-3696 |

It is hard to avoid a flourish of "B's" when describing Babson, the Boston-area college best known for business. Babson is unique among business schools because it exists outside the context of a university, although its 1,700 undergraduates are joined by nearly as many graduate students. Babson's track record of turning out titans of industry is a big draw, and so, too, is its location. Marketing, economics, and finance are Babson's three most popular majors. It seems as if everyone wants to be in the Boston area, and the nearby suburb of Wellesley (technically Babson Park) fits the bill. Babson is need-blind and says it meets the vast majority of need, although its average debt per aid recipient is a high $19,500. Babson offers one lone merit scholarship: the $5,000 Presidential Scholars Award, which honors "exceptional academic and co-curricular accomplishments." There are also a number of named merit-within-need scholarships, including some for minority and disadvantaged students that range up to full tuition.

*Deadlines:*
  EARLY DECISION AND ACTION: Dec. 1
  REGULAR ADMISSION: Feb. 1
  FAFSA: Feb. 15
  CSS PROFILE: Feb. 15

# BARD COLLEGE ◆ Annandale-on-Hudson, NY 12504

| | |
|---|---|
| ENROLLMENT: | 1,100 |
| UNDERGRADUATE: | 1,100 |
| ACCEPTANCE RATE: | 54% |
| SAT RANGE: | 530–700 Verbal |
| | 540–670 Math |
| STICKER PRICE: | $30,000+ |
| NEED-BLIND: | Yes |
| NEED MET: | 90% |
| AVERAGE STUDENT DEBT: | NA |
| MERIT SCHOLARSHIPS: | Many |
| RANGE: | Up to full tuition |
| ATHLETIC SCHOLARSHIPS: | No |
| ROTC: | No |
| WEB SITE: | www.bard.edu |
| PHONE: | (914) 758-7472 |

At a time when many alternative colleges are up to their nose-rings in trouble, Bard is prospering as a mecca for nonconformists of all stripes. Enrollment is robust, and today's Bard is as selective as it ever was. A celebrated president with a knack for raising money is part of the equation, and so, too, is Bard's strategic location two hours north of New York City. And let's not forget Bard's innovative cost-cutters to attract top students, most notably the Excellence and Equal Cost Scholarship, which gives students in the top 10 percent of their high school class the same price for a Bard education as they would pay for a public university in their home state. In hopes of attracting a few top scientists, Bard offers ten full-tuition Distinguished Scientist Scholarships. A similar rationale applies for the Jerome Levy Economics Institute Scholarship. Other merit awards include the Trustee Leader Scholarships, which honor academic excellence and community service. There is also a merit-within-need scholarship of up to $8,000 for students who live in the Hudson Valley.

*Deadlines:*
  EARLY ACTION: Dec. 1
  REGULAR ADMISSION: Jan. 31
  FAFSA: Feb. 15
  CSS PROFILE: Feb. 15

# BARNARD COLLEGE ◆ New York, NY 10027

| | |
|---|---|
| ENROLLMENT: | 2,300 |
| UNDERGRADUATE: | 2,300 |
| ACCEPTANCE RATE: | 40% |
| SAT RANGE: | 620–700 Verbal |
| | 610–680 Math |
| STICKER PRICE: | $30,000+ |
| NEED-BLIND: | Yes |
| NEED MET: | 100% |
| AVERAGE STUDENT DEBT: | $12,800 |
| MERIT SCHOLARSHIPS: | None |
| ATHLETIC SCHOLARSHIPS: | No |
| ROTC: | No |
| WEB SITE: | www.barnard.columbia.edu |
| PHONE: | (212) 854-2014 |

It's official: Barnard is the hottest women's college in the nation. Riding the crest of New York City's popularity, the college's applications have shot up more than 100 percent in the 1990s. Barnard's prosperity is vindication of its decision twenty years ago to decline a merger with brother school Columbia College. Still a part of Columbia University, Barnard combines the benefits of a small women's college with the resources of the great university across the street. Barnard women tend to be more liberal and more connected to the city than their female counterparts at Columbia. English and psychology are the most heavily subscribed majors. The college is particularly strong in the performing arts, due in part to ties with Juilliard and Manhattan School of Music. In keeping with Ivy League policies, Barnard offers no merit scholarships. But it does meet full need, and aid recipients graduate with a relatively modest average debt of $12,800. First year aid recipients are expected to borrow approximately $2,600, take a term-time job, and contribute $1,500 of summer earnings.

*Deadlines:*
　EARLY DECISION: Nov. 15, Dec. 15
　REGULAR ADMISSION: Jan. 15
　FAFSA: Feb. 1
　CSS PROFILE: Feb. 1

# BATES COLLEGE ◆ Lewiston, ME 04240

| | |
|---|---|
| ENROLLMENT: | 1,600 |
| UNDERGRADUATE: | 1,600 |
| ACCEPTANCE RATE: | 34% |
| SAT RANGE: | 590–680 Verbal |
| | 600–680 Math |
| STICKER PRICE: | $30,000+ |
| NEED-BLIND: | Yes |
| NEED MET: | 100% |
| AVERAGE STUDENT DEBT: | $12,600 |
| MERIT SCHOLARSHIPS: | None |
| ATHLETIC SCHOLARSHIPS: | No |
| ROTC: | No |
| WEB SITE: | www.bates.edu |
| PHONE: | (207) 786-6000 |

Bates College's tradition of equality and fair play dates back to its founding by abolitionists on the eve of the Civil War. Today, as one after another of its competitors tries to rid itself of social fraternities, Bates can take pride in the fact that it never had them. Bates is one of a handful of elite colleges that does not require submission of any standardized testing. The main drawback to Bates is its location in the postindustrial, seen-better-days town of Lewiston. The college's personal approach to education carries over into admission, where contacts from prospective students are meticulously logged. (It never hurts to show interest.) Applications have held steady in recent years with the admit rate at approximately one-third. In keeping with its egalitarian ethos, Bates offers financial aid based only on need. The college's policy on outside scholarships is more generous than many other highly competitive colleges, allowing students to reduce their expected family contribution where possible.

*Deadlines:*
　EARLY DECISION: Nov. 15, Jan. 1
　REGULAR ADMISSION: Jan. 15
　FAFSA: Feb. 10
　CSS PROFILE: Jan. 15

# BAYLOR UNIVERSITY ✦ Waco, TX 76798

| | |
|---|---|
| ENROLLMENT: | 12,500 |
| UNDERGRADUATE: | 10,600 |
| ACCEPTANCE RATE: | 87% |
| SAT RANGE: | 520–620 Verbal |
| | 530–640 Math |
| STICKER PRICE: | $15,000+ |
| NEED-BLIND: | Yes |
| NEED MET: | 79% |
| AVERAGE STUDENT DEBT: | NA |
| MERIT SCHOLARSHIPS: | Many |
| RANGE: | Up to full tuition |
| ATHLETIC SCHOLARSHIPS: | Yes |
| ROTC: | Air Force |
| WEB SITE: | www.baylor.edu |
| PHONE: | (800) BAYLORU |

As the largest Baptist university in the world, Baylor combines down-home Texas pride with dyed-in-the-wool commitment to conservative Christian ideals. The college of arts and sciences is Baylor's largest division, and students flock to programs which will prepare them for health-related fields. Business is the university's other primary drawing card. With a sticker price under $16,000, Baylor is a bargain by national standards but pricey next to Texas's low-cost public institutions. Baylor's biggest merit scholarship is a full tuition award made to National Merit Finalists. Three other layers of awards ranging from $13,000 to $4,000 per year are aimed at top students, the lower amount available to students who rank in the top half of their high school class with a combined SAT I of 1200 or an ACT of 27. The School of Music has an extensive scholarship program (students should contact it directly), and various academic departments sponsor their own awards. A number of scholarships are earmarked for Baptists who have won recognition in high school.

*Deadlines:*
   ADMISSION: Rolling
   FAFSA: Mar. 1

# BELOIT COLLEGE ✦ Beloit, WI 53511

| | |
|---|---|
| ENROLLMENT: | 1,300 |
| UNDERGRADUATE: | 1,300 |
| ACCEPTANCE RATE: | 72% |
| SAT RANGE: | 580–690 Verbal |
| | 550–650 Math |
| STICKER PRICE: | $24,000+ |
| NEED-BLIND: | Yes |
| NEED MET: | 100% |
| AVERAGE STUDENT DEBT: | $11,600 |
| MERIT SCHOLARSHIPS: | Many |
| RANGE: | Up to $8,000 |
| ATHLETIC SCHOLARSHIPS: | No |
| ROTC: | No |
| WEB SITE: | www.beloit.edu |
| PHONE: | (800) 356-0751 |

The most popular major at Beloit College is anthropology—an unconventional choice by most standards, but perfectly in keeping with life at this liberal, open-minded, international little college. Beloit is a slight underdog in the competition for students with rivals Macalester, Carleton, Oberlin, and Grinnell. With only 1,300 students, it is smaller than all but Grinnell and offers an exceptional degree of interaction between students and faculty. Southern Wisconsin is not a drawing card, but students who get stir-crazy can take advantage of one of the best study-abroad programs in the nation. Beloit's top merit award is the $8,000 Presidential Scholarship, which goes to selected students with at least a 3.5 GPA or a top 10 percent class rank who score 1200 on the SAT I or 25 on the ACT. An application for admission is due by January 15. National Merit Finalists are eligible for $4,000, and the Charles Winter Wood Scholarships give top African Americans up to $8,000. Other awards are reserved for Wisconsin and Illinois residents ($5,000), musicians ($2,500), and those who have studied abroad ($2,000).

*Deadlines:*
   EARLY DECISION: Dec. 1
   REGULAR ADMISSION: Feb.1
   FAFSA: Apr. 1

# BENNINGTON COLLEGE ✦ Bennington, VT 05201

| | |
|---|---|
| ENROLLMENT: | 500 |
| UNDERGRADUATE: | 400 |
| ACCEPTANCE RATE: | 81% |
| SAT RANGE: | 550–650 Verbal |
| | 500–600 Math |
| STICKER PRICE: | $27,000+ |
| NEED-BLIND: | Yes |
| NEED MET: | 82% |
| AVERAGE STUDENT DEBT: | $16,300 |
| MERIT SCHOLARSHIPS: | Many |
| RANGE: | Up to $10,000 |
| ATHLETIC SCHOLARSHIPS: | No |
| ROTC: | No |
| WEB SITE: | www.bennington.edu |
| PHONE: | (800) 833-6845 |

Bennington adds a splash of artsy flair to the picturesque countryside of southern Vermont. Students learn by doing at Bennington; there are no official academic departments and students design their own majors. Drama, dance, the visual arts, and creative writing are the major drawing cards, and a high percentage of Bennington faculty are professionals in their fields rather than merely teachers. Bennington is still trying to live down the days when it was known as the nation's most expensive college. Since a dramatic restructuring in the early '90s, the college has kept a lid on the price increases. Enrollment, which had slumped, is now rebounding. A total of 24 freshmen received a non-need scholarship in a recent year. Bennington's top merit scholarship, Bennington Scholars, ranges from $5,000 to $10,000 per year but requires a separate essay and an application by December 1. The Brockway Scholarship, worth up to $7,000, requires no special application. A merit-within-need award, the Ellen Knowles Harcourt Scholarship, is also worth $7,500.

*Deadlines:*
   EARLY DECISION: Dec. 1
   REGULAR ADMISSION: Feb. 1
   FAFSA: Feb. 1

# BEREA COLLEGE ✦ Berea, KY 40404

| | |
|---|---|
| ENROLLMENT: | 1,500 |
| UNDERGRADUATE: | 1,500 |
| ACCEPTANCE RATE: | 35% |
| SAT AVERAGE: | 563 Verbal |
| | 526 Math |
| STICKER PRICE: | $4,000+ |
| NEED-BLIND: | No |
| NEED MET: | 81% |
| AVERAGE STUDENT DEBT: | $3,000 |
| MERIT SCHOLARSHIPS: | Full tuition for all students |
| ATHLETIC SCHOLARSHIPS: | No |
| ROTC: | No |
| WEB SITE: | www.berea.edu |
| PHONE: | (800) 326-5948 |

If the idea of free tuition perks up your interest, there's a little college in rural Kentucky where nobody pays a dime. With a larger endowment per student than Stanford, MIT, and most of the Ivy League, Berea College uses its money to aid students who could not otherwise afford college. Berea is open only to low- and middle-income families; the maximum qualifying income for a family of four in 1998–99 was $44,000 (assuming one student in college). Residents of Appalachia, a region that covers parts of nine states from Alabama to Ohio, are given preference in admission. Freshmen pay an average of only $850 toward the sticker price of their living expenses, but all students are expected to work at least ten hours per week in the college's Labor Program, which includes farm work, crafts and ceramics, and jobs in a college-owned hotel. Though Berea enrolls only 1,500 students, it offers an impressive variety in its curriculum, including the liberal arts, business, education, and nursing.

*Deadlines:*
   ADMISSION: Feb. 1 (priority)
   FAFSA: Feb. 15

## BIRMINGHAM-SOUTHERN COLLEGE ✦ Birmingham, AL 35254

| | |
|---|---|
| ENROLLMENT: | 1,400 |
| UNDERGRADUATE: | 1,400 |
| ACCEPTANCE RATE: | 96% |
| SAT RANGE: | 540–670 Verbal |
| | 530–660 Math |
| STICKER PRICE: | $20,000+ |
| NEED-BLIND: | Yes |
| NEED MET: | 87% |
| AVERAGE STUDENT DEBT: | $12,000 |
| MERIT SCHOLARSHIPS: | Many |
| RANGE: | Up to full costs |
| ATHLETIC SCHOLARSHIPS: | Yes |
| ROTC: | Army, Air Force |
| WEB SITE: | www.bsc.edu |
| PHONE: | (800) 523-5793 |

Want merit scholarships? Birmingham-Southern is Deep South scholarship central. There is something for everyone: academic merit scholarships for students who are in the top 20 percent of their class and scored a 1050 or above on the SAT I or a 26 on the ACT; awards for future health professionals, Birmingham residents, those who can write an essay titled "Why I Would Like a Career in Small Business;" scholarships for art, music, dance, and theater based on in-person auditions and portfolio presentations; scholarships for Eagle Scouts, Girl Scout Gold Award recipients, and members of the United Methodist Church; and last but not least, a $3,000 award for any winner of the Miss Alabama Pageant, along with $1,500 for any of the ten runners-up, and a similar program for Junior Miss winners and runners-up. The latter two might raise eyebrows on some campuses, but not at this small liberal arts college in the heart of Dixieland. Some scholarships require separate forms or an application for admission as early as January 15. About 86 percent of the freshmen in a recent year received a non-need award.

*Deadlines:*
    ADMISSION: Jan. 15
    FAFSA: Mar. 1

## BOSTON COLLEGE ✦ Chestnut Hill, MA 02167

| | |
|---|---|
| ENROLLMENT: | 14,700 |
| UNDERGRADUATE: | 8,900 |
| ACCEPTANCE RATE: | 38% |
| SAT RANGE: | 520–620 Verbal |
| | 610–700 Math |
| STICKER PRICE: | $30,000+ |
| NEED-BLIND: | Yes |
| NEED MET: | NA |
| AVERAGE STUDENT DEBT: | NA |
| MERIT SCHOLARSHIPS: | Few |
| RANGE: | Half tuition |
| ATHLETIC SCHOLARSHIPS: | Yes |
| ROTC: | Army, Navy, Air Force |
| WEB SITE: | www.bc.edu |
| PHONE: | (617) 552-3100 |

Boston College has become the Northeast's version of Notre Dame. Vaulted to prominence by its football team in the 1980s, BC has stayed hot because of Boston's powerful allure. BC's secluded campus is a quick subway ride away from the bustle of downtown. Despite its location in one of the nation's most liberal regions, BC attracts a conservative breed of student, just over three-quarters of whom are Catholic. Not really a college, BC is in fact a large university with nearly as many graduate students as undergraduates. BC offers primarily need-based aid, with the exception of ten half-tuition Presidential Scholarships that are awarded to early action applicants on the basis of "academic excellence, personal accomplishments and future potential." BC's policy for considering the finances of noncustodial parents when making need-based aid awards is typical of many highly selective private colleges: "We feel very strongly that both parents have an obligation to contribute towards your cost of education, and a divorce or separation does not change that obligation."

*Deadlines:*
    EARLY ACTION: Nov. 1
    REGULAR ADMISSION: Jan. 15
    FAFSA: Feb. 1
    CSS PROFILE: Feb. 1

# BOSTON CONSERVATORY • Boston, MA 02215

| | |
|---|---|
| ENROLLMENT: | 300 |
| UNDERGRADUATE: | 300 |
| ACCEPTANCE RATE: | 47% |
| SAT AVERAGE: | 460 Verbal |
| | 483 Math |
| STICKER PRICE: | $25,000+ |
| NEED-BLIND: | Yes |
| NEED MET: | NA |
| AVERAGE STUDENT DEBT: | NA |
| MERIT SCHOLARSHIPS: | Few |
| RANGE: | Up to full tuition |
| ATHLETIC SCHOLARSHIPS: | No |
| ROTC: | No |
| WEB SITE: | www.bostonconservatory.edu |
| PHONE: | (617) 536-6340 |

There could hardly be a better spot for a music conservatory than the bustling arts scene of Boston's Back Bay. Boston University, Berklee College of Music, and New England Conservatory are all in the neighborhood, and beyond are the resources of America's favorite college town. A pioneer in the teaching of musical theater, Boston Conservatory also offers degree programs in music performance, education and composition, and dance. A total of twelve faculty members are either present or past members of the Boston Symphony Orchestra. A limited number of Conservatory Talent Scholarships of up to full tuition are awarded to the most promising students with the stipulation they participate in "performance activities as might be required by the Conservatory." There are also assistantships available for students to earn while they learn. A number of named honor scholarships are also available. The Conservatory supplements federal loans with an endowed program of its own for "those who have exhausted all other forms of financial aid."

*Deadlines:*
  ADMISSION: Mar. 1 (priority)
  FAFSA: Feb. 15

# BOSTON UNIVERSITY • Boston, MA 02215

| | |
|---|---|
| ENROLLMENT: | 29,400 |
| UNDERGRADUATE: | 18,900 |
| ACCEPTANCE RATE: | 55% |
| SAT RANGE: | 580–680 Verbal |
| | 580–680 Math |
| STICKER PRICE: | $31,000+ |
| NEED-BLIND: | Yes |
| NEED MET: | 94% |
| AVERAGE STUDENT DEBT: | $17,000 |
| MERIT SCHOLARSHIPS: | Many |
| RANGE: | Up to full tuition |
| ATHLETIC SCHOLARSHIPS: | Yes |
| ROTC: | Army, Navy, Air Force |
| WEB SITE: | www.bu.edu |
| PHONE: | (617) 353-2300 |

After decades as the Rodney Dangerfield of Boston's college scene, BU is finally getting some respect. Applications are up, the city is chic, and BU has a richly deserved reputation for excellence in the arts, media, and journalism. Other strong programs include business, engineering, and pre-med, and applications pour in for the combined B.A./M.D. program. BU has a wide range of merit scholarships, highlighted by the Trustee Scholarship that offers full tuition and fees to selected students at the top of their high school class with approximately 1490 on the SAT I or 32 on the ACT. Application materials are due December 1. A number of other university-wide scholarship programs are available, down to the $5,000 Founders' Grant, for which average recipients have a 3.3 GPA with a score of 1240 or 27. The college of engineering offers a minimum of six full tuition scholarships that are awarded at regional contests held in the late fall. Scholarships are also offered in the arts, classics, education, and to those who live in the Boston area. Some merit scholarships require the FAFSA and PROFILE.

*Deadlines:*
  EARLY DECISION: Nov. 1
  REGULAR ADMISSION: Jan. 15
  FAFSA: Feb. 15
  CSS PROFILE: Feb. 15

# BOWDOIN COLLEGE ◆ Brunswick, ME 04011

| | |
|---|---|
| ENROLLMENT: | 1,600 |
| UNDERGRADUATE: | 1,600 |
| ACCEPTANCE RATE: | 34% |
| SAT RANGE: | 620–710 Verbal |
| | 620–710 Math |
| STICKER PRICE: | $31,000+ |
| NEED-BLIND: | Yes |
| NEED MET: | 100% |
| AVERAGE STUDENT DEBT: | $14,900 |
| MERIT SCHOLARSHIPS: | None |
| ATHLETIC SCHOLARSHIPS: | No |
| ROTC: | No |
| WEB SITE: | www.bowdoin.edu |
| PHONE: | (207) 725-3101 |

Bowdoin is a quiet member of the elite private college group. Often mentioned in the same breath as Amherst, Swarthmore, and Williams, Bowdoin is not easily pigeonholed. It was among the first private liberal arts colleges to declare standardized testing optional, yet Bowdoin has also been among the slowest to eject Greek letter fraternities. The latter will be gone by 2000, replaced with a "house" system in which students will be assigned to a particular house when they enroll. Academically, Bowdoin is best known in the sciences, and its location within arm's length of the Atlantic coast makes for abundant field work opportunities. Government is Bowdoin's most popular department, and its tradition in English dates back to the nineteenth century when students included the likes of Nathaniel Hawthorne and Henry Wadsworth Longfellow. Bowdoin is need-blind in admissions and meets the full need of all accepted students, *sans* merit scholarships. Bowdoin's endowment per student places it near the top, but not at the rarified heights of Grinnell or Swarthmore.

*Deadlines:*
    EARLY DECISION: Nov. 15
    REGULAR ADMISSION: Jan. 1
    FAFSA: Feb. 15
    CSS PROFILE: Feb. 15

# BRADFORD COLLEGE ◆ Haverhill, MA 01835

| | |
|---|---|
| ENROLLMENT: | 600 |
| UNDERGRADUATE: | 600 |
| ACCEPTANCE RATE: | 78% |
| SAT RANGE: | NA |
| STICKER PRICE: | $24,000+ |
| NEED-BLIND: | NA |
| NEED MET: | 93% |
| AVERAGE STUDENT DEBT: | $22,000 |
| MERIT SCHOLARSHIPS: | Many |
| RANGE: | Up to full tuition |
| ATHLETIC SCHOLARSHIPS: | No |
| ROTC: | No |
| WEB SITE: | www.bradford.edu |
| PHONE: | (800) 336-6448 |

How did a tiny Massachusetts liberal arts college become one of the most innovative institutions in all of higher education? The secret is in the Bradford Plan, which allows students to combine broad-based liberal arts training with practical internships and minors in job-related fields such as marketing or management. The plan features an interdisciplinary core curriculum that includes subjects such as Individual and Community and Global Perspectives. Students leave Bradford with both an education for life and skills for the world of work. Bradford's menu of merit scholarships includes awards up to full tuition as well as half-tuition awards for any student ranked in the top 10 percent of their high school class. Scholarships of $5,000 are available for excellence in leadership, and artists can vie for $5,000 awards in graphic design, visual arts, and performing arts. There are also half-tuition awards available for older students going back to school. Bradford's high student debt average of $22,000 is due in part to the fact that many students show high financial need.

*Deadlines:*
    ADMISSION: Rolling
    FAFSA: Feb. 15

## BRADLEY UNIVERSITY • Peoria, IL 61625

| | |
|---|---|
| ENROLLMENT: | 5,800 |
| UNDERGRADUATE: | 4,900 |
| ACCEPTANCE RATE: | 89% |
| ACT RANGE: | 22–28 |
| STICKER PRICE: | $18,000+ |
| NEED-BLIND: | Yes |
| NEED MET: | 90% |
| AVERAGE STUDENT DEBT: | $14,000 |
| MERIT SCHOLARSHIPS: | Many |
| RANGE: | Up to full tuition |
| ATHLETIC SCHOLARSHIPS: | Yes |
| ROTC: | Army |
| WEB SITE: | www.bradley.edu |
| PHONE: | (800) 447-6460 |

Bradley University doesn't mind sharing the fact that nearly 200 National Merit Finalists have enrolled in the past five years. Some of them were probably seduced by the Midwestern charm of Peoria; others may have been drawn to Bradley's wide-ranging curriculum that includes the liberal arts, business, communications, education, engineering, fine arts, and health sciences. No doubt there are a few who like the fact that Bradley is a major university but small enough to offer personal attention. But the real reason why they enroll probably lies in the full-tuition scholarship that Bradley offers to all National Merit Finalists. Other top students can aspire to the Dean's Scholarship, which gives half-tuition to those who rank in the top 10 percent with 1240 on the SAT I or a 28 on the ACT. Valedictorians also get a half-tuition discount. In celebration of its recent 100-year anniversary, Bradley inaugurated the Legacy Scholarships, which offer up to $6,000 to children and grandchildren of alumni. Scholarship hopefuls must complete the university's Competitive Scholarship application by January 15.

*Deadlines:*
ADMISSION: Rolling
FAFSA: Mar.1

## BRANDEIS UNIVERSITY • Waltham, MA 02254

| | |
|---|---|
| ENROLLMENT: | 4,300 |
| UNDERGRADUATE: | 3,100 |
| ACCEPTANCE RATE: | 54% |
| SAT RANGE: | 620–700 Verbal |
| | 610–700 Math |
| STICKER PRICE: | $31,000+ |
| NEED-BLIND: | Yes |
| NEED MET: | NA |
| AVERAGE STUDENT DEBT: | NA |
| MERIT SCHOLARSHIPS: | Many |
| RANGE: | Up to $18,000 |
| ATHLETIC SCHOLARSHIPS: | No |
| ROTC: | Army, Air Force |
| WEB SITE: | www.brandeis.edu |
| PHONE: | (781) 736-3500 |

If a major merit award is on your wish list, Brandeis has plenty. The university was founded under Jewish auspices in the wake of World War II and still attracts a student body that is more than 60 percent Jewish. But there is much at Brandeis to appeal to students of all faiths: a liberal atmosphere, a suburban Boston location, and strong programs in the natural sciences. Brandeis is a world leader in anything related to Judiasm and the Middle East. With competitors that include the likes of Harvard and the University of Pennsylvania, Brandeis uses merit money to lure its share of the crème de la crème. Approximately ninety scholarships of up to $18,000 are given in honor of university namesake Justice Louis Brandeis, and the Norman S. Rabb, Annenberg, and Gilbert scholarships also feature $18,000 awards. More than 100 Presidential Scholarships of $10,000 are also available, along with one award for three-quarters of tuition that memorializes the Challenger astronauts. The university also earmarks money for National Merit Finalists. About 20 percent of each class receives a merit award.

*Deadlines:*
EARLY DECISION: Jan. 1
REGULAR ADMISSION: Feb. 1
FAFSA: Feb. 1
CSS PROFILE: Feb. 1

# BRIGHAM YOUNG UNIVERSITY ◆ Provo, UT 84602

| | |
|---|---|
| ENROLLMENT: | 32,200 |
| UNDERGRADUATE: | 28,500 |
| ACCEPTANCE RATE: | 71% |
| ACT RANGE: | 24–29 |
| STICKER PRICE: | Church members, $7,000+ |
| | Nonmembers, $8,000+ |
| NEED-BLIND: | NA |
| NEED MET: | NA |
| AVERAGE STUDENT DEBT: | $11,500 |
| MERIT SCHOLARSHIPS: | Many |
| RANGE: | Up to full tuition |
| ATHLETIC SCHOLARSHIPS: | Yes |
| ROTC: | Army, Air Force |
| WEB SITE: | www.byu.edu |
| PHONE: | (801) 378-2507 |

Most Americans get their introduction to BYU from watching the exploits of its football and basketball teams. But for Mormons across the nation, BYU means something much more: it's the intellectual hub of the Church of Jesus Christ of Latter Day Saints. BYU is an institution of 32,200 students, united in its commitment to clean living, traditional values, and the tenets of the church. BYU provides every conceivable academic program, with particular quality in foreign language. A sticker price below $8,000 for church members makes BYU a bargain even by public university standards. The university's most prestigious merit awards, the Gordon B. Hinckley Presidential Scholarships, offer full tuition to church members with a minimum SAT I score of 1430 (or an ACT of 33) and a high school GPA of 3.90 or a top 5 percent ranking. The deadline is January 15. Many other academic scholarships, including one for National Merit Finalists, are also available. Other awards honor artistic talent and residence in a particular state or country.

*Deadlines:*
ADMISSION: Feb. 15
FAFSA: Apr. 15

# BROWN UNIVERSITY ◆ Providence, RI 02912

| | |
|---|---|
| ENROLLMENT: | 7,600 |
| UNDERGRADUATE: | 6,000 |
| ACCEPTANCE RATE: | 18% |
| SAT RANGE: | 640–740 Verbal |
| | 650–740 Math |
| STICKER PRICE: | $31,000+ |
| NEED-BLIND: | No |
| NEED MET: | 100% |
| AVERAGE STUDENT DEBT: | $17,500 |
| MERIT SCHOLARSHIPS: | None |
| ATHLETIC SCHOLARSHIPS: | No |
| ROTC: | Army |
| WEB SITE: | www.brown.edu |
| PHONE: | (401) 863-2378 |

Brown will go down in history as the comeback kid of college admissions. Few would have imagined that this Ivy League also-ran of the 1950s and '60s would one day vault to so near the top of the heap. It took savvy marketing and a student love affair with the thirty-year-old "new" curriculum, which eliminates distribution requirements and offers a generous pass/fail option. Alternately praised for its open-mindedness and condemned as permissive and politically correct, Brown seems to thrive on the cutting edge. Though the equal of Yale in selectivity and nearly so of Harvard and Princeton, Brown's endowment is only about one-fifth as large. Brown is the only Ivy to consider financial need when making some borderline admission decisions. Brown has no merit scholarships, but top applicants may find extra grant money in their need-based package along with a University Scholar designation. After students are enrolled, Brown offers a number of paid fellowships for academic study and community service, notably the Royce Fellowship Program, which features a stipend of up to $4,000.

*Deadlines:*
EARLY ACTION: Nov. 1
REGULAR ADMISSION: Jan. 1
FAFSA: Mar. 1
CSS PROFILE: Feb. 1

## BRYN MAWR COLLEGE ✦ Bryn Mawr, PA 19010

ENROLLMENT:            1,700
UNDERGRADUATE:         1,200
ACCEPTANCE RATE:       58%
SAT RANGE:             630–700 Verbal
                       630–710 Math
STICKER PRICE:         $31,000+
NEED-BLIND:            No
NEED MET:              100%
AVERAGE STUDENT DEBT:  $13,000
MERIT SCHOLARSHIPS:    None
ATHLETIC SCHOLARSHIPS: No
ROTC:                  Navy
WEB SITE:              www.brynmawr.edu
PHONE:                 (610) 526-5153

Bryn Mawr has always reflected the feisty individualism of its most famous alumna, Katharine Hepburn. Usually viewed as the most intellectually serious of the one-time Seven Sisters, Bryn Mawr has adapted well to a world in which most colleges are coed. Strong ties remain with Haverford College, a hop, skip, and jump down Philadelphia's Main Line, although Haverford has admitted women of its own for more than two decades. Bryn Mawr's production of students who ultimately earn a Ph.D. has always ranked near the top for institutions of all types, and if one considers female Ph.D.s in the natural sciences, BMC's percentage is off the charts. (Biology is the college's most popular major followed by English and psychology.) Rival Wellesley has the chic of Boston on its side, but Bryn Mawr is probably the more diverse of the two. With an undergraduate enrollment of only 1,200, Bryn Mawr is smaller than most of its competitors, although course offerings are supplemented by those at Haverford. The college offers aid based only on need—meeting 100 percent—and the average total debt of graduating aid recipients is a moderate $13,000.

*Deadlines:*
   EARLY DECISION: Nov. 15
   REGULAR ADMISSION: Jan. 15
   FAFSA: Jan. 15

## BUCKNELL UNIVERSITY ✦ Lewisburg, PA 17837

ENROLLMENT:            3,500
UNDERGRADUATE:         3,300
ACCEPTANCE RATE:       54%
SAT RANGE:             570–650 Verbal
                       600–680 Math
STICKER PRICE:         $28,000+
NEED-BLIND:            No
NEED MET:              100%
AVERAGE STUDENT DEBT:  $16,000
MERIT SCHOLARSHIPS:    None
ATHLETIC SCHOLARSHIPS: No
ROTC:                  Army
WEB SITE:              www.bucknell.edu
PHONE:                 (717) 524-1101

The typical Bucknellian is conservative and well-rounded—not as intellectual as an Ivy Leaguer, but just as likely to reach the top rung of the corporate ladder. Often associated with Colgate, Hamilton, and Lafayette, Bucknell is really more like Lehigh—a small university combining the liberal arts with top-notch preprofessional programs in business and engineering. Biology and economics head the list of most popular majors. Though the campus is gorgeous, central Pennsylvania can seem remote for those accustomed to city life. Bucknell remains a holdout against merit scholarships, despite their growth at competitor colleges. The one exception is Army ROTC, which offers more than $16,000 per year and preferential packaging from the university to meet any additional need. Bucknell's Scholarship Security program ensures that every student's need is projected for the entire four years and offers a guarantee that aid packages will rise to meet future increases in need that can be predicted at enrollment. Bucknell requires submission of the CSS PROFILE by the unusually early date of January 1.

*Deadlines:*
   EARLY DECISION: Dec. 1
   REGULAR ADMISSION: Jan. 1
   FAFSA: MAY 1
   CSS PROFILE: Jan. 1

## BUTLER UNIVERSITY • Indianapolis, IN 46208

| | |
|---|---|
| ENROLLMENT: | 3,900 |
| UNDERGRADUATE: | 3,100 |
| ACCEPTANCE RATE: | 87% |
| SAT RANGE: | 520–620 Verbal |
| | 520–630 Math |
| STICKER PRICE: | $21,000+ |
| NEED-BLIND: | Yes |
| NEED MET: | 86% |
| AVERAGE STUDENT DEBT: | $21,000 |
| MERIT SCHOLARSHIPS: | Many |
| ATHLETIC SCHOLARSHIPS: | Yes |
| ROTC: | Army, Air Force |
| WEB SITE: | www.butler.edu |
| PHONE: | (317) 940-8100 |

Butler is a small university in suburban Indianapolis, best known for its programs in the fine arts. Drama, dance, and music are all well-respected, and telecommunication arts students have the benefit of a college-run public television station. Business and pharmacy are also popular. Butler takes better care of its 3,100 undergraduates than most universities; under its Learning Initiative program, students get extra support when they choose a major, which continues as they plan for the job market. The university ensures that liberal arts students have access to internships similar to those in the professional schools. Merit scholarship applicants should be aware that Butler has early deadlines. A variety of departmental awards are available for students who apply for admission by December 1, and university-wide scholarships of up to $7,600 require an application by February 1, although earlier is preferred. Valedictorians, salutatorians, and National Merit Semifinalists are guaranteed an award if they apply by February 1. Audition-based awards are available in the fine arts.

*Deadlines:*
    EARLY ACTION: Dec. 1, Feb. 1
    REGULAR ADMISSION: Rolling
    FAFSA: Feb. 20

## CALIFORNIA INSTITUTE OF THE ARTS • Valencia, CA 91355

| | |
|---|---|
| ENROLLMENT: | 1,100 |
| UNDERGRADUATE: | 700 |
| ACCEPTANCE RATE: | 40% |
| SAT RANGE: | NA |
| STICKER PRICE: | $24,000+ |
| NEED-BLIND: | Yes |
| NEED MET: | 79% |
| AVERAGE STUDENT DEBT: | $22,300 |
| MERIT SCHOLARSHIPS: | Few |
| ATHLETIC SCHOLARSHIPS: | No |
| ROTC: | No |
| WEB SITE: | www.calarts.edu |
| PHONE: | (800) 292-2787 (in-state) |
| | (800) 545-2787 (out-of-state) |

Cal Arts has as much glitz and variety as one would expect from a school founded by Walt Disney. Art, dance, drama, and all kinds of music are here, as well as the excellence to be expected in film/video. But Cal Arts is far from a corporate subsidiary; it has always been one of the most innovative schools of its kind. Experimentation is the norm, as in the new Integrated Media Program that allows students to explore new combinations in an increasingly multimedia world. The school is also committed to multicultural artistic experiences. In the Community Arts Partnership, students work with inner-city communities to plan and execute a wide variety of arts programs. Nestled in a desert valley on the northern fringe of Los Angeles, the school's sixty-acre campus features spacious lawns and housing for 450 students. The vast majority of aid at Cal Arts is reserved for those who have need. However, the school notes that "the dollar amount of your award may vary based on your merit placement," and a small number of awards are based on merit alone.

*Deadlines:*
    ADMISSION: Feb. 1 (priority)
    FAFSA: Mar. 2

# CALIFORNIA INSTITUTE OF TECHNOLOGY ✦
## Pasadena, CA 91125

| | |
|---|---|
| ENROLLMENT: | 1,900 |
| UNDERGRADUATE: | 900 |
| ACCEPTANCE RATE: | 23% |
| SAT RANGE: | 680–770 Verbal |
| | 740–800 Math |
| STICKER PRICE: | $25,000+ |
| NEED-BLIND: | Yes |
| NEED MET: | 100% |
| AVERAGE STUDENT DEBT: | $12,600 |
| MERIT SCHOLARSHIPS: | Few |
| RANGE: | Up to full tuition |
| ATHLETIC SCHOLARSHIPS: | No |
| ROTC: | Army, Air Force |
| WEB SITE: | www.caltech.edu |
| PHONE: | (800) 568-8324 |

With an average SAT score that even Harvard and MIT can't match, there is little doubt that Caltech enrolls the highest per capita concentration of science geniuses on the planet. Caltech is all about the creativity unleashed by so much brain power packed into such a small space. Engineering and physics, the two most popular majors, are where Caltech's reputation lies. Unencumbered by an army of graduate students or layers of bureaucracy, Caltechies are free to be their zany, off-beat, distractedly brilliant selves. Students have unparalleled access to facilities; Caltech operates on an honor code, and everybody gets a key to every building. Notwithstanding its location near downtown Pasadena, many doors remain unlocked twenty-four hours a day. Although Caltech puts its emphasis on need-based aid, a small number of merit scholarships worth $10,000, $15,000, or full tuition are quietly parceled out to the best of the best. Some awards are made to enhance campus diversity. More scholarships are available for upperclassmen, including some sponsored by particular academic departments.

*Deadlines:*
  EARLY ACTION: Nov. 1
  REGULAR ADMISSION: Jan. 1
  FAFSA: Jan. 15
  CSS PROFILE: Jan. 15

# CALIFORNIA POLYTECHNIC
## STATE UNIVERSITY/SAN LUIS OBISPO ✦
## San Luis Obispo, CA 93407

| | |
|---|---|
| ENROLLMENT: | 16,700 |
| UNDERGRADUATE: | 15,800 |
| ACCEPTANCE RATE: | 38% |
| SAT RANGE: | 450–600 Verbal |
| | 475–650 Math |
| STICKER PRICE: | In-state, $8,000+ |
| | Out-of-state, $14,000+ |
| NEED-BLIND: | Yes |
| NEED MET: | 74% |
| AVERAGE STUDENT DEBT: | $14,200 |
| MERIT SCHOLARSHIPS: | Many |
| ATHLETIC SCHOLARSHIPS: | Yes |
| ROTC: | Army |
| WEB SITE: | www.calpoly.edu |
| PHONE: | (805) 756-2311 |

The rugged beauty of California's central coast is home to the jewel of its state university system, Cal Poly/San Luis Obispo. With strong programs across a broad range of preprofessional and technical fields, Cal Poly has a simple philosophy that is the school's unofficial motto: "Learn by Doing." That means, among other things, an extensive cooperative education program that places students in six-month internships related to their majors. Although best known for its technical programs, the university's largest major is business administration, and it offers degrees in everything from music to teacher education. Cal Poly uses a formula of grade point average and test scores as the primary basis for admission decisions, and with only 38 percent of the applicants accepted, competition is stiff. The filing of Cal Poly's scholarship application by March 2 allows students to be considered for scores of awards, most of which are worth $3,000 or less and offered by the various academic divisions.

*Deadlines:*
  ADMISSION: Nov. 30
  FAFSA: MAR. 1

166

## UNIVERSITY OF CALIFORNIA/BERKELEY ♦
## Berkeley, CA 94720

| | |
|---|---|
| ENROLLMENT: | 30,300 |
| UNDERGRADUATE: | 21,700 |
| ACCEPTANCE RATE: | 31% |
| SAT RANGE: | 580–710 Verbal |
| | 620–730 Math |
| STICKER PRICE: | In-state, $12,000+ |
| | Out-of-state, $21,000+ |
| NEED-BLIND: | Yes |
| NEED MET: | 87% |
| AVERAGE STUDENT DEBT: | $10,100 |
| MERIT SCHOLARSHIPS: | Many |
| ATHLETIC SCHOLARSHIPS: | Yes |
| ROTC: | Army, Navy, Air Force |
| WEB SITE: | www.berkeley.edu |
| PHONE: | (510) 642-3175 |

Berkeley is a realm of mythic proportions in the world of higher education. As both a great university and a magnet for free-thinkers of every conceivable stripe, Berkeley is perhaps the greatest intellectual crossroads in the United States. Yet a host of problems threaten to make Berkeley's future less distinguished than its past: state-mandated budget cuts, the rampant overcrowding of the UC system, and the new statewide policy against consideration of race in admission that has drastically curtailed the presence of underrepresented minority groups. With an in-state sticker price one-third the cost of elite private institutions, Berkeley remains a tremendous bargain. The university awards approximately 250 academic scholarships to freshmen each year, most notably the Regents and Chancellor's awards, which offer a minimum stipend of $1,000 per year and up to full tuition for those with need. Alumni Leadership Scholarships are available to students from California and other selected states. Berkeley also gives scholarships to National Merit Finalists, and additional awards are made in various categories.

*Deadlines:*
   ADMISSION: Nov. 30
   FAFSA: Mar. 2

## UNIVERSITY OF CALIFORNIA/DAVIS ♦
## Davis, CA 95616

| | |
|---|---|
| ENROLLMENT: | 23,100 |
| UNDERGRADUATE: | 18,800 |
| ACCEPTANCE RATE: | 73% |
| SAT RANGE: | 503–620 Verbal |
| | 545–650 Math |
| STICKER PRICE: | In-state, $11,000+ |
| | Out-of-state, $21,000+ |
| NEED-BLIND: | Yes |
| NEED MET: | NA |
| AVERAGE STUDENT DEBT: | $10,500 |
| MERIT SCHOLARSHIPS: | Many |
| ATHLETIC SCHOLARSHIPS: | Yes |
| ROTC: | Army, Air Force |
| WEB SITE: | www.ucdavis.edu |
| PHONE: | (916) 752-2971 |

UC/Davis has come a long way since its founding in 1905 as the "University Farm." Though still an aggie school at heart, Davis has emerged as a national leader in fields like biology, biotechnology, and environmental sciences. Like all UC campuses, Davis has been weighed down by the state's budget cuts in recent years. One unique offering at Davis is the Integrated Studies residential honors program, which provides small classes, interdisciplinary courses, and hands-on learning opportunities to a limited number of first-year students. In addition to its modest sticker price, Davis gives non-need scholarships to approximately 1,500 new and returning students. Eligibility for University of California Regents awards is based primarily on a GPA-SAT score formula. The Cal Aggie Alumni Scholarship requires a minimum GPA of 3.5, a one page essay on leadership, and an interview after the application is filed. The univerisity also sponsors awards for National Merit Finalists, and additional scholarships are based on merit and/or need.

*Deadlines:*
   ADMISSION: Nov. 30
   FAFSA: Mar. 2

## UNIVERSITY OF CALIFORNIA/IRVINE •
## Irvine, CA 92717

ENROLLMENT:           17,800
UNDERGRADUATE:        14,100
ACCEPTANCE RATE:      66%
SAT RANGE:            465–580 Verbal
                      525–640 Math
STICKER PRICE:        In-state, $11,000+
                      Out-of-state, $21,000+
NEED-BLIND:           Yes
NEED MET:             NA
AVERAGE STUDENT DEBT: NA
MERIT SCHOLARSHIPS:   Many
ATHLETIC SCHOLARSHIPS: Yes
ROTC:                 Army, Air Force
WEB SITE:             www.ucop.edu/pathways
PHONE:                (714) 824-6703

Founded in 1965, Irvine is the babe of the University of California system, but it has grown quickly into a mature research institution. Irvine is best known as a pre-med factory, and biological sciences is the most popular major. Located in sunny Southern California within a few miles of the Pacific, the 1,500-acre campus combines modern architecture with exotic subtropical vegetation. The Campuswide Honors Program provides top students with special classes, research opportunities, and enhanced advising. As elsewhere in the UC system, top students can aspire to a Regents Scholarship, which at Irvine covers full in-state tuition. For consideration, students must have a 3.75 GPA and minimum of 1340 on the SAT I. University Scholarships provide renewable awards of $1,000, while the Chancellors Club award gives top students a total of $4,000 spread over two years. A small number of National Merit Finalists also receive funding, and small nonrenewable awards are also available via a number of programs.

*Deadlines:*
ADMISSION: Nov. 30
FAFSA: Mar. 2

## UNIVERSITY OF CALIFORNIA/LOS ANGELES •
## Los Angeles, CA 90095

ENROLLMENT:           35,600
UNDERGRADUATE:        23,900
ACCEPTANCE RATE:      36%
SAT RANGE:            550–660 Verbal
                      590–700 Math
STICKER PRICE:        In-state, $11,000+
                      Out-of-state, $21,000+
NEED-BLIND:           Yes
NEED MET:             NA
AVERAGE STUDENT DEBT: $14,700
MERIT SCHOLARSHIPS:   Many
ATHLETIC SCHOLARSHIPS: Yes
ROTC:                 Army, Navy, Air Force
WEB SITE:             www.ucla.edu
PHONE:                (310) 825-3101

It is a measure of UCLA's fame that many Americans don't immediately connect the acronym with the University of California/Los Angeles. UCLA is less an academic institution than a cultural icon—a home to big-time athletic teams, a set for Hollywood movies, and alma mater to the rich and famous. The University of California/Los Angeles is a highly selective public university, second only in the UC system to Berkeley, with superior academic programs in many areas and perhaps the nation's best in media and the arts. UCLA has been damaged by recent California budget cuts like the other UC campuses. UC Regents Scholarships, which generally require a 4.0 GPA for consideration, offer $500 for those without need and meet the full need of those who do. The university also sponsors approximately 60 National Merit Finalists every year with awards of up to $2,000. Alumni scholarships are earmarked for California residents and minority students, and other university scholarships target a range of special categories.

*Deadlines:*
ADMISSION: Nov. 30
FAFSA: Mar. 2

# UNIVERSITY OF CALIFORNIA/RIVERSIDE ◆
## Riverside, CA 92521

| | |
|---|---|
| ENROLLMENT: | 9,900 |
| UNDERGRADUATE: | 8,400 |
| ACCEPTANCE RATE: | 84% |
| SAT RANGE: | 450–570 Verbal |
| | 490–620 Math |
| STICKER PRICE: | In-state, $11,000+ |
| | Out-of-state, $20,000+ |
| NEED-BLIND: | Yes |
| NEED MET: | NA |
| AVERAGE STUDENT DEBT: | NA |
| MERIT SCHOLARSHIPS: | Many |
| ATHLETIC SCHOLARSHIPS: | Yes |
| ROTC: | Army, Air Force |
| WEB SITE: | www.ucr.edu |
| PHONE: | (909) 787-4531 |

Among UC/Riverside's recent contributions to modern science is a variant of grapefruit hailed as "the sweetest, juiciest and quickest to ripen ever picked from a tree." Fruit isn't the only thing ripening at UCR; so, too, is its reputation as a leading research university. UCR is home to research institutions for everything from planetary physics to insect pest research, and its combined B.S./M.D. program is a major draw for top premed students. And as the smallest of the UC campuses, Riverside has always prided itself on the quality of its undergraduate teaching. Proof of that commitment can be found in its honors program, which features small seminars, a Freshman Colloquium, and a senior project completed in conjunction with a faculty mentor. Applicants for the UC Regents Scholarships must generally have a minimum GPA of 3.65 and a combined SAT I score of 1300. Alumni Scholarships, also based on merit, have slightly less stringent standards. A small number of awards honor National Merit Finalists, and other awards are available.

*Deadlines:*
ADMISSION: Nov. 30
FAFSA: Mar. 2

# UNIVERSITY OF CALIFORNIA/
## SANTA BARBARA ◆ Santa Barbara, CA 93106

| | |
|---|---|
| ENROLLMENT: | 18,900 |
| UNDERGRADUATE: | 16,700 |
| ACCEPTANCE RATE: | 78% |
| SAT RANGE: | 500–600 Verbal |
| | 520–620 Math |
| STICKER PRICE: | In-state, $11,000+ |
| | Out-of-state, $20,000+ |
| NEED-BLIND: | Yes |
| NEED MET: | NA |
| AVERAGE STUDENT DEBT: | NA |
| MERIT SCHOLARSHIPS: | Many |
| ATHLETIC SCHOLARSHIPS: | Yes |
| ROTC: | Army |
| WEB SITE: | www.ucsb.edu |
| PHONE: | (805) 893-2485 |

Set amid palm and eucalyptus trees on a plateau overlooking the Pacific, UC/Santa Barbara is as close to paradise as a college campus can get. It takes willpower to hit the books when you'd rather hit the beach, but students at UCSB seem able to cope. Business economics tops the list of most popular majors, and the programs in environmental studies and marine biology are buoyed by the presence of a graduate-level School of Environmental Science and Management. Perhaps the most unique facet of UCSB is its College of Creative Studies, which allows students to pursue original degree programs that culminate in creative or scientific projects. UCSB is not immune from the financial pressures that are squeezing public higher education in California, but its all-around reputation is definitely on the rise. As at other UC institutions, the university offers Regents Scholarships to its ablest admitted students, as well as some for National Merit Finalists. Other scholarships are available with various stipulations.

*Deadlines:*
ADMISSION: Nov. 30
FAFSA: Mar. 2

## UNIVERSITY OF CALIFORNIA/SANTA CRUZ ✦
## Santa Cruz, CA 95064

| | |
|---|---|
| ENROLLMENT: | 10,100 |
| UNDERGRADUATE: | 9,100 |
| ACCEPTANCE RATE: | 83% |
| SAT AVERAGE: | 572 Verbal |
| | 567 Math |
| STICKER PRICE: | In-state, $11,000+ |
| | Out-of-state, $20,000+ |
| NEED-BLIND: | Yes |
| NEED MET: | NA |
| AVERAGE STUDENT DEBT: | $14,200 |
| MERIT SCHOLARSHIPS: | Many |
| ATHLETIC SCHOLARSHIPS: | No |
| ROTC: | No |
| WEB SITE: | www.ucsc.edu |
| PHONE: | (408) 459-4452 |

In a state known for its UCLA Bruins and USC Trojans, UC/Santa Cruz selected the banana slug as its official mascot. The choice was a parody on big-time sports and typical of UCSC's penchant for nonconformity. Once a mecca for granola types, today's Santa Cruz is more practical and pragmatic. Students live in one of eight residential colleges designed to break down the university into smaller units. Each has an academic emphasis and core courses of its own; all provide students with a homebase and a variety of support services. UCSC has fine programs in environmental science, marine science, and astronomy, and it is working to expand a fledgling engineering program. With enrollment on the rise, Santa Cruz will be challenged to retain its distinctive flavor and emphasis on undergraduates. The university's standards for Regents Scholarships vary with each year's applicant pool, and a handful of awards are given to National Merit Finalists. Other awards with varying criteria are available.

*Deadlines:*
    ADMISSION: Nov. 30
    FAFSA: Mar. 2

## UNIVERSITY OF CALIFORNIA/SAN DIEGO ✦
## La Jolla, CA 92093

| | |
|---|---|
| ENROLLMENT: | 18,700 |
| UNDERGRADUATE: | 15,100 |
| ACCEPTANCE RATE: | 53% |
| SAT AVERAGE: | 593 Verbal |
| | 632 Math |
| STICKER PRICE: | In-state, $11,000+ |
| | Out-of-state, $21,000+ |
| NEED-BLIND: | Yes |
| NEED MET: | NA |
| AVERAGE STUDENT DEBT: | NA |
| MERIT SCHOLARSHIPS: | Many |
| ATHLETIC SCHOLARSHIPS: | No |
| ROTC: | No |
| WEB SITE: | www.ucsd.edu |
| PHONE: | (619) 534-4831 |

Behind Berkeley and UCLA, San Diego is the third-most selective school in the UC system. A picturesque location on the Pacific shore may be part of the allure, but so, too, is an innovative academic program that divides students into colleges with their own unique flavor. Thurgood Marshall College draws its name from the distinguished Supreme Court Justice and features a year-long core titled Dimensions of Culture—Diversity, Justice, Imagination. John Muir College, named for the famous conservationist, encourages nontraditional study and concentrations in areas such as women's studies and environmental studies. Other colleges honor Earl Warren, Eleanor Roosevelt, and one of UCSD's founders who was a noted scientist. Standards for the UC Regents Scholarships are based on an elaborate formula that includes high school GPA and SAT I and II scores. A variety of other scholarships dependent on merit and need are available, including a handful for National Merit Finalists.

*Deadlines:*
    ADMISSION: Nov. 30
    FAFSA: Mar. 2

# CALVIN COLLEGE ✦ Grand Rapids, MI 49546

| | |
|---|---|
| ENROLLMENT: | 4,100 |
| UNDERGRADUATE: | 4,000 |
| ACCEPTANCE RATE: | 98% |
| SAT RANGE: | 530–680 Verbal |
| | 540–660 Math |
| STICKER PRICE: | $17,000+ |
| NEED-BLIND: | Yes |
| NEED MET: | 85% |
| AVERAGE STUDENT DEBT: | $16,000 |
| MERIT SCHOLARSHIPS: | Many |
| RANGE: | Up to $8,500 |
| ATHLETIC SCHOLARSHIPS: | No |
| ROTC: | No |
| WEB SITE: | www.calvin.edu |
| PHONE: | (800) 688-0122 |

At a college where the motto is "My heart I offer to you, Lord," there is no fuzziness about its mission. Calvin is one of the best-known evangelical colleges in the nation, although it must share the Michigan market for conservative Christians with neighboring Hope and Hillsdale. A 98 percent acceptance rate leaves little room for choosiness in admissions. Calvin is named one of the best bargains in higher education annually, with a sticker price of less than $18,000 in 1998–99. Business ranks as the most popular major on campus, followed by English and biology. Merit scholarships abound, with the richest offering $8,500 to any National Merit Finalist with a 3.5 high school GPA. Four other levels of collegewide awards bottom out at $1,500 per year, and the college reports that a GPA of 3.5 with an ACT of 25 or SAT I of 1150 is typically the minimum for consideration. A variety of special interest awards are available with criteria ranging from leadership and musical ability to attendance at a particular high school. Scholarship candidates should apply for admission by February 1.

*Deadlines:*
ADMISSION: Mar. 1 (priority)
FAFSA: Feb. 15

# CARLETON COLLEGE ✦ Northfield, MN 55057

| | |
|---|---|
| ENROLLMENT: | 1,900 |
| UNDERGRADUATE: | 1,900 |
| ACCEPTANCE RATE: | 51% |
| SAT RANGE: | 630–730 Verbal |
| | 630–710 Math |
| STICKER PRICE: | $27,000+ |
| NEED-BLIND: | No |
| NEED MET: | 100% |
| AVERAGE STUDENT DEBT: | $13,900 |
| MERIT SCHOLARSHIPS: | Few |
| RANGE: | Up to $2,000 |
| ATHLETIC SCHOLARSHIPS: | No |
| ROTC: | No |
| WEB SITE: | www.carleton.edu |
| PHONE: | (800) 995-2275 |

The town of Northfield styles itself "Home of Cows, Colleges and Contentment," a perfect place for Carleton's brand of unpretentious liberal arts excellence. Though not a household name to the general public, Carleton is highly esteemed in academic circles and attracts many sons and daughters of professors. In a recent ten-year period, Carleton produced the highest number of students who went on to earn a Ph.D. in the sciences of any college in the nation. Biology tops the list of popular majors. Carleton is a predominantly liberal place, but with a less alternative atomosphere than rivals like Oberlin, Grinnell, or Macalester. Carleton is the most selective of the group, though the others are close on its heels. Carleton is among the colleges that has acknowledged that financial need may play a role in some borderline admission decisions, although its commitment to diversity remains strong. The college does not offer major merit money, but approximately eighty National Merit Finalists get awards of up to $2,000. Carleton is among the few remaining colleges that does not use preferential packaging in awarding need-based aid.

*Deadlines:*
EARLY DECISION: Nov. 15, Jan. 15
REGULAR ADMISSION: Jan. 15
FAFSA: FEB. 15
CSS PROFILE: Jan. 15

# CARNEGIE MELLON UNIVERSITY ◆
## Pittsburgh, PA 15213

| | |
|---|---|
| ENROLLMENT: | 7,900 |
| UNDERGRADUATE: | 4,900 |
| ACCEPTANCE RATE: | 43% |
| SAT RANGE: | 590–710 Verbal |
| | 660–750 Math |
| STICKER PRICE: | $28,000+ |
| NEED-BLIND: | Yes |
| NEED MET: | 88% |
| AVERAGE STUDENT DEBT: | $23,800 |
| MERIT SCHOLARSHIPS: | Many |
| RANGE: | Up to full tuition |
| ATHLETIC SCHOLARSHIPS: | No |
| ROTC: | Army, Navy, Air Force |
| WEB SITE: | www.cmu.edu |
| PHONE: | (412) 268-2082 |

Carnegie Mellon stands alone with its combination of world-class engineering programs and equally distinguished offerings in the fine arts. Since CMU divides its admissions by program and major, standards range from moderately difficult to intensely competitive. Chalk up electrical and computer engineering to the latter category, as well as the entire School of Computer Science, which accepts less than a quarter of its applicants. On the other hand, the College of Humanities and Social Sciences accepts two-thirds. CMU is candid about its willingness to consider an appeal for more aid, and also about the fact that some of its need-based awards don't meet full need. Thirty percent of students get non-need awards, including the half-tuition Andrew Carnegie (for all around achievement) and Judith Resnick Awards (for women in science or engineering). The Carnegie Mellon is a half-tuition scholarship for minority students, and the $10,000 Presidential Scholarship is a general excellence award which requires that applicants apply for need-based assistance. Academic scholarships are renewable for a total of five years (instead of four) for architecture students.

*Deadlines:*
    EARLY DECISION: Nov. 15 (Fine Arts, Nov. 1)
    REGULAR ADMISSION: Jan. 15
    FAFSA: Feb. 15

# CASE WESTERN RESERVE UNIVERSITY ◆
## Cleveland, OH 44106

| | |
|---|---|
| ENROLLMENT: | 9,900 |
| UNDERGRADUATE: | 3,600 |
| ACCEPTANCE RATE: | 79% |
| SAT RANGE: | 580–690 Verbal |
| | 620–720 Math |
| STICKER PRICE: | $25,000+ |
| NEED-BLIND: | Yes |
| NEED MET: | 100% |
| AVERAGE STUDENT DEBT: | $19,400 |
| MERIT SCHOLARSHIPS: | Many |
| RANGE: | Up to full tuition |
| ATHLETIC SCHOLARSHIPS: | No |
| ROTC: | Army, Air Force |
| WEB SITE: | www.cwru.edu |
| PHONE: | (216) 368-4450 |

Case Western Reserve University gets its off-beat name from the merger of an engineering institute and a liberal arts college in the 1960s. Technology is Case's calling card; often overlooked is its strength in the arts, which comes from a location near Cleveland's cultural hub. Case has fought an uphill battle for students against the likes of Northwestern, Carnegie Mellon, and the University of Rochester; its fortunes may improve with Cleveland's highly publicized renaissance. A sizable 40 percent of entering students get some sort of merit award, topped by the full-tuition Trustee Scholarships for those with a combined SAT I of at least 1500 (ACT of 35) who ranked in the top 10 percent of their high school class. Students who score at least 1300 or 31 and rank in the top 15 percent get $9,200 per year. Other awards for study in particular academic areas carry up to full-tuition, and Creative Achievement Awards offer $9,200 to students in art, creative writing, music, and theater. Awards are also available for leadership, minority students, and residents of Ohio.

*Deadlines:*
    EARLY DECISION: Jan. 1
    REGULAR ADMISSION: Feb. 1
    FAFSA: Feb. 1
    CSS PROFILE: Feb. 1

## THE CATHOLIC UNIVERSITY OF AMERICA ✦ Washington, DC 20064

| | |
|---|---|
| ENROLLMENT: | 5,600 |
| UNDERGRADUATE: | 2,300 |
| ACCEPTANCE RATE: | 69% |
| SAT RANGE: | 530–630 Verbal |
| | 510–620 Math |
| STICKER PRICE: | $24,000+ |
| NEED-BLIND: | No |
| NEED MET: | 90% |
| AVERAGE STUDENT DEBT: | $18,200 |
| MERIT SCHOLARSHIPS: | Many |
| RANGE: | Up to $18,000 |
| ATHLETIC SCHOLARSHIPS: | No |
| ROTC: | Army, Navy, Air Force |
| WEB SITE: | www.cua.edu |
| PHONE: | (800) 673-2772 |

The official name of Catholic University dates from the late nineteenth century when it really was the only Catholic university in America. CUA is still the only one with direct ties to the Vatican, giving it a more conservative outlook than most of its counterparts. Though a relatively small university, Catholic offers preprofessional programs in architecture, engineering, music, and nursing, as well as business in the school of arts and sciences. Catholic's D.C. location accounts for the fact that politics is its second-most popular major, and those seeking international study benefit from the university's extensive overseas contacts. Catholic gives away about $8 million in non-need-based aid per year, a tidy sum for a university with only 2,300 undergraduates. CUA offers merit awards in six categories, beginning with the Archdiocesan Scholarship that delivers an average of $18,000. Other awards are offered in stair-step increments down to the Achievement/Leadership Awards, which provide a minimum of $2,500.

*Deadlines:*
  EARLY ACTION: Nov. 15
  REGULAR ADMISSION: Feb. 15
  FAFSA: Jan. 15

## CENTRE COLLEGE ✦ Danville, KY 40422

| | |
|---|---|
| ENROLLMENT: | 1,000 |
| UNDERGRADUATE: | 1,000 |
| ACCEPTANCE RATE: | 85% |
| SAT RANGE: | 560–660 Verbal |
| | 550–660 Math |
| STICKER PRICE: | $20,000+ |
| NEED-BLIND: | Yes |
| NEED MET: | NA |
| AVERAGE STUDENT DEBT: | $11,200 |
| MERIT SCHOLARSHIPS: | Many |
| RANGE: | Up to full costs |
| ATHLETIC SCHOLARSHIPS: | No |
| ROTC: | Army, Air Force |
| WEB SITE: | www.centre.edu |
| PHONE: | (800) 423-6236 |

The tiny town of Danville, Kentucky, isn't the place you'd expect to find two Supreme Court Justices, thirteen Senators, forty-three U.S. Representatives, and eleven governors. They were never on campus at the same time, but all attended Centre College at one time during its illustrious 170-year history. With a rich tradition of turning out Kentucky's most distinguished citizens, Centre inspires a near-fanatical loyalty among its graduates, partly because the conservative tenor at Centre is a throwback to college life as the alumni remember it. Fraternities and sororities dominate the social scene, with approximately two-thirds of the students joining. Centre's curriculum is pure liberal arts, with English ranking as the most popular major. The college's sticker price is low by national standards, and in addition to need-based aid, nearly half the students receive an academic scholarship. General ones come in five categories ranging from the full-ride Trustee Scholarship down to Honor Scholarships worth a minimum of $2,500. Additional awards target minority and Appalachian students, and those who have shown commitment to volunteerism.

*Deadlines:*
  EARLY DECISION: Nov. 15
  EARLY ACTION: Nov. 15
  REGULAR ADMISSION: Feb. 1 (priority)
  FAFSA: Feb. 15

## COLLEGE OF CHARLESTON •
## Charleston, SC 29424

| | |
|---|---|
| ENROLLMENT: | 10,900 |
| UNDERGRADUATE: | 9,300 |
| ACCEPTANCE RATE: | 69% |
| SAT RANGE: | 530–610 Verbal |
| | 510–600 Math |
| STICKER PRICE: | In-state, $7,000+ |
| | Out-of-State, $10,000+ |
| NEED-BLIND: | Yes |
| NEED MET: | 72% |
| AVERAGE STUDENT DEBT: | $13,500 |
| MERIT SCHOLARSHIPS: | Many |
| RANGE: | Up to $6,000 |
| ATHLETIC SCHOLARSHIPS: | Yes |
| ROTC: | Air Force |
| WEB SITE: | www.cofc.edu |
| PHONE: | (843) 953-5670 |

In the city that started the Civil War, College of Charleston is making some noise of its own as one of the South's best bargains for a liberal arts education. Set in the genteel splendor of the city's historic district, C of C's popularity has grown rapidly among comparison shoppers seeking a private university education at a public university price. The college is an especially good deal for students in the honors program, who generally rank in the top 10 percent of their high school class, with a 1300 on the SAT I. The program features small classes, a Colloquium in Western Civilization, and a senior essay. Students who apply for admission by January 15 are considered for the college's merit scholarships, which have the same minimum standards as the honors program. C of C's top award is the Presidential Scholarship, which is worth up to $6,000. Other scholarships of varying amounts recognize all-around academic excellence, leadership and community involvement, and various specialized traits.

*Deadlines:*
ADMISSION: Apr. 1
FAFSA: Apr. 1

## UNIVERSITY OF CHICAGO •
## Chicago, IL 60637

| | |
|---|---|
| ENROLLMENT: | 11,800 |
| UNDERGRADUATE: | 3,700 |
| ACCEPTANCE RATE: | 33% |
| SAT RANGE: | 620–730 Verbal |
| | 630–730 Math |
| STICKER PRICE: | $31,000+ |
| NEED-BLIND: | Yes |
| NEED MET: | 100% |
| AVERAGE STUDENT DEBT: | $13,800 |
| MERIT SCHOLARSHIPS: | Few |
| RANGE: | Up to full tuition |
| ATHLETIC SCHOLARSHIPS: | No |
| ROTC: | Army, Air Force |
| WEB SITE: | www.uchicago.edu |
| PHONE: | (773) 702-8650 |

The University of Chicago is the Midwest's great liberal arts university. Intellectual yet unpretentious, U of C is revered in academic circles as the "teacher of teachers" and has turned out more Nobel prize winners than any other institution on the planet. (At last count there were six on the faculty.) The rigor of its curriculum is legendary, including a Common Core that spans the waterfront of liberal learning. One thing U of C doesn't have is the social cachet of the Ivy League, and though students have always taken pride in their nerdiness, the current administration is working hard to soften that image in a bid to increase undergraduate enrollment. Economics is the most popular major on Chicago's campus, followed by biology and English. The university offers one of the most prestigious merit scholarships in the country, the full-tuition College Honor Scholarship, to approximately thirty-five of its ablest applicants. Dean's grants in the amount of $5,000 allow selected students to complete projects ranging from art to community service. Awards of up to $2,000 go to National Merit Finalists.

*Deadlines:*
EARLY ACTION: Nov. 15
REGULAR ADMISSIONS: Jan. 1
FAFSA: Feb. 1
CSS PROFILE: Feb. 1

# UNIVERSITY OF CINCINNATI ✦
## Cincinnati, OH 45221

| | |
|---|---|
| ENROLLMENT: | 28,200 |
| UNDERGRADUATE: | 21,000 |
| ACCEPTANCE RATE: | 85% |
| SAT RANGE: | 480–600 Verbal |
| | 480–620 Math |
| STICKER PRICE: | In-state, $11,000+ |
| | Out-of-state, 18,000+ |
| NEED-BLIND: | Yes |
| NEED MET: | NA |
| AVERAGE STUDENT DEBT: | NA |
| MERIT SCHOLARSHIPS: | Many |
| ATHLETIC SCHOLARSHIPS: | Yes |
| ROTC: | Army, Air Force |
| WEB SITE: | www.uc.edu |
| PHONE: | (513) 556-1105 |

The University of Cincinnati has a right to feel good about itself. Enrollment is up, and campus pride has swelled with the exploits of a nationally ranked men's basketball team. UC's College of Engineering pioneered cooperative education (the placement of students in jobs related to their course of study) at the turn of the century and is still among UC's biggest draws. Enrollment in the College of Design, Architecture, Art, and Planning has recently surged. (Communication arts is the most popular major on campus.) UC's most coveted merit scholarships are bestowed via the Cincinnatus Scholarship Competition, which requires students to submit a completed application for admission by January 15. (December 15 is recommended.) In order to be in the running, a student must rank in the top 5 percent of the high school class and have an SAT I of 1250 or an ACT of 28. Scholarships range from $15,000 to $1,500. A variety of additional awards recognizing academic or artistic ability in a particular field, racial diversity, or depending on other criteria are available.

*Deadlines:*
   ADMISSION: Rolling (Dec. 15 priority)
   FAFSA: Rolling

# CITY UNIVERSITY OF NEW YORK/
## BROOKLYN COLLEGE ✦ Brooklyn, NY 11210

| | |
|---|---|
| ENROLLMENT: | 15,000 |
| UNDERGRADUATE: | 11,000 |
| ACCEPTANCE RATE: | 83% |
| SAT RANGE: | 430–560 Verbal |
| | 440–580 Math |
| STICKER PRICE (COMMUTER): | In-state, $4,000+ |
| | Out-of-state, $7,000+ |
| NEED-BLIND: | Yes |
| NEED MET: | 100% |
| AVERAGE STUDENT DEBT: | $5,700 |
| MERIT SCHOLARSHIPS: | Many |
| RANGE: | Up to $5,000 |
| ATHLETIC SCHOLARSHIPS: | No |
| ROTC: | No |
| WEB SITE: | www.brooklyn.cuny.edu |
| PHONE: | (718) 951-5001 |

For generations of Brooklynites working toward a better life, Brooklyn College has been the gateway to higher education and success in the business world. According to a Standard and Poor's Survey, Brooklyn is among the nation's leaders in producing corporate executives, and it also ranks high in the number of graduates who earn a Ph.D. In a borough that by itself is one of the nation's largest cities, Brooklyn College is the only prominent institution of higher learning devoted to the liberal arts. The college has drawn national attention for innovative core curriculum, which features interdisciplinary courses and incorporates culturally diverse perspectives. Approximately three-quarters of the students receive need-based aid, and about 150 entering freshmen get merit scholarships of up to $5,000. Awards for general academic merit are available, as well as scholarships for minority students and those with special talents or interests. Scholarship deadlines come as early as mid-December.

*Deadlines:*
   ADMISSION: Jan. 15 (priority)
   FAFSA: Apr. 1

## CITY UNIVERSITY OF NEW YORK/ CITY COLLEGE ✦ New York, NY 10031

| | |
|---|---|
| ENROLLMENT: | 12,100 |
| UNDERGRADUATE: | 9,100 |
| ACCEPTANCE RATE: | 70% |
| SAT AVERAGE | 481 Verbal |
| | 517 Math |
| STICKER PRICE (COMMUTER): | In-state, $4,000+ |
| | Out-of-state, $7,000+ |
| NEED-BLIND: | Yes |
| NEED MET: | NA |
| AVERAGE STUDENT DEBT: | NA |
| MERIT SCHOLARSHIPS: | Few |
| RANGE: | Up to $5,000 |
| ATHLETIC SCHOLARSHIPS: | No |
| ROTC: | No |
| WEB SITE: | www.ccny.cuny.edu |
| PHONE: | (212) 650-6977 |

CCNY proudly bears the nickname "Harvard of the Poor." With a list of alumni that includes eight Nobel Prize winners and luminaries from Ira Gershwin to Colin Powell, City's past is as distinguished as any elite college. City College, and the City University as a whole, is among the most diverse institutions of higher learning in the nation. Yet today CCNY is struggling with the challenges that come with that diversity, including the controversial systemwide elimination of remedial courses that is likely to hike selectivity and may substantially decrease enrollment. Although known as City College, CCNY is actually a university in its own right, with schools of architecture, communications, film and video, education, engineering, music, and biomedical education. The compact 35-acre campus stretches along Convent Avenue from 131st to 141st Streets in Manhattan. CCNY awards a limited number of academic merit scholarships of up to $5,000 per year "based on academic achievement, potential for advanced work, leadership and service."

*Deadlines:*
ADMISSION: Jan. 15
FAFSA: May 1

## CITY UNIVERSITY OF NEW YORK/ HUNTER COLLEGE ✦ New York, NY 10021

| | |
|---|---|
| ENROLLMENT: | 19,700 |
| UNDERGRADUATE: | 15,400 |
| ACCEPTANCE RATE: | 55% |
| SAT RANGE: | 430–560 Verbal |
| | 440–550 Math |
| STICKER PRICE (COMMUTER): | In-state, $4,000+ |
| | Out-of-state, $7,000+ |
| NEED-BLIND: | Yes |
| NEED MET: | NA |
| AVERAGE STUDENT DEBT: | NA |
| MERIT SCHOLARSHIPS: | Few |
| RANGE: | Up to $10,000 |
| ATHLETIC SCHOLARSHIPS: | No |
| ROTC: | No |
| WEB SITE: | www.hunter.cuny.edu |
| PHONE: | (212) 772-4490 |

Set on a piece of prime real estate at 68th Street and Lexington Avenue, Hunter's main campus consists of four buildings interconnected by a sky-walk. The college is best known for its schools of nursing and health sciences, located at East 25th Street. Other areas of strength include education, social work, and liberal arts. Hunter was formerly the women's campus of the City University system, and women still outnumber men by more than two to one. Like all the CUNY campuses, Hunter is keeping an eye on the possible impact of higher admission standards and drastically lower enrollment that may come with its board-mandated end of remedial courses. The college offers only a handful of merit scholarships, most notably the new Athena Award, which carries with it a whopping $10,000-per-year stipend. Runners-up in the Athena contest may qualify for a Hunter College Scholars award, which includes full tuition. To be in the race for either, students must have a 90 high school average and a 1200 on the SAT I.

*Deadlines:*
ADMISSION: Jan. 15
FAFSA: Apr. 1

# CITY UNIVERSITY OF NEW YORK/ JOHN JAY COLLEGE OF CRIMINAL JUSTICE ✦ New York, NY 10019

| | |
|---|---|
| ENROLLMENT: | 10,900 |
| UNDERGRADUATE: | 9,900 |
| ACCEPTANCE RATE: | 94% |
| SAT RANGE: | 400–510 Verbal |
| | 380–480 Math |
| STICKER PRICE (COMMUTER): | In-state, $4,000+ |
| | Out-of-state, $7,000+ |
| NEED-BLIND: | Yes |
| NEED MET: | NA |
| AVERAGE STUDENT DEBT: | $8,000 |
| MERIT SCHOLARSHIPS: | Few |
| ATHLETIC SCHOLARSHIPS: | No |
| ROTC: | No |
| WEB SITE: | www.jjay.cuny.edu |
| PHONE: | (212) 237-8865 |

John Jay is one of a kind in the world of higher education: a liberal arts college dedicated to criminal justice and public affairs. About 20 percent of the student body already serves in uniformed criminal justice and fire service agencies; the rest aspire to careers in public service. The college strives for a balance between study of core liberal arts disciplines and practical work-related training. John Jay is home to a variety of research institutes devoted to violence, ethics, toxicology, substance abuse, and other specialties. With a high percentage of its students already in the work force, the college offers flexible day and night scheduling. Located at 59th Street and 10th Avenue, John Jay is within easy reach of Lincoln Center, Carnegie Hall, Times Square, and the midtown business district. Total enrollment currently stands at 10,900, but that number may fall with a planned tightening of admission standards. Although the vast majority of aid at John Jay is need-based, a limited number of merit scholarships are available.

*Priority Deadlines:*
    ADMISSION: Jan. 1
    FAFSA: Jun. 1 -

# CITY UNIVERSITY OF NEW YORK/ QUEENS COLLEGE ✦ Flushing, NY 11367

| | |
|---|---|
| ENROLLMENT: | 16,400 |
| UNDERGRADUATE: | 12,500 |
| ACCEPTANCE RATE: | 67% |
| SAT RANGE: | 430–560 Verbal |
| | 450–570 Math |
| STICKER PRICE (COMMUTER): | In-state, $4,000+ |
| | Out-of-state, $7,000+ |
| NEED-BLIND: | Yes |
| NEED MET: | NA |
| AVERAGE STUDENT DEBT: | NA |
| MERIT SCHOLARSHIPS: | Many |
| RANGE: | Up to $5,000 |
| ATHLETIC SCHOLARSHIPS: | No |
| ROTC: | Army |
| WEB SITE: | www.qc.edu |
| PHONE: | (718) 997-5600 |

In the borough known to most Americans as Archie Bunker's home, an outsider might not expect to find the best college in the entire CUNY system. But that's exactly what Queens College is—an excellent liberal arts university that also offers strong programs in education and music. Though far from small, Queens makes an extra effort to nurture undergraduates with programs like the Freshman Year Initiative, which divides selected first year students into small groups to promote interaction with faculty. Queens also offers a rarity in New York City: a 1,600-acre site for environmental research and teaching at Caumsett State Park, equipped with dormitories and classrooms. Queens provides a variety of merit awards of up to $5,000; students with an A average and SAT I scores of approximately 1250 or better are encouraged to apply. Included are a number of full-tuition awards for students planning to be secondary school math teachers. Scholarship applicants are advised to take at least two SAT II subject tests.

*Deadlines:*
    ADMISSION: Jan. 1
    FAFSA: Rolling

# CLAREMONT MCKENNA COLLEGE ✦ Claremont, CA 91711

| | |
|---|---|
| TOTAL ENROLLMENT: | 1,000 |
| UNDERGRADUATE: | 1,000 |
| ACCEPTANCE RATE: | 33% |
| SAT RANGE: | 680–710 Verbal |
| | 640–710 Math |
| STICKER PRICE: | $27,000+ |
| NEED-BLIND: | Yes |
| NEED MET: | 100% |
| AVERAGE STUDENT DEBT: | $15,700 |
| MERIT SCHOLARSHIPS: | Few |
| RANGE: | Up to $5,000 |
| ATHLETIC SCHOLARSHIPS: | No |
| ROTC: | Army, Navy, Air Force |
| WEB SITE: | www.mckenna.edu |
| PHONE: | (909) 621-8088 |

Claremont McKenna has put the world on notice that Pomona isn't the only top-shelf liberal arts college in Southern California. With a healthy endowment and a focus on public affairs that is in tune with the times, McKenna now attracts students every bit as strong as its better-known rival down the block. Both colleges are members of the Claremont Colleges Consortium, along with Harvey Mudd, Pitzer, and Scripps, and no other location in the U.S. boasts so many premier institutions in such a small space. Economics, government, and accounting are the most popular majors on campus. Claremont is an upscale town without much to offer students, but Los Angeles and the San Gabriel Mountains are both close by. CMC snags some of its best and brightest with the McKenna Achievement Scholarship, offered in amounts of $3,000 and $5,000 to thirty students per year. National Merit Finalists also get renewable awards of up to $2,000, and a single Chevron Merit Award of $2,000 is offered in alternating years.

*Deadlines:*
EARLY DECISION: Nov. 15
REGULAR ADMISSION: Jan. 15
FAFSA: Feb. 1
CSS PROFILE: Feb. 1

# CLARK UNIVERSITY ✦ Worcester, MA 01610

| | |
|---|---|
| ENROLLMENT: | 3,100 |
| UNDERGRADUATE: | 2,300 |
| ACCEPTANCE RATE: | 77% |
| SAT RANGE: | 520—620 Verbal |
| | 520–620 Math |
| STICKER PRICE: | $26,000+ |
| NEED-BLIND: | NA |
| NEED MET: | 93% |
| AVERAGE STUDENT DEBT: | $16,900 |
| MERIT SCHOLARSHIPS: | Many |
| RANGE: | Up to $10,000 |
| ATHLETIC SCHOLARSHIPS: | No |
| ROTC: | Army, Navy, Air Force |
| WEB SITE: | www.clarku.edu |
| PHONE: | (800) GO-CLARK |

The Clark admission office produces a poster emblazened with the message: "Categorizing People Is Not Something You Can Do Here." That spirit of tolerance is a shining attribute of Clark, a small university best-known as the place where Sigmund Freud delivered his lectures introducing psychoanalysis to the American public at the turn of the century. Psychology is still the most popular major at Clark today, followed by government and international relations. Clark is a world leader in the study of geography, and its Environmental School is an umbrella for a variety of related majors. An innovative cost-cutter at Clark is the Fifth-Year Free Program which allows high-achieving students an extra year at no cost to complete a master's degree. Clark gave merit scholarships to approximately 12 percent of its entering class in a recent year but has expanded its offerings for 1999–2000. The President's Scholarship Program guarantees a $10,000 scholarship to all applicants with a 3.7 GPA or a class rank in the top 10 percent and an SAT I score of 1300. Students who have a 3.4 GPA or rank in the top 20 percent and have a score of 1200 or more get $7,000.

*Deadlines:*
EARLY DECISION: Nov. 15, Dec. 15
REGULAR ADMISSION: Feb. 1
FAFSA: Feb. 1
CSS PROFILE: Feb. 1

# CLARKSON UNIVERSITY ✦ Potsdam, NY 13699

| | |
|---|---|
| ENROLLMENT: | 2,700 |
| UNDERGRADUATE: | 2,400 |
| ACCEPTANCE RATE: | 81% |
| SAT AVERAGE: | 575 Verbal |
| | 626 Math |
| STICKER PRICE: | $27,000+ |
| NEED-BLIND: | NA |
| NEED MET: | 90% |
| AVERAGE STUDENT DEBT: | $21,600 |
| MERIT SCHOLARSHIPS: | Many |
| RANGE: | Up to $10,000 |
| ATHLETIC SCHOLARSHIPS: | Yes |
| ROTC: | Army, Air Force |
| WEB SITE: | www.clarkson.edu |
| PHONE: | (315) 268-6479 |

Located a mere twenty miles from the Canadian border in the northernmost reaches of New York State, Clarkson College isn't the kind of place one stumbles upon by accident. Nor is it the sort you find every day: a small, student-oriented college devoted to science, engineering, and business. All but about 300 of Clarkson's students are undergraduates, and they have access to faculty beyond the wildest dreams of counterparts at larger institutions. Also absent is the hypercompetition for grades typical of many technical institutes. At Clarkson, the emphasis is on teamwork. For its strongest applicants, Clarkson offers merit scholarships ranging up to $10,000, and the Clarkson Leadership Award bestows $8,000 on students nominated by their schools in eleventh grade on the basis of leadership and achievement. Students selected for the honors program garner an extra $1,000 grant, and approximately fifty students get a $1,000 to $2,000 grant for the combination of merit and a recommendation from an alumnus. Athletic scholarships are available only for the powerhouse men's hockey team.

*Deadlines:*
  EARLY DECISION: Dec. 1, Jan. 15
  REGULAR ADMISSION: Mar. 1
  FAFSA: Feb 15

# CLEMSON UNIVERSITY ✦ Clemson, SC 29634

| | |
|---|---|
| ENROLLMENT: | 16,400 |
| UNDERGRADUATE: | 11,900 |
| ACCEPTANCE RATE: | 74% |
| SAT RANGE: | 510–610 Verbal |
| | 520–630 Math |
| STICKER PRICE: | In-state, $8,000+ |
| | Out-of-state, $13,000+ |
| NEED-BLIND: | Yes |
| NEED MET: | 74% |
| AVERAGE STUDENT DEBT: | $13,500 |
| MERIT SCHOLARSHIPS: | Many |
| RANGE: | Up to $7,000 |
| ATHLETIC SCHOLARSHIPS: | Yes |
| ROTC: | Army, Air Force |
| WEB SITE: | www.clemson.edu |
| PHONE: | (864) 656-2287 |

The back country of South Carolina isn't the most likely place to find a major research university, but Clemson has beaten the odds. Formerly a humble cousin to the down-state aristocracy at the University of South Carolina, Clemson has developed first-rate engineering programs that give Georgia Tech a run for its money as the region's best. (Mechanical engineering is the largest major.) Business and education are also big draws, but nothing rivals the popularity of the football team on fall weekends. Rather than feature a few big-ticket merit scholarships, Clemson offers a potpourri of awards based on all-around excellence, plans to major in a particular subject, and place of residence. A number of Diversity Scholarships are available for minorities. Scholarships are generally in the $1,000–$3,000 range, though many come with a waiver of the out-of-state tuition and fee differential for those from outside South Carolina. Students are automatically considered for relevant merit awards with one major caveat: They must apply early, by December 31.

*Deadlines:*
  ADMISSION: May 1
  FAFSA: Apr. 1

## CLEVELAND INSTITUTE OF MUSIC ✦ Cleveland, OH 44106

| | |
|---|---|
| ENROLLMENT: | 360 |
| UNDERGRADUATE: | 360 |
| ACCEPTANCE RATE: | 33% |
| SAT AVERAGE: | 640 Verbal |
| | 590 Math |
| STICKER PRICE: | $24,000+ |
| NEED-BLIND: | NA |
| NEED MET: | 84% |
| AVERAGE STUDENT DEBT: | $20,500 |
| MERIT SCHOLARSHIPS: | Few |
| RANGE: | Up to full tuition |
| ATHLETIC SCHOLARSHIPS: | No |
| ROTC: | No |
| WEB SITE: | www.cwru.edu/CIM/cimhome.html |
| PHONE: | (216) 795-3107 |

If Cleveland isn't the first city that comes to mind when you think of music, maybe it should be. The Cleveland Orchestra is world famous, and many of its players are on CIM's faculty. The campus has a perfect location adjacent to Cleveland's concert hall, art museum, and other artistic resources, and it is also contiguous with the campus of Case Western Reserve, a major university. Though CIM is not part of Case in the same way that Peabody is a division of Johns Hopkins and Eastman belongs to University of Rochester, the benefit is similar. In addition to enjoying access to Case's extensive facilities, students can take courses in its music department. With a total enrollment of only 360, CIM's admission standards depend partly on the institute's effort to maintain a balance among students in the various instruments. Most aid is need-based, though a limited number of merit scholarships of up to full tuition are awarded to outstanding candidates whose instrumental specialty fills a need.

*Deadlines:*
   ADMISSION: Nov. 15 (priority)
   FAFSA: Mar. 1
   CSS PROFILE: Mar. 1

## COLBY COLLEGE ✦ Waterville, ME 04901

| | |
|---|---|
| ENROLLMENT: | 1,800 |
| UNDERGRADUATE: | 1,800 |
| ACCEPTANCE RATE: | 34% |
| SAT RANGE: | 610–680 Verbal |
| | 610–690 Math |
| STICKER PRICE: | $31,000+ |
| NEED-BLIND: | No |
| NEED MET: | 100% |
| AVERAGE STUDENT DEBT: | $14,800 |
| MERIT SCHOLARSHIPS: | None |
| ATHLETIC SCHOLARSHIPS: | No |
| ROTC: | Army |
| WEB SITE: | www.colby.edu |
| PHONE: | (800) 723-3032 |

Colby is the northernmost of Maine's trio of selective private colleges, set on a hilltop in the small town of Waterville. The college is strong across a broad range of liberal arts disciplines and perhaps best known for its outstanding study abroad opportunities. Colby offers its own programs in France, Germany, Spain, England, Ireland, Mexico, and Russia and approximately two-thirds of the students go abroad at some point during their college careers. Biology, English, and economics are Colby's three most popular majors. Colby has always attracted an upscale clientele even by the standards of selective private colleges; only 34 percent of a recent entering class qualified for need-based aid. Colby is now among the colleges that consider financial need when making some borderline admission decisions, though it meets the full need of those who are admitted. All aid is need-based, although the Ralph J. Bunche Scholars Program eliminates loans from aid packages of particularly strong minority students. A similar award is available to returning students on the basis of academic excellence.

*Deadlines:*
   EARLY DECISION: Nov. 15, Jan. 1
   REGULAR ADMISSION: Jan. 15
   FAFSA: Feb. 1

# COLGATE UNIVERSITY ◆ Hamilton, NY 13346

| | |
|---|---|
| ENROLLMENT: | 2,800 |
| UNDERGRADUATE: | 2,800 |
| ACCEPTANCE RATE: | 42% |
| SAT RANGE: | 600–690 Verbal |
| | 600–690 Math |
| STICKER PRICE: | $30,000+ |
| NEED-BLIND: | No |
| NEED MET: | 98% |
| AVERAGE STUDENT DEBT: | $14,000 |
| MERIT SCHOLARSHIPS: | None |
| ATHLETIC SCHOLARSHIPS: | No |
| ROTC: | No |
| WEB SITE: | www.colgate.edu |
| PHONE: | (315) 228-7401 |

William Colgate went down in history for two things, one of which was giving his name—and some cash—to Colgate University. (He also founded a certain well-known toothpaste company.) Colgate has traditionally ranked near the top of a list of smallish institutions, including Bucknell and Hamilton, which are just below the Ivy League on the prestige pyramid. Colgate attracts a traditional breed of student and has plenty of athletes jogging its picturesque campus. Rather than eliminate fraternities and sororities like some other elite private colleges, Colgate has kept the Greeks while beefing up social alternatives. With 2,800 students, Colgate is bigger than most small colleges. The university considers financial need when making some borderline admission decisions but meets the full need of most students who are admitted. Colgate engages in less preferential packaging than most private colleges; 11 percent of the hottest prospects in a recent entering class got a bonus of more grants and less loans in their aid packages.

*Deadlines:*
   EARLY DECISION: Nov. 15, Jan. 15
   FAFSA: Feb. 1
   CSS PROFILE: Feb.1

# COLORADO COLLEGE ◆ Colorado Springs, CO 80903

| | |
|---|---|
| ENROLLMENT: | 2,000 |
| UNDERGRADUATE: | 2,000 |
| ACCEPTANCE RATE: | 48% |
| SAT RANGE: | 590–680 Verbal |
| | 590–680 Math |
| STICKER PRICE: | $26,000+ |
| NEED-BLIND: | Yes |
| NEED MET: | 100% |
| AVERAGE STUDENT DEBT: | $13,300 |
| MERIT SCHOLARSHIPS: | Few |
| RANGE: | Up to full tuition |
| ATHLETIC SCHOLARSHIPS: | Yes |
| ROTC: | Army |
| WEB SITE: | www.cc.colorado.edu |
| PHONE: | (800) 542-7214 |

Colorado College's allure boils down to two things: the Rocky Mountain peaks that rise a few miles from campus, and an innovative academic program in which students study one course at a time. The latter is called The Block Plan and requires students to immerse themselves in one subject for three-and-a-half week intervals instead of carrying four or five classes for a traditional semester. The Block Plan is especially suited to labs and field work; it also promotes contact with faculty. A steady supply of well-heeled applicants puts CC in a stronger financial position than most private colleges. The majority of aid is need-based, though the college offers a total of approximately ten full-tuition merit scholarships for students majoring in chemistry or biochemistry, and for those majoring in other natural sciences or math. Both require an additional application after the regular deadline. CC also gives scholarships of up to $2,000 to National Merit Finalists. Athletic scholarships are available only in men's hockey and women's soccer.

*Deadlines:*
   EARLY ACTION: Nov. 15
   REGULAR ADMISSION: Jan. 15
   FAFSA: Feb. 15
   CSS PROFILE: Feb. 15

## COLORADO SCHOOL OF MINES ✦
## Golden, CO 80401

| | |
|---|---|
| ENROLLMENT: | 3,200 |
| UNDERGRADUATE: | 2,400 |
| ACCEPTANCE RATE: | 80% |
| SAT RANGE: | 540–650 Verbal |
| | 600–690 Math |
| STICKER PRICE: | In-state, $10,000+ |
| | Out-of-state, $20,000+ |
| NEED-BLIND: | Yes |
| NEED MET: | 100% |
| AVERAGE STUDENT DEBT: | $14,300 |
| MERIT SCHOLARSHIPS: | Many |
| RANGE: | Up to full costs |
| ATHLETIC SCHOLARSHIPS: | Yes |
| ROTC: | Army, Air Force |
| WEB SITE: | www.mines.edu |
| PHONE: | (800) 446-9488 |

Perched high atop a peak of 6,900 feet, the most prominent symbol of Colorado School of Mines is a 10,000-square-foot letter "M" built into the mountain side. The "M" is certainly the most visible example of CSM students' engineering prowess, but far from the only one. Colorado School of Mines is the nation's premier university devoted mainly to the study of geological, geophysical, mining, petroleum, and metallurgical and materials engineering. The university's innovative honors program addresses the "moral and social" implications of engineering through offerings in the humanities and social sciences. The school provides an array of academic scholarships that range up to full tuition for both in- and out-of-staters. (Mines is a public institution.) Scholarships of one-quarter to one-half tuition are available for students who excel in band or chorus, and Mines beefs up ROTC scholarships to include full tuition and fees plus an allowance for books and personal expenses. Children of alumni can qualify for a $1,000 award.

*Deadlines:*
    ADMISSION: Rolling
    FAFSA: Mar. 1

## UNIVERSITY OF COLORADO ✦
## Boulder, CO 80309

| | |
|---|---|
| ENROLLMENT: | 25,100 |
| UNDERGRADUATE: | 20,400 |
| ACCEPTANCE RATE: | 83% |
| SAT RANGE: | 520–620 Verbal |
| | 540–640 Math |
| STICKER PRICE: | In-state, $8,000+ |
| | Out-of-state, $21,000+ |
| NEED-BLIND: | Yes |
| NEED MET: | NA |
| AVERAGE STUDENT DEBT: | $12,300 |
| MERIT SCHOLARSHIPS: | Many |
| RANGE: | Up to full costs |
| ATHLETIC SCHOLARSHIPS: | Yes |
| ROTC: | Army, Navy, Air Force |
| WEB SITE: | www.colorado.edu |
| PHONE: | (303) 492-6301 |

Boulder has taken its place along side Berkeley and Ann Arbor as one of the hippest college towns in America. Set against the backdrop of the Rockies, Boulder is a sun-drenched paradise where downtown is a thriving pedestrian mall and bikes are the preferred mode of transportation. Nearly twice as many out-of-staters as in-staters apply to the university, with more than 80 percent admitted in both categories. Environmental biology and environmental studies both rank in the top ten most popular majors. The university has a variety of merit scholarships, most in the range of $1,000 to $2,000 with some that require a special application. Sixty $2,000 President's Leadership Class awards are given for "academic excellence, leadership potential, and community service" and require a special application. Students in the program get two years of enriched study focused on public affairs that includes hands-on involvement in the wider community. The College of Engineering offers scholarships of up to $4,000 based on high school grades and test scores. Other academic divisions also sponsor awards.

*Deadlines:*
    ADMISSION: Feb. 15
    FAFSA: Apr. 1

# COLUMBIA UNIVERSITY ✦
## NEW YORK, NY 10027

| | |
|---|---|
| ENROLLMENT: | 19,900 |
| UNDERGRADUATE: | 7,300 |
| ACCEPTANCE RATE: | 17% |
| SAT RANGE: | 640–740 Verbal |
| | 630–730 Math |
| STICKER PRICE: | $31,000+ |
| NEED-BLIND: | Yes |
| NEED MET: | 100% |
| AVERAGE STUDENT DEBT: | NA |
| MERIT SCHOLARSHIPS: | None |
| ATHLETIC SCHOLARSHIPS: | No |
| ROTC: | No |
| WEB SITE: | www.columbia.edu |
| PHONE: | (212) 854-2522 |

Considering the fact that Columbia was founded in 1754, it isn't exactly a new kid on the block. Yet Columbia has recently been discovered by a new generation of high school students, and applications have nearly doubled in the 1990s. The much-heralded comeback of New York City is part of the reason for the newfound popularity, though Columbia's world-class academic programs must get their due. With 3,800 students, Columbia College is the largest undergraduate division of Columbia University, which also encompasses 1,200 undergraduates in its School of Engineering and Applied Science and 2,300 more across the street at all-female Barnard. The hallmark of Columbia College is its famous core curriculum, which features a year-long Contemporary Civilization and Humanities sequence taught in small discussion classes. Like all the Ivy League institutions, Columbia offers financial aid only on the basis of need. Columbia University's endowment per student ranks in the middle of the Ivy League, ahead of Brown, Cornell, and the University of Pennsylvania but far behind Harvard, Yale, and Princeton.

*Deadlines:*
  EARLY DECISION: Nov. 1
  REGULAR ADMISSION: Jan. 1
  FAFSA: Feb. 10
  CSS PROFILE: Feb. 15

# CONNECTICUT COLLEGE ✦
## New London, CT 06320

| | |
|---|---|
| ENROLLMENT: | 1,900 |
| UNDERGRADUATE: | 1,800 |
| ACCEPTANCE RATE: | 40% |
| SAT RANGE: | 592–686 Verbal |
| | 581–664 Math |
| STICKER PRICE: | $30,000+ |
| NEED-BLIND: | No |
| NEED MET: | 100% |
| AVERAGE STUDENT DEBT: | $12,200 |
| MERIT SCHOLARSHIPS: | None |
| ATHLETIC SCHOLARSHIPS: | No |
| ROTC: | No |
| WEB SITE: | camel.conncoll.edu |
| PHONE: | (860) 439-2200 |

Many colleges talk about their commitment to the liberal arts, but few back it up with as much energy and idealism as Connecticut College. At the core of a Conn College education is the Foundation, which requires students to take at least one course in seven broad categories ranging from mathematics and logic to the creative arts. Another sign that Conn College takes education more seriously than most: a summer reading list is assigned to all students that dovetails with a yearly campus-wide theme. Government and history top the list of most popular majors. Conn College has one of the best study abroad programs in the nation, including programs of its own in twenty-three countries. With a strong philosophical commitment to need-based aid, Conn offers no merit scholarships. However, approximately seventy enrolling freshmen are designated Lawrence Scholars with the promise of $3,000 to pursue a summer internship after their junior year. Under its Access to a Connecticut Education Scholarships program, the college offers loan-free aid packages to selected minority students with family incomes below $25,000.

*Deadlines:*
  EARLY DECISION: Nov. 15
  REGULAR DECISION: Jan. 15
  FAFSA: Jan. 15
  CSS PROFILE: Feb. 1

## UNIVERSITY OF CONNECTICUT ◆ Storrs, CT 06269

ENROLLMENT: 15,800
UNDERGRADUATE: 11,300
ACCEPTANCE RATE: 70%
SAT RANGE: 500–600 Verbal
500–610 Math
STICKER PRICE: In-state, $11,000+
Out-of-state, 20,000+
NEED-BLIND: Yes
NEED MET: 61%
AVERAGE STUDENT DEBT: NA
MERIT SCHOLARSHIPS: Many
RANGE: Up to full costs
ATHLETIC SCHOLARSHIPS: Yes
ROTC: Army, Air Force
WEB SITE: www.uconn.edu
PHONE: (860) 486-3137

Everybody knows that U Conn is located in the East, but the more crucial fact is the university's membership in the Big East. The latter is synonymous with basketball, and U Conn is riding a wave of popularity fueled in part by the success of its teams. The state of Connecticut also enjoys a top ranking when it comes to producing well-qualified high school graduates—more and more of whom are choosing U Conn over the high-priced private college competition. The university's ample menu of merit scholarships is highlighted by two exclusive programs, the Day of Pride and Nutmeg Scholarships, which offer a full ride to several dozen Connecticut residents. (Both require a special application due December 19 and November 3, respectively.) Other awards ranging from $1,500 to $8,000 per year include: The Presidential Scholarship, for students headed to the honors program; The Leadership Scholarship, for contributions to the community; and the Chancellor and Dean's Scholarship, for academic excellence. Most academic divisions also have their own awards.

*Deadlines:*
    ADMISSION: Mar. 1
    FAFSA: Mar. 1

## COOPER UNION ◆ New York, NY 10003

ENROLLMENT: 900
UNDERGRADUATE: 900
ACCEPTANCE RATE: 13%
SAT RANGE: 620–720 Verbal
700–780 Math
STICKER PRICE: $7,000+
NEED-BLIND: Yes
NEED MET: 100%
AVERAGE STUDENT DEBT: $11,400
MERIT SCHOLARSHIPS: Full tuition for all students
ATHLETIC SCHOLARSHIPS: No
ROTC: No
WEB SITE: www.cooper.edu
PHONE: (212) 353-4120

Cooper Union was founded by a nineteenth century entrepreneur who believed that education should be "as free as water and air." Today, students at the institution that bears his name pay no tuition for some of the nation's finest training in art, architecture, and engineering. Located in New York City's thriving East Village, Cooper Union is both an educational institution and a cultural landmark, and presidents from Lincoln to Clinton have made major addresses in its famed Great Hall. Engineering is by far the largest of Cooper Union's divisions, accounting for more than half the student body. Competition for admission is intense—CU's combined acceptance rate is only 13 percent. Cooper Union students are legendary for their work ethic and include a high proportion of native New Yorkers. To help ensure that its legacy will endure, Cooper Union boasts an endowment per student that is among the largest in the nation. The tuition scholarship given to each student is valued at over $8,000, and students can apply for need-based aid to help with additional expenses.

*Deadlines:*
    EARLY DECISION: Dec. 1
    REGULAR ADMISSION: Jan./Feb. (varies by program)
    FAFSA: May 1
    CSS PROFILE: May 1

# CORNELL COLLEGE ✦ Mount Vernon, IA 52314

| | |
|---|---|
| ENROLLMENT: | 1,100 |
| UNDERGRADUATE: | 1,100 |
| ACCEPTANCE RATE: | 81% |
| SAT RANGE: | 550–670 Verbal |
| | 520–630 Math |
| STICKER PRICE: | $24,000+ |
| NEED-BLIND: | Yes |
| NEED MET: | 97% |
| AVERAGE STUDENT DEBT: | $16,500 |
| MERIT SCHOLARSHIPS: | Many |
| RANGE: | Up to $15,000 |
| ATHLETIC SCHOLARSHIPS: | No |
| ROTC: | No |
| WEB SITE: | www.cornell-iowa.edu |
| PHONE: | (800) 747-1112 |

Cornell College is not to be confused with the Ivy League upstart by the same name. That Cornell may be ten times bigger and a tad more famous, but this one was founded twelve years earlier and could probably teach its younger sibling a thing or two about undergraduate education. Cornell College and Colorado College are the nation's only selective institutions to operate on a one-course-at-a-time calendar. Instead of conventional semesters, the school year features blocks of three and a half weeks that are divided by four-day breaks. In addition to promoting close interaction between students and faculty, one-course-at-a-time study is a boon to labs, field work, and travel. Psychology, history, and business are Cornell's most popular majors. Cornell has a full bankroll of merit scholarships for good and excellent students. Those with a 3.4 GPA and/or a rank in the top 20 percent and strong standardized test scores are eligible for academic scholarships, which range up to $15,000. There are also scholarships for achievement in the visual and performing arts. Three quarters of the entering students received a non-need award in a recent year.

*Deadlines:*
  EARLY DECISION: Dec. 1
  ADMISSION: Mar. 1 (priority)
  FAFSA: Mar. 1

# CORNELL UNIVERSITY ✦ Ithaca, NY 14853

| | |
|---|---|
| ENROLLMENT: | 18,400 |
| UNDERGRADUATE: | 13,300 |
| ACCEPTANCE RATE: | 34% |
| SAT RANGE: | 610–710 Verbal |
| | 640–730 Math |
| STICKER PRICE: | Private Divisions: $31,000+ |
| | Public Divisions: |
| | In-state, 18,000+ |
| | Out-of-state, $27,000+ |
| NEED-BLIND: | Yes |
| NEED MET: | 100% |
| AVERAGE STUDENT DEBT: | $14,000 |
| MERIT SCHOLARSHIPS: | None |
| ATHLETIC SCHOLARSHIPS: | No |
| ROTC: | Army, Navy, Air Force |
| WEB SITE: | www.cornell.edu |
| PHONE: | (607) 255-5241 |

High above Cayuga Lake in New York's picturesque Finger Lakes district, Cornell combines an Ivy League liberal arts college with elite programs in hotel administration, architecture and engineering—topped off by New York State–sponsored offerings in agriculture and life sciences, human ecology, and industrial and labor relations. For all its greatness, Cornell still has an inferiority complex next to the Harvards and Princetons of the world, though students seem intent on making up the difference with a few extra hours per day in the library. Other Ivy institutions don't offer merit scholarships, and neither does Cornell...er...at least not exactly. For outstanding students who also show need, the university has several pot sweeteners, known as the Tradition Fellowships, Presidential Research Scholars, and National Scholars. All three allow selected students to replace a portion of their financial aid loans with grant money. The Presidential Research Scholars also provides $3,000 for summer study.

*Deadlines:*
  REGULAR ADMISSION: Jan. 1
  FAFSA: Feb. 15
  CSS PROFILE: Feb. 15

# CREIGHTON UNIVERSITY ✦ Omaha, NE 68178

| | |
|---|---|
| Enrollment: | 6,300 |
| Undergraduate: | 3,800 |
| Acceptance Rate: | 92% |
| SAT Range: | 510–610 Verbal |
| | 520–650 Math |
| Sticker Price: | $19,000+ |
| Need-Blind: | Yes |
| Need Met: | 90% |
| Average Student Debt: | $20,500 |
| Merit Scholarships: | Many |
| Range: | Up to full tuition |
| Athletic Scholarships: | Yes |
| ROTC: | Army, Air Force |
| Web site: | www.creighton.edu |
| Phone: | (800) 282-5835 |

Omaha isn't the most likely place to find a Catholic university, and Creighton is like a small-town cousin of institutions such as Marquette (Milwaukee) and Depaul (Chicago). Typical of many Jesuit schools, Creighton is strongest in health-related fields such as pre-med, pre-dental, nursing, and pharmacy. Business is also popular. The Midwest is a land of inexpensive public universities (with winning football teams), and Creighton faces a major challenge in attracting students to a smallish university that costs thousands more. How to do it? One way is to offer eight different classifications of non-need scholarships. The Scott Scholarships are the richest, providing full tuition for top business students. Presidential Scholarships give three-quarters of tuition plus $1,000 to students based on test scores, grades, and leadership. Lesser scholarships vary and include an award for children of Mutual of Omaha employees and a discount when a family member is enrolled full-time. ROTC scholarship recipients get a sweetener for the equivalent of the annual cost of a room. Scholarship applicants should apply by February 1.

*Deadlines:*
  Admission: Aug. 1
  FAFSA: Apr. 1

# CURRY COLLEGE ✦ Milton, MA 02186

| | |
|---|---|
| Enrollment: | 1,900 |
| Undergraduate: | 1,900 |
| Acceptance Rate: | 84% |
| SAT Average: | 420 Verbal |
| | 420 Math |
| Sticker Price: | $23,000+ |
| Need-Blind: | Yes |
| Need Met: | 80% |
| Average Student Debt: | $18,000 |
| Merit Scholarships: | None |
| Athletic Scholarships: | No |
| ROTC: | No |
| Web site: | www.curry.edu:8080 |
| Phone: | (800) 669-0686 |

Curry is a small college in suburban Boston and a pioneer in the education of learning disabled (LD) students. Nearly thirty years ago, Curry created the Program for Advancement of Learning (PAL), which gives comprehensive support services to LD students who are mainstreamed in Curry's degree programs. In addition to their regular courses in fields such as business, education, nursing, and the liberal arts, PAL students work closely with faculty members in individual and small group sessions to understand their own learning styles and develop coping strategies for long-term success. About one-third of Curry students enroll in the PAL, which costs approximately $3,500 in addition to the standard tuition and fees. Curry offers aid only on the basis of need, and more than 70 percent of students qualified in a recent year. In addition to the standard application materials, students applying to the PAL must submit the results of a recently administered Wechsler Adult Intelligence Scale test. Curry's most popular programs include criminal justice, nursing, and business administration.

*Priority Deadlines:*
  Early Decision: Dec. 1
  Regular Admission: Apr. 1
  FAFSA: Mar. 15

# CURTIS INSTITUTE OF MUSIC ◆ Philadelphia, PA 19103

| | |
|---|---|
| ENROLLMENT: | 160 |
| UNDERGRADUATE: | 160 |
| ACCEPTANCE RATE: | 6% |
| SAT AVERAGE: | NA |
| STICKER PRICE: | $695 (fees only) |
| NEED-BLIND: | Yes |
| NEED MET: | NA |
| AVERAGE STUDENT DEBT: | NA |
| MERIT SCHOLARSHIPS: | Full tuition for all students |
| ATHLETIC SCHOLARSHIPS: | No |
| ROTC: | No |
| WEB SITE: | www.curtis.edu |
| PHONE: | (215) 893-5252 |

Most people think that Harvard is the nation's most selective institution of higher learning, but that honor actually belongs to the Curtis Institute of Music. With the nation's most talented musicians lined up at its door, a microscopic 6 percent are admitted. The reasons for its popularity are not hard to figure out: Curtis is among the most prestigious conservatories in the world, and it offers free tuition to every student. With the fifth largest endowment per student of any institution in the nation, Curtis can afford to lavish attention and resources on its students. There are nearly half as many teachers as students at Curtis, and the latter can stay indefinitely until the faculty decides they are ready to graduate. Enrollment is purposely limited to one full orchestra and an opera department, with a small number of additional students in areas such as composition, conducting, and keyboard instruments. Curtis provides no housing, and students who need assistance with living expenses can apply for financial aid.

*Deadlines:*
ADMISSION: Jan. 15
FAFSA: Rolling

# UNIVERSITY OF DALLAS ◆ Irving, TX 75062

| | |
|---|---|
| ENROLLMENT: | 2,900 |
| UNDERGRADUATE: | 1,100 |
| ACCEPTANCE RATE: | 94% |
| SAT AVERAGE: | 627 Verbal |
| | 606 Math |
| STICKER PRICE: | $19,000+ |
| NEED-BLIND: | Yes |
| NEED MET: | 87% |
| AVERAGE STUDENT DEBT: | $16,800 |
| MERIT SCHOLARSHIPS: | Many |
| RANGE: | Up to full tuition |
| ATHLETIC SCHOLARSHIPS: | No |
| ROTC: | Army, Air Force |
| WEB SITE: | www.udallas.edu |
| PHONE: | (800) 628-6999 |

Not just any college would send its whole sophomore class trooping off for a semester in Rome. But that's the plan at the University of Dallas, a Catholic-affiliated institution where the Western tradition forms the foundation of all that is taught. Along with the program at the university's Rome campus, the heart of a UD education is its extensive core curriculum, which includes requirements in philosophy, English, math, science, U.S. history, European history, politics, economics, fine arts, theology, and foreign language. With tough competition for students among the many private and public institutions in Texas, UD offers a wide variety of merit scholarships. Valedictorians, salutatorians, and National Merit finalists get full tuition awards. Other scholarships are given for academic excellence and leadership, and to distinguished Catholic students. In November, the college gives an on-campus exam that can qualify students for a partial scholarship. Academic departments that sponsor scholarships include art, math, modern and classical languages, physics, and theater. Students who apply by the priority deadline are automatically considered for scholarships.

*Deadlines:*
ADMISSIONS: Dec. 1 (priority)
FAFSA: Feb. 1

# DARTMOUTH COLLEGE ✦ Hanover, NH 03755

| | |
|---|---|
| ENROLLMENT: | 5,300 |
| UNDERGRADUATE: | 4,300 |
| ACCEPTANCE RATE: | 22% |
| SAT RANGE: | 660–760 Verbal |
| | 680–760 Math |
| STICKER PRICE: | $31,000+ |
| NEED-BLIND: | Yes |
| NEED MET: | 100% |
| AVERAGE STUDENT DEBT: | NA |
| MERIT SCHOLARSHIPS: | None |
| ATHLETIC SCHOLARSHIPS: | No |
| ROTC: | Army |
| WEB SITE: | www.dartmouth.edu |
| PHONE: | (603) 646-2875 |

Throughout the 1980s and '90s, Dartmouth was ground zero in the academic culture wars. On one side was a liberal president, determined to remake Dartmouth in a more scholarly image while enhancing campus diversity and tolerance of differences. On the other side were the forces of old Dartmouth, intent on holding out against political correctness while preserving the unique camaraderie that has always been Dartmouth's hallmark. The former president's campaign was largely successful, and today's Dartmouth is a more civil place while retaining its traditional academic excellence. Women now comprise 48 percent of the student body and applications are on the rise. One measure of Dartmouth's diversity is the fact that 55 percent of undergraduates qualify for need-based aid, a higher proportion than at many competitors. Dartmouth is among the elite institutions that recently enhanced its need-based aid. Loans have been eliminated for families with less than $30,000 in income and reduced for those below $60,000. The college is also more lenient in its consideration of assets and outside scholarships.

*Deadlines:*
  EARLY DECISION: Nov. 1
  REGULAR ADMISSION: Jan. 1
  FAFSA: Feb. 1
  CSS PROFILE: Feb. 1

# DAVIDSON COLLEGE ✦ Davidson, NC 28036

| | |
|---|---|
| ENROLLMENT: | 1,600 |
| UNDERGRADUATE: | 1,600 |
| ACCEPTANCE RATE: | 36% |
| SAT RANGE: | 610–710 Verbal |
| | 620–710 Math |
| STICKER PRICE: | $28,000+ |
| NEED-BLIND: | Yes |
| NEED MET: | 100% |
| AVERAGE STUDENT DEBT: | $13,800 |
| MERIT SCHOLARSHIPS: | Many |
| RANGE: | Up to full costs |
| ATHLETIC SCHOLARSHIPS: | Yes |
| ROTC: | Army |
| WEB SITE: | www.davidson.edu |
| PHONE: | (800) 768-0380 |

Davidson has often been described as the Dartmouth of the South. This name is both a tip of the cap to Davidson's status as the premier private liberal arts college in the region and an indication of its heritage as a bastion of traditionalism. Like Dartmouth, Davidson is set in a small college town with social life dominated by fraternities. (Davidson's equivalent of sororities are known as "eating clubs.") Academically, Davidson is known for its unusual degree of interaction between students and faculty. About 15 percent of each entering class receives a merit scholarship, the most lucrative of which are grouped under the heading of Special Competition Scholarships and range from $15,000 to the full costs of attendance. Other awards honor leadership, artistic talent, accomplishment in a particular academic subject, and membership in the Presbyterian Church. A college of 1,600 is an improbable place to find athletic scholarships, but Davidson is among the smallest colleges in the nation to field Division I athletic teams.

*Deadlines:*
  EARLY DECISION: Nov. 15
  REGULAR ADMISSION: Jan. 2
  FAFSA: Feb. 15
  CSS PROFILE: Feb. 15

# UNIVERSITY OF DAYTON ◆ Dayton, OH 45469

| | |
|---|---|
| ENROLLMENT: | 10,200 |
| UNDERGRADUATE: | 6,700 |
| ACCEPTANCE RATE: | 93% |
| SAT RANGE: | 500–610 Verbal |
| | 510–630 Math |
| STICKER PRICE: | $20,000+ |
| NEED-BLIND: | Yes |
| NEED MET: | 93% |
| AVERAGE STUDENT DEBT: | $16,500 |
| MERIT SCHOLARSHIPS: | Many |
| RANGE: | Up to full tuition |
| ATHLETIC SCHOLARSHIPS: | Yes |
| ROTC: | Army, Air Force |
| WEB SITE: | www.udayton.edu |
| PHONE: | (800) 837-7433 |

UD is a middle-sized university that combines solid preprofessional programs and down-to-earth Midwestern charm. Dayton is the major Catholic-affliated institution in its region and nearly half the students graduated from parochial schools. Academic divisions include arts and sciences, business, education, and engineering; engineering is the most selective and where Dayton's strongest reputation lies. Several hundred top students in each class are named University Scholars and offered access to specially designated courses and events. The Honors Program is even more elite and features a variety of privileges. Surrounded by less expensive public universities, Dayton offers a truck-load of merit scholarships to even the playing field. A scholarship chart plots award levels for various combinations of class rank and SAT I or ACT scores. Most students in the top 15 percent with at least 1100 or 24 get $2,500 or more. Awards range up to full tuition. Additional scholarships are available for music, visual arts, leadership, National Merit Finalist status, and numerous other categories. Scholarship applicants should apply by January 15.

*Deadlines:*
  ADMISSION: Rolling
  FAFSA: Mar. 31

# DEEP SPRINGS COLLEGE ◆ Deep Springs, CA (mail: Dyer, NV 89010)

| | |
|---|---|
| ENROLLMENT: | 26 |
| UNDERGRADUATE: | 26 |
| ACCEPTANCE RATE: | 5% |
| SAT AVERAGE: | 750 Verbal |
| | 750 Math |
| STICKER PRICE: | No tuition or fees |
| NEED-BLIND: | Yes |
| NEED MET: | 100% |
| AVERAGE STUDENT DEBT: | NA |
| MERIT SCHOLARSHIPS: | Full costs for all students |
| ATHLETIC SCHOLARSHIPS: | No |
| ROTC: | No |
| WEB SITE: | praxis.deepsprings.edu |
| PHONE: | (760) 872-2000 |

Why would twenty-six of the nation's best students turn down Ivy League acceptances to spend two years living in the California desert? The answer is Deep Springs College, a tiny outpost of remarkable intellect where students live, learn, and work as a self-sufficient community. Only men are admitted, but the tenor of life is much more introspective than macho. Surrounded by stark desert beauty, Deep Springers do their chores, talk about the meaning of life, and take courses that in recent years have ranged from "History of Franciscan and Sufi Spirituality" to "Non-Linear Dynamics." The curriculum covers a broad range of disciplines and changes yearly according to the interests of the students and faculty. Part of Deep Springs's appeal is the fact that tuition and living expenses are paid for by the college. Students are merely required to labor twenty hours per week on a variety of tasks related to the upkeep of their desert home. Deep Springs is a two year program, and most students transfer to highly selective institutions to complete a bachelor's degree.

*Deadlines:*
  ADMISSION: Nov. 15

# UNIVERSITY OF DELAWARE ◆ Newark, DE 19716

| | |
|---|---|
| ENROLLMENT: | 18,200 |
| UNDERGRADUATE: | 15,000 |
| ACCEPTANCE RATE: | 65% |
| SAT RANGE: | 520–610 Verbal |
| | 530–610 Math |
| STICKER PRICE: | In-state, $10,000+ |
| | Out-of-state, $18,000+ |
| NEED-BLIND: | Yes |
| NEED MET: | 79% |
| AVERAGE STUDENT DEBT: | $13,500 |
| MERIT SCHOLARSHIPS: | Many |
| RANGE: | Up to full tuition |
| Athletic Scholarships: | Yes |
| ROTC: | Army, Air Force |
| WEB SITE: | www.udel.edu |
| PHONE: | (302) 831-8123 |

Never seen a Blue Hen before? There are about 18,000 of them walking the campus of the University of Delaware—and not one has laid an egg. Goofy mascot aside, Delaware has developed a strong reputation throughout the East and attracts more than its share of out-of-staters. Engineering is the biggest draw for top students, and Delaware is known as one of the nation's most-wired campuses. A beautiful 1,000-acre campus evokes the aura of a private college. The university offers a wide range of merit awards, the most lucrative of which include 10–12 Eugene du Pont Memorial awards that provide full tuition and fees plus a stipend for books. The music department sponsors a significant number of awards, and scholarships for achievement and interest in a variety of academic disciplines are available. Some academic scholarships give preference to students from under-represented groups. Merit scholarship candidates must complete the application for admission by January 1. Approximately 15 percent of a recent freshman class received a non-need award.

*Deadlines:*
    ADMISSION: Jan. 15 (priority)
    FAFSA: Feb. 15

# DENISON UNIVERSITY ◆ Granville, OH 43023

| | |
|---|---|
| ENROLLMENT: | 2,000 |
| UNDERGRADUATE: | 2,000 |
| Acceptance Rate: | 78% |
| SAT AVERAGE: | 540–640 Verbal |
| | 540–640 Math |
| STICKER PRICE: | $27,000+ |
| NEED-BLIND: | Yes |
| NEED MET: | 97% |
| AVERAGE STUDENT DEBT: | $11,600 |
| MERIT SCHOLARSHIPS: | Many |
| RANGE: | Up to full tuition |
| ATHLETIC SCHOLARSHIPS: | No |
| ROTC: | No |
| WEB SITE: | www.denison.edu |
| PHONE: | (800) 336-4766 |

In a state full of excellent colleges and universities, Denison University has been among the most aggressive in using merit scholarships and tuition discounts to recruit the best students. More than a third of entering students get an academic scholarship from a total of eighteen separate programs. Denison tends to attract a conventional breed of student; economics is the most popular major on campus. The university's reputation for social carousing has waned in recent years, due partly to its decision to shut down Greek houses. (Students can still join fraternities and sororities but must live in the dorms or off campus.) Today's emphasis is on the honors program, and nearly a third of each entering class receives an invitation. Two full-tuition awards, the Wells Science and Dunbar Humanities Scholarships, require a special application. Additional scholarships are based on academic merit, including several for minority students. Alumni Awards of up to one-third of tuition go to good students who have shown "evidence of leadership, special talent, or commitment to community service." Applicants for all scholarships must apply by January 1.

*Deadlines:*
    EARLY DECISION: Jan. 1
    REGULAR ADMISSION: Feb. 1
    FAFSA: Feb. 15

# UNIVERSITY OF DENVER • Denver, CO 80208

| | |
|---|---|
| ENROLLMENT: | 9,100 |
| UNDERGRADUATE: | 3,500 |
| ACCEPTANCE RATE: | 84% |
| SAT RANGE: | 490–610 Verbal |
| | 500–610 Math |
| STICKER PRICE: | $25,000+ |
| NEED-BLIND: | Yes |
| NEED MET: | NA |
| AVERAGE STUDENT DEBT: | NA |
| MERIT SCHOLARSHIPS: | Many |
| RANGE: | Up to full costs |
| ATHLETIC SCHOLARSHIPS: | Yes |
| ROTC: | Army, Air Force |
| WEB SITE: | www.du.edu |
| PHONE: | (800) 525-9495 |

As the only private university in Colorado, the University of Denver is ideally positioned to capitalize on the state's burgeoning popularity. Enrollment has risen about 25 percent in the past decade, and DU has acquired national prominence in a number of areas. The business college, well known for its international program, is among the most noted of DU's divisions. DU is a national leader in the education of learning disabled students via its Learning Effectiveness Program, and the unique Pioneer Leadership Program provides special housing, courses in leadership, and community service opportunities. DU's bountiful merit scholarship program includes a number that cover full costs or full tuition, based on academic excellence, minority status, or Colorado residency. The University of Denver Merit Awards offer $2,000 to $8,000 for selected students in the top 30 percent of their high school class who scored at least 1100 on the SAT I or 24 on the ACT. Awards are also available in theater, music, forensics, and a variety of academic fields.

*Deadlines:*
  EARLY DECISION: Dec. 1
  REGULAR ADMISSION: Feb. 15
  FAFSA: Feb. 20

# DEPAUL UNIVERSITY • Chicago, IL 60604

| | |
|---|---|
| ENROLLMENT: | 15,800 |
| UNDERGRADUATE: | 10,700 |
| ACCEPTANCE RATE: | 81% |
| SAT RANGE: | 530–640 Verbal |
| | 510–530 Math |
| STICKER PRICE: | $20,000+ |
| NEED-BLIND: | Yes |
| NEED MET: | NA |
| AVERAGE STUDENT DEBT: | NA |
| MERIT SCHOLARSHIPS: | Many |
| RANGE: | Up to $9,000 |
| ATHLETIC SCHOLARSHIPS: | Yes |
| ROTC: | Army |
| WEB SITE: | www.depaul.edu |
| PHONE: | (312) 362-9300 |

The story of Depaul University reads like one of Horatio Alger's rags-to-riches tales. In the span of a generation, Depaul has transformed itself from a humble commuter school to a major university. Undergraduate enrollment has nearly doubled, selectivity has increased, and Depaul finds itself looking more and more like Chicago's version of Boston University or NYU. The bustling neighborhood of Lincoln Park, home to the university's main campus, is a perfect location for students who want the charms of city nightlife without an overdose of the urban jungle. Academic scholarships range up to $9,000, with minimum eligibility requirements that include a top 10 percent high school class rank and an SAT I of 1220 or an ACT of 27. Talent-based awards are offered in art, debate, and theater, and additional scholarships are available for community service and membership in a minority group. Since most Depaul Scholarships are awarded on a rolling basis beginning in early December, an early application for admission is crucial.

*Deadlines:*
  EARLY DECISION: Nov. 15
  REGULAR ADMISSION: Rolling
  FAFSA: May 1

# DEPAUW UNIVERSITY ✦ Greencastle, IN 46135

| | |
|---|---|
| ENROLLMENT: | 2,300 |
| UNDERGRADUATE: | 2,300 |
| ACCEPTANCE RATE: | 88% |
| SAT RANGE: | 520–640 Verbal |
| | 530–630 Math |
| STICKER PRICE: | $24,000+ |
| NEED-BLIND: | Yes |
| NEED MET: | NA |
| AVERAGE STUDENT DEBT: | $12,000 |
| MERIT SCHOLARSHIPS: | Many |
| RANGE: | Up to full costs |
| ATHLETIC SCHOLARSHIPS: | No |
| ROTC: | Army, Air Force |
| WEB SITE: | www.depauw.edu |
| PHONE: | (800) 447-2495 |

Tucked away in the heartland of central Indiana, Depauw serves up a hearty helping of the liberal arts with a preprofessional twist. The popular Management Fellows Program offers a business curriculum that features a paid internship in the junior year. A similar program is available for students in Depauw's Center for Contemporary Media, and Depauw is also home to one of the oldest music schools in the Midwest. The university offers many merit scholarships to help take the sting out of private college tuition. The Holton Scholarship Program covers full costs for students from selected Midwestern states who demonstrate outstanding leadership or community service. Merit awards are also dispensed to all students with qualifying GPAs and test scores down to a minimum level of approximately 3.0 and 1100 for the SAT I. A Science and Mathematics Scholarship of $11,000 rewards top scorers on an exam administered on Depauw's campus each fall, and numerous other special scholarships are available for everything from musical talent to community service to being the son or daughter of an alumnus.

*Deadlines:*
   EARLY ACTION: Dec. 1
   EARLY DECISION: Dec. 1
   REGULAR ADMISSION: Feb. 15
   FAFSA: Feb. 15
   CSS PROFILE: Feb. 15

# DICKINSON COLLEGE ✦ Carlisle, PA 17013

| | |
|---|---|
| ENROLLMENT: | 1,800 |
| UNDERGRADUATE: | 1,800 |
| ACCEPTANCE RATE: | 79% |
| SAT RANGE: | 540–640 Verbal |
| | 530–620 Math |
| STICKER PRICE: | $29,000+ |
| NEED-BLIND: | Yes |
| NEED MET: | 97% |
| AVERAGE STUDENT DEBT: | $16,900 |
| MERIT SCHOLARSHIPS: | Few |
| RANGE: | Up to $10,000 |
| ATHLETIC SCHOLARSHIPS: | No |
| ROTC: | Army |
| WEB SITE: | www.dickinson.edu |
| PHONE: | (800) 644-1773 |

Dickinson's challenge is to maintain its selectivity against the likes of Bucknell, Franklin and Marshall, Gettysburg, Lafayette, and the 800-pound gorilla otherwise known as Penn State. Central Pennsylania is not a major drawing card, but Dickinson has an answer with one of the nation's finest study abroad programs. From Beijing to Yaoundé, Dickinson students travel the world with unusual flexibility made possible by the college's 4-1-4 calendar. Although Dickinson has thus far resisted the temptation to dispense major merit money, the Benjamin Rush Scholarships offer up to $10,000 to top students, either as a non-need award or to sweeten need-based packages. ROTC scholarship winners can come close to a full ride with a combination of Dickinson and Army money. The Dickinson Grant Guarantee Plan ensures that any accepted applicant who applies by December 1 and submits the College Board PROFILE will be guaranteed that the grant portion of the aid package will not decrease for any reason during the entire four years.

*Deadlines:*
   EARLY DECISION: Feb. 1
   REGULAR ADMISSION: Feb. 15
   FAFSA: Feb. 15
   CSS PROFILE: Feb. 15

# DREW UNIVERSITY ✦ Madison, NJ 07940

| | |
|---|---|
| ENROLLMENT: | 2,300 |
| UNDERGRADUATE: | 1,500 |
| ACCEPTANCE RATE: | 74% |
| SAT RANGE: | 572–681 Verbal |
| | 558–664 Math |
| STICKER PRICE: | $29,000+ |
| NEED-BLIND: | Yes |
| NEED MET: | 86% |
| AVERAGE STUDENT DEBT: | $13,400 |
| MERIT SCHOLARSHIPS: | Many |
| RANGE: | Up to full tuition |
| ATHLETIC SCHOLARSHIPS: | No |
| ROTC: | No |
| WEB SITE: | www.drew.edu |
| PHONE: | (201) 408-DREW |

Drew University combines a campus of wooded seclusion with a strategic location approximately thirty miles from New York City. Technically a university because of its theological seminary and small graduate school, Drew is really a small college. Political science is Drew's biggest draw, and upperclassmen have the chance for a semester either at the United Nations or on Wall Street. With a popular former governor of New Jersey as its president, Drew also has plenty of political connections at the state level. Drew dispenses more than six million dollars in non-need-based aid every year, a princely sum for such a small institution. For selected applicants with at least 1450 on the SAT I who rank at the top of their high school class, the Drew Scholars Program offers a full-tuition award. At the lower end, the Drew Recognition Award offers $6,000 or more to applicants who "have academic credentials above the median of the entering class." A scholarship of up to $10,000 per year recognizes talent in theater, music, art, or creative writing, and another targets minority students.

*Deadlines:*
  EARLY DECISION: Dec. 1, Jan. 15
  REGULAR ADMISSION: Feb. 15
  FAFSA: Mar. 1

# DREXEL UNIVERSITY ✦ Philadelphia, PA 19104

| | |
|---|---|
| ENROLLMENT: | 10,500 |
| UNDERGRADUATE: | 7,700 |
| ACCEPTANCE RATE: | 69% |
| SAT RANGE: | 500–600 Verbal |
| | 530–630 Math |
| STICKER PRICE: | $23,000+ |
| NEED-BLIND: | Yes |
| NEED MET: | NA |
| AVERAGE STUDENT DEBT: | NA |
| MERIT SCHOLARSHIPS: | Many |
| RANGE: | Up to $8,000 |
| ATHLETIC SCHOLARSHIPS: | Yes |
| ROTC: | Army, Navy, Air Force |
| WEB SITE: | www.drexel.edu |
| PHONE: | (215) 895-2400 |

Drexel University is so excited about its cooperative education program that it trademarked a name: The Ultimate Internship. By the time students graduate, most have spent eighteen months in jobs related to their majors and/or career interests. Though graduation generally takes five years, students rake in an average of about $12,000 for each six-month period of work to help soften the financial blow. Engineering and computer science are where Drexel's reputation lies, but it offers good programs in other preprofessional fields as well. Located in downtown Philadelphia, Drexel is still primarily a regional school, though its appeal is expanding. A new 500-student dorm will help speed Drexel's transition to a residential university. Approximately 38 percent of Drexel's entering students get some sort of merit award. The most prestigious is the A.J. Drexel Scholarship, worth up to $8,000 per year. Awards are also offered for excellence in the peforming arts (up to $2,000), and to children of alumni and National Merit Finalists, among others.

*Deadlines:*
  ADMISSION: Feb. 1
  FAFSA: Mar. 1

## DUKE UNIVERSITY • Durham, NC 27708

| | |
|---|---|
| ENROLLMENT: | 11,600 |
| UNDERGRADUATE: | 6,300 |
| ACCEPTANCE RATE: | 30% |
| SAT RANGE: | 640–730 Verbal |
| | 660–750 Math |
| STICKER PRICE: | $31,000+ |
| NEED-BLIND: | Yes |
| NEED MET: | 100% |
| AVERAGE STUDENT DEBT: | $13,700 |
| MERIT SCHOLARSHIPS: | Few |
| RANGE: | Up to full tuition |
| ATHLETIC SCHOLARSHIPS: | Yes |
| ROTC: | Army, Navy, Air Force |
| WEB SITE: | www.duke.edu |
| PHONE: | (919) 684-3214 |

The only bad thing about a Duke education is suffering through four years known as a "Blue Devil." But it could be worse—just ask the Texas Christian "Purple Horned Frogs"—and if a decade of surging applications is any indication, Dukies don't mind a bit. Duke is like the Harvard, Yale, and Princeton of the South rolled into one. Although its endowment is only a third the size of rival Emory and half that of Rice, Duke offers excellent need-based aid. The university is also home to one of the most coveted merit awards in higher education: the Angier B. Duke Memorial Scholarship Program, which features a full tuition grant and summer study at Oxford University in England. Five scholarships for three-quarters of tuition are earmarked for African Americans, and two music scholarships, one for $7,500 and the other for $3,500, require a separate application. In a recent year, 40 freshmen out of a total of 1600 received a non-need-based award. Other programs sweeten need-based packages, including one that converts loans to grants for residents of the Carolinas.

*Deadlines:*
EARLY DECISION: Nov. 1
REGULAR ADMISSION: Jan. 2
FAFSA: Feb. 1
CSS PROFILE: Feb. 1

## DUQUESNE UNIVERSITY • Pittsburgh, PA 15282

| | |
|---|---|
| ENROLLMENT: | 9,500 |
| UNDERGRADUATE: | 5,500 |
| ACCEPTANCE RATE: | 65% |
| SAT RANGE: | 500–600 Verbal |
| | 490—600 Math |
| STICKER PRICE: | $21,000+ |
| NEED-BLIND: | NA |
| NEED MET: | 80% |
| AVERAGE STUDENT DEBT: | $21,200 |
| MERIT SCHOLARSHIPS: | Many |
| ATHLETIC SCHOLARSHIPS: | Yes |
| ROTC: | Army, Air Force |
| WEB SITE: | www.duq.edu |
| PHONE: | (800) 456-0590 |

Fort Duquesne was the original name of Pittsburgh back in the days before the French and Indian War. Two hundred and fifty years later, Duquesne University appears to be winning its battle for regional and national recognition. Enrollment is rising and applications have nearly doubled from ten years ago. The School of Natural and Environmental Sciences is among the hottest of Duquesne's eight undergraduate divisions. The School of Health Sciences includes popular majors in physical therapy and physician assistance, which require an application by December 1. The school of pharmacy also has a strong reputation. In part because of its Catholic affiliation, Duquesne places extra emphasis on moral and spiritual life, and its liberal arts curriculum stresses the Western heritage. Duquesne offers a formidible array of academic scholarships, headlined by the full-tuition Chancellor's Merit Award. Two other scholarships for general academic excellence are worth $6,500 and $4,000. Many other awards are available, including some targeted specifically to minority students, musicians, and members of churches in the Pittsburgh Diocese.

*Deadlines:*
EARLY DECISION: Nov. 15
REGULAR ADMISSION: Jul. 1
FAFSA: May 1

# EARLHAM COLLEGE ✦ Richmond, IN 47374

| | |
|---|---|
| ENROLLMENT: | 1,100 |
| Undergraduate: | 1,000 |
| ACCEPTANCE RATE: | 83% |
| SAT RANGE: | 550–690 Verbal |
| | 510–650 Math |
| STICKER PRICE: | $23,000+ |
| NEED-BLIND: | Yes |
| NEED MET: | 88% |
| AVERAGE STUDENT DEBT: | $8,700 |
| MERIT SCHOLARSHIPS: | Many |
| RANGE: | Up to $7,500 |
| ATHLETIC SCHOLARSHIPS: | No |
| ROTC: | No |
| WEB SITE: | www.earlham.edu |
| PHONE: | (800) 327-5426 |

It is fitting that Peace and Global Studies is one of Earlham College's best-known programs. Founded by the Society of Friends more than 150 years ago, Earlham stands for the ancient Quaker principles of social justice, consensus-seeking, and nonviolence. One measure of the prevailing mind-set is the fact that sociology/anthropology, a niche major on most campuses, is the second-most popular at Earlham. Earlham shares applicants with other Midwestern bastions of progressivism such as Grinnell and Oberlin, although it is less than half the size of the latter. Earlham has an international focus; it enjoys a strong reputation abroad and enrolls a large contingent of foreign students. For the top candidates in its applicant pool, Earlham offers merit scholarships ranging from $2,500 to $7,500. National Merit finalists get at least $5,000 when they designate Earlham as their first choice college. Other awards recognize minority students, community service, and students who intend to major in chemistry. Students who earn an Indiana Honors diploma get $2,000.

*Deadlines:*
EARLY DECISION: Dec. 1
REGULAR ADMISSION: Feb. 15
FAFSA: Mar. 1

# EASTMAN SCHOOL OF MUSIC ✦ Rochester, NY 14604

| | |
|---|---|
| ENROLLMENT: | 800 |
| UNDERGRADUATE: | 500 |
| ACCEPTANCE RATE: | 35% |
| SAT RANGE: | NA |
| STICKER PRICE: | $28,000+ |
| NEED-BLIND: | Yes |
| NEED MET: | NA |
| AVERAGE STUDENT DEBT: | NA |
| MERIT SCHOLARSHIPS: | Few |
| RANGE: | Up to $7,500 |
| ATHLETIC SCHOLARSHIPS: | No |
| ROTC: | NA |
| WEB SITE: | www.rochester.edu/Eastman |
| PHONE: | (716) 274-1088 |

Eastman is doing its best to bring the highbrow image of classical music down to earth. Most music conservatories tend to be, er, a bit conservative, but the new Eastman Initiatives program represents genuinely bold innovation in this normally staid world. Fueled by concern over the declining appeal of classical music to the general public, Eastman's initiatives include teaching students how to interact with audiences and how to succeed in the business of music. Community outreach is also a new emphasis, and Eastman students are active in bringing music to various local organizations. There's even some rock 'n' roll and other kinds of contemporary music in the curriculum. Lest there be any confusion, Eastman remains one of the premier conservatories in the nation with world-renown in the traditional staples of music training. A number of merit scholarships, ranging from approximately $2,000 to $7,500 per year, are available to outstanding students on the basis of musical talent and academic achievement. Eastman is a division of the University of Rochester, thus giving students access to all the resources of a major university.

*Deadlines:*
ADMISSION: Jan. 1
FAFSA: As soon as possible after Jan. 1

## ECKERD COLLEGE ✦ St. Petersburg, FL 33711

| | |
|---|---|
| ENROLLMENT: | 1,500 |
| UNDERGRADUATE: | 1,500 |
| ACCEPTANCE RATE: | 76% |
| SAT RANGE: | 520–650 Verbal |
| | 520–640 Math |
| STICKER PRICE: | $23,000+ |
| NEED-BLIND: | Yes |
| NEED MET: | 83% |
| AVERAGE STUDENT DEBT: | $16,600 |
| MERIT SCHOLARSHIPS: | Many |
| RANGE: | Up to full tuition |
| ATHLETIC SCHOLARSHIPS: | Yes |
| ROTC: | Army, Air Force |
| WEB SITE: | www.eckerd.edu |
| PHONE: | (800) 456-9009 |

With a waterfront campus at the point where Tampa Bay meets the Gulf of Mexico, Eckerd College can be forgiven for a little smugness about providing "the right climate for learning." The appeal of its seaside location is powerful, especially for the dozens of aspiring marine scientists that descend on its campus every year. The international business program is also a major draw. Twenty-five of Eckerd's ablest freshmen receive a Presidential Scholarship, valued at up to $10,000 per year, and honorees in the various National Merit programs can compete for full-tuition awards. The former requires a separate application; the deadline for both is February 15. Church and Campus Scholarships recognize members of the Presbyterian Church with up to $7,000, and Special Talent Scholarships of $5,000 honor academic prowess in a particular subject or extracurricular achievement. Florida residents get an automatic $5,000 award, and more if they qualify for state-sponsored merit scholarships. A $1,500 scholarship is available for incoming students who want to do research with a faculty member.

*Deadlines:*
  ADMISSION: Rolling
  FAFSA: Apr. 1

## EMORY UNIVERSITY ✦ Atlanta, GA 30322

| | |
|---|---|
| ENROLLMENT: | 11,100 |
| UNDERGRADUATE: | 6,000 |
| ACCEPTANCE RATE: | 45% |
| SAT RANGE: | 630–700 Verbal |
| | 650–710 Math |
| STICKER PRICE: | $30,000+ |
| NEED-BLIND: | Yes |
| NEED MET: | 93% |
| AVERAGE STUDENT DEBT: | $16,100 |
| MERIT SCHOLARSHIPS: | Few |
| RANGE: | Up to full costs |
| ATHLETIC SCHOLARSHIPS: | No |
| ROTC: | Air Force |
| WEB SITE: | www.emory.edu |
| PHONE: | (800) 727-6036 |

The time may come when Emory overtakes Duke as the southeast's premier private university. It hasn't happened yet, but keep watching. Set in the region's leading city with an endowment-per-student topped only by Harvard, Yale, Princeton, and Rice among major universities, Emory has been zooming up the selectivity charts. As heir to part of the Coca Cola fortune, Emory can afford huge investments in state-of-the-art facilities, such as the new $25 million home of the business school. Emory has always attracted a national student body, so much so that administrators once worried about enrolling too many Yankees and not enough Southerners. Emory is home to one of the most prestigious merit programs in higher education, the Emory Scholars, which annually selects seventy students for awards of at least full tuition. Applicants must secure a school nomination and apply by November 15. There are also two scholarships for outstanding debaters, and National Merit Finalists are eligible for up to $2,000. The financial aid office also gives a scholarship for as much as one-third tuition to top candidates who show need.

*Deadlines:*
  EARLY DECISION: Nov. 1
  ADMISSION: Jan. 15
  FAFSA: Feb. 15
  CSS PROFILE: Feb. 15

# EUGENE LANG COLLEGE ◆ New York, NY 10011

| | |
|---|---|
| ENROLLMENT: | 400 |
| UNDERGRADUATE: | 400 |
| ACCEPTANCE RATE: | 80% |
| SAT AVERAGE: | 590 Verbal |
| | 520 Math |
| STICKER PRICE: | $28,000+ |
| NEED-BLIND: | Yes |
| NEED MET: | NA |
| AVERAGE STUDENT DEBT: | $10,000 |
| MERIT SCHOLARSHIPS: | None |
| ATHLETIC SCHOLARSHIPS: | No |
| ROTC: | No |
| WEB SITE: | www.newschool.edu |
| PHONE: | (212) 229-5665 |

There is no mistaking Eugene Lang for a typical college—not with a student body of 400 and a campus that consists of New York City sidewalks. Part of New School University, the nation's largest supplier of evening classes for adults, Eugene Lang features small seminars and self-designed interdisciplinary majors (known as "concentrations of study"). Lang's curriculum is largely limited to the arts, humanities, and social sciences, supplemented somewhat by courses in the New School's other divisions, which include Parson's School of Design, a school of management, and a social sciences graduate school. Although library resources are scant, students have access to the massive collection at New York University just a few blocks to the south. Lang doesn't have a campus in the traditional sense of the word; the main academic building is at Eleventh Street between Fifth and Sixth Avenues, and there is also a student center and a handful of dorms a few blocks to the east. Lang gives financial aid only on the basis of need.

*Deadlines:*
  EARLY DECISION: Nov. 15
  REGULAR ADMISSION: Feb. 1
  FAFSA: Apr. 1
  CSS PROFILE: Apr. 1

# EVERGREEN STATE COLLEGE ◆ Olympia, WA 98505

| | |
|---|---|
| ENROLLMENT: | 4,100 |
| UNDERGRADUATE: | 3,800 |
| ACCEPTANCE RATE: | 88% |
| SAT RANGE: | 530–650 Verbal |
| | 490–600 Math |
| STICKER PRICE: | In-state, $7,000+ |
| | Out-of-state, $14,000+ |
| NEED-BLIND: | Yes |
| NEED MET: | 89% |
| AVERAGE STUDENT DEBT: | $12,000 |
| MERIT SCHOLARSHIPS: | Few |
| RANGE: | Up to $3,000 |
| ATHLETIC SCHOLARSHIPS: | No |
| ROTC: | No |
| WEB SITE: | www.evergreen.edu |
| PHONE: | (360) 866-6000 |

Evergreen is not the kind of place where students spend time worrying about GPAs or making the dean's list. Evergreen students have no GPAs—the faculty provides narrative evaluations instead of grades—and the entire academic program is designed to replace individual competition with group collaboration. Instead of traditional courses that focus on a single subject, Evergreen offers team-taught, interdisciplinary programs in which students study a range of subjects as an interconnected whole. Classes are generally small, emphasizing participation and hands-on work. Established in 1971 in a picturesque forest near Washington State's Puget Sound, Evergreen is a state institution where the ambience bears a striking resemblance to nonconformist havens of the East such as Bard and Sarah Lawrence. It should come as no surprise that one of Evergreen's largest merit awards is the $2,500 Democratic Socialist Peace Award, which requires an essay about "political action you have taken." Only a handful of merit and merit-within-need awards are available, a significant number of which are targeted to minority students. Most are less than $1,000.

*Deadlines:*
  ADMISSION: Mar. 1
  FAFSA: Feb. 15

# FAIRFIELD UNIVERSITY ◆ Fairfield, CT 06430

| | |
|---|---|
| ENROLLMENT: | 5,200 |
| UNDERGRADUATE: | 4,300 |
| ACCEPTANCE RATE: | 68% |
| SAT RANGE: | 520–600 Verbal |
| | 520–610 Math |
| STICKER PRICE: | $27,000+ |
| NEED-BLIND: | Yes |
| NEED MET: | 80% |
| AVERAGE STUDENT DEBT: | $17,100 |
| MERIT SCHOLARSHIPS: | Many |
| RANGE: | Up to $10,000 |
| ATHLETIC SCHOLARSHIPS: | Yes |
| ROTC: | No |
| WEB SITE: | www.fairfield.edu |
| PHONE: | (203) 254-4100 |

Founded in 1942, Fairfield is a twentieth-century incarnation of the ancient Jesuit tradition of education. Strategically located on the Connecticut coast within easy striking distance of New York City, Fairfield is perhaps best known for its business program, which is riding high in a new facility. The business curriculum has been revitalized in recent years to include more interdisciplinary, team-taught courses and to increase the number of internships. English and psychology are the most heavily subscribed programs in the liberal arts, and the nursing program is also popular. In keeping with the Jesuit tradition, ethics and community service are major points of emphasis. The $10,000 University Fellowship Scholarship highlights the list of merit awards; students need a top 10 percent class rank and a 1300 on the SAT I or 29 on the ACT for consideration. A separate application by December 1 is required. The Presidential Scholarship offers $8,500 to those who score 1200 or 27, and the Dean's Scholarship of $6,000 is awarded on the basis of academic and nonacademic criteria.

*Deadlines:*
 EARLY DECISION: Dec. 1
 REGULAR ADMISSION: Feb. 1
 FAFSA: Feb. 15
 CSS PROFILE: Feb. 15

# FLORIDA A&M UNIVERSITY ◆ Tallahassee, FL 32307

| | |
|---|---|
| ENROLLMENT: | 11,100 |
| UNDERGRADUATE: | 8,800 |
| ACCEPTANCE RATE: | 66% |
| SAT AVERAGE: | 1141 combined |
| STICKER PRICE: | In-state, $7,000+ |
| | Out-of-state, $15,000+ |
| NEED-BLIND: | Yes |
| NEED MET: | NA |
| AVERAGE STUDENT DEBT: | NA |
| MERIT SCHOLARSHIPS: | Many |
| RANGE: | Up to full costs |
| ATHLETIC SCHOLARSHIPS: | Yes |
| ROTC: | Army, Navy, Air Force |
| WEB SITE: | www.famu.edu |
| PHONE: | (850) 599-3796 |

Florida A&M is rising swiftly among the ranks of the nation's top historically black universities. Enrollment has more than doubled since the mid-1980s, and the university is still on a roll from being chosen as the Time/Princeton Review College of the Year in 1997–98. The colleges of business, pharmacy, and health sciences include most of the university's best-known programs; A&M also offers degrees in arts and sciences, education, engineering, and journalism/media. A&M is a terrific deal by private university standards, and much of its success has been due to aggressive recruiting of top students with merit scholarships. Several programs are targeted to honorees in the National Merit Program or the affiliated National Achievement Scholarship Program for African American students. Among those programs is the Life-Gets-Better Award, which offers a full-costs free ride plus a paid internship. The Sloan Scholars Program gives a full scholarship to science students with a 3.5 GPA and an SAT I of 1200 or an ACT of 27 who plan to pursue a Ph.D.

*Deadlines:*
 EARLY DECISION: Feb. 1
 REGULAR ADMISSION: May 1
 FAFSA: Apr. 1

# FLORIDA INSTITUTE OF TECHNOLOGY ◆
## Melbourne, FL 32901

| | |
|---|---|
| ENROLLMENT: | 4,100 |
| UNDERGRADUATE: | 1,800 |
| ACCEPTANCE RATE: | 85% |
| SAT RANGE: | 510–610 Verbal |
| | 540–630 Math |
| STICKER PRICE: | $22,000+ |
| NEED-BLIND: | No |
| NEED MET: | 81% |
| AVERAGE STUDENT DEBT: | $21,000 |
| MERIT SCHOLARSHIPS: | Many |
| RANGE: | Up to $7,500 |
| ATHLETIC SCHOLARSHIPS: | Yes |
| ROTC: | Army |
| WEB SITE: | www.fit.edu |
| PHONE: | (800) 888-4348 |

The Kennedy Space Center is famous for sending forth rockets and space shuttles, but it also launched Florida Tech, which was founded in 1958 to provide education for the people in the space program. Today, FIT is a full-fledged private university. Engineering is by far FIT's largest division; also notable are its offerings in aeronautics and marine biology. Set on 130 tropical acres in central Florida, FIT is within easy reach of fun spots ranging from the Atlantic beaches to Disney World. As FIT does not mind repeating, its average SAT I scores are the highest among Florida's major universities (just in case any Gators in Gainesville are listening). The state of Florida is unusually generous with merit money for in-staters, and many FIT students get their tuition paid for by the state. The school itself also hands out more than 100 merit scholarships per year, highlighted by the $7,500 Presidential Award. Scholarship candidates should apply for admission by February 1.

*Deadlines:*
    ADMISSION: Rolling
    FAFSA: Mar. 15

# FLORIDA STATE UNIVERSITY ◆
## Tallahassee, FL 32306

| | |
|---|---|
| ENROLLMENT: | 30,400 |
| UNDERGRADUATE: | 23,700 |
| ACCEPTANCE RATE: | 72% |
| SAT RANGE: | 510–620 Verbal |
| | 510–610 Math |
| Sticker Price: | In-state, $7,000+ |
| | Out-of-state, $14,000+ |
| NEED-BLIND: | Yes |
| NEED MET: | 48% |
| AVERAGE STUDENT DEBT: | $20,900 |
| MERIT SCHOLARSHIPS: | Many |
| RANGE: | Up to full costs |
| ATHLETIC SCHOLARSHIPS: | Yes |
| ROTC: | Army, Navy, Air Force |
| WEB SITE: | www.fsu.edu |
| PHONE: | (850) 644-6200 |

Any list of Florida State's nationally ranked programs must begin with the one that plays its games on fall Saturday afternoons. But the football field isn't the only place where FSU comes out a winner. Florida State has developed a national reputation across a host of areas, with particularly notable programs in the arts and media. Music, theater, visual arts, and dance are nationally respected, and a new School of Motion Picture, Television, and Recording Arts has bolstered offerings in both the arts and communications. The College of Business is by far FSU's largest professional school. FSU gives awards covering 90 percent of tuition, room, and board to National Merit Finalists, National Achievement Finalists, and National Hispanic Scholars who designate the university as their first choice. Other scholarships of up to $2,500 include one for outstanding Florida residents and another for minority students. A $500 stipend is available for honorees at the state science fair, and various awards are given for artistic talent and through the academic departments. Students should apply by December 15 to ensure full consideration for scholarships.

*Deadlines:*
    ADMISSION: Mar. 2
    FAFSA: Mar. 1

## UNIVERSITY OF FLORIDA ✦ Gainsville, FL 32611

ENROLLMENT: 41,700
UNDERGRADUATE: 31,500
ACCEPTANCE RATE: 64%
SAT RANGE: 560–670 Verbal
580–680 Math
STICKER PRICE: In-state, $7,000+
Out-of-state, $14,000+
NEED-BLIND: Yes
NEED MET: NA
AVERAGE STUDENT DEBT: NA
MERIT SCHOLARSHIPS: Many
RANGE: Up to $6,000
ATHLETIC SCHOLARSHIPS: Yes
ROTC: Army, Navy, Air Force
WEB SITE: www.ufl.edu
PHONE: (352) 392-1365

Gator pride runs deep at the University of Florida—even its financial aid and scholarships are known as "Gator Aid." With 41,700 students in 23 colleges and schools, UF alone has as many academic offerings as some states. Students studying everything from anthropology to zoology will find quality programs, although the university's reputation is particularly strong in business, engineering, fine arts, and journalism/communications. The football team is famous for its annual exploits in the nation's top ten, and UF gives UCLA a run for its money as the best all-around athletic program in NCAA Division I. With the state's new Bright Futures Scholarship Program, many Florida residents have a merit scholarship in hand before they apply. National Merit Finalists who designate UF as their first choice receive a $4,000 award, and National Achievement Finalists get at least $6,000 per year. In-state valedictorians get a one-time $500 award, and fifty top out-of-staters get a $2,500 reduction in their bill that may or may not be renewed. Numerous other merit and merit-within-need awards are available.

*Deadlines:*
    ADMISSION: Jan. 30
    FAFSA: Apr. 15

## FORDHAM UNIVERSITY ✦ New York, NY 10458

ENROLLMENT: 13,700
UNDERGRADUATE: 6,100
ACCEPTANCE RATE: 69%
SAT RANGE: 520–620 Verbal
500–590 Math
STICKER PRICE: $27,000+
NEED-BLIND: Yes
NEED MET: NA
AVERAGE STUDENT DEBT: $9,900
MERIT SCHOLARSHIPS: Many
RANGE: Up to full costs
ATHLETIC SCHOLARSHIPS: Yes
ROTC: Army, Navy, Air Force
WEB SITE: www.fordham.edu
PHONE: (718) 817-4000

In the city that never sleeps, more and more people are waking up to the fact that Columbia and NYU aren't the only major private universities in town. With one campus at Lincoln Center in Manhattan and another in the Bronx, Fordham allows students to sample the bustle of midtown or retreat to the more collegiate atmosphere of Rose Hill. The latter is home to the business school and liberal arts offerings. The Lincoln Center campus also offers liberal arts with an emphasis on studio art, theater, and media. True to the Jesuit model, all students complete a core curriculum that includes philosophy and theology along with a range of other disciplines. Fordham's most prestigious merit scholarship is the Presidential, which offers full tuition plus the cost of a room for four years. Students with slightly less highfallutin credentials get the Dean's Scholarship, worth $7,500. Other scholarships honor community involvement and students with an interest in Italian Studies, among others.

*Deadlines:*
    EARLY DECISION: Nov. 1
    REGULAR ADMISSION: Feb. 1
    FAFSA: Feb. 1
    CSS PROFILE: Feb. 1

# FRANKLIN AND MARSHALL COLLEGE ◆ Lancaster, PA 17604

| | |
|---|---|
| ENROLLMENT: | 1,800 |
| UNDERGRADUATE: | 1,800 |
| ACCEPTANCE RATE: | 54% |
| SAT RANGE: | 580–670 Verbal |
| | 580–678 Math |
| STICKER PRICE: | $29,000+ |
| NEED-BLIND: | No |
| NEED MET: | 100% |
| AVERAGE STUDENT DEBT: | $14,400 |
| MERIT SCHOLARSHIPS: | Many |
| RANGE: | Up to $12,500 |
| ATHLETIC SCHOLARSHIPS: | No |
| ROTC: | No |
| WEB SITE: | www.fandm.edu |
| PHONE: | (717) 291-3951 |

Benjamin Franklin helped build a nation on the values of hard work and practicality. More than 200 years later, the students at his namesake college are following in his footsteps. Career-oriented majors such as pre-med, pre-law, and business are where the aspirations of many F&M students lie, and they're willing to pull a few all-nighters to get there. Government is the most popular major on campus, and the college is known for its strong connections in Washington, D.C. F&M competes with larger rivals such as Bucknell, Colgate, and Lehigh but is closer in size to Hamilton and Lafayette. The John Marshall Scholarship heads the list of merit awards and includes a package that totals over $7,500 (with $5,000 more tacked on for National Merit Semifinalists). Presidential Scholars get a $5,000 award, and the Gray Scholarships give selected African Americans and Latinos a need-based aid package without loans. The $4,000 Buchanan Scholars program recognizes public service, and another $4,000 award goes to top applicants from Pennsylvania. Sixty freshmen received a non-need award in a recent year.

*Deadlines:*
  EARLY DECISION: Dec. 1
  REGULAR ADMISSION: Feb. 1
  FAFSA: Feb. 1
  CSS PROFILE: Feb. 1

# FURMAN UNIVERSITY ◆ Greenville, SC 29613

| | |
|---|---|
| ENROLLMENT: | 2,800 |
| UNDERGRADUATE: | 2,600 |
| ACCEPTANCE RATE: | 80% |
| SAT RANGE: | 560–670 Verbal |
| | 570–670 Math |
| STICKER PRICE: | $22,000+ |
| NEED-BLIND: | No |
| NEED MET: | 76% |
| AVERAGE STUDENT DEBT: | $12,900 |
| MERIT SCHOLARSHIPS: | Many |
| RANGE: | Up to full costs |
| ATHLETIC SCHOLARSHIPS: | Yes |
| ROTC: | Army |
| WEB SITE: | www.furman.edu |
| PHONE: | (864) 294-2034 |

No matter what else Furman may be known for, the first thing people mention is the beauty of its sprawling 750-acre campus, which includes everything from an 18-hole golf course to a Japanese garden. With its warm glow of Southern hospitality, the Furman atmosphere is enough to put even the most overprotective parent's mind at ease. Though "university" is part of its name, Furman is a small liberal arts college that specializes in training South Carolina's doctors, lawyers, and businesspeople. It is a conservative place, although Furman has severed ties to the fundamentalist-dominated South Carolina Baptist Convention. With an entering class of 750, Furman awards approximately 100 renewable merit scholarships that range up to full costs. Students designated by participating high schools as Furman Scholars get at least $3,500 and can compete for more. Other scholarships for students interested in business, computer science, economics, math or pre-engineering require a separate application to be filed by February 1. Music scholarships require an audition to be scheduled in December or January.

*Deadlines:*
  EARLY DECISION: Dec. 1
  REGULAR ADMISSION: Feb. 1
  FAFSA: Feb. 1

## GEORGE MASON UNIVERSITY ✦
### Fairfax, VA 22030

| | |
|---|---|
| ENROLLMENT: | 23,800 |
| UNDERGRADUATE: | 13,900 |
| ACCEPTANCE RATE: | 68% |
| SAT RANGE: | 460–570 Verbal |
| | 460–570 Math |
| STICKER PRICE: | In-state, $11,000+ |
| | Out-of-state, $19,000+ |
| NEED-BLIND: | Yes |
| NEED MET: | 63% |
| AVERAGE STUDENT DEBT: | $11,700 |
| MERIT SCHOLARSHIPS: | Few |
| RANGE: | Up to $5,000 |
| ATHLETIC SCHOLARSHIPS: | Yes |
| ROTC: | Army |
| WEB SITE: | www.gmu.edu |
| PHONE: | (703) 993-2400 |

In a region that includes Georgetown, George Washington, and James Madison within a 100-mile radius, a little confusion about the identity of George Mason University is inevitable. Located in the Virginia suburbs outside Washington, D.C., GMU is a relative newcomer that has vaulted to prominence with the rapid growth of the northern Virginia suburbs. There are 13,900 undergraduates at GMU, most of them commuters. The university is developing its residential life, but it will need a few more years to match the resources at more established institutions like UVA or Virginia Tech. GMU is home to the innovative New Century College, which offers freshmen an interdisciplinary core and then allows them to branch off to small-group work and a self-designed major. Top billing among GMU's merit awards goes to the University Scholars Program, which offers $5,000 per year and a variety of enrichment programs. The $1,500 Dean's Scholarship is also awarded on the basis of all-around academic achievement. Students should apply by January 5 for full scholarship consideration.

*Deadlines:*
  EARLY ACTION: Dec. 1
  REGULAR ADMISSION: Feb. 1
  FAFSA: Mar. 1

## GEORGE WASHINGTON UNIVERSITY ✦
### Washington, DC 20052

| | |
|---|---|
| ENROLLMENT: | 19,400 |
| UNDERGRADUATE: | 7,800 |
| ACCEPTANCE RATE: | 49% |
| SAT RANGE: | 570–670 Verbal |
| | 570—660 Math |
| STICKER PRICE: | $31,000+ |
| NEED-BLIND: | Yes |
| NEED MET: | NA |
| AVERAGE STUDENT DEBT: | $14,400 |
| MERIT SCHOLARSHIPS: | Many |
| RANGE: | Up to $15,000 |
| ATHLETIC SCHOLARSHIPS: | Yes |
| ROTC: | Army, Navy, Air Force |
| WEB SITE: | www.gwu.edu |
| PHONE: | (800) 447-3765 |

Next door to the World Bank, down the street from the State Department, and four blocks from the White House, George Washington University is a crossroads for talented and ambitious souls seeking their fortune in the nation's capital. Less a campus than a collection of buildings, GW lacks the collegiate ambience of American or Georgetown, offering instead the bustle of nearby restaurants and night spots. GW has a strong reputation in the arts, natural sciences, and anything related to politics. Surging applications mean admission is getting tougher. The threshold to compete for GW's top merit awards is approximately a 3.7 GPA and SAT I of 1350 or ACT of 30. (Check programs for details.) Those eligible for awards of $10,000 include top science students, those admitted to the honors program, and those in one of GW's elite combined-degree programs in law, medicine, and/or engineering. Outstanding artists get up to $8,000 based partly on a portfolio or audition. Other awards are available, including half off tuition for students with a GW sibling.

*Deadlines:*
  EARLY DECISION: Nov. 1, Dec. 1
  REGULAR ADMISSION: Feb. 1
  FAFSA: Feb. 1
  CSS PROFILE: Feb. 1

# GEORGETOWN UNIVERSITY ◆
## Washington, DC 20057

| | |
|---|---|
| ENROLLMENT: | 12,500 |
| UNDERGRADUATE: | 6,200 |
| ACCEPTANCE RATE: | 21% |
| SAT RANGE: | 610–730 Verbal |
| | 620–710 Math |
| STICKER PRICE: | $31,000+ |
| NEED-BLIND: | Yes |
| NEED MET: | 100% |
| AVERAGE STUDENT DEBT: | $17,300 |
| MERIT SCHOLARSHIPS: | None |
| ATHLETIC SCHOLARSHIPS: | Yes |
| ROTC: | Army, Navy, Air Force |
| WEB SITE: | www.georgetown.edu |
| PHONE: | (202) 687-3600 |

When John Carroll decided to found an academy "at George-Town on the Patowmack River," the choice could not have been more fortuitous. Little did he know that a piece of nearby swampland would soon be selected as the site of the nation's capital. Today, Georgetown's runaway popularity is due largely to its location. Lost in the minds of some applicants is the fact that Georgetown is a Jesuit institution, and the university continues an internal tug-of-war between preservation of its Catholic identity and its leadership position in the secular world. Georgetown is more conservative than most elite institutions and more liberal than most Catholic ones. Georgetown offers no merit scholarships but several merit-within-need awards. Students with need who are selected as John Carroll Scholars get extra grants in their aid packages. The Bellarmine and Ignatian programs offer a similar deal to students from Jesuit high schools who are valedictorians or rank in the top 5 percent and show all-around merit.

*Deadlines:*
  EARLY ACTION: Nov. 1
  REGULAR ADMISSION: Jan. 10
  FAFSA: Feb.1
  CSS PROFILE: Feb.1

# GEORGIA INSTITUTE OF TECHNOLOGY ◆
## Atlanta, GA 30332

| | |
|---|---|
| ENROLLMENT: | 13,000 |
| UNDERGRADUATE: | 9,500 |
| ACCEPTANCE RATE: | 61% |
| SAT RANGE: | 620–630 Verbal |
| | 680–690 Math |
| STICKER PRICE: | In-state, $8,000+ |
| | Out-of-state, $15,000+ |
| NEED-BLIND: | Yes |
| NEED MET: | 75% |
| AVERAGE STUDENT DEBT: | $11,500 |
| MERIT SCHOLARSHIPS: | Few |
| RANGE: | Up to full tuition |
| ATHLETIC SCHOLARSHIPS: | Yes |
| ROTC: | Army, Navy, Air Force |
| WEB SITE: | www.gatech.edu |
| PHONE: | (404) 894-4154 |

It is not immediately clear why an engineering school would want to be known as "The Ramblin' Wreck," but the name is worn with pride at Georgia Tech. Whatever you call her, Ma Tech reigns as the leading science and technology institution in the Southeast and also one of its best educational bargains. Most in-staters have their tuition costs covered by Georgia's HOPE Scholarship, and a high percentage of them earn extra money with a co-op job related to their majors. Engineering is far and away Tech's best known division, but Tech also offers strong programs in business, the natural sciences, and architecture. The school's prestigious Presidential Scholarship annually gives 75 outstanding students a half- or full-tuition free ride. Typical qualifications include a 3.9 GPA and SAT I scores of 1380–1510, and applicants must apply for admission by October 31. Tech also gives a small award to National Merit Finalists who designate the institute as their first choice. A variety of other awards are available.

*Deadlines:*
  ADMISSION: Jan. 15
  FAFSA: Mar. 1

## UNIVERSITY OF GEORGIA ✦
## Athens, GA 30602

| | |
|---|---|
| ENROLLMENT: | 29,700 |
| UNDERGRADUATE: | 23,200 |
| ACCEPTANCE RATE: | 73% |
| SAT RANGE: | 550–650 Verbal |
| | 550–640 Math |
| STICKER PRICE: | In-state, $8,000+ |
| | Out-of-state, $15,000+ |
| NEED-BLIND: | Yes |
| NEED MET: | 82% |
| AVERAGE STUDENT DEBT: | $13,000 |
| MERIT SCHOLARSHIPS: | Many |
| RANGE: | Up to full costs |
| ATHLETIC SCHOLARSHIPS: | Yes |
| ROTC: | Army, Air Force |
| WEB SITE: | www.uga.edu |
| PHONE: | (706) 542-2112 |

Georgia's Bulldogs are strutting a little prouder these days. The state's HOPE Scholarship has brought a flood of well-qualified applicants, and the university's reputation is soaring. Major attractions include a nationally acclaimed School of Journalism and Mass Communication, a first-rate business school, and some of the best arts facilities in the South. Since every aspiring student in the state with 3.0 high school GPA gets a tuition scholarship plus an allowance for fees and books, a whopping 97 percent of the in-staters pay for nothing except room and board. About 20–25 top students are selected for the Foundation Fellowship program, which covers all university expenses and adds money for travel and independent study. Applicants should have at least a 1300 on the SAT I or 31 on the ACT with a 3.7 GPA, and the application is due November 30. Students in the top 5 percent of each entering class are granted a Charter Scholarship, which gives in-staters $1,000 and out-of-staters a package totaling $8,000. Many other awards are available.

*Deadlines:*
  ADMISSION: Feb. 1
  FAFSA: Mar. 1

## GETTYSBURG COLLEGE ✦
## Gettysburg, PA 17325

| | |
|---|---|
| ENROLLMENT: | 2,200 |
| UNDERGRADUATE: | 2,200 |
| ACCEPTANCE RATE: | 72% |
| SAT RANGE: | 550–645 Verbal |
| | 550–645 Math |
| STICKER PRICE: | $29,000+ |
| NEED-BLIND: | Yes |
| NEED MET: | 100% |
| AVERAGE STUDENT DEBT: | $12,200 |
| MERIT SCHOLARSHIPS: | Many |
| RANGE: | Up to $7,000 |
| ATHLETIC SCHOLARSHIPS: | No |
| ROTC: | No |
| WEB SITE: | www.gettysburg.edu |
| PHONE: | (800) 431-0803 |

With the greatest battle in our nation's history raging at its doorstep, Gettysburg College's administration building served as a field hospital. Today's Gettysburg attracts its share of history buffs, but the most popular degree program is business. Though the students are career-oriented, the college itself has a traditional liberal arts focus with extensive distribution requirements in nine categories ranging from quantitative reasoning to non-Western culture. In a state rich with small private colleges, Gettysburg competes on even footing with Dickinson, just thirty miles down the road, but faces a tougher time wresting students from the likes of Bucknell, Franklin and Marshall, and Lafayette. While many private colleges have gone whole hog for tuition discounting, Gettysburg has maintained need-based aid as its primary emphasis. The college does offer merit scholarships worth $7,000 under its Presidential Scholars Program to students who generally rank in the top 10 percent of their high school class with SAT scores to match. In a recent year, the college offered non-need awards to 74 of approximately 650 entering freshmen.

*Deadlines:*
  EARLY DECISION: Feb. 1
  REGULAR ADMISSION: Feb. 15
  FAFSA: Feb. 15
  CSS PROFILE: Feb. 15

# GODDARD COLLEGE ✦ Plainfield, VT 05667

| | |
|---|---|
| ENROLLMENT: | 500 |
| UNDERGRADUATE: | 300 |
| ACCEPTANCE RATE: | 81% |
| SAT AVERAGE: | 500 Verbal |
| | 490 Math |
| STICKER PRICE: | $21,000+ |
| NEED-BLIND: | Yes |
| NEED MET: | NA |
| AVERAGE STUDENT DEBT: | NA |
| MERIT SCHOLARSHIPS: | None |
| ATHLETIC SCHOLARSHIPS: | No |
| ROTC: | No |
| WEB SITE: | www.goddard.edu |
| PHONE: | (800) 468-4888 |

With about 300 undergraduates, 25 faculty, and 250 acres of countryside in central Vermont, Goddard is like a 1960s commune updated for the new century. Educationally, Goddard is as progressive as it gets—no grades, no majors, and few of the traditional academic trappings. Instead, students work with faculty to develop an individualized Study Plan that includes both what will be learned and how the learning will take place. What other colleges call courses are styled "Group Studies" at Goddard, and most consist of a handful of students with a teacher. The offerings tend toward the arts, humanities, and biological/environmental sciences; recent titles have included Activists and Activism, On Being Male, and Experimental Creativity. In addition to their studies, all students participate in the college's work program and play a role in community governance. Many of Goddard's students are transfers who want something different after sampling life in a traditional academic setting. True to its egalitarian philosophy, Goddard gives financial aid only to those with need.

*Deadlines:*
  ADMISSION: Rolling
  FAFSA: Rolling

# GORDON COLLEGE ✦ Wenham, MA 01984

| | |
|---|---|
| ENROLLMENT: | 1,400 |
| UNDERGRADUATE: | 1,400 |
| ACCEPTANCE RATE: | 80% |
| SAT RANGE: | 530–640 Verbal |
| | 500–620 Math |
| STICKER PRICE: | $21,000+ |
| NEED-BLIND: | Yes |
| NEED MET: | 81% |
| AVERAGE STUDENT DEBT: | $12,900 |
| MERIT SCHOLARSHIPS: | Many |
| RANGE: | Up to full tuition |
| ATHLETIC SCHOLARSHIPS: | No |
| ROTC: | Air Force |
| WEB SITE: | www.gordonc.edu |
| PHONE: | (800) 343-1379 |

Gordon is indisputably New England's premier evangelical Christian college. Located within a stone's throw of the North Shore of Massachusetts, Gordon's quiet campus is only twenty-five miles up the coast from Boston. Students choose majors just as they would at any other college—English, biology, and psychology are the most popular—but everything is taught from a Christian perspective. In addition to participation in regular chapel and other worship services, Gordon students are unusually active in community service and outreach ministries. The A.J. Gordon Scholarship offers $10,000 per year to the college's most outstanding candidates who apply by February 1, and National Merit Finalists are eligible for a full tuition award. Awards for general excellence range down to the Challenge Scholars, which offers $5,000 to students in the top 15 percent of their high school class with a combined SAT I of at least 1140. Other scholarships target students from Christian high schools, those who have contributed to their community and its spiritual life, and outstanding musicians.

*Deadlines:*
  EARLY DECISION: Dec. 1
  REGULAR ADMISSION: Mar. 15
  FAFSA: Mar. 15
  CSS PROFILE: Mar. 1

# GOUCHER COLLEGE ✦ Baltimore, MD 21204

| | |
|---|---|
| ENROLLMENT: | 1,400 |
| UNDERGRADUATE: | 1,100 |
| ACCEPTANCE RATE: | 78% |
| SAT RANGE: | 550–650 Verbal |
| | 510–620 Math |
| STICKER PRICE: | $27,000+ |
| NEED-BLIND: | Yes |
| NEED MET: | 100% |
| AVERAGE STUDENT DEBT: | NA |
| MERIT SCHOLARSHIPS: | Many |
| RANGE: | Up to full tuition |
| ATHLETIC SCHOLARSHIPS: | No |
| WEB SITE: | www.goucher.edu |
| PHONE: | (410) 337-6100 |

In the past dozen years, Goucher has executed a remarkable about-face. Once a traditional women's college in the mold of Sweet Briar or Randolph-Macon, Goucher admitted men in 1987 and gave itself a personality transplant in the process. Today's Goucher is artsy, hip, and much more like Sarah Lawrence or Skidmore of New York than any college south of the Mason-Dixon. Goucher gives the liberal arts a preprofessional emphasis with internships, field work, and study abroad. Goucher distributes nearly $5.5 million in non-need-based aid every year, a substantial total for a college with only 1,000 undergraduates. At the top of the heap are the Dean's Scholarships, which cover full tuition for fifteen outstanding students who typically rank in the top 10 percent with SAT I scores averaging about 1350. The Marvin Perry Scholarships give $10,000 to all students who apply with at least a 3.0 academic GPA and a score of 1200 (or an ACT of 27); students with 3.0 and 1100 or 24 get $8,500. Goucher also gives special achievement awards in dance, music, theater, and the visual arts.

*Deadlines:*
  EARLY ACTION: Dec. 1
  REGULAR ADMISSION: Feb. 1
  FAFSA: Feb. 15
  CSS PROFILE: Feb. 15

# GRINNELL COLLEGE ✦ Grinnell, IA 50112

| | |
|---|---|
| TOTAL ENROLLMENT: | 1,400 |
| UNDERGRADUATE | 1,400 |
| ACCEPTANCE RATE: | 69% |
| SAT RANGE: | 630–740 Verbal |
| | 630–710 Math |
| STICKER PRICE: | $24,000+ |
| NEED-BLIND: | Yes |
| NEED MET: | 100% |
| AVERAGE STUDENT DEBT: | $7,500 |
| MERIT SCHOLARSHIPS: | Many |
| RANGE: | Up to $10,000 |
| ATHLETIC SCHOLARSHIPS: | No |
| ROTC: | No |
| WEB SITE: | www.grinnell.edu |
| PHONE: | (800)247-0113 |

If it weren't for the cornfields that stretch hundreds of miles in any direction, Grinnell College could easily be mistaken for a trendy neighborhood in Chicago or New York. Liberal, intellectual, and popular among city dwellers, Grinnell competes with close cousins Carleton and Macalester for honors as the top liberal arts college in the upper Midwest. It's a tough sell to lure all those urbanites to Iowa, but with one of the largest endowments per student of any college in the nation, Grinnell combines a bargain basement sticker price and plenty of financial aid. Grinnell's need-based packages frequently top those of competitors, and students on aid emerge with an average debt of only $7,500. Grinnell is among the few elite institutions that offer a signficant number of merit scholarships. The most lucrative of these is the Grinnell Trustee Honor Scholarship, which tops out at $10,000 per year. National Merit Scholars get up to $2,000 per year and other awards target those who contribute to the community. Approximately 42 percent of a recent freshman class received a non-need award.

*Deadlines:*
  EARLY DECISION: Dec. 1
  REGULAR ADMISSION: Feb. 1
  FAFSA: Feb. 1

# GROVE CITY COLLEGE ◆ Grove City, PA 16127

| | |
|---|---|
| ENROLLMENT: | 2,300 |
| UNDERGRADUATE: | 2,300 |
| ACCEPTANCE RATE: | 42% |
| SAT RANGE: | 590–650 Verbal |
| | 600–650 Math |
| STICKER PRICE: | $11,000+ |
| NEED-BLIND: | Yes |
| NEED MET: | 79% |
| AVERAGE STUDENT DEBT: | $12,200 |
| MERIT SCHOLARSHIPS: | Few |
| RANGE: | Up to full tuition |
| ATHLETIC SCHOLARSHIPS: | No |
| ROTC: | No |
| WEB SITE: | www.gcc.edu |
| PHONE: | (412) 458-2100 |

Grove City is best known for a David-and-Goliath battle against federal regulation that culminated in its withdrawal from federal aid programs. The college is also unabashed in its commitment to individual freedom, traditional values, and a Christian outlook. The combination has made Grove City the darling of social conservatives and sent its popularity soaring. The foundation of a Grove City education is a three-year humanities sequence dedicated to "truth, morality and freedom" within the Western tradition. With a sticker price of less than $12,000, Grove City is remarkably inexpensive for a private college. It is an even better deal for students who are selected for the full-tuition Trustee Academic Scholarship; applicants must sit for a college-administered test in the winter of twelfth grade. Students who were valedictorians or salutatorians of their high school classes get $1,500, and top engineering students vie for four $2,500 awards. Grove City offers some need-based aid, though less than one in five aid recipients in a recent class had full need met. An institutional aid form is required in lieu of the FAFSA.

*Deadlines:*
  EARLY DECISION: Nov. 15
  REGULAR ADMISSION: Feb. 15

# GUILFORD COLLEGE ◆ Greensboro, NC 27410

| | |
|---|---|
| ENROLLMENT: | 1,100 |
| UNDERGRADUATE: | 1,100 |
| ACCEPTANCE RATE: | 81% |
| SAT RANGE: | 520–640 Verbal |
| | 460–610 Math |
| STICKER PRICE: | $22,000+ |
| NEED-BLIND: | Yes |
| NEED MET: | NA |
| AVERAGE STUDENT DEBT: | $12,100 |
| MERIT SCHOLARSHIPS: | Many |
| Range: | Up to full costs |
| ATHLETIC SCHOLARSHIPS: | No |
| ROTC: | Army, Air Force |
| WEB SITE: | www.guilford.edu |
| PHONE: | (800) 992-7759 |

Guilford is one of the few Southern schools that puts the "liberal" back into liberal arts. Founded by the Society of Friends and still imbued with Quaker principles, Guilford attracts progressive-minded students from across the Southeast and beyond. The list of Guilford values includes "justice, simplicity, team building, and conflict resolution through non-violent means." With few close cousins in the South, Guilford has more in common with Midwestern schools such as Earlham and Oberlin. At the high end of Guilford's merit awards is the Guilford Scholars, which delivers full costs plus books and a $1,000 travel stipend to five recipients per year. The Honors Scholarship offers $7,500 to full tuition for selected students in the top 10 percent of their high school class with a GPA of 3.5 and a combined SAT I of 1300 or ACT of 29. Additional awards honor those with lesser credentials, and scholarships of $1,500 to $2,000 are available for leadership, community service, and interest in a business career. Scholarship hopefuls are "encouraged" to apply for admission by January 1.

*Deadlines:*
  EARLY DECISION: Dec. 1
  REGULAR ADMISSION: Feb. 1
  FAFSA: Mar. 1
  CSS PROFILE: Mar. 1

## GUSTAVUS ADOLPHUS COLLEGE ◆ St. Peter, MN 56082

| | |
|---|---|
| ENROLLMENT: | 2,400 |
| UNDERGRADUATE: | 2,400 |
| ACCEPTANCE RATE: | 83% |
| SAT RANGE: | 540–660 Verbal |
| | 560–660 Math |
| STICKER PRICE: | $21,000+ |
| NEED-BLIND: | Yes |
| NEED MET: | NA |
| AVERAGE STUDENT DEBT: | $16,000 |
| MERIT SCHOLARSHIPS: | Many |
| RANGE: | Up to $10,000 |
| ATHLETIC SCHOLARSHIPS: | No |
| ROTC: | Army |
| WEB SITE: | www.gustavus.edu |
| PHONE: | (800) 487-8288 |

Gustavus Adolphus owes its distinctive name to a seventeenth-century Swedish king who won fame and glory in the Thirty Years War. The college's ancient Lutheran heritage is still alive today in its emphasis on Western history and culture, and in its notable Scandinavian studies program. Gustavus prides itself on close interaction between students and faculty and the unusually large number of undergraduates who do their own research. Located in southern Minnesota, Gustavus competes head-to-head with the state's other notable Lutheran liberal arts college, St. Olaf. The college's Partners in Scholarship program gives awards of $7,500 to thirty-five top incoming students with at least a 1400 on the SAT I or an ACT of 32. National Merit Finalists can receive up to $10,000, and Trustee Scholarships give $1,000 to $5,000 to other students with a strong academic record. Awards of up to $2,000 are given for music, theater, and dance, a $1,500 award is available for community service, and $2,500 is awarded to children and grandchildren of alumni who show academic achievement.

*Deadlines:*
    EARLY DECISION: Dec. 1
    EARLY ACTION: Feb. 15
    REGULAR ADMISSION: Apr. 15
    FAFSA: Apr. 15

## HAMILTON COLLEGE ◆ Clinton, NY 13323

| | |
|---|---|
| TOTAL ENROLLMENT: | 1,700 |
| UNDERGRADUATE: | 1,700 |
| ACCEPTANCE RATE: | 42% |
| SAT AVERAGES: | 642 Verbal |
| | 644 Math |
| STICKER PRICE: | $30,000+ |
| NEED-BLIND: | No |
| NEED MET: | 100% |
| AVERAGE STUDENT DEBT: | $16,500 |
| MERIT SCHOLARSHIPS: | Few |
| RANGE: | Up to $10,000 |
| ATHLETIC SCHOLARSHIPS: | No |
| ROTC: | Army |
| WEB SITE: | www.hamilton.edu |
| PHONE: | (315) 859-4421 |

Set on a secluded hilltop in upstate New York, Hamilton College maintains a quietly prestigious aura. Hamilton is a 150-year-old bastion of the tried and true in liberal arts education with a progressive streak dating from its merger in the late '70s with artsy sister school Kirkland College. With an enrollment of 1,700, Hamilton is slightly smaller than competitors such as Colgate (2,800), Middlebury (2,200), and Williams (2,100) and emphasizes the personal touch. Hamilton's biggest academic draw is government, with economics and history runners-up in popularity. After years of offering aid only on the basis of need, Hamilton now gives merit money via the Bristol Scholars Program, which provides ten outstanding students up to $10,000 per year, a research stipend, and other special treatment. The Schambach Scholars Program gives ten other students need-based aid packages without loans for all four years. There is also $2,000 per year for National Merit Finalists who designate Hamilton as their first choice. The college maintains a financial aid waiting list for a handful of borderline candidates at the end of the admission process.

*Deadlines:*
    EARLY DECISION: Nov. 15, Jan. 10
    REGULAR ADMISSION: Jan. 15
    FAFSA: Feb. 1
    CSS PROFILE: Feb. 1

## HAMPDEN-SYDNEY COLLEGE ◆ Hampden-Sydney, VA 23943

| | |
|---|---|
| ENROLLMENT: | 1,000 |
| UNDERGRADUATE: | 1,000 |
| ACCEPTANCE RATE: | 85% |
| SAT RANGE: | 510–610 Verbal |
| | 510–630 Math |
| STICKER PRICE: | $20,000+ |
| NEED-BLIND: | Yes |
| NEED MET: | 92% |
| AVERAGE STUDENT DEBT: | $13,800 |
| MERIT SCHOLARSHIPS: | Many |
| RANGE: | Up to $15,000 |
| ATHLETIC SCHOLARSHIPS: | No |
| ROTC: | Army |
| WEB SITE: | www.hsc.edu |
| PHONE: | (800) 755-0733 |

Though "Carry Me Back to Old Virginny" is no longer its official state song, the spirit of old Virginia is alive and well at Hampden-Sydney College. Founded in 1776, Hampden-Sydney remains true to its original mission "to form good men and good citizens." Along with Wabash in Indiana, Hampden-Sydney is the last of the traditional, selective, nonmilitary all-male colleges. Set on 820 acres in the heart of Virginia's rural south side, the college has turned out generations of doctors, lawyers, and businessmen. (Biology and economics are the most popular majors.) Hampden-Sydney's most lucrative merit award is the Allan Scholarship, which gives $15,000 to students in the top 5 percent of their high school class who score 1400 or better on the SAT I. Two additional scholarship levels give $11,250 and $7,500, respectively, to students with slightly lesser credentials; the latter requires a top 15 percent rank and an SAT score 1250 or better. The college also offers Achievement Awards of $3,000 to those in the top 30 percent who score at least 1200. About 20 percent of the entering students get a non-need scholarship.

*Deadlines:*
EARLY DECISION: Nov. 15
REGULAR ADMISSION: Mar. 1
FAFSA: Mar. 1
CSS PROFILE: Mar. 1

## HAMPSHIRE COLLEGE ◆ Amherst, MA 01002

| | |
|---|---|
| ENROLLMENT: | 1,200 |
| UNDERGRADUATE: | 1,200 |
| ACCEPTANCE RATE: | 66% |
| SAT RANGE: | 590–690 Verbal |
| | 540–650 Math |
| STICKER PRICE: | $31,000+ |
| NEED-BLIND: | Yes |
| NEED MET: | 100% |
| AVERAGE STUDENT DEBT: | $15,300 |
| MERIT SCHOLARSHIPS: | Many |
| RANGE: | Up to $7,500 |
| ATHLETIC SCHOLARSHIPS: | No |
| ROTC: | No |
| WEB SITE: | www.hampshire.edu |
| PHONE: | (413) 559-5471 |

The word "experimental" pops up frequently in descriptions of Hampshire College, a child of the 1960s that has been nurtured to adulthood by membership in the prestigious Five College Consortium that includes Amherst, Mount Holyoke, Smith, and the University of Massachusetts. All Hampshire students design their own academic programs, and interdisciplinary learning is a prime emphasis. Hampshire's Experimental School of Cognitive Science, for instance, examines "the mind, the brain, and computing technology" from a variety of perspectives. The arts are Hampshire's main draw, and the film program is basking in the fame of alumnus Ken Burns. About 15 percent of Hampshire's entering students receive a non-need award. Up to ten students of color get $7,500, and ten more top students get $5,000 to $7,500. Other awards include $2,500 for an outstanding female student, two awards of $3,000 to $5,000 to students from Springfield, Massachusetts, and $5,000 to a participant in the A Better Chance program. The college also offers matching funds for National Service Education Award recipients.

*Deadlines:*
EARLY DECISION: Nov. 15
EARLY ACTION: Jan. 1
REGULAR ADMISSION: Feb. 1
FAFSA: Feb. 1
CSS PROFILE: Feb. 1

## HAMPTON UNIVERSITY ✦ Hampton, VA 23368

| | |
|---|---|
| ENROLLMENT: | 5,700 |
| UNDERGRADUATE: | 4,600 |
| ACCEPTANCE RATE: | 49% |
| SAT RANGE: | NA |
| STICKER PRICE: | $15,000+ |
| NEED-BLIND: | Yes |
| NEED MET: | NA |
| AVERAGE STUDENT DEBT: | $17,100 |
| MERIT SCHOLARSHIPS: | Many |
| RANGE: | Up to full costs |
| ATHLETIC SCHOLARSHIPS: | Yes |
| ROTC: | Army, Navy |
| WEB SITE: | www.hamptonu.edu |
| PHONE: | (800) 624-3328 |

Founded in the aftermath of the Civil War, Hampton is one of the leading historically black institutions in the nation. The university occupies a picturesque location near the mouth of the Chesapeake Bay across from Norfolk. The city of Hampton is notable for its annual jazz festival, which is co-sponsored by the university. Hampton offers degrees in the liberal arts and sciences, as well as in professional fields such as architecture, pharmacy, and business. Accounting is the largest major. With a sticker price of less than $16,000, Hampton is a sweet deal by private university standards. Heading the list of merit scholarships is the Presidential Scholars Award, which gives up to full tuition and room and board to exceptional students in the top 10 percent of their high school class with scores of 1200 on the SAT I or 28 on the ACT. Academic Achievers Awards offer $1,000 to $3,500 to those in the top 20 percent with 1100 or 24. Students should apply for both by February 28. Other awards with various stipulations are available.

*Deadlines:*
  ADMISSION: Mar. 15
  FAFSA: Mar. 1

## HANOVER COLLEGE ✦ Hanover, IN 47243

| | |
|---|---|
| ENROLLMENT: | 1,100 |
| UNDERGRADUATE: | 1,100 |
| ACCEPTANCE RATE: | 86% |
| SAT RANGE: | 500–610 Verbal |
| | 520–620 Math |
| STICKER PRICE: | $15,000+ |
| NEED-BLIND: | Yes |
| NEED MET: | NA |
| AVERAGE STUDENT DEBT: | $8,800 |
| MERIT SCHOLARSHIPS: | Many |
| RANGE: | Up to full costs |
| ATHLETIC SCHOLARSHIPS: | No |
| ROTC: | No |
| WEB SITE: | www.hanover.edu |
| PHONE: | (800) 213-2178 |

Set on 650 acres that overlook the Ohio River in southern Indiana, Hanover is a Midwestern bastion of traditional liberal arts education. The cornerstone of a Hanover education is the unusually close relationship between students and faculty; nearly half the latter reside with their families on school grounds. Hanover's calendar includes a month-long term at the end of the school year that facilitates internships and study abroad, and the college offers a special fund to support student-designed individual projects. With a sticker price under $16,000, Hanover makes the list of best private college bargains, with help from an endowment per student that ranks ahead of such titans as Cornell, Duke, and Johns Hopkins. Hanover offers seven categories of merit scholarships for various degrees of academic excellence that range from full costs to $1,500. The most prestigious of these require a top 10 percent high school ranking and at least a 1200 on the SAT I or 27 on the ACT for consideration, as well as an application for admission by January 15. A $2,000 scholarship is available for musicians.

*Deadlines:*
  EARLY ACTION: Dec. 1
  ADMISSION: Mar. 1
  FAFSA: Feb. 15
  CSS PROFILE: Feb. 15

# HARTWICK COLLEGE ◆ Oneonta, NY 13820

| | |
|---|---|
| ENROLLMENT: | 1,500 |
| UNDERGRADUATE: | 1,500 |
| ACCEPTANCE RATE: | 90% |
| SAT RANGE: | 510–620 Verbal |
| | 500–610 Math |
| STICKER PRICE: | $29,000+ |
| NEED-BLIND: | Yes |
| NEED MET: | 90% |
| AVERAGE STUDENT DEBT: | $19,600 |
| MERIT SCHOLARSHIPS: | Many |
| RANGE: | Up to $20,000 |
| ATHLETIC SCHOLARSHIPS: | Yes |
| ROTC: | No |
| WEB SITE: | www.hartwick.edu |
| PHONE: | (888) HARTWICK |

There is no such thing as a money-back guarantee in higher education, but Hartwick College comes close. Under its Guaranteed Placement Program, any student who maintains a 3.0 GPA and completes designated co-curricular activities will get a paid internship courtesy of the board of trustees if he or she is unemployed six months after graduation. That sort of commitment is typical of this small institution in upstate New York, which offers a main course of the liberal arts with side dishes in business and nursing. For students at the top of the class with standardized test scores to match, Hartwick offers merit scholarships that range up to $20,000 per year. Valedictorians and salutatorians automatically get at least $10,000. Faculty Recognition Scholarships offer up to $8,000 to students who have at least a 3.0 average and rank in the top half of their class. Additional awards target children and grandchildren of alumni and those who have demonstrated leadership. Athletic scholarships are available only in men's soccer.

*Deadlines:*
  EARLY DECISION: Dec. 1, Jan. 15
  REGULAR ADMISSION: Feb. 15
  FAFSA: Feb. 15
  CSS PROFILE: Feb. 15

# HARVARD UNIVERSITY ◆ Cambridge, MA 02138

| | |
|---|---|
| ENROLLMENT: | 18,200 |
| UNDERGRADUATE: | 6,600 |
| ACCEPTANCE RATE: | 13% |
| SAT RANGE: | 700–790 Verbal |
| | 690–790 Math |
| STICKER PRICE: | $31,000+ |
| NEED-BLIND: | Yes |
| NEED MET: | 100% |
| AVERAGE STUDENT DEBT: | $15,200 |
| MERIT SCHOLARSHIPS: | None |
| ATHLETIC SCHOLARSHIPS: | No |
| ROTC: | Army, Navy, Air Force |
| WEB SITE: | www.harvard.edu |
| PHONE: | (617) 495-1551 |

The most telling statistic about Harvard University isn't the average SAT score of its students or the number of Nobel Laureates strolling its campus. With more top students in its applicant pool than any other university in the solar system, the real eye-opener is that fully 80 percent of those who are admitted decide to enroll. Not many students have the moxie to turn down a Harvard acceptance. Part of Harvard's appeal lies in the bustle of Cambridge and its assortment of restaurants, book stores, and watering holes. Beyond, there is Boston. A galaxy of opportunities awaits in the classroom, where the most popular majors include economics, government, and biology. Harvard gives away nearly $40 million of financial aid per year, but only on the basis of need. In response to similar moves by other Ivys, Harvard recently decided to add $2,000 per year to every need-based grant it awards. And those on financial aid who win outside scholarships now get to keep the full amount of their Harvard grant, where possible, with the outside scholarship used to reduce loans.

*Deadlines:*
  EARLY ACTION: Nov. 1 (Oct. 15 recommended)
  REGULAR ADMISSION: Jan. 1 (Dec. 15 recommended)
  FAFSA: Feb. 1
  CSS PROFILE: Feb. 1

## HARVEY MUDD COLLEGE ◆ Claremont, CA 91711

| | |
|---|---|
| ENROLLMENT: | 700 |
| UNDERGRADUATE: | 700 |
| ACCEPTANCE RATE: | 43% |
| SAT RANGE: | 660–770 Verbal |
| | 720–790 Math |
| STICKER PRICE: | $29,000+ |
| NEED-BLIND: | No |
| NEED MET: | 100% |
| AVERAGE STUDENT DEBT: | $15,800 |
| MERIT SCHOLARSHIPS: | Few |
| RANGE: | Up to $5,000 |
| ATHLETIC SCHOLARSHIPS: | No |
| ROTC: | Army, Air Force |
| WEB SITE: | www.hmc.edu |
| PHONE: | (909) 621-8011 |

Harvey Mudd is the greatest institution devoted to science and engineering that most people have never heard of. With average SAT scores that trump the Ivy League, Harvey Mudd attracts an elite corps of science geniuses who experience first-hand the benefits of small classes with no graduate students. Though it enrolls only 700 students, Harvey Mudd shares its Claremont location with four siblings—Claremont McKenna, Pitzer, Pomoma, and Scripps—which bring total enrollment in the neighborhood to approximately 5,000. Primarily a tech school, HMC places more emphasis on the humanities and social sciences than most of its competitors. Since its founding in 1955, a higher percentage of Harvey Mudd students have gone for a Ph.D. than at any other institution in the nation. Most aid at HMC is based on need, but exceptionally high achievers are awarded a $5,000 Harvey Mudd Scholarship. The college also gives National Merit Finalists an award of $750 to $2,000 depending on need. A total of 50 non-need scholarships were given to freshmen in a recent year.

*Deadlines:*
   EARLY DECISION: Nov. 15
   REGULAR ADMISSION: Jan. 15
   FAFSA: Feb. 1
   CSS PROFILE: Feb. 1

## HAVERFORD COLLEGE ◆ Haverford, PA 19041

| | |
|---|---|
| ENROLLMENT: | 1,100 |
| UNDERGRADUATE: | 1,100 |
| ACCEPTANCE RATE: | 34% |
| SAT RANGE: | 640–720 Verbal |
| | 630–730 Math |
| STICKER PRICE: | $31,000+ |
| NEED-BLIND: | Yes |
| NEED MET: | 100% |
| AVERAGE STUDENT DEBT: | $13,300 |
| MERIT SCHOLARSHIPS: | None |
| ATHLETIC SCHOLARSHIPS: | No |
| ROTC: | No |
| WEB SITE: | www.haverford.edu |
| PHONE: | (610) 896-1350 |

Between feminist Bryn Mawr and quirky intellectual Swarthmore, Haverford is the down-to-earth sibling among Philadelphia's trio of outstanding liberal arts colleges. Haverford is only a mile from Bryn Mawr, and the two continue close ties that began in the days when Haverford was a men's college, though Haverford itself now enrolls more women than men. Students can take courses or major at either one. Haverford's self-contained 204-acre campus looks like a park and comes complete with a duck pond, nature walk, Zen garden, and 400 species of trees and shrubs. In keeping with its Quaker heritage, the college has an air of easy informality and a century-old honor code that allows for self-proctored exams and gives students a voice in college governance. All financial aid at Haverford is based on need, and the college meets the full need of all admitted applicants. In keeping with the spirit of the honor code, applicants who express their intention to enroll are not required to make a deposit before the tuition bill arrives.

*Deadlines:*
   EARLY DECISION: Nov. 15
   REGULAR ADMISSION: Jan. 15
   FAFSA: Jan. 31
   CSS PROFILE: Jan. 31

# UNIVERSITY OF HAWAII • Honolulu, HI 96822

| | |
|---|---|
| ENROLLMENT: | 17,400 |
| UNDERGRADUATE: | 17,400 |
| ACCEPTANCE RATE: | 69% |
| SAT RANGE: | 460–560 Verbal |
| | 510–610 Math |
| STICKER PRICE: | In-state, $9,000 |
| | Out-of-state, $15,000 |
| NEED-BLIND: | Yes |
| NEED MET: | 98% |
| AVERAGE STUDENT DEBT: | $9,800 |
| MERIT SCHOLARSHIPS: | Many |
| ATHLETIC SCHOLARSHIPS: | Yes |
| ROTC: | Army, Air Force |
| WEB SITE: | www.hawaii.edu/uhinfo.html |
| PHONE: | (808) 956-8975 |

A lot of mainlanders fantasize about going to college in Hawaii, and for the few who actually follow through, the University of Hawaii at Manoa is probably the best bet. As Hawaii's flagship public institution, the university styles itself "the premier institution of higher learning and research in the Pacific Basin." Located on 300 acres in Honolulu, Manoa offers leading programs in marine sciences, evolutionary biology, international business, and Asian/Pacific studies. Elementary education and accounting top the list of most popular majors. The remarkably diverse student body includes roughly equal numbers of Caucasians, Japanese, Filipinos, and native Hawaiians, and Manoa gives instruction in more foreign languages than any university in the nation. With Manoa's low in-state tuition, less than a third of the students qualify for need-based aid. The university offers a range of merit and merit-within-need awards, most for modest sums. Bigger money is available in the form of approximately 300 athletic scholarships, which average approximately $3,500 per year.

*Deadlines:*
   ADMISSION: May 1
   FAFSA: Mar. 1

# HENDRIX COLLEGE • Conway, AR 72032

| | |
|---|---|
| ENROLLMENT: | 1,000 |
| UNDERGRADUATE: | 1,000 |
| ACCEPTANCE RATE: | 89% |
| SAT RANGE: | 560–680 Verbal |
| | 540–650 Math |
| STICKER PRICE: | $15,000+ |
| NEED-BLIND: | Yes |
| NEED MET: | 87% |
| AVERAGE STUDENT DEBT: | $13,200 |
| MERIT SCHOLARSHIPS: | Many |
| RANGE: | Up to full costs |
| ATHLETIC SCHOLARSHIPS: | No |
| ROTC: | Army |
| WEB SITE: | www.hendrix.edu |
| PHONE: | (800) 277-9017 |

Situated in an Arkansas town best-known for its annual Toad Suck Daze Festival, Hendrix is a lot more progressive than an outsider might expect. With an enrollment of only 1,000, Hendrix has become a regional magnet for bright and ambitious students who don't fit the cookie-cutter mold that prevails at nearby state universities. With a sticker price under $16,000 per year, Hendrix is roughly half the price of the most expensive private colleges, and the college's ample supply of merit scholarships and discounts can help lower the out-of-pocket expense even further. Priority for academic merit scholarships is given to those who apply for admission by January 15, and all candidates must interview with a faculty member. Scholarships come at a variety of levels ranging up to full costs; students with approximately a 3.0 GPA and an SAT I of 1140 or ACT of 25 are encouraged to compete. Other awards are available for leadership ($2,000), performing arts (up to $1,000) and those active in United Methodist Youth ministries ($3,000). National Merit Finalists who name Hendrix as their first choice are guaranteed $6,500.

*Deadlines:*
   ADMISSION: Apr. 1
   FAFSA: Feb. 15

# HILLSDALE COLLEGE ✦ Hillsdale, MI 49242

| | |
|---|---|
| ENROLLMENT: | 1,200 |
| UNDERGRADUATE: | 1,200 |
| ACCEPTANCE RATE: | 83% |
| SAT RANGE: | 570–690 Verbal |
| | 520–660 Math |
| STICKER PRICE: | $19,000+ |
| NEED-BLIND: | Yes |
| NEED MET: | 73% |
| AVERAGE STUDENT DEBT: | $18,000 |
| MERIT SCHOLARSHIPS: | Many |
| RANGE: | Up to full tuition |
| ATHLETIC SCHOLARSHIPS: | Yes |
| ROTC: | No |
| WEB SITE: | www.hillsdale.edu |
| PHONE: | (517) 437-7341 |

Fiercely independent and unabashedly conservative, Hillsdale appeals to students who are disillusioned with political correctness and multiculturalism. Hillsdale's curriculum emphasizes "modern man's intellectual and spiritual inheritance from the Judeo-Christian faith and Greco-Roman culture." Though Hillsdale is independent of any particular denomination, evangelicals comprise a significant fraction of the student body. When it comes to choosing a major, business administration is Hillsdale's most popular. Like counterpart Grove City, Hillsdale refuses to accept government funding of any kind. That includes money for financial aid, but the college puts $6 million of its own money into need-based grants and offers both loans and work-study. Academic scholarships are available to those in the top 10 percent of their high school class with comparable standardized test scores. Scholarship candidates must submit an application for admission by January 1, and awards range from $1,000 up to full tuition. Top scholarships require an on-campus interview with the Scholarship Selection Committee.

*Deadlines:*
  ADMISSION: July 15
  FAFSA: Mar. 15
  CSS PROFILE: Mar. 15

# HIRAM COLLEGE ✦ Hiram, OH 44234

| | |
|---|---|
| ENROLLMENT: | 800 |
| UNDERGRADUATE: | 800 |
| ACCEPTANCE RATE: | 88% |
| SAT RANGE: | 510–630 Verbal |
| | 500–630 Math |
| STICKER PRICE: | $23,000+ |
| NEED-BLIND: | Yes |
| NEED MET: | 97% |
| AVERAGE STUDENT DEBT: | $16,200 |
| MERIT SCHOLARSHIPS: | Many |
| RANGE: | Up to $12,000 |
| ATHLETIC SCHOLARSHIPS: | No |
| ROTC: | No |
| WEB SITE: | www.hiram.edu |
| PHONE: | (800) 362-5280 |

Nestled in a quiet corner of northeast Ohio about thirty-five miles from Cleveland, Hiram specializes in Midwestern friendliness and close relationships between students and professors. Students are paired with their faculty advisors during a week-long orientation program before classes begin, and the association continues throughout the year in a required seminar taught by the advisor. Hiram's unusual calendar includes two twelve-week semesters that are each followed by three-week sessions, and the latter provide additional opportunity for independent and small group work with professors. Hiram offers a bushel of merit scholarships for good and excellent students, highlighted by the $12,000-per-year Trustee Scholarships. Some awards target students who plan to major in specific fields (up to $10,000); others recognize musical talent ($1,400), residency in a particular geographical area (up to $3,000), membership in a minority group ($2,000), and students chosen by their high schools as Hugh O'Brien Youth Ambassadors ($2,000). Priority consideration for merit awards is given to students who apply by February 1.

*Deadlines:*
  ADMISSION: Mar. 15
  FAFSA: Feb. 15

# HOBART AND WILLIAM SMITH COLLEGES ♦
## Geneva, NY 14456

| | |
|---|---|
| TOTAL ENROLLMENT | 1,800 |
| UNDERGRADUATE: | 1,800 |
| ACCEPTANCE RATE: | 76% |
| SAT RANGE: | 520–610 Verbal |
| | 520–610 Math |
| STICKER PRICE: | $31,000+ |
| NEED-BLIND: | Yes |
| NEED MET: | 90% |
| AVERAGE STUDENT DEBT: | $14,300 |
| MERIT SCHOLARSHIPS: | Many |
| RANGE: | Up to full tuition |
| ATHLETIC SCHOLARSHIPS: | No |
| ROTC: | No |
| WEB SITE: | www.hws.edu |
| PHONE: | (800) 852-2256 (Hobart) |
| | (800) 245-0100 (William Smith) |

Hobart and William Smith are two coordinate colleges, one for men and one for women, that preserve separate identities while jointly offering most academic programs from a shared campus in upstate New York. The separation gives HWS a more traditional atmosphere than the typical coed campus. Male camaraderie and Greek letter fraternities flourish on the Hobart side; William Smith women partake of traditions and support services typical of women's colleges. The men's lacrosse team, a perennial national championship contender, is the focal point of campus spirit.(A separate application is due January 1.) Students in the top 10 percent of their class with 1250 or higher on the SAT I can compete for the Trustee Scholarship, which offers $10,000 to full tuition. Students with slightly lower credentials are eligible for awards of $3,000 to $8,000, and Presidential Leaders Scholarships offer a similar amount to students with "exemplary leadership skills and personal qualities." Outstanding artists who file a separate application by January 1 are eligible for awards of $7,500. Roughly one-fourth of entering HWS students get a merit scholarship.

*Deadlines:*
EARLY DECISION: Nov. 15, Jan. 1
REGULAR ADMISSION: Feb. 1
FAFSA: Feb. 15
CSS PROFILE: Feb. 15

# HOFSTRA UNIVERSITY ♦
## Hempstead, NY 11549

| | |
|---|---|
| TOTAL ENROLLMENT: | 12,600 |
| UNDERGRADUATE: | 8,700 |
| ACCEPTANCE RATE: | 83% |
| SAT RANGE: | 490–580 Verbal |
| | 490–590 Math |
| STICKER PRICE: | $22,000+ |
| NEED-BLIND: | Yes |
| NEED MET: | 53% |
| AVERAGE STUDENT DEBT: | NA |
| MERIT SCHOLARSHIPS: | Many |
| RANGE: | Up to full tuition |
| ATHLETIC SCHOLARSHIPS: | Yes |
| ROTC: | Army |
| WEB SITE: | www.hofstra.edu |
| PHONE: | (800) HOFSTRA |

A relative newcomer to the ranks of major universities, Hofstra has carved its niche by delivering preprofessional training to students from Long Island and Queens. Hofstra's school of communications is well-regarded and known for its offerings in television and media. The School of Business is home to popular programs in accounting and marketing, and the performing arts have a strong reputation. Hofstra's top merit award is the Distinguished Academic Scholar Program, which offers full tuition to students with a minimum of 1300 on the SAT I or 29 on the ACT. Four other programs extend scholarships of at least $2,000 to those who rank in the top 30 percent of their high school class with scores of at least 1380 or 31, and to those with a higher rank (top 10 percent) and minimum scores of 1170 or 23. Variable grants are offered to those who excel in art, athletics, communications, dance, drama, or music, and Middle Income Awards of $500 to $1,000 give modest relief to families making $18,000 to $35,000 a year.

*Deadlines:*
EARLY DECISION: Dec. 1
ADMISSION: Feb. 15
FAFSA: Rolling

## HOLLINS UNIVERSITY ✦ Roanoke, VA 24020

| | |
|---|---|
| TOTAL ENROLLMENT: | 1,100 |
| UNDERGRADUATE: | 900 |
| ACCEPTANCE RATE: | 85% |
| SAT RANGE: | 530–650 Verbal |
| | 480–590 Math |
| STICKER PRICE: | $22,000+ |
| NEED-BLIND: | Yes |
| NEED MET: | 98% |
| AVERAGE STUDENT DEBT: | $17,000 |
| MERIT SCHOLARSHIPS: | Many |
| RANGE: | Up to $15,000 |
| ATHLETIC SCHOLARSHIPS: | No |
| ROTC: | No |
| WEB SITE: | www.hollins.edu |
| PHONE: | (800) 456-9595 |

After 156 years as a small women's college, Hollins recently became a "university" to call attention to its tiny graduate program. But the essence of Hollins is still small classes and close working relationships between students and faculty. Set on a beautiful 475-acre campus on the outskirts of a medium-sized city, Hollins is best known for its creative writing program that has produced a number of noted authors including Pulitzer Prize–winner Annie Dillard. The Hollins Scholars program gives $8,000 to $15,000 to at least ten outstanding freshmen who are in the top 10 percent of their high school class with at SAT I score of 1300. (The deadline is February 1.) The most talented music students who plan to major in voice have the chance for a special deal: a half-tuition scholarship that includes funds for lessons, an accompanist and summer study. Additional scholarships of up to $7,500 a year are parceled out to students who excel in everything from community service to the creative arts, and a $5,000 award targets those who have shown leadership ability.

*Deadlines:*
    EARLY DECISION: Dec. 1
    REGULAR ADMISSION: Feb. 15
    FAFSA: Mar. 1

## COLLEGE OF THE HOLY CROSS ✦ Worcester, MA 01610

| | |
|---|---|
| TOTAL ENROLLMENT: | 2,700 |
| UNDERGRADUATE: | 2,700 |
| ACCEPTANCE RATE: | 50% |
| SAT AVERAGE: | 628 Verbal |
| | 623 Math |
| STICKER PRICE: | $29,000+ |
| NEED-BLIND: | Yes |
| NEED MET: | 100% |
| AVERAGE STUDENT DEBT: | $17,500 |
| MERIT SCHOLARSHIPS: | Few |
| RANGE: | Up to full tuition |
| ATHLETIC SCHOLARSHIPS: | Yes |
| ROTC: | Army, Navy, Air Force |
| WEB SITE: | www.holycross.edu |
| PHONE: | (800) 442-2421 |

Though founded in 1843, Holy Cross traces its lineage back 300 years earlier to Ignatius of Loyola, famed founder of the Jesuits. Holy Cross is the smallest of the leading Catholic institutions—Boston College, Georgetown, and Notre Dame are all three times as large—and HC is known for its strong sense of community and fierce alumni loyalty. Religious life also plays a more prominent role at Holy Cross than elsewhere, although academic requirements are limited to one course in religion and one in philosophy. HC's picturesque campus is set high on a hill overlooking the city of Worcester, a nondescript industrial city with the saving grace of being an hour from Boston. The overwhelming majority of financial aid at Holy Cross is based on need, but full-tuition merit scholarships are available for a few top students interested in classics or music. The only other avenue to merit money is via ROTC. Navy ROTC is offered on campus, and Army and Air Force programs are within easy reach at nearby Worcester Polytechnic Institute.

*Deadlines:*
    EARLY DECISION: Dec. 15
    REGULAR ADMISSION: Jan. 15
    FAFSA: Feb. 1
    CSS PROFILE: Feb. 1

# HOPE COLLEGE ◆ Holland, MI 49422

| | |
|---|---|
| TOTAL ENROLLMENT: | 2,900 |
| UNDERGRADUATE: | 2,900 |
| ACCEPTANCE RATE: | 92% |
| SAT RANGE: | 1090–1310 combined |
| STICKER PRICE: | $21,000+ |
| NEED-BLIND: | Yes |
| NEED MET: | 90% |
| AVERAGE STUDENT DEBT: | $16,100 |
| MERIT SCHOLARSHIPS: | Many |
| RANGE: | Up to $12,000 |
| ATHLETIC SCHOLARSHIPS: | No |
| ROTC: | No |
| WEB SITE: | www.hope.edu |
| PHONE: | (800) 968-7850 |

It is no accident that Hope College offers a study abroad program in Jerusalem. As one of the foremost evangelical colleges in the nation, Hope maintains a twin commitment to Christian faith and academic excellence. With 2,900 undergraduates, Hope is smaller than archrival Calvin, but its curriculum includes a broad range of offerings from engineering to nursing. Business administration is the most popular major. Hope offers a flotilla of merit awards, notably the $12,000 Trustee Scholarship that requires an application for admission filed by January 20. Students with a 3.5 GPA and a combined SAT I of 1140 or an ACT of 25 are eligible for an Alumni Honors Scholarship of $3,000. Five other categories of scholarships are available, including $12,000 for National Merit Finalists and $5,000 for high school valedictorians. The Distinguished Artist Awards bestow $2,500 per year to students in the visual arts, dance, music, and theatre, and the Biomedical Scholarship gives $8,000 to one Michigan minority student interested in medicine.

*Deadlines:*
  ADMISSION: Feb. 1 (priority)
  FAFSA: Feb. 15
  CSS PROFILE: Feb. 15

# HOUGHTON COLLEGE ◆ Houghton, NY 14744

| | |
|---|---|
| TOTAL ENROLLMENT: | 1,400 |
| UNDERGRADUATE: | 1,400 |
| ACCEPTANCE RATE: | 85% |
| SAT RANGE: | 540–660 Verbal |
| | 500–640 Math |
| STICKER PRICE: | $18,000+ |
| NEED-BLIND: | Yes |
| NEED MET: | 86% |
| AVERAGE STUDENT DEBT: | $13,900 |
| MERIT SCHOLARSHIPS: | Many |
| RANGE: | Up to $11,000 |
| ATHLETIC SCHOLARSHIPS: | Yes |
| ROTC: | Army |
| WEB SITE: | www.houghton.edu |
| PHONE: | (800) 777-2556 |

The rolling hills of western New York are home to Houghton College, a devoutly Christian liberal arts college affiliated with the Wesleyan Church. While old-time religion is the bedrock of a Houghton education, the latest technology is also evident in its requirement that all first-year students acquire a laptop. Perhaps Houghton's most innovative offering is its First Year Honors Program, which takes participants to London for the spring semester. The Houghton Heritage Scholarships of up to $11,000 are bestowed on three students who are at the top of their high school class with an SAT I of at least 1300 or an ACT of 29. Students who are above 1200 or 26 and rank in the top 15 percent are eligible for awards up to $5,000. Other scholarships are available for artists, members of the Wesleyan Church, and those whose parents are in full-time Christian service. There is also a Three-in-Family Grant of approximately $1,650. As a carrot for those north of the border, Houghton accepts Canadian currency at par.

*Deadlines:*
  REGULAR ADMISSION: Mar. 15
  FAFSA: Mar. 15

## UNIVERSITY OF HOUSTON ◆
## Houston, TX 77204

| | |
|---|---|
| TOTAL ENROLLMENT: | 31,600 |
| UNDERGRADUATE: | 23,600 |
| ACCEPTANCE RATE: | 70% |
| SAT RANGE: | 440–570 Verbal |
| | 460–590 Math |
| STICKER PRICE: | In-state, $7,000+ |
| | Out-of-state, $12,000+ |
| NEED-BLIND: | Yes |
| NEED MET: | NA |
| AVERAGE STUDENT DEBT: | NA |
| MERIT SCHOLARSHIPS: | Many |
| RANGE: | Up to full costs |
| ATHLETIC SCHOLARSHIPS: | Yes |
| ROTC: | Army |
| WEB SITE: | www.uh.edu |
| Phone: | (713) 743-1010 |

The University of Houston's moment in the sun occurred in the early 1980s, when basketball greats Hakeem Olajuwon and Clyde Drexler soared for slam dunks. UH's academic prowess is less well known, though strong programs are available in engineering, business, and hotel and restaurant management (the latter funded by millions from Conrad Hilton). The best bet in the liberal arts is UH's honors program, which emphasizes Western cultural heritage. In-staters get a rare deal at UH—tuition and fees under $2,000—and even out-of-staters pay only a fraction of what they might at a private university. UH gives National Merit Finalists a full ride when they designate the university as their first choice, and students who rank in the top 10 percent and score at least 1180 on the SAT I or 26 on the ACT can compete for up to $3,000. The Cullen Leadership Scholarship of up to $4,000 honors students with exceptional all-around achievement, and children of alumni get a $1,000 award. Students seeking a scholarship must apply by April 1.

*Deadlines:*
  ADMISSION: July 1
  FAFSA: Apr. 1

## HOWARD UNIVERSITY ◆
## Washington, DC 20059

| | |
|---|---|
| TOTAL ENROLLMENT: | 10,400 |
| UNDERGRADUATE: | 6,700 |
| ACCEPTANCE RATE: | 58% |
| SAT AVERAGE: | 513 Verbal |
| | 494 Math |
| STICKER PRICE: | $15,000+ |
| NEED-BLIND: | Yes |
| NEED MET: | 61% |
| AVERAGE STUDENT DEBT: | NA |
| MERIT SCHOLARSHIPS: | Many |
| RANGE: | Up to full costs |
| ATHLETIC SCHOLARSHIPS: | No |
| ROTC: | Army, Air Force |
| WEB SITE: | www.howard.edu |
| PHONE: | (202) 806-2763 |

With alumni ranging from Thurgood Marshall to Toni Morrison, Howard has turned out generations of leading African Americans since its founding in the aftermath of the Civil War. Unlike other historically black institutions that were created to offer technical training, Howard was chartered as a liberal arts institution and has remained true to the spirit of leading black intellectuals such as Frederick Douglass and W. E. B. DuBois. The university's merit awards are highlighted by the Presidential Scholarship, which offers full tuition, room and board, $900 for books, and a laptop computer to academic whiz kids with at least 1500 on the SAT I (or 34 on the ACT) and a 3.75 GPA. National Achievement Scholar Finalists who designate Howard as their first choice get the same loot. Other sizable awards are available for candidates with lesser credentials; those with at least 1100 or 24 and a GPA of 3.0 can compete for full tuition awards. Scholarships are awarded on a first-come, first-served basis, and hopefuls should apply for admission by November.

*Deadlines:*
  EARLY DECISION: Nov. 30
  REGULAR ADMISSION: Apr. 15
  FAFSA: Apr. 1

# ILLINOIS INSTITUTE OF TECHNOLOGY ✦
## Chicago, IL 60616

| | |
|---|---|
| TOTAL ENROLLMENT: | 6,100 |
| UNDERGRADUATE: | 1,800 |
| ACCEPTANCE RATE: | 68% |
| SAT RANGE: | 570–670 Verbal |
| | 620–720 Math |
| STICKER PRICE: | $22,000+ |
| NEED-BLIND: | Yes |
| NEED MET: | 90% |
| AVERAGE STUDENT DEBT: | $12,700 |
| MERIT SCHOLARSHIPS: | Many |
| RANGE: | Up to full costs |
| ATHLETIC SCHOLARSHIPS: | Yes |
| ROTC: | Army, Navy, Air Force |
| WEB SITE: | www.iit.edu |
| PHONE: | (800) 448-2329 |

IIT began in 1893 with a gift from famed Chicago meat packer Philip Armour, who was inspired by a church sermon to start a school where students from all backgrounds could get a higher education. Located on the city's South Side near Comiskey Park, IIT is remarkably diverse for a school with only 1,800 undergraduates. Engineering is the largest and most prominent program, but IIT also offers architecture, business, design, and a somewhat unusual Institute of Psychology. Even more notable is the bonanza of big-ticket merit awards available through a variety of programs, including eighty scholarships for engineering and computer science students that range up to full tuition plus room and board for five years. Nearly as generous awards are offered in applied sciences, architecture, pre-med, and pre-law. Scholarships of up to full tuition are also available for women and minority students. Most of the top scholarships require a supplemental application due January 15, though others are given on a rolling basis.

*Deadlines:*
   ADMISSION: Rolling
   FAFSA: Mar. 15

# ILLINOIS WESLEYAN UNIVERSITY ✦
## Bloomington, IL 61702

| | |
|---|---|
| TOTAL ENROLLMENT: | 2,000 |
| UNDERGRADUATE: | 2,000 |
| ACCEPTANCE RATE: | 59% |
| SAT RANGE: | 560–670 Verbal |
| | 570–680 Math |
| STICKER PRICE: | $23,000+ |
| NEED-BLIND: | Yes |
| NEED MET: | 100% |
| AVERAGE STUDENT DEBT: | $16,300 |
| MERIT SCHOLARSHIPS: | Many |
| RANGE: | Up to full tuition |
| ATHLETIC SCHOLARSHIPS: | No |
| ROTC: | Army |
| WEB SITE: | www.iwu.edu |
| PHONE: | (800) 332-2498 |

Famed explorer John Wesley Powell once served on the faculty at Illinois Wesleyan, but IWU has only recently been discovered as one of the Midwest's leading liberal arts colleges. IWU is now the most prominent small college alternative in the Land of Lincoln to major universities like Northwestern and the University of Illinois. The liberal arts account for the bulk of IWU's enrollment, although the most popular major is business administration. The university is perhaps best-known for its College of Fine Arts, which includes schools of art, theater, and music. There is also a small school of nursing. IWU operates on a 4-4-1 calendar that features a month-long term in May that is ideal for travel and internships. The university offers Alumni Scholarships ranging from $3,000 to $11,500 to students who rank in the top quarter of their high school class and get at least a 1240 on the SAT I or 28 on the ACT. Fine arts awards generally range from $3,200 to $7,000, though a limited number of full tuition awards are available for top musicians.

*Deadlines:*
   ADMISSION: Rolling
   FAFSA: Mar. 1
   CSS PROFILE: Mar. 1

# UNIVERSITY OF ILLINOIS/CHICAGO ✦
## Chicago, IL 60607

| | |
|---|---|
| TOTAL ENROLLMENT: | 24,500 |
| UNDERGRADUATE: | 16,300 |
| ACCEPTANCE RATE: | 56% |
| SAT AVERAGE: | 540 Verbal |
| | 570 Math |
| STICKER PRICE: | In-state, $10,000+ |
| | Out-of-state, $17,000+ |
| NEED-BLIND: | Yes |
| NEED MET: | 80% |
| AVERAGE STUDENT DEBT: | $10,000 |
| MERIT SCHOLARSHIPS: | Many |
| RANGE: | Up to full costs |
| ATHLETIC SCHOLARSHIPS: | Yes |
| ROTC: | Army, Navy, Air Force |
| WEB SITE: | www.uic.edu |
| PHONE: | (312) 996-4350 |

Located just west of Chicago's famed Loop, the University of Illinois/Chicago is the epitome of a streetwise urban institution. With 24,500 students in 16 colleges and schools, it is the largest university in the city and second only to Urbana-Champaign in the state. Business is UIC's best-known offering, though health-related programs are also strong. With such a strategic location, it should come as no surprise that the university offers extensive co-op and internship opportunities. Many of UIC's merit awards are parceled out by the various academic departments, but some are available to all students based on leadership, minority status, attendance at Chicago public school, and other miscellaneous criteria. The largest prize is the University Scholar Award, given through the Honors College, which covers full tuition and fees. (A separate application is required by January 22.) Applicants must be in the top 10 percent of their high school class with a 1240 on the SAT I or a 28 on the ACT, and only Illinois residents are eligible. Additional awards have various criteria.

*Deadlines:*
  ADMISSION: Feb.1 (priority)
  FAFSA: Mar. 1

# UNIVERSITY OF ILLINOIS/URBANA-CHAMPAIGN ✦ Urbana, IL 61801

| | |
|---|---|
| TOTAL ENROLLMENT: | 36,000 |
| UNDERGRADUATE: | 26,900 |
| ACCEPTANCE RATE: | 68% |
| SAT AVERAGE: | 600 Verbal |
| | 640 Math |
| STICKER PRICE: | In-state, $10,000+ |
| | Out-of-state, $17,000+ |
| NEED-BLIND: | Yes |
| NEED MET: | 94% |
| AVERAGE STUDENT DEBT: | $13,400 |
| MERIT SCHOLARSHIPS | Many |
| ATHLETIC SCHOLARSHIPS: | Yes |
| ROTC: | Army, Navy, Air Force |
| WEB SITE: | www.uiuc.edu |
| PHONE: | (217) 333-0302 |

Along with its counterparts in Michigan and Wisconsin, the University of Illinois heads the list of premier public universities in the Midwest. Business, communications, engineering, and the arts are particularly strong, and the Campus Honors Program competes on an even footing with Northwestern, the University of Chicago, and the Ivy League for top in-state talent. One of the university's most distinctive divisions is the College of Applied Life Sciences, which combines everything from leisure studies to speech and hearing science under the unifying theme of health and wellness. Most UI freshman merit scholarships are awarded by the academic departments and colleges, and admitted students are notified automatically if they qualify. Miscellaneous awards include a YMCA-sponsored scholarship of up to $1,200 for those who "demonstrate concern for others and help make our society better," and a $1,000 award that recognizes academic excellence and participation in amateur sports. Students admitted to the honors program get a small tuition discount.

*Deadlines:*
  ADMISSION: Jan. 1
  FAFSA: Mar. 15

# INDIANA UNIVERSITY ✦ Bloomington, IN 47405

| | |
|---|---|
| TOTAL ENROLLMENT: | 34,900 |
| UNDERGRADUATE: | 27,100 |
| ACCEPTANCE RATE: | 83% |
| SAT RANGE: | 490–610 Verbal |
| | 500–620 Math |
| STICKER PRICE: | In-state, $9,000+ |
| | Out-of-state, $18,000+ |
| NEED-BLIND: | Yes |
| NEED MET: | 72% |
| AVERAGE STUDENT DEBT: | NA |
| MERIT SCHOLARSHIPS: | Many |
| RANGE: | Up to full costs |
| ATHLETIC SCHOLARSHIPS: | Yes |
| ROTC: | Army, Air Force |
| WEB SITE: | www.indiana.edu |
| PHONE: | (812) 855-0661 |

The Hoosier state is best known for basketball, bike races, and the Indianapolis 500, but it is also home to one of the nation's leading research universities. With a sprawling 1,800-acre campus and seven satellite locations throughout the state, Indiana University dominates nontechnical higher education in its home state. IU's programs in the fine arts are among the best in the nation, and the schools of business and communications are exceptionally strong. Foreign languages are another specialty. The majority of merit scholarships are offered through particular departments and schools, with a chunk of more than 200 available through the Honors Division. The most prestigious is the Wells Scholars Program, which covers full expenses plus a living stipend. (Students from selected high schools are nominated by their high school in the fall of twelfth grade.) Other awards fund student research, summer activities, and teaching internships. Applicants for Honors Division Scholarships should rank in the top 10 percent with an SAT I of 1300 or an ACT of 30.

*Deadlines:*
  ADMISSION: Feb. 15
  FAFSA: Mar. 1

# IOWA STATE UNIVERSITY ✦ Ames, IA 50011

| | |
|---|---|
| TOTAL ENROLLMENT: | 25,400 |
| UNDERGRADUATE: | 20,400 |
| ACCEPTANCE RATE: | 91% |
| SAT RANGE: | 500–650 Verbal |
| | 540–680 Math |
| STICKER PRICE: | In-state, $7,000+ |
| | Out-of-state, $13,000+ |
| NEED-BLIND: | Yes |
| NEED MET: | 95% |
| AVERAGE STUDENT DEBT: | $16,600 |
| MERIT SCHOLARSHIPS: | Many |
| RANGE: | Up to full costs |
| ATHLETIC SCHOLARSHIPS: | Yes |
| ROTC: | Army, Navy, Air Force |
| WEB SITE: | www.iastate.edu |
| PHONE: | (800) 262-3810 |

Founded as a training ground for Iowa farm boys, ISU's transition from cows to computers began in the late 1930s when university researchers pioneered development of the first electronic digital computing machines. Today, Iowa State is a leading high tech research center with top programs in engineering, computer science, and the natural sciences. Veterinary medicine is also a big draw, and though no longer at center stage, the College of Agriculture will remain among the nation's best for as long as there is corn in Iowa fields. ISU offers scholarships ranging from $6,000 to full costs for National Merit Finalists, and forty more awards of $2,500 are given to top students who apply for admission by March 1. Thirty entering students are part of the President's Leadership Class; the program features a $1,000 stipend and weekly group meetings with the university president. Additional scholarships target minorities, in-staters, and former 4-H members, among others. A host of awards are also available through the various academic divisions.

*Deadlines:*
  ADMISSION: Rolling
  FAFSA: Mar. 1

# UNIVERSITY OF IOWA ✦ Iowa City, IA 52242

TOTAL ENROLLMENT: 27,900
UNDERGRADUATE: 18,800
ACCEPTANCE RATE: 84%
SAT RANGE: 520–640 Verbal
530–650 Math
STICKER PRICE: In-state, $7,000+
Out-of-state, $15,000+
NEED-BLIND: Yes
NEED MET: NA
AVERAGE STUDENT DEBT: $13,000
MERIT SCHOLARSHIPS: Many
RANGE: Up to $7,000
ATHLETIC SCHOLARSHIPS: Yes
ROTC: Army, Air Force
WEB SITE: www.uiowa.edu
PHONE: (319) 335-3847

True to its reputation as the most literate state in the nation, Iowa needed less than two months of statehood to found the University of Iowa back in 1847. World famous for its writing programs, UI is also notable for business, health-related professions, and the arts. The university prides itself on being the least expensive university in the Big Ten, and approximately a third of the students hail from out-of-state. Psychology, English, and finance rate as the most popular majors. UI's Presidential Scholarship offers $7,000 per year to fifty top students who score at least 1290 on the SAT I or 30 on the ACT and rank in the top 5 percent of their high school class. Students must apply by December 1. An additional seventy runners-up get a $1,000 consolation prize. A $3,000 Enrichment Scholarship is granted to twenty-five entering freshmen who will contribute to "diversity of opinion, life experience, and perspective." Additional scholarships target National Merit Finalists, minority students, and those who live in a particular geographical area, and numerous awards are offered through the various academic divisions.

*Deadlines:*
ADMISSION: May 15
FAFSA: As soon as possible after Jan. 1

# ITHACA COLLEGE ✦ Ithaca, NY 14850

TOTAL ENROLLMENT: 5,900
UNDERGRADUATE: 5,600
ACCEPTANCE RATE: 69%
SAT RANGE: 520–620 Verbal
520–620 Math
STICKER PRICE: $26,000
NEED-BLIND: Yes
NEED MET: 81%
AVERAGE STUDENT DEBT: NA
MERIT SCHOLARSHIPS: Many
RANGE: Up to $11,000
ATHLETIC SCHOLARSHIPS: No
ROTC: Army, Air Force
WEB SITE: www.ithaca.edu
PHONE: (800) 429-4274

Ithaca has come a long way since its founding as a conservatory of music, but 100 years later its forte is still the fine arts. Communications is another of Ithaca's strengths, especially the broadcast media. The School of Health Sciences and Human Performance is home to popular programs ranging from physical therapy, one of the most selective on campus, to sport management and speech pathology. With the waters of Cayuga Lake lapping at the edge of campus, Ithaca is widely noted for its beauty. The college offers a complete line of merit scholarships, topped by an $11,000 award for National Merit Finalists, along with additional awards in increments down to $3,000. A Leadership Scholarship of $6,000 is also available, and the Premier Talent Scholarship bestows $10,000 on Ithaca's top artistic applicants. An award of up to $5,000 is available for minority students, and $1,000 discounts go to children of alumni and students with siblings currently enrolled. Early decision applicants are required to file the CSS PROFILE by November 1.

*Deadlines:*
EARLY DECISION: Nov. 1
REGULAR ADMISSION: Mar. 1 (PHYSICAL THERAPY: Nov. 1)
FAFSA: FEB. 1

## JAMES MADISON UNIVERSITY ✦
## Harrisonburg, VA 22807

| | |
|---|---|
| TOTAL ENROLLMENT: | 14,100 |
| UNDERGRADUATE: | 12,900 |
| ACCEPTANCE RATE: | 55% |
| SAT RANGE: | 540–630 Verbal |
| | 540–630 Math |
| STICKER PRICE: | In-state, $10,000+ |
| | Out-of-state, $15,000+ |
| NEED-BLIND: | Yes |
| NEED MET: | 75% |
| AVERAGE STUDENT DEBT: | $10,700 |
| MERIT SCHOLARSHIPS: | Many |
| ATHLETIC SCHOLARSHIPS: | Yes |
| ROTC: | Army |
| WEB SITE: | www.jmu.edu |
| PHONE: | (540) 568-6147 |

James Madison was a sleepy teacher's college until the 1970s, when it became a full-fledged university and rose to prominence under the leadership of a dynamic president. Located midway down Virginia's scenic Shenandoah Valley, Madison is especially noted for its programs in business, communications, and health-related fields. An innovative general education program requires students to take clusters of courses with an emphasis on writing, oral communication, and use of technology. The university's honors program features small classes, independent study opportunities, and a variety of enrichment activities. Many of JMU's merit scholarships are given by particular departments (students should contact them directly), but some university-wide awards are available, generally "in the $1,000 range." James Madison Scholarships recognize students in the top 10 percent of their high school class with a combined SAT I of at least 1200. Others target minority students, leaders, and students from particular regions in Virginia. Applicants for nondepartmental awards must submit a one-page letter outlining their qualifications to the director of scholarships.

*Deadlines:*
  EARLY ACTION: Nov. 15
  REGULAR ADMISSION: Jan. 15
  FAFSA: Feb. 15

## JOHN CARROLL UNIVERSITY ✦
## Cleveland, OH 44118

| | |
|---|---|
| TOTAL ENROLLMENT: | 4,400 |
| UNDERGRADUATE: | 3,400 |
| ACCEPTANCE RATE: | 89% |
| SAT RANGE: | 520–630 Verbal |
| | 510–630 Math |
| STICKER PRICE: | $21,000+ |
| NEED-BLIND: | YES |
| NEED MET: | NA |
| AVERAGE STUDENT DEBT: | NA |
| MERIT SCHOLARSHIPS: | Many |
| ATHLETIC SCHOLARSHIPS: | No |
| ROTC: | Army |
| WEB SITE: | www.jcu.edu |
| PHONE: | (216) 397-4294 |

John Carroll is a small university that proudly bills itself as "Jesuit in Every Aspect." Set on a quiet campus in suburban Cleveland, JCU emphasizes traditional values, such as academic rigor, character-building, and community service. The conservative tenor of life is reflected in the popularity of preprofessional programs such as business, pre-med, and pre-law. Students with a GPA of 3.5 or better can apply for the President's Honor Award, which comes in variable amounts and requires a special application by February 15. Top students who expect to major in math, biology, chemistry, or physics can aim for the $10,000 Mastin Scholarship, which is open to students who are National Merit honorees or who score 27 or better on the ACT. Full-tuition scholarships are earmarked for selected students who have taken at least three years of Latin and plan to major in classics. Smaller merit scholarships are available to graduates of Catholic high schools in Cleveland, and a merit-within-need award honors leadership and/or community service.

*Deadlines:*
  ADMISSION: Mar. 15
  FAFSA: Mar. 1

## JOHNS HOPKINS UNIVERSITY •
## Baltimore, MD 21218

| | |
|---|---|
| TOTAL ENROLLMENT: | 5,000 |
| UNDERGRADUATE: | 3,700 |
| ACCEPTANCE RATE: | 41% |
| SAT RANGE: | 620–720 Verbal |
| | 670–740 Math |
| STICKER PRICE: | $30,000+ |
| NEED-BLIND: | No |
| NEED MET: | 100% |
| AVERAGE STUDENT DEBT: | $16,000 |
| MERIT SCHOLARSHIPS: | Few |
| RANGE: | Up to $17,000 |
| ATHLETIC SCHOLARSHIPS: | Yes |
| ROTC: | Army, Air Force |
| WEB SITE: | www.jhu.edu |
| PHONE: | (410) 516-8171 |

Administrators will tell you that John Hopkins's reputation for having the nation's most high-powered pre-med program is a mixed blessing. A modest-sized university of only 5,000 students, Hopkins offers a top-notch school of engineering and quality programs throughout the liberal arts. A notable example is international studies, which ranks behind biology as the second-most popular major. Though the school of engineering is heavily male, women now outnumber men in the arts and sciences. The biggest prize for Hopkins applicants is the Beneficial-Hodson Scholarship, which gives $17,000 per year to fifteen of the very best. (Applicants must be nominated by January 1.) Selected National Merit and National Achievement Finalists are eligible for awards of $500 to $2,000, depending on need. Early decision applicants should note that Hopkins reserves preferential need-based packages for those in the regular pool. Applicants in the humanities are likely to get better need-based packages as Hopkins works to attract top students to those programs. Athletic scholarships are offered only in men's lacrosse.

*Deadlines:*
  EARLY DECISION: Nov. 15
  REGULAR ADMISSION: Jan. 1
  FAFSA: Feb. 1

## JUILLIARD SCHOOL •
## New York, NY 10023

| | |
|---|---|
| TOTAL ENROLLMENT: | 800 |
| UNDERGRADUATE: | 450 |
| ACCEPTANCE RATE: | 8% |
| SAT RANGE: | NA |
| STICKER PRICE: | $24,000+ |
| NEED-BLIND: | Yes |
| NEED MET: | NA |
| AVERAGE STUDENT DEBT: | NA |
| MERIT SCHOLARSHIPS: | Many |
| ATHLETIC SCHOLARSHIPS: | No |
| ROTC: | No |
| WEB SITE: | www.juilliard.edu |
| PHONE: | (212) 799-5000 |

Juilliard is the stuff that dreams are made of. Located adjacent to the legendary venues of Lincoln Center and featuring a list of alumni that includes Itzhak Perlman, Wynton Marsalis, and Robin Williams (to name but a few), Juilliard enrolls an elite group of the finest young musicians, dancers, and actors in the world. With 1,522 applications for 85 spaces in a recent freshman class, admission is a realistic possibility for only a rare few with extraordinary talent and single-minded devotion. Performers are often solitary individuals, but Juilliard's Community Fellowship Program ensures that students share their talent with those at area nursing homes and hospitals. Juilliard also benefits from a cross-registration arrangement with Columbia University for liberal arts courses. With an endowment per student that is nearly as impressive as its artistic reputation, Juilliard provides more financial aid than most arts schools. Awards are made for a combination of need and merit depending on "the student's artistic promise and school record, and on the financial circumstances" of each student.

*Deadlines:*
  ADMISSION: Dec. 1 (some programs later)
  FAFSA: Six weeks prior to audition

# KALAMAZOO COLLEGE ✦
## Kalamazoo, MI 49006

| | |
|---|---|
| TOTAL ENROLLMENT: | 1,200 |
| UNDERGRADUATE: | 1,200 |
| ACCEPTANCE RATE: | 88% |
| SAT RANGE: | 570–670 Verbal |
| | 570–680 Math |
| STICKER PRICE: | $24,000+ |
| NEED-BLIND: | Yes |
| NEED MET: | NA |
| AVERAGE STUDENT DEBT: | $11,600 |
| MERIT SCHOLARSHIPS: | Many |
| RANGE: | Up to $10,000 |
| ATHLETIC SCHOLARSHIPS: | No |
| ROTC: | No |
| WEB SITE: | www.kzoo.edu |
| PHONE: | (800) 253-3602 |

Though Kalamazoo sounds like a place dreamed up by Dr. Seuss, it is a real college in southern Michigan. Actually, Dr. Seuss would have loved Kalamazoo, a leading educational innovator where 85 percent of the students study abroad and all complete an individualized senior project. The heart of Kalamazoo is the "K" Plan, in which students alternate terms of on-campus study with career-oriented internships. The college's merit scholarships come in two varieties. The Honors Scholarships are open to students who either rank in the top 25 percent, have a 3.5 GPA, or score 1140 on the SAT I or 25 on the ACT. Based on academic record, leadership, and personal accomplishment, the awards range from $3,000 to $10,000. (Early applicants get priority consideration.) Competitive Scholarships of $1,500 to $3,000 are awarded based on exams administered at the college in January and February. Students may choose to enter in science and math, history and social science, foreign language, writing, or fine arts.

*Deadlines:*
   ADMISSION: Feb. 15 (priority)
   FAFSA: Feb. 15
   CSS PROFILE: Feb. 15

# KANSAS STATE UNIVERSITY ✦
## Manhattan, KS 66506

| | |
|---|---|
| TOTAL ENROLLMENT: | 20,300 |
| UNDERGRADUATE: | 16,900 |
| ACCEPTANCE RATE: | 66% |
| ACT AVERAGE: | 23 |
| STICKER PRICE: | In-state, $7,000+ |
| | Out-of-state, $13,000+ |
| NEED-BLIND: | Yes |
| NEED MET: | NA |
| AVERAGE STUDENT DEBT: | $15,500 |
| MERIT SCHOLARSHIPS: | Many |
| ATHLETIC SCHOLARSHIPS: | Yes |
| ROTC: | Army, Air Force |
| WEB SITE: | www.ksu.edu |
| PHONE: | (785) 532-6250 |

When folks in Kansas want to go to Manhattan, they don't need to cross the George Washington Bridge. This Manhattan is in the rolling hills of northeast Kansas and home to K State, one of the nation's oldest land-grant universities. Founded as an agriculture school, K State's other notable offerings include architecture, business, engineering, veterinary medicine, and a distinctive College of Technology and Aviation. K State offers an abundance of merit scholarships, many of which are given based on specific criteria, such as intended major or place of residence. The highlight of university-wide awards is the Presidential Scholarship which offers a four-year total of up to $15,000 to honorees in the National Merit Scholarship Corporation's various programs. Other awards include a $1,500 Leadership Scholarship, a $900 scholarship for extracurricular achievement, and a one-time $5,000 award for students who have shown all-around achievement. Major scholarships require submission of the university scholarship application by November 1.

*Deadlines:*
   ADMISSION: Rolling
   FAFSA: Mar. 15

## UNIVERSITY OF KANSAS ◆
## Lawrence, KS 66044

| | |
|---|---|
| TOTAL ENROLLMENT: | 27,600 |
| UNDERGRADUATE: | 18,900 |
| ACCEPTANCE RATE: | 61% |
| ACT RANGE: | 21–28 |
| STICKER PRICE: | In-state, $7,000+ |
| | Out-of-state, $13,000+ |
| NEED-BLIND: | Yes |
| NEED MET: | 55% |
| AVERAGE STUDENT DEBT: | $13,800 |
| MERIT SCHOLARSHIPS: | Many |
| ATHLETIC SCHOLARSHIPS: | Yes |
| ROTC: | Army, Navy, Air Force |
| WEB SITE: | www.ukans.edu |
| PHONE: | (888) 686-7323 |

"Rock Chalk, Jayhawk" is the ancient chant that stirs the blood of every University of Kansas loyalist. As one of the Midwest's top public universities—and one of the least expensive—KU has plenty to cheer about. The university offers a full lineup of preprofessional programs, most notably architecture, business, journalism, and mass communications, and various health-related fields. KU's honors program offers tutorial classes, enhanced advising, and independent projects that can be funded up to $1,000. With in-state tuition only about $2,000, most of KU's merit scholarships carry modest dollar amounts. The Summerfield/Watkins-Berger Scholarships give a renewable $2,500 award to in-staters in the top 5 percent of their high school class with an ACT score of 30 or higher. The Freshman Honor Scholarships offer $500 to in-staters in the top 20 percent with a 24. Other awards are given on the basis of leadership, place of residence, and to National Merit honorees. A host of scholarships are also available through KU's academic divisions. The priority deadline for the Application for Freshman Scholarships is January 15.

*Deadlines:*
   ADMISSION: Apr. 1
   FAFSA: Mar. 1

## UNIVERSITY OF KENTUCKY ◆
## Lexington, KY 40506

| | |
|---|---|
| TOTAL ENROLLMENT: | 23,500 |
| UNDERGRADUATE: | 17,000 |
| ACCEPTANCE RATE: | 78% |
| SAT AVERAGE: | 1040 combined |
| STICKER PRICE: | In-state, $7,000+ |
| | Out-of-state, $12,000+ |
| NEED-BLIND: | Yes |
| NEED MET: | NA |
| AVERAGE STUDENT DEBT: | NA |
| MERIT SCHOLARSHIPS: | Many |
| RANGE: | Up to full costs |
| ATHLETIC SCHOLARSHIPS: | Yes |
| ROTC: | Army, Air Force |
| WEB SITE: | www.uky.edu |
| PHONE: | (606) 257-2000 |

The University of Kentucky's biggest claim to fame is its storied men's basketball program, which has brought numerous national championships to legendary Rupp Arena. With nearly 40 percent of Kentucky college students in attendance, UK is easily the dominant institution in the bluegrass state. UK's array of seventeen academic divisions covers everything from agriculture to social work; the strongest programs tend to be in preprofessional fields such as business, engineering, and health-related fields. One of the university's biggest merit prizes is the Otis A. Singletary Scholarship, which offers $6,400 to twenty freshmen with a minimum GPA of 3.75 and 31 on the ACT. Students with at least 3.3 and 28 can vie for both the President's and Chancellor's Scholarships, which offer in-state tuition and $1,000, respectively. All three programs require an application by the first Friday in January, and the general scholarship deadline is January 15. Additional awards are aimed at National Merit Finalists, Kentucky valedictorians, and minority students, and hundreds more are available from various university offices.

*Deadlines:*
   ADMISSION: Feb. 15 (priority)
   FAFSA: Rolling

## KENYON COLLEGE ✦ Gambier, OH 43022

| | |
|---|---|
| TOTAL ENROLLMENT: | 1,500 |
| UNDERGRADUATE: | 1,500 |
| ACCEPTANCE RATE: | 70% |
| SAT RANGE: | 610–710 Verbal |
| | 580–660 Math |
| STICKER PRICE: | $28,000+ |
| NEED-BLIND: | Yes |
| NEED MET: | 95% |
| AVERAGE STUDENT DEBT: | $15,900 |
| MERIT SCHOLARSHIPS: | Many |
| RANGE: | Up to full tuition |
| ATHLETIC SCHOLARSHIPS: | No |
| ROTC: | No |
| WEB SITE: | www.kenyon.edu |
| PHONE: | (800) 848-2468 |

Unlike some colleges that dress up preprofessional courses in liberal-artsy garb, Kenyon remains true to the original vision of a liberal arts college. An outstanding English department has always been Kenyon's cornerstone, with its famed *Kenyon Review*. Other programs across the liberal arts are strong, and Kenyon's drama department has been a magnet for budding thespians at least since Paul Newman put it on the map. Because of its location in rural Ohio, Kenyon is less selective than other colleges of comparable quality, such as Hamilton or Bowdoin, though it outdraws in-state rivals such as Denison and the College of Wooster. Top applicants can vie for the Kenyon Honor and Science Scholarships, which offer up to full tuition to twelve outstanding students but require a special application by December 15. The same deadline applies to equally generous awards earmarked for African Americans and Latinos. A $6,000 scholarship is automatically awarded to top applicants in the regular admission pool, and Kenyon also funds National Merit Finalists up to $2,000.

*Deadlines:*
EARLY DECISION: Dec. 1, Feb. 1
REGULAR ADMISSION: Feb. 1
FAFSA: Feb. 15
CSS PROFILE: Feb. 15

## KETTERING UNIVERSITY ✦ Flint, MI 48504

| | |
|---|---|
| TOTAL ENROLLMENT: | 3,200 |
| UNDERGRADUATE: | 2,500 |
| ACCEPTANCE RATE: | 76% |
| SAT RANGE: | 540–640 Verbal |
| | 590–690 Math |
| STICKER PRICE: | $18,000+ |
| NEED-BLIND: | Yes |
| NEED MET: | NA |
| AVERAGE STUDENT DEBT: | $25,000 |
| MERIT SCHOLARSHIPS: | Few |
| ATHLETIC SCHOLARSHIPS: | No |
| ROTC: | No |
| WEB SITE: | www.kettering.edu |
| PHONE: | (800) 955-4464 |

Few names rank higher than that of Charles Kettering on the honor roll of American industry. In 1998, the GMI Engineering and Management Institute decided to rename itself in honor of the longtime General Motors executive who invented the electric starting system and high-octane gasoline. Independent from GM since 1982, the school offers programs in business and management, engineering, and math and science. The cornerstone of a Kettering education is its mandatory co-op program, in which students alternate twelve weeks on campus with twelve at work (while earning an average of $50,000 by the time they graduate). Before they set foot on campus, students arrange a co-op job (with Kettering's help) and generally stay with the same employer for most or all of their undergraduate years. Kettering offers only a handful of merit scholarships, including one for mechanical engineering students with an automotive specialty and another based on general excellence for students who show need. Other awards target residents of particular regions in Michigan and Ohio. Scholarship applicants must apply by March 1.

*Deadlines:*
ADMISSION: Rolling
FAFSA: Feb. 1

# KNOX COLLEGE • Galesburg, IL 61401

| | |
|---|---|
| TOTAL ENROLLMENT: | 1,200 |
| UNDERGRADUATE: | 1,200 |
| ACCEPTANCE RATE: | 79% |
| SAT RANGE: | 540–660 Verbal |
| | 650–660 Math |
| STICKER PRICE: | $24,000+ |
| NEED-BLIND: | Yes |
| NEED MET: | 100% |
| AVERAGE STUDENT DEBT: | $14,400 |
| MERIT SCHOLARSHIPS: | Many |
| RANGE: | Up to full tuition |
| ATHLETIC SCHOLARSHIPS: | No |
| ROTC: | No |
| WEB SITE: | www.knox.edu |
| PHONE: | (800) 678-5669 |

Knox was a fledgling institution in 1858 when Abraham Lincoln raised his voice against slavery from the steps of its Old Main building, but more than 140 years later Knox still uses Lincoln as its touchstone. A small college in rural Illinois, Knox prides itself on openmindedness and diversity. Two unique programs allow students to spend an entire term as full-time artists or at work on a major theatrical production. Knox has an unusually large stash of major merit awards. Six to eight full-tuition Lincoln Scholarships are awarded to top applicants by a faculty-student committee, and National Merit, National Achievement, and National Hispanic Scholar honorees get at least $6,000 per year. Other scholarships are aimed at residents of metro New York ($1,500) and Colorado ($1,500), prospective majors in chemistry and math ($4,000), and those who have participated in an American Field Service (AFS) foreign study program. Social Concerns Scholarships honor those who have been active in the community ($3,000), and there are also $3,000 awards for students with special talent in the creative arts.

*Deadlines:*
   EARLY ACTION: Dec. 1
   REGULAR ADMISSION: Feb. 15
   FAFSA: MAR. 1

# LAFAYETTE COLLEGE • Easton, PA 18042

| | |
|---|---|
| TOTAL ENROLLMENT: | 2,200 |
| UNDERGRADUATE: | 2,200 |
| ACCEPTANCE RATE: | 58% |
| SAT RANGE: | 530–620 Verbal |
| | 560–660 Math |
| STICKER PRICE: | $28,000+ |
| NEED-BLIND: | Yes |
| NEED MET: | 95% |
| AVERAGE STUDENT DEBT: | $13,400 |
| MERIT SCHOLARSHIPS: | Few |
| RANGE: | Up to $10,000 |
| ATHLETIC SCHOLARSHIPS: | Yes |
| ROTC | Army |
| WEB SITE: | www.lafayette.edu |
| PHONE: | (610) 250-5100 |

Lafayette is among a smattering of small colleges that combine the liberal arts with engineering. Any of the college's programs in the sciences is likely to be strong, although the most popular majors are economics/business and government/law. More traditional than many of its highly selective peers, Lafayette's social life is dominated by fraternities and sororities. The college is often mentioned in the same breath with nearby Lehigh—a much larger university—but is more comparable in scale to places like Franklin and Marshall, Colgate, and Bucknell. Lafayette offers one of the largest merit awards of any of its close competitors, the Marquis Scholarship, which features a $10,000 stipend (up to full costs for those with need) plus funding for study abroad. About 150 per year are offered to top applicants with a high school class rank in the top 5 percent and an SAT I of 1350 or higher. For students on need-based aid, Lafayette supplements federal loan programs with its own HELP loans of up to $7,000 per year, which are interest- and payment-free until after graduation.

*Deadlines:*
   EARLY DECISION: Feb. 15
   REGULAR ADMISSION: Jan. 1
   FAFSA: Feb. 1
   CSS PROFILE: Feb. 1

# LAKE FOREST COLLEGE ✦
## Lake Forest, IL 60045

| | |
|---|---|
| TOTAL ENROLLMENT: | 1,200 |
| UNDERGRADUATE: | 1,200 |
| ACCEPTANCE RATE: | 78% |
| SAT RANGE: | 520–620 Verbal |
| | 500–610 Math |
| STICKER PRICE: | $25,000+ |
| NEED-BLIND: | Yes |
| NEED MET: | 100% |
| AVERAGE STUDENT DEBT: | $11,500 |
| MERIT SCHOLARSHIPS: | Many |
| RANGE: | Up to full tuition |
| ATHLETIC SCHOLARSHIPS: | No |
| ROTC: | No |
| WEB SITE: | www.lfc.edu |
| PHONE: | (800) 828-4751 |

Set on a wooded campus that evokes the air of a grand estate, Lake Forest combines a secluded suburban location with easy access to nearby Chicago via a commuter railroad. Lake Forest likes to refer to Chicago as its second campus, and numerous internship programs ensure that students get hands-on experience there. Lake Forest is smaller than many of its competitors and emphasizes close contact between students and professors. The college's Presidential Scholarship bestows full- and half-tuition scholarships on students with a minimum of 1240 on the SAT I or 28 on the ACT and a 3.5 GPA. Students must apply by January 29 and participate in an on-campus competition. Deerpath Scholarships offer $3,000 to $9,000 to students who excel in leadership or the arts. Illinois residents can compete for the Founders' Scholarships of up to full tuition if they have a top 20 percent rank and minimum test scores of 1170 or 28. (Be mindful of a November 26 deadline.) Children and grandchildren of alumni qualify for a tuition discount.

*Deadlines:*
 EARLY DECISION: Jan. 1
 REGULAR ADMISSION: Mar.1
 FAFSA: Mar. 1

# LAWRENCE UNIVERSITY ✦
## Appleton, WI 54912

| | |
|---|---|
| TOTAL ENROLLMENT: | 1,200 |
| UNDERGRADUATE: | 1,200 |
| ACCEPTANCE RATE: | 80% |
| SAT RANGE: | 580–700 Verbal |
| | 580–680 Math |
| STICKER PRICE: | $25,000+ |
| NEED-BLIND: | Yes |
| NEED MET: | 100% |
| AVERAGE STUDENT DEBT: | NA |
| MERIT SCHOLARSHIPS: | Many |
| RANGE: | Up to $10,000 |
| ATHLETIC SCHOLARSHIPS: | No |
| ROTC: | No |
| WEB SITE: | www.lawrence.edu |
| PHONE: | (920) 832-6500 |

If Lawrence were located in Boston or Colorado Springs, it would probably be deluged with applicants. A central Wisconsin address ensures that Lawrence will remain a well-kept secret—all the better for those who discover the college's uniquely student-centered brand of higher education. Small classes are a given, and there is unusual opportunity for independent study and one-on-one work with faculty. Along with Oberlin, Lawrence is among the few colleges that combine liberal arts with a nationally known conservatory of music. Merit scholarships abound. Via a competition in January and February, Lawrence gives awards of $5,000 to $10,000 to more than a third of the entering class, including students with at least 1100 on the SAT I or 24 on the ACT who have a strong academic record. Scholarships are available for minority students, residents of particular places, and those who plan to major in the natural sciences, government, or economics. The conservatory has a full stable of awards ranging up to $12,000.

*Deadlines:*
 EARLY DECISION: Nov. 15, Jan. 1
 REGULAR ADMISSION: Feb. 1
 FAFSA: Mar. 1

# LEHIGH UNIVERSITY ✦ Bethlehem, PA 18015

| | |
|---|---|
| TOTAL ENROLLMENT: | 6,300 |
| UNDERGRADUATE: | 4,500 |
| ACCEPTANCE RATE: | 54% |
| SAT RANGE: | 550–644 Verbal |
| | 587–679 Math |
| STICKER PRICE: | $29,000+ |
| NEED-BLIND: | No |
| NEED MET: | 98% |
| AVERAGE STUDENT DEBT: | $15,300 |
| MERIT SCHOLARSHIPS: | Many |
| RANGE: | Up to $7,000 |
| ATHLETIC SCHOLARSHIPS: | Yes |
| ROTC | Army |
| WEB SITE: | www.lehigh.edu |
| PHONE: | (610) 758-3100 |

Founded by a railroad magnate in the aftermath of the Civil War, Lehigh has always thrived on the boundary of technology and business. The university is best known for its College of Engineering and Applied Science, which recently received a shot in the arm from a $25-million donation. The College of Business and Economics is also strong, and Lehigh is noted for interdisciplinary offerings that combine business and engineering. Lehigh's other strength is the natural sciences, including its ultracompetitive six year combined B.A./M.D. program. About a tenth of Lehigh's entering students receive merit scholarships, which are highlighted by the $7,000 Dean's Scholar Award. Students in music and theater can compete for $2,500 scholarships, and National Merit Finalists who designate Lehigh has their first choice get awards of up to $2,000, depending on need. Most notable of all, students who finish Lehigh with a 3.5 average or above can study for an additional year free to complete a second bachelor's degree or work toward a master's.

*Deadlines:*
  EARLY DECISION: Dec. 1
  REGULAR ADMISSION: Jan. 15
  FAFSA: Jan. 15
  CSS PROFILE: Jan. 15

# LEWIS AND CLARK COLLEGE ✦ Portland, OR 97219

| | |
|---|---|
| TOTAL ENROLLMENT: | 3,000 |
| UNDERGRADUATE: | 1,900 |
| ACCEPTANCE RATE: | 66% |
| SAT RANGE: | 570–680 Verbal |
| | 570–660 Math |
| STICKER PRICE: | $25,000+ |
| NEED-BLIND: | Yes |
| NEED MET: | 91% |
| AVERAGE STUDENT DEBT: | $17,000 |
| MERIT SCHOLARSHIPS: | Many |
| RANGE: | Up to full tuition |
| ATHLETIC SCHOLARSHIPS: | No |
| ROTC | No |
| WEB SITE: | www.lclark.edu |
| PHONE: | (800) 444-4111 |

Named for the intrepid explorers who first charted the North American continent, Lewis and Clark College is famous for sending its students on voyages of exploration. More than half participate in study abroad during their academic careers, to destinations ranging from Beijing to Zimbabwe. Set on a beautiful wooded campus in suburban Portland, the college combines proximity to a major city with easy access to beaches and mountains. Lewis and Clark gives ten full-tuition scholarships to its most outstanding freshmen, along with fifteen half-tuition awards for the runners-up. Though the primary criteria relate to all-around achievement, preference is given to students interested in math or science and those with demonstrated interest in world cultures. Dean's Scholarships of up to $7,000 go to those with slightly less stellar qualifications, and students who excel in music and forensics are in contention for awards of up to $2,500 and $5,000, respectively. National Merit Finalists get up to $2,000, and a handful of awards are available for students from Oregon and Idaho.

*Deadlines:*
  EARLY ACTION: Dec. 1
  REGULAR ADMISSION: Feb. 1
  FAFSA: Feb. 15

## LOUISIANA STATE UNIVERSITY ✦ Baton Rouge, LA 70803

| | |
|---|---|
| TOTAL ENROLLMENT: | 28,100 |
| UNDERGRADUATE: | 22,700 |
| ACCEPTANCE RATE: | 79% |
| ACT RANGE: | 20–27 |
| STICKER PRICE: | In-state, $7,000+ |
| | Out-of-state, 11,000+ |
| NEED-BLIND: | Yes |
| NEED MET: | 75% |
| AVERAGE STUDENT DEBT: | $17,700 |
| MERIT SCHOLARSHIPS: | Many |
| ATHLETIC SCHOLARSHIPS: | Yes |
| ROTC: | Army, Navy, Air Force |
| WEB SITE: | www.lsu.edu |
| PHONE: | (504) 388-1175 |

As the dominant public university in Louisiana, LSU is both an educational institution and rallying point for state pride. With 22,700 undergraduates on its Baton Rouge campus, LSU offers the liberal arts plus a full selection of preprofessional programs including agriculture, architecture, business, communications and journalism, education, engineering, the performing arts, and veterinary medicine. The Chancellor's Alumni Scholarships are among LSU's richest campus-wide awards, covering full tuition and fees for selected students with at least 1450 on the SAT I or 33 on the ACT and an A average. The 100 students with the highest combination of grades and scores in each entering class get a $1,000 award, National Merit Finalists get up to $2,000, and top students from out-of-state can get exemptions from paying out-of-state prices. Students with intended majors in technology-related fields can qualify for up to $5,000 per year, and approximately 100 non-renewable scholarships of $1,000 are earmarked for students who demonstrate leadership. Applicants for these and numerous other scholarships should apply by December 15.

*Deadlines:*
  ADMISSION: Jun. 1
  FAFSA: Apr. 1

## LOYOLA COLLEGE ✦ Baltimore, MD 21210

| | |
|---|---|
| TOTAL ENROLLMENT: | 6,200 |
| UNDERGRADUATE: | 3,300 |
| ACCEPTANCE RATE: | 70% |
| SAT RANGE: | 540–640 Verbal |
| | 540–650 Math |
| STICKER PRICE: | $24,000+ |
| NEED-BLIND: | Yes |
| NEED MET: | 97% |
| AVERAGE STUDENT DEBT: | $13,500 |
| MERIT SCHOLARSHIPS: | Many |
| RANGE: | Up to full tuition |
| ATHLETIC SCHOLARSHIPS: | No |
| ROTC: | Army, Air Force |
| WEB SITE: | www.loyola.edu |
| PHONE: | (800) 221-9107 |

Loyola of Maryland is far from the only American college named in honor of the illustrious founder of the Jesuits, but it was the first. True to the Jesuit philosophy, Loyola is dedicated to educating "the whole person" while encouraging a commitment to the wider community. Approximately two-thirds of the students participate in the college's community service programs, and an extensive core curriculum accounts for nearly half of every student's program. Students who want to delve deeply into the Western tradition should consider the honors program, which features small classes and special housing. Loyola is perhaps best known for its business school, in which approximately one-third of its students are enrolled. Loyola's Presidential Scholarships give awards to top students that range up to full tuition, and a second program offers stipends of $2,500–$3,500 to those of somewhat lesser distinction. A full-tuition scholarship is available for Catholic students who live in the Archdiocese of Baltimore, and a $2,500 award is reserved for students who commute.

*Deadlines:*
  ADMISSION: Jan. 15
  FAFSA: Feb. 1
  CSS PROFILE: Feb. 1

## LOYOLA MARYMOUNT UNIVERSITY ◆
## Los Angeles, CA 90045

| | |
|---|---|
| TOTAL ENROLLMENT: | 5,600 |
| UNDERGRADUATE: | 4,300 |
| ACCEPTANCE RATE: | 70% |
| SAT RANGE: | 500–590 Verbal |
| | 510–600 Math |
| STICKER PRICE: | $25,000+ |
| NEED-BLIND: | Yes |
| NEED MET: | NA |
| AVERAGE STUDENT DEBT: | NA |
| MERIT SCHOLARSHIPS: | Many |
| RANGE: | Up to $7,500 |
| ATHLETIC SCHOLARSHIPS: | Yes |
| ROTC: | Army, Navy, Air Force |
| WEB SITE: | www.lmu.edu |
| PHONE: | (310) 338-2750 |

Set in southwest Los Angeles near the beach, the mountains, and the airport, Loyola Marymount is a medium-sized Jesuit university with undergraduate programs in the liberal arts, business, science and engineering, and communication and fine arts. The latter includes majors ranging from dance to animation and is the beneficiary of LMU's location in the entertainment capital of the world. To be considered for an academic scholarship, students must have at least a 3.6 GPA, a score of 1300 or better on the SAT I (including 650 on both verbal and math), or an ACT of 29. The crème de la crème are invited to campus in the early spring to compete for ten full-tuition scholarships and twenty awards of $7,500. An additional twenty Leadership Scholarships of $6,000 are available with a preference for students from disadvantaged backgrounds. Students from Catholic high schools can compete for a $5,000 award that has a separate application, and a $7,500 scholarship goes to top graduates of Jesuit or Marymount schools. Scholarship applicants are required to file the FAFSA.

*Deadlines:*
  ADMISSION: Feb. 1 (priority)
  FAFSA: Feb. 15
  CSS PROFILE: Feb. 15

## LOYOLA UNIVERSITY/CHICAGO ◆
## Chicago, IL 60611

| | |
|---|---|
| TOTAL ENROLLMENT: | 13,600 |
| UNDERGRADUATE: | 7,500 |
| ACCEPTANCE RATE: | 89% |
| SAT RANGE: | 520–630 Verbal |
| | 510–620 Math |
| STICKER PRICE: | $23,000+ |
| NEED-BLIND: | YES |
| NEED MET: | 50% |
| AVERAGE STUDENT DEBT: | $13,400 |
| MERIT SCHOLARSHIPS: | Many |
| RANGE: | Up to full tuition |
| ATHLETIC SCHOLARSHIPS: | YES |
| ROTC: | Army, Navy, Air Force |
| WEB SITE: | www.luc.edu |
| PHONE: | (312) 915-6500 |

With 3 campuses, 13,600 students, and 11 colleges and schools, Loyola is among the most diverse of the nation's Jesuit universities. With its main campus along Lake Michigan on Chicago's far north side, Loyola also has a downtown branch on the city's Magnificent Mile that includes the business school, which recently moved into a new multi-million-dollar facility. Loyola is strong in health-related fields and offers a variety of preprofessional majors for particular career paths. Chicago provides an endless variety of academic and personal opportunities, and for those who want to venture farther afield, Loyola operates its own permanent center in Rome. Top liberal arts students can aim for the honors program, which features small classes, independent research opportunities, and the chance to vie for three full tuition scholarships. (A special application is required by March 15.) Loyola's university-wide merit program includes awards at three different levels: the Presidential Scholarship ($10,000), the Damen Scholarship ($7,000), and the Loyola Scholarship ($5,000).

*Deadlines:*
  ADMISSION: Apr.1
  FAFSA: Mar. 1
  CSS PROFILE: Mar. 1

## LOYOLA UNIVERSITY/NEW ORLEANS ✦ New Orleans, LA 70118

| | |
|---|---|
| TOTAL ENROLLMENT: | 3,800 |
| UNDERGRADUATE: | 2,800 |
| ACCEPTANCE RATE: | 91% |
| SAT RANGE: | 550–640 Verbal |
| | 510–620 Math |
| STICKER PRICE: | $20,000+ |
| NEED-BLIND: | Yes |
| NEED MET: | 87% |
| AVERAGE STUDENT DEBT: | $17,200 |
| MERIT SCHOLARSHIPS: | Many |
| RANGE: | Up to full costs |
| ATHLETIC SCHOLARSHIPS: | No |
| ROTC: | Army, Navy, Air Force |
| WEB SITE: | www.loyno.edu |
| PHONE: | (800) 4LOYOLA |

Set in an upscale neighborhood, Loyola is a quick trolley ride from the legendary French Quarter, and students enjoy an appealing blend of warm temperatures, freewheeling city life, and Jesuit education. Loyola's primary undergraduate divisions are arts and sciences, business, and music; communication ranks as the most popular major. Among Loyola's 450 merit awards designated for incoming freshmen and transfers, the most prestigious is the Ignatian Scholarship for Academic Excellence, which covers full tuition plus the cost of a room for ten students who have a minimum GPA of 3.5 in academic courses and a combined SAT I of 1300 or an ACT of 29. Lower on the totem pole is the Loyola Scholarship, which goes to students with at least a 3.2 GPA and "competitive" test scores. Partial tuition scholarships are available for top business students, those with demonstrated commitment to social justice, and those planning to major in drama, music, and visual arts. All scholarship applicants must apply for admission by December 1.

*Deadlines:*
  ADMISSION: May 1
  FAFSA: May 1

## MACALESTER COLLEGE ✦ St. Paul, MN 55105

| | |
|---|---|
| TOTAL ENROLLMENT: | 1,800 |
| UNDERGRADUATE: | 1,800 |
| ACCEPTANCE RATE: | 54% |
| SAT RANGE: | 620–710 Verbal |
| | 600–700 Math |
| STICKER PRICE: | $26,000+ |
| NEED-BLIND: | Yes |
| NEED MET: | 100% |
| AVERAGE STUDENT DEBT: | $13,900 |
| MERIT SCHOLARSHIPS: | Few |
| RANGE: | Up to $5,000 |
| ATHLETIC SCHOLARSHIPS: | No |
| ROTC: | Navy, Air Force |
| WEB SITE: | www.macalester.edu |
| PHONE: | (800) 231-7974 |

While most other elite liberal arts colleges are surrounded by cows and cornfields, Macalester's home is one of the most vibrant metropolitan areas in the Midwest. It is no coincidence that Mac's selectivity has remained strong as other small colleges have been forced to scramble for applicants. Like its close cousins Carleton, Grinnell, and Oberlin, the college attracts a liberal clientele, and Mac is particularly noted for its international outlook. With an endowment per student among the largest in the nation, Mac has spent approximately $100 million on enhancing its facilities in the past twelve years. The college combines abundant need-based aid with a limited number of merit scholarships. National Merit Finalists who designate Mac as their first choice get $5,000, and middle-income students with top academic records are eligible for awards that begin at $3,000. A similar program targets African American, Latino, and Native American students, with larger amounts going to those who are National Achievement and National Hispanic Scholar honorees.

*Deadlines:*
  EARLY DECISION: Nov. 1, Jan. 15
  REGULAR ADMISSION: Jan. 15
  FAFSA: Feb. 1
  CSS PROFILE: Feb. 1

# UNIVERSITY OF MAINE ◆ Orono, ME 04469

| | |
|---|---|
| TOTAL ENROLLMENT: | 8,900 |
| UNDERGRADUATE: | 7,000 |
| ACCEPTANCE RATE: | 75% |
| SAT RANGE: | 490–600 Verbal |
| | 490–600 Math |
| STICKER PRICE: | In-state, $10,000+ |
| | Out-of-state, 17,000+ |
| NEED-BLIND: | Yes |
| NEED MET: | 87% |
| AVERAGE STUDENT DEBT: | $11,000 |
| MERIT SCHOLARSHIPS: | Many |
| RANGE: | Up to full tuition |
| ATHLETIC SCHOLARSHIPS: | Yes |
| ROTC: | Army, Navy |
| WEB SITE: | www.umaine.edu |
| PHONE: | (207) 581-1561 |

Set on a spacious campus near the outskirts of Bangor, the University of Maine has one foot in the populous coastal corridor and the other in the vast rural expanses that lie to the north. Maine has a total enrollment of only 8,900 and does not attract the interest of out-of-staters in the manner of the University of New Hampshire or the University of Vermont. But small can be beautiful; a case in point is the honors program, which enrolls 200 students and offers seminars with twelve students or less. Maine's Top Scholar Awards offer full tuition to in-staters who rank number one or two in their high school class, and a second program also gives a tuition award to in-staters or covers the differential between in-state and out-of-state tuition for those from beyond Maine's borders. The Distinguished Student Awards range from $1,000 up to the nonresident differential for students who "exhibit diversity—culturally, personally, or through achievement in the visual and performing arts." The application deadline for scholarships is February 1.

*Deadlines:*
    ADMISSION: Rolling
    FAFSA: Mar. 1

# MANHATTAN SCHOOL OF MUSIC ◆ New York, NY 10027

| | |
|---|---|
| TOTAL ENROLLMENT: | 800 |
| UNDERGRADUATE: | 400 |
| ACCEPTANCE RATE: | 40% |
| SAT RANGE: | NA |
| STICKER PRICE: | $28,000+ |
| NEED-BLIND: | No |
| NEED MET: | 50% |
| AVERAGE STUDENT DEBT: | $17,100 |
| MERIT SCHOLARSHIPS: | Few |
| ATHLETIC SCHOLARSHIPS: | No |
| ROTC: | No |
| WEB SITE: | www.msmnyc.edu |
| PHONE: | (212) 749-2802 |

Situated at 122nd Street and Broadway beside Columbia University, Manhattan School of Music combines outstanding conservatory education with access to a great university and the nation's leading city for the arts. Unlike some competitors, Manhattan offers both classical training and programs in contemporary music and jazz. The latter is among the largest areas of enrollment, along with piano and voice. The distinguished faculty includes many players from the city's foremost institutions, such as the New York Philharmonic and the Metropolitan Opera. The school places major emphasis on performance opportunities for students in a variety of orchestras and ensembles. Though not as insanely competitive as Juilliard, Manhattan accepts only about 40 percent of the applicants from a strong pool. Financial aid is awarded on the basis of both demonstrated need and artistic talent, with a fraction of the money bestowed on the basis of merit alone. Funds are limited, and only fourteen of fifty-four aid applicants had their need fully met in a recent year.

*Deadlines:*
    ADMISSION: Dec. 15 (priority)
    FAFSA: Mar. 15
    CSS PROFILE: Mar. 15

# MANHATTANVILLE COLLEGE ✦ Purchase, NY 10577

| | |
|---|---|
| TOTAL ENROLLMENT: | 1,900 |
| UNDERGRADUATE: | 1,100 |
| ACCEPTANCE RATE: | 73% |
| SAT RANGE: | 410–490 Verbal |
| | 430–560 Math |
| STICKER PRICE: | $26,000+ |
| NEED-BLIND: | Yes |
| NEED MET: | 82% |
| AVERAGE STUDENT DEBT: | $17,500 |
| MERIT SCHOLARSHIPS: | Many |
| RANGE: | Up to $10,000 |
| ATHLETIC SCHOLARSHIPS: | No |
| ROTC: | No |
| WEB SITE: | www.manhattanville.edu |
| PHONE: | (800) 328-4553 |

To paraphrase Mark Twain, the difference between Manhattan and Manhattanville is like the difference between lightning and a lightning bug. Manhattanville is indeed located near New York City, but in the open countryside of affluent Westchester County. The cornerstone of a Manhattanville education is a required student portfolio, developed from the first year on campus, where students illustrate what they have learned and outline plans for future study. Economics and management head the list of most popular majors, and with numerous Fortune 500 companies headquartered in the area, there are abundant opportunities for hands-on experience. All students begin their Manhattanville careers with the freshman Preceptorial, an interdisciplinary seminar that emphasizes reading and writing and provides an introduction to college life. A whopping 80 percent of entering students get a merit award at one of three levels: Board of Trustees Scholarship, $8,500 to $10,000; President's Scholarship, $7,500; or a Merit Award of $5,500. Additional scholarships are available for transfers and returning students.

*Deadlines:*
ADMISSION: Mar. 1 (priority)
FAFSA: Mar. 1
CSS PROFILE: Rolling

# MARLBORO COLLEGE ✦ Marlboro, VT 05344

| | |
|---|---|
| TOTAL ENROLLMENT: | 300 |
| UNDERGRADUATE: | 300 |
| ACCEPTANCE RATE: | 75% |
| SAT RANGE: | 560–680 Verbal |
| | 500–610 Math |
| STICKER PRICE: | $27,000+ |
| NEED-BLIND: | Yes |
| NEED MET: | 98% |
| AVERAGE STUDENT DEBT: | $15,700 |
| MERIT SCHOLARSHIPS: | Few |
| RANGE: | Up to $3,000 |
| ATHLETIC SCHOLARSHIPS: | No |
| ROTC: | No |
| WEB SITE: | www.marlboro.edu |
| PHONE: | (800) 343-0049 |

At most colleges, administrative higher-ups make the policy decisions and students follow along. Not so at Marlboro, where everyone down to the lowliest first-year student has a vote at the town meetings that govern the college. Marlboro's communal ethic dates to its founding in 1946, when a handful of faculty and students came together to remodel two dairy farms into a college. Marlboro's unique brand of education allows students to work in small groups and one-on-one with faculty as they design their own courses of study. Students must be self-motivated to succeed, though the college provides structure with features like the Clear Writing Requirement, which stipulates that students complete a twenty-page portfolio by the end their first year to demonstrate "clear, concise, grammatical, expository writing." Seniors complete a thesis that is evaluated by outside examiners in addition to college faculty. Marlboro awards most of its financial aid to students who have need, though about thirty top applicants get a merit-based scholarship of $3,000.

*Deadlines:*
EARLY DECISION: Nov. 15
EARLY ACTION: Jan. 15
REGULAR ADMISSION: Mar. 1 (priority)
FAFSA: Mar. 1
CSS PROFILE: Mar. 1

## MARQUETTE UNIVERSITY ◆
## Milwaukee, WI 53201

| | |
|---|---|
| TOTAL ENROLLMENT: | 10,600 |
| UNDERGRADUATE: | 7,300 |
| ACCEPTANCE RATE: | 81% |
| SAT RANGE: | 510–620 Verbal |
| | 520–640 Math |
| STICKER PRICE: | $22,000+ |
| NEED-BLIND: | Yes |
| NEED MET: | 97% |
| AVERAGE STUDENT DEBT: | $18,000 |
| MERIT SCHOLARSHIPS: | Many |
| RANGE: | Up to full tuition |
| ATHLETIC SCHOLARSHIPS: | Yes |
| ROTC: | Army, Navy, Air Force |
| WEB SITE: | www.marquette.edu |
| PHONE: | (800) 222-6544 |

Famous for breweries and the escapades of television's *Laverne & Shirley*, Milwaukee is also home to Marquette University, which sits on eighty acres at the heart of the city. Marquette has a broad spectrum of academic programs, including business, communication, education, engineering, and health-related fields. The university's co-operative education program is among the nation's oldest. Marquette offers the full-tuition Raynor Distinguished Scholar Award to selected students who rank in the top 5 percent of their class with an SAT I of 1300 or an ACT of 30. An additional full-tuition award is available for Wisconsin residents. Other scholarships for all-around excellence are offered at levels of $7,500, $6,500, and $4,500; awards of $3,500 are given to students who excel in leadership or community service. The deadline for all is February 1. Each of Marquette's colleges also holds an on-campus scholarship exam for awards of $5,000. Other programs include two NASA Scholarships of $6,500 for students planning a career in space-related fields and one for National Merit Finalists of up to $2,000.

*Deadlines:*
  ADMISSION: Rolling
  FAFSA: Mar. 1

## MARY WASHINGTON COLLEGE ◆
## Fredericksburg, VA 22401

| | |
|---|---|
| Total Enrollment: | 3,800 |
| UNDERGRADUATE: | 3,800 |
| ACCEPTANCE RATE: | 58% |
| SAT RANGE: | 550–640 Verbal |
| | 530–620 Math |
| STICKER PRICE: | In-state, $9,000+ |
| | Out-of-state, $15,000+ |
| NEED-BLIND: | Yes |
| NEED MET: | 65% |
| AVERAGE STUDENT DEBT: | $10,000 |
| MERIT SCHOLARSHIPS: | Few |
| RANGE: | Up to full tuition |
| ATHLETIC SCHOLARSHIPS: | No |
| ROTC: | No |
| WEB SITE: | www.mwc.edu |
| PHONE: | (800) 468-5614 |

Named for George Washington's mother and built on one of the Civil War's bloodiest battlefields, Mary Washington is steeped in history. But it is also among the leaders of a new breed in higher education, the public liberal arts college, offering the look and feel of a private institution at a fraction of the cost. Even the out-of-state sticker price of $15,000 is roughly half that of many private colleges that offer a similar education. Business administration, English, and psychology top the list of most popular majors, and Mary Washington features a notable program in historic preservation. Most of Mary Washington's freshman merit awards are delivered via the Alumni Scholarship Program; typical stipends range from $500 to $1,000, but a few of the most outstanding students get awards equal to full in-state tuition and fees. Winners are selected from those who apply by January 15. Special scholarships based on merit and need go to students in various majors or who live in particular geographic areas.

*Deadlines:*
  EARLY DECISION: Nov. 1
  REGULAR ADMISSION: Feb. 1
  FAFSA: MAR. 1

# MARYLAND INSTITUTE, COLLEGE OF ART ✦
## Baltimore, MD 21217

| | |
|---|---|
| TOTAL ENROLLMENT: | 1,100 |
| UNDERGRADUATE: | 1,000 |
| ACCEPTANCE RATE: | 50% |
| SAT AVERAGE: | 590 Verbal |
| | 550 Math |
| STICKER PRICE: | $24,000+ |
| NEED-BLIND: | Yes |
| NEED MET: | 70% |
| AVERAGE STUDENT DEBT: | $17,000 |
| MERIT SCHOLARSHIPS: | Many |
| RANGE: | Up to $7,500 |
| ATHLETIC SCHOLARSHIPS: | No |
| ROTC: | No |
| WEB SITE: | www.mica.edu |
| PHONE: | (410) 225-2222 |

Maryland Institute is the oldest art college in the nation and also one of the best. Located in a historic neighborhood near downtown Baltimore, MICA's undergraduate degree programs include design, illustration, interior architecture, painting, and sculpture. Students are required to take a third of their courses in the liberal arts, and they can also study at participating area institutions such as Goucher and Johns Hopkins. MICA has an unusually wide variety of merit scholarships which are parceled in various competitions. Examples include the Fanny B. Thalheimer Scholarship, which features thirty-eight renewable grants ranging from $2,500 to $6,250. Eight $2,500 awards are available for international students, and twenty $1,000 scholarships go to students who are members of the National Art Honor Society. Two other competitions bestow scholarships on the basis of talent and need; awards also target residents of Baltimore, Catholics from Baltimore, and winners of the State of Maryland's Distinguished Scholar Award in the visual arts. For all programs, a short scholarship application is required.

*Deadlines:*
EARLY DECISION: Nov. 15
REGULAR ADMISSION: Feb. 1
FAFSA: Mar. 1

# UNIVERSITY OF MARYLAND ✦
## College Park, MA 20742

| | |
|---|---|
| TOTAL ENROLLMENT: | 32,700 |
| UNDERGRADUATE: | 24,500 |
| ACCEPTANCE RATE: | 65% |
| SAT RANGE: | 540–650 Verbal |
| | 560–670 Math |
| STICKER PRICE: | In-state, $11,000+ |
| | Out-of-state, $17,000+ |
| NEED-BLIND: | Yes |
| NEED MET: | 71% |
| AVERAGE STUDENT DEBT: | $14,300 |
| MERIT SCHOLARSHIPS: | Many |
| RANGE: | Up to full costs |
| ATHLETIC SCHOLARSHIPS: | Yes |
| ROTC: | Army, Navy, Air Force |
| WEB SITE: | www.umd.edu |
| PHONE: | (800) 422-5867 |

If you're the kind of person who has a mental picture of what a college campus should look like, chances are that it closely resembles the classic colonial look of the University of Maryland. Located in arm's length of the nation's capital, within one of the nation's highest concentrations of well-educated people, Maryland has never gotten the respect it deserves vis-à-vis institutions like Penn State or the University of Virginia. A particularly fine option for top students is the College Park Scholars, a residential learning community with numerous enrichment programs. The university's most outstanding applicants are chosen for the Banneker/Key and Regents Scholarships, which cover full costs plus an additional stipend. A third program offers awards of $2,000 to $4,500 per year, and those with unusual talent in art, dance, music, or theater can audition for awards up to full in-state tuition. Smaller scholarships are offered by various academic divisions. In order to get full consideration for merit awards and special programs, students must apply for admission by December 1.

*Deadlines:*
EARLY ACTION: Dec. 1
REGULAR ADMISSION: FEB. 15
FAFSA: Feb. 15

## MASSACHUSSETTS INSTITUTE OF TECHNOLOGY ✦ Cambridge, MA 02139

| | |
|---|---|
| TOTAL ENROLLMENT: | 9,900 |
| UNDERGRADUATE: | 4,400 |
| ACCEPTANCE RATE: | 25% |
| SAT RANGE: | 660–760 Verbal |
| | 730–800 Math |
| STICKER PRICE: | $31,000+ |
| NEED-BLIND: | Yes |
| NEED MET: | 100% |
| AVERAGE STUDENT DEBT: | $22,600 |
| MERIT SCHOLARSHIPS: | None |
| ATHLETIC SCHOLARSHIPS: | No |
| ROTC: | Army, Navy, Air Force |
| WEB SITE: | web.mit.edu |
| PHONE: | (617) 253-4791 |

In high schools from coast to coast, wherever there is a math genius or a science whiz, you'll find students whose fondest dream is to attend MIT. The sum of MIT's brain power creates dazzling opportunities, although freshmen must quickly learn to cope with being another face in the crowd rather than the smartest person in the class. The MIT mystique is enhanced by its location in Boston—a.k.a. the Hub of the Universe—and the fact that Harvard shares the same neighborhood. The "tute" is tops in just about anything related to science and technology; its most popular majors include electrical engineering/computer science, mechanical engineering, and biology. Not content with mere technical wizardry, MIT also excels in the social sciences, notably economics and political science. MIT is among the elite institutions that beefed up need-based aid in 1998; the change increased grants in many aid packages by $1,000 while lowering the standard amount of loans and work study. MIT offers no merit scholarships aside from ROTC.

*Deadlines:*
  EARLY ACTION: Nov. 15
  REGULAR ADMISSION: Jan. 1
  FAFSA: Jan. 15
  CSS PROFILE: Jan. 15

## UNIVERSITY OF MASSACHUSETTS/AMHERST ✦ Amherst, MA 01003

| | |
|---|---|
| TOTAL ENROLLMENT: | 24,900 |
| UNDERGRADUATE: | 19,000 |
| ACCEPTANCE RATE: | 73% |
| SAT RANGE: | 500–610 Verbal |
| | 510–610 Math |
| STICKER PRICE: | In-state, $10,000+ |
| | Out-of-state, $17,000+ |
| NEED-BLIND: | Yes |
| NEED MET: | NA |
| AVERAGE STUDENT DEBT: | $12,700 |
| MERIT SCHOLARSHIPS: | Many |
| RANGE: | Up to full costs |
| ATHLETIC SCHOLARSHIPS: | Yes |
| ROTC: | Army, Air Force |
| WEB SITE: | www.umass.edu |
| PHONE: | (413) 545-0222 |

New England has traditionally been the domain of elite private universities, but as tuition continues to zoom skyward, more and more top students are discovering the virtues of public institutions like UMass. The university is ideally situated in a cosmopolitan town in the foothills of the Berkshires and enjoys the benefits of a coordinate relationship with four elite private colleges: Amherst, Hampshire, Smith, and Mount Holyoke. In addition to small classes and other perks, the honors program offers students the chance to do independent research, for which they can receive fellowship funding. Massachusetts students in the top 5 percent of their class who score at least 1400 on the SAT I may be considered for the Commonwealth Scholars Program, which covers full costs. A second $8,000-per-year program honors Massachusetts valedictorians and salutatorians. A $5,000 award is aimed at minority students, and additional grants honor students who have shown achievement in academics or the arts. Other awards are available with varying criteria.

*Deadlines:*
  ADMISSION: Feb. 1
  FAFSA: Feb. 15

## McGILL UNIVERSITY ✦ Montreal, Quebec H3A 2T5

| | |
|---|---|
| TOTAL ENROLLMENT: | 29,400 |
| UNDERGRADUATE: | 21,300 |
| ACCEPTANCE RATE: | 58% |
| SAT RANGE: | NA |
| STICKER PRICE: | In-province, $10,000+ (Canadian) |
| | Out-of-province, $12,000+ (Canadian) |
| | International, $11,000+ (U.S. dollars) |
| NEED-BLIND: | NA |
| NEED MET: | NA |
| AVERAGE STUDENT DEBT: | NA |
| MERIT SCHOLARSHIPS: | Many |
| RANGE: | Up to $10,000 |
| ATHLETIC SCHOLARSHIPS: | No |
| ROTC: | No |
| WEB SITE: | www.mcgill.ca |
| PHONE: | (514) 398-3910 |

Going to Canada was popular in the 1960s to avoid the Vietnam War, but today 18-year-olds have a different reason for heading north of the border: college education at a bargain price. Canadian universities are comparable to state institutions in the United States, and more and more are aggressively recruiting Americans. McGill is often referred to as the Harvard of Canada and offers the full gamut of liberal arts programs with pre-professional offerings that include architecture, commerce, education, engineering, nursing and health professions, and social work. U.S. citizens make up about 10 percent of the student body. Montreal is one of North America's most exciting and cosmopolitan cities, and because of its location in Quebec, proficiency in French is a must. (English is McGill's language of instruction.) McGill offers a wide variety of merit scholarships, which range from $2,000 to $10,000 (Canadian); about a tenth of a recent entering class received one. Most scholarships are open to U.S. applicants, and a few target them directly.

*Deadlines:*
  ADMISSION: Jan. 15
  FAFSA: Rolling

## MIAMI UNIVERSITY ✦ Oxford, OH 45056

| | |
|---|---|
| TOTAL ENROLLMENT: | 16,300 |
| UNDERGRADUATE: | 14,700 |
| ACCEPTANCE RATE: | 77% |
| SAT RANGE: | 540–630 Verbal |
| | 560–650 Math |
| STICKER PRICE: | In-state, $11,000+ |
| | Out-of-state, $17,000+ |
| NEED-BLIND: | Yes |
| NEED MET: | 70% |
| AVERAGE STUDENT DEBT: | $14,100 |
| MERIT SCHOLARSHIPS: | Many |
| RANGE: | Up to full costs |
| ATHLETIC SCHOLARSHIPS: | Yes |
| ROTC: | Army, Navy, Air Force |
| WEB SITE: | www.muohio.edu |
| PHONE: | (513) 529-2531 |

Mention Miami University and most people think of surfer dudes or the nationally ranked Hurricane football team. Such is the understandable confusion with Florida's University of Miami, but *this* Miami is 1,000 miles north, in Ohio, and has a ranking of its own as one of the nation's premier public universities. With the aura of a private college and a sticker price thousands less, Miami attracts plenty of upscale students whose families are doubtful of getting need-based aid at more expensive colleges. The highly sought-after Harrison Scholarship, which covers full costs, goes to ten students with an SAT I of at least 1310 or ACT of 30. But mark your calendar: the deadline is October 1. The Miami Scholars award gives up to $3,000 to students with a 1200 on the SAT I or 27 on the ACT. Other awards are available for high school valedictorians, National Merit Finalists, minority students, and those who enroll in the honors program. Over 650 Miami freshmen got a merit or merit-within-need award in a recent year, with most scholarships in the $1,000 to $2,000 range.

*Deadlines:*
  EARLY DECISION: Nov. 1
  REGULAR ADMISSION: Jan. 31
  FAFSA: Feb. 15

# UNIVERSITY OF MIAMI ◆
## Coral Gables, FL 33124

| | |
|---|---|
| TOTAL ENROLLMENT: | 13,200 |
| UNDERGRADUATE: | 8,000 |
| ACCEPTANCE RATE: | 60% |
| SAT RANGE: | 1040–1240 combined |
| STICKER PRICE: | $27,000+ |
| NEED-BLIND: | Yes |
| NEED MET: | NA |
| AVERAGE STUDENT DEBT: | NA |
| MERIT SCHOLARSHIPS: | Many |
| RANGE: | Up to full tuition |
| ATHLETIC SCHOLARSHIPS: | Yes |
| ROTC: | Army, Air Force |
| WEB SITE: | www.miami.edu |
| PHONE: | (305) 284-4323 |

With nearly as many palm trees as people on its 260-acre campus, the University of Miami is a Shangri-la that most students can only dream about. But the reason for Miami's surging popularity has more to do with its academic climate. Among Miami's strongest programs are architecture, business, international studies, marine science, and performing arts. Perhaps the biggest draw of all may be Miami's huge merit scholarship program, which annually bestows awards on nearly half of the entering class. Topping the list is the full-tuition Singer Scholarship for those with a 4.0 GPA and matching test scores; runners-up qualify for a three-quarter tuition award. More than a fifth of each class gets the half-tuition Stanford Scholarship, which requires a top 10 percent class rank and 1270 on the SAT I or 28 on the ACT. Students in the top 20 percent with 1180 or 26 get a one-third tuition discount. Scholarship programs of up to full tuition are available for music students and those of African descent.

*Deadlines:*
  EARLY DECISION: Nov. 15
  EARLY ACTION: Nov. 15
  REGULAR ADMISSION: Mar. 1
  FAFSA: Feb. 15

# MICHIGAN STATE UNIVERSITY ◆
## East Lansing, MI 48824

| | |
|---|---|
| TOTAL ENROLLMENT: | 42,600 |
| UNDERGRADUATE: | 33,300 |
| ACCEPTANCE RATE: | 81% |
| SAT RANGE: | 480–610 Verbal |
| | 500–620 Math |
| STICKER PRICE: | In-state, $9,000+ |
| | Out-of-state, $16,000+ |
| NEED-BLIND: | Yes |
| NEED MET: | 100% |
| AVERAGE STUDENT DEBT: | $15,800 |
| MERIT SCHOLARSHIPS: | Many |
| RANGE: | Up to full costs |
| ATHLETIC SCHOLARSHIPS: | Yes |
| ROTC: | Army, Air Force |
| WEB SITE: | www.msu.edu |
| PHONE: | (517) 355-8332 |

The University of Michigan is often viewed as the quintessential mega-university, but people forget that Michigan State actually has nearly 10,000 more undergraduates. MSU offers the huge array of programs that only a super-sized university could provide, yet some of the best of them manage to create a small-college atmosphere. Particularly notable are the innovative James Madison and Lyman Briggs programs, which offer integrated living/learning experiences for students in the social sciences (Madison) or the natural sciences and math (Briggs). MSU recently vowed to limit tuition increases to no more than the rate of inflation. The Alumni Distinguished Scholarship is MSU's biggest merit prize, offering full costs plus a $1,000 stipend to ten top scorers on an exam held in February. Even runners-up can qualify for full-tuition awards, but aspirants must apply for admission by November 1. Other scholarships are aimed at Honors College participants, out-of-staters, children of alumni, 4-H participants, National Merit and National Achievement honorees, and students in particular academic fields.

*Deadlines:*
  ADMISSION: Jul. 20
  FAFSA: Rolling

## MICHIGAN TECHNOLOGICAL UNIVERSITY •
## Houghton, MI 49931

| | |
|---|---|
| TOTAL ENROLLMENT: | 6,200 |
| UNDERGRADUATE: | 5,500 |
| ACCEPTANCE RATE: | 97% |
| ACT RANGE: | 23–28 |
| STICKER PRICE: | In-state, $9,000+ |
| | Out-of-state, $15,000+ |
| NEED-BLIND: | Yes |
| NEED MET: | NA |
| AVERAGE STUDENT DEBT: | $10,700 |
| MERIT SCHOLARSHIPS: | Many |
| RANGE: | Up to full costs |
| ATHLETIC SCHOLARSHIPS: | Yes |
| ROTC: | Army, Air Force |
| WEB SITE: | www.mtu.edu |
| PHONE: | (906) 487-2335 |

Michigan Tech is the upper-Midwest's only major university devoted to science and technology. Founded in 1885 as the Michigan Mining School, MTU has the nation's largest enrollment in metallurgical and materials engineering. Well over half the students major in technical fields, although the university also offers programs in arts and sciences, business, and forestry. In-staters account for nearly three-quarters of the students, and the University Scholar Awards cover full costs for outstanding Michigan residents who are nominated by a math or science teacher. (The deadline is in early October.) Runners-up in the competition may qualify for Board of Control Scholarships, worth up to full tuition. A full-tuition scholarship is available for underrepresented minorities from the Detroit area, and National Merit Scholars get an award of up to $2,000 depending on need. Other academic scholarships of $5,100 per year go to out-of-staters with a high school class rank in the top 15 percent, and to out-of-state sons and daughters of alumni in the top 20 percent.

*Deadline:*
  ADMISSION: Rolling
  FAFSA: Feb.10

## UNIVERSITY OF MICHIGAN •
## Ann Arbor, MI 48104

| | |
|---|---|
| TOTAL ENROLLMENT: | 37,000 |
| UNDERGRADUATE: | 23,900 |
| ACCEPTANCE RATE: | 69% |
| SAT RANGE: | 560–660 Verbal |
| | 600–700 Math |
| STICKER PRICE: | In-state, $12,000+ |
| | Out-of-state, $25,000+ |
| NEED-BLIND: | Yes |
| NEED MET: | 90% |
| AVERAGE STUDENT DEBT: | $13,200 |
| MERIT SCHOLARSHIPS: | Many |
| RANGE: | Up to full tuition |
| ATHLETIC SCHOLARSHIPS: | Yes |
| ROTC: | Army, Navy, Air Force |
| WEB SITE: | www.umich.edu |
| PHONE: | (734) 764-7433 |

The University of Michigan stands second to none in the pantheon of great public universities. With a galaxy of strong departments in dozens of fields, Michigan is at its best in the special programs that it styles "learning communities." Particularly notable is the Residential College, which gives 1,000 liberal arts students the chance to live and learn together while working closely with faculty. With out-of-state tuition about $20,000, UM is barely less expensive for non-Michiganders than the elite private universities where they also apply. Michigan's top merit awards include the Bentley Scholarship, which offers $10,000 per year to four outstanding in-state liberal arts students, and the Shipman Scholarship, which bestows $7,500 plus room and board. Both require students to be admitted by January 15. Scholarships for underrepresented minorities go up to full tuition, and other merit-based awards are designated for both in- and out-of-staters. Numerous scholarships are also available through the university's various academic divisions.

*Deadlines:*
  ADMISSION: Feb. 1
  FAFSA: Feb. 1

# MIDDLEBURY COLLEGE ✦ Middlebury, VT 05753

| | |
|---|---|
| TOTAL ENROLLMENT: | 2,200 |
| UNDERGRADUATE: | 2,200 |
| ACCEPTANCE RATE: | 31% |
| SAT RANGE: | 670–730 Verbal |
| | 640–720 Math |
| STICKER PRICE: | $31,000+ |
| NEED-BLIND: | Yes |
| NEED MET: | 100% |
| AVERAGE STUDENT DEBT: | NA |
| MERIT SCHOLARSHIPS: | None |
| ATHLETIC SCHOLARSHIPS: | No |
| ROTC: | No |
| WEB SITE: | www.middlebury.edu |
| PHONE: | (802) 443-3000 |

With a picture-postcard campus nestled between the Adirondacks and the Green Mountains in central Vermont, Middlebury is rising in the ranks of prestigious private colleges. The college is especially strong in two of today's hottest majors—international studies and environmental studies—and is known far and wide for its outstanding foreign language programs. Nearly two-thirds of Middlebury students study abroad, many of them at college programs in France, Germany, Italy, Russia, and Spain. Middlebury has always been popular among those who love winter sports; the college has its own ski bowl in the nearby mountains, and the men's ice hockey team is a perennial Division III national champion. Middlebury is among the colleges that have made the SAT I optional, and students can substitute scores from the SAT II, Advanced Placement exams, International Baccalaureate exams, or the ACT. (About 20 percent of accepted applicants do so.) With an endowment that ranks near the top among selective private colleges, Middlebury offers abundant need-based aid but no merit scholarships.

*Deadlines:*
    EARLY DECISION: Nov. 15, Dec. 15
    REGULAR ADMISSION: Jan. 15
    FAFSA: Jan. 15
    CSS PROFILE: Jan. 15

# MILLS COLLEGE ✦ Oakland, CA 94613

| | |
|---|---|
| TOTAL ENROLLMENT: | 1,100 |
| UNDERGRADUATE: | 1,100 |
| ACCEPTANCE RATE: | 82% |
| SAT RANGE: | 520–640 Verbal |
| | 480–580 Math |
| STICKER PRICE: | $25,000+ |
| NEED-BLIND: | Yes |
| NEED MET: | NA |
| AVERAGE STUDENT DEBT: | NA |
| MERIT SCHOLARSHIPS: | Few |
| ATHLETIC SCHOLARSHIPS: | No |
| ROTC: | No |
| WEB SITE: | www.mills.edu |
| PHONE: | (800) 87-MILLS |

Mills is a small California women's college that almost decided to go coed in the late 1980s, but changed course when fierce protests greeted the announcement. Mills women have always had an independent streak, and with an average class size of only fifteen students, they get plenty of opportunities to express themselves. Mills is best-known in the arts and humanities; special programs include a Center for Contemporary Music, which specializes in electronic and computer music, and a working elementary school. Mills offers several merit scholarship programs, but the total number of awards is modest. Three "freshwomen" receive $10,000 Trustee Scholarships, given on the basis of merit and need, and ten awards of $2,000 are offered on merit alone. Applicants for there awards should have at least a 3.5 GPA and an SAT I score of 1200 or better. Ten Regional Scholarships of $5,000 go to students who show all-around excellence and contribute to regional diversity, two $5,000 awards go to outstanding musicians, and one $2,000 targets those in math/science.

*Deadlines:*
    ADMISSION: Feb. 15 (priority)
    FAFSA: Feb. 15

# MILLSAPS COLLEGE ✦ Jackson, MS 39210

| | |
|---|---|
| TOTAL ENROLLMENT: | 1,400 |
| UNDERGRADUATE: | 1,200 |
| ACCEPTANCE RATE: | 81% |
| SAT RANGE: | 540–680 Verbal |
| | 560–660 Math |
| STICKER PRICE: | $20,000+ |
| NEED-BLIND: | Yes |
| NEED MET: | 94% |
| AVERAGE STUDENT DEBT: | $17,300 |
| MERIT SCHOLARSHIPS: | Many |
| RANGE: | Up to $13,000 |
| ATHLETIC SCHOLARSHIPS: | No |
| ROTC: | Army |
| WEB SITE: | www.millsaps.edu |
| PHONE: | (800) 352-1050 |

Reuben Millsaps rose from the backwoods of Mississippi to attend Harvard Law School, and in 1890 he founded a small college where a little of his spirit is still alive today. Along with Hendrix in Arkansas and Rhodes in Tennessee, Millsaps is among the leading liberal arts colleges in the geographic triangle between Georgia, Texas, and southern Missouri. Though not a hotbed of liberalism by national standards, Millsaps is far more progressive than the rest of Mississippi and is located in Jackson, the state capital. Millsaps has a wide-ranging merit scholarship program, and students with a 3.2 GPA, an SAT I of 1150, or an ACT of 26 are encouraged to apply. The Second Century Scholars Program offers awards of up $13,000 with an emphasis on out-of-school activities as well as academics. Other stipends go to students in the fine arts (up to $10,000), those planning a business major ($3,000), Mississippi residents, and those active in a United Methodist church. Scholarship consideration requires a separate application filed by the priority regular admission deadline.

*Deadlines:*
EARLY DECISION: Nov. 15
REGULAR ADMISSION: Feb. 1 (priority)
FAFSA: Mar. 1

# UNIVERSITY OF MINNESOTA/MORRIS ✦ Morris, MN 56267

| | |
|---|---|
| TOTAL ENROLLMENT: | 1,900 |
| UNDERGRADUATE: | 1,900 |
| ACCEPTANCE RATE: | 87% |
| SAT RANGE: | 560–670 Verbal |
| | 520–660 Math |
| STICKER PRICE: | In-state, $9,000+ |
| | Out-of-state, $13,000+ |
| NEED-BLIND: | Yes |
| NEED MET: | 85% |
| AVERAGE STUDENT DEBT: | $10,300 |
| MERIT SCHOLARSHIPS: | Many |
| RANGE: | Up to half tuition |
| ATHLETIC SCHOLARSHIPS: | No |
| ROTC: | No |
| WEB SITE: | www.mrs.umn.edu.edu |
| PHONE: | (800) 992-8863 |

The prairie of western Minnesota is the improbable home for one of higher education's most unusual institutions—a remote outpost of the University of Minnesota dedicated to the liberal arts. Minnesota/Morris offers the amenities of a small private college, most notably small classes and close interaction with faculty, but at a price tag that will be music to the ears of even the most penny-pinching parents. Under the terms of the Freshman Academic Scholarships, students in the top 5 percent of their high school class are automatically awarded a half-tuition scholarship, while those in the top 10 percent get one-quarter tuition. Presidential Scholarships of $2,000 require a special application due February 15. An additional scholarship of up to $3,000 targets minority students, and tuition for Native Americans is waived due to Morris's heritage as an Indian boarding school in the 1880s. Along with an award for National Merit Finalists, Morris offers $1,000 to a limited number of National Merit Commended students on a first-come, first-served basis.

*Deadlines:*
EARLY ACTION: Dec. 1, Feb. 1
REGULAR ADMISSION: Mar. 15
FAFSA: Apr. 1

## UNIVERSITY OF MINNESOTA/TWIN CITIES ✦
## Minneapolis, MN 55455

| | |
|---|---|
| TOTAL ENROLLMENT: | 37,600 |
| UNDERGRADUATE: | 24,300 |
| ACCEPTANCE RATE: | 80% |
| SAT RANGE: | 510–640 Verbal |
| | 530–670 Math |
| STICKER PRICE: | In-state, $9,000+ |
| | Out-of-state, $16,000+ |
| NEED-BLIND: | YES |
| NEED MET: | 100% |
| AVERAGE STUDENT DEBT: | NA |
| MERIT SCHOLARSHIPS: | Many |
| ATHLETIC SCHOLARSHIPS: | Yes |
| ROTC: | Army, Navy, Air Force |
| WEB SITE: | www.umn.edu/tc |
| PHONE: | (800) 752-1000 |

The combined resources of the University of Minnesota/Twin Cities include 19 colleges, 161 bachelor's degree programs, and all the attractions of one of America's most cosmopolitan urban areas. To avoid being submerged in a sea of humanity, top students should check out the honors programs, which are run by the separate colleges and generally require a first-rate high school record and a score of 1260 or better on the SAT I or 28 on the ACT. Merit awards include the U2000 Scholarship which offers $5,000 to selected students who graduate in the top 3 percent of their high school class in Minnesota and other nearby states. The deadline is January 15. Other awards are available for Minnesota residents in the top 10 percent, and the Gopher State Scholarships offer a $1,000 stipend renewable for one year to out-of-staters in the top 5 percent. Scholarships of up to $5,000 are available to students of color, and a variable award is given to selected students who are at least one-quarter Native American.

*Deadlines:*
  ADMISSION: Dec. 15 (priority)
  FAFSA: Feb. 15

## UNIVERSITY OF MISSOURI/COLUMBIA ✦
## Columbia, MO 65211

| | |
|---|---|
| TOTAL ENROLLMENT: | 22,600 |
| UNDERGRADUATE: | 17,300 |
| ACCEPTANCE RATE: | 79% |
| ACT RANGE: | 24–29 |
| STICKER PRICE: | In-state, $9,000+ |
| | Out-of-state, $17,000+ |
| NEED-BLIND: | Yes |
| NEED MET: | 90% |
| AVERAGE STUDENT DEBT: | $14,800 |
| MERIT SCHOLARSHIPS: | Many |
| ATHLETIC SCHOLARSHIPS: | Yes |
| ROTC: | Army, Navy, Air Force |
| WEB SITE: | www.missouri.edu |
| PHONE: | (800) 225-6075 |

As the flagship public university of the Show Me state, Mizzou is a major research university. But it also emphasizes undergraduate teaching to an unusual degree for a school its size. The university is notable for its development of Freshman Interest Groups (FIGs), which allow students with shared concerns to live in common housing. Journalism is Mizzou's most famous academic division, and business administration is the most popular major. The university has more than 100 general scholarship programs, and many more sponsored by its academic divisions. Among the most lucrative is the Curators Scholars Award, which goes to Missouri students in the top 5 percent of their high school class who score at least 1240 on the SAT I or 28 on the ACT. Chancellor's Scholars awards of $2,500 honor students with slightly lesser qualifications, and top minority students can garner up to $8,500. A Nonresident Scholars Award offers up to $5,500 to out-of-staters in the top 25 percent who score at least 1200 or 27. The application deadline for scholarships is December 1.

*Deadlines:*
  ADMISSION: May 1
  FAFSA: Mar. 1

## UNIVERSITY OF MISSOURI/ROLLA ✦
## Rolla, MO 65409

| | |
|---|---|
| TOTAL ENROLLMENT: | 5,000 |
| UNDERGRADUATE: | 4,100 |
| ACCEPTANCE RATE: | 97% |
| SAT RANGE: | 570–670 Verbal |
| | 600–700 Math |
| STICKER PRICE: | In-state, $9,000+ |
| | Out-of-state, $17,000+ |
| NEED-BLIND: | Yes |
| NEED MET: | 81% |
| AVERAGE STUDENT DEBT: | $11,000 |
| MERIT SCHOLARSHIPS: | Many |
| RANGE: | Up to $12,000 |
| ATHLETIC SCHOLARSHIPS: | Yes |
| ROTC: | Army, Air Force |
| WEB SITE: | www.umr.edu |
| PHONE: | (800) 522-0938 |

The fact that Missouri/Rolla was founded as Missouri School of Mines and Metallurgy is the first hint that UMR is not your typical state university. With as many techies per capita as any school in the country, UMR offers programs ranging from electromagnetics to explosives engineering—and a few liberal arts programs mixed in for good measure. The university has an extensive cooperative education program that allows students to earn while they learn. UMR has an early bird priority deadline of November 1 for scholarships. The elite Master Student Fellowship, worth $12,000 for out-of-staters and $8,000 for in-staters, goes to students in the top 5 percent of their high school class with an SAT I of 1320 or an ACT of 30. The UMR Chancellor's Scholarship offers $9,000 to selected Missouri residents in the top 10 percent with an ACT of 30 or above. Other scholarships are aimed at women and minority engineers. There is a $2,000 award for National Merit Finalists and many more offered by particular departments.

*Deadlines:*
   ADMISSION: Rolling
   FAFSA: Mar. 1

## MONTANA TECH OF THE UNIVERSITY OF
## MONTANA ✦ Butte, MT 59701

| | |
|---|---|
| TOTAL ENROLLMENT: | 1,800 |
| UNDERGRADUATE: | 1,700 |
| ACCEPTANCE RATE: | 99% |
| SAT AVERAGE: | 526 Verbal |
| | 555 Math |
| STICKER PRICE: | In-state, $6,000+ |
| | Out-of-state, $11,000+ |
| NEED-BLIND: | Yes |
| NEED MET: | 80% |
| AVERAGE STUDENT DEBT: | $10,000 |
| MERIT SCHOLARSHIPS: | Many |
| ATHLETIC SCHOLARSHIPS: | Yes |
| ROTC: | Army, Air Force |
| WEB SITE: | www.mtech.edu |
| PHONE: | (800) 445-8324 |

In the Big Sky country of Montana, the mountains are high, the air is clear, and the ground is full of virtually every precious metal in the periodic table. Founded as Montana School of Mines in 1900, Montana Tech has been teaching students how to extract that treasure for the past 100 years. In addition to mining-related fields, the school offers other engineering and science disciplines, math, computer science, and business. The school's most popular majors are environmental engineering and environmental science. Though a Montana Tech education is rigorous, admission standards are not. Of 468 applicants in a recent year, only two were denied admission. In addition to being a great place to study mining and engineering, Butte is near a myriad of mountain playgrounds for hiking, backpacking, and skiing enthusiasts. Approximately one-third of entering freshmen at Montana Tech get one of more than 100 scholarships designated for new students, most of which are based on academic merit and leadership. Scholarship applicants are advised to apply by February 15.

*Deadlines:*
   ADMISSION: Jul. 1
   FAFSA: Apr. 1

# MOREHOUSE COLLEGE ✦ Atlanta, GA 30314

| | |
|---|---|
| TOTAL ENROLLMENT: | 3,000 |
| UNDERGRADUATE: | 3,000 |
| ACCEPTANCE RATE: | 69% |
| SAT AVERAGE: | 527 Verbal |
| | 529 Math |
| STICKER PRICE: | $17,000+ |
| NEED-BLIND: | Yes |
| NEED MET: | NA |
| AVERAGE STUDENT DEBT: | $18,000 |
| MERIT SCHOLARSHIPS: | Many |
| RANGE: | Up to full costs |
| ATHLETIC SCHOLARSHIPS: | Yes |
| ROTC: | Army, Navy, Air Force |
| WEB SITE: | www.morehouse.edu |
| PHONE: | (800) 851-1254 |

It is an ironic twist that the campus of Morehouse College sits on a spot of ground that was once a fortification of the Confederate army during the Civil War. Today, Morehouse and its fellow institutions in the Atlanta University Center comprise the nation's leading center for the education of African Americans. Morehouse maintains close ties with neighboring all-female Spelman College; the two were often likened to Harvard and Radcliffe in the days when Radcliffe had a separate identity. The college annually awards nearly 100 merit scholarships to deserving students on the basis of academic ability and leadership potential. Among the most notable is the McNair Scholarship, which gives awards of up to full costs to students with at least a 3.0 GPA and 1000 on the SAT I who plan to major in math, physics, computer science, or engineering. The program also includes summer internships at NASA and other enrichment opportunities. Talent awards in band and music are also available, as well as scholarships sponsored by individual departments.

*Deadlines:*
EARLY DECISION: Feb. 15
REGULAR ADMISSION: Feb. 15
FAFSA: Feb. 15

# MORGAN STATE UNIVERSITY ✦ Baltimore, MD 21251

| | |
|---|---|
| TOTAL ENROLLMENT: | 5,900 |
| UNDERGRADUATE: | 5,500 |
| ACCEPTANCE RATE: | 55% |
| SAT AVERAGE: | 476 Verbal |
| | 463 Math |
| STICKER PRICE: | In-state, $9,000+ |
| | Out-of-state, 14,000+ |
| NEED-BLIND: | Yes |
| NEED MET: | NA |
| AVERAGE STUDENT DEBT: | NA |
| MERIT SCHOLARSHIPS: | Many |
| RANGE: | Up to full costs |
| ATHLETIC SCHOLARSHIPS: | Yes |
| ROTC: | Army |
| WEB SITE: | www.morgan.edu |
| PHONE: | (800) 332-6674 |

Morgan State is a historically black institution that is known to the general public for its marching band, the Magnificent Marching Machine, which has won fame entertaining U.S. presidents and NFL crowds. In academic circles, Morgan is recognized as one of the foremost producers of African American students who ultimately get a Ph.D. Located in northeast Baltimore and designated the state's "Public Urban University," Morgan's primary academic divisions include architecture, arts and sciences, business, engineering, education, and social work. Morgan offers hundreds of merit awards for entering students in two categories: the Regents Scholars, which covers full costs for students with at least a 3.2 high school GPA and an SAT I of at least 1200 (at least 1100 for in-staters); and the Honors Associates, which gives full tuition to those with a 3.0 and 1100 (1000 for in-staters). A small number of Incentive Awards are available for students with strong credentials who don't make the cut for the other two. Scholarships are awarded to qualifying students on a first-come, first-served basis.

*Deadlines:*
ADMISSION: Jul. 15
FAFSA: Apr. 1

# MOUNT HOLYOKE COLLEGE ✦
## South Hadley, MA 01075

| | |
|---|---|
| TOTAL ENROLLMENT: | 1,900 |
| UNDERGRADUATE: | 1,900 |
| ACCEPTANCE RATE: | 61% |
| SAT RANGE: | 570–690 Verbal |
| | 560–670 Math |
| STICKER PRICE: | $31,000+ |
| NEED-BLIND: | No |
| NEED MET: | 100% |
| AVERAGE STUDENT DEBT: | $15,000 |
| MERIT SCHOLARSHIPS: | None |
| ATHLETIC SCHOLARSHIPS: | No |
| ROTC: | Army, Air Force |
| WEB SITE: | www.mtholyoke.edu |
| PHONE: | (413) 538-2023 |

The oldest of the storied Seven Sisters, Mount Holyoke is a child of the first American women's movement (the one that began in the 1830s). Holyoke's 800-acre campus combines pastoral beauty with ready access to the vast resources offered by fellow members of the Five College Consortium, which includes Amherst, Hampshire, Smith, and the University of Massachusetts. Though Holyoke students are a predominantly liberal group, they are less so than those at rival Smith. The college is distinguished by two innovative curricular initiatives: the Speaking, Arguing, and Writing Program, an unusually focused effort to enhance student communication skills; and the Center for Leadership and Public Interest Advocacy, which helps equip students with the skills they need to become involved citizens. Holyoke has a middle-sized endowment among schools of its caliber and is now among the schools that consider financial need when making some borderline admission decisions, although it meets 100 percent of need for those who do get in.

*Deadlines:*
    EARLY DECISION: Dec. 1, Jan. 1
    REGULAR ADMISSION: Jan. 15
    FAFSA: Feb. 1

# MUHLENBERG COLLEGE ✦
## Allentown, PA 18104

| | |
|---|---|
| TOTAL ENROLLMENT: | 2,100 |
| UNDERGRADUATE: | 2,100 |
| ACCEPTANCE RATE: | 66% |
| SAT RANGE: | 523–617 Verbal |
| | 535–619 Math |
| STICKER PRICE: | $25,000+ |
| NEED-BLIND: | Yes |
| NEED MET: | NA |
| AVERAGE STUDENT DEBT: | $12,700 |
| MERIT SCHOLARSHIPS: | Many |
| Range: | Up to $8,000 |
| ATHLETIC SCHOLARSHIPS: | No |
| ROTC: | Army |
| WEB SITE: | www.muhlenberg.edu |
| PHONE: | (610) 821-3200 |

Muhlenberg enrolls bright, career-oriented students and gives them what they want: practical programs in areas such as business, pre-law, and pre-health professions. Theater arts is also excellent, and Muhlenberg has an unusually strong sense of community that encompasses both students and faculty. The 'Berg also has a refreshing emphasis on student participation rather than mind-numbing lectures. The college faces an uphill battle to wrest students away from competitors such as Franklin and Marshall and Lafayette, but more often wins against Gettysburg or Dickinson. Approximately one-fifth of the students receive a merit scholarship, which ranges from $1,000 to $8,000. Hopefuls must generally be in the top 10 percent with a 1250 or better on the SAT I. Fifteen students per year are chosen for the Muhlenberg Scholars Program, which offers a $3,000 renewable award, sweetened need-based packages, four years of small classes, and independent study opportunities. The Dana Associates Program, also with a $3,000 scholarship, is similar but emphasizes opportunities in the "real world."

*Deadlines:*
    EARLY DECISION: Jan. 15
    REGULAR ADMISSION: Feb. 15
    FAFSA: Feb. 15
    CSS PROFILE: Feb. 15

## MUSKINGUM COLLEGE ◆
### New Concord, OH 43762

| | |
|---|---|
| TOTAL ENROLLMENT: | 1,400 |
| UNDERGRADUATE: | 1,400 |
| ACCEPTANCE RATE: | 81% |
| SAT RANGE: | 470–590 Verbal |
| | 450–580 Math |
| STICKER PRICE: | $16,000+ |
| NEED-BLIND: | Yes |
| NEED MET: | 87% |
| AVERAGE STUDENT DEBT: | $16,300 |
| MERIT SCHOLARSHIPS: | Many |
| RANGE: | Up to full tuition |
| ATHLETIC SCHOLARSHIPS: | No |
| ROTC: | No |
| WEB SITE: | www.muskingum.edu |
| PHONE: | (800) 752-6082 |

Muskingum is a small college in rural Ohio that did the right thing at the right time. By slashing $4,000 off its tuition in 1996, the college made national headlines, shot to the top of the value rankings in national publications, and increased its enrollment by a third. Though a liberal arts college, Muskingum is best-known for business and education, and for its work with students who have learning disabilities. The lower sticker price has theoretically meant less tuition discounting, but an abundance of merit and non-need awards remain. The $25,000 John Glenn Scholarship offers full tuition for outstanding students, and smaller stipends ranging from $2,000 to $9,000 are given to the runners-up. Awards are available for scientists ($1,500), musicians (up to $2,000), and those interested in art, speech, and theater ($1,500). Additional groups that qualify for awards of $1,000 or less include minority students, children and grandchildren of alumni, and members of the Presbyterian Church (U.S.A). Students with a brother or sister enrolled get a 25 percent tuition reduction.

*Deadlines:*
  ADMISSION: Jun. 1
  FAFSA: Mar. 15

## UNIVERSITY OF NEBRASKA ◆
### Lincoln, NE 68588

| | |
|---|---|
| TOTAL ENROLLMENT: | 22,800 |
| UNDERGRADUATE: | 18,200 |
| ACCEPTANCE RATE: | 81% |
| SAT RANGE: | 500–630 Verbal |
| | 510–650 Math |
| STICKER PRICE: | In-state, $7,000+ |
| | Out-of-state, $11,000+ |
| NEED-BLIND: | Yes |
| NEED MET: | 75% |
| AVERAGE STUDENT DEBT: | $14,500 |
| MERIT SCHOLARSHIPS: | Many |
| RANGE: | Up to full costs |
| ATHLETIC SCHOLARSHIPS: | Yes |
| ROTC: | Army, Navy, Air Force |
| WEB SITE: | www.unl.edu |
| PHONE: | (402) 472-2023 |

The University of Nebraska is technically located in the city of Lincoln—but why not call it "Football Town USA"? The gridiron exploits of the Cornhuskers are always front-page news, but UNL also has reason to take pride in its academic offerings. Easily the state's leading university, UNL offers professional training in agriculture, architecture, business, education, engineering, fine arts, and journalism, plus a wide menu of programs in the arts and sciences. The Regents Scholarship provides a full-tuition scholarship to outstanding in-staters based on class rank and test scores, and National Merit Finalists get the same. Nonresidents can qualify for an award that covers the differential between in-state and out-of-state tuition. Other awards of up to full costs target top minority students, and the Chancellor's Leadership Class Scholarship bestows a one-time $1,000 award on students who have shown leadership in high school. Many scholarships are available through the various academic divisions, and students must apply by January 15 for "full scholarship consideration."

*Deadlines:*
  ADMISSION: Jun. 30
  FAFSA: Rolling

## NEW COLLEGE OF THE UNIVERSITY OF SOUTH FLORIDA ✦ Sarasota, FL 34243

| | |
|---|---|
| TOTAL ENROLLMENT: | 600 |
| UNDERGRADUATE: | 600 |
| ACCEPTANCE RATE: | 62% |
| SAT RANGE: | 670–740 Verbal |
| | 600–680 Math |
| STICKER PRICE: | In-state, $7,000+ |
| | Out-of-state, $15,000+ |
| NEED-BLIND: | Yes |
| NEED MET: | 80% |
| AVERAGE STUDENT DEBT: | $12,900 |
| MERIT SCHOLARSHIPS: | Many |
| RANGE: | Up to $7,500 |
| ATHLETIC SCHOLARSHIPS: | No |
| ROTC: | Army, Air Force |
| WEB SITE: | www.newcollege.usf.edu |
| PHONE: | (941) 359-4269 |

Picture yourself lazing on the sun-baked shore of Sarasota Bay—not on vacation, but attending a nationally renowned college that costs a tiny fraction of the price charged at schools of similar quality. Sound too good to be true? Students at New College live the dream every day, and get one of the best bargains in higher education in the process. New College is the honors college of the state of Florida, but it functions like a progressive private college. Instead of letter grades, New College students get narrative assessments of their work, and the emphasis is on individual exploration and hands-on learning. National Merit Finalists who designate New College as their first choice qualify for the biggest merit award ($7,500 for out-of-staters and $5,000 for in-staters), and National Achievement and National Hispanic Scholars also get $5,000. Waivers of the differential between in-state and out-of-state costs are available for top non-Floridians, and additional awards include two that recognize leadership ($2,000) and members of minority groups ($2,000).

*Deadlines:*
  ADMISSION: Mar. 1 (priority)
  FAFSA: Mar. 1

## NEW ENGLAND CONSERVATORY OF MUSIC ✦ Boston, MA 02115

| | |
|---|---|
| TOTAL ENROLLMENT: | 800 |
| UNDERGRADUATE: | 800 |
| ACCEPTANCE RATE: | 45% |
| SAT RANGE: | NA |
| STICKER PRICE: | $29,000+ |
| NEED-BLIND: | Yes |
| NEED MET: | 93% |
| AVERAGE STUDENT DEBT: | $19,100 |
| MERIT SCHOLARSHIPS: | Few |
| RANGE: | Up to full tuition |
| ATHLETIC SCHOLARSHIPS: | No |
| ROTC: | No |
| WEB SITE: | www.newenglandconservatory.edu |
| PHONE: | (617) 262-1120 |

For an idea of New England Conservatory's prominence in the Boston music scene, consider that nearly half the players of the Boston Symphony Orchestra are either NEC faculty or alumni. NEC is one of the nation's oldest conservatories, and it was also the first to introduce a jazz performance program, which is among the most popular majors along with voice and piano. In addition to their performance work, all students complete core requirements that include music history, music theory, and the liberal arts. A five-year dual degree program with Tufts University requires that students be admitted simultaneously to both schools. Mindful of the extremely tight job market for musicians, NEC requires a course in career skills during the junior year that covers everything from auditions to freelancing, and the school also has an active placement office. Most NEC financial aid is awarded on a combination of "financial need, musical ability, and academic achievement." A limited number of awards are based solely on merit, ranging from $1,000 to full tuition.

*Deadlines:*
  ADMISSION: Dec. 1 (priority)
  FAFSA: Feb. 2

## UNIVERSITY OF NEW HAMPSHIRE ✦
## Durham, NH 03824

| | |
|---|---|
| TOTAL ENROLLMENT: | 12,200 |
| UNDERGRADUATE: | 10,400 |
| ACCEPTANCE RATE: | 76% |
| SAT RANGE: | 505–605 Verbal |
| | 505–610 Math |
| STICKER PRICE: | In-state, $11,000+ |
| | Out-of-state, $20,000+ |
| NEED-BLIND: | Yes |
| NEED MET: | 81% |
| AVERAGE STUDENT DEBT: | $16,100 |
| MERIT SCHOLARSHIPS: | Many |
| ATHLETIC SCHOLARSHIPS: | Yes |
| ROTC: | Army. Air Force |
| WEB SITE: | www.unh.edu |
| PHONE: | (603) 862-1360 |

UNH is a public university on a human scale that attracts approximately 40 percent of its student body from outside the state. Its location has all the charm of small-town New Hampshire, yet is only twenty minutes from the Atlantic coast and an hour from Boston. The university's major academic divisions include liberal arts, business and economics, engineering and physical sciences, and health and human services. An Undergraduate Research Opportunities Program offers students the chance to get funding for independent work and summer study. Approximately one-tenth of UNH's entering freshmen are in the honors program and first in line for its merit scholarships. The Granite State Scholarship gives $7,500 per year to in-state honors students and the Dean's and University Honors Scholarships bestow $5,000 and $1,500, respectively, on out-of-state honors students. The Presidential Scholarship offers $2,600 for in-staters and $7,000 for out-of-staters who rank in the top 10 percent of their high school class and score at least 1350 on the SAT I or 31 on the ACT.

*Deadlines:*
  EARLY ACTION: Dec. 1
  REGULAR ADMISSION: Feb. 1
  FAFSA: Mar. 1

## NEW JERSEY INSTITUTE OF TECHNOLOGY ✦
## Newark, NJ 07102

| | |
|---|---|
| TOTAL ENROLLMENT: | 8,100 |
| UNDERGRADUATE: | 5,000 |
| ACCEPTANCE RATE: | 66% |
| SAT RANGE: | 470–580 Verbal |
| | 530–630 Math |
| STICKER PRICE: | In-state, $13,000+ |
| | Out-of-state, $18,000+ |
| NEED-BLIND: | Yes |
| NEED MET: | 92% |
| AVERAGE STUDENT DEBT: | $10,000 |
| MERIT SCHOLARSHIPS: | Many |
| ATHLETIC SCHOLARSHIPS: | No |
| ROTC: | Air Force |
| WEB SITE: | www.njit.edu |
| PHONE: | (973) 596-3300 |

As New Jersey's public university dedicated to technology, NJIT offers hands-on education with a practical emphasis. Though its programs include architecture, management, and liberal arts, NJIT is best-known for engineering. Students enjoy the benefits of a sticker price that is significantly lower than at private competitors, and work opportunities through NJIT's co-op program can slice thousands more from the bill. An honors college offers preferred housing and enhanced research opportunities, plus the chance at combined degree programs that include medicine, dentistry, or optometry. All students admitted to the honors college get a scholarship of at least one-half tuition, and top out-of-staters may be eligible for an award that bridges the gap between in-state and out-of-state costs. The Environmental Scholars Program gives top students access to summer research programs and a master's degree after five years. Alumni Association Scholarships are awarded on the basis of both merit and need, and particular academic departments sponsor a variety of awards.

*Deadlines:*
  ADMISSION: Apr. 1 (priority)
  FAFSA: Mar. 15

## COLLEGE OF NEW JERSEY ✦ Ewing, NJ 08628

| | |
|---|---|
| TOTAL ENROLLMENT: | 6,800 |
| UNDERGRADUATE: | 5,900 |
| ACCEPTANCE RATE: | 57% |
| SAT RANGE: | 570–650 Verbal |
| | 570–670 Math |
| STICKER PRICE: | In-state, $11,000+ |
| | Out-of-state, $14,000+ |
| NEED-BLIND: | Yes |
| NEED MET: | NA |
| AVERAGE STUDENT DEBT: | $12,500 |
| MERIT SCHOLARSHIPS: | Many |
| RANGE: | Up to $8,500 |
| ATHLETIC SCHOLARSHIPS: | No |
| ROTC: | Army, Air Force |
| WEB SITE: | www.tcnj.edu |
| PHONE: | (609) 771-2131 |

Formerly known as Trenton State, the College of New Jersey is a public institution that could easily be mistaken for a pricey private college. That fact has not been lost on college ratings guides such as *U.S. News & World Report*, which have vaulted CNJ to prominence as one of the nation's best bargains. With 5,900 undergraduates, CNJ offers degrees in arts and sciences, business, education, engineering, and nursing. The college is also notable for its First-Year Experience program, which features an extensive orientation program and centralized housing for freshmen. A unique general education program requires, among other things, that students contribute ten hours to community service. The college's merit scholarships range from $1,500 to $8,500 per year and are based on a formula of class rank and test scores. In-staters with at least 1200 on the SAT I and a high school class rank in the top 5 percent, or 1350 with a rank in the top 15 percent, qualify for a minimum of $2,500. Out-of-staters face slightly higher thresholds and a maximum award of $4,500. Departmental awards are available.

*Deadlines:*
  EARLY DECISION: Nov. 15
  REGULAR ADMISSION: Feb.15
  FAFSA: Mar. 1

## NEW MEXICO INSTITUTE OF MINING AND TECHNOLOGY ✦ Socorro, NM 87801

| | |
|---|---|
| TOTAL ENROLLMENT: | 1,400 |
| UNDERGRADUATE: | 1,100 |
| ACCEPTANCE RATE: | 76% |
| ACT RANGE: | 24–29 |
| STICKER PRICE: | In-state, $6,000+ |
| | Out-of-state, 11,000+ |
| NEED-BLIND: | Yes |
| NEED MET: | 98% |
| AVERAGE STUDENT DEBT: | $14,000 |
| MERIT SCHOLARSHIPS: | Many |
| RANGE: | Up to $5,000 |
| ATHLETIC SCHOLARSHIPS: | No |
| ROTC: | No |
| WEB SITE: | www.nmt.edu |
| PHONE: | (800) 428-TECH |

New Mexico Tech's ingenuity was recently on display when researchers there figured out how to use chili pepper extract to repel aquatic pests such as zebra mussels. With a total enrollment of 1,400 and only a smattering of graduate students, Tech is a place where undergraduates can experience innovative research firsthand. Many of its programs relate to mining, but Tech also features a range of strong offerings across engineering and the natural sciences. Tech's sun-drenched campus is located in a small town in the Rio Grande Valley about 75 miles south of Albuquerque. General academic merit scholarships are available at four levels with the $5,000 Gold Merit Scholarship going to National Merit Finalists with at least a 3.0 GPA. On the lower end, students with a 3.0 and an SAT I of 1130 or an ACT of 25 get $2,000. Smaller awards are available for students from New Mexico, including one that grants $1,500 to those who are nominated by their high school counselor. Another modest award targets out-of-staters.

*Deadlines:*
  ADMISSION: Mar. 1
  FAFSA: Mar. 1 (priority)

## UNIVERSITY OF NEW MEXICO ✦ Albuquerque, NM 87131

| | |
|---|---|
| TOTAL ENROLLMENT: | 24,000 |
| UNDERGRADUATE: | 15,800 |
| ACCEPTANCE RATE: | 69% |
| SAT RANGE: | 480–610 Verbal |
| | 470–600 Math |
| STICKER PRICE: | In-state, $7,000+ |
| | Out-of-state, 14,000+ |
| NEED-BLIND: | Yes |
| NEED MET: | 74% |
| AVERAGE STUDENT DEBT: | NA |
| MERIT SCHOLARSHIPS: | Many |
| RANGE: | Up to Full Costs |
| ATHLETIC SCHOLARSHIPS: | Yes |
| ROTC: | Navy, Air Force |
| WEB SITE: | www.unm.edu |
| PHONE: | (505) 277-2446 |

If location is everything, the University of New Mexico has it all. In the major city of Albuquerque, surrounded by the natural beauty and temperate climate of The Land of Enchantment, UNM has appeal for urbanites and outdoor enthusiasts alike. The university offers undergraduate programs in architecture and planning, arts and sciences, education, engineering, fine arts, health sciences, and management. Top students should investigate the General Honors Program, which provides a variety of enriched opportunities for students with a strong high school record and at least 1250 on the SAT I or 29 on the ACT. The Regents' Scholars is UNM's most elite merit program, covering full costs plus books on the basis of class rank, test scores, citizenship, leadership, and an interview. With similar criteria but no interview, the Presidential Scholars program offers a full tuition and books stipend for in-staters. The deadline for both is December 1. An additional full-tuition award has a February 1 deadline, and a program earmarked for out-of-staters has no deadline. Other awards include many sponsored by individual departments.

*Deadlines:*
ADMISSION: Rolling
FAFSA: Mar. 1

## NEW YORK UNIVERSITY ✦ New York, NY 10011

| | |
|---|---|
| TOTAL ENROLLMENT: | 36,700 |
| UNDERGRADUATE: | 17,500 |
| ACCEPTANCE RATE: | 40% |
| SAT RANGE: | 600–690 Verbal |
| | 590–690 Math |
| STICKER PRICE: | $31,000+ |
| NEED-BLIND: | Yes |
| NEED MET: | 66% |
| AVERAGE STUDENT DEBT: | $16,500 |
| MERIT SCHOLARSHIPS: | Many |
| RANGE: | Up to $15,000 |
| ATHLETIC SCHOLARSHIPS: | No |
| ROTC: | Army |
| WEB SITE: | www.nyu.edu |
| PHONE: | (212) 998-4500 |

Along with the city whose name it bears, NYU has experienced a grand reversal of fortune. Twenty years ago, New York was going down the drain and NYU was perceived as an underdog institution for students who couldn't get into Columbia. Today, the city is on a roll and NYU is among the hottest places in higher education. (Unfortunately, that means NYU now accepts 40 percent of its applicants instead of 60 percent.) Though strong in many areas, NYU is preeminent in the media and performing arts disciplines of its famed Tisch School. Business naturally benefits from the proximity to Wall Street, and the independent-minded should check out the unusual Gallatin School of Individualized Study, which combines a Great Books curriculum with self-designed majors. NYU does not make a big deal out of its merit scholarships, but approximately 10 percent of the entering freshmen receive one, ranging from $1,000 to $15,000. Students are automatically considered for these awards based on the application for admission.

*Deadlines:*
EARLY DECISION: Nov. 15
REGULAR ADMISSION: Jan. 15
FAFSA: Feb. 15

# NORTH CAROLINA SCHOOL OF THE ARTS ◆
## Winston-Salem, NC 27117

| | |
|---|---|
| TOTAL ENROLLMENT: | 800 |
| UNDERGRADUATE: | 800 |
| ACCEPTANCE RATE: | 32% |
| SAT AVERAGE: | Verbal 551 |
| | Math 586 |
| STICKER PRICE: | In-state, $6,000+ |
| | Out-of-state, $15,000+ |
| NEED-BLIND: | Yes |
| NEED MET: | 54% |
| AVERAGE STUDENT DEBT: | $15,900 |
| MERIT SCHOLARSHIPS: | Many |
| ATHLETIC SCHOLARSHIPS: | No |
| ROTC: | No |
| WEB SITE: | www.ncarts.edu |
| PHONE: | (336) 770-3291 |

North Carolina School of the Arts is like a child prodigy of the education world. Founded in 1963, NCSA has yet to reach middle age and is already the outstanding arts specialty school in the South. As a state institution, NCSA is one of several entrées on the bargain menu for North Carolina college shoppers, and the price is reasonable for out-of-staters, too. NCSA offers programs in dance, music, drama, filmmaking, and theatrical design and production, with the latter being the most popular major. Unlike many arts schools, NCSA is a residential institution that requires freshmen and sophomores to live on campus, thereby adding an important element of community. All students must complete a General Studies program that requires proficiency in reading, writing, oral communication, and coursework in the social/behavioral sciences and math/natural sciences. In addition to need-based aid, scholarships are awarded on the basis of artistic talent or talent and need. In a recent year, approximately 30 percent of the entering class received a non-need award.

*Deadlines:*
ADMISSION: Mar. 1 (priority)
FAFSA: Mar. 1

# NORTH CAROLINA STATE UNIVERSITY ◆
## Raleigh, NC 27695

| | |
|---|---|
| TOTAL ENROLLMENT: | 28,300 |
| UNDERGRADUATE: | 21,800 |
| ACCEPTANCE RATE: | 75% |
| SAT RANGE: | 510–620 Verbal |
| | 530–640 Math |
| STICKER PRICE: | In-state, $6,000+ |
| | Out-of-state, $15,000+ |
| NEED–BLIND: | Yes |
| NEED MET: | NA |
| AVERAGE STUDENT DEBT: | $6,300 |
| MERIT SCHOLARSHIPS: | Many |
| RANGE: | Up to full costs |
| ATHLETIC SCHOLARSHIPS: | Yes |
| ROTC: | Army, Navy, Air Force |
| WEB SITE: | www.ncsu.edu |
| PHONE: | (919) 515-2434 |

NC State may lack some of the panache of its high-brow neighbors, Duke and UNC/Chapel Hill, but it still has plenty to interest prospective students. Science and technology are State's strengths; premed is a major draw and the College of Engineering is among the largest in the Southeast. The most prestigious of NC State's merit awards is the Park Scholarship, which covers full costs and provides a personal computer for students nominated by their high schools. A notch down is the Caldwell Scholarship, which offers $4,000 for in-staters and $7,500 for out-of-staters plus a $1,500 stipend for a summer experience. Other awards of $1,000 to $4,000 are available, including ones for winners of state contests in math and writing. To be considered for university scholarships, applicants must generally be in the top 5 percent of their high-school class with a 1300 on the SAT I or 30 on the ACT and apply for admission by November 15. Other awards are sponsored by particular academic divisions. About 400 future teachers get a $5,000 scholarship if they agree to teach in North Carolina public schools.

*Deadlines:*
EARLY ACTION: Nov. 15
REGULAR ADMISSION: Feb. 1
FAFSA: Mar. 1

# NORTH CAROLINA WESLEYAN UNIVERSITY ◆
## Rocky Mount, NC 27804

| | |
|---|---|
| TOTAL ENROLLMENT: | 900 |
| UNDERGRADUATE: | 900 |
| ACCEPTANCE RATE: | 74% |
| SAT RANGE: | 400–549 Verbal |
| | 400–499 Math |
| STICKER PRICE: | 13,000+ |
| NEED-BLIND: | Yes |
| NEED MET: | NA |
| AVERAGE STUDENT DEBT: | $17,000 |
| MERIT SCHOLARSHIPS: | Few |
| ATHLETIC SCHOLARSHIPS: | No |
| ROTC: | No |
| WEB SITE: | www.ncwc.edu |
| PHONE: | (919) 985-5200 |

North Carolina Wesleyan is a small regional college that made national headlines in 1996 by chopping 23 percent off its tuition. Already inexpensive by most standards, Wesleyan's sticker price (now just over $13,000) is among the lowest of small private colleges. With only 900 students, the college delivers education with a personal touch — even the president teaches an introductory freshman course. Business administration tops the list of most popular majors, and Wesleyan has strong programs in criminal justice and hotel management. All freshmen get an introduction to life on their own via College 101, a course that covers basic skills ranging from time management and public speaking to the ability to use educational technology. Wesleyan's highest merit award is the Presidential Scholarship, which offers $2,500 based on academic excellence and contributions to the high school community. An Honors Scholarship of $1,500 goes to students who are accepted into the honors program, and other merit-within-need awards have various criteria.

*Deadlines:*
  ADMISSION: Rolling
  FAFSA: As soon as possible after Jan. 1

# UNIVERSITY OF NORTH CAROLINA/ASHEVILLE
## ◆ Asheville, NC 28804

| | |
|---|---|
| TOTAL ENROLLMENT: | 3,200 |
| UNDERGRADUATE: | 3,100 |
| ACCEPTANCE RATE: | 60% |
| SAT RANGE: | 530–640 Verbal |
| | 510–610 Math |
| STICKER PRICE: | In-state, $6,000+ |
| | Out-of-state, $12,000+ |
| NEED-BLIND: | Yes |
| NEED MET: | 79% |
| AVERAGE STUDENT DEBT: | $12,500 |
| MERIT SCHOLARSHIPS: | Many |
| RANGE: | Up to full in-state tuition |
| ATHLETIC SCHOLARSHIPS: | Yes |
| ROTC: | No |
| WEB SITE: | www.unca.edu |
| PHONE: | (704) 251-6480 |

Nestled in the Blue Ridge Mountains overlooking a historic resort city, UNC/Asheville would get more recognition were it not for its big-name sister school in Chapel Hill. Asheville is the designated public liberal arts university of North Carolina, and its modest enrollment and small classes give it the atmosphere of a private institution. The university founded the National Conference on Undergraduate Research and remains a leader in encouraging independent work. Many of UNCA's merit scholarships are included under the umbrella of the University Laurels Scholarships, which offer full or partial coverage of in-state tuition. Included among them is the Undergraduate Fellows and Scholars program, which funds one-on-one study with faculty mentors. The application deadline for all is December 4. UNCA also offers North Carolina Teaching Fellowships, worth $5,000 annually for students who agree to teach in the state's public schools. Another award is reserved for students from western North Carolina who have "a solid school record and a keen interest in developing leadership skills and public service experience."

*Deadlines:*
  EARLY ACTION: Oct. 15
  ADMISSION: Apr. 15
  FAFSA: Mar. 1

## UNIVERSITY OF NORTH CAROLINA/ CHAPEL HILL ◆ Chapel Hill, NC 27599

| | |
|---|---|
| TOTAL ENROLLMENT: | 24,200 |
| UNDERGRADUATE: | 15,300 |
| ACCEPTANCE RATE: | 37% |
| SAT RANGE: | 550–670 Verbal |
| | 560–670 Math |
| STICKER PRICE: | In-state, $7,000+ |
| | Out-of-state, $16,000+ |
| NEED-BLIND: | Yes |
| NEED MET: | 97% |
| AVERAGE STUDENT DEBT: | $12,500 |
| MERIT SCHOLARSHIPS: | Many |
| RANGE: | Up to full costs |
| ATHLETIC SCHOLARSHIPS: | Yes |
| ROTC: | Army, Navy, Air Force |
| WEB SITE: | www.unc.edu |
| PHONE: | (919) 966-3621 |

Maybe it is because of Michael Jordan — or the fact that God made the sky Carolina blue. For whatever reason, the University of North Carolina/Chapel Hill continues to ride a wave of immense popularity among the nation's top students. With less than 20 percent of its places reserved for out-of-staters, applicants from beyond North Carolina's borders face Ivy League–style competition for the few coveted letters of acceptance. The situation is a lot better for in-staters, who can attend an elite public university in their backyard at a bargain price. UNC's Morehead Scholars Program ranks as one of the nation's most prestigious, covering full costs plus a summer stipend, but applicants must attend a participating high school and secure a nomination in the fall of 12th grade. (A handful of students from the regular applicant pool are considered.) Other merit awards range up to $10,000 and require an application for admission by November 15 and a separate scholarship application by December 15. All applicants who apply for need-based aid are considered for two merit-within-need awards of up to $12,000.

*Deadlines:*
ADMISSION: Jan. 15
FAFSA: Mar. 1
CSS PROFILE: Mar. 1

## UNIVERSITY OF NORTH CAROLINA/ GREENSBORO ◆ Greensboro, NC 27412

| | |
|---|---|
| TOTAL ENROLLMENT: | 12,300 |
| UNDERGRADUATE: | 9,700 |
| ACCEPTANCE RATE: | 76% |
| SAT RANGE: | 460–570 Verbal |
| | 450–560 Math |
| STICKER PRICE: | In-state, $6,000+ |
| | Out-of-state, $15,000+ |
| NEED-BLIND: | Yes |
| NEED MET: | 65% |
| AVERAGE STUDENT DEBT: | $17,800 |
| MERIT SCHOLARSHIPS: | Many |
| RANGE: | Up to $12,000 |
| ATHLETIC SCHOLARSHIPS: | Yes |
| ROTC: | Army, Air Force |
| WEB SITE: | www.uncg.edu |
| PHONE: | (336) 334-5243 |

Situated on 190 acres in the medium-sized city of Greensboro, UNCG was once North Carolina's public women's college before going coed in 1961. Education is a traditional strength, and the university also includes professional schools in business and economics, health and human performance, human environmental sciences, music, and nursing. In addition to regular housing options, UNCG offers two residential colleges that create a shared living/learning community. Approximately one-tenth of UNCG freshmen receive a merit award, which range from $2,000 to $12,000. Applicants must score at least 1100 on the SAT I and have an overall high school GPA of 3.5. North Carolina residents are eligible for the Reynolds Scholarship, which offers $5,000 per year plus two $1,250 stipends for community work and $2,500 for study abroad in the junior year. Others include an award for students nominated by their school superintendent and another for participants in the International Baccalaureate program. Applicants for merit scholarships must complete a separate application by January 15.

*Deadlines:*
ADMISSION: Mar. 1 (priority)
FAFSA: Mar. 1

## NORTHEASTERN UNIVERSITY ✦
## Boston, MA 02115

| | |
|---|---|
| TOTAL ENROLLMENT: | 24,300 |
| UNDERGRADUATE: | 19,700 |
| ACCEPTANCE RATE: | 70% |
| SAT RANGE: | 480–590 Verbal |
| | 490–600 Math |
| STICKER PRICE: | $25,000+ |
| NEED-BLIND: | Yes |
| NEED MET: | 61% |
| AVERAGE STUDENT DEBT: | $14,800 |
| MERIT SCHOLARSHIPS: | Many |
| RANGE: | Up to full costs |
| ATHLETIC SCHOLARSHIPS: | Yes |
| ROTC: | Army, Navy, Air Force |
| WEB SITE: | www.neu.edu |
| PHONE: | (617) 373-2200 |

Northeastern University could easily change its name to Real World U. Located in the heart of Boston, Northeastern is best-known for a cooperative education program that sends forth thousands of students to supplement their classroom learning with job experience. About 40 percent of graduates take a permanent job where they co-op. Criminology tops the list of Northeastern's most popular majors, followed by nursing and physical therapy. University-wide merit awards include the Ell Scholarship, which covers full costs for selected students who are in the top 5 percent of their high school class with an SAT I of 1250 or better. A similar award goes to National Merit Finalists from New England. Two additional scholarships cover full costs for minority students with top grades who score at least 1150. A $6,500 award targets Bostonians who have shown leadership and service, and a one-time half-tuition scholarship rewards exceptional foreign students. Scholarship candidates should apply for admission by January 1.

*Deadlines:*
    ADMISSION: Mar. 1 (priority)
    FAFSA: Mar. 1
    CSS PROFILE: Mar. 1

## NORTHWESTERN UNIVERSITY ✦
## Evanston, IL 60208

| | |
|---|---|
| TOTAL ENROLLMENT: | 15,500 |
| UNDERGRADUATE: | 7,600 |
| ACCEPTANCE RATE: | 29% |
| SAT RANGE: | 620–720 Verbal |
| | 650–730 Math |
| STICKER PRICE: | $30,000+ |
| NEED-BLIND: | Yes |
| NEED MET: | 100% |
| AVERAGE STUDENT DEBT: | $13,300 |
| MERIT SCHOLARSHIPS: | Few |
| ATHLETIC SCHOLARSHIPS: | Yes |
| ROTC: | Army, Navy, Air Force |
| WEB SITE: | www.nwu.edu |
| PHONE: | (847) 491-7271 |

Northwestern ranks high on the list of universities that are much harder to get into now than ten years ago. Unlike the Ivy League and the nearby University of Chicago, Northwestern has made its name on preprofessional programs rather than the liberal arts. The School of Journalism rates among the nation's elite, and many pre-meds would give their first-born child (if they had one) for admission to NU's Honors Program in Medical Education. Other strong programs are available across the curriculum in arts and sciences, education and social policy, engineering and applied science, music, and speech (which includes performing arts and media). The ultimate proof that Northwestern is on a roll is the resurgence of its football program, which overcame a legendary losing streak to become a contender among the titans of the Big Ten. Aside from athletic scholarships and ROTC, the overwhelming majority of financial aid at Northwestern goes to students with need, though the university does offer athletic and ROTC scholarships, and merit awards for students entering the School of Music. Northwestern also funds National Merit and National Achievement awards for qualifying students who demonstrate need.

*Deadlines:*
    EARLY DECISION: Nov. 1
    REGULAR ADMISSION: Jan. 1
    FAFSA: Feb. 1
    CSS PROFILE: Feb. 1

# UNIVERSITY OF NOTRE DAME ✦
# Notre Dame, IN 46556

| | |
|---|---|
| TOTAL ENROLLMENT: | 10,300 |
| UNDERGRADUATE: | 7,800 |
| ACCEPTANCE RATE: | 40% |
| SAT RANGE: | 600–630 Verbal |
| | 700–710 Math |
| STICKER PRICE: | $29,000+ |
| NEED-BLIND: | Yes |
| NEED MET: | 88% |
| AVERAGE STUDENT DEBT: | $16,300 |
| MERIT SCHOLARSHIPS: | None |
| ATHLETIC SCHOLARSHIPS: | Yes |
| ROTC: | Army, Navy, Air Force |
| WEB SITE: | www.nd.edu |
| PHONE: | (219) 631-7505 |

For thousands of Catholic boys and girls across the nation, one of life's greatest ambitions is to spend four years under Notre Dame's fabled golden dome. It is a tradition passed down from generation to generation, and one that has grown stronger with Notre Dame's development as a leading academic institution. The atmosphere at ND is predominantly conservative, and students are more likely to be dedicated preprofessionals than connoisseurs of the liberal arts. (Accounting and finance are the most popular majors.) Notre Dame probably has the highest proportion of scholar/jocks in the nation, and many of its intramural teams could probably knock off the varsity squads at other colleges. Though the football team has not equaled its past glory in recent years, the Fighting Irish are still a strong source of campus pride. Aside from its athletic scholarships and a full slate of ROTC programs, Notre Dame awards financial aid only to students with need, although it does have several merit-within-need scholarship programs.

*Deadlines:*
  EARLY ACTION: Nov. 1
  REGULAR ADMISSION: Jan. 8
  FAFSA: Feb. 15
  CSS PROFILE: Feb. 15

# OBERLIN COLLEGE ✦ Oberlin, OH 44074

| | |
|---|---|
| TOTAL ENROLLMENT: | 2,900 |
| UNDERGRADUATE: | 2,900 |
| ACCEPTANCE RATE: | 62% |
| SAT RANGE: | 620–720 Verbal |
| | 580–690 Math |
| STICKER PRICE: | $30,000+ |
| NEED-BLIND: | No |
| NEED MET: | 100% |
| AVERAGE STUDENT DEBT: | $15,200 |
| MERIT SCHOLARSHIPS: | Few |
| RANGE: | Up to $10,000 |
| ATHLETIC SCHOLARSHIPS: | No |
| ROTC: | No |
| WEB SITE: | www.oberlin.edu |
| PHONE: | (800) 622-6243 |

If this generation of college students really is more conservative than its elders, you'd never guess it from a visit to Oberlin College. Unabashedly liberal, Oberlin is proud of its heritage as the first college to admit women and African Americans and is determined to remain in the vanguard of social change. Oberlin has strong departments throughout the liberal arts; English, history, and biology rank as the most popular majors. The college also boasts one of the nation's top music conservatories. With a total of 2,900 undergraduates, Oberlin is more than twice as large as traditional rival Grinnell and 50 percent bigger than Carleton and Macalester. The overwhelming majority of Oberlin's financial aid is based on need, but some merit scholarships are available. Approximately 5 percent of admitted students are offered the John Frederick Oberlin award for either $10,000 or $5,000. A second $10,000 award goes to five outstanding Ohio students, and National Merit Finalists are funded at up to $2,000. Oberlin's conservatory offers Dean's Talent Awards based on "audition ratings and ensemble needs."

*Deadlines:*
  EARLY DECISION: Nov. 15, Jan. 2
  REGULAR ADMISSION: Jan. 15
  FAFSA: Feb. 15
  CSS PROFILE: Feb. 15

# OCCIDENTAL COLLEGE ✦
## Los Angeles, CA 90041

| | |
|---|---|
| TOTAL ENROLLMENT: | 1,600 |
| UNDERGRADUATE: | 1,600 |
| ACCEPTANCE RATE: | 77% |
| SAT RANGE: | 530–650 Verbal |
| | 540–650 Math |
| STICKER PRICE: | $28,000+ |
| NEED-BLIND: | Yes |
| NEED MET: | 99% |
| AVERAGE STUDENT DEBT: | $16,100 |
| MERIT SCHOLARSHIPS: | Many |
| RANGE: | Up to $15,000 |
| ATHLETIC SCHOLARSHIPS: | No |
| ROTC: | Army, Air Force |
| WEB SITE: | www.oxy.edu |
| PHONE: | (800) 852-5262 |

Lots of colleges wax poetic about the diversity of their campuses, but Occidental College lives the ideal. With a student body that is 16 percent Asian American, 14 percent Latino, 7 percent African American, and 5 percent international students, Oxy is a remarkable mosaic. Add in twenty-three study abroad programs in fifteen countries, plus a fellowship program to fund summer research abroad, and Oxy gives its students as big a slice of the world as any private college in the country. Situated on a hilltop in northeast Los Angeles, the college is a stone's throw from Hollywood, and not coincidentally offers a strong program in film and video art. Oxy does not tout any named merit scholarships, but approximately a quarter of admitted students were offered one in a recent year. Amounts range from $7,000 to $15,000. Under the college's Graduation Guarantee program, any student who does not graduate on time because of the college's failure to offer required courses will not be charged additional tuition.

*Deadlines:*
EARLY DECISION: Nov. 15
REGULAR ADMISSION: Jan. 15
FAFSA: Feb. 1
CSS PROFILE: Feb. 1

# OGLETHORPE UNIVERSITY ✦
## Atlanta, GA 30319

| | |
|---|---|
| TOTAL ENROLLMENT: | 1,200 |
| UNDERGRADUATE: | 1,100 |
| ACCEPTANCE RATE: | 81% |
| SAT RANGE: | 570–670 Verbal |
| | 540–640 Math |
| STICKER PRICE: | $21,000+ |
| NEED-BLIND: | No |
| NEED MET: | 91% |
| AVERAGE STUDENT DEBT: | $15,900 |
| MERIT SCHOLARSHIPS: | Many |
| RANGE: | Up to full costs |
| ATHLETIC SCHOLARSHIPS: | No |
| ROTC: | Army |
| WEB SITE: | www.oglethorpe.edu |
| PHONE: | (404) 364-8307 |

Though Oglethorpe bears the name of Georgia's eighteenth-century founder, the college draws its identity less from the state than the city of Atlanta. With a rapid transit station at its doorstep, Oglethorpe combines a comfortable suburban campus with easy access to the Southeast's most vibrant metropolitan area. In addition to all its social and artistic opportunities, the city is a fertile source of internships. Oglethorpe's curriculum takes its shape from an unusual core program that requires a sequence of interdisciplinary courses, one per year, that give students a shared experience with classmates from enrollment to graduation. Top applicants are eligible for the James Edward Oglethorpe Scholarship, which covers full costs. Runners-up get a $9,000 award. Three additional levels of scholarships are based on a GPA/standardized test formula: those with a 3.6 and 1250 on the SAT I or 28 on the ACT get $8,000; those with a 3.4 and 1180 or 26 qualify for $5,000; and those with a 3.2 and 1120 or 24 get $3,000.

*Deadlines:*
EARLY DECISION: Nov. 30
EARLY ACTION: Dec. 30
REGULAR ADMISSION: Feb. 1
FAFSA: Mar. 1

## OHIO NORTHERN UNIVERSITY ✦
## Ada, OH 45810

| | |
|---|---|
| TOTAL ENROLLMENT: | 2,900 |
| UNDERGRADUATE: | 2,500 |
| ACCEPTANCE RATE: | 94% |
| ACT RANGE: | 21–27 |
| STICKER PRICE: | $25,000 |
| NEED-BLIND: | Yes |
| NEED MET: | 96% |
| AVERAGE STUDENT DEBT: | $14,000 |
| MERIT SCHOLARSHIPS: | Many |
| RANGE: | Up to $20,000 |
| ATHLETIC SCHOLARSHIPS: | No |
| ROTC: | Army, Air Force |
| WEB SITE: | www.onu.edu |
| PHONE: | (419) 772-2260 |

Ohio Northern may sound like just another regional public university, but it is actually a private institution known for one of the largest pharmacy schools in the Midwest. Affiliated with the United Methodist church, ONU also offers programs in business, engineering, and the liberal arts. Set in rural Ohio, ONU has the friendly and conservative flavor of the Midwestern heartland. Strong students who apply by December 15 are invited to one of a series of on-campus scholarship competitions. The $20,000 Presidential Scholar award is given to one student in each of ONU's four colleges who has at least a 3.6 GPA (and/or top 5 percent high school class rank) and a score of 1250 on the SAT I or 28 on the ACT. Other competition scholarships have less lofty criteria and range between $12,500 and $16,000. A Dean's Scholarship worth up to $10,000 is awarded to students with at least a 3.3 and 1150 or 25 who apply by May 1. Talent Awards of up to $6,000 are awarded in art, music, and communication arts. Smaller discounts go to United Methodists and those with siblings at ONU.

*Deadlines:*
  ADMISSION: Mar. 1 (priority)
  FAFSA: Apr. 1

## OHIO STATE UNIVERSITY ✦
## Columbus, OH 43210

| | |
|---|---|
| ENROLLMENT: | 48,300 |
| UNDERGRADUATE: | 30,300 |
| ACCEPTANCE RATE: | 80% |
| SAT RANGE: | 503–627 Verbal |
| | 511–647 Math |
| STICKER PRICE: | In-state, $9,000+ |
| | Out-of-state, $16,000+ |
| NEED-BLIND: | Yes |
| NEED MET: | 80% |
| AVERAGE STUDENT DEBT: | $12,500 |
| MERIT SCHOLARSHIPS: | Many |
| RANGE: | Up to full costs |
| ATHLETIC SCHOLARSHIPS: | Yes |
| ROTC: | Army, Navy, Air Force |
| WEB SITE: | www.osu.edu |
| PHONE: | (614) 292-3980 |

With a student body the size of most Balkan republics, Ohio State gives new meaning to the phrase "cast of thousands." Try 48,000, give or take a few hundred. Ohio State is BIG, but if you take out your magnifying glass and look closely, you'll find quality programs. Business, the natural sciences, and engineering draw many of the top students. Notable for small classes and good teaching, the honors program enrolls approximately 1,000. OSU's leading merit awards are distributed via the University Scholar Maximus program, which offers 120 scholarships at 3 levels up to a full ride. The deadline is December 15. Students who rank in the top 15 percent with 1120 on the SAT I or a 25 on the ACT get a $600 Trustee Scholarship, and the Cooperative Scholarship Housing program allows students to work off part of their room and board costs. National Merit and National Achievement Finalists are in the running for awards of full tuition plus $3,000, and more awards are available through the departments and colleges.

*Deadlines:*
  ADMISSION: Feb. 15
  FAFSA: Feb. 15

259

# OHIO UNIVERSITY • Athens, OH 45701

| | |
|---|---|
| TOTAL ENROLLMENT: | 19,200 |
| UNDERGRADUATE: | 16,100 |
| ACCEPTANCE RATE: | 75% |
| SAT RANGE: | 500–600 Verbal |
| | 510–600 Math |
| STICKER PRICE: | In-state, $10,000+ |
| | Out-of-state, $15,000+ |
| NEED-BLIND: | Yes |
| NEED MET: | NA |
| AVERAGE STUDENT DEBT: | $13,200 |
| MERIT SCHOLARSHIPS: | Many |
| RANGE: | Up to full tuition |
| ATHLETIC SCHOLARSHIPS: | Yes |
| ROTC: | Army, Air Force |
| WEB SITE: | www.ohiou.edu |
| PHONE: | (740) 593-4100 |

Without the football fanfare of Ohio State or "public Ivy" status like Miami University, OU is the quietest of Ohio's big three public universities. Yet OU has been making some noise of late. Applications have surged, and competition has become downright fierce in leading divisions such as business, journalism, and engineering. A major attraction for top students is the Honors Tutorial College, which is based on the British model of one-on-one interaction. For all students in the top 10 percent who score at least 1460 on the SAT I or 33 on the ACT, OU offers the Distinguished Scholars award, which covers full in-state tuition. Two more scholarships, one worth full tuition and the other $2,500, are awarded on a competitive basis to those in the top 10 percent who score above 1310 or 30, and another full-tuition award targets underrepresented minorities. (Students seeking scholarships in the fine arts should contact the respective departments.) OU has a scholarship search program on its Web site that allows students to enter personal criteria for matches with over 500 university awards.

*Deadlines:*
  ADMISSION: Feb. 1
  FAFSA: Mar. 1

# OHIO WESLEYAN UNIVERSITY • Delaware, OH 43015

| | |
|---|---|
| TOTAL ENROLLMENT: | 1,900 |
| UNDERGRADUATE: | 1,900 |
| ACCEPTANCE RATE: | 82% |
| SAT RANGE: | 520–650 Verbal |
| | 530–670 Math |
| STICKER PRICE: | $27,000+ |
| NEED-BLIND: | Yes |
| NEED MET: | 98% |
| AVERAGE STUDENT DEBT: | $16,800 |
| MERIT SCHOLARSHIPS: | Many |
| RANGE: | Up to full tuition |
| ATHLETIC SCHOLARSHIPS: | No |
| ROTC: | Army |
| WEB SITE: | www.owu.edu |
| PHONE: | (800) 922-8953 |

Ohio Wesleyan is strong in the liberal arts from A to Z—zoology is the most popular major on campus. Therein lies testament to the college's quality in the life sciences, where botany/microbiology also has a loyal following. Economics is another student favorite. Wesleyan is among a cluster of liberal arts colleges in central Ohio who compete gamely for top students, and merit scholarships are the weapon of choice. The full-tuition Presidential Scholarship goes to the college's top applicants, and students with slightly lesser credentials can get a three-quarter- or half-tuition award. (A total of 100 are available across the 3 categories.) Students from Ohio get an automatic $5,000 discount, and those from the Northeast, Southeast, or far West get $4,000. Other awards are available for community service (up to $7,500), minority students (up to full tuition), children of alumni ($5,000), and Methodists ($4,000). Departmental awards are available (mainly in the fine arts), and early decision candidates pocket a $4,000 discount.

*Deadlines:*
  EARLY DECISION: Dec. 1
  REGULAR ADMISSION: Mar. 1
  FAFSA: Feb. 1

## UNIVERSITY OF OKLAHOMA ◆
## Norman, OK 73019

| | |
|---|---|
| TOTAL ENROLLMENT: | 20,500 |
| UNDERGRADUATE: | 16,200 |
| ACCEPTANCE RATE: | 88% |
| SAT AVERAGE: | 1154 combined |
| STICKER PRICE: | In-state, $7,000+ |
| | Out-of-state, $10,000+ |
| NEED-BLIND: | Yes |
| NEED MET: | 99% |
| AVERAGE STUDENT DEBT: | $16,500 |
| MERIT SCHOLARSHIPS: | Many |
| RANGE: | Up to full tuition |
| ATHLETIC SCHOLARSHIPS: | Yes |
| ROTC: | Army, Navy, Air Force |
| WEB SITE: | www.ou.edu |
| PHONE: | (405) 325-2251 |

Before the federal government gave the go-ahead to settle the Oklahoma Territory back in 1891, a few enterprising souls sneaked in ahead of time to grab the best land. Oklahoma Sooners they were, and today 20,500 of their descendents attend the state's flagship university. Savvy Sooners with top grades should make a beeline for the Honors College, where students not only get small classes but a variety of other benefits, ranging from preferred library privileges to opportunities for funded research. When it comes to OU's top merit scholarships, students are advised to apply Sooner rather than later. The OU Scholars Selection Committee begins meeting November 1 to distribute awards of up to $1,500 in five categories, and applicants should file a scholarship application by that date (or soon thereafter). Honorees in all of the National Merit programs can get a full-tuition award, and the President's Leadership Class offers a $1,000 scholarship to seventy-five students based on high school activities. Many other awards are available, mostly through particular academic departments.

*Deadlines:*
  ADMISSION: Jul. 15
  FAFSA: Mar. 1

## OREGON STATE UNIVERSITY ◆
## Corvallis, OR 97331

| | |
|---|---|
| TOTAL ENROLLMENT: | 16,100 |
| UNDERGRADUATE: | 13,200 |
| ACCEPTANCE RATE: | 85% |
| SAT AVERAGE: | 446 Verbal |
| | 551 Math |
| STICKER PRICE: | In-state, $9,000+ |
| | Out-of-state, $18,000+ |
| NEED-BLIND: | Yes |
| NEED MET: | NA |
| AVERAGE STUDENT DEBT: | NA |
| MERIT SCHOLARSHIPS: | Many |
| RANGE: | Up to full tuition |
| ATHLETIC SCHOLARSHIPS: | Yes |
| ROTC: | Army, Navy, Air Force |
| WEB SITE: | www.orst.edu |
| PHONE: | (541) 737-4411 |

With 14,100 students and degree programs in 12 colleges, Oregon State excels in a variety of pre-professional fields. Agriculture and science-related disciplines are strong, and OSU's most popular major is business administration. The university is among the few with a full-fledged college devoted to oceanic and atmospheric sciences. OSU encourages interdisciplinary work and offers programs such as Peace Studies, Natural Resources, and Twentieth-Century Studies. Merit scholarships are offered on a university-wide and departmental basis with minimum eligibility standards of at least a 3.0 GPA and an SAT I of 1100 or an ACT of 24. Heading the list of general excellence awards for Oregon residents is the Presidential Scholarship, worth $3,000. In-staters from underrepresented minority groups can qualify for a full-tuition scholarship, and National Merit Finalists are eligible for up to $2,000 depending on need. Students whose parents attended OSU get a $1,000 discount. The university also gives about 100 merit-within-need awards of up to $3,500. Scholarship deadlines are "as early as January."

*Deadlines:*
  ADMISSION: Mar. 1
  FAFSA: Mar. 1

## UNIVERSITY OF OREGON ◆ Eugene, OR 97403

| | |
|---|---|
| TOTAL ENROLLMENT: | 17,200 |
| UNDERGRADUATE: | 13,800 |
| ACCEPTANCE RATE: | 90% |
| SAT RANGE: | 490–607 Verbal |
| | 492–607 Math |
| STICKER PRICE: | In-state, $9,000+ |
| | Out-of-state, $18,000+ |
| NEED-BLIND: | Yes |
| NEED MET: | 90% |
| AVERAGE STUDENT DEBT: | $17,400 |
| MERIT SCHOLARSHIPS: | Many |
| ATHLETIC SCHOLARSHIPS: | Yes |
| ROTC: | Army |
| WEB SITE: | www.uoregon.edu |
| PHONE: | (800) 232-3825 |

Set in the scenic Willamette Valley, University of Oregon combines easy access to the playgrounds of the Pacific Northwest with a location in one of America's most active college towns. Major academic divisions include architecture and allied sciences, arts and sciences, business, education, journalism and communications, and music. UO's campus is no less beautiful than the surrounding area and features more than 2,000 varieties of trees. General-University scholarships range from $1,500 to $4,100 and are awarded on the basis of both academic and personal qualifications. Without "exceptional circumstances," students must have a GPA of 3.5 and an SAT I of 1100 or an ACT of 24 for consideration. Fifty Presidential Scholarships of $3,000 are awarded to top in-staters. National Merit Finalists are funded up to $2,000 depending on need, and many more scholarships are offered through the various departments. Scholarship applicants must apply for admission and submit the scholarship application by February 1, with early notification to those who apply by November 1.

*Deadlines:*
ADMISSION: Mar. 1
FAFSA: Feb. 1

## COLLEGE OF THE OZARKS ◆ Point Lookout, MO 65726

| | |
|---|---|
| TOTAL ENROLLMENT: | 1,600 |
| UNDERGRADUATE: | 1,600 |
| ACCEPTANCE RATE: | 14% |
| SAT RANGE: | NA |
| STICKER PRICE: | $2,000+ |
| NEED-BLIND: | No |
| NEED MET: | 81% |
| AVERAGE STUDENT DEBT: | $1,500 |
| MERIT SCHOLARSHIPS: | Full tuition for all students |
| ATHLETIC SCHOLARSHIPS: | No |
| ROTC: | Army |
| WEB SITE: | www.cofo.edu |
| PHONE: | (800) 222-0525 |

College of the Ozarks likes to call itself "Hard Work U," and with good reason. All students must work fifteen hours per week in a campus job that can range from office work to manual labor in the college's meat processing plant. If that sounds harsh, consider that students at C of O pay not a dime in tuition for an education that includes the liberal arts and a variety of preprofessional fields. One important detail: admission is limited primarily to students "whose families would have a difficult time financing a college education." C of O places a strong emphasis on traditional values and counts among its goals the nurturing of both patriotic and spiritual growth. Though the college is nondenominational, attendance at some Christian convocations is mandatory. In addition to term-time jobs, the college also sponsors a summer work program that helps cash-strapped students cover room and board. C of O's average student debt figure of $1,500 is among the nation's lowest.

*Deadlines:*
ADMISSION: Jan. 15 (priority)
FAFSA: Mar. 15

# PACIFIC LUTHERAN UNIVERSITY ✦
## Tacoma, WA 98447

| | |
|---|---|
| TOTAL ENROLLMENT: | 3,600 |
| UNDERGRADUATE: | 3,300 |
| ACCEPTANCE RATE: | 86% |
| SAT RANGE: | 480–610 Verbal |
| | 490–610 Math |
| STICKER PRICE: | $21,000+ |
| NEED-BLIND: | Yes |
| NEED MET: | 84% |
| AVERAGE STUDENT DEBT: | NA |
| MERIT SCHOLARSHIPS: | Many |
| RANGE: | Up to full tuition |
| ATHLETIC SCHOLARSHIPS: | No |
| ROTC: | Army |
| WEB SITE: | www.plu.edu |
| PHONE: | (800) 274-6758 |

Founded in 1890 by a hardy band of transplanted Norwegian Lutherans, PLU has grown up with the Pacific Northwest. Though modest in size, the university offers degrees in the liberal arts and five professional schools, including arts, business, education, nursing, and physical education. PLU is rooted in Christian faith and an international outlook, and its month-long January term provides many opportunities for study abroad. The Regents' Scholarship gives full tuition to three outstanding students with at least a 3.8 GPA and 1200 on the SAT I or 27 on the ACT. Other academic awards are available in various increments down to the Academic Excellence Award, worth $3,500–$4,500. National Merit Finalists are guaranteed a total of $7,000 per year, and a $1,500 discount goes to children of alumni with strong academic records. A distinctive leadership award gives $2,000 for "active involvement in a multi-ethnic context," and dependents of Christian clergy qualify for $1,000. Applicants for the Regents' must apply for admission by January 10. Other programs have a March 1 deadline.

*Deadlines:*
  EARLY ACTION: Nov. 15
  REGULAR ADMISSION: Rolling
  FAFSA: Jan. 31

# UNIVERSITY OF THE PACIFIC ✦
## Stockton, CA 95211

| | |
|---|---|
| TOTAL ENROLLMENT: | 5,600 |
| UNDERGRADUATE: | 2,800 |
| ACCEPTANCE RATE: | 84% |
| SAT RANGE: | 480–610 Verbal |
| | 500–630 Math |
| STICKER PRICE: | $25,000+ |
| NEED-BLIND: | Yes |
| NEED MET: | NA |
| AVERAGE STUDENT DEBT: | NA |
| MERIT SCHOLARSHIPS: | Many |
| RANGE: | Up to 90 percent of tuition |
| ATHLETIC SCHOLARSHIPS: | Yes |
| ROTC: | Air Force |
| WEB SITE: | www.uop.edu |
| PHONE: | (800) 959-2867 |

University of the Pacific sounds like a grandiose name for a smallish university—until you consider that Pacific is California's oldest chartered college. Founded in 1851, Pacific is unusually diverse for an institution of its size, offering undergraduate programs in arts and sciences, business, education, engineering, and pharmacy and health sciences. A noteworthy School of International Studies brings together faculty from disciplines across the curriculum and requires students to study abroad. Merit awards begin with the Pacific Scholarships, which cover 90 percent of tuition for selected freshmen with at least a 3.85 GPA and an SAT I score of 1350 or an ACT of 31. Valedictorians are eligible for a 75 percent tuition discount, and two other scholarships are worth 50 percent and 33 percent. (Minimums to be considered for the latter are 3.33 and 1170 or 26.) Dean's Scholarships worth 25 percent of tuition are offered by each academic division. All awards require filing of a scholarship application from the admission packet. The university makes its own calculation of GPA in determining eligibility.

*Deadlines:*
  EARLY ACTION: Dec. 15
  REGULAR ADMISSION: Feb. 15
  FAFSA: Feb. 15

# PARSONS SCHOOL OF DESIGN ◆
## New York, NY 10011

| | |
|---|---|
| TOTAL ENROLLMENT: | 2,000 |
| UNDERGRADUATE: | 1,800 |
| ACCEPTANCE RATE: | 49% |
| SAT AVERAGE: | 540 Verbal |
| | 520 Math |
| STICKER PRICE: | $29,000+ |
| NEED-BLIND: | Yes |
| NEED MET: | 40% |
| AVERAGE STUDENT DEBT: | $17,100 |
| MERIT SCHOLARSHIPS: | None |
| ATHLETIC SCHOLARSHIPS: | No |
| ROTC: | No |
| WEB SITE: | www.parsons.newschool.edu |
| PHONE: | (800) 252-0852 |

The advantage of Parsons over other leading schools of design can be summarized in one word: Manhattan. Located in Greenwich Village on legendary Fifth Avenue, Parsons offers unparalleled access to the design world. Fashion design, communication design, and illustration top the list of most popular majors. Fashion students study in a program based at Fortieth Street in the heart of New York's fashion district, and for the ultimate fashion experience, Parsons also operates a program in Paris. The school offers an unusual program in design merchandising that leads to a business degree and features internships with industry leaders. Parsons is a division of New School University, which offers a combined degree program with its Eugene Lang College and access to a myriad of courses in its continuing education division. Financial aid at Parsons is limited to students who show need, though an average of only 40 percent was met in a recent year. Parsons accepts about half of its applicants, slightly more than Rhode Island School of Design but fewer than cross-town competitor Pratt.

*Deadlines:*
  ADMISSION: Mar. 1 (priority)
  FAFSA: Apr. 1
  CSS PROFILE: Apr. 1

# PEABODY CONSERVATORY OF MUSIC ◆
## Baltimore, MD 21202

| | |
|---|---|
| TOTAL ENROLLMENT: | 600 |
| UNDERGRADUATE: | 300 |
| ACCEPTANCE RATE: | 57% |
| SAT RANGE: | NA |
| STICKER PRICE: | $27,000+ |
| NEED-BLIND: | Yes |
| NEED MET: | 65% |
| AVERAGE STUDENT DEBT: | $15,000 |
| MERIT SCHOLARSHIPS: | Few |
| RANGE: | Up to full tuition |
| ATHLETIC SCHOLARSHIPS: | No |
| WEB SITE: | www.peabody.jhu.edu |
| PHONE: | (410) 659-8110 |

Set on a compact campus in urban Baltimore, Peabody combines the resources of one of the nation's oldest conservatories with those of parent institution Johns Hopkins, a major research university. Peabody's primary emphasis is classical music, and every student must be admitted to one of its performance majors. Categories include composition, early musical instruments, guitar, keyboard instruments, orchestral instruments, and voice. The conservatory has only limited offerings in jazz studies and computer music. Interested students can complete a teacher certification program. Peabody's offerings in the liberal arts are supplemented by those at Johns Hopkins, and it does not hurt to have the Hopkins name on the diploma when graduation rolls around. Admission to Peabody is more competitive than its 57 percent acceptance rate would suggest because only outstanding musicians are encouraged to apply. Peabody offers merit scholarships "usually in the range of $1,000 to $6,000," though full tuition awards are made on rare occasions "to help keep Peabody balanced in various instruments and voices." Other aid is awarded for a combination of merit and need.

*Deadlines:*
  ADMISSION: Dec. 15
  FAFSA: Feb. 1

## PENNSYLVANIA STATE UNIVERSITY ◆
### University Park, PA 16802

| | |
|---|---|
| TOTAL ENROLLMENT: | 40,500 |
| UNDERGRADUATE: | 34,300 |
| ACCEPTANCE RATE: | 56% |
| SAT RANGE: | 540–640 Verbal |
| | 560–660 Math |
| STICKER PRICE: | In-state, $11,000+ |
| | Out-of-state, $17,000+ |
| NEED-BLIND: | Yes |
| NEED MET: | NA |
| AVERAGE STUDENT DEBT: | $16,500 |
| MERIT SCHOLARSHIPS: | Many |
| ATHLETIC SCHOLARSHIPS: | Yes |
| ROTC: | Army, Navy, Air Force |
| WEB SITE: | www.psu.edu |
| PHONE: | (814) 865-5471 |

With 24 campuses, 80,000 students, and nearly 400,000 living alumni, Penn State could probably secede from the union and declare independence if it took a notion to do so. The University Park campus (the one actually located in State College) is the headquarters of the entire operation and among the most selective public universities in the nation. The same is true of its Schreyer Honors College, which offers the usual honors trimmings plus an Academic Excellence Scholarship worth $2,000–$3,000, travel grants for study abroad, and opportunities to complete a combined degree program. The priority deadline for consideration is November 30. The majority of Penn State's merit scholarships are available through its various academic divisions. For example, the College of the Liberal Arts offers awards that "typically range from $500 to $1,500." The College of Earth and Mineral Sciences gives about sixty Dean's Freshman Scholarships of up to $2,500. Many of the colleges have scholarships that augment the Schreyer awards. Deadlines and procedures vary.

*Deadlines:*
   ADMISSION: Nov. 30 (priority)
   FAFSA: Feb. 15

## UNIVERSITY OF PENNSYLVANIA ◆
### Philadelphia, PA 19104

| | |
|---|---|
| TOTAL ENROLLMENT: | 21,600 |
| UNDERGRADUATE: | 11,400 |
| ACCEPTANCE RATE: | 31% |
| SAT RANGE: | 620–720 Verbal |
| | 650–740 Math |
| STICKER PRICE: | $31,000+ |
| NEED-BLIND: | Yes |
| NEED MET: | 100% |
| AVERAGE STUDENT DEBT: | $19,100 |
| MERIT SCHOLARSHIPS: | None |
| ATHLETIC SCHOLARSHIPS: | No |
| ROTC: | Army, Navy, Air Force |
| WEB SITE: | www.upenn.edu |
| PHONE: | (215) 898-7507 |

It is no coincidence that the statue of Benjamin Franklin on the Penn campus is wearing a contented smile. As the founder of Penn more than three centuries ago, he would surely be pleased at the surge of interest from top students that has pushed applications to record levels. Franklin was a serious man but he also knew how to have a good time, and today's Penn students have the same reputation in comparison with their more uptight Ivy League brethren. The author of *Poor Richard's Almanac* was also a practical man who would be delighted that Penn is home to the finest undergraduate business school in the nation and top schools in nursing and engineering. Like the rest of the Ivy League, Penn offers financial aid only on the basis of need. But it does entice approximately 140 incoming freshmen with selection to the Benjamin Franklin Scholars Program, which offers small classes with the university's top professors and funding for summer research. The merit-within-need Trustee Scholars program provides up to $4,000, and Penn also offers a package of borrowing and payment options called The Penn Plan.

*Deadlines:*
   EARLY DECISION: Nov. 1
   REGULAR ADMISSION: Jan. 1
   FAFSA: Feb. 15
   CSS PROFILE: Feb. 15

# PEPPERDINE UNIVERSITY ◆
## Malibu, CA 90263

| | |
|---|---|
| TOTAL ENROLLMENT: | 7,800 |
| UNDERGRADUATE: | 3,300 |
| ACCEPTANCE RATE: | 54% |
| SAT RANGE: | 550–640 Verbal |
| | 552–650 Math |
| STICKER PRICE: | $29,000+ |
| NEED-BLIND: | Yes |
| NEED MET: | NA |
| AVERAGE STUDENT DEBT: | NA |
| MERIT SCHOLARSHIPS: | Many |
| ATHLETIC SCHOLARSHIPS: | Yes |
| ROTC: | Army, Air Force |
| WEB SITE: | www.pepperdine.edu |
| PHONE: | (310) 456-4392 |

Perched atop the sun-drenched bluffs where the Santa Monica Mountains meet the Pacific Ocean, Pepperdine has the most stunning backdrop imaginable for a college campus. The opulence of Malibu adds to the aura, and with Santa Monica and Beverly Hills just down the road, there is plenty of city bustle close at hand. Along with physical beauty, Pepperdine is known for its conservatism and commitment to the Christian faith. (The university is affiliated with the Churches of Christ.) Business administration heads the list of most popular majors; telecommunications is second. Students seeking a merit scholarship must have a 3.75 high school GPA with a 1320 SAT I or a 30 on the ACT. Scholarships go "almost exclusively" to students who are in the top 10 percent of Pepperdine's applicant pool and had an average value of $10,000 in a recent year. Special achievement awards are also available from the various academic divisions in art, forensics, music, student publications, journalism, television and radio production, and theater. Students are advised to contact the relevant departments.

*Deadlines:*
EARLY ACTION: Nov. 15
REGULAR ADMISSION: Jan. 15
FAFSA: Feb. 15

# UNIVERSITY OF PITTSBURGH ◆
## Pittsburgh, PA 15260

| | |
|---|---|
| TOTAL ENROLLMENT: | 25,500 |
| UNDERGRADUATE: | 16,200 |
| ACCEPTANCE RATE: | 78% |
| SAT AVERAGE: | 500—610 Verbal |
| | 500—610 Math |
| STICKER PRICE: | In-state, $12,000+ |
| | Out-of-state, $19,000+ |
| NEED-BLIND: | Yes |
| NEED MET: | 85% |
| AVERAGE STUDENT DEBT: | $15,000 |
| MERIT SCHOLARSHIPS: | Many |
| RANGE: | Up to full costs |
| ATHLETIC SCHOLARSHIPS: | Yes |
| ROTC: | Army, Navy, Air Force |
| WEB SITE: | www.pitt.edu |
| PHONE: | (412) 624-PITT |

Pitt is home to one of higher education's most enduring symbols—the 42-story Cathedral of Learning that towers over its 132-acre campus. More than just a show piece, the Cathedral is home to many of the university's offices and classrooms. A major draw for top students is the chance for guaranteed admission to graduate programs in law, medicine, physical therapy, and dentistry. (Admission standards are steep.) Nearly 20 percent of Pitt freshmen receive a merit scholarship, and the university guarantees an award of at least $1,000 for any student who scores 1300 on the SAT I or 29 on the ACT with a high school class rank in the top 20 percent. Fifteen Chancellor's Scholarships, covering full costs, top the list. Full-ride scholarships are also available for African Americans in business, engineering, and arts and sciences. University Scholarships of $1,000 and up account for the bulk of Pitt's awards. The priority deadline for scholarships and the combined degree programs is January 15.

*Deadlines:*
ADMISSION: Rolling
FAFSA: Mar. 1

# PITZER COLLEGE ✦ Claremont, CA 91711

| | |
|---|---|
| TOTAL ENROLLMENT: | 900 |
| UNDERGRADUATE: | 900 |
| ACCEPTANCE RATE: | 65% |
| SAT AVERAGE: | 602 Verbal |
| | 584 Math |
| STICKER PRICE: | $30,000+ |
| NEED-BLIND: | No |
| NEED MET: | 100% |
| AVERAGE STUDENT DEBT: | $18,600 |
| MERIT SCHOLARSHIPS: | Few |
| RANGE: | Up to $10,000 |
| ATHLETIC SCHOLARSHIPS: | No |
| ROTC: | No |
| WEB SITE: | www.pitzer.edu |
| PHONE: | (909) 621-8129 |

General education courses at most colleges can be a drag, but at Pitzer they have names like "L.A. as Film Noir" and "Youth Rebellion: Reggae, Rap and Beyond." These two recent classes from Pitzer's interdisciplinary Freshman Seminar series are examples of academic life at this innovative, slightly off-beat younger sibling of the Claremont Colleges. Best known for its programs in the social and behavioral sciences, Pitzer gives students extra freedom to design their own course of study. The college also stresses off-campus opportunities, including nine study abroad programs that emphasize cultural immersion. Though Pitzer has an alternative flavor, it does not have a hard-core anti-establishment atmosphere. Located thirty-five miles from Los Angeles, Pitzer shares its Claremont location with four other outstanding undergraduate institutions: Claremont McKenna, Harvey Mudd, Pomona, and Scripps. Pitzer's merit awards are limited to twenty Trustee-Community Scholarships of $10,000 per year, which are based on academic excellence plus leadership, talent, or service.

*Deadlines:*
  EARLY DECISION: Dec. 1
  EARLY ACTION: Dec. 1
  REGULAR ADMISSION: Feb.1
  FAFSA: Feb. 1
  CSS PROFILE: Feb. 1

# POLYTECHNIC UNIVERSITY ✦ Brooklyn, NY 11201

| | |
|---|---|
| TOTAL ENROLLMENT: | 3,000 |
| UNDERGRADUATE: | 1,500 |
| ACCEPTANCE RATE: | 72% |
| SAT RANGE: | 400–540 Verbal |
| | 570–670 Math |
| STICKER PRICE: | $25,000+ |
| NEED-BLIND: | Yes |
| NEED MET: | NA |
| AVERAGE STUDENT DEBT: | $19,300 |
| MERIT SCHOLARSHIPS: | Many |
| RANGE: | Up to full tuition |
| ATHLETIC SCHOLARSHIPS: | No |
| ROTC: | Army, Air Force |
| WEB SITE: | www.poly.edu |
| PHONE: | (718) 260-3100 |

There was a time when Polytechnic University considered moving out of Brooklyn—but it decided to stay and help spearhead an urban renaissance instead. Today, Polytechnic stands at the center of a thriving industrial park, with leading programs in electrical engineering, polymer chemistry, aerospace and microwave engineering, and other engineering fields. Nearly 60 percent of Polytechnic students get an academic scholarship, and the university offers no less than eight award programs of up to $10,000. Full-tuition scholarships are available for National Merit Finalists and Semifinalists, outstanding New Yorkers, and those majoring in engineering or computer science. Among the $10,000 programs are awards for outstanding minority students and top achievers of Arab descent, and a $4,000 scholarship goes to students of Italian ancestry. Once enrolled, students from New York City or Long Island in good academic standing are guaranteed a Tuition Savings Award of at least $5,000. In addition to the main campus, Polytechnic operates a satellite location on Long Island.

*Deadlines:*
  EARLY ACTION: Nov. 1
  REGULAR ADMISSION: Feb. 1 (priority)
  FAFSA: Feb. 1

# POMONA COLLEGE ✦ Claremont, CA 91711

| | |
|---|---|
| TOTAL ENROLLMENT: | 1,400 |
| UNDERGRADUATE: | 1,400 |
| ACCEPTANCE RATE: | 31% |
| SAT RANGE: | 670–750 Verbal |
| | 670–740 Math |
| STICKER PRICE: | $29,000+ |
| NEED-BLIND: | Yes |
| NEED MET: | 100% |
| AVERAGE STUDENT DEBT: | $15,500 |
| MERIT SCHOLARSHIPS: | Few |
| RANGE: | Up to $2,000 |
| ATHLETIC SCHOLARSHIPS: | No |
| ROTC: | No |
| WEB SITE: | www.pomona.edu |
| PHONE: | (909) 621-8134 |

In a state dominated by the University of California system and Stanford, Pomona is the leading exemplar of East Coast–style liberal arts excellence—a bit like if Williams or Wesleyan were transplanted to southern California. But sunny weather isn't Pomona's only advantage. Nestled amid four other outstanding schools that collectively make up the Claremont colleges—Claremont McKenna, Harvey Mudd, Pitzer, and Scripps—Pomona combines the atmosphere of a small college with the resources of a major university. (Among elite coed private colleges, only Amherst's position in the Five College Consortium is comparable.) Like most California institutions, Pomona is far more diverse than Eastern schools, with an enrollment that is about 20 percent Asian, 10 percent Latino, and 4 percent African American. Popular majors include psychology, economics, and English. Pomona maintains a need-blind admissions policy and meets full need. The only non-need scholarships, valued at up to $2,000 depending on need, go to six National Merit Finalists among the dozens of such students who enroll.

*Deadlines:*
    EARLY DECISION: Nov. 15
    REGULAR ADMISSION: Jan. 1
    FAFSA: Feb. 1
    CSS PROFILE: Feb. 1

# PRATT INSTITUTE ✦ Brooklyn, NY 11205

| | |
|---|---|
| TOTAL ENROLLMENT: | 3,700 |
| UNDERGRADUATE: | 2,400 |
| ACCEPTANCE RATE: | 56% |
| SAT RANGE: | 470–580 Verbal |
| | 420–560 Math |
| STICKER PRICE: | $27,000+ |
| NEED-BLIND: | NA |
| NEED MET: | NA |
| AVERAGE STUDENT DEBT: | NA |
| MERIT SCHOLARSHIPS: | Many |
| RANGE: | Up to $8,000 |
| ATHLETIC SCHOLARSHIPS: | No |
| ROTC: | No |
| WEB SITE: | www.pratt.edu |
| PHONE: | (800) 331-0834 |

Don't let the fact that Pratt is an "institute" fool you. Pratt's specialties are art, design, and architecture. Pratt occupies twenty-five acres in the Clinton Hill section of Brooklyn—the only East Coast art school with an enclosed campus, the administration points out—and housing is guaranteed to all who want it. The school has a satellite location in Manhattan, a quick subway ride away, and many internship opportunities are available there, too. Architecture heads the list of most popular majors, followed by communication design and fine arts. All students must complete a liberal arts core that includes humanities, social sciences, math, and science. Pratt is among a number of art schools that have beefed up academic standards for admission instead of relying solely on a portfolio. High school GPA and test scores are considered along with portfolios in granting the Presidential Merit Scholarship, which gives top freshmen an award ranging from $3,000 to $8,000. Other scholarships are available with specific criteria from Pratt's various academic divisions.

*Deadlines:*
    EARLY DECISION: Nov. 15
    REGULAR ADMISSION: Feb. 1 (priority)
    FAFSA: Feb. 1
    CSS PROFILE: Feb. 1

# PRESBYTERIAN COLLEGE ✦ Clinton, SC 29325

| | |
|---|---|
| TOTAL ENROLLMENT: | 1,100 |
| UNDERGRADUATE: | 1,100 |
| ACCEPTANCE RATE: | 84% |
| SAT RANGE: | 500–600 Verbal |
| | 550–650 Math |
| STICKER PRICE: | $20,000+ |
| NEED-BLIND: | Yes |
| NEED MET: | 89% |
| AVERAGE STUDENT DEBT: | $13,600 |
| MERIT SCHOLARSHIPS: | Many |
| RANGE: | Up to full costs |
| ATHLETIC SCHOLARSHIPS: | Yes |
| ROTC: | Army |
| WEB SITE: | www.presby.edu |
| PHONE: | (864) 833-8230 |

Presbyterian is a small college in rural South Carolina that competes with Furman and Wofford for liberal arts students in the Palmetto state. Affiliated with the Presbyterian Church (U.S.A.), the college places a strong emphasis on values, which are embodied in the college's Honor Code. Fifteen percent of Presbyterian freshmen receive academic scholarships, which are highlighted by the full-ride Quattlebaum Scholarship for two superior applicants. Three other scholarship packages cover 66 percent, 50 percent, or 33 percent of tuition based on high school grades and standardized test scores. (The latter of the three requires a 3.0 GPA with a combined SAT 1 of 1000 or an ACT of 22.) All of the aforementioned awards require an application for admission by December 5. Other programs target students who have shown leadership ($7,500 and $2,000), superior achievement in math or science ($2,000), and musical talent (variable), or who are Presbyterian church members ($1,000) or children of almuni ($1,000). Georgians who would have qualified for the HOPE Scholarship get $3,000.

*Deadlines:*
  ADMISSION: Apr. 1
  FAFSA: Mar. 1

# PRESCOTT COLLEGE ✦ Prescott, AZ 86301

| | |
|---|---|
| TOTAL ENROLLMENT: | 450 |
| UNDERGRADUATE: | 450 |
| ACCEPTANCE RATE: | 68% |
| SAT AVERAGE: | 1070 combined |
| STICKER PRICE (COMMUTER): | $12,000+ |
| NEED-BLIND: | Yes |
| NEED MET: | 38% |
| AVERAGE STUDENT DEBT: | $12,800 |
| MERIT SCHOLARSHIPS: | None |
| ATHLETIC SCHOLARSHIPS: | No |
| ROTC: | No |
| WEB SITE: | www.prescott.edu |
| PHONE: | (520) 776-5180 |

Surrounded by 1.4 million acres of national forest in the mountains of central Arizona, Prescott is like an academic version of Outward Bound. A three-week Wilderness Orientation for all new arrivals sets the tone; students spend the rest of their Prescott years exploring the importance of self-reliance, experiential learning, group collaboration, and stewardship of the environment. Students complete learning contracts with their professors that outline their plan of study, and grades are deemphasized in favor of narrative assessments. Adventure education ranks as the most popular major on campus, followed by environmental studies. Many students complete interdisciplinary majors such as Peace Studies or Human Development. A large percentage of Prescott students are transfers who have tried conventional institutions and found them wanting. In keeping with the theme of independence, Prescott provides no housing, but the college notes that there is plenty available in the area. Financial aid funds are limited but include a small amount of merit-within-need money.

*Deadlines:*
  ADMISSION: Feb. 1 (priority)
  FAFSA: May 12

# PRINCETON UNIVERSITY ✦
## Princeton, NJ 08544

| | |
|---|---|
| TOTAL ENROLLMENT: | 6,300 |
| UNDERGRADUATE: | 4,600 |
| ACCEPTANCE RATE: | 15% |
| SAT RANGE: | 620–710 Verbal |
| | 680–770 Math |
| STICKER PRICE: | $31,000+ |
| NEED-BLIND: | Yes |
| NEED MET: | 100% |
| AVERAGE STUDENT DEBT: | $15,000 |
| MERIT SCHOLARSHIPS: | None |
| ATHLETIC SCHOLARSHIPS: | No |
| ROTC: | Army, Air Force |
| WEB SITE: | www.princeton.edu |
| PHONE: | (609) 258-3060 |

As Yale weathered a run of bad publicity in the 1990s, Princeton emerged as the preferred alternative to Harvard among the tiny handful of super-achievers with the power to choose such things. Though Princeton's undergraduate enrollment of 4,600 is not significantly less than the other two, a crucial distinction lies in Princeton's total of only 1,700 graduate and professional students. (Yale has 5,400 undergraduates and 5,700 graduate students; Harvard has 6,600 and 11,600, respectively.) Faculty attention and independent scholarship are the hallmarks of a Princeton education, and all students complete a junior-year independent project and a senior thesis. The university's most popular majors are history and politics. With the largest endowment per student in the nation, Princeton can afford to give need-based aid packages that trump those of most competitors. The university set off a chain reaction in 1998 when it announced that it would modify its need-based aid formula: no more loans for families whose income is below $40,000, less loans for those below $57,000, and home equity out of the aid equation for most families below $90,000.

*Deadlines:*
   EARLY DECISION: Nov. 1
   REGULAR ADMISSION: Jan. 2
   FAFSA: Feb. 1
   CSS PROFILE: Feb. 1

# PROVIDENCE COLLEGE ✦
## Providence, RI 02918

| | |
|---|---|
| TOTAL ENROLLMENT: | 5,500 |
| UNDERGRADUATE: | 4,600 |
| ACCEPTANCE RATE: | 67% |
| SAT RANGE: | 500–600 Verbal |
| | 500–600 Math |
| STICKER PRICE: | $24,000+ |
| NEED-BLIND: | Yes |
| NEED MET: | 85% |
| AVERAGE STUDENT DEBT: | $20,000 |
| MERIT SCHOLARSHIPS: | Many |
| ATHLETIC SCHOLARSHIPS: | Up to full costs |
| ROTC: | Army |
| WEB SITE: | www.providence.edu |
| PHONE: | (401) 865-2535 |

Providence College traces its heritage back to the year 1216 and the founding of the Dominican Order of the Catholic Church. With nearly a millenium of history to draw on, Providence has a steadfast commitment to the study of Western civilization and backs it up with a core curriculum covering more than 40 percent of the requirements for a degree. Business takes first place on the list of most popular majors. The Presidential Scholarship offers a full-tuition award to selected students who rank at the top of their high school class with at least 1400 on the SAT I. Those in the top 10 percent with 1250 or better are in contention for the half-tuition Dean's Scholarship. Women and minority students are considered for a full-costs award with the same academic criteria as the Dean's, and a Martin Luther King, Jr. Scholarship for minority students requires a separate application. Additional awards are offered for community service ($2,000) and to those who are interested in medicine (up to full costs).

*Deadlines:*
   EARLY ACTION: Nov. 15
   REGULAR ADMISSION: Jan. 15
   FAFSA: Feb. 1
   CSS PROFILE: Feb. 1

# UNIVERSITY OF PUGET SOUND ✦
## Tacoma, WA 98416

| | |
|---|---|
| TOTAL ENROLLMENT: | 3,000 |
| UNDERGRADUATE: | 2,700 |
| ACCEPTANCE RATE: | 79% |
| SAT RANGE: | 570–670 Verbal |
| | 570–660 Math |
| STICKER PRICE: | $25,000+ |
| NEED-BLIND: | Yes |
| NEED MET: | 87% |
| AVERAGE STUDENT DEBT: | $18,400 |
| MERIT SCHOLARSHIPS: | Many |
| RANGE: | Up to full tuition |
| ATHLETIC SCHOLARSHIPS: | No |
| ROTC: | Army |
| WEB SITE: | www.ups.edu |
| PHONE: | (800) 396-7191 |

Ask anyone in Tacoma about UPS—the university, not the parcel service—and they'll tell you that Puget Sound delivers an unusual blend of interdisciplinary majors within the liberal arts. Surrounded by the natural beauty of the Pacific Northwest, UPS is best-known for its pioneering work in Asian studies. Other showcase programs include International Political Economy and Science in Context, the latter combining science and public policy. About 20 percent of incoming students receive merit scholarships that average nearly $6,000. Those who apply for admission by February 1 are in contention for awards based on academic records and test scores that range from $3,000 to $11,000. Students in art, forensics, music, and theater can vie for scholarships averaging $1,500 to $4,000 per year, the latter two requiring an audition on tape or in person. Students should contact the departments. A third category includes miscellaneous awards based on intended major, leadership, religious affiliation, place of residence, and other criteria. A separate application, due March 1, is required.

*Deadlines:*
  EARLY DECISION: Nov. 15
  REGULAR ADMISSION: Feb. 1
  FAFSA: Jan. 20

# PURDUE UNIVERSITY ✦
## West Lafayette, IN 47907

| | |
|---|---|
| TOTAL ENROLLMENT: | 35,700 |
| UNDERGRADUATE: | 29,100 |
| ACCEPTANCE RATE: | 89% |
| SAT RANGE: | 480–540 Verbal |
| | 500–630 Math |
| STICKER PRICE: | In-state, $9,000+ |
| | Out-of-state, $17,000+ |
| NEED-BLIND: | Yes |
| NEED MET: | NA |
| AVERAGE STUDENT DEBT: | $13,800 |
| MERIT SCHOLARSHIPS: | Many |
| RANGE: | Up to full tuition |
| ATHLETIC SCHOLARSHIPS: | Yes |
| ROTC: | Army, Navy, Air Force |
| WEB SITE: | www.purdue.edu |
| PHONE: | (765) 494-1776 |

Purdue is the state university of Indiana devoted primarily to science and technology. The university prides itself on having launched the careers of more astronauts than any other university, and aviation remains one of its strengths. (The flight technology and nursing programs have a recommended application deadline of November 15.) Computer/electrical engineering ranks as the most popular major on campus. A $1,000 scholarship for valedictorians and an award for National Merit Finalists top the list of university-wide merit programs, though most scholarships come via the academic divisions. Examples include the School of Science's Distinguished Scholar Award, which includes eight stipends of up to $4,000 per year. Selection of recipients begins December 1. In the School of Management, Freshman Year Scholarships of up to $6,000 (some renewable) have a March 1 deadline, and the engineering school sponsors a Women in Engineering scholarship of up to $5,000, with a deadline of February 1. Students should contact the school in their area of interest for scholarship information.

*Deadlines:*
  ADMISSION: Rolling
  FAFSA: Mar. 1

# RANDOLPH-MACON WOMAN'S COLLEGE ◆
## Lynchburg, VA 24503

| | |
|---|---|
| TOTAL ENROLLMENT: | 700 |
| UNDERGRADUATE: | 700 |
| ACCEPTANCE RATE: | 89% |
| SAT RANGE: | 550–660 Verbal |
| | 510–610 Math |
| STICKER PRICE: | $24,000+ |
| NEED-BLIND: | Yes |
| NEED MET: | 92% |
| AVERAGE STUDENT DEBT: | $16,600 |
| MERIT SCHOLARSHIPS: | Many |
| RANGE: | Up to full tuition |
| ATHLETIC SCHOLARSHIPS: | No |
| ROTC: | No |
| WEB SITE: | www.rmwc.edu |
| PHONE: | (800) 745-7692 |

Randolph-Macon calls itself a woman's college—singular—to highlight its attention to the needs of every student. With only 700 students and an average class size of 13, the college delivers on that promise. RMWC has a proud heritage of liberal arts excellence and is among a trio of women's colleges in west-central Virginia (along with Hollins and Sweet Briar) that compete directly for many of the same students. More than half of accepted applicants are offered a merit scholarship, most notably the Gottwald Scholarship, which offers full tuition plus a $2,500 fellowship for study abroad to three of the college's star freshmen. A special application is required by December 15. Awards of up to $10,000 honor all-around achievement, and scholarships are available to top math students (up to $3,000), high achieving minority students (up to $5,000), those whose parents are United Methodist clergy ($1,000), and those who live in Lynchburg, Washington, D.C., and other areas. Additional awards include a $2,000 stipend for those active in community service.

*Deadlines:*
  EARLY DECISION: Nov. 15
  REGULAR ADMISSION: Feb. 15
  FAFSA: Feb. 1

# UNIVERSITY OF REDLANDS ◆
## Redlands, CA 92373

| | |
|---|---|
| TOTAL ENROLLMENT: | 1,500 |
| UNDERGRADUATE: | 1,400 |
| ACCEPTANCE RATE: | 80% |
| SAT RANGE: | 510–620 Verbal |
| | 500–620 Math |
| STICKER PRICE: | $27,000+ |
| NEED-BLIND: | Yes |
| NEED MET: | 94% |
| AVERAGE STUDENT DEBT: | $19,100 |
| MERIT SCHOLARSHIPS: | Many |
| RANGE: | Up to full tuition |
| ATHLETIC SCHOLARSHIPS: | No |
| ROTC: | Army, Air Force |
| WEB SITE: | www.redlands.edu |
| PHONE: | (800) 455-5064 |

Framed against a stunning tableau of palm trees superimposed on snow-covered peaks, Redlands is a traditional undergraduate college with a nonconformist twist. The latter comes in the form of the Johnston Center for Integrative Studies, an unusual college-within-a-college that Redlands describes as "a community of independent, atypical and adventurous students who talk about ideas." But most of Redlands is more standard fare. Popular majors include business, pre-med, government, and education. Redlands also includes a well-regarded school of music. Located about an hour's drive east of Los Angeles, Redlands offers easy access to mountains, the ocean, the desert, and the rest of southern California's charms. The university offers Awards of Merit up to full tuition to selected National Merit Finalists. Other scholarships based on academic achievement provide up to $7,000, and Talent Awards of up to $4,000 are available in art, writing, debate, and music. Scholarship candidates should apply by December 15.

*Deadlines:*
  ADMISSION: Feb. 1 (priority)
  FAFSA: Feb. 15

# REED COLLEGE ◆ Portland, OR 97202

| | |
|---|---|
| TOTAL ENROLLMENT: | 1,300 |
| UNDERGRADUATE: | 1,300 |
| ACCEPTANCE RATE: | 70% |
| SAT RANGE: | 640–730 Verbal |
| | 600–690 Math |
| STICKER PRICE: | $30,000+ |
| NEED-BLIND: | Yes |
| NEED MET: | NA |
| AVERAGE STUDENT DEBT: | $13,200 |
| MERIT SCHOLARSHIPS: | None |
| ATHLETIC SCHOLARSHIPS: | No |
| ROTC: | Army |
| WEB SITE: | www.reed.edu |
| PHONE: | (800) 547-4750 |

Reed is a four letter word for the purest form of intellectual striving yet invented by an American college. Reed students are warriors who eagerly embrace the pleasure and pain that comes from all-out commitment to the life of the mind. The students are a nonconformist breed and sometimes a little quirky, but Reed should not be mistaken for an artsy alternative school. The curriculum is traditional liberal arts, and the college produces just as many students who ultimately earn a Ph.D. in the sciences as English. Reed has fought a high-profile battle with *U.S. News and World Report* over its place in the annual rankings; the magazine has judged Reed a "second tier" school, partly because of its high attrition rate. (The kind of student who chooses Reed probably would not care about such things.) The college offers no merit scholarships, and at this writing, outside scholarships merely reduce Reed's institutional grant for need-based students, though it is possible to petition for an exemption. In a recent year, 137 out of 161 freshman with financial need received packages that covered it fully.

*Deadlines:*
  EARLY DECISION: Dec. 1, Jan. 15
  REGULAR ADMISSION: Feb. 1
  FAFSA: Feb. 1
  CSS PROFILE: Feb. 1

# RENSSELAER POLYTECHNIC INSTITUTE ◆ Troy, NY 12180

| | |
|---|---|
| TOTAL ENROLLMENT: | 6,400 |
| UNDERGRADUATE: | 4,300 |
| ACCEPTANCE RATE: | 83% |
| SAT RANGE: | 550–660 Verbal |
| | 610–710 Math |
| STICKER PRICE: | $30,000+ |
| NEED-BLIND: | Yes |
| NEED MET: | 91% |
| AVERAGE STUDENT DEBT: | $20,300 |
| MERIT SCHOLARSHIPS: | Many |
| RANGE: | Up to $10,000 |
| ATHLETIC SCHOLARSHIPS: | Yes |
| ROTC: | Army, Navy, Air Force |
| WEB SITE: | www.rpi.edu |
| PHONE: | (518) 276-6216 |

Aside from a few thousand graduate students, the primary difference between Rensselaer and MIT is that one is located near Harvard in Boston and the other in Troy, New York. Rensselaer has less cachet, but the technical education is at least as good. RPI is a pioneer in the use of interactive technology to create hands-on, team-oriented classrooms. Engineering is where Rensselaer's primary reputation lies; its most popular majors are mechanical and electrical engineering. RPI's schools of architecture and science are also strong, and its School of Management and Technology has a unique program in technological entrepreneurship. Merit scholarships include the Rensselaer Medal, awarded to outstanding eleventh graders at 2,300 participating high schools, which gives $10,000 to those who enroll at RPI. The Emily Roebling Scholarship gives $7,500 to leading female engineers, and a Dean's Award of $3,000 goes to top freshmen. All are awarded based on the application for admission. The school gives a total of eighteen athletic scholarships exclusively in men's hockey.

*Deadlines:*
  EARLY DECISION: Dec. 1
  REGULAR ADMISSION: Jan. 1
  FAFSA: Feb. 15

## RHODE ISLAND SCHOOL OF DESIGN •
## Providence, RI 02903

| | |
|---|---|
| TOTAL ENROLLMENT: | 2,000 |
| UNDERGRADUATE: | 1,800 |
| ACCEPTANCE RATE: | 43% |
| SAT AVERAGE: | 593 Verbal |
| | 581 Math |
| STICKER PRICE: | $28,000+ |
| NEED-BLIND: | Yes |
| NEED MET: | NA |
| AVERAGE STUDENT DEBT: | $19,000 |
| MERIT SCHOLARSHIPS: | Few |
| ATHLETIC SCHOLARSHIPS: | No |
| ROTC: | No |
| WEB SITE: | www.risd.edu |
| PHONE: | (401) 454-6300 |

RISD is the closest thing to a household name in the world of art and design education. It certainly has the most famous acronym. (Pronounce it "Riz-dee.") Set on the edge of a historic district near downtown Providence, RISD's two main divisions are architecture and design, and fine arts. Illustration, graphic design, and architecture comprise the list of most popular majors. Students begin their RISD careers with Foundation Studies, which covers drawing, 2-D and 3-D design, art, architectural history, and English. Approximately a third of each student's coursework takes place in the liberal arts, and RISD's own programs are bolstered by cross-registration with adjacent Brown University. Leading students are eligible for the European Honors Program, which allows them to spend a year in Italy doing independent work with a faculty member. RISD offers only a handful of merit awards under the heading of Trustee Scholarships, which average about $3,000. In a recent year, less than 10 percent of students with need had it met in full.

*Deadlines:*
EARLY ACTION: Dec. 15
REGULAR ADMISSION: Feb. 15
FAFSA: Feb. 15
CSS PROFILE: Feb. 15

## UNIVERSITY OF RHODE ISLAND •
## Kingston, RI 02881

| | |
|---|---|
| TOTAL ENROLLMENT: | 13,400 |
| UNDERGRADUATE: | 10,200 |
| ACCEPTANCE RATE: | 79% |
| SAT RANGE: | 490–590 Verbal |
| | 490–590 Math |
| STICKER PRICE: | In-state, $11,000+ |
| | Out-of-state, $19,000+ |
| NEED-BLIND: | Yes |
| NEED MET: | NA |
| AVERAGE STUDENT DEBT: | NA |
| MERIT SCHOLARSHIPS: | Many |
| RANGE: | Up to full tuition |
| ATHLETIC SCHOLARSHIPS: | Yes |
| ROTC: | Army |
| WEB SITE: | www.uri.edu |
| PHONE: | (401) 874-7000 |

URI is among the few public universities that enroll more students from out-of-state than its home turf. With a total enrollment of 13,400, Rhode Island is bigger than some state school counterparts (including the Universities of New Hampshire, Maine, and Vermont) but far from a mega-university. All freshmen enroll in a seminar called URI 101 that helps ease the transition to college life with work on basic skills and discussion of majors and career paths. Rhode Island's primary academic divisions include arts and sciences, business, engineering, environmental and life sciences, human science and services, nursing, and pharmacy; a graduate school of oceanography ensures that programs related to marine science are strong. URI's primary method of attracting top students is through its Early Action and Centennial Scholarship programs, which offer hundreds of awards ranging from $1,000 to full tuition. Applicants must apply for admission by December 15.

*Deadlines:*
EARLY ACTION: Dec. 15
REGULAR ADMISSION: Mar. 1
FAFSA: Mar. 1

# RHODES COLLEGE ✦ Memphis, TN 38112

| | |
|---|---|
| TOTAL ENROLLMENT: | 1,400 |
| UNDERGRADUATE: | 1,400 |
| ACCEPTANCE RATE: | 75% |
| SAT RANGE: | 600–690 Verbal |
| | 600–680 Math |
| STICKER PRICE: | $23,000+ |
| NEED-BLIND: | No |
| NEED MET: | NA |
| AVERAGE STUDENT DEBT: | $15,200 |
| MERIT SCHOLARSHIPS: | Many |
| RANGE: | Up to full costs |
| ATHLETIC SCHOLARSHIPS: | No |
| ROTC: | Army, Air Force |
| WEB SITE: | www.rhodes.edu |
| PHONE: | (800) 844-5969 |

Rhodes stands alongside the University of the South, Hendrix, and Millsaps among fine small colleges in the lower Mississippi River region. Unlike the others, it is located in a major metropolitan area, Memphis, the birthplace of blues. Rhodes spent most of its 150-year history known as Southwestern at Memphis. Approximately 40 percent of the students in each incoming class receive a merit award. A total of four of its most outstanding freshmen receive the Bellingrath and Hyde Scholarships, which cover the full costs of attendance. Applicants must be nominated by a school official, minister, or alumnus before December 1. Eight other categories of merit awards are available, ranging from the full tuition Morse Scholarships down to the Rhodes Awards, which offer up to $5,000 to selected students with at least a 3.6 GPA and an SAT I score of 1210 or an ACT of 27. Fine arts awards of $10,000 are available in music, theater, and art, and merit-within-need scholarships are given for leadership, community service, and to top African American applicants.

*Deadlines:*
EARLY DECISION: Nov. 15
REGULAR ADMISSION: Feb. 1
FAFSA: Mar. 1

# RICE UNIVERSITY ✦ Houston, TX 77005

| | |
|---|---|
| TOTAL ENROLLMENT: | 4,200 |
| UNDERGRADUATE: | 2,800 |
| ACCEPTANCE RATE: | 27% |
| SAT RANGE: | 650–760 Verbal |
| | 680–770 Math |
| STICKER PRICE: | $22,000+ |
| NEED-BLIND: | Yes |
| NEED MET: | 100% |
| AVERAGE STUDENT DEBT: | $11,500 |
| MERIT SCHOLARSHIPS: | Many |
| RANGE: | Up to full tuition |
| ATHLETIC SCHOLARSHIPS: | Yes |
| ROTC: | Army, Navy |
| WEB SITE: | www.rice.edu |
| PHONE: | (800) 527-OWLS |

Top faculty and outstanding facilities notwithstanding, Rice owes much of its greatness to a little thing called compound interest. A handsome bequest of $4.6 million in 1904 put Rice on the road to greatness. Today, its multibillion-dollar endowment allows Rice to offer a world class education at a savings of roughly $10,000 vis-a-vis comparable private universities. Though Rice made its reputation in science, architecture, and engineering, the humanities and social sciences are also strong and the university boasts an outstanding school of music. With tuition skyrocketing elsewhere, small wonder that Rice has become ultracompetitive in admission, accepting only 27 percent in a recent year. For need-based aid recipients, Rice places a cap of approximately $2,500 on loans in its aid packages. It also guarantees that tuition increases will not exceed inflation between enrollment and graduation. Rice offers merit scholarships of up to full tuition for extraordinarily strong applicants, including seventy-five awards for National Merit Finalists that range from $750 to $2,000, depending on need.

*Deadlines:*
EARLY DECISION: Nov. 1
EARLY ACTION: Dec. 1
REGULAR ADMISSION: Jan. 2
FAFSA: Rolling

## UNIVERSITY OF RICHMOND ✦ Richmond, VA 23173

| | |
|---|---|
| TOTAL ENROLLMENT: | 4,400 |
| UNDERGRADUATE: | 3,600 |
| ACCEPTANCE RATE: | 45% |
| SAT RANGE: | 580–670 Verbal |
| | 600–670 Math |
| STICKER PRICE: | $23,000+ |
| NEED-BLIND: | Yes |
| NEED MET: | 90% |
| AVERAGE STUDENT DEBT: | $13,500 |
| MERIT SCHOLARSHIPS: | Many |
| RANGE: | Up to full costs |
| ATHLETIC SCHOLARSHIPS: | Yes |
| ROTC: | Army |
| WEB SITE: | www.richmond.edu |
| PHONE: | (800) 700-1662 |

Though the city of Richmond was once the capital of the Confederacy, don't go looking for the ghost of Jefferson Davis on this campus. The University of Richmond is a creation of the New South—with plenty of Yankees thrown in for good measure. Set on 350 secluded acres, Richmond combines the liberal arts and business with the nation's only School of Leadership Studies. High-powered merit scholarships are a Richmond specialty, beginning with the Oldham Scholars program, which covers full costs along with a $1,500 stipend for summer activities. A similar program gives outstanding science students a full-costs scholarship plus a research stipend. The deadline for both is January 2. The University Scholars program offers half tuition to top students with at least 1350 on the SAT I, and other major awards target African Americans (half tuition, January 15 deadline) and Virginia Baptists. Scholarships from the music department range up to $12,000, National Merit Finalists get up to half tuition, and a unique merit-within-need program honors commitment to community service.

*Deadlines:*
  EARLY DECISION: Nov. 15
  REGULAR ADMISSION: Feb. 1
  FAFSA: Feb. 25

## RIPON COLLEGE ✦ Ripon, WI 54971

| | |
|---|---|
| TOTAL ENROLLMENT: | 700 |
| UNDERGRADUATE: | 700 |
| ACCEPTANCE RATE: | 88% |
| SAT RANGE: | 510–610 Verbal |
| | 490–580 Math |
| STICKER PRICE: | $23,000+ |
| NEED-BLIND: | Yes |
| NEED MET: | 97% |
| AVERAGE STUDENT DEBT: | $10,500 |
| MERIT SCHOLARSHIPS: | Many |
| RANGE: | Up to full tuition |
| ATHLETIC SCHOLARSHIPS: | No |
| ROTC: | Army |
| WEB SITE: | www.ripon.edu |
| PHONE: | (800) 94-RIPON |

By an improbable twist of fate, Ripon College was founded in 1851 in the same tiny hamlet that three years later spawned the Republican Party. Fittingly, politics and history are the college's most popular majors, and Ripon has one of the oldest forensics programs in the nation (which features an $8,000 scholarship for entering freshmen). Ripon has a substantial merit scholarship program, and about half of the entering freshmen received a non-need award in a recent year. Top applicants are selected for scholarships ranging from $10,000 to full tuition on Scholarship Days held in December and March. Additional awards are given in thousand-dollar increments from $8,000 to $5,000 on the basis of GPA and test scores, with the lowest going to students who have at least a 3.2 GPA with an SAT I of 1110 or an ACT of 24. Performance/Recognition scholarships include an $11,000 award for prospective physics majors and $5,000 awards in art, music, and theater that require an audition. Children of alumni can qualify for a $2,000 award. The college takes pride in its low average student debt of $10,500.

*Deadlines:*
  EARLY DECISION: Dec. 1
  REGULAR ADMISSION: Mar. 15
  FAFSA: Apr. 15

# ROCHESTER INSTITUTE OF TECHNOLOGY ◆
## Rochester, NY 14623

| | |
|---|---|
| TOTAL ENROLLMENT: | 13,200 |
| UNDERGRADUATE: | 11,100 |
| ACCEPTANCE RATE: | 78% |
| SAT RANGE: | 520–630 Verbal |
| | 540–650 Math |
| STICKER PRICE: | $24,000+ |
| NEED-BLIND: | Yes |
| NEED MET: | NA |
| AVERAGE STUDENT DEBT: | NA |
| MERIT SCHOLARSHIPS: | Many |
| RANGE: | Up to full tuition |
| ATHLETIC SCHOLARSHIPS: | No |
| ROTC: | Army, Navy, Air Force |
| WEB SITE: | www.rit.edu |
| PHONE: | (716) 475-6631 |

The fact that RIT employs twenty-three people in its co-op and career services office sends a loud-and-clear message. At RIT, the focus is on practical problem-solving, marketable skills, and experience in the real world. In addition to programs in arts and sciences, business, and engineering, RIT features a College of Applied Science and Technology that includes everything from food management to software engineering, and a College of Imaging Arts and Sciences that offers a blend of artsy and techie influences. RIT awards Presidential Scholarships ranging from $1,000 to $7,000 on the basis of all-around excellence, which may include a portfolio review for applicants in art and design. In a recent year, approximately 300 students received a Presidential Scholarship. National Merit, National Achievement, and National Hispanic Scholar Finalists or Semifinalists are guaranteed at least $7,000, and the Kate Gleason Scholarship offers full tuition to an outstanding female engineer. Students seeking scholarships should apply for admission by February 1.

*Deadlines:*
  EARLY DECISION: Dec. 1
  REGULAR ADMISSION: Mar. 1 (priority)
  FAFSA: Mar. 15

# UNIVERSITY OF ROCHESTER ◆
## Rochester, NY 14627

| | |
|---|---|
| TOTAL ENROLLMENT: | 8,500 |
| UNDERGRADUATE: | 3,400 |
| ACCEPTANCE RATE: | 54% |
| SAT RANGE: | 590–690 Verbal |
| | 600–700 Math |
| STICKER PRICE: | $30,000+ |
| NEED-BLIND: | Yes |
| NEED MET: | 93% |
| AVERAGE STUDENT DEBT: | $18,900 |
| MERIT SCHOLARSHIPS: | Many |
| RANGE: | Up to $10,000 |
| ATHLETIC SCHOLARSHIPS: | No |
| ROTC: | Army, Navy, Air Force |
| WEB SITE: | www.rochester.edu |
| PHONE: | (888) 822-2256 |

When someone mentions the University of Rochester, the next synapse to fire generally includes the word "pre-med." Rochester's Undergraduate Program in Biology and Medicine is well known, as is its ultracompetitive B.S./M.D. program. Rochester is a medium-sized university with a full range of liberal arts and professional programs, cut from similar cloth as places like Carnegie Mellon, Case Western Reserve, Johns Hopkins, and Washington U. The Rush Rhees Scholarship is awarded in the amount of either $5,000 or $10,000 to students with a minimum of 1350 on the SAT I or 31 on the ACT. Winners of high school recognition programs from Bausch & Lomb, Xerox, and Kodak get a $6,000 scholarship, and all New York state residents and children of alumni get a $5,000 discount. Other scholarships come courtesy of the National Merit program ($2,000) and the Urban League ($6,000). The university's Take Five program allows selected students to complete a fifth year of study tuition-free. An application for admission brings automatic scholarship consideration.

*Deadlines:*
  EARLY DECISION: Nov. 15
  REGULAR ADMISSION: Jan. 1
  FAFSA: Feb. 1
  CSS PROFILE: Feb. 1

# ROLLINS COLLEGE ◆ Winter Park, FL 32789

| | |
|---|---|
| TOTAL ENROLLMENT: | 2,200 |
| UNDERGRADUATE: | 1,500 |
| ACCEPTANCE RATE: | 70% |
| SAT RANGE: | 520–620 Verbal |
| | 520–620 Math |
| STICKER PRICE: | $28,000+ |
| NEED-BLIND: | Yes |
| NEED MET: | 88% |
| AVERAGE STUDENT DEBT: | $14,000 |
| MERIT SCHOLARSHIPS: | Many |
| RANGE: | Up to $15,000 |
| ATHLETIC SCHOLARSHIPS: | Yes |
| ROTC: | No |
| WEB SITE: | www.rollins.edu |
| PHONE: | (407) 646-2161 |

Rollins is proof that you don't need to be eighty years old to move south for the winter. Located in sunny Orlando, Rollins draws plenty of northerners looking for a small college in more temperate climes. Along with the liberal arts, they find excellent programs in business (bolstered by a graduate school) and the performing arts. Those among the top 10 percent of entering freshmen are strong candidates for the Alonzo Rollins Scholarship, which offers up to $15,000 per year plus a laptop computer. The Presidential Scholarship, also awarded for academic achievement, provides up to $6,000 and a laptop. Artists, musicians, and actors can compete for $10,000 awards, and a $5,000 scholarship is available to students planning a major in math, the physical sciences, or computer science. A $3,000 scholarship goes to good students who have contributed to their school or community. Scholarship candidates should apply by February 1. With only 1,500 undergraduates, Rollins competes in NCAA Division II and gives more than 100 athletic scholarships.

*Deadlines:*
  EARLY DECISION: Nov. 15, Jan. 15
  REGULAR ADMISSION: Feb. 15
  FAFSA: Mar. 1

# ROSE-HULMAN INSTITUTE OF TECHNOLOGY ◆ Terre Haute, IN 47803

| | |
|---|---|
| TOTAL ENROLLMENT: | 1,700 |
| UNDERGRADUATE: | 1,700 |
| ACCEPTANCE RATE: | 62% |
| SAT RANGE: | 540–650 Verbal |
| | 650–800 Math |
| STICKER PRICE: | $25,000+ |
| NEED-BLIND: | Yes |
| NEED MET: | 88% |
| AVERAGE STUDENT DEBT: | $22,000 |
| MERIT SCHOLARSHIPS: | Many |
| RANGE: | Up to $8,000 |
| ATHLETIC SCHOLARSHIPS: | No |
| ROTC: | Army, Air Force |
| WEB SITE: | www.rose-hulman.edu |
| PHONE: | (800) 248-7448 |

The Rose-Hulman Institute is a unique phenomenon—a tiny engineering school in the Midwestern heartland that until a few years ago was all-male. Electrical, mechanical, and chemical engineering are the majors of choice; other offerings include the physical sciences, computer science, economics, and applied optics. As one of the few technical institutions where professors do all the teaching, Rose-Hulman takes pride in its hands-on style that heavily emphasizes lab work. Students are required to take about 20 percent of their courses in the humanities and social sciences. Merit scholarships based on academic excellence are available for up to $8,000, and the college also funds National Merit Finalists up to $2,000. About 60 percent of the incoming freshmen are given a merit scholarship. A whopping 90 percent of incoming students have financial need, of which just over one-third received a package that fully met need in a recent year. The institute's sticker price includes $1,300 for a lease-to-own laptop computer that is required for all students.

*Deadlines:*
  ADMISSION: Dec. 1 (priority)
  FAFSA: Mar. 1

## RUTGERS, THE STATE UNIVERSITY OF NEW JERSEY ✦ New Brunswick, NJ 08903

| | |
|---|---|
| TOTAL ENROLLMENT: | 47,800 |
| UNDERGRADUATE: | 35,100 |
| ACCEPTANCE RATE: | 57% |
| SAT RANGE: | 500–620 Verbal |
| | 520–640 Math |
| STICKER PRICE: | In-state, $11,000+ |
| | Out-of-state, $16,000+ |
| NEED-BLIND: | Yes |
| NEED MET: | 80% |
| AVERAGE STUDENT DEBT: | $12,600 |
| MERIT SCHOLARSHIPS: | Many |
| ATHLETIC SCHOLARSHIPS: | Yes |
| ROTC: | Army, Air Force |
| WEB SITE: | www.rutgers.edu |
| PHONE: | (732) 932-INFO |

From its origins in a street-corner tavern in 1766, Rutgers has grown to encompass 48,000 students spread across three campuses. The biggest of the three is the New Brunswick campus, which includes Rutgers College (the original), Douglass (the nation's largest women's college), Cook (life sciences), and Livingston (social sciences). Other divisions include arts, business, communications, engineering, and pharmacy. University-wide merit awards begin with the Outstanding Scholars Recruitment Program, which offers $2,500 to $7,500 to in-staters who rank in the top 15 percent of their high school class with at least a 1350 on the SAT I. (The amount depends on a combination of scores and grades.) Scholarships for underrepresented minorities are worth up to $5,000, and National Merit and National Achievement Finalists get $1,000. Students should apply by December 15 to be considered for university merit awards. Additional merit scholarships go to students admitted to the honors programs of the various colleges. Students should contact those offices directly.

*Deadlines:*
  ADMISSION: Dec. 15 (priority)
  FAFSA: Mar. 15

## ST. JOHN'S COLLEGE ✦ Annapolis, MD 21404 Santa Fe, NM 87501

| | |
|---|---|
| TOTAL ENROLLMENT: | 550 |
| UNDERGRADUATE: | 500 |
| ACCEPTANCE RATE: | 85% |
| SAT RANGE: | 630–740 Verbal |
| | 550–640 Math |
| STICKER PRICE: | $28,000+ |
| NEED-BLIND: | Yes |
| NEED MET: | 90% |
| AVERAGE STUDENT DEBT: | $17,100 |
| MERIT SCHOLARSHIPS: | None |
| ATHLETIC SCHOLARSHIPS: | No |
| ROTC: | No |
| WEB SITE: | www.sjca.edu (MD) |
| | www.sjcsf.edu (NM) |
| PHONE: | (800) 727-9238 (MD) |
| | (800) 331-5232 (NM) |

If you ever see a St. John's College student on the street, the odds are good that he or she will be carrying a book. Maybe two or three. At St. John's, the entire curriculum consists of reading the Great Books. From Homer to Heidegger, Kant to Kafka, Descartes to Dostoyevsky—you name it, they read it. There are no lecture classes, nor even any professors. The teachers at St. John's are called tutors, and their purpose is to guide discussion rather than dispense answers. Everybody reads the books in the same sequence for four years. Then they talk about it. St. John's is unique in another way because it has two campuses, one in historic Annapolis (where the college was founded in 1696) and the other in Santa Fe, recreation hub of the Southwest. Both campuses enroll about 400 students and share an identical curriculum. (The statistics above are from the Annapolis campus, though Santa Fe's are similar.) St. John's financial aid is as pure as its curriculum; everything is based on need.

*Deadlines:*
  ADMISSION: Mar. 1
  FAFSA: Feb. 15
  CSS PROFILE: Feb. 15

## ST. JOHN'S UNIVERSITY ✦ Collegeville, MN 56321

## COLLEGE OF ST. BENEDICT ✦ St. Joseph, MN 56374

| | |
|---|---|
| TOTAL ENROLLMENT: | 3,800 |
| UNDERGRADUATE: | 3,700 |
| ACCEPTANCE RATE: | 87% (St. John's) |
| | 92% (St. Benedict) |
| SAT AVERAGE: | 572 Verbal |
| | 593 Math (St. John's) |
| | 545 Verbal |
| | 564 Math (St. Benedict) |
| STICKER PRICE: | $20,000+ |
| NEED-BLIND: | Yes |
| NEED MET: | 94% |
| AVERAGE STUDENT DEBT: | $14,900 |
| MERIT SCHOLARSHIPS: | Many |
| RANGE: | Up to $7,500 |
| ATHLETIC SCHOLARSHIPS: | No |
| ROTC: | Army |
| WEB SITE: | www.csbsju.edu |
| PHONE: | (800) 544-1489 |

Saint John's and Saint Benedict offer a throwback to the kind of college life that many parents remember. As two cooperating single-sex colleges (St. John's for men and St. Benedict for women), they offer coed classes and a host of common activities but house their students on separate campuses about five miles apart. Students of both sexes begin their college careers with an interdisciplinary seminar limited to sixteen students (eight males and eight females) that is taught by a professor who doubles as the freshman advisor. The Regents'/Trustees' Scholarships of $7,500 honor students with a minimum GPA of 3.6 or a high school class rank in the top 5 percent who have an SAT I of 1320 or an ACT of 30. Two other general awards are offered in lesser amounts, and demonstrated leadership is a factor in all three. Performing and fine arts awards are worth up to $2,000, and Girl Scout Gold Award recipients earn $1,000. Three different categories of awards for students of color yield up to $6,000. All scholarships have a priority deadline of February 1.

*Deadlines:*
  ADMISSION: May 1
  FAFSA: Mar. 1 (SJU), Apr. 1 (CSB)

## ST. JOHN'S UNIVERSITY ✦ Jamaica, NY 11439

| | |
|---|---|
| TOTAL ENROLLMENT: | 18,500 |
| UNDERGRADUATE: | 13,900 |
| ACCEPTANCE RATE: | 86% |
| SAT RANGE: | 420–540 Verbal |
| | 420–550 Math |
| STICKER PRICE (COMMUTER): | $14,000+ |
| NEED-BLIND: | Yes |
| NEED MET: | 100% |
| AVERAGE STUDENT DEBT: | $12,700 |
| MERIT SCHOLARSHIPS: | Many |
| RANGE: | Up to full tuition |
| ATHLETIC SCHOLARSHIPS: | Yes |
| ROTC: | Army |
| WEB SITE: | www.stjohns.edu |
| PHONE: | (718) 990-6114 |

With two campuses in New York City and a graduate center in Rome, St. John's is the largest Catholic university in the nation. It is also among the largest commuter schools, although in 1999 St. John's opens three new dorms, beginning a transition toward becoming a full-fledged residential university. St. John's academic divisions include liberal arts, business administration, education and human services, and pharmacy and allied health, and its St. Vincent's College offers a potpourri of programs ranging from sports management to funeral service administration. Freshman merit awards range from the full-tuition Presidential Scholarship down to the $2,500 Academic Merit Scholarship. A $2,500 scholarship is offered to a student from each Catholic high school in specified dioceses in the New York area, and a partial-tuition Women in Science Scholarship is available to those pursuing computer science, math, or the sciences. Merit-within-need awards are available for special talents, and any family with three full-time students gets a half-tuition discount on the third.

*Deadlines:*
  ADMISSION: Rolling
  FAFSA: Apr. 1

## ST. LAWRENCE UNIVERSITY ◆
## Canton, NY 13617

| | |
|---|---|
| TOTAL ENROLLMENT: | 2,000 |
| UNDERGRADUATE: | 1,900 |
| ACCEPTANCE RATE: | 71% |
| SAT RANGE: | 510–620 Verbal |
| | 520–610 Math |
| STICKER PRICE: | $29,000+ |
| NEED-BLIND: | No |
| NEED MET: | 87% |
| AVERAGE STUDENT DEBT: | $12,000 |
| MERIT SCHOLARSHIPS: | Many |
| RANGE: | Up to $10,000 |
| ATHLETIC SCHOLARSHIPS: | Yes |
| ROTC: | Army, Air Force |
| WEB SITE: | www.stlawu.edu |
| PHONE: | (800) 285-1856 |

Closer to the Canadian capital than to any major U.S. city, St. Lawrence is a liberal arts college on the nation's northern frontier. With the vast expanses of Adirondack Park on its southern flank, St. Lawrence is an ideal setting for winter sports enthusiasts and environmental science majors. Perhaps because it occupies such a remote corner of the world, St. Lawrence has an especially strong sense of community that is accentuated by its First-Year Program, which divides freshmen into living/learning communities with affiliated faculty. St. Lawrence is also known for its strong international and study abroad programs. Most of St. Lawrence's merit awards come via the University Scholar Program, which included about 150 stipends of $10,000 and $7,500 in a recent year. A $10,000 award is aimed at residents of northern New York and part of Canada, and a Community Service Scholarship of $7,500 is also available. All awards are based on the application for admission. St. Lawrence offers athletic scholarships only in men's hockey.

*Deadlines:*
  EARLY DECISION: Dec. 15
  REGULAR ADMISSION: Feb. 15
  FAFSA: Feb. 15

## SAINT LOUIS UNIVERSITY ◆
## St. Louis, MO 63103

| | |
|---|---|
| TOTAL ENROLLMENT: | 14,200 |
| UNDERGRADUATE: | 7,800 |
| ACCEPTANCE RATE: | 71% |
| SAT AVERAGE: | 1178 combined |
| STICKER PRICE: | $22,000+ |
| NEED-BLIND: | Yes |
| NEED MET: | 45% |
| AVERAGE STUDENT DEBT: | $15,500 |
| MERIT SCHOLARSHIPS: | Many |
| RANGE: | Up to full costs |
| ATHLETIC SCHOLARSHIPS: | Yes |
| ROTC: | Army, Air Force |
| WEB SITE: | www.slu.edu |
| PHONE: | (314) 977-2500 |

Located in downtown St. Louis a few miles from the famed Gateway Arch, Saint Louis University is the oldest institution of higher learning west of the Mississippi, dating back to 1818. Health fields are the featured attraction at this Jesuit university, and top students are drawn to the pre-med program by the prospect of early admission to the university's medical school. Physical therapy is highly competitive and has a December 15 deadline. Students with at least a 3.85 GPA and a score of 1320 on the SAT I or 30 on the ACT are in the running for one of ten Presidential Scholarships, which cover full costs. Those judged to be in the top 5 percent of admitted applicants get an $8,500 scholarship, and those in the fifth to the tenth percentile (with at least 3.5 and 1170 or 26) get $6,800. Outstanding African American students can vie for twenty-six scholarships valued at up to $9,350, and twenty Ignatian Service awards honor community service. Other scholarships are available, including one for National Merit and Achievement Finalists. Priority for all awards goes to students who apply for admission by December 1.

*Deadlines:*
  ADMISSION: Aug. 1
  FAFSA: As soon as possible after Jan. 1

# ST. MARY'S COLLEGE OF MARYLAND ✦
## St. Mary's City, MD 20686

| | |
|---|---|
| TOTAL ENROLLMENT: | 1,700 |
| UNDERGRADUATE: | 1,700 |
| ACCEPTANCE RATE: | 61% |
| SAT RANGE: | 590–690 Verbal |
| | 570–660 Math |
| STICKER PRICE: | In-state, $13,000+ |
| | Out-of-state, $17,000+ |
| NEED-BLIND: | Yes |
| NEED MET: | 82% |
| AVERAGE STUDENT DEBT: | $14,500 |
| MERIT SCHOLARSHIPS: | Many |
| RANGE: | Up to full tuition |
| ATHLETIC SCHOLARSHIPS: | No |
| ROTC: | No |
| WEB SITE: | www.smcm.edu |
| PHONE: | (800) 492-7181 |

St. Mary's probably sounds like just another small Catholic women's college. The part about being small is true enough, but St. Mary's is actually a state-supported honors college with a name that dates back to Maryland's founding by Catholics in the 1600s. Occupying 275 acres along the shore of the historic St. Mary's River near Chesapeake Bay, the college is becoming a hot commodity as word spreads about its private-college approach to education and moderate price tag. St. Mary's small honors program features interdisciplinary seminars and an independent project dealing with leadership. Merit scholarships of up to full tuition are available for selected students with at least a 3.5 GPA and an SAT I of 1350. A second program offers awards of up to $5,500 "based on academic promise, leadership potential, special talent, diversity, and a thorough review of a writing sample." Students are automatically considered for scholarships but must file the FAFSA in order to qualify. Approximately 10 percent of each entering class gets a merit scholarship.

*Deadlines:*
  EARLY DECISION: Dec. 1
  REGULAR ADMISSION: Jan. 15
  FAFSA: Mar. 1

# ST. OLAF COLLEGE ✦ Northfield, MN 55057

| | |
|---|---|
| TOTAL ENROLLMENT: | 3,000 |
| UNDERGRADUATE: | 3,000 |
| ACCEPTANCE RATE: | 78% |
| SAT RANGE: | 550–670 Verbal |
| | 560–670 Math |
| STICKER PRICE: | $22,000+ |
| NEED-BLIND: | Yes |
| NEED MET: | 100% |
| AVERAGE STUDENT DEBT: | $16,000 |
| MERIT SCHOLARSHIPS: | Many |
| RANGE: | Up to $6,000 |
| ATHLETIC SCHOLARSHIPS: | No |
| ROTC: | No |
| WEB SITE: | www.stolaf.edu |
| PHONE: | (800) 800-3025 |

Higher education's version of the odd couple resides in the tiny town of Northfield, Minnesota. That's where the liberal grunge of Carleton College meets the clean-cut wholesomeness of St. Olaf, a liberal arts college affiliated with the Evangelical Lutheran Church. One thing the two colleges share is academic excellence. St. Olaf is well known for its study abroad programs, in which about two-thirds of the students participate, and its music program is also outstanding. (Approximately one-third of the students play in an ensemble or take lessons.) The Buntrock Academic Scholarship offers stipends of up to $6,000 to nearly 300 entering students; recipients typically have at least a 3.6 GPA or a high school class rank in the top 10 percent. Community service awards of $2,000 are also available, with winners expected to donate five hours per week of their time once enrolled. Students with outstanding musical talent can compete for $3,000 scholarships. National Merit Finalists designating St. Olaf as their first choice get no less than $5,000, and a $2,000 award goes to Lutherans who have been active in the church.

*Deadlines:*
  EARLY DECISION: Nov. 15
  REGULAR ADMISSION: Feb. 1
  FAFSA: Mar. 1

## SAN FRANCISCO CONSERVATORY OF MUSIC ✦
### San Francisco, CA 94122

| | |
|---|---|
| TOTAL ENROLLMENT: | 250 |
| UNDERGRADUATE: | 200 |
| ACCEPTANCE RATE: | 53% |
| SAT RANGE: | 510–710 Verbal |
| | 450–650 Math |
| STICKER PRICE (COMMUTER): | $18,000+ |
| NEED-BLIND: | Yes |
| NEED MET: | 70% |
| AVERAGE STUDENT DEBT: | $20,300 |
| MERIT SCHOLARSHIPS: | None |
| ATHLETIC SCHOLARSHIPS: | No |
| ROTC | No |
| WEB SITE: | www.sfcm.edu |
| PHONE: | (415) 759-3431 |

SFCM is what might be called a high performance conservatory of music. The conservatory prides itself on creating opportunities for students to perform, with nearly 400 public events per year, ranging from solo recitals to full-fledged operas and symphonies. Located in a residential neighborhood near Golden Gate Park, SFCM is the only major independent conservatory in the West. Undergraduate degree programs include keyboard instruments, orchestral instruments, composition, classical guitar, and voice. The latter two were among the most popular majors in a recent year, along with piano. A community service program gives academic credit to students who participate in performances at hospitals and retirement homes. As with most arts specialty schools, there is no campus housing. Though all financial aid is distributed to students with need, more generous awards (including named scholarships) are awarded on the basis of musical ability and the instrumental needs of the school. Such awards go automatically to students who complete the admission process.

*Deadlines:*
    ADMISSION: Mar.1
    FAFSA: Mar. 1

## UNIVERSITY OF SAN FRANCISCO ✦
### San Francisco, CA 94117

| | |
|---|---|
| TOTAL ENROLLMENT: | 8,000 |
| UNDERGRADUATE: | 4,700 |
| ACCEPTANCE RATE: | 76% |
| SAT RANGE: | 480–598 Verbal |
| | 480–600 Math |
| STICKER PRICE: | $25,000+ |
| NEED-BLIND: | Yes |
| NEED MET: | 70% |
| AVERAGE STUDENT DEBT: | $19,800 |
| MERIT SCHOLARSHIPS: | Many |
| ATHLETIC SCHOLARSHIPS: | Yes |
| ROTC: | Army, Air Force |
| WEB SITE: | www.usfca.edu |
| PHONE: | (800) CALLUSF |

USF combines a location in one of America's most progressive cities with a firm commitment to the time-honored Jesuit tradition. Business and nursing are among the university's best-known professional programs, and communications is also popular. USF is international in its outlook, with notable centers for Pacific Rim and Latino Studies. Students can major in the fine arts by completing a joint degree program with the California College of Arts and Crafts, a leading arts specialty school. USF has comprehensive general education requirements, which include theology and ethics, and students who want a deeper exposure to the Western tradition can opt for the Great Books–based St. Ignatius Institute. The University Scholars is USF's primary merit program for entering students; those with an academic GPA of 3.8 and a 1320 on the SAT I or 30 on the ACT get a renewable scholarship worth 75 percent of tuition. Students must apply by December 1. Other awards are available, many for continuing students or those who show need.

*Deadlines:*
    EARLY ACTION: Dec. 1
    REGULAR ADMISSION: Feb. 1
    FAFSA: Feb. 15

# SANTA CLARA UNIVERSITY ✦ Santa Clara, CA 95053

| | |
|---|---|
| TOTAL ENROLLMENT: | 7,900 |
| UNDERGRADUATE: | 4,300 |
| ACCEPTANCE RATE: | 66% |
| SAT RANGE: | 530–620 Verbal |
| | 550–650 Math |
| STICKER PRICE: | $25,000+ |
| NEED-BLIND: | Yes |
| NEED MET: | NA |
| AVERAGE STUDENT DEBT: | $21,200 |
| MERIT SCHOLARSHIPS: | Many |
| ATHLETIC SCHOLARSHIPS: | Yes |
| ROTC: | Army, Air Force |
| WEB SITE: | www.scu.edu |
| PHONE: | (408) 554-4700 |

Santa Clara combines the ancient Jesuit tradition with a location in futuristic Silicon Valley. Its sunsplashed campus sits near the southern tip of San Francisco Bay, an especially strategic place for its colleges of engineering and business. Santa Clara stays connected to its surroundings with a strong emphasis on internships and community service, which sometimes provide academic credit. Like most of its Jesuit brethren, Santa Clara has detailed core requirements, which entail a spectrum of liberal arts subjects, including three courses in religion and one in ethics. Santa Clara awards a Dean's Scholarship of up to $3,000 to the twenty top students in its divisions of arts and sciences, business, and engineering. The same amount goes to fifty outstanding graduates of Jesuit high schools. The engineering school has its own awards of up to $2,500, and students invited to the honors program should contact it directly about awards of up to $3,500. Talent awards are available in theater, dance, and music with an audition required.

*Deadlines:*
ADMISSION: Jan. 15
FAFSA: Feb. 1
CSS PROFILE: Feb. 1

# COLLEGE OF SANTA FE ✦ Santa Fe, NM 87505

| | |
|---|---|
| TOTAL ENROLLMENT: | 1,400 |
| UNDERGRADUATE: | 1,200 |
| ACCEPTANCE RATE: | 84% |
| SAT RANGE: | 540–650 Verbal |
| | 490–590 Math |
| STICKER PRICE: | $19,000+ |
| NEED-BLIND: | Yes |
| NEED MET: | 82% |
| AVERAGE STUDENT DEBT: | $17,100 |
| MERIT SCHOLARSHIPS: | Many |
| RANGE: | Up to $5,000 |
| ATHLETIC SCHOLARSHIPS: | No |
| ROTC: | No |
| WEB SITE: | www.csf.edu |
| PHONE: | (800) 456-2673 |

College of Santa Fe has come a long way from its beginnings in an adobe hut on the Pecos Trail in what was then the New Mexico Territory. One hundred twenty-five years later, CSF is a regional center for the performing arts in one of America's premier resort cities. Moving image arts (filmmaking) and theater head the list of most popular majors, and CSF productions are an important part of Santa Fe's thriving arts scene. The visual arts programs are also strong and recently moved into new facilities. The college provides programs in the liberal arts, business, and education, and when the work is done, Santa Fe's sunny skies and nearby mountain peaks beckon outdoor enthusiasts. Top incoming freshman are considered for the Presidential Scholarship, worth up to $5,000. To be eligible, students must have a 3.5 GPA and an SAT I score of at least 1100 or an ACT of 24. The $3,000 Dean's Scholarship has minimums of 3.0 and 1000 or 22 and places more emphasis on community service. Talent Awards in the arts of up to $2,500 are also available.

*Deadlines:*
EARLY DECISION: Nov. 15
REGULAR ADMISSION: Feb. 15 (priority)
FAFSA: Mar. 1

# SARAH LAWRENCE COLLEGE •
## Bronxville, NY 10708

| | |
|---|---|
| TOTAL ENROLLMENT: | 1,400 |
| UNDERGRADUATE: | 1,100 |
| ACCEPTANCE RATE: | 46% |
| SAT RANGE: | 620–720 Verbal |
| | 540–630 Math |
| STICKER PRICE: | $30,000+ |
| NEED-BLIND: | No |
| NEED MET: | 100% |
| AVERAGE STUDENT DEBT: | $12,300 |
| MERIT SCHOLARSHIPS: | None |
| ATHLETIC SCHOLARSHIPS: | No |
| ROTC: | No |
| WEB SITE: | www.slc.edu |
| PHONE: | (800) 888-2858 |

Intellectual, sophisticated, streetwise, sometimes aloof, always independent, Sarah Lawrence College is bursting at the seams with creativity. A trendy neighborhood in Greenwich Village would seem the ideal place for SLC, but the college is actually located fifteen miles outside the city in the Westchester suburbs. The performing arts and creative writing are signature programs, and so, too, is the college's highly individualized curriculum in which students work with a faculty "don" to develop their course of study. (Grades are deemphasized in favor of written narratives, but in a bow to practicality, grades are recorded for graduate school.) Applications have doubled since the 1980s, and SLC's acceptance rate is far lower than it was a decade ago (46 percent in a recent year). Though Sarah Lawrence has been coed for more than three decades, the sex ratio is still 2 to 1 with females in the majority. Sarah Lawrence is among the colleges that consider ability to pay in making some borderline admission decisions. Those admitted get packages that meet 100 percent of need.

*Deadlines:*
  EARLY DECISION: Nov. 15, Jan. 1
  REGULAR ADMISSION: Feb. 1
  FAFSA: Feb. 1
  CSS PROFILE: Feb. 1

# UNIVERSITY OF SCRANTON •
## Scranton, PA 18510

| | |
|---|---|
| TOTAL ENROLLMENT: | 4,800 |
| UNDERGRADUATE: | 4,100 |
| ACCEPTANCE RATE: | 78% |
| SAT RANGE: | 510–610 Verbal |
| | 510–610 Math |
| STICKER PRICE: | $25,000+ |
| NEED-BLIND: | Yes |
| NEED MET: | 77% |
| AVERAGE STUDENT DEBT: | $13,700 |
| MERIT SCHOLARSHIPS: | Many |
| RANGE: | Up to full tuition |
| ATHLETIC SCHOLARSHIPS: | No |
| ROTC: | Army, Air Force |
| WEB SITE: | www.uofs.edu |
| PHONE: | (717) 941-7540 |

The University of Scranton is a smallish Jesuit university with undergraduate programs in the liberal arts, business, education, and health-related fields. A Faculty/Student Research Program involves students (including freshmen) in research with professors across all majors, and an internship program helps place students in career-related fields to complement their academic work. The university occupies fifty acres near the center of Scranton, a city of approximately 80,000 within a metropolitan area of 750,000. Twelve incoming freshmen get the prestigious Ignatian Scholarship, worth full tuition. Successful candidates generally rank at the top of the class with at least 1400 on the SAT I. Loyola Scholarships of up to $10,000 go to an additional 400 freshmen who usually rank in the top fifth with at least 1100. Two merit-within-need programs account for more than 500 additional awards, and when two or more students are enrolled from the same family, all get a 10 percent discount. There are also a number of scholarships for students from the Scranton area.

*Deadlines:*
  ADMISSION: Mar. 1 (priority)
  FAFSA: Feb. 15
  CSS PROFILE: Feb. 15

# SCRIPPS COLLEGE ◆ Claremont, CA 91711

| | |
|---|---|
| TOTAL ENROLLMENT: | 700 |
| UNDERGRADUATE: | 700 |
| ACCEPTANCE RATE: | 70% |
| SAT RANGE: | 580–680 Verbal |
| | 560–640 Math |
| STICKER PRICE: | $28,000+ |
| NEED-BLIND: | Yes |
| NEED MET: | 100% |
| AVERAGE STUDENT DEBT: | $20,700 |
| MERIT SCHOLARSHIPS: | Many |
| RANGE: | Up to $7,500 |
| ATHLETIC SCHOLARSHIPS: | No |
| ROTC: | Army, Air Force |
| WEB SITE: | www.scrippscol.edu |
| PHONE: | (800) 770-1333 |

It is no mystery why Scripps College included an aerial photo in its recent brochure. One of the biggest selling points of this small women's college is its location smack in the middle of four other outstanding small colleges—Claremont McKenna, Harvey Mudd, Pitzer, and Pomona—that are known collectively as the Claremonts. With only 700 students, Scripps provides all-female camaraderie inside a coed college community of nearly 5,000 undergraduates. The advantages of the latter include intercollegiate athletic teams (with Claremont McKenna and Harvey Mudd), cross-registration, and the chance to complete B.A./M.A. degrees through the Claremont Graduate University. The college is proud of its team-taught core curriculum in Interdisciplinary Humanities, which links subject matter across the liberal arts. Psychology, biology, and international relations are the most popular majors. Merit awards at Scripps are limited to approximately twenty-five James E. Scripps Scholarships, awarded for all-around excellence in the amount of $7,500.

*Deadlines:*
   EARLY DECISION: Nov. 15
   REGULAR ADMISSION: Feb. 1
   FAFSA: Feb. 1
   CSS PROFILE: Feb. 1

# SETON HALL UNIVERSITY ◆ South Orange, NJ 07079

| | |
|---|---|
| TOTAL ENROLLMENT: | 9,300 |
| UNDERGRADUATE: | 4,900 |
| ACCEPTANCE RATE: | 80% |
| SAT RANGE: | 400–480 Verbal |
| | 440–550 Math |
| STICKER PRICE: | $24,000+ |
| NEED-BLIND: | Yes |
| NEED MET: | NA |
| AVERAGE STUDENT DEBT: | $16,600 |
| MERIT SCHOLARSHIPS: | Many |
| RANGE: | Up to full tuition |
| ATHLETIC SCHOLARSHIPS: | Yes |
| ROTC: | Army, Air Force |
| WEB SITE: | www.shu.edu |
| PHONE: | (973) 761-9332 |

A lot of universities talk big on the subject of technology, but few back it up like Seton Hall. Under its Mobile Computing Program, every incoming freshman gets a specially formatted IBM ThinkPad and spends the next four years plugged in. The technology is integrated with the curriculum in a systematic way, beginning with first-year core courses. Seton Hall offers an impressive variety of liberal arts and preprofessional programs for an institution its size, as well as a broad array of full-tuition merit scholarships. Chancellor's and Provost's Scholarships are given to Catholics and non-Catholics, respectively, based on nominations from school officials. Martin Luther King, Jr. Scholarships offer full tuition to selected African Americans and require a special application by January 10; Clare Boothe Luce Scholarships give the same to women interested in math or science. Smaller academic scholarships are available to those who apply for admission by February 15, and sons and daughters of alumni are eligible for an additional scholarship.

*Deadlines:*
   ADMISSION: Mar. 1
   FAFSA: Apr. 1

# SIENA COLLEGE ✦ Loudonville, NY 12211

| | |
|---|---|
| TOTAL ENROLLMENT: | 3,100 |
| UNDERGRADUATE: | 3,100 |
| ACCEPTANCE RATE: | 77% |
| SAT AVERAGE: | 553 Verbal |
| | 555 Math |
| STICKER PRICE: | $20,000+ |
| NEED-BLIND: | Yes |
| NEED MET: | 74% |
| AVERAGE STUDENT DEBT: | $13,400 |
| MERIT SCHOLARSHIPS: | Many |
| ATHLETIC SCHOLARSHIPS: | Yes |
| ROTC: | Army, Air Force |
| WEB SITE: | www.siena.edu |
| PHONE: | (888) AT-SIENA |

Siena is a small college in upstate New York known for its preprofessional programs and relatively modest sticker price. Operated by the Franciscan order of the Catholic Church, Siena's primary offerings include the liberal arts and business. Marketing, management, accounting, and finance head the list of most popular majors, and programs in pre-law and pre–health professions are also heavily subscribed. As freshmen, all students enroll in a Foundations Sequence, consisting of a year-long seminar that explores human behavior, religion, and the American experience. Top applicants can aspire to the Siena Presidential Scholarship, which ranges upward from a minimum of $2,500 to full tuition for those who show need. Students must file a special application by January 15. Other good students can qualify for an Honorary Scholarship, which ranges from $500 to $3,000. There is also a $4,000 award for students admitted to Siena's accelerated medical program with Albany Medical College.

*Deadlines:*
 EARLY DECISION: Dec. 1
 EARLY ACTION: Dec. 1
 REGULAR ADMISSION: Mar. 1
 FAFSA: Feb. 1

# SIMMONS COLLEGE ✦ Boston, MA 02115

| | |
|---|---|
| Total Enrollment: | 3,500 |
| Undergraduate: | 1,200 |
| Acceptance Rate: | 68% |
| SAT RANGE: | 430–540 Verbal |
| | 440–560 Math |
| STICKER PRICE: | $27,000+ |
| NEED-BLIND: | Yes |
| NEED MET: | 90% |
| AVERAGE STUDENT DEBT: | $14,200 |
| MERIT SCHOLARSHIPS: | Many |
| RANGE: | Up to full tuition |
| ATHLETIC SCHOLARSHIPS: | No |
| ROTC: | Army |
| WEB SITE: | www.simmons.edu |
| PHONE: | (800) 345-8468 |

While many women's colleges are squirreled away in the pristine countryside, Simmons is in the heart of America's most exciting city for students. Sharing Boston's Back Bay with numerous other institutions (including some that share cross-registration via the Colleges of the Fenway Consortium), Simmons combines the liberal arts with business, communications, and the health professions. Independence is not just a buzzword at Simmons. All students are required to complete an independent learning experience that often entails an internship in the city. About 15 percent of entering students receive a merit scholarship, including half-tuition Honors Scholarships that go to students entering the honors program. Half-tuition awards are available to students from underrepresented minority groups, and two full-tuition Simmons Boston Scholarships reward outstanding graduates of city public schools. Simmons also has scholarships for leadership, extracurricular activities, and community service, as well as a program for daughters and granddaughters of alumnae.

*Deadlines:*
 EARLY DECISION: Nov. 15, Jan. 1
 REGULAR ADMISSION: Feb. 1
 FAFSA: Feb. 1

## SIMON'S ROCK OF BARD COLLEGE ✦
## Great Barrington, MA 01230

| | |
|---|---|
| TOTAL ENROLLMENT: | 350 |
| UNDERGRADUATE: | 350 |
| ACCEPTANCE RATE: | 62% |
| SAT AVERAGE: | 660 Verbal |
| | 600 Math |
| STICKER PRICE: | $29,000+ |
| NEED-BLIND: | Yes |
| NEED MET: | 85% |
| AVERAGE STUDENT DEBT: | $17,000 |
| MERIT SCHOLARSHIPS: | Many |
| RANGE: | Up to full costs |
| ATHLETIC SCHOLARSHIPS: | No |
| ROTC: | No |
| WEB SITE: | www.simons-rock.edu |
| PHONE: | (800) 235-7186 |

Many a world-weary high school student has fantasized about leaving early for college. Simon's Rock enrolls about 350 intrepid souls who actually do it, generally after the tenth or eleventh grade. Parents may tremble at the thought, but Simon's Rock offers a high-quality, structured curriculum for students who have either outgrown high school or never fit the mold. A core program accounts for about half of each student's classes, and distinctive elements include a week-long Writing and Thinking Workshop and a First Year Seminar that covers classics of literature. All students earn an associate's degree in liberal arts, and most transfer to Bard College or elsewhere to complete a B.A. (Bard is located about fifty miles away and rescued Simon's Rock from bankruptcy in the late 1970s.) Simon's Rock offers twenty Acceleration to Excellence scholarships that cover full costs, and approximately thirty more awards that range from $5,000 to $10,000. Applicants must have at least a 3.5 GPA, be enrolled in tenth grade, and participate in extracurricular activites. The deadline to apply is January 30.

*Deadlines:*
    ADMISSION: Jun. 15
    FAFSA: Jun. 15
    CSS PROFILE: Jun. 15

## SKIDMORE COLLEGE ✦
## Saratoga Springs, NY 12866

| | |
|---|---|
| TOTAL ENROLLMENT: | 2,200 |
| UNDERGRADUATE: | 2,200 |
| ACCEPTANCE RATE: | 48% |
| SAT RANGE: | 540–640 Verbal |
| | 540–630 Math |
| STICKER PRICE: | $30,000+ |
| NEED-BLIND: | No |
| NEED MET: | 90% |
| AVERAGE STUDENT DEBT: | $12,300 |
| MERIT SCHOLARSHIPS: | Few |
| RANGE: | Up to $10,000 |
| ATHLETIC SCHOLARSHIPS: | No |
| ROTC: | Army, Navy, Air Force |
| WEB SITE: | www.skidmore.edu |
| PHONE: | (800) 867-6007 |

Set on 850 acres outside a famous resort town in upstate New York, Skidmore belongs to the group of former women's colleges that includes Connecticut College, Vassar, and Wheaton. Such schools generally offer strong programs in the arts and humanities—as Skidmore does—but Skidmore also has a strong tradition in business. Popular majors include English, studio art, government, and psychology. Skidmore's architecture is modern rather than classic collegiate, but nature buffs will appreciate its densely wooded ambience. Skidmore considers ability to pay in some borderline admission decisions. The vast majority of Skidmore's aid goes to students who show need, but five $10,000 scholarships are awarded to students who excel in math and/or science. Four more worth $6,000 are awarded via the Filene Music Scholarships program, for which applicants must submit a tape to the music department by the application deadline. Finalists are invited to the college to audition.

*Deadlines:*
    EARLY DECISION: Dec. 1, Jan. 15
    REGULAR ADMISSION: Feb. 1
    FAFSA: Feb. 1
    CSS PROFILE: Feb. 1

# SMITH COLLEGE ◆ Northampton, MA 01063

| | |
|---|---|
| TOTAL ENROLLMENT: | 2,600 |
| UNDERGRADUATE: | 2,500 |
| ACCEPTANCE RATE: | 56% |
| SAT RANGE: | 610–710 Verbal |
| | 580–670 Math |
| STICKER PRICE: | $30,000+ |
| NEED-BLIND: | No |
| NEED MET: | 100% |
| AVERAGE STUDENT DEBT: | $16,200 |
| MERIT SCHOLARSHIPS: | None |
| ATHLETIC SCHOLARSHIPS: | No |
| ROTC: | Army, Air Force |
| WEB SITE: | www.smith.edu |
| PHONE: | (413) 585-2500 |

With alumnae that include Betty Friedan and Gloria Steinem, Smith College has a history of turning out bright women who know how to push the envelope. Today's generation is no exception: they're liberal, independent, and right at home in the town of Northampton in western Massachusetts, a haven for artists, intellectuals, and other nonconformists. Smith is the largest of the select group once known as the Seven Sisters, and it offers a bonanza of additional resources via its membership in the Five College Consortium, which includes Amherst, Hampshire, Mount Holyoke, and the University of Massachusetts. Government ranks as the most popular major on campus, and a new program guarantees a funded internship to all students in the junior year. Smith's curriculum is notable for an absence of requirements outside the student's major. The college reports that admission is need-blind for "96 to 99 percent" of the applicant pool and that it meets 100 percent of need for those accepted. Smith's aid process requires parental tax returns from the two years prior to enrollment.

*Deadlines:*
EARLY DECISION: Nov. 15, Jan. 1
REGULAR ADMISSION: Feb. 1
FAFSA: Feb. 1
PROFILE: Feb. 15

# UNIVERSITY OF THE SOUTH ◆ Sewanee, TN 37383

| | |
|---|---|
| TOTAL ENROLLMENT: | 1,400 |
| UNDERGRADUATE: | 1,300 |
| ACCEPTANCE RATE: | 64% |
| SAT RANGE: | 580–680 Verbal |
| | 570–670 Math |
| STICKER PRICE: | $24,000+ |
| NEED-BLIND: | Yes |
| NEED MET: | 100% |
| AVERAGE STUDENT DEBT: | $12,800 |
| MERIT SCHOLARSHIPS: | Many |
| RANGE: | Up to full costs |
| ATHLETIC SCHOLARSHIPS: | No |
| ROTC: | No |
| WEB SITE: | www.sewanee.edu |
| PHONE: | (800) 522-2234 |

Close your eyes on the campus of the University of the South and you could swear it was Oxford or Cambridge. The resemblance is no accident. Known to all as Sewanee, the university has patterned itself after the two great titans of English education ever since they donated books to help found its library nearly 150 years ago. All faculty and honor students wear traditional academic gowns to class every day, and students still observe an informal dress code: jacket and tie for men and skirt or dress for women. Approximately 10 percent of Sewanee students receive a merit scholarship. The elite Benedict Scholars Program covers the entire cost of a Sewanee education for three outstanding freshmen, and twenty-five more receive a Wilkins Scholarship of at least half tuition. Regents Scholarships in the same amount target outstanding minority students, and an additional award is reserved for students from Montgomery County, Alabama. Those seeking merit scholarships must apply by January 1. A unique program sweetens need-based aid packages with up to $3,000 in additional grants (substituted for loans) for returning students who maintain a 3.0 GPA.

*Deadlines:*
EARLY DECISION: Nov. 15
REGULAR ADMISSION: Feb. 1
FAFSA: Mar. 1

# UNIVERSITY OF SOUTH CAROLINA •
## Columbia, SC 29208

| | |
|---|---|
| TOTAL ENROLLMENT: | 25,400 |
| UNDERGRADUATE: | 15,800 |
| ACCEPTANCE RATE: | 77% |
| SAT RANGE: | 480–600 Verbal |
| | 470–600 Math |
| STICKER PRICE: | In-state, $8,000+ |
| | Out-of-state, $13,000+ |
| NEED-BLIND: | Yes |
| NEED MET: | 72% |
| AVERAGE STUDENT DEBT: | $17,200 |
| MERIT SCHOLARSHIPS: | Many |
| ATHLETIC SCHOLARSHIPS: | Yes |
| ROTC: | Army, Navy, Air Force |
| WEB SITE: | www.sc.edu |
| PHONE: | (800) 868-5872 |

The University of South Carolina knows that the typical freshman can be overwhelmed on a campus with 26,000 students, 19 colleges and schools, and 75 majors. That's why it created University 101, a small seminar that gives counseling and support to help new arrivals get off to a good start. USC attracts top freshmen with more than 800 scholarships each year, though candidates should apply by November 1 and submit a separate application. Twenty in-state students receive the $7,000 Carolina Scholars award, and ten out-of-staters get $12,000, along with designation as a McNair Scholar. The alumni association gives a merit scholarship of $3,500 to students who generally have at least a 3.8 GPA and 1300 on the SAT I, and another $1,500 stipend is available for students with similar qualifications. In-state valedictorians get $3,000, National Merit and National Achievement Finalists garner up to $6,000, and a $3,000 award recognizes academic excellence with special consideration to minority students. A $500 scholarship is available for children of active alumni. Many of the scholarship programs allow out-of-staters to pay in-state rates.

*Deadlines:*
  ADMISSION: Rolling
  FAFSA: Apr. 15

# UNIVERSITY OF SOUTHERN CALIFORNIA •
## Los Angeles, CA 90089

| | |
|---|---|
| TOTAL ENROLLMENT: | 27,700 |
| UNDERGRADUATE: | 14,800 |
| ACCEPTANCE RATE: | 46% |
| SAT RANGE: | 540–650 Verbal |
| | 570–680 Math |
| STICKER PRICE: | $29,000+ |
| NEED-BLIND: | Yes |
| NEED MET: | NA |
| AVERAGE STUDENT DEBT: | NA |
| MERIT SCHOLARSHIPS: | Many |
| RANGE: | Up to full tuition |
| ATHLETIC SCHOLARSHIPS: | Yes |
| ROTC: | Army, Navy, Air Force |
| WEB SITE: | www.usc.edu |
| PHONE: | (213) 740-1111 |

In the state with the nation's best system of public universities—all of which are available at a bargain price—it takes a little extra umph to be a front-rank private university. USC delivers with its world-renowned School of Cinema-Television and strong programs in business, architecture, engineering, journalism, fine arts, and health professions, to name a few. A host of merit and merit-within-need awards are available, but to ensure priority consideration students should file an application for admission and the Competitive Scholarship Application by December 10. Elite students may enter the chase for 80 full-tuition Trustee Scholarships and 100 Presidential Scholarships valued at half tuition. About 200–250 Deans' awards worth $6,000 go to students in the top 5 percent with matching SAT scores. Other scholarship programs target Los Angeles residents, students from USC's neighborhood, National Merit and National Achievement Finalists, sons and daughters of alumni, Southern Californians, international students, and members of various minority groups.

*Deadlines:*
  ADMISSION: Jan. 31
  FAFSA: Feb. 15

## SOUTHERN METHODIST UNIVERSITY ◆ Dallas, TX 75275

| | |
|---|---|
| TOTAL ENROLLMENT: | 9,700 |
| UNDERGRADUATE: | 5,400 |
| ACCEPTANCE RATE: | 88% |
| SAT RANGE: | 510–630 Verbal |
| | 520–630 Math |
| STICKER PRICE: | $25,000+ |
| NEED-BLIND: | Yes |
| NEED MET: | NA |
| AVERAGE STUDENT DEBT: | NA |
| MERIT SCHOLARSHIPS: | Many |
| RANGE: | Up to full tuition |
| ATHLETIC SCHOLARSHIPS: | Yes |
| ROTC: | Army, Air Force |
| WEB SITE: | www.smu.edu |
| PHONE: | (800) 323-0672 |

The citizens of Dallas gave 600 acres and $300,000 to help found SMU in 1915, and ever since the university has been populating the city—and the entire region—with doctors, lawyers, and other professionals. A nondenominational institution despite its name, SMU's main attractions include a strong business program and nationally renowned offerings in the arts. Up to twenty entering students are awarded a full-tuition Presidential Scholarship. Minimum credentials include a high school class rank in the top 10 percent and an SAT I of 1350 or an ACT of 31, and runners-up get the half-tuition Dean's Scholar Award. Twenty-five outstanding leaders get a scholarship equal to the differential between SMU's cost and that of the leading public university in their state. (A separate essay is required.) Other university-wide awards for general excellence range up to $12,000, and scholarships are also available for United Methodists and students who will play in the university band. Additional scholarships are provided through SMU's academic divisions. Scholarship applicants should apply for admission by January 15.

*Deadlines:*
   EARLY ACTION: Nov. 1
   REGULAR ADMISSION: Apr. 1
   FAFSA: Feb. 1

## SOUTHWESTERN UNIVERSITY ◆ Georgetown, TX 78626

| | |
|---|---|
| TOTAL ENROLLMENT: | 1,200 |
| UNDERGRADUATE: | 1,200 |
| ACCEPTANCE RATE | 73% |
| SAT RANGE: | 550–660 Verbal |
| | 550–660 Math |
| STICKER PRICE: | $20,000+ |
| NEED-BLIND: | Yes |
| NEED MET: | 99% |
| AVERAGE STUDENT DEBT: | $15,000 |
| MERIT SCHOLARSHIPS: | Many |
| RANGE: | Up to full costs |
| ATHLETIC SCHOLARSHIPS: | No |
| ROTC: | No |
| WEB SITE: | www.southwestern.edu |
| PHONE: | (800) 252-3166 |

In a state that seems to prefer everything supersized, Southwestern University is a small college dedicated to individualized education and Methodist values. Located on the outskirts of Austin, Southwestern combines the liberal arts and fine arts. Despite its modest size, Southwestern has a healthy bank account. Its endowment per student is larger than that of Cornell, Columbia, and Duke, to name a few, and the fact that the college recently pumped $50 million into its physical plant is no coincidence. For students who rank at the top of the heap, Southwestern offers three scholarships—Brown Scholars (full costs), President's Scholars ($10,000), and National Scholars ($7,500)—that require an application and interview by February 1. Other scholarships, worth $5,000 and $3,000, are open to students with top grades and scores of at least 1200 on the SAT I or 27 on the ACT. An award of up to $3,000 goes to students with special talent in the arts, and funds are also available for United Methodists.

*Deadlines:*
   EARLY DECISION: Nov. 1, Jan. 1
   REGULAR DECISION: Feb. 15
   FAFSA: Mar. 1

# SPELMAN COLLEGE ✦ Atlanta, GA 30314

| | |
|---|---|
| TOTAL ENROLLMENT: | 1,900 |
| UNDERGRADUATE: | 1,900 |
| ACCEPTANCE RATE: | 50% |
| SAT RANGE: | 500–590 Verbal |
| | 480–570 Math |
| STICKER PRICE: | $17,000+ |
| NEED-BLIND: | Yes |
| NEED MET: | 40% |
| AVERAGE STUDENT DEBT: | $17,500 |
| MERIT SCHOLARSHIPS: | Many |
| RANGE: | Up to full costs |
| ATHLETIC SCHOLARSHIPS: | No |
| ROTC: | Army, Navy, Air Force |
| WEB SITE: | www.spelman.edu |
| PHONE: | (800) 982-2411 |

In no particular order, Spelman is (a) an outstanding liberal arts college, (b) one of the best bargains in higher education, and (c) the most prestigious historically black college for women in the nation. Along with brother school Morehouse, Spelman is part of the Atlanta University Center, which provides the resources of a major university complex. In addition to the standard requirements, Spelman's core curriculum features a two-semester course on The African Diaspora in the World. Five incoming freshmen are honored with the Presidential Scholarship, which covers full costs and is based on academic excellence, leadership potential, and community service. Approximately sixty-five more freshmen get the Dean's Scholarship, which ranges up to full tuition. For students who plan to major in engineering, math, or the physical sciences, the Women in Science and Engineering Scholarship gives half tuition plus room, board, and expenses, and features a ten-week summer program at a NASA facility. Other scholarships are available to international students and to those who show commitment to community service.

*Deadlines:*
    EARLY ACTION: Nov. 15
    REGULAR ADMISSION: Feb. 1
    FAFSA: Mar. 1

# SPRING HILL COLLEGE ✦ Mobile, AL 36608

| | |
|---|---|
| TOTAL ENROLLMENT: | 1,500 |
| UNDERGRADUATE: | 1,200 |
| ACCEPTANCE RATE: | 90% |
| SAT RANGE: | 430–520 Verbal |
| | 470–580 Math |
| STICKER PRICE: | $19,000+ |
| NEED-BLIND: | Yes |
| NEED MET: | 71% |
| AVERAGE STUDENT DEBT: | NA |
| MERIT SCHOLARSHIPS: | Many |
| RANGE: | Up to $7,000 |
| ATHLETIC SCHOLARSHIPS: | Yes |
| ROTC: | Army, Air Force |
| WEB SITE: | www.shc.edu |
| PHONE: | (800) 742-6704 |

Spring Hill's finest hour came in 1954: it was the first college in Alabama to enact racial integration. Set on a spacious 500-acre campus within arm's length of the Gulf of Mexico, Spring Hill is the nation's third-oldest college affiliated with the Jesuit order of the Catholic Church. Given its small size, the college's academic offerings are remarkably diverse and include liberal arts, business, communication, fine and performing arts, and nursing. More than two-thirds of the students are out-of-staters. The Presidential Honors Scholarship offers $7,000 to students with a high school GPA of 3.4 or better who score at least 1220 on the SAT I or 27 on the ACT. The $4,000 Academic Honors Scholarship gives $4,000 to those with a 3.2 and 1030 or 22. A Metropolitan Service Award of $2,200 goes to Mobile residents with a commitment to community service, and the Jesuit Service Award in the same amount targets students who are graduates of Jesuit high schools. Merit scholarship applicants must complete the college's Application for Scholarship and Financial Assistance.

*Deadlines:*
    ADMISSION: Rolling
    FAFSA: Mar. 1

# STANFORD UNIVERSITY • Stanford, CA 94305

| | |
|---|---|
| TOTAL ENROLLMENT: | 13,800 |
| UNDERGRADUATE: | 6,600 |
| ACCEPTANCE RATE: | 19% |
| SAT RANGE: | 590–690 Verbal |
| | 660–750 Math |
| STICKER PRICE: | $31,000+ |
| NEED-BLIND: | Yes |
| NEED MET: | 100% |
| AVERAGE STUDENT DEBT: | $12,800 |
| MERIT SCHOLARSHIPS: | None |
| ATHLETIC SCHOLARSHIPS: | Yes |
| ROTC: | Army, Navy, Air Force |
| WEB SITE: | www.stanford.edu |
| PHONE: | (415) 723-2091 |

Railroad magnate Leland Stanford personally drove the golden spike to complete the transcontinental railroad in 1869, and twenty-two years later he struck a blow for higher education by founding Stanford University on his 8,000-acre farm. Today, Stanford stands alone as the leading private university west of the Mississippi and the counterpart to the Ivy League. Stanford has always faced questions about whether its intellectual climate is the equal of the top Eastern schools; there is no doubt that Stanford has less neurotic energy. Much of the university's character comes from its strength in science and engineering, and its close ties to the high-tech Silicon Valley. Stanford's endowment per student ranks near the top and its need-based aid is plentiful. The university recently changed its aid eligibility formula to cap the dollar value of home equity that is considered in the asset equation at three times the level of family income. Outside scholarships won by students who receive need-based aid now reduce the loan portion of the package rather than the grant.

*Deadlines:*
    EARLY DECISION: Nov. 1
    REGULAR ADMISSION: Dec. 15
    FAFSA: Feb. 1
    CSS PROFILE: Feb. 1

# STATE UNIVERSITY OF NEW YORK/ALBANY • Albany, NY 12222

| | |
|---|---|
| TOTAL ENROLLMENT: | 16,100 |
| UNDERGRADUATE: | 11,000 |
| ACCEPTANCE RATE: | 61% |
| SAT RANGE: | 510–610 Verbal |
| | 520–620 Math |
| STICKER PRICE: | In-state, $10,000+ |
| | Out-of-state, $15,000+ |
| NEED-BLIND: | Yes |
| NEED MET: | 83% |
| AVERAGE STUDENT DEBT: | $15,000 |
| MERIT SCHOLARSHIPS: | Many |
| ATHLETIC SCHOLARSHIPS: | Yes |
| ROTC: | Army, Air Force |
| WEB SITE: | www.albany.edu |
| PHONE: | (518) 442-5435 |

Any description of SUNY/Albany must begin with the unique design of its campus, which features a giant rectangular complex of buildings ringed by dorm quadrangles with high-rise towers. Along with its interesting architecture, Albany offers programs in arts and sciences, business, education, public health, and public affairs and policy, the latter of which includes a well-known school of criminal justice. Albany delivers most of its university-wide merit awards through its Presidential Scholars honors program. Students with at least 1270 on the SAT I and a 91 academic average are eligible for awards ranging from $1,000 to $5,000, and all Presidential Scholars also get a personal computer courtesy of the university. (A supplemental scholarship application is required.) The Frederick Douglass Scholars program honors top in-state minority students, and additional awards come through the various academic divisions. A total of 353 students received a non-need award in a recent year. Freshmen seeking merit scholarships are encouraged to apply by December 1.

*Deadlines:*
    EARLY DECISION: Nov. 15
    EARLY ACTION: Dec. 1
    REGULAR ADMISSION: Mar. 1
    FAFSA: Mar. 15

## STATE UNIVERSITY OF NEW YORK/ BINGHAMTON ◆ Binghamton, NY 13902

| | |
|---|---|
| TOTAL ENROLLMENT: | 12,200 |
| UNDERGRADUATE: | 9,500 |
| ACCEPTANCE RATE: | 42% |
| SAT AVERAGE: | 589 Verbal |
| | 618 Math |
| STICKER PRICE: | In-state, $10,000+ |
| | Out-of-state, $15,000+ |
| NEED-BLIND: | Yes |
| NEED MET: | NA |
| AVERAGE STUDENT DEBT: | $22,000 |
| MERIT SCHOLARSHIPS: | Few |
| RANGE: | Up to $4,000 |
| ATHLETIC SCHOLARSHIPS: | No |
| ROTC: | Air Force |
| WEB SITE: | www.binghamton.edu |
| PHONE: | (607) 777-2171 |

Binghamton lacks the ivy-covered mystique of the elite private universities, and it does not have a bigtime sports program like the UCLAs and UVAs of the world. But from humble beginnings barely more than fifty years ago, Binghamton has grown to become one of the nation's front-rank universities. The hallmark of Binghamton is its strong commitment to undergraduate education. The campus is divided into residential colleges that integrate living and learning, and Binghamton's mentoring program for freshmen ensures that newcomers get the assistance they need. Binghamton's allure has much to do with a price tag that is thousands less than private university competitors. The university offers only a handful of merit awards, including twenty Presidential Scholarships worth half of instate tuition. A single Morris Gitlitz Memorial Scholarship of $4,000 goes to a student who excels in both academics and extracurriculars. A variety of merit-within-need awards are available. Binghamton requires early decision applicants who are seeking financial aid to file the CSS PROFILE by December 1.

*Deadlines:*
   EARLY DECISION: Nov. 1
   REGULAR ADMISSION: Jan. 15 (priority)
   FAFSA: Mar. 1

## STATE UNIVERSITY OF NEW YORK/BUFFALO ◆ Buffalo, NY 14260

| | |
|---|---|
| TOTAL ENROLLMENT: | 23,400 |
| UNDERGRADUATE: | 15,600 |
| ACCEPTANCE RATE: | 73% |
| SAT RANGE: | 500–600 Verbal |
| | 520–630 Math |
| STICKER PRICE: | In-state, $11,000+ |
| | Out-of-state, $16,000+ |
| NEED-BLIND: | Yes |
| NEED MET: | 63% |
| AVERAGE STUDENT DEBT: | $15,100 |
| MERIT SCHOLARSHIPS: | Many |
| RANGE: | Up to full costs |
| ATHLETIC SCHOLARSHIPS: | Yes |
| ROTC: | Army |
| WEB SITE: | www.buffalo.edu |
| PHONE: | (716) 645-6900 |

History buffs remember Millard Fillmore as the most obscure President in U.S. history, but he was also the founding chancellor of what is now SUNY/Buffalo. Fillmore went from the Oval Office to oblivion, but his university's reputation has continued to grow throughout its 150-year existence. As the largest of the institutions in the SUNY system, Buffalo offers a full slate of liberal arts and preprofessional programs, including the only SUNY programs in architecture and pharmacy. Business administration heads the list of most popular majors. Twenty Distinguished Honors Scholars awards are available for oustanding students who file a separate application by January 10. More than 500 other students received a scholarship of at least $2,500 in a recent year, including a handful for distinction in the creative and performing arts. Many scholarships are reserved for students admitted to the University Honors Program, whose minimum standards include an SAT I score of 1300 or an ACT of 31. Approximately 15 percent of entering students receive a merit award.

*Deadlines:*
   EARLY DECISION: Nov. 1
   REGULAR ADMISSION: Rolling
   FAFSA: Mar. 1

# STATE UNIVERSITY OF NEW YORK COLLEGE/ GENESEO ◆ Geneseo, NY 14454

| | |
|---|---|
| TOTAL ENROLLMENT: | 5,600 |
| UNDERGRADUATE: | 5,200 |
| ACCEPTANCE RATE: | 54% |
| SAT RANGE: | 560–650 Verbal |
| | 570–640 Math |
| STICKER PRICE: | In-state, $9,000+ |
| | Out-of-state, $14,000+ |
| NEED-BLIND: | Yes |
| NEED MET: | 75% |
| AVERAGE STUDENT DEBT: | $12,100 |
| MERIT SCHOLARSHIPS: | Many |
| RANGE: | Up to full tuition |
| ATHLETIC SCHOLARSHIPS: | No |
| ROTC: | Army, Air Force |
| WEB SITE: | www.geneseo.edu |
| PHONE: | (716) 245-5571 |

With an enrollment of 5,600 and only a smattering of graduate students, Geneseo offers SUNY education with a personal touch. Set in a small town approximately twenty miles south of Rochester, Geneseo includes programs in the liberal arts, business, education, and the fine arts. Barely more than half of the applicants are accepted, and Geneseo is second only to Binghamton in selectivity among the SUNY universities. The university's general education requirements are notable for the inclusion of non-Western culture along with the humanities, social sciences, natural sciences, math, and fine arts. About twenty incoming students per year who are invited to join the honors program get a $1,400 renewable scholarship. Other merit awards are given through the alumni association or the academic divisions based on various criteria. The School of Performing Arts has a range of scholarships in music, theater, musical theater, and dance, though most are worth $1,000 or less. Early decision applicants must file the CSS PROFILE by December 1.

*Deadlines:*
  EARLY DECISION: Nov. 15
  REGULAR ADMISSION: Jan. 15
  FAFSA: Feb. 15

# STATE UNIVERSITY OF NEW YORK/ PURCHASE COLLEGE ◆ Purchase, NY 10577

| | |
|---|---|
| TOTAL ENROLLMENT: | 3,300 |
| UNDERGRADUATE: | 3,200 |
| ACCEPTANCE RATE: | 54% |
| SAT RANGE: | 480–600 Verbal |
| | 450–570 Math |
| STICKER PRICE: | In-state, $10,000+ |
| | Out-of-state, $15,000+ |
| NEED-BLIND: | Yes |
| NEED MET: | 76% |
| AVERAGE STUDENT DEBT: | $11,000 |
| MERIT SCHOLARSHIPS: | Many |
| RANGE: | Up to full tuition |
| ATHLETIC SCHOLARSHIPS: | No |
| ROTC: | No |
| WEB SITE: | www.purchase.edu |
| PHONE: | (914) 251-6300 |

Founded in 1969, Purchase is the artsy younger sibling of the SUNY system. As one of the few major public institutions in the nation devoted largely to the arts, Purchase offers preprofessional programs in art and design, dance, music, and theater arts and film along with a College of Liberal Arts and Sciences. An enrollment of only 3,300 gives Purchase the air of a small private college and allows abundant one-on-one contact with faculty, many of whom are practicing artists. Purchase occupies a 400-acre campus on the outskirts of New York City near the prosperous suburb of White Plains. In the liberal arts, merit scholarships require a separate application and an academic average of at least 86 with a score of 1200 on the SAT I. A faculty committee matches students with scholarships, which average in high school about $1,500 but include a few awards up to full tuition. Significant scholarship money is also available in the arts on the basis of an audition or portfolio. All students (and especially scholarship applicants) are advised to apply by December 1.

*Deadlines:*
  ADMISSION: Jan. 1
  FAFSA: Dec. 1 (priority)

## STATE UNIVERSITY OF NEW YORK/ STONY BROOK ✦ Stony Brook, NY 11790

| | |
|---|---|
| TOTAL ENROLLMENT: | 17,800 |
| UNDERGRADUATE: | 11,800 |
| ACCEPTANCE RATE: | 57% |
| SAT RANGE: | 470–580 Verbal |
| | 510–620 Math |
| STICKER PRICE: | In-state, $10,000+ |
| | Out-of-state, $15,000+ |
| NEED-BLIND: | Yes |
| NEED MET: | 11% |
| AVERAGE STUDENT DEBT: | $13,800 |
| MERIT SCHOLARSHIPS: | Many |
| RANGE: | Up to full tuition |
| ATHLETIC SCHOLARSHIPS: | Yes |
| ROTC: | No |
| WEB SITE: | www.sunysb.edu |
| PHONE: | (800) USB-SUNY |

Founded in 1956, Stony Brook needed only a few decades to establish itself as a major university. As the second-largest institution in the SUNY system, Stony Brook includes divisions of arts and sciences, engineering and applied sciences, management and policy, and health sciences. The university occupies 1,100 acres near the midpoint of Long Island and offers easy access to Manhattan (sixty miles to the west) and plenty of outdoor recreation spots. The Presidential Achievement Scholarships are the crown jewel of Stony Brook's merit program, providing up to full in-state tuition for those with at least a 90 academic average in high school, combined SAT scores of 1200 or higher, and extracurricular achievement. Students must apply for admission by December 30. A few top students who submit credentials to the Honors College by January 1 are rewarded with full-tuition scholarships, and every Honors student gets a one-time $2,000 award. The Women in Science and Engineering Program also offers a $2,000 scholarship for the first year, and more awards are available through the academic divisions.

*Deadlines:*
EARLY DECISION: Nov. 1
REGULAR ADMISSION: Rolling
FAFSA: Mar. 1

## STETSON UNIVERSITY ✦ Deland, FL 32720

| | |
|---|---|
| TOTAL ENROLLMENT: | 2,900 |
| UNDERGRADUATE: | 1,900 |
| ACCEPTANCE RATE: | 88% |
| SAT RANGE: | 510–620 Verbal |
| | 500–610 Math |
| STICKER PRICE: | $23,000+ |
| NEED-BLIND: | Yes |
| NEED MET: | 85% |
| AVERAGE STUDENT DEBT: | $16,000 |
| MERIT SCHOLARSHIPS: | Many |
| RANGE: | Up to full costs |
| ATHLETIC SCHOLARSHIPS: | Yes |
| ROTC: | Army |
| WEB SITE: | www.stetson.edu |
| PHONE: | (800) 688-0101 |

Stetson is a small university in central Florida that combines the liberal arts with schools of business and music. Sun worshipers will be happy to learn that Daytona Beach is only twenty-five miles away, and Orlando is also within easy reach. Business administration is the most popular major on campus. The J. Ollie Edmunds Distinguished Scholarship, Stetson's most coveted prize, covers full costs and is given to four entering students per year on the basis of all-around excellence. Students must secure the nomination of a school official by January 15. Presidential Scholar awards of up to $10,000 are based on leadership and service in addition to academic achievement, as are the Faculty Merit Scholarships worth $3,500 to $5,000. The Hollis Scholars program gives up to $5,500 to good students who have served as volunteers in the school and community, and the Special Achievement Scholars awards honor Hispanics and African Americans with $1,000 to $3,000. The music school gives talent awards worth up to full tuition, and National Merit Finalists qualify for up to $2,000.

*Deadlines:*
EARLY DECISION: Nov. 1
REGULAR ADMISSION: Mar. 1
FAFSA: Apr. 15

# STEVENS INSTITUTE OF TECHNOLOGY ◆
## Hoboken, NJ 07030

| | |
|---|---|
| TOTAL ENROLLMENT: | 3,200 |
| UNDERGRADUATE: | 1,400 |
| ACCEPTANCE RATE: | 67% |
| SAT AVERAGE: | 620 Verbal |
| | 670 Math |
| STICKER PRICE: | $28,000+ |
| NEED-BLIND: | Yes |
| NEED MET: | 95% |
| AVERAGE STUDENT DEBT: | $12,100 |
| MERIT SCHOLARSHIPS: | Many |
| RANGE: | Up to full tuition |
| ATHLETIC SCHOLARSHIPS: | No |
| ROTC: | Army, Air Force |
| WEB SITE: | www.stevens-tech.edu |
| PHONE: | (800) 458-5323 |

It is no surprise that Stevens Institute of Technology requires students to own a personal computer. More remarkable is the fact that the policy was implemented in 1982, a time when students at most universities were still hunting and pecking on typewriters. Stevens remains on the cutting edge today with its emphasis on partnerships with business and government, and a noteworthy program in engineering management trains students to deal with issues on the boundary of business and technology. The most popular degree programs include engineering, computer science, and chemical biology. Located in Hoboken, New Jersey, Stevens is a quick subway ride from Midtown Manhattan. Stevens bestowed more than $5 million in non-need-based aid in a recent year, and a substantial majority of the first-year students received an award. Academic scholarships in varying amounts up to full tuition are given to the strongest applicants. Awards of up $1,500 are reserved for National Merit Finalists. Stevens requires an interview for students who live within 250 miles of campus.

*Deadlines:*
  EARLY DECISION: Dec. 1
  REGULAR ADMISSION: Mar. 1
  FAFSA: Mar. 1

# SUSQUEHANNA UNIVERSITY ◆
## Selinsgrove, PA 17870

| | |
|---|---|
| TOTAL ENROLLMENT: | 1,700 |
| UNDERGRADUATE: | 1,700 |
| ACCEPTANCE RATE: | 75% |
| SAT RANGE: | 520–610 Verbal |
| | 510–610 Math |
| STICKER PRICE: | $25,000+ |
| NEED-BLIND: | Yes |
| NEED MET: | 85% |
| AVERAGE STUDENT DEBT: | $13,200 |
| MERIT SCHOLARSHIPS: | Many |
| RANGE: | Up to $10,000 |
| ATHLETIC SCHOLARSHIPS: | No |
| ROTC: | Army |
| WEB SITE: | www.susqu.edu |
| PHONE: | (800) 326-9672 |

Central Pennsylvania is home to Susquehanna University, which sits in a small town along the mighty river whose name it bears. With a mere 1,700 students, Susquehanna includes three major divisions: arts and sciences, business, and fine arts and communications. The $10,000 University Assistantships comprise Susquehanna's richest merit program and include "a creative work experience" under the tutelage of a faculty member. Valedictorians and salutatorians get an $8,000 award, and additional $8,000 stipends are designated for those who plan to major in business, science, or math. A $6,500 scholarship is available for students who rank in the top 15 percent of their high school class with at least 1100 on the SAT I. A variety of music scholarships yield up to $5,000, and a Dean's Scholarship with an emphasis on extracurriculars is worth up to $5,000. Additional awards are aimed at minority groups, children of alumni, international students, and children of Lutheran clergy. Consideration for all scholarships is automatic with an application for admission.

*Deadlines:*
  EARLY DECISION: Dec. 15
  REGULAR ADMISSION: Mar. 1
  FAFSA: Mar. 1
  CSS PROFILE: Mar. 1

# SWARTHMORE COLLEGE ✦
## Swarthmore, PA 19081

| | |
|---|---|
| TOTAL ENROLLMENT: | 1,400 |
| UNDERGRADUATE: | 1,400 |
| ACCEPTANCE RATE: | 24% |
| SAT RANGE: | 670–770 Verbal |
| | 660–750 Math |
| STICKER PRICE: | $31,000+ |
| NEED-BLIND: | Yes |
| NEED MET: | 100% |
| AVERAGE STUDENT DEBT: | $13,700 |
| MERIT SCHOLARSHIPS: | Few |
| RANGE: | Up to full tuition |
| ATHLETIC SCHOLARSHIPS: | No |
| ROTC: | Navy |
| WEB SITE: | www.swarthmore.edu |
| PHONE: | (610) 328-8300 |

Even among the nation's most selective colleges, Swarthmore commands an extra measure of respect. A few others have the same surpassing commitment to intellectual life, and a handful are just as selective, but none attract so many outstanding students who are so dedicated to the life of the mind. Swarthmore ranks with Amherst and Williams as the most selective of the small liberal arts colleges, though Swat's personality is more progressive than the other two. The college grades its freshmen on a pass-fail basis during their first semester. Swarthmore is among the few elite small colleges with an engineering program—about ninety students are enrolled. The college also offers an unusual prize for a handful of fortunate superachievers: two McCabe Scholarships worth full tuition, and several more in the same amount reserved for residents of Delaware County, Pennsylvania and the Delmarva Peninsula. No separate application is required. The Lang Opportunity Scholarships are awarded to six to twelve incoming freshman who are committed to social service; the pay-off includes enhanced need-based packages, a $1,500 grant, and the chance to qualify for $10,000 to fund a service project.

*Deadlines:*
EARLY DECISION: Nov. 15, Jan. 1
REGULAR ADMISSION: Jan. 1
FAFSA: Feb. 1
CSS PROFILE: Feb. 1

# SWEET BRIAR COLLEGE ✦
## Sweet Briar, VA 24595

| | |
|---|---|
| TOTAL ENROLLMENT: | 800 |
| UNDERGRADUATE: | 700 |
| ACCEPTANCE RATE: | 94% |
| SAT RANGE: | 530–640 Verbal |
| | 480–600 Math |
| STICKER PRICE: | $23,000+ |
| NEED-BLIND: | Yes |
| NEED MET: | 83% |
| AVERAGE STUDENT DEBT: | $15,000 |
| MERIT SCHOLARSHIPS: | Many |
| RANGE: | Up to $15,000 |
| ATHLETIC SCHOLARSHIPS: | No |
| ROTC: | No |
| WEB SITE: | www.sbc.edu |
| PHONE: | (800) 381-6142 |

All-female Sweet Briar occupies 3,300 sprawling acres deep in the woods of central Virginia, and it should come as no surprise that SBC has one of the best equestrian programs in the nation. Less expected, perhaps, is a top ranking from *Yahoo! Internet Life* as one of the nation's most wired campuses. Leadership is another Sweet Briar emphasis, and perhaps not coincidentally, government and international relations are among the most popular majors. The Founders' and Prothro Scholarships, worth up to $15,000, are Sweet Briar's most prestigious merit scholarships. The Commonwealth Scholarship gives up to $13,000 to Virginia residents, and the Sweet Briar Scholarship of up to $9,000 is based on "overall academic record as well as special talent in a particular area." International students can vie for a $12,500 award. Smaller discounts are available for residents of Jacksonville ($3,000) and Altanta ($1,000), those planning a career in medicine, and those who have shown unusual creativity and musical talent. Scholarship seekers must apply for admission by January 15.

*Deadlines:*
EARLY DECISION: Dec. 1
REGULAR ADMISSION: Feb. 15
FAFSA: Mar. 1

# SYRACUSE UNIVERSITY ✦
## Syracuse, NY 13244

| | |
|---|---|
| TOTAL ENROLLMENT: | 14,600 |
| UNDERGRADUATE: | 10,400 |
| ACCEPTANCE RATE: | 60% |
| SAT RANGE: | 530–630 Verbal |
| | 540–640 Math |
| STICKER PRICE: | $27,000+ |
| NEED-BLIND: | Yes |
| NEED MET: | NA |
| AVERAGE STUDENT DEBT: | $17,700 |
| MERIT SCHOLARSHIPS: | Many |
| RANGE: | Up to $6,000 |
| ATHLETIC SCHOLARSHIPS: | Yes |
| ROTC: | Army, Air Force |
| WEB SITE: | www.syr.edu |
| PHONE: | (315) 443-3611 |

If it looks like an alien spacecraft has landed in the middle of the Syracuse campus, don't bother calling Gillian Anderson. The huge white blob is known to sports fans as the Carrier Dome, famed venue of the university's top-ranked football and basketball teams. The closest thing to a national champion among Syracuse's academic programs is the Newhouse School of Public Communications, which attracts some of the best budding journalists in the nation. Aside from arts and sciences, the College of Visual and Performing Arts is the largest undergraduate division on campus. The top merit award for freshmen at Syracuse is the Chancellor's Scholarship, worth $6,000, and those with slightly less exalted credentials may qualify for the Dean's Scholarship valued at $4,000. An additional $6,000 award is available for students at local high schools who have excelled in courses offered under the auspices of the university's Project Advance program. In a recent year, approximately 13 percent of the freshmen received a non-need award.

*Deadlines:*
  EARLY DECISION: Nov. 15
  REGULAR ADMISSION: Jan. 15
  FAFSA: Feb. 15

# TEMPLE UNIVERSITY ✦
## Philadelphia, PA 19122

| | |
|---|---|
| TOTAL ENROLLMENT: | 27,700 |
| UNDERGRADUATE: | 18,100 |
| ACCEPTANCE RATE: | 69% |
| SAT RANGE: | 446–560 Verbal |
| | 438–550 Math |
| STICKER PRICE: | In-state, $12,000+ |
| | Out-of-state, $17,000+ |
| NEED-BLIND: | Yes |
| NEED MET: | 66% |
| AVERAGE STUDENT DEBT: | NA |
| MERIT SCHOLARSHIPS: | Many |
| RANGE: | Up to full tuition |
| ATHLETIC SCHOLARSHIPS: | Yes |
| ROTC: | Army, Navy, Air Force |
| WEB SITE: | www.temple.edu |
| PHONE: | (888) 267-5870 |

The Temple Owls earned their nickname because of all the night classes logged by generations of hard-working students who used Temple as the stepping-stone to a better life. Temple is the major public university in Philadelphia, serving students in eleven undergraduate schools. In a recent year, more than 20 percent of Temple freshmen received a non-need scholarship. For students who are generally in the top 15 percent of their high school class, the Temple Scholar Awards are worth up to full tuition. National Merit and National Achievement Finalists are eligible for a full-tuition award, as are outstanding students from Philadelphia high schools who receive a nomination by January 1. Students from New Jersey and Delaware are considered for scholarships of $2,500. Five half-tuition awards are available to those who attended Pennsylvania Governor's School. A variety of awards are available from the College of Music, and stipends for participation in one of Temple's bands range up to $2,000. Most scholarship programs require that students apply for admission by March 1.

*Deadlines:*
  REGULAR ADMISSION: May 1
  FAFSA: Mar. 31

# UNIVERSITY OF TENNESSEE ✦
## Knoxville, TN 37996

| | |
|---|---|
| TOTAL ENROLLMENT: | 25,400 |
| UNDERGRADUATE: | 19,100 |
| ACCEPTANCE RATE: | 76% |
| SAT RANGE: | 490–610 Verbal |
| | 490–610 Math |
| STICKER PRICE: | In-state, $7,000+ |
| | Out-of-state, $12,000+ |
| NEED-BLIND: | Yes |
| NEED MET: | 74% |
| AVERAGE STUDENT DEBT: | $6,600 |
| MERIT SCHOLARSHIPS: | Many |
| RANGE: | Up to $7,000 |
| ATHLETIC SCHOLARSHIPS: | Yes |
| ROTC: | Army, Air Force |
| WEB SITE: | www.utk.edu |
| PHONE: | (423) 974-2184 |

As the flagship public university of the Volunteer state, UTK offers more than 100 majors in 10 undergraduate colleges. Located by the shores of the Tennessee River adjacent to downtown Knoxville, the university combines an urban location with easy access to the Smoky Mountains. UTK prides itself on an unusually low average debt for aid recipients of only $6,600. It also offers more than 1,400 scholarship programs—a hefty total, though many are small, need-based, and/or reserved for returning students. All Tennessee residents with a 3.75 high school GPA and a 1360 on the SAT I or 31 on the ACT qualify for a full-tuition Bicentennial Scholarship. Outstanding students nominated by January 1 can compete for one of ten Whittle Scholarships, which offer $7,000 per year, a waiver of out-of-state tuition for non-Tennessee residents, and a $3,500 stipend for study abroad. Runners-up in the Whittle program get $4,000. Other scholarships target minority students, National Merit Finalists, and those who show leadership along with academic excellence. Most scholarships have a February 1 deadline.

*Deadlines:*
  ADMISSION: Jun. 1
  FAFSA: Mar. 2

# TEXAS A&M UNIVERSITY ✦
## College Station, TX 77843

| | |
|---|---|
| TOTAL ENROLLMENT: | 41,500 |
| UNDERGRADUATE: | 33,900 |
| ACCEPTANCE RATE: | 73% |
| SAT RANGE: | 520–560 Verbal |
| | 550–650 Math |
| STICKER PRICE: | In-state, $7,000+ |
| | Out-of-state, $13,000+ |
| NEED-BLIND: | Yes |
| NEED MET: | NA |
| AVERAGE STUDENT DEBT: | NA |
| MERIT SCHOLARSHIPS: | Many |
| ATHLETIC SCHOLARSHIPS: | Yes |
| ROTC: | Army, Navy, Air Force |
| WEB SITE: | www.tamu.edu |
| PHONE: | (409) 845-3741 |

Texas A&M started out as a military school for Texas farm boys, and though today it is one of the nation's largest and most comprehensive universities, a healthy dose of the Aggie spirit remains. "Texas A&M is not going to become a school of nerds," says its president, "I don't ever want to get to the point where test scores count more than leadership." But test scores do count for something, as demonstrated by a $6,000 scholarship awarded to all National Merit Finalists. Those students, along with others who score 1300 on the SAT I or 30 on the ACT and show personal distinction (including leadership), can compete for additional awards that range up to full costs. Some have the added bonus of a $1,000 stipend for study abroad. A scholarship application due January 8 is the gateway to these and 200 more awards offered by the various academic divisions. Three programs offer scholarships of up to $2,500 for students in the Corps of Cadets, and an Opportunity Award of up to $2,500 for all-around achievement has a January 15 deadline.

*Deadlines:*
  EARLY ACTION: Dec. 1
  REGULAR ADMISSION: Mar. 1
  FAFSA: Apr. 1

# TEXAS CHRISTIAN UNIVERSITY ✦ Fort Worth, TX 76129

| | |
|---|---|
| TOTAL ENROLLMENT: | 7,300 |
| UNDERGRADUATE: | 6,200 |
| ACCEPTANCE RATE: | 79% |
| SAT RANGE: | 500–610 Verbal |
| | 510–620 Math |
| STICKER PRICE: | $16,000+ |
| NEED-BLIND: | Yes |
| NEED MET: | 83% |
| AVERAGE STUDENT DEBT: | NA |
| MERIT SCHOLARSHIPS: | Many |
| RANGE: | Up to full tuition |
| ATHLETIC SCHOLARSHIPS: | Yes |
| ROTC: | Army, Air Force |
| WEB SITE: | www.tcu.edu |
| PHONE: | (817) 257-7490 |

Texas Christian is a medium-sized university that emphasizes its cozy atmosphere compared to the massive public universities of the Lone Star State. TCU is affiliated with the Christian Church (Disciples of Christ) but offers a nondenominational atmosphere that is respectful of all faiths. Students who rank in the top 10 percent of their high school class with 1300 on the SAT I or 30 on the ACT are eligible for TCU's premier merit award, the Chancellor's Scholarship, which covers full tuition. Runners-up can receive a Dean's ($5,000) or Faculty ($3,000) Scholarship. Those in the top 15 percent with 1180 or 27 can garner the $1,800 TCU Scholarship, and National Merit Finalists qualify for awards ranging from $3,000 to full tuition. An Emerging Leader Award offers up to $2,000 to those active outside the classroom. Consideration for academic awards is automatic with an application for admission by January 15. Talent awards in the fine arts go up to $6,000, and those who excel in band, chorus, or orchestra should contact the respective directors about stipends that range up to full tuition.

*Deadlines:*
  EARLY ACTION: Nov. 15
  REGULAR ADMISSION: Feb. 15
  FAFSA: May 1

# UNIVERSITY OF TEXAS ✦ Austin, TX 78712

| | |
|---|---|
| TOTAL ENROLLMENT: | 48,900 |
| UNDERGRADUATE: | 36,900 |
| ACCEPTANCE RATE: | 78% |
| SAT RANGE: | 540–650 Verbal |
| | 560–660 Math |
| STICKER PRICE: | In-state, $8,000+ |
| | Out-of-state, $14,000+ |
| NEED-BLIND: | No |
| NEED MET: | 85% |
| AVERAGE STUDENT DEBT: | $12,000 |
| MERIT SCHOLARSHIPS: | Many |
| ATHLETIC SCHOLARSHIPS: | Yes |
| ROTC: | Army, Navy, Air Force |
| WEB SITE: | www.utexas.edu |
| PHONE: | (512) 475-7399 |

Beneath the famed clock tower that is its most recognizable symbol, the UT campus pulses with the energy of nearly 49,000 students. Always included among the nation's top public universities, UT offers just about everything to be found under the hot Texas sun—except agriculture, which is left to a certain school down the road in College Station. Architecture, business, communications, and engineering are UT's most competitive divisions, and the Plan II liberal arts honors program offers a complete academic/extracurricular experience to 800 Ivy League–caliber students. UT grants a staggering 13,000 academic scholarships with a combined value of more than $20 million. To be eligible, students must file the Application for Freshman Scholarships by December 1. Most awards are bestowed through the academic divisions. Texas residents who are National Merit Finalists receive $4,000 and out-of-staters are allowed to pay in-state tuition and get a $1,000 stipend. The President's Achievement Scholarship offers up to $5,000 to Texans who have overcome adversity.

*Deadlines:*
  ADMISSION: Feb. 1 (priority)
  FAFSA: Mar. 31

# THOMAS AQUINAS COLLEGE ✦
## Santa Paula, CA 93060

| | |
|---|---|
| TOTAL ENROLLMENT: | 200 |
| UNDERGRADUATE: | 200 |
| ACCEPTANCE RATE: | 84% |
| SAT RANGE: | 590–670 Verbal |
| | 540–630 Math |
| STICKER PRICE: | $19,000+ |
| NEED-BLIND: | Yes |
| NEED MET: | 92% |
| AVERAGE STUDENT DEBT: | $13,300 |
| MERIT SCHOLARSHIPS: | None |
| ATHLETIC SCHOLARSHIPS: | No |
| ROTC: | No |
| WEB SITE: | www.thomasaquinas.edu |
| PHONE: | (800) 634-9797 |

Students looking for a conventional college experience will find a few surprises at Thomas Aquinas, such as the absence of textbooks, professors, lectures, majors, and distribution requirements. At Aquinas, the Great Books are teachers, from the ancient Greeks to twentieth century giants such as Einstein and Freud. Every class in the entire college has less than twenty students, everyone studies the same list of books, and the purpose of the faculty (called tutors) is to facilitate discussion rather than to give answers. Academic life at Aquinas has much in common with that of St. John's College, but while the latter is a secular (and liberal) institution, Aquinas is firmly rooted in the Catholic tradition. Optional mass is offered thrice daily, and 63 percent of the students graduated from a private school or were homeschooled. With a sticker price of less than $20,000, Aquinas is remarkably inexpensive given its highly personalized brand of education. (For reference, the tuition at St. John's is nearly twice as much.) All financial aid is based on need.

*Deadlines:*
  ADMISSION: Rolling
  FAFSA: Sept. 1

# UNIVERSITY OF TORONTO ✦
## Ontario, CA M5S1A3

| | |
|---|---|
| TOTAL ENROLLMENT: | 53,500 |
| UNDERGRADUATE: | 43,400 |
| ACCEPTANCE RATE: | 33% |
| SAT RANGE: | NA |
| STICKER PRICE: | Canadian, $9,000+ |
| | (Canadian dollars) |
| | U.S., $9,000+ (U.S. dollars) |
| NEED-BLIND: | Yes |
| NEED MET: | NA |
| AVERAGE STUDENT DEBT: | NA |
| MERIT SCHOLARSHIPS: | Many |
| ATHLETIC SCHOLARSHIPS: | No |
| WEB SITE: | www.utoronto.ca |
| PHONE: | (416) 978-2190 |

With 53,500 students spread across three campuses, the University of Toronto is on par with the biggest American universities. Generally viewed as the top research university in Canada, Toronto offers 300 undergraduate majors, from actuarial science to zoology. United States citizens have always beaten a path to Toronto for graduate school, and in recent years the university has become more attractive to American undergraduates because of its low sticker price. (Note that tuition varies significantly from program to program, and that the sticker price figures above are minimums.) All students are eligible for Toronto's 1,000 merit and merit-within-need scholarships for entering students, which have an average value of about $2,000. Included in the total are 150 University of Toronto Scholars awards worth $3,000 apiece, which are given on the basis of academic achievement "with particular emphasis on the most recent results." Students are automatically considered for scholarships with an application for admission.

*Deadlines:*
  ADMISSION: Mar. 1 (priority)
  FAFSA: Rolling

# TRINITY COLLEGE ◆ Hartford, CT 06016

| | |
|---|---|
| TOTAL ENROLLMENT: | 2,200 |
| UNDERGRADUATE: | 2,100 |
| ACCEPTANCE RATE: | 43% |
| SAT RANGE: | 570–660 Verbal |
| | 570–670 Math |
| STICKER PRICE: | $30,000+ |
| NEED-BLIND: | Yes |
| NEED MET: | 100% |
| AVERAGE STUDENT DEBT: | $15,500 |
| MERIT SCHOLARSHIPS: | None |
| ATHLETIC SCHOLARSHIPS: | No |
| ROTC: | Army |
| WEB SITE: | www.trincoll.edu |
| PHONE: | (860) 297-2180 |

Trinity's best-known symbol is a Gothic tower that soars majestically above its main quadrangle. The campus is similar to those of other top liberal arts colleges, except that Trinity is located in the heart of a major city. Hartford offers the bustle of a state capital and nearly 1,000,000 people, though the neighborhood around Trinity has seen better days. (The college is working with the city to spruce it up.) Along with places such as Lafayette, Swarthmore, and Union, Trinity is among the few small liberal arts colleges that include engineering in the curriculum. Economics ranks as the most popular major on campus, followed by English and psychology. Trinity has a strong program to acclimate first-year students, which features seminars of 12–15 students that introduce freshmen to college-level work and include an upperclass student mentor as well as a professor. Nearly half the students study abroad, and Trinity has a campus of its own in Rome. All financial aid at Trinity is based on need except for two small non-need awards for applicants from Illinois and the San Francisco area.

*Deadlines:*
    EARLY DECISION: Nov. 15, Feb. 1
    REGULAR ADMISSION: Jan. 15
    FAFSA: Feb. 1
    CSS PROFILE: Feb. 1

# TRINITY UNIVERSITY ◆ San Antonio, TX 78212

| | |
|---|---|
| TOTAL ENROLLMENT: | 2,600 |
| UNDERGRADUATE: | 2,300 |
| ACCEPTANCE RATE: | 77% |
| SAT RANGE: | 515–615 Verbal |
| | 585–675 Math |
| STICKER PRICE: | $21,000+ |
| NEED-BLIND: | NA |
| NEED MET: | 100% |
| AVERAGE STUDENT DEBT: | $21,500 |
| MERIT SCHOLARSHIPS: | Many |
| RANGE: | Up to $10,000 |
| ATHLETIC SCHOLARSHIPS: | No |
| ROTC: | Army, Air Force |
| WEB SITE: | www.trinity.edu |
| PHONE: | (800) TRINITY |

High atop a hill overlooking the San Antonio skyline, Trinity is a small college that combines the liberal arts with career-oriented programs in business, communications, and engineering science. A Common Curriculum requires all students to take courses in six broad categories and to demonstrate proficiency in a foreign language, math, computer skills, and a lifetime sport, such as golf. Trinity has the biggest national reputation among the Texas liberal arts colleges, and with an endowment per student that ranks near the top, it has plenty of money to spend on both need-based and merit awards. Approximately 25 percent of the freshmen in a recent class received one of the latter, which are highlighted by twenty Murchison Scholarships valued at $10,000 each. (Winners typically rank at the top of their high school class with at least 1400 on the SAT I or 32 on the ACT.) National Merit Finalists who don't win the Murchison can garner up to $8,000, and the President's Scholarship of up to $5,000 goes to students who score over 1300 or 29. Music students may audition for a scholarship of up $2,500. Consideration for merit awards is automatic.

*Deadlines:*
    EARLY DECISION: Nov. 15
    REGULAR ADMISSION: Feb. 1
    FAFSA: Feb. 1

# TRUMAN STATE UNIVERSITY ◆ Kirksville, MO 63501

| | |
|---|---|
| Total Enrollment: | 6,400 |
| Undergraduate: | 6,100 |
| Selectivity: | 81% |
| SAT Range: | 550–670 Verbal |
| | 550–650 Math |
| Sticker Price: | In-state, $8,000+ |
| | Out-of-state, $11,000+ |
| Need-Blind: | Yes |
| Need Met: | 67% |
| Average Student Debt: | $13,400 |
| Merit Scholarships: | Many |
| Range: | Up to full costs |
| Athletic Scholarships: | Yes |
| ROTC: | Army |
| Web site: | www.truman.edu |
| Phone: | (660) 785-4114 |

Known until recently as Northeast Missouri State, Truman adopted the new name to signify its transition from a sleepy regional school into a nationally known liberal arts university. Truman has feasted on rankings from *Money* magazine and *U.S. News & World Report* that compare its low sticker price with more expensive private institutions. Twelve outstanding freshmen enter with Pershing Scholarships, which cover full costs and offer a $4,000 stipend for study abroad. In-staters who show outstanding leadership are eligible for the Truman Leadership Award, another full-costs scholarship that enrolls winners in a for-credit leadership course. Other awards are available for National Merit Finalists, members of the National Honor Society, and those who excel in a foreign language. Students with top grades and test scores automatically get scholarships of up to $2,000 based on a sliding scale, and artistic talent awards are available via the Division of Fine Arts. Most major scholarships have a deadline of January 15, although some endowed awards have a priority deadline of November 15.

*Deadlines:*
  Early Action: Nov. 15
  Regular Admission: Mar. 1
  FAFSA: Apr. 1

# TUFTS UNIVERSITY ◆ Medford, MA 02155

| | |
|---|---|
| Total Enrollment: | 8,700 |
| Undergraduate: | 4,700 |
| Selectivity: | 32% |
| SAT Range: | 610–700 Verbal |
| | 630–710 Math |
| Sticker Price: | $30,000+ |
| Need-Blind: | NA |
| Need Met: | 100% |
| Average Student Debt: | $14,400 |
| Merit Scholarships: | None |
| Athletic Scholarships: | No |
| ROTC: | Army, Navy, Air Force |
| Web site: | www.tufts.edu |
| Phone: | (617) 627-3170 |

Tufts won fame a century ago as the home of Jumbo the elephant, a gift of legendary showman and Tufts trustee Phineas T. Barnam. (Sadly, Jumbo's stuffed body was destroyed by fire in 1975.) Today, Tufts' burgeoning popularity has more to do with its combination of liberal arts and engineering—and its location in suburban Boston. Applications were up more than 60 percent in a recent five year period, putting Tufts in a class with Northwestern and Duke on the near–Ivy League hot college list. International relations is a campus specialty, in part because of the influence of the graduate-level Fletcher School of Law and Diplomacy. (More than 50 percent of the undergraduates study abroad during their four years.) One unique Tufts program is the Experimental College, which offers credit courses taught by people ranging from outside experts to undergraduates. Recent titles include Do Animals Think? and The Life of John Coltrane. There are no merit scholarships at Tufts, but merit-within-need awards include a full-tuition program for outstanding African Americans.

*Deadlines:*
  Early Decision: Nov. 15, Jan. 1
  Regular Admission: Jan. 1
  FAFSA: Feb. 1
  CSS PROFILE: Jan. 1

## TULANE UNIVERSITY ◆ New Orleans, LA 70118

| | |
|---|---|
| TOTAL ENROLLMENT: | 10,900 |
| UNDERGRADUATE: | 6,600 |
| ACCEPTANCE RATE: | 76% |
| SAT RANGE: | 580–690 Verbal |
| | 580–680 Math |
| STICKER PRICE: | $30,000+ |
| NEED-BLIND: | Yes |
| NEED MET: | 93% |
| AVERAGE STUDENT DEBT: | $16,000 |
| MERIT SCHOLARSHIPS: | Many |
| RANGE: | Up to full tuition |
| ATHLETIC SCHOLARSHIPS: | Yes |
| ROTC: | Army, Navy, Air Force |
| WEB SITE: | www.tulane.edu |
| PHONE: | (504) 865-5731 |

It is only by a quirk of geography that Tulane is in the Deep South. With more students from New York than any other state except Louisiana, Tulane draws over two-thirds of its enrollment from outside the Southeast. The combination of strong academics, warm weather, and the urban funkiness of New Orleans is apparently more irresistible than ever to students all over the map. Like close competitors Emory and Washington U, Tulane has seen applications rise significantly in recent years. Tulane offers about 120 full-tuition Dean's Honor Scholarships to its most prized applicants, who generally rank in the top 5 percent of their high school class with 1400 on the SAT I or 31 on the ACT. A special application is required by December 1. Roughly 500 more applicants with a top 5 percent class rank and 1300 are offered a Distinguished Scholars Award in or the Founders Scholarship both valued at $8,000 to $10,000. Other scholarships target National Merit Finalists, musicians, and international students. Residents of New Orleans and Louisiana can get a tuition scholarship with a nomination by the Mayor or a state legislator.

*Deadlines:*
  EARLY ACTION: Nov. 1
  REGULAR ADMISSION: Jan. 15
  FAFSA: Feb. 1
  CSS PROFILE: Feb. 1

## UNIVERSITY OF TULSA ◆ Tulsa, OK 74104

| | |
|---|---|
| TOTAL ENROLLMENT: | 4,200 |
| UNDERGRADUATE: | 2,900 |
| ACCEPTANCE RATE: | 83% |
| SAT RANGE: | 550–650 Verbal |
| | 530–660 Math |
| STICKER PRICE: | $17,000+ |
| NEED-BLIND: | Yes |
| NEED MET: | 46% |
| AVERAGE STUDENT DEBT: | $18,600 |
| MERIT SCHOLARSHIPS: | Many |
| RANGE: | Up to full costs |
| ATHLETIC SCHOLARSHIPS: | Yes |
| ROTC: | No |
| WEB SITE: | www.utulsa.edu |
| PHONE: | (800) 331-3050 |

From an unlikely beginning as the Presbyterian School for Indian Girls back in the days when Oklahoma was still a territory, the University of Tulsa has evolved into a comprehensive university with divisions of arts and sciences, business administration, and engineering and applied sciences. Students who rank in the top 10 percent of their high school class with a 1400 on the SAT I or 32 on the ACT are considered for the Presidential Scholarship, which offers up to $6,000. National Merit Finalists, National Achievement Finalists, and National Hispanic Scholar honorees get scholarships that cover a minimum of full tuition. Students admitted to the honors program receive $1,100 with "best consideration" given to those who apply by February 15. Awards are also available for alumni children ($1,000) and High O'Brien Youth Leadership honorees (up to $6,000). Performing arts scholarships of up to full tuition are offered in music, theater, and musical theater with auditions beginning in January; a $2,500 award is reserved for winners in the Scholastic Arts Competition.

*Deadlines:*
  ADMISSION: Rolling
  FAFSA: Apr. 1

# UNION COLLEGE • Schenectady, NY 12308

| | |
|---|---|
| TOTAL ENROLLMENT: | 2,400 |
| UNDERGRADUATE: | 2,100 |
| ACCEPTANCE RATE: | 52% |
| SAT RANGE: | 560–640 Verbal |
| | 580–660 Math |
| STICKER PRICE: | $30,000+ |
| NEED-BLIND: | No |
| NEED MET: | 100% |
| AVERAGE STUDENT DEBT: | NA |
| MERIT SCHOLARSHIPS: | None |
| ATHLETIC SCHOLARSHIPS: | No |
| ROTC: | Army, Navy, Air Force |
| WEB SITE: | www.union.edu |
| PHONE: | (888) 843-6688 |

Union was the first college to combine liberal arts and engineering, and today it is among the few that maintain an equal commitment to both. Enrollment is split 50/50 between the two, and all students must complete the same general education program which features distribution requirements in four categories plus a discussion-oriented Freshman Preceptorial. The college is noted for joint degree offerings that include the highly selective Leadership in Medicine Program, which enrolls twenty students per year in a B.S./M.D. curriculum with Albany Medical College. Another drawing card is Union's extensive study abroad program; more than half of Union students spend a term outside the United States before graduation. Among other selective small colleges, Union most closely resembles Lafayette, but it also competes with geographically nearer neighbors such as Hamilton and Colgate. All financial aid at Union goes to students with need, though the college's unusual CAUSE program provides loans that can be forgiven for students who enter public service after graduation.

*Deadlines:*
    EARLY DECISION: Nov. 15, Jan. 15
    REGULAR ADMISSION: Feb. 1
    FAFSA: Feb. 1
    CSS PROFILE: Feb. 1

# URSINUS COLLEGE • Collegeville, PA 19426

| | |
|---|---|
| TOTAL ENROLLMENT: | 1,200 |
| UNDERGRADUATE: | 1,200 |
| ACCEPTANCE RATE: | 71% |
| SAT RANGE: | 550–635 Verbal |
| | 530–640 Math |
| STICKER PRICE: | $25,000+ |
| NEED-BLIND: | Yes |
| NEED MET: | 85% |
| AVERAGE STUDENT DEBT: | $14,500 |
| Merit Scholarships: | Many |
| RANGE: | Up to full tuition |
| ATHLETIC SCHOLARSHIPS: | No |
| ROTC: | No |
| WEB SITE: | www.ursinus.edu |
| PHONE: | (610) 409-3200 |

Ursinus is a small college located twenty-five miles from Philadelphia that prides itself on turning out students headed for careers in business and the professions. Nearly 20 percent of the students major in biology, and economics and psychology are also popular. Ursinus offers an extensive study abroad program with more than a dozen options ranging from Scotland to Senegal. With an enrollment of only 1,200, Ursinus stresses small classes and hands-on learning. Almost 15 percent of the freshmen in a recent class received a non-need scholarship. The Tower Scholarships offer full tuition to Latino and African American students planning graduate work in a professional field, and National Merit Finalists also qualify for a tuition stipend. The Steinway Scholarships give full tuition to one resident from each of six neighboring counties in eastern Pennsylvania. The Ursinus Scholarships, worth from $3,000 to half tuition, are awarded after finalists have come to the college for an interview. There is no separate application for merit scholarships.

*Deadlines:*
    EARLY DECISION: Jan. 15
    REGULAR ADMISSION: Feb. 15
    FAFSA: Feb. 15
    CSS PROFILE: Feb. 15

# UNIVERSITY OF UTAH ✦
## Salt Lake City, UT 84112

| | |
|---|---|
| TOTAL ENROLLMENT: | 26,200 |
| UNDERGRADUATE: | 19,700 |
| ACCEPTANCE RATE: | 90% |
| SAT RANGE: | 460–620 Verbal |
| | 470–630 Math |
| STICKER PRICE: | In-state, $9,000+ |
| | Out-of-state, $14,000+ |
| NEED-BLIND: | No |
| NEED MET: | 54% |
| AVERAGE STUDENT DEBT: | NA |
| MERIT SCHOLARSHIPS: | Many |
| ATHLETIC SCHOLARSHIPS: | Yes |
| ROTC: | Army, Navy, Air Force |
| WEB SITE: | www.utah.edu |
| PHONE: | (801) 581-7281 |

For those who love mountain getaways but can't bear to give up the charms of city life, the University of Utah provides the best of both worlds. Salt Lake City is within arm's length of the majestic Wasatch Mountains, which provide a picturesque backdrop for the university's 1,500-acre campus. Utah's academic offerings cover the entire waterfront of liberal arts and preprofessional majors, and along with them come hundreds of merit scholarships. The President's Scholarship gives $12,000 to 50 top in-state students who have a high school GPA of at least a 3.9, an ACT of 28, or National Merit Finalist status, and 250 runners-up get a full tuition award. Fifty Leadership Scholarships of full-tuition go to in-staters with a 3.0 GPA or higher. A smaller number of awards are available for out-of-staters, ranging up to full out-of-state tuition plus a $1,800 stipend. Ten Leadership Scholarships are available for nonresidents. Candidates for university-wide scholarships should complete a separate application by February 1 and contact the department of their intended major to learn about additional awards.

*Deadlines:*
  ADMISSION: Feb. 15 (priority)
  FAFSA: Feb. 15
  INSTITUTIONAL: Feb. 15

# VALPARAISO UNIVERSITY ✦
## Valparaiso, IN 46383

| | |
|---|---|
| TOTAL ENROLLMENT: | 3,600 |
| UNDERGRADUATE: | 2,900 |
| ACCEPTANCE RATE: | 86% |
| SAT Range: | 510–640 Verbal |
| | 510–650 Math |
| STICKER PRICE: | $20,000+ |
| NEED-BLIND: | Yes |
| NEED MET: | 95% |
| AVERAGE STUDENT DEBT: | $16,800 |
| MERIT SCHOLARSHIPS: | Many |
| RANGE: | Up to full cost |
| ATHLETIC SCHOLARSHIPS: | Yes |
| ROTC: | No |
| WEB SITE: | www.valpo.edu |
| PHONE: | (800) GO-VALPO |

Valparaiso is known to one and all as Valpo, a perfect nickname for a small university in a friendly Midwestern town. An independent Lutheran institution, Valpo offers degrees in arts and sciences, business, engineering, and nursing. The university also has one of the nation's largest non-need scholarship programs. Major merit awards are bestowed based on a combination of standardized test scores and high school class rank. Students with an SAT I of at least 1510 (or an ACT of 34) who rank in the top 5 percent of their high school class qualify for the full-tuition Founders Scholarship if they apply by January 15. Partial tuition awards (75 percent, 50 percent, 35 percent, and 20 percent) go to students who rank in the top 20 percent and score at least 1100 or 24. (Students with a rank in the top 40 percent and higher test scores also qualify.) Diversity awards of up to $4,000 go to top minority students, and discounts are available for sons and daughters of alumni (up to $500), Lutherans (up to 25 percent of tuition), and those with siblings enrolled ($500). Additional awards are available in the fine arts and from the academic departments.

*Deadlines:*
  ADMISSION: Rolling
  FAFSA: Mar. 1

# VANDERBILT UNIVERSITY ◆ Nashville, TN 37240

| | |
|---|---|
| TOTAL ENROLLMENT: | 10,200 |
| UNDERGRADUATE: | 5,800 |
| ACCEPTANCE RATE: | 58% |
| SAT RANGE: | 590–680 Verbal |
| | 610–690 Math |
| STICKER PRICE: | $31,000+ |
| NEED-BLIND: | Yes |
| NEED MET: | 96% |
| AVERAGE STUDENT DEBT: | $17,500 |
| MERIT SCHOLARSHIPS: | Many |
| RANGE: | Up to full tuition |
| ATHLETIC SCHOLARSHIPS: | Yes |
| ROTC: | Army, Navy, Air Force |
| WEB SITE: | www.vanderbilt.edu |
| PHONE: | (615) 322-2561 |

Cornelius Vanderbilt was one of the notorious Robber Barons who ruled late nineteenth-century America, but he did at least one good deed by founding Vanderbilt University in 1871. Traditonally a more "Southern" institution than Emory and Tulane, Vandy has broadened its appeal and raised its selectivity in recent years. For the most outstanding students, Vandy bestows twelve Harold Stirling Vanderbilt Honor Scholarships that cover full tuition with a stipend for summer study abroad. Top minority students can get the same deal from a similar scholarship, and a third program gives a full-tuition award to an aspiring sports writer. The half-tuition Ingram Scholarship is aimed at strong students with an interest in community service and includes $3,000 for summer projects that must "address significant societal needs." Other awards are available for residents of Georgia and Tennessee, and the academic divisions sponsor additional ones that go up to full tuition. All scholarship applicants must apply for admission by January 1, and several of the major awards require a special application.

*Deadlines:*
　EARLY DECISION: Nov. 1
　REGULAR ADMISSION: Jan. 15
　FAFSA: Feb. 1
　CSS PROFILE: Feb. 1

# VASSAR COLLEGE ◆ Poughkeepsie, NY 12604

| | |
|---|---|
| TOTAL ENROLLMENT: | 2,400 |
| UNDERGRADUATE: | 2,400 |
| ACCEPTANCE RATE: | 42% |
| SAT AVERAGE: | 666 Verbal, |
| | 641 Math |
| STICKER PRICE: | $30,000+ |
| NEED-BLIND: | No |
| NEED MET: | 100% |
| AVERAGE STUDENT DEBT: | $13,700 |
| MERIT SCHOLARSHIPS: | None |
| ATHLETIC SCHOLARSHIPS: | No |
| ROTC: | No |
| WEB SITE: | www.vassar.edu |
| PHONE: | (914) 437-7300 |

Vassar has successfully made the transition from a distinguished women's college to an equally distinguished coed institution. But the fact that women were there first—and still comprise 60 percent of the students—gives Vassar a liberal and feminist flavor. It also means particularly strong programs in the arts and humanities; English is the most popular major, and the art history program is among the best in the nation. Interdisciplinary work is a Vassar specialty, and more than a third of its majors cross traditional departmental lines. Curricular requirements are minimal, though students must show proficiency in a foreign language and quantitative reasoning. They also take a Freshman Course which is taught in seminar format on topics ranging from Perspectives on the Global Village to Russia and the Short Story. The beauty of Vassar's campus is legendary, though its homebase in postindustrial Poughkeepsie is not a garden spot. Vassar meets the full financial need of all students who are accepted, but like a number of selective private colleges, it does consider financial need in a few (5 percent or less) of the admission decisions.

*Deadlines:*
　EARLY DECISION: Nov. 15, Jan. 1
　REGULAR ADMISSION: Jan. 1
　FAFSA: Jan. 15
　CSS PROFILE: Jan. 15

# UNIVERSITY OF VERMONT •
## Burlington, VT 05401

| | |
|---|---|
| TOTAL ENROLLMENT: | 9,100 |
| UNDERGRADUATE: | 7,500 |
| ACCEPTANCE RATE: | 85% |
| SAT RANGE: | 510–610 Verbal |
| | 510–610 Math |
| STICKER PRICE: | In-state, $13,000+ |
| | Out-of-state, $24,000+ |
| NEED-BLIND: | Yes |
| NEED MET: | 90% |
| AVERAGE STUDENT DEBT: | $21,000 |
| MERIT SCHOLARSHIPS: | Few |
| RANGE: | Up to full tuition |
| ATHLETIC SCHOLARSHIPS: | Yes |
| ROTC: | Army, Air Force |
| WEB SITE: | www.uvm.edu |
| PHONE: | (802) 656-3370 |

UVM's initials stand for Universitas Viridis Montis, which Latin buffs will recognize as "University of the Green Mountain." The allure of those mountains that loom in the distance, combined with the charms of cosmopolitan Burlington, make UVM a popular destination for students from across the nation. UVM's enrollment of only 7,100 gives it the ambience of a private university; unfortunately the feeling is heightened by an out-of-state comprehensive fee of more than $24,000. Most UVM Scholarships are awarded to students who show need. The Vermont Scholars Program meets the full financial need of top in-staters without loans (a work-study job is required), and winners who do not show need get a $500 stipend. A similar deal goes to Vermonters who have demonstrated commitment to leadership and community service. A lone Green Mountain Power Centennial Scholarship offers full tuition to an outstanding in-stater, and merit-within-need awards are available with various criteria, including several programs for underrepresented minorities.

*Deadlines:*
  EARLY DECISION: Nov. 1
  REGULAR ADMISSION: Feb. 1
  FAFSA: Feb. 10

# VILLANOVA UNIVERSITY •
## Villanova, PA 19085

| | |
|---|---|
| TOTAL ENROLLMENT: | 10,000 |
| UNDERGRADUATE: | 7,100 |
| ACCEPTANCE RATE: | 61% |
| SAT RANGE: | 560–630 Verbal |
| | 580–650 Math |
| STICKER PRICE: | $28,000+ |
| NEED-BLIND: | Yes |
| NEED MET: | 84% |
| AVERAGE STUDENT DEBT: | $16,500 |
| MERIT SCHOLARSHIPS: | Many |
| RANGE: | Up to full costs |
| ATHLETIC SCHOLARSHIPS: | Yes |
| ROTC: | Army, Navy, Air Force |
| WEB SITE: | www.vill.edu |
| PHONE: | (800) 338-7927 |

Villanova occupies a comfortable 222-acre campus in the suburbs of Philadelphia, an easy commute away from Center City. Affiliated with the Augustinian order of the Catholic Church, 'Nova features colleges of liberal arts and sciences, commerce and finance, engineering, and nursing. Finance and accountancy head the list of most popular majors. The full-tuition Presidential Scholarship is bestowed upon fifty outstanding applicants each year who rank in the top 5 percent of their high school class and score at least 1350 on the SAT I. Students must apply by December 1. Villanova Scholars awards of up to $12,500 are awarded to other superior students (top 10 percent and 1300) with leadership and community involvement among the criteria. In a recent year, 840 of these were offered. An additional award of up to $12,500 is reserved for commuters, and a scholarship covering the full cost of attendance is available for the strongest applicants from underrepresented minority groups. National Merit Finalists are offered up to $2,000, and the university sweetens many ROTC scholarships with money from its own coffers.

*Deadlines:*
  EARLY ACTION: Dec. 1
  REGULAR ADMISSION: Jan. 15
  FAFSA: Feb. 15

# VIRGINIA TECH • Blacksburg, VA 24061

| | |
|---|---|
| TOTAL ENROLLMENT: | 25,200 |
| UNDERGRADUATE: | 21,000 |
| ACCEPTANCE RATE: | 73% |
| SAT RANGE: | 520–620 Verbal |
| | 540–650 Math |
| STICKER PRICE: | In-state, $8,000+ |
| | Out-of-state, $16,000+ |
| NEED-BLIND: | Yes |
| NEED MET: | NA |
| AVERAGE STUDENT DEBT: | $8,500 |
| MERIT SCHOLARSHIPS: | Many |
| ATHLETIC SCHOLARSHIPS: | Yes |
| ROTC: | Army, Navy, Air Force |
| WEB SITE: | www.vt.edu |
| PHONE: | (540) 231-6267 |

An essay question on one of Virginia Tech's scholarship applications poses a frequently asked question: "What does it mean to be a Hokie?" The technical answer has to do with a line from the school's fight song, but most students at Tech would say it involves the pride of attending Virginia's largest research university. (Tech's official name is a tongue-twister: Virginia Polytechnic Institute and State University.) With seventy undergraduate degree programs in seven colleges, Tech is best-known for engineering. The Pamplin Leadership Award offers a one-time, $1,000 stipend to a single student from each public high school in Virginia. Applicants must have a high school class rank in the top 10 percent (or a 3.75 GPA), get the nomination of their high school, and submit a special application by February 15. National Merit Finalists qualify for up to $2,000, and Academic Merit scholarships are bestowed on applicants who score around 1350 on the SAT I and apply for admission by January 15. A separate class of merit-within-need General Scholarships requires a minimum SAT I score of 1100 and a special application by March 1, and the Corps of Cadets also sponsors scholarships.

*Deadlines:*
  EARLY DECISION: Nov. 1
  REGULAR ADMISSION: Feb. 1
  FAFSA: Mar. 1

# UNIVERSITY OF VIRGINIA • Charlottesville, VA 22903

| | |
|---|---|
| TOTAL ENROLLMENT: | 21,900 |
| UNDERGRADUATE: | 13,200 |
| ACCEPTANCE RATE: | 36% |
| SAT AVERAGE: | 590–700 Verbal |
| | 610–710 Math |
| STICKER PRICE: | In-state, $10,000+ |
| | Out-of-state, 21,000+ |
| NEED-BLIND: | Yes |
| NEED MET: | 82% |
| AVERAGE STUDENT DEBT: | $15,200 |
| MERIT SCHOLARSHIPS: | Few |
| RANGE: | Up to full costs |
| ATHLETIC SCHOLARSHIPS: | Yes |
| ROTC: | Army, Navy, Air Force |
| WEB SITE: | www.virginia.edu |
| PHONE: | (804) 982-3200 |

Call it the UVA aura. Or the mystique of Mr. Jefferson. When college applicants come under the spell of the University of Virginia, they want nothing more than to follow in the footsteps of the man who wrote the Declaration of Independence, but considered the founding of UVA his greatest achievement. Many hear the call but few are chosen: only 24 percent of the out-of-state applicants and 46 percent of the Virginians were admitted in a recent year. A strong Greek system sets the tenor of social life, and UVA's most popular major is commerce. The Jefferson Scholars Program is a prize plum for twenty-five top freshmen, covering the full cost of four years with a stipend for foreign travel. Students must secure a nomination if they attend one of 1,300 participating high schools, and if they do not, they are considered on an at-large basis. Runners-up in the competition get a $1,000 consolation prize. Five outstanding African American students get a $10,000 award, and fifty more in-staters receive full tuition. The school of engineering also awards a number of scholarships to high-achieving minority students and those chosen for the Rodman Scholars honors program.

*Deadlines:*
  EARLY DECISION: Nov. 1
  REGULAR ADMISSION: Jan. 2
  FAFSA: Mar. 1

# SCHOOL OF VISUAL ARTS ◆ New York, NY 10010

| | |
|---|---|
| TOTAL ENROLLMENT: | 5,200 |
| UNDERGRADUATE: | 2,800 |
| ACCEPTANCE RATE: | 61% |
| SAT AVERAGE: | 470–590 Verbal |
| | 450–550 Math |
| STICKER PRICE: | $23,000+ |
| NEED-BLIND: | Yes |
| NEED MET: | 78% |
| AVERAGE STUDENT DEBT: | $14,000 |
| MERIT SCHOLARSHIPS: | Many |
| ATHLETIC SCHOLARSHIPS: | No |
| ROTC: | No |
| WEB SITE: | www.schoolofvisualarts.edu |
| PHONE: | (212) 592-2100 |

Founded as The Cartoonists and Illustrators School in 1947, School of Visual Arts has needed only fifty years to become the largest independent college of art in the nation. Available majors include advertising and graphic design, art education, computer art, film and video animation, fine arts, illustration and cartooning, interior design, and photography. With five academic buildings and three dorms on the southern edge of Midtown Manhattan, SVA pioneered the use of working art professionals as faculty. Nearly two-thirds of the students hail from the New York City area. The Silas H. Rhodes Scholarships, named for SVA's founder, give an average of $6,500 to as many as ten incoming students in each department based on "meritorious achievement in art and academics." Students must apply by February 1. The Chairman's Merit Award recognizes top students who also demonstrate need, and the Scholastic Art Awards provide an average of $6,500 to students identified as scholarship nominees in the National Portfolio Competition with SVA as their first choice.

*Deadlines:*
   EARLY DECISION: Dec. 19
   REGULAR ADMISSION: Varies by program
   FAFSA: Rolling

# WABASH COLLEGE ◆ Crawfordsville, IN 47933

| | |
|---|---|
| TOTAL ENROLLMENT: | 800 |
| UNDERGRADUATE: | 800 |
| ACCEPTANCE RATE: | 77% |
| SAT AVERAGE: | 530–640 Verbal |
| | 540–680 Math |
| STICKER PRICE: | $22,000+ |
| NEED-BLIND: | Yes |
| NEED MET: | 100% |
| AVERAGE STUDENT DEBT: | $7,600 |
| MERIT SCHOLARSHIPS: | Many |
| RANGE: | Up to full costs |
| ATHLETIC SCHOLARSHIPS: | No |
| ROTC: | No |
| WEB SITE: | www.wabash.edu |
| PHONE: | (800) 345-5385 |

Since its founding in 1832, Wabash has had only one rule: "A Wabash man will conduct himself at all times, both on and off campus, as a gentleman and responsible citizen." That may seem a little old-fashioned, but it is the cornerstone of Wabash, one of the last remaining all-male institutions in the nation. Wabash ranks ninth among liberal arts colleges in the endowment per student ranking, a fact that may account for the unusually low debt of its financial aid recipients. The Lilly Fellowships cover full costs with a $1,000 travel stipend for up to ten outstanding students with superior personal qualities. An $11,000 Fine Arts Scholarship is offered in four areas, and Honor Scholarships worth $12,000 are up for grabs at an on-campus examination. President's Scholarships of $5,000–$10,000 go automatically to students who meet grade and test score cut-offs, with the lowest award requiring a rank in the top 20 percent and an SAT I of 1100 or an ACT of 24. Stipends of up to $10,000 are also available for leaders and outstanding minority students. The priority deadline for the President's Scholarships is December 1; other programs require an application by February 1.

*Deadlines:*
   EARLY DECISION: Nov. 1
   EARLY ACTION: Dec. 1
   REGULAR ADMISSION: Mar. 1
   FAFSA: Feb. 15
   CSS PROFILE: Feb. 15

# WAKE FOREST UNIVERSITY ✦
## Winston-Salem, NC 27109

| | |
|---|---|
| TOTAL ENROLLMENT: | 6,100 |
| UNDERGRADUATE: | 4,000 |
| ACCEPTANCE RATE: | 44% |
| SAT AVERAGE: | 600–690 Verbal |
| | 610–700 Math |
| STICKER PRICE: | $26,000+ |
| NEED-BLIND: | Yes |
| NEED MET: | 98% |
| AVERAGE STUDENT DEBT: | $14,100 |
| MERIT SCHOLARSHIPS: | Many |
| RANGE: | Up to full costs |
| ATHLETIC SCHOLARSHIPS: | Yes |
| ROTC: | Army |
| WEB SITE: | www.wfu.edu |
| PHONE: | (336) 758-5201 |

As the smallest of the South's leading private universities, Wake Forest puts undergraduates front and center. In 1996, Wake began implementation of a new Undergraduate Plan that has meant more faculty, smaller classes, a university-wide seminar for first-year students, dramatically expanded funding for study abroad and student research, and laptop computers for the entire student body. Though a tuition hike accompanied the initiative, Wake's sticker price remains significantly lower than those at Duke or Vanderbilt. The most lucrative prize for entering students is the Reynolds Scholarship, which covers the full costs of attendance for up to five outstanding students. The deadline is December 1. Other merit and merit-within-need awards of up to full tuition are available with various criteria. North Carolinians who show need and strong leadership skills can compete for a $2,600 award, and an $8,000 scholarship for in-state Baptists has a December 15 deadline. Scholarships are also available for the performing arts, debate, community service, and other activities. Most require a separate application.

*Deadlines:*
  EARLY DECISION: Nov. 15
  REGULAR ADMISSION: Jan. 15
  FAFSA: Apr. 15
  CSS PROFILE: Mar. 1

# WARREN WILSON COLLEGE ✦
## Asheville, NC 28815

| | |
|---|---|
| TOTAL ENROLLMENT: | 700 |
| UNDERGRADUATE: | 700 |
| ACCEPTANCE RATE: | 83% |
| SAT AVERAGE: | 540–630 Verbal |
| | 490–600 Math |
| STICKER PRICE: | $18,000+ |
| NEED-BLIND: | Yes |
| NEED MET: | 82% |
| AVERAGE STUDENT DEBT: | $16,800 |
| MERIT SCHOLARSHIPS: | Many |
| RANGE: | Up to $4,000 |
| ATHLETIC SCHOLARSHIPS: | No |
| ROTC: | No |
| WEB SITE: | www.warren-wilson.edu |
| PHONE: | (704) 298-3325 |

In the supermarket of higher education, look for Warren Wilson in the all-natural aisle. With a scenic location in North Carolina's western mountains, Warren Wilson is firmly committed to both the study and stewardship of the environment. But what sets it apart are two unique requirements: all students must work at least 15 hours per week in an on-campus job, and all must complete 100 hours of community service before graduation. In addition to its moderate sticker price, Warren Wilson offers students the prospect of earning approximately $2,500 in their campus jobs. A lone Wilson Honor Scholarship of $4,000 is the top merit award. Others include $3,000 for National Merit Finalists, $2,000 for valedictorians and salutatorians, and $1,000 for the first thirty admitted North Carolina residents who rank in the top 25 percent of their high school class with either 1050 on the SAT I or 24 on the ACT. Additional scholarships based on academic excellence, special work skills, and commitment to community service are available to students who apply for admission and submit the financial aid and scholarship application by February 28.

*Deadlines:*
  EARLY DECISION: Nov. 15
  REGULAR ADMISSION: Mar. 15
  FAFSA: Mar. 15

## WASHINGTON AND JEFFERSON COLLEGE ❖
## Washington, PA 15301

| | |
|---|---|
| TOTAL ENROLLMENT: | 1,100 |
| UNDERGRADUATE: | 1,100 |
| SELECTIVITY: | 83% |
| SAT AVERAGE: | 510–620 Verbal |
| | 520–620 Math |
| STICKER PRICE: | $23,000+ |
| NEED-BLIND: | Yes |
| NEED MET: | 100% |
| AVERAGE STUDENT DEBT: | $14,000 |
| MERIT SCHOLARSHIPS: | Many |
| RANGE: | Up to full tuition |
| ATHLETIC SCHOLARSHIPS: | No |
| ROTC: | Army |
| WEB SITE: | www.washjeff.edu |
| PHONE: | (412) 223-6025 |

Hidden away in western Pennsylvania about twenty-five miles south of Pittsburgh, Washington and Jefferson gets its name from the merger of two small colleges in the wake of the Civil War. Business administration and biology rank first and second among the largest majors, and the popularity of the latter is indicative of the high percentage of students who pursue careers in the health professions. Five outstanding students who emerge successfully from an on-campus evaluation get full-tuition scholarships, and others with a high school class rank in the top 10 percent and an SAT I of 1200 or an ACT of 27 are awarded $10,000. Those with scores of at least 1000 or 23 and a top 10 percent rank are considered for an $8,000 scholarship. Sons and daughters of alumni are eligible for a $5,000 stipend, and the $3,000 Dean's Award is based on "academic performance, achievement outside the classroom, and citizenship." The Eagle Scholarship is reserved for students enrolling in the Entrepreneurial Studies program and varies depending on need. About a third of the entering students receive a non-need award.

*Deadlines:*
   EARLY DECISION: Nov. 1
   REGULAR ADMISSION: Mar. 1
   FAFSA: Mar. 15

## WASHINGTON AND LEE UNIVERSITY ❖
## Lexington, VA 24450

| | |
|---|---|
| TOTAL ENROLLMENT: | 2,100 |
| UNDERGRADUATE: | 1,700 |
| ACCEPTANCE RATE: | 31% |
| SAT AVERAGE: | 630–710 Verbal |
| | 620–700 Math |
| STICKER PRICE: | $24,000+ |
| NEED-BLIND: | Yes |
| NEED MET: | 97% |
| AVERAGE STUDENT DEBT: | $14,000 |
| MERIT SCHOLARSHIPS: | Many |
| RANGE: | Up to full tuition |
| ATHLETIC SCHOLARSHIPS: | No |
| ROTC: | Army |
| WEB SITE: | www.wlu.edu |
| PHONE: | (540) 463-8710 |

Generations of Southerners have heard the story of how Robert E. Lee came back from the Civil War to live out his days as president of what is now Washington and Lee. One hundred and thirty years later, the general is still talked about as if he just went out for a ride on Traveler and will return presently. On a campus steeped in tradition, history is the most popular major, and the university is also strong in the disciplines of its School of Commerce, Economics, and Politics. W&L's popularity has soared since it went coed in 1985 (women now make up 43 percent of the students), and today the university is the southeast's most selective liberal arts college. Though W&L wears its Southern identity on its sleeve, the university has always attracted plenty of Yankees, too. W&L offers several dozen merit awards of up to full tuition each year via its Honor Scholarship program. Many are based on all-around excellence; others include stipulations related to place of residence or intended major. A special application is required by December 15. National Merit Finalists get a minimum of $750 and more if they show need.

*Deadlines:*
   EARLY DECISION: Dec. 1
   REGULAR ADMISSION: Jan. 15
   FAFSA: Feb. 1
   CSS PROFILE: Feb. 1

## WASHINGTON UNIVERSITY IN ST. LOUIS ◆ St. Louis, MO 63130

| | |
|---|---|
| TOTAL ENROLLMENT: | 11,600 |
| UNDERGRADUATE: | 6,100 |
| ACCEPTANCE RATE: | 40% |
| SAT AVERAGE: | 590–680 Verbal |
| | 620–710 Math |
| STICKER PRICE: | $30,000+ |
| NEED-BLIND: | No |
| NEED MET: | 100% |
| AVERAGE STUDENT DEBT: | NA |
| MERIT SCHOLARSHIPS: | Many |
| RANGE: | Up to full tuition, plus $2,500 |
| ATHLETIC SCHOLARSHIPS: | No |
| ROTC: | Army, Air Force |
| WEB SITE: | www.wustl.edu |
| PHONE: | (800) 638-0700 |

If Northwestern is the Duke of the Midwest, Washington U qualifies as the Emory of the region. (Then again, maybe Emory is the Wash U of the South.) Like the other three, Washington U is a midsized private institution that has surged in popularity on the strength of its reputation in fields such as pre-med, business, engineering, and the arts. With an endowment per student in the top ten among major universities, Wash U has plenty of financial firepower. Approximately thirty awards worth at least full tuition are available through nine separate programs for students who plan to study science and math, social sciences, humanities, music, writing, architecture, art, business, and engineering. An additional award of full tuition plus a $2,500 stipend is reserved for outstanding black students. The colleges of engineering and arts and sciences also give about twenty-five half-tuition scholarships apiece, and the latter has a scholarship that pays for a campus summer program in biology and biomedical research. All programs except the School of Art's full tuition award require a separate application.

*Deadlines:*
  EARLY DECISION: Nov. 15, Jan. 1
  REGULAR ADMISSION: Jan. 15
  FAFSA: Feb. 15
  CSS PROFILE: Feb. 15

## WEBB INSTITUTE ◆ Glen Cove, NY 11542

| | |
|---|---|
| TOTAL ENROLLMENT: | 90 |
| UNDERGRADUATE: | 90 |
| ACCEPTANCE RATE: | 48% |
| SAT AVERAGE: | 620–730 Verbal |
| | 680–720 Math |
| STICKER PRICE: | $6,000+ |
| NEED-BLIND: | Yes |
| NEED MET: | 58% |
| AVERAGE STUDENT DEBT: | $4,000 |
| MERIT SCHOLARSHIPS: | Full tuition for all students |
| ATHLETIC SCHOLARSHIPS: | No |
| ROTC: | No |
| WEB SITE: | www.webb-institute.edu |
| PHONE: | (516) 671-2213 |

Not many schools can guarantee graduates a job after graduation, but Webb Institute does it without thinking twice. If that sounds like a good deal, get this: Webb students pay no tuition, and they live and learn on a picturesque former estate on the north shore of Long Island. With a total of only 90 handpicked students, Webb is the only institution in the nation devoted solely to naval architecture and marine engineering (known in less fastidious circles as ship building). In addition to excellent academics, Webb offers an exceptionally strong sense of community accentuated by an honor code. Founded by a nineteenth-century shipping magnate, Webb has the highest endowment per student of any institution in the nation except Princeton. Along with the tuition waiver, students have a chance to generate income via the school's Winter Work Term, a two-month period during which students take paid internships in various aspects of the shipping industry. A personal interview is part of the process of applying for admission, and Webb's standardized test requirement includes three SAT II Subject Tests (writing, math, and chemistry or physics).

*Deadlines:*
  EARLY DECISION: Oct. 15
  REGULAR ADMISSION: Feb. 15
  FAFSA: Rolling

# WELLESLEY COLLEGE ✦ Wellesley, MA 02181

| | |
|---|---|
| TOTAL ENROLLMENT: | 2,300 |
| UNDERGRADUATE: | 2,300 |
| ACCEPTANCE RATE: | 43% |
| SAT AVERAGE: | 630–720 Verbal |
| | 620–700 Math |
| STICKER PRICE: | $30,000+ |
| NEED-BLIND: | Yes |
| NEED MET: | 100% |
| AVERAGE STUDENT DEBT: | $15,500 |
| MERIT SCHOLARSHIPS: | None |
| ATHLETIC SCHOLARSHIPS: | No |
| ROTC: | Army, Air Force |
| WEB SITE: | www.wellesley.edu |
| PHONE: | (781) 283-2270 |

There may be a more beautiful campus than Wellesley's, but not on this planet. And if a typical prospective student were to pick the perfect location for a college, suburban Boston would be a prime choice. The campus, the location, and a well-deserved reputation for academic excellence are all part of what makes Wellesley the nation's most selective women's college. Wellesley women are a more traditional group than their counterparts at Barnard, Bryn Mawr, and Smith—witness the fact that economics is the most popular major on campus. Wellesley's reputation is particularly strong among Asian Americans, who account for nearly a quarter of the student body. African Americans and Hispanics both comprised 7 percent of the entering freshmen in a recent year. Wellesley's endowment per student ranks near the top of the charts, and the college continues to be need-blind in admissions while meeting the full need of all accepted applicants. (There are no merit scholarships.) The college reports that aid is available for waitlisted candidates "more often than not."

*Deadlines:*
   EARLY DECISION: Nov. 1
   REGULAR DECISION: Jan. 15
   FAFSA: Feb. 1
   CSS PROFILE: Feb. 1

# WELLS COLLEGE ✦ Aurora, NY 13026

| | |
|---|---|
| TOTAL ENROLLMENT: | 300 |
| UNDERGRADUATE: | 300 |
| ACCEPTANCE RATE: | 84% |
| SAT AVERAGE: | 540–640 Verbal |
| | 500–610 Math |
| STICKER PRICE: | $18,000+ |
| NEED-BLIND: | Yes |
| NEED MET: | 92% |
| AVERAGE STUDENT DEBT: | $17,100 |
| MERIT SCHOLARSHIPS: | Few |
| RANGE: | Up to $10,000 |
| ATHLETIC SCHOLARSHIPS: | No |
| ROTC: | Air Force |
| WEB SITE: | www.wells.edu |
| PHONE: | (800) 952-9355 |

There is finally some good news in the tuition wars courtesy of Wells College, which recently decided to slice more than $5,000 off its sticker price. After charging $17,540 for tuition in 1998–1999, the figure for 1999–2000 is only $12,300. Such innovation is typical of Wells, a women's college in the Finger Lakes region of upstate New York that emphasizes small classes, collaborative learning, and internships. Entering students enroll in an interdisciplinary Twenty-First Century Issues class that covers everything from quantitative methods to multicultural sensitivity, and a Leadership Week at the beginning of the second semester offers the chance to build skills in a conference-style format. A handful of merit awards include the Reiche Legacy Scholarships, which offer $10,000 to daughters and granddaughters of Wells alumni. Every admitted student with an academic average of 90 and a score of 1150 on the SAT I or 28 on the ACT is designated a Henry Wells Scholar and guaranteed two internships or comparable experiences and a stipend of $3,000.

*Deadlines:*
   EARLY ACTION: Dec. 15
   EARLY DECISION: Dec. 15
   REGULAR ADMISSION: Feb. 15
   FAFSA: Feb. 15
   CSS PROFILE: Feb. 15

# WESLEYAN UNIVERSITY ✦
## Middletown, CT 06459

| | |
|---|---|
| TOTAL ENROLLMENT: | 3,300 |
| UNDERGRADUATE: | 2,800 |
| ACCEPTANCE RATE: | 33% |
| SAT AVERAGE: | 620–720 Verbal |
| | 620–710 Math |
| STICKER PRICE: | $31,000+ |
| NEED-BLIND: | Yes |
| NEED MET: | 100% |
| AVERAGE STUDENT DEBT: | $17,000 |
| MERIT SCHOLARSHIPS: | None |
| ATHLETIC SCHOLARSHIPS: | No |
| ROTC: | Army, Navy, Air Force |
| WEB SITE: | www.wesleyan.edu |
| PHONE: | (860) 685-3000 |

When administrators at Wesleyan University decided to dub it "the Independent Ivy," the plan hit a snag. Wesleyan students are an independent-minded group, and many rose up to protest the idea of defining the university in terms of its Ivy League competitors. The Independent Un-Ivy would probably be a better name for Wesleyan, a school that stands out among the nation's elite for its historic commitment to diversity and free thinking. Technically a university because of a few small graduate programs (including a novel specialty in ethnomusicology), Wesleyan is actually a plus-sized small college. Bigger than either Amherst or Williams, Wesleyan is also the most progressive of the three. English ranks as Wesleyan's most popular major, followed by government and economics. Though Wesleyan's pockets are not as deep as some of its peers, it has maintained a need-blind/meet-full-need policy. There are no merit scholarships for domestic students, but Wesleyan does give twenty Freeman Asian Scholarships that cover full costs to students from ten Asian countries.

*Deadlines:*
> EARLY DECISION: Nov. 15, Jan. 1
> REGULAR ADMISSION: Jan. 1
> FAFSA: Feb. 1
> CSS PROFILE: Feb. 1

# WEST VIRGINIA UNIVERSITY ✦
## Morgantown, WV 26506

| | |
|---|---|
| TOTAL ENROLLMENT: | 22,200 |
| UNDERGRADUATE: | 15,000 |
| ACCEPTANCE RATE: | 89% |
| SAT AVERAGE: | 470–560 Verbal |
| | 470–570 Math |
| STICKER PRICE: | In-state, $8,000+ |
| | Out-of-state, $13,000+ |
| NEED-BLIND: | Yes |
| NEED MET: | 72% |
| AVERAGE STUDENT DEBT: | $12,100 |
| MERIT SCHOLARSHIPS: | Many |
| RANGE: | Up to full costs |
| ATHLETIC SCHOLARSHIPS: | Yes |
| ROTC: | Army, Air Force |
| WEB SITE: | www.wvu.edu |
| PHONE: | (800) 344-WVU1 |

WVU is the only major university in the Mountaineer State and offers a complete line of undergraduate programs in fourteen colleges and schools. Business administration and journalism are two of the most popular majors, and WVU also excels in engineering and health-related fields. WVU's vast merit scholarship program begins with the Foundation Scholarship, which covers full costs and provides an additional $2,000 stipend for five outstanding in-staters. Minimums include a 3.8 GPA and an SAT I score of 1320 or 30 on the ACT. Twelve runners-up get awards nearly as rich, and 125 more full-tuition scholarships with the same criteria are open to in-staters and out-of-staters alike. Five hundred $1,000 awards go to students with at least a 3.0 and scores of 1010 or 22, and 400 more one-time $1,000 awards are given to students who demonstrate leadership. Other awards honor African Americans, valedictorians, National Merit Finalists, and students who attended the Governor's Honors Academy. February 15 is the scholarship application deadline, although awards are made on a rolling basis beginning October 15.

*Deadlines:*
> ADMISSION: Mar. 1 (priority)
> FAFSA: Feb. 15

# WHEATON COLLEGE ✦ Wheaton, IL 60187

| | |
|---|---|
| TOTAL ENROLLMENT: | 2,700 |
| UNDERGRADUATE: | 2,300 |
| ACCEPTANCE RATE: | 55% |
| SAT AVERAGE: | 600–710 Verbal |
| | 600–700 Math |
| STICKER PRICE: | $20,000+ |
| NEED-BLIND: | Yes |
| NEED MET: | 85% |
| AVERAGE STUDENT DEBT: | $18,800 |
| MERIT SCHOLARSHIPS: | Many |
| RANGE: | Up to $2,500 |
| ATHLETIC SCHOLARSHIPS: | No |
| ROTC: | Army |
| WEB SITE: | www.wheaton.edu |
| PHONE: | (800) 222-2419 |

Many colleges in the United States were founded by evangelical Christians, but Wheaton is among the few that has stayed the course. As the most prestigious of the nation's Christ-centered schools, Wheaton requires applicants to show both strong academic credentials and a Christian commitment. The college's popularity has increased in recent years with its growing reputation for traditional academics at a reasonable price. Along with the liberal arts, Wheaton features a conservatory of music and religion-oriented majors such as fine arts ministries and Christian education. About 125 freshmen receive the President's Award, which offers $1,000 to students with a minimum GPA of 3.6 and an SAT I of 1400 or an ACT of 32. National Merit Finalists take home up to $2,000, and a Special Achievement Award in Music tops out at $2,500. Minority students with a 3.5 GPA and 1150 or 25 are eligible for the $2,500 Burr Scholarship, though a special application must be filed by March 1. National Hispanic Scholar and National Achievement honorees also qualify for up to $2,000.

*Deadlines:*
   EARLY ACTION: Nov. 1
   REGULAR ADMISSION: Jan. 15
   FAFSA: Feb. 15

# WHEATON COLLEGE ✦ Norton, MA 02766

| | |
|---|---|
| TOTAL ENROLLMENT: | 1,500 |
| UNDERGRADUATE: | 1,500 |
| ACCEPTANCE RATE: | 74% |
| SAT AVERAGE: | 560–650 Verbal |
| | 520–630 Math |
| STICKER PRICE: | $29,000+ |
| NEED-BLIND: | Yes |
| NEED MET: | 94% |
| AVERAGE STUDENT DEBT: | $15,300 |
| MERIT SCHOLARSHIPS: | Few |
| RANGE: | Up to $7,000 |
| ATHLETIC SCHOLARSHIPS: | No |
| ROTC: | No |
| WEB SITE: | www.wheatonma.edu |
| PHONE: | (800) 394-6003 |

Formerly a cousin to the Seven Sisters, Wheaton recently celebrated its tenth anniversary of coeducation after 122 years as an all-female institution. Men now comprise a third of the student body as Wheaton follows the path of Skidmore, Vassar, and Connecticut College toward successful coeducation. Wheaton's proximity to Boston (forty-five minutes away) is a major selling point, and the college's Center for Work and Learning finds opportunities for students that include internships, community service, and opportunities jobs. The Balfour Scholars program rewards the college's strongest applicants with a $7,000 scholarship, a personal computer, and a one-time $400 textbook voucher. The Trustee Scholars program offers a $6,000 award and a one-time $4,000 stipend for research or other projects during the sophomore and junior years. The Community Scholars program recognizes a combination of academic achievement and service with a $5,000 scholarship and a one-time $3,000 allowance for summer service work. No separate scholarship application is required.

*Deadlines:*
   EARLY DECISION: Nov. 15
   EARLY ACTION: Dec. 15
   REGULAR ADMISSION: Feb. 1
   FAFSA: Feb. 1
   CSS PROFILE: Feb. 1

# WHITMAN COLLEGE ✦ Walla Walla, WA 99362

| | |
|---|---|
| TOTAL ENROLLMENT: | 1,400 |
| UNDERGRADUATE: | 1,400 |
| ACCEPTANCE RATE: | 51% |
| SAT AVERAGE: | 590–690 Verbal |
| | 580–680 Math |
| STICKER PRICE: | $26,000+ |
| NEED-BLIND: | Yes |
| NEED MET: | 89% |
| AVERAGE STUDENT DEBT: | $13,900 |
| MERIT SCHOLARSHIPS: | Many |
| RANGE: | Up to full costs |
| ATHLETIC SCHOLARSHIPS: | No |
| ROTC: | No |
| WEB SITE: | www.whitman.edu |
| PHONE: | (509) 527-5176 |

Whitman College is named for a husband-and-wife team of frontier missionaries who met an untimely death on the Oregon Trail in the 1840s. The natural beauty of southeastern Washington remains awe-inspiring 150 years later, and the college offers easy access to backpacking, skiing, rock-climbing, and whitewater rafting, to name a few. Whitman is known for its unusually loyal alumni, and rising applications in the 1990s have made the college much more selective. The Eells Scholarship covers full tuition and fees along with a research stipend for one top entering student, and three other programs provide funding up to the full cost of attendance for students with need and give a $2,500 stipend to those without need. Whitman Merit Scholarships offer up to $7,500 based on all-around excellence. The $6,000 Higley Scholarship goes to an outstanding musician. Other awards are available for leadership ($2,000), diversity (variable), music (up to $2,000), and Hugh O'Brien Youth Ambassadors ($1,500). Scholarships are also earmarked for residents of Washington and Idaho.

*Deadlines:*
  EARLY DECISION: Nov. 15, Jan. 15
  REGULAR DECISION: Feb. 1
  FAFSA: Feb. 1
  CSS PROFILE: Feb. 1

# WHITTIER COLLEGE ✦ Whittier, CA 90608

| | |
|---|---|
| TOTAL ENROLLMENT: | 2,100 |
| UNDERGRADUATE: | 1,300 |
| ACCEPTANCE RATE: | 87% |
| SAT AVERAGE: | 460–590 Verbal |
| | 450–590 Math |
| STICKER PRICE: | $26,000+ |
| NEED-BLIND: | Yes |
| NEED MET: | 91% |
| AVERAGE STUDENT DEBT: | $21,600 |
| MERIT SCHOLARSHIPS: | Many |
| RANGE: | Up to full tuition |
| ATHLETIC SCHOLARSHIPS: | No |
| ROTC: | Army, Air Force |
| WEB SITE: | www.whittier.edu |
| PHONE: | (562) 907-4238 |

The streets bordering Whittier's campus have names like Bryn Mawr Way, Penn Street, Earlham Drive, and Guilford Way. Got the pattern? You don't need to be John Greenleaf Whittier to figure out that Whittier College was founded by transplanted Quakers who wanted to bring Eastern-style liberal arts education to the West Coast. The Quaker legacy lives on in the close interaction between students and faculty, and in the college's commitment to diversity, community service and respect for the individual. Though liberal arts is the primary fare, business administration tops the list of most popular majors. Students with a 3.5 GPA and a score of 1200 on the SAT I or 27 on the ACT can compete for John Greenleaf Whittier Scholarships of up to full tuition. Contestants are chosen from among those who apply for admission by October 15. Academic merit scholarships range from $2,000 to full tuition, and sons and daughters of alumni get a $1,000 discount. Talent Scholarships of $5,000 to $10,000 per year are also available in art, music, and theater arts.

*Priority Deadlines:*
  EARLY ACTION: Dec. 1
  REGULAR ADMISSION: Feb. 1
  FAFSA: Feb. 15
  CSS PROFILE: Feb. 1

# WILLAMETTE UNIVERSITY ✦
## Salem, OR 97301

| | |
|---|---|
| TOTAL ENROLLMENT: | 2,500 |
| UNDERGRADUATE: | 1,700 |
| ACCEPTANCE RATE: | 81% |
| SAT AVERAGE: | 560–670 Verbal |
| | 570–670 Math |
| STICKER PRICE: | $27,000+ |
| NEED-BLIND: | Yes |
| NEED MET: | 84% |
| AVERAGE STUDENT DEBT: | $16,600 |
| MERIT SCHOLARSHIPS: | Many |
| RANGE: | Up to full tuition |
| ATHLETIC SCHOLARSHIPS: | No |
| ROTC: | Air Force |
| WEB SITE: | www.willamette.edu |
| PHONE: | (503) 370-6303 |

Willamette is a small university in Oregon's capital city with undergraduate programs in the liberal arts and graduate schools of business, education, and law. It also offers something not found every day: an adjacent branch campus of a Japanese institution, Tokyo International University, with which Willamette has had a coordinate relationship for more than thirty years. (Exchange opportunities are available on both sides of the Pacific.) Economics, politics, and psychology rank as Willamette's most popular majors. About 18 percent of the students receive a merit award, including twenty-five Smith Scholarships of up to full tuition for students who generally have a 3.8 GPA, an SAT I score of 1350 or an ACT of 30, and show strength in leadership and community service. Goudy Scholarships worth $10,000 go to students with minimums of 3.7 and 1300 or 29. Awards of up to full tuition are available for honorees in the National Merit Scholarship Corporation's various programs. Multicultural awards are valued at up to $5,000, as are nearly forty Talent Scholarships in music, forensics, and theater.

*Deadlines:*
   EARLY DECISION: Nov. 1
   REGULAR ADMISSION: Feb. 1
   FAFSA: Feb. 1
   CSS PROFILE: Feb. 1

# COLLEGE OF WILLIAM AND MARY ✦
## Williamsburg, VA 23187

| | |
|---|---|
| TOTAL ENROLLMENT: | 7,600 |
| UNDERGRADUATE: | 5,600 |
| ACCEPTANCE RATE: | 46% |
| SAT AVERAGE: | 600–710 Verbal |
| | 590–680 Math |
| STICKER PRICE: | In-state, $10,000+ |
| | Out-of-state, $21,000+ |
| NEED-BLIND: | Yes |
| NEED MET: | 80% |
| AVERAGE STUDENT DEBT: | NA |
| MERIT SCHOLARSHIPS: | Few |
| RANGE: | Up to full costs |
| ATHLETIC SCHOLARSHIPS: | Yes |
| ROTC: | Army |
| WEB SITE: | www.wm.edu |
| PHONE: | (757) 221-4223 |

If William and Mary seldom makes the list of outstanding public universities, it is only because everybody thinks it is a private college. Set on 1,200 acres next door to Colonial Williamsburg, William and Mary is the second-oldest institution of higher learning in the nation and the place that invented the Phi Beta Kappa honor society. Though still known as a "college," William and Mary is actually a medium-sized university with programs in arts and sciences, business, and education. Just over 60 percent of the places in each class are reserved for Virginians. The school offers few merit scholarships, but 10 percent of each entering class is designated as Monroe Scholars, giving them access to special programs and a $2,000 summer enrichment stipend. About twenty-five students receive the William and Mary Scholars Award, which ranges up to full costs and is offered for a combination of academic excellence and financial need, or to those who have overcome adversity or will enhance campus diversity. Early decision applicants must file the CSS PROFILE.

*Deadlines:*
   EARLY DECISION: Nov. 1
   REGULAR ADMISSION: Jan. 15
   FAFSA: Feb. 15

# WILLIAMS COLLEGE ◆
## Williamstown, MA 01267

| | |
|---|---|
| TOTAL ENROLLMENT: | 2,100 |
| UNDERGRADUATE: | 2,100 |
| ACCEPTANCE RATE: | 26% |
| SAT AVERAGE: | 650–770 Verbal |
| | 660–750 Math |
| STICKER PRICE: | $31,000+ |
| NEED-BLIND: | Yes |
| NEED MET: | 100% |
| AVERAGE STUDENT DEBT: | $14,200 |
| MERIT SCHOLARSHIPS: | None |
| ATHLETIC SCHOLARSHIPS: | No |
| ROTC: | No |
| WEB SITE: | www.williams.edu |
| PHONE: | (413) 597-2211 |

Nathaniel Hawthorne once described Williams students as "unpolished bumpkins who had grown up as farmer boys." The college has tightened its admissions standards since then, and today Williams ranks as one of the premier small colleges in the nation. Williams was founded when western Massachusetts was a wilderness, and though some people still think Williams is isolated, it is certainly a splendid isolation in the beauty of the Berkshire Mountains. History, biology, and English are the three most popular majors at Williams, and the art and art history programs are bolstered by one of the best college art galleries in the nation. Williams students also have a reputation for athletic prowess, and about half play intercollegiate sports. With an endowment per student that ranks in the nation's top twenty, Williams has the deep pockets one would expect from a college of its stature. In addition to meeting the full need of all admitted applicants, Williams has two named merit-within-need scholarship programs that reward all-around excellence and outstanding minority students.

*Deadlines:*
EARLY DECISION: Nov. 15
REGULAR ADMISSION: Jan. 1
FAFSA: Feb. 1
CSS PROFILE: Feb. 1

# UNIVERSITY OF WISCONSIN ◆
## Madison, WI 53706

| | |
|---|---|
| TOTAL ENROLLMENT: | 40,200 |
| UNDERGRADUATE: | 29,500 |
| ACCEPTANCE RATE: | 77% |
| SAT AVERAGE: | 520–650 Verbal |
| | 550–670 Math |
| STICKER PRICE: | In-state, $9,000+ |
| | Out-of-state, $17,000+ |
| NEED-BLIND: | Yes |
| NEED MET: | NA |
| AVERAGE STUDENT DEBT: | $15,800 |
| MERIT SCHOLARSHIPS: | Many |
| ATHLETIC SCHOLARSHIPS: | Yes |
| ROTC: | Army, Navy, Air Force |
| WEB SITE: | www.wisc.edu |
| PHONE: | (608) 262-3961 |

The University of Wisconsin describes itself as a city within a city, and the sheer size of the place accounts for much of its allure. Nevertheless, UW is at its best with small programs that break down the university into manageable units. Savvy students should consider the Bradley Learning Center and the Chadbourne Residential College, two living/learning options that provide a sense of community amid the multitudes. Two university-wide scholarship programs offer one-time awards of up to $2,000 to 200 Wisconsin residents based on a formula of grades and test scores. The Chancellor's Scholarship program recognizes the achievements of underrepresented minorities, and National Merit Finalists are eligible for up to $2,000, depending on need. But the vast majority of UW's scholarships are awarded by the academic divisions. Students should contact the particular colleges directly for more information. Deadlines can come as early as December 15, and some scholarships require a separate application. Four divisions—agriculture, engineering, music, and arts and letters—offer awards for out-of-state freshmen. Additional scholarships are available through the university's alumni clubs.

*Deadlines:*
ADMISSION: Feb. 1
FAFSA: Mar. 1

# WITTENBERG UNIVERSITY ✦ Springfield, OH 45501

| | |
|---|---|
| TOTAL ENROLLMENT: | 2,000 |
| UNDERGRADUATE: | 2,000 |
| ACCEPTANCE RATE: | 88% |
| SAT AVERAGE: | 560–640 Verbal |
| | 555–630 Math |
| STICKER PRICE: | $25,000+ |
| NEED-BLIND: | Yes |
| NEED MET: | NA |
| AVERAGE STUDENT DEBT: | $14,000 |
| MERIT SCHOLARSHIPS: | Many |
| RANGE: | Up to full tuition |
| ATHLETIC SCHOLARSHIPS: | No |
| ROTC: | Army, Air Force |
| WEB SITE: | www.wittenberg.edu |
| PHONE: | (800) 677-7558 |

Wittenberg quotes a parent as saying, "If we were this friendly in New York City, we'd be arrested." An extra helping of Midwestern charm is what you'll get at Wittenberg, a college noted for its strong sense of community and close relationships between students and faculty. Business administration is first on the list of most popular majors, followed by biology and education. Witt's substantial merit program is headlined by the Distinguished Faculty Scholar Award, which offers full tuition based on all-around achievement. A half-tuition scholarship targets African American students, and an award of up to $8,000 is aimed at underrepresented minorities. A Community Service Award includes an $8,500 scholarship and a $1,500 employment stipend (and also requires a separate application). Variable awards are available for students in the arts, and other scholarships recognize citizenship (up to $7,500), children and grandchildren of alumni ($5,000), and Hugh O'Brien Youth Ambassadors (up to $7,500). Students should apply by February 15 for full scholarship consideration.

*Deadlines:*
  EARLY DECISION: Nov. 15
  REGULAR ADMISSION: Mar. 15
  FAFSA: Mar. 15

# WOFFORD COLLEGE ✦ Spartanburg, SC 29303

| | |
|---|---|
| TOTAL ENROLLMENT: | 1,100 |
| UNDERGRADUATE: | 1,100 |
| ACCEPTANCE RATE: | 82% |
| SAT AVERAGE: | 550–640 Verbal |
| | 530–600 Math |
| STICKER PRICE: | $21,000+ |
| NEED-BLIND: | Yes |
| NEED MET: | NA |
| AVERAGE STUDENT DEBT: | $15,000 |
| MERIT SCHOLARSHIPS: | Many |
| RANGE: | Up to full costs |
| ATHLETIC SCHOLARSHIPS: | Yes |
| ROTC: | Army |
| WEB SITE: | www.wofford.edu |
| PHONE: | (864) 597-4130 |

Located in the South Carolina foothills of the Appalachian Mountains, Wofford has educated generations of students beneath the twin towers of its venerable Old Main Building. Business economics is Wofford's most popular major, and the college is a national leader in the number of students who earn academic credit abroad. The scholarship process at Wofford begins when high school counselors are solicited for nominations. The nominees who apply for admission by December 1 are eligible for the Wofford Scholars Program, with scholarships ranging up to full costs. In addition to awards based on general excellence, there are scholarships for students pursuing a health-related field, those planning a career in economics and business, and those who show leadership and service. Separate programs offer awards of up to $10,000 based on various criteria, and $1,000 grants are available for children of Methodist ministers and those who plan to be ministers themselves. Twenty students active in community service get up to $3,700 through the national Bonner Scholars Program.

*Deadlines:*
  EARLY DECISION: Nov. 15
  EARLY ACTION: Dec. 1
  REGULAR ADMISSION: Feb. 1
  FAFSA: Mar. 15
  CSS PROFILE: Mar. 15

# COLLEGE OF WOOSTER • Wooster, OH 44691

| | |
|---|---|
| TOTAL ENROLLMENT: | 1,700 |
| UNDERGRADUATE: | 1,700 |
| ACCEPTANCE RATE: | 86% |
| SAT AVERAGE: | 540–660 Verbal |
| | 520–650 Math |
| STICKER PRICE: | $26,000+ |
| NEED-BLIND: | Yes |
| NEED MET: | 93% |
| AVERAGE STUDENT DEBT: | $14,500 |
| MERIT SCHOLARSHIPS: | Many |
| RANGE: | Up to $16,000 |
| ATHLETIC SCHOLARSHIPS: | No |
| ROTC: | No |
| WEB SITE: | www.wooster.edu |
| PHONE: | (800) 877-9905 |

Wooster is one of the few institutions that began as a university and then decided to ditch its graduate programs to focus on undergraduates. Though not as selective as its quality would merit, Wooster takes good students and gives them the tools to become outstanding ones. Highly respected in academic circles and well-known abroad, Wooster caps its program with a three-term Independent Study that gives students a taste of graduate-level work. Wooster gives away scholarships of up to $16,000 via the College Scholar competition held on-campus in January and February. Students must have a 3.4 GPA and score 1270 on the SAT I (or 670 on the verbal portion) or earn a 28 on the ACT. A similar program rewards African Americans, and the Compton Scholarship offers up to $14,000 for all-around excellence and requires a separate application. A $10,000 scholarship targets history and English majors, Presbyterians can qualify for $8,000, and Wooster's $6,000 performing arts scholarships include awards for its famed Scot Marching Band. Those seeking scholarships should apply for admission by January 15.

*Deadines:*
   EARLY DECISION: Dec. 1, Jan. 15
   REGULAR ADMISSION: Feb. 15
   FAFSA: Feb. 15
   CSS PROFILE: Feb. 15

# WORCESTER POLYTECHNIC INSTITUTE • Worcester, MA 01609

| | |
|---|---|
| TOTAL ENROLLMENT: | 3,800 |
| UNDERGRADUATE: | 2,700 |
| ACCEPTANCE RATE: | 78% |
| SAT AVERAGE: | 570–670 Verbal |
| | 610–710 Math |
| STICKER PRICE: | $28,000+ |
| NEED-BLIND: | Yes |
| NEED MET: | 89% |
| AVERAGE STUDENT DEBT: | $17,800 |
| MERIT SCHOLARSHIPS: | Many |
| RANGE: | Up to full tuition |
| ATHLETIC SCHOLARSHIPS: | No |
| ROTC: | Army, Navy, Air Force |
| WEB SITE: | www.wpi.edu |
| PHONE: | (508) 831-5286 |

With a hands-on curriculum and touch of self-effacing humor, WPI does its best to smash the prevailing stereotypes about technical institutes. Undergraduates outnumber graduate students by nearly 4 to 1, and unlike some of its well-known brethren, WPI puts at least as much emphasis on teaching as research. A unique project-based curriculum lets students build, tinker, and make connections instead of consigning them to the back of a lecture hall. WPI offers over 200 academic scholarships to entering freshmen, including 10 Trustees' Scholarships worth full tuition, 60 Presidential Scholarships of $10,000 apiece, and 125 Dean's Scholarships that carry a $5,000 stipend. Eligible students generally rank in the top 5 percent of their high school class (or have a GPA of 3.5 at schools that don't rank) and bring scores of at least 1350 on the SAT I or 30 on the ACT. National Merit Finalists get an automatic $10,000 if they name WPI as their first choice. Thirty students enrolling in WPI's Medical Professions Scholars or Chemistry and Biochemistry Scholars Programs receive $5,000.

*Deadlines:*
   EARLY DECISION: Dec. 1
   REGULAR ADMISSION: Feb. 15
   FAFSA: Mar. 1
   CSS PROFILE: Mar. 1

# YALE UNIVERSITY ✦ New Haven, CT 06520

| | |
|---|---|
| TOTAL ENROLLMENT: | 11,100 |
| UNDERGRADUATE: | 5,400 |
| ACCEPTANCE RATE: | 18% |
| SAT AVERAGE: | 670–770 Verbal |
| | 670–760 Math |
| STICKER PRICE: | $31,000+ |
| NEED-BLIND: | Yes |
| NEED MET: | 100% |
| AVERAGE STUDENT DEBT: | $15,700 |
| MERIT SCHOLARSHIPS: | None |
| ATHLETIC SCHOLARSHIPS: | No |
| ROTC: | Army, Air Force |
| WEB SITE: | www.yale.edu |
| PHONE: | (203) 432-9300 |

Yale was founded by religious leaders intent on showing Harvard the error of its decadent ways, a task that has taken the better part of 300 years. With Harvard's unquestioned supremacy as a research institution, Yale aims to be the place where undergraduates are front and center. Its residential college system, which divides the student body into twelve intimate living/learning units, has been copied far and wide. Yale's greatest fame is in the arts and humanities, but biology is the most popular major. Yale's location in the city center of New Haven is a turn-off, though the city provides a ready outlet for student activism and community service. Yale weathered some belt-tightening in the 1990s but retains the fourth-largest endowment per student among major universities behind Princeton, Harvard, and Rice. The university recently adjusted its need-based aid formula to exempt up to $150,000 in parental assets (including home equity) from the aid equation. It is also more lenient in its expectations for income from summer work to allow students to take low-paying internships or study abroad.

*Deadlines:*
  EARLY DECISION: Nov. 1
  REGULAR ADMISSION: Dec. 31
  FAFSA: Feb. 1
  CSS PROFILE: Feb. 1

# YESHIVA UNIVERSITY ✦ New York, NY 10033

| | |
|---|---|
| TOTAL ENROLLMENT: | 5,300 |
| UNDERGRADUATE: | 2,300 |
| ACCEPTANCE RATE: | 84% |
| SAT AVERAGE: | 557 Verbal |
| | 634 Math |
| STICKER PRICE: | $22,000+ |
| NEED-BLIND: | Yes |
| NEED MET: | NA |
| AVERAGE STUDENT DEBT: | $26,100 |
| MERIT SCHOLARSHIPS: | Many |
| RANGE: | Up to $10,000 |
| ATHLETIC SCHOLARSHIPS: | No |
| ROTC: | No |
| WEB SITE: | www.yu.edu |
| PHONE: | (212) 960-5277 |

Yeshiva University is dedicated to combining the ancient traditions of Judaism with academic programs in the liberal arts and business. The most popular majors at Yeshiva are similar to those at any other college—psychology, biology, and accounting are among them—but all students simultaneously complete a rigorous program in Jewish studies. Consistent with the tenets of the faith, the sexes live and learn separately. The men inhabit Yeshiva's main campus in upper Manhattan on West 185th Street; the women are enrolled in Stern College for Women in the Murray Hill section of Midtown. Both have benefit of classes in Yeshiva's business school. Outstanding students can apply for the Distinguished Scholars program, which offers a $10,000 stipend along with enriched seminars and special events. Applicants must score at least 1400 on the SAT I, and a special application is required. Applicants are automatically considered for the Academic Scholars program, which offers up to $5,000 to students with slightly less outstanding credentials.

*Deadlines:*
  ADMISSION: Feb. 15
  FAFSA: Apr. 15

# ACKNOWLEDGMENTS

I am grateful to a host of people for their help in the preparation of this book. First and foremost, I would like to thank the hundreds of college administrators who responded to my requests for information. I am particularly grateful to Tom Anthony, Peter Van Buskirk, and Dr. Nancy Dye for their candor in the interviews that are transcribed in chapters 2 and 4. Tom Anthony was gracious in offering extensive comments on several of the chapters in Part I. I am also indebted to a number of colleagues who reviewed portions of Part I, including Bill Conley, dean of undergraduate admission at Case Western Reserve University; Pan Fay-Williams, director of college counseling at Columbus School for Girls; Anne Ferguson, director of college counseling at Hathaway Brown School; Chuck Lundholm, director of college advising at Maumee Valley Country Day School; and David Miller, director of financial aid at the College of Wooster. For a presidential perspective on college admission and financial aid, I am grateful for the insights offered by Dr. Mary Brown Bullock, president of Agnes Scott College, and Dr. John Wilson, former president of Washington and Lee University. My father, Guy Hammond, patiently read the entire manuscript and offered useful comments. The good people at Lake Ridge Academy were supportive of my early efforts on the book, especially Joe Ferber and Susan Sour, who have done much to further my growth as an educator. This project would not have gotten off the ground without the work of Nancy Evans and Warren Cook of iVillage.com, the parent company of Parent Soup, who saw the potential of this book and gave me timely encouragement. Susan Weaver and Susan Hahn were also a constant source of support. The book owes much to the thousands of parents that make Parent Soup such a vibrant on-line community, especially Kathy Hume and her group of dedicated moms. Thanks also go to my editor, Cassie Jones, for her patience and goodwill. Finally, I am indebted to my mentor and friend Ted Fiske, from whom I have learned much about education and how to produce a college guide. Though I extend deep thanks to all, the ultimate responsibility for this book is mine alone.